CORPORATE AMERICA

$$

This bibliography was conceived and compiled from the periodicals database of the American Bibliographical Center by editors at ABC-Clio Information Services.

Lance Klass and Susan Kinnell, project coordinators

Robert deV. Brunkow
Jeffery B. Serena

Pamela R. Byrne
Gail Schlachter

CORPORATE AMERICA

$$$

A Historical Bibliography

ABC-Clio Information Services

Santa Barbara, California
Oxford, England

Library of Congress Cataloging in Publication Data
Main entry under title:

Corporate America: a historical bibliography

    Includes index.
    1. Corporations–United States–History–Bibliography.
I. ABC-Clio Information Services.
Z7164.T87C66 1983 [HD2785] 016.3387'4'0973 83-11232
ISBN 0-87436-362-4

ABC-Clio Information Services
2040 Alameda Padre Serra, Box 4397
Santa Barbara, California 93103

Clio Press Ltd.
55 St. Thomas Street
Oxford 0X1 1JG, England

Cover design and graphics by Lance Klass
Printed and bound in the United States of America

ABC-CLIO RESEARCH GUIDES

The ABC-Clio Research Guides are a new generation of annotated bibliographies that provide comprehensive control of the recent journal literature on high-interest topics in history and related social sciences. These publications are created by editor/historians and other subject specialists who examine every article entry in ABC-Clio Information Services' vast history database and select abstracts of all citations published during the past decade that relate to the particular topic of study.

Each entry selected from this database—the largest history database in the world—has been reedited to ensure consistency in treatment and completeness of coverage. The extensive subject profile index (ABC-SPIndex) accompanying each volume has also been reassessed, specifically in terms of the particular subject presented, to allow precise and rapid access to the entries.

The titles in this series are prepared to save researchers, students, and librarians the considerable time and expense usually associated with accessing materials manually or through online searching. ABC-Clio's Research Guides offer unmatched access to significant scholarly articles on the topics of most current interest to historians and social scientists.

ABC-CLIO RESEARCH GUIDES

Gail Schlachter, Editor
Pamela R. Byrne, Executive Editor

1.
World War II from an American Perspective
1982   LC 82-22823   ISBN 0-87436-035-8

2.
The Jewish Experience in America
1982   LC 82-24480   ISBN 0-87436-034-x

3.
Nuclear America
1983   LC 83-12227   ISBN 0-87436-360-8

4.
The Great Depression
1983   LC 83-12234   ISBN 0-87436-361-6

5.
Corporate America
1983   LC 83-11232   ISBN 0-87436-362-4

6.
Crime and Punishment in America
1983   LC 83-12248   ISBN 0-87436-363-2

7.
The Democratic and Republican Parties
1983   LC 83-12230   ISBN 0-87436-364-0

8.
The American Electorate
1983   LC 83-12229   ISBN 0-87436-372-1

CONTENTS

LIST OF ABBREVIATIONS

A.	Author-prepared Abstract	*Illus.*	Illustrated, Illustration
Acad.	Academy, Academie, Academia	*Inst.*	Institute, Institut-.
Agric.	Agriculture, Agricultural	*Int.*	International, Internacional,
AIA	Abstracts in Anthropology		Internationaal, Internationaux,
Akad.	Akademie		Internazionale
Am.	America, American	*J.*	Journal, Journal-prepared Abstract
Ann.	Annals, Annales, Annual, Annali	*Lib.*	Library, Libraries
Anthrop.	Anthropology, Anthropological	*Mag.*	Magazine
Arch.	Archives	*Mus.*	Museum, Musee, Museo
Archaeol.	Archaeology, Archaeological	*Nac.*	Nacional
Art.	Article	*Natl.*	National, Nationale
Assoc.	Association, Associate	*Naz.*	Nazionale
Biblio.	Bibliography, Bibliographical	*Phil.*	Philosophy, Philosophical
Biog.	Biography, Biographical	*Photo.*	Photograph
Bol.	Boletim, Boletin	*Pol.*	Politics, Political, Politique, Politico
Bull.	Bulletin	*Pr.*	Press
c.	century (in index)	*Pres.*	President
ca.	circa	*Pro.*	Proceedings
Can.	Canada, Canadian, Canadien	*Publ.*	Publishing, Publication
Cent.	Century	*Q.*	Quarterly
Coll.	College	*Rev.*	Review, Revue, Revista, Revised
Com.	Committee	*Riv.*	Rivista
Comm.	Commission	*Res.*	Research
Comp.	Compiler	*RSA*	Romanian Scientific Abstracts
DAI	Dissertation Abstracts	*S.*	Staff-prepared Abstract
	International	*Sci.*	Science, Scientific
Dept.	Department	*Secy.*	Secretary
Dir.	Director, Direktor	*Soc.*	Society, Societe, Sociedad,
Econ.	Economy, Econom-.		Societa
Ed.	Editor, Edition	*Sociol.*	Sociology, Sociological
Educ.	Education, Educational	*Tr.*	Transactions
Geneal.	Genealogy, Genealogical,	*Transl.*	Translator, Translation
	Genealogique	*U.*	University, Universi-.
Grad.	Graduate	*US*	United States
Hist.	History, Hist-.	*Vol.*	Volume
IHE	Indice Historico Espanol	*Y.*	Yearbook

INTRODUCTION

"The chief business of the American people is business." Calvin Coolidge in 1925 thus reduced to elegant epigram the driving force of American society. Since the early 19th century, when Jefferson's vision of an agrarian America was lost amid the smoke and din of the industrial revolution, American business and its corporate infrastructure have been at the heart of the nation's development.

Recognition of the fundamental role of business in American history has given rise to a vast body of historical scholarship that is both venerable and dynamic. During the past decade, scholars have focused on American businesses as social institutions, emphasizing the inter-relationships among corporations, government, and the culture and social organization of workers. Business history has been transformed into social history.

Corporate America: A Historical Bibliography brings together this modern scholarship on corporations in American history. It is a compendium of 1,368 abstracts of articles on American business history published during 1973-82. The abstracts are drawn from the database of ABC-Clio Information Services—the largest history database in the world—which includes abstracts of articles from more than 2,000 journals in 42 languages, published in 90 countries.

Access to the abstracts in this volume is provided by ABC-SPIndex, one of the most advanced and comprehensive indexing systems in the world. ABC-SPIndex links together the key subject terms and the chronology of each abstract to form a composite index entry that furnishes a complete subject profile of the journal article. Each set of index terms is rotated so that the complete profile appears in the index under every subject term. In this way, the number of access points is increased severalfold over conventional hierarchical indexes, and irrelevant works can be eliminated early in the search process.

Additional access to the abstracts is provided by the internal division of the bibliography into 10 chapters. Each of these chapters focuses on a particular aspect of business history or segment of American industry. Scholars concerned with specific issues or topics as diverse as the growth of multinationals, price supports for agribusiness, or the evolution of the automobile industry can turn immediately to the relevant chapter to gain a broad insight into the scope, thrust, and basic issues of modern scholarship on these subjects.

Chapter 1, "Multinationals, Conglomerates, and Big Business," focuses on the nature of the American corporation and the internationalizing tendencies of the largest firms. The seven chapters that follow comprise abstracts of scholarly works on the growth and influence of particular industries. Chapter 2 encompasses the banking, investments, and service industries; Chapters 3 and 4, transportation and communication; Chapter 5, the energy industries; Chapter 6, agriculture and textile industries; Chapter 7, mining; and Chapter 8, manufacturing and merchandising. Chapter 9, "Social Effects and Environmental Impacts," summarizes scholarship on the controversial issue of corporate social responsibility. The final chapter, "Government Regulation and Intervention," focuses on the adversary relationship between business and government that has developed in the context of 20th-century government regulation.

The article abstracts were selected by the editors, who examined every abstract in the database for 1973-82. This careful selection process has provided very thorough coverage of the modern periodical literature of American business history. The result far exceeds in breadth of coverage what is obtainable through an online search of the database or even an extensive manual search using the database's subject index. Great care has been taken to ensure consistency and precision in the index terms. In addition, cross-references have been added to the subject index to facilitate rapid and accurate searching. These editorial labors have produced a bibliography that combines readability, easy accessability, and thorough coverage of the modern scholarship on corporate America.

1

MULTINATIONALS, CONGLOMERATES, AND BIG BUSINESS

1. Abrams, Matthew J. THE COMPANY CAMP IN LATIN AMERICA: A CHANGE IN UNITED STATES MINING AND PETROLEUM COMPANY POLICY. *Land Econ. 1966 42(4): 523-526.*

2. Abrams, Richard W. THE MODERN CORPORATION. *Society 1979 16(3): 44-51.* Discusses the social responsibilities of private business since colonial times, and focuses on modern corporate power and the fear that the United States government is unable to assure that corporations be held accountable for their actions in light of the best interests of society.

3. Allen, Michael Patrick. ECONOMIC INTEREST GROUPS AND THE CORPORATE ELITE STRUCTURE. *Social Sci. Q. 1978 58(4): 597-615.* Examines the 10 principal interlocking groups among the 250 major corporations of 1935 and 1970 in terms of their characteristics as economic interest groups. Indicates that family and financial interest groups with centers of common control have declined relative to geographical interest groups without centers of common control, although family and financial interest groups have not been entirely eliminated.								J

4. Astapovich, A. AMERIKANSKOE MEZHDUNARODNYE KORPORATSII I GOSUDARSTVO [The American international corporations and the state]. *Mirovaia Ekonomika i Mezhdunarodnye Otnosheniia [USSR] 1977 (7): 45-57.* The rise of large multinational corporations in the United States has brought about a situation where the traditional methods of bourgeois governments for controlling the economy have become inadequate.

5. Baughman, James P. AMERICAN MULTINATIONALS: WHO, WHAT, WHEN, WHERE, AND HOW? *Rev. in Am. Hist. 1975 3(3): 343-347.* Review article prompted by Mira Wilkins' *The Maturing of Multinational Enterprise: American Business Abroad from 1914 to 1970* (Cambridge, Mass.: Harvard U. Pr., 1974).

6. Becker, James F. THE RISE OF THE MANAGERIAL ECONOMICS. *Marxist Perspectives 1979 2(2): 34-54.* The productive worker and the social scientist in Europe and in America have come to be progressively subjugated to the practice and to the "science" of the entrepreneurial technician.

7. Becker, William H. CONTRIBUTIONS DURING THE 1960S TO THE HISTORY OF AMERICAN BUSINESS. *Rev. Int. d'Hist. de la Banque [Italy] 1974 8: 216-224.* Business history in the 1960's differed from earlier decades in the sheer volume produced and in the variety of methodology used. Writers were also more interested in developing abstract or theoretical explanations of the growth of business enterprise, the study of strategy and structure by Alfred D. Chandler being one of the best examples of this tendency. Finally the relationship between business and the federal government became a focal point of study. On the whole, the 1960's affirmed the conclusions of the earlier decades regarding the close interrelationship between government and business enterprise. Secondary sources; 19 notes.   D. McGinnis

8. Benjamin, Thomas. INTERNATIONAL HARVESTER AND THE HENEQUEN MARKETING SYSTEM IN YUCATAN, 1898-1915: A NEW PERSPECTIVE. *Inter-American Econ. Affairs 1977 31(3): 3-19.* Argues that contrary to popular theory, the International Harvester Company (IHC) and the marketing house of Molina-Montes did not manipulate the henequen market in Yucatán. Concludes that reduced henequen prices after IHC entered the market in 1903 resulted from world market conditions. 3 tables, 51 notes.
D. A. Franz

9. Berger, Henry W. UNIONS AND EMPIRE: ORGANIZED LABOR AND AMERICAN CORPORATIONS ABROAD. *Peace and Change 1976 3(4): 34-48.* Discusses the AFL's (and later AFL-CIO's) role in, and attitudes toward, US multinational corporations 1880's-1970's, emphasizing employment, economic expansionism, and foreign policy.

10. Bloomfield, Maxwell. THE MUNICIPAL CORPORATION REVISITED. *Rev. in Am. Hist. 1976 4(1): 27-31.* Review article prompted by Jon C. Teaford's *The Municipal Revolution in America: Origins of Modern Urban Government, 1650-1825* (Chicago: U. of Chicago Pr., 1975).

11. Bluestone, Barry and Harrison, Bennett. WHY CORPORATIONS CLOSE PROFITABLE PLANTS. *Working Papers for a New Society 1980 7(3): 15-23.* Claims that major corporations of the last two decades take the profits from subsidiary corporations, mismanage them, and then terminate them for the sake of efficiency.

12. Bock, Peter G. THE TRANSNATIONAL CORPORATION AND PRIVATE FOREIGN POLICY. *Society 1974 11(2): 44-49.* Examines the foreign policy of the International Telephone and Telegraph Company in Chile.   S

13. Bol'shakova, I. and Kochetov, E'. STRATEGIIA MONOPOLII I PROTIVORECHIIA KAPITALISTICHESKOGO MEZHDUNARODNOGO RAZDELENIIA TRUDA [The strategy of monopolies and the contradictions of the capitalist international division of labor]. *Mirovaia Ekonomika i Mezhdunarodnye Otnosheniia [USSR] 1977 (12): 28-38.* Argues that the contradiction between the conditions of production of value added and the conditions of its realization is increasingly manifested in the intensifying struggle among the multinational corporations for markets, and that the capitalist international division of labor is essentially a chaotic process.

14. Bowen, Richard A. MULTINATIONAL CORPORATIONS. *US Naval Inst. Pro. 1973 99(1): 54-64.* As the world moves from an age of geopolitics to one of "ecopolitics," the remarkable growth of multinational enterprise, if properly guided and controlled, can reinforce American national power. But to take advantage of the strength and opportunity created by this development, the United States must tailor its grand strategy to accommodate multinational enterprise and resolve the dilemma of atomization at the economic policy level. Illus., map. J. K. Ohl

15. Brower, Michael. EXPERIENCE WITH SELF-MANAGEMENT AND PARTICIPATION IN UNITED STATES INDUSTRY. *Administration and Soc. 1975 7(1): 65-84.* Examines cases of self-management of small firms since the 1920's and recent experiments of large capitalist firms, speculating on the future of self-managed institutions. S

16. Brown, D. E. CORPORATIONS AND SOCIAL CLASSIFICATION. *Current Anthrop. 1974 15(1): 29-41.* The classification of corporations is an important theoretical task. A recent classification by M. G. Smith is critically reviewed. Although corporations are institutions, they are much less boundless in form than the totality of institutions. Corporations are classifiable in terms of eight characteristics. Since further classification rests on precise definitions of principles of incorporation, the method of isolating such principles is examined. Finally it is argued that corporate analysis readily promotes the generation and testing of hypotheses. J/S

17. Bueno, Clodoaldo. FERROVIAS E PENETRACAO CAPITALISTA NORTEAMERICANA NA AMERICA LATINA: UN DOCUMENTO SIGNIFICATIVO [Railroads and North American capitalist penetration in Latin America: a significant document]. *Estudos Hist. [Brazil] 1977 16: 101-184.* Reproduces Charles M. Pepper's *The Pan-American Railway* (1904), a report written when the United States reshaped its foreign policy and displaced Great Britain from a dominant role in controlling transport in Latin America. Portuguese.

18. Buxbaum, Richard M. THE RELATION OF THE LARGE CORPORATION'S STRUCTURE TO THE ROLE OF SHAREHOLDERS AND DIRECTORS: SOME AMERICAN HISTORICAL PERSPECTIVES. Horn, Norbert and Kocka, Jürgen, ed. *Recht und Entwicklung der Grossunternehmen im 19. und frühen 20. Jahrhundert* (Göttingen: Vandenhoeck & Ruprecht, 1979): 243-254. Reviews the promotional role of investment banking in corporate structure development, 1865-1914. While the shareholders, board of directors, and management were accommodated within the preexisting framework, the legal order had to be changed to conform to financial realities. It was this which allowed for the dominance of investment bankers. 45 notes, biblio. German summary. S

19. Calderwood, Stanford. THE ROLE OF THE AMERICAN CORPORATION. *Current Hist. 1975 69(410): 175-178, 198-200.* Discusses the role of corporations in the problem of capital formation, inflation, and unemployment during the 1970's.

20. Calleo, David P. BUSINESS CORPORATIONS AND THE NA-
TIONAL STATE. *Social Res. 1974 41(4): 702-718.* Situates the multinational
corporation in regard to the nation state.   S

21. Capitman, William G. CORPORATION LOGIC. *Center Mag. 1975
8(3): 23-27.* Discusses current economic conditions within corporations.   S

22. Carl, Robert. THE BANANA NAVY. *US Naval Inst. Pro. 1976
102(12): 55-67.* Numerous photographs and a short narrative tell the story of "the
Great White Fleet of the giant United Fruit Company . . . an almost legendary
commercial enterprise that rose to prominence from inconspicuous beginnings."
Lorenzo Dow Baker began the enterprise in 1870 at Port Antonio, Jamaica. He
was joined in 1876 by Andrew Preston of Boston to form the Boston Fruit
Company. They were joined later by Minor Keith, and on 30 March 1899 formed
the United Fruit Company. By the 1930's, the Great White Fleet had grown to
the size of a small navy. "The year 1955 marked the apex and the beginning of
the demise of the United Fruit Company. . . . today, the . . . Company operates
no U.S. ship." 39 photos.   A. N. Garland

23. Caroselli, Maria Raffaella. I FATTORI DELLA SECONDA RIVOLUZ-
IONE INDUSTRIALE [The factors of the second industrial revolution]. *Econ.
e Storia [Italy] 1978 25(3): 389-418.* Changes revolutionized industry at the close
of the 19th century and resulted in an impressive mechanization and in a better
organization of work. Frederick Taylor and Henry Ford led public opinion
toward a scientific approach to social problems. Secondary sources; 40 notes.
                                                                    F. Busachi

24. Caves, Richard E. and Murphy, William F., II. FRANCHISING:
FIRMS, MARKETS, AND INTANGIBLE ASSETS. *Southern Econ. J. 1976
42(4): 572-586.* Explains the occurrence and economic performance of franchised
businesses between 1969 and 1973.

25. Caves, Richard E. INDUSTRIAL ORGANIZATION, CORPORATE
STRATEGY AND STRUCTURE. *J. of Econ. Literature 1980 18(1): 64-92.*
Synthesizes and reports interdisciplinary research on the relations between the
firm and its market environment in the United States, and presents opportunities
for further empirical and theoretical research.

26. Chandler, Alfred. INSTITUTIONAL INTEGRATION: AN AP-
PROACH TO COMPARATIVE STUDIES OF THE HISTORY OF LARGE-
SCALE BUSINESS ENTERPRISE. *Rev. Econ. [France] 1976 27(2): 177-199.*
The concept of institutional aggregation and integration in business history provides a more relevant approach to the study of the development of large-scale
modern enterprise than does that of institutional specialization and disintegra-
tion. A focus on the division of labour is largely misleading in respect to the
history of business enterprise. Many analysts fail to realize that large-scale enterprises never went through a stage of pure competition and that the first oligopo-
lists were also the nation's first multinationals. Historical evidence comes from
the main industrial and transportation sectors of the American economy. The
author asserts the hypothesis that, despite important differences, the same analysis would fit the Western European cases or even the Japanese one.   J

27. Chandler, Alfred D.   THE GROWTH OF THE TRANSNATIONAL INDUSTRIAL FIRM IN THE UNITED STATES AND THE UNITED KINGDOM: A COMPARATIVE ANALYSIS. *Econ. Hist. Rev. [Great Britain] 1980 33(3): 346-410.* Compares the large multinational corporations that emerged in both Great Britain and the United States after 1880 and traces developments to the present. Managerial enterprise appeared much more rapidly in the United States. Managerial failure—the continuing existence of the family firm—helped deprive Britain of a class of trained managers with the technological skills essential in the technological age.   B. L. Crapster

28. Chandler, Alfred D., Jr. and Daems, Herman.   ADMINISTRATIVE CO-ORDINATION, ALLOCATION AND MONITORING: CONCEPTS AND COMPARISONS.   Horn, Norbert and Kocka, Jürgen, ed. *Recht und Entwicklung der Grossunternehmen im 19. und frühen 20. Jahrhundert* (Göttingen: Vandenhoeck & Ruprecht, 1979): 28-54. Examines the divergent development of modern hierarchical business administration in Western Europe and the United States through the accounting systems and organizational structures. The greatest difference occurred in manufacturing "where technology and markets encouraged the integration of production with distribution." The British used holding companies, while the Germans had cartels. In the United States trade associations first carried out interagency agreements, but with antitrust legislation holding companies similar to those in Great Britain arose. Covers 1850's-1920's. 3 charts, 29 notes, ref. German summary.   S

29. Chandler, Alfred D., Jr.   DECISION MAKING AND MODERN INSTITUTIONAL CHANGE.   *J. of Econ. Hist. 1973 33(1): 1-15.* Considers the reshaping of business institutions, the processes of decisionmaking, and how they helped reform business structure over the past 150 years. The result was the emergence in the 20th century of large-scale organizations run by a managerial class. The processes of decisionmaking are much the same for generals, government officials, or presidents of large corporations. The contrast is seen between generations rather than between occupations. Presidential address at the 32nd annual meeting of the Economic History Association.   C. W. Olson

30. Cieślik, Jerzy.   MULTINATIONAL CORPORATIONS AND THE CHOICE OF TECHNOLOGY IN DEVELOPING COUNTRIES. *Studies on the Developing Countries [Poland] 1978 (9): 110-122.* Examines the role of multinational corporations in developing nations from 1960 to 1976 and concludes that the developing countries cannot count on the assistance of the MNC's in the research and adaptation work aimed at broadening the spectrum of available technologies, for MNC's favor modern capital-intensive technologies, and in addition their sophisticated advertising techniques have an insidious effect on inhabitants of developing countries.

31. Clairmonte, Frederick F.   UNITED STATES FOOD MULTINATIONALS: LESSONS FOR THE THIRD WORLD.   *J. of Contemporary Asia [Sweden] 1981 11(1): 62-90.* Oligopolistic capitalism in its conglomerate phase has become omnidirectional predation. This explains rocketing prices at the supermarket matched by plummeting farm incomes. Such a paradox is the result of the imbrications of the industrial and food complexes of the multinationals in all principal food intersects: farming, agrichemicals, farm machinery, food pro-

cessing, wholesaling and retailing, with multinational banking and the giant food traders. The food complexes are part of a wider social and economic system geared not to the satisfaction of needs but to the aggrandizement of corporate capital. 73 notes.   J. V. Coutinho

32. Clairmonte, Frederick F. and Cavanagh, John. WORLD CHEMICALS: THE ANATOMY OF CORPORATE POWER. *J. of Contemporary Asia [Sweden] 1980 10(4): 444-452.* In 1979 13 companies produced three-fifths of the world's synthetic fibers, comprising 80 to 90% of the world trade. Discusses the research and development and marketing techniques that have made this oligopolistic structure possible. Primary sources; 2 tables, 17 notes.   J. Powell

33. Clairmonte, Frederick F. WORLD TOBACCO: THE DYNAMICS OF OLIGOPOLISTIC ANNEXATIONISM. *J. of Contemporary Asia [Sweden] 1979 9(3): 255-273.* Analyzes the structure and practices of the international tobacco conglomerate. No more than seven companies control the bulk of the world market. Small and developing nations produce more than half of the world raw output, but virtually none of the finished product, nor have they a say in the finished product. Through mass production and marketing techniques, the oligopoly has effected significant world control, but such moments of control have, historically, been brief. 3 fig., 32 notes.   V. L. Human

34. Cochran, Thomas C. THE BUSINESS REVOLUTION. *Am. Hist. R. 1974 79(5): 1449-1466.* Business structure can be the equivalent of a leading sector in stimulating rapid economic growth, and this structure is a part of the general social system and values. The thesis seems clearly illustrated in the United States from 1790 to 1840. According to recent econometric evidence the United States during this period had the world's most rapid rate of economic growth, chiefly induced not by the introduction of new technology, but by increasing division of functions and labor in business offices. Early state exploitation of the possibilities of the chartered corporation was an outstanding feature of this business development.   A

35. Collins, Robert M. AMERICAN CORPORATISM: THE COMMITTEE FOR ECONOMIC DEVELOPMENT, 1942-1964. *Historian 1982 44(2): 151-173.* Recent historical emphasis upon organization as a dominant factor in the shaping of modern American society provides a new conceptual window through which to view the process of state building in US history. Examines the Committee for Economic Development (CED) and its influence on national macroeconomic policy to trace the development of American corporatism. CED contributed in three ways: contributors to economic thought, activities of its personnel, and relationships as an institution to other agencies. Corporatists, as evidenced by the CED, did very well. Primary sources; 81 notes.
                                                                    R. S. Sliwoski

36. Cox, Robert W. LABOR AND THE MULTINATIONALS. *Foreign Affairs 1975 54(2): 344-365.* " . . .the expansion of the multinational corporation is a major, perhaps *the* major, phenomenon of the international economy today . . .labor today has managed to generate only a confused, partial and lopsided response . . ." in exercising its options in this critical situation. 12 notes.
                                                                    R. Riles

37. Craypo, Charles. COLLECTIVE BARGAINING IN THE CON-GLOMERATE, MULTINATIONAL FIRM: LITTON'S SHUTDOWN OF ROYAL TYPEWRITER. *Industrial and Labor Relations R. 1975 29(1): 3-25.* Discusses the new multinational corporations that have emerged in the 1960's and 1970's, and labor unions' reaction to management's cross-subsidization of funds.

38. Cuddy, D. L. AMERICAN BUSINESS AND PRIVATE INVEST-MENT IN AUSTRALIA. *Australia J. of Pol. and Hist. [Australia] 1980 26(1): 45-56.* The first major influx of American business and capital came after 1946 when Canada severed itself from the sterling bloc, preventing US firms from entering Australia via Canadian affiliates. By 1955 US investment in Australia equaled Britain's, and by the 1970's there were calls for curbs on American control of large sectors of the economy. The reasons for American investment were a mass market second only to the United States and Canada, tax incentives, low labor costs, weak competition, saturation of the US market, security, and a compatible language and legal environment. American companies grew from 800 in 1955 to 2,000 in 1970. Car production led, followed by minerals and land development and the pastoral industry. By 1978 cumulative private investment had reached $6.4 billion. Based on newspapers, commercial journals, and mono-graphs; 59 notes.   W. D. McIntyre

39. Cuff, Robert D. FROM MARKET TO MANAGER. *Can. Rev. of Am. Studies [Canada] 1979 10(1): 47-54.* Since the early 1960's, entrepreneurial and business history studies increasingly have stressed the management phase of modern commercial activity in which the interaction of technology and corporate management structures and systems of control and communication predominate. Among the sophisticated treatises of this historical genre is *The Visible Hand: The Managerial Revolution in American Business* (Cambridge: Harvard U. Pr., 1977) by Alfred D. Chandler, Jr. 7 notes.   H. T. Lovin

40. Dalton, James A. and Esposito, Louis. THE IMPACT OF LIQUIDITY ON MERGER ACTIVITY. *Q. R. of Econ. and Business 1973 13(1): 15-26.* "The decision to merge is a product of the interworkings of a number of motives. This article addresses the underlying conditions for merger by going beyond the particular circumstances to the necessary conditions. The purpose is to test the hypothesis that excess internal firm liquidity is a cause of mergers. The results suggest that there is a positive association between firm liquidity and the degree of merger activity. The study does not find a statistically significant association between merger activity and stock prices."   J

41. De Alessi, Louis. DO BUSINESS FIRMS GAIN FROM INFLATION? REPRISE. *J. of Business 1975 48(2): 264-266.* Common stocks may not provide a hedge against changes in general price levels, while gains from inflation depend upon net-debtor status. The proportion of American corporations in that condi-tion during 1934-56 fluctuated from 40 to 60 percent and promised little gain. During 1948-56 about 80 percent of British firms were net debtors and should have gained. Secondary sources; 16 notes.   J. W. Williams

42. Demsétz, Harold. INDUSTRY STRUCTURE, MARKET RIVALRY, AND PUBLIC POLICY. *J. of Law and Econ. 1973 16(1): 1-9.* A critical analysis of the current preoccupation with monopoly in quantitative work on industrial organization, presenting "data which suggests that this doctrine offers a dangerous base upon which to build a public policy towards business." The point of analysis is "an explanation of industry structure and profitability based on competitive superiority." Based on secondary sources; 4 tables, 6 notes.

C. A. Gallacci

43. Drucker, Peter F. MULTINATIONALS AND DEVELOPING COUN-TRIES: MYTHS AND REALITIES. *Foreign Affairs 1974 53(1): 121-134.* The myths are: 1) the developing nations are the mainstay of the multinational corpo-ration as a major source of sales, revenues, profits, and growth, 2) only foreign capital can supply the funds necessary for economic development, 3) the multina-tional subordinates the best national interest to that of global exploitation, and 4) the multinational's organization follows that of the 19th-century corporation with a parent company and wholly-owned branches abroad. The realities lie on the other side. The developing countries need the multinational for investment technology, managerial competence, and marketing and export abilities. They are "a most effective means to constructive nationhood for the developing world." 4 notes.

C. W. Olson

44. DuBoff, Richard B. THE "BIAS" OF TECHNOLOGY: CORPORATE CAPITAL AND THE ENGINEERS, 1880-1930. *Monthly Rev. 1978 30(5): 19-28.* Discusses David F. Noble's *America by Design: Science, Technology, and the Rise of Corporate Capitalism* (1977) which explains the transformation of the American economy by big business during 1880-1930.

45. Dye, Thomas R. and Pickering, John W. GOVERNMENTAL AND CORPORATE ELITES: CONVERGENCE AND DIFFERENTIATION. *J. of Pol. 1974 36(4): 900-925.* The purposes of "Governmental and Corporate Elites: Convergence and Differentiation" are to define and identify a national institutional "elite" in America and then to examine the degree of convergence and differentiation among corporate, governmental, and public interest elites. Authors Thomas R. Dye and John W. Pickering describe concentration in institu-tional resources; the extent of interlocking and specialization in officeholding; the differences in recruitment paths to top positions in governmental, corporate, and public interest organizations; and the degree of differentiation in social back-grounds between top officeholders in these separate types of institutions. J

46. Eisenberg, William M. MEASURING THE PRODUCTIVITY OF NONFINANCIAL CORPORATIONS. *Monthly Labor Rev. 1974 97(11): 21-34.* Analysis of productivity in nonfinancial corporations in the United States, including the US operations of multinational corporations, between 1948 and 1973, shows that trends were similar to those in the total private economy.

47. Erickson, Rodney A. THE SPATIAL PATTERN OF INCOME GEN-ERATION IN LEAD FIRM, GROWTH AREA LINKAGE SYSTEMS. *Econ. Geography 1975 51(1): 17-26.* Using the Boeing Company in the Puget Sound area as an example, analyzes the ways a lead firm exerts growth-generating forces which are transferred to other elements in the firm's economic system by interindustry and income-multiplier linkages. S

48. Fernandez, Raul A. THE BORDER INDUSTRIAL PROGRAM ON THE UNITED STATES-MEXICO BORDER. *R. of Radical Pol. Econ. 1973 5(1): 37-52.* Examines the economic impact of multinational corporations on the US-Mexico border region, 1940-70.

49. Fletcher, Thomas W. and McGwire, John M. GOVERNMENT AND PRIVATE BUSINESS: NEW RELATIONSHIPS EMERGING. *Natl. Civic Rev. 1980 69(9): 491-496.* A central fact of modern business life is that the private corporation is increasingly being viewed as a public institution. Through court decisions, legislation and citizen action, rather than simply by governmental regulations, corporations are being forced to consider many public issues. Government and business are coming to realize that they have common stakes in responding to these pressures.   J

50. Freeman, Orville. THE WORKHORSE OF THE WORLD. *Foreign Service J. 1976 53(7): 14, 18-22.* Compares the growing internationalization of production through multinational corporations to the unification of the American economy that went on during World War II; despite different currencies, countless tariffs, and other restrictions to investment, the unification of the world economy is leading to human interdependence and world survival.

51. Freeman, Susan. CANADA'S CHANGING POSTURE TOWARD MULTINATIONAL CORPORATIONS: AN ATTEMPT TO HARMONIZE NATIONALISM WITH CONTINUED ECONOMIC GROWTH. *New York U. J. of Internat. Law and Pol. 1974 7(2): 271-315.* Analyzes Canada's special relationship with the United States and her recent attempts to "foster a sense of nationhood in the face of cultural divisiveness, great economic disparities among the provinces and pervasive American corporate power and American cultural influences on their society. Discusses Canada's recent economic concerns and policies, concluding that "Canadian compromises with nationalism and ambivalence toward American investment endure" and that Canada's first concern is with a high standard of living, not with foreign investment. Primary and secondary sources; 252 notes.   M. L. Frey

52. Galey, John. INDUSTRIALIST IN THE WILDERNESS: HENRY FORD'S AMAZON VENTURE. *J. of Interamerican Studies and World Affairs 1979 21(2): 261-289.* Henry Ford's efforts (1920's-40's) to initiate a major rubber plantation system in Brazil were hindered and ultimately stymied by factors such as Brazil's suspicion of foreign investments, particularly in the northern Amazonia region. Ford also insisted on following a predetermined, US model for building and administering the plantation. He chose engineers and naval people rather than agronomists to head the operation. These problems, disease and insect problems, Ford's inability to recognize alternative sources of cash crops from the project, and the development of synthetic rubber, prompted the abandonment of the project in 1945. Based on manuscripts and printed primary and secondary materials; 13 notes, ref.   T. D. Schoonover

53. García, Alejandro and Zanetti, Oscar. LOS MONOPOLIOS NORTEAMERICANOS Y LA LEY TARAFA [US monopolies and the Tarafa law]. *Rev. de la Biblioteca Nac. José Martí [Cuba] 1980 22(2): 57-89.* The law sponsored by José M. Tarafa laid the groundwork for US monopolization of public railroads in Cuba. 64 notes.   J. A. Lewis

54.   Gauzner,   N.   EKSPANSIIA   TRANSNATSIONAL'NIKH   KOR-
PORATSII I ZANIATOST'RABOCHEGO KLASSA   [Expansion of transnational corporations and employment of the working class]. *Mirovaia Ekonomika
i Mezhdunarodnye Otnosheniia [USSR] 1979 (8): 82-95.* Discusses the problem
of the influence of international monopolies on the level of employment of working class elements of contemporary capitalism. Tables, biblio.

55.   Gerlach,   Luther   P.   THE   FLEA   AND   THE   ELEPHANT: INFANT
FORMULA CONTROVERSY.   *Society 1980 17(6): 51-57.* Examines the controversy over the promotion and marketing of infant formula in the developing
nations, specifically the response of the food industry to charges by protest groups
and the implications which go beyond the infant formula protest and symbolize
concern about the world food supply and the gap between rich and poor.

56.   Gervasi,   Sean.   STAGNATION,   FORCED   GROWTH,   AND   CRISIS.
Social Policy 1975 6(2): 71-78. Business strategies used by US corporations
1900-75 have failed to prevent depressions.

57.   Giback,   Thomas   H.   FILM   AS   INTERNATIONAL   BUSINESS.
J. of Communication 1974 24(1): 90-101. Examines the American film industry
as a multinational corporation.   S

58.   Gilpin,   Robert.   THE   POLITICAL   ECONOMY   OF   THE   MULTINA-
TIONAL   CORPORATION: THREE   CONTRASTING   PERSPECTIVES.
Am. Pol. Sci. Rev. 1976 70(1): 184-191. A review essay covering Kari Levitt,
Silent Surrender: The American Economic Empire in Canada (New York: Live-
right Press, 1970), Jagdish Bhagwati, ed., *Economics and World Order: From the
1970's to the 1990's* (Macmillan, 1972) and Raymond Vernon, *Sovereignty at
Bay: The Multinational Spread of U.S. Enterprises* (Basic Books, 1971). These
publications differ fundamentally with respect to multinational corporations as
representing the "liberal conception," the "Marxist conception," and the "mer-
cantilist conception." 15 notes.   R. V. Ritter

59.   Goldberg,   Lawrence   G.   THE   EFFECT   OF   CONGLOMERATE
MERGERS ON COMPETITION.   *J. of Law and Econ. 1973 16(1): 137-158.*
Examines the allegation that conglomerate mergers are harmful to competition.
The results of an analysis based on 44 mergers in 15 different industries provide
no evidence in support of this allegation. "Conglomerate mergers should not be
prohibited as a general policy based on supposed harmful competitive effects as
has been proposed by the Neal Task Force." Based on secondary sources; 9 tables,
36 notes.   C. A. Gallacci

60.   Gresham,   Perry E.   THE BELEAGUERED BUSINESSMAN.   *Freeman
1974 24(9): 536-544.* "The case for business needs to be made as long as antibusiness groups are advocating socialism."   J

61.   Griliches,   Zvi.   R & D AND THE PRODUCTIVITY SLOWDOWN.
Am. Econ. Rev. 1980 70(2): 343-348. The slowdown in research and development
(R & D) did not cause the current productivity slowdown. In fact the influence
has been just the opposite with the R & D to GNP ratio peaking to 2.9% in 1964
but declining to 2.37% in 1975. Edward F. Denison's discussion (pp. 354-355)
questions the statistical effectiveness of using correlation analysis to estimate the
contribution of R & D to growth. Covers 1959-77. 2 tables, 16 ref.
                                                                                  D. K. Pickens

62.   Groff-Smith, Geoffrey.   THE MULTINATIONAL CORPORATION: A
NEW FORCE IN AMERICAN FOREIGN RELATIONS.   *Naval War Coll.
R. 1973 25(3): 60-69.* "U.S. business has long been recognized as a significant
element in America's relations abroad. Whether seen as a beneficent influence or
as part of an imperialist conspiracy to dominate the world, commercial ties
between American businessmen and foreign nations have had as notable an
influence on the conduct of U.S. foreign policy as considerations of ideology and
national defense. The rapidly growing part played by multinational corporations
in international commercial relations, however, will necessarily add new dimensions to the international community of the future, perhaps altering in a fundamental way political as well as economic links between peoples. For if any
institutions are building effective foundations for a greater sense of world community and interdependence in the future, they are to be found today in business and
not within diplomatic circles."   J

63.   Grubel, Herbert G.   TAXATION AND THE RATES OF RETURN
FROM SOME U.S. ASSET HOLDINGS ABROAD, 1960-1969.   *J. of Pol.
Econ. 1974 82(3): 469-487.* "The paper shows theoretically that US tax laws are
designed to induce equalization of private rates of return from investment in the
United States and abroad but that, unless the marginal government expenditures
on investment equal tax payments by the investment, there is a difference between
private and social rates of return to US foreign investment. Calculations covering
the period 1960-69 for developed countries and US holdings of bonds, equities,
and direct investment in manufacturing showed that private rates of return
generally were positive but that social rates of return from investing abroad rather
than domestically were strongly negative, assuming zero marginal government
expenditures and disregarding all externalities."   J

64.   Hannah, Leslie.   MERGERS, CARTELS, AND CONCENTRATION:
LEGAL FACTORS IN THE U.S. AND EUROPEAN EXPERIENCE.
Horn, Norbert and Kocka, Jürgen, ed. *Recht und Entwicklung der Grossunternehmen im 19. und frühen 20. Jahrhundert* (Göttingen: Vandenhoeck & Ruprecht, 1979): 306-316. The growth of large modern corporations generally
requires the existence of laws enabling the creation of limited liability companies,
although some family enterprises have been able to grow quite large without
relinquishing financial control. In the United States there was generally a trend
toward joint-stock companies and mergers as antitrust laws were enacted, but
France, Germany, and Great Britain permitted cartels until World War II or
later, so that, while the trend in Europe was also toward large limited liability
corporations, the pattern was different. The model necessary to explain the
relationship between corporate development and business law is extremely complicated and has not yet been constructed. Covers 1880-1914. 26 ref. German
summary.   S

65.   Harker, John.   TRADE UNIONS AND A CODE OF CONDUCT FOR
MULTINATIONALS.   *Can. Labour [Canada] 1977 22(1): 8-11.* Discusses the
principal bases for the commitment of trade unions to the development of and
enforcement of a code of conduct for multinational corporations, and describes
the evolution of code guidelines by the Organization for Economic Cooperation
and Development (OECD).

66. Harwood, Edwin. THE ENTREPRENEURIAL RENAISSANCE AND ITS PROMOTERS. *Society 1979 16(3): 27-31.* Discusses the success of business entrepreneurs in the United States in the 1970's, and traces the rise of business and profits since the early 1940's.

67. Hawley, Ellis W. THE DISCOVERY AND STUDY OF A "CORPORATE LIBERALISM." *Business Hist. Rev. 1978 52(3): 309-320.* Argues that the classic liberal and conservative interpretations of American history do not accurately reflect the ways in which the modern nation has been organized. Rather than a continual business-government conflict, there has been the development of an "organizational sector" between the private enterprise and the public sectors. Introduces a special issue devoted to the study of "corporate liberalism," the attempt to find a "liberal but not-statist alternative to laissez-faire prescriptions" to recurring economic crises. Secondary works; 11 notes.
C. J. Pusateri

68. Heise, Paul A. THE MULTINATIONAL CORPORATION AND INDUSTRIAL RELATIONS: THE AMERICAN APPROACH. *Industrial Relations [Canada] 1973 28(1): 34-53.* "The special problems that the MNC presents in the context of the American industrial relations system has led the U.S. unions to respond with a call for controls on trade. Europeans, in a different context, are responding to the integration of Europe and the imposition of some aspects of the U.S. system by U.S. corporations in Europe. The problems of understanding each other's goals will be difficult, but controls on the MNCs could serve both."
J

69. Helleiner, G. K. STRUCTURAL ASPECTS OF THIRD WORLD TRADE: SOME TRENDS AND SOME PROSPECTS. *J. of Development Studies [Great Britain] 1979 15(3): 70-88.* Examines the role of multinational corporations in the economic development of third world nations and the adaptability of the corporation and labor to changing political attitudes, using US data, 1966-75.

70. Helleiner, G. K. TRANSNATIONAL ENTERPRISES AND THE NEW POLITICAL ECONOMY OF U.S. TRADE POLICY. *Oxford Econ. Papers [Great Britain] 1977 29(1): 102-116.* Examines the political influence of transnational enterprises and organized labor on US trade policy, particularly during 1966-74.

71. Hewson, Barbara C. INFLUENCING MULTINATIONAL CORPORATIONS: THE INFANT FORMULA MARKETING CONTROVERSY. *New York U. J. of Int. Law and Pol. 1977 10(1): 125-170.* Alarm over the results of distribution of breastmilk substitutes marketed by US corporations in developing nations, 1970's, poses questions of the possibility of federal regulation of multinationals' foreign activities, the power which shareholders wield in influencing overseas activities, the rights of the host country to regulate advertising, and the authority of the UN Commission on Transnational Corporations to regulate such activity.

72. Hildebrand, George H. PROBLEMS AND POLICIES AFFECTING LABOR'S INTERESTS. *Am. Econ. R. 1974 64(2): 283-288.* Examines the impact of multinational corporations on labor in the world economy.

73. Hoernel, David. LAS GRANDES CORPORACIONES Y LA POLÍTICA DEL GRAN GARROTE EN CUBA Y A MÉXICO [Large corporations and the Big Stick policy in Cuba and Mexico]. *Hist. Mexicana [Mexico] 1980 30(2): 209-246.* During the late 19th century, the interests and overseas activities of many financial and industrial corporations frequently clashed with those of their governments. The rhythm of these clashes affected US policy in Cuba and Mexico. Theodore Roosevelt's Big Stick policy was the fruit of his alliance with financial and industrial groups opposed to the largest trusts. Taft's "Dollar Diplomacy" reflected his effort to restore domestic financial stability by cultivating the largest trusts. Wilson's reaction to the Madero assassination reflected not only moral outrage but the widening rift between the US government and US financial interests allied to German financial interests. Based on documents in the National Archives and secondary works.   F. J. Shaw, Jr.

74. Holland, Daniel M. and Meyers, Stewart C. PROFITABILITY AND CAPITAL COSTS FOR MANUFACTURING CORPORATIONS AND ALL NONFINANCIAL CORPORATIONS. *Am. Econ. Rev. 1980 70(2): 320-325.* Over time, both nonfinancial corporations and manufacturing corporations demonstrate the same behavior with strong activity in the 1960's but weaker performance in the last decade. With the real cost of capital and business risk being stable for most of the postwar years, manufacturing corporations are richer than the larger nonfinancial corporations; however, manufacturing corporations have higher rates of return. Covers 1945-78. 3 tables, 5 ref.   D. K. Pickens

75. Horowitz, Irving Louis. CAPITALISM, COMMUNISM AND MULTI-NATIONALISM. *Society 1974 11(2): 32-43.* Multinational corporations have altered the dimensions of the ideological struggle between capitalism and Communism.   S

76. Horst, Thomas. AMERICAN MULTINATIONALS AND THE U.S. ECONOMY. *Am. Econ. Rev. 1976 66(2): 149-155.* After providing a summary of trade, tax, and antitrust issues, Horst finds that multinational corporations may have competitive advantages over their domestic competitors because their foreign operations might be, not just a cause of, but a solution to the problem of market power. Notes.   D. K. Pickens

77. Howe, Carolyn. MULTINATIONALS AND LABOR UNITY: BOTH SIDES. *Southwest Econ. and Soc. 1978 4(1): 43-74.* Examines theoretical and objective bases for labor solidarity in American-Mexican border areas; discusses multinational corporations and the Mexican Border Industry Program, 1966-78.

78. Hufbauer, G. C. MULTINATIONAL CORPORATIONS AND THE INTERNATIONAL ADJUSTMENT PROCESS. *Am. Econ. R. 1974 64(2): 271-275.* Discusses possible international and national policy responses to structural changes in multinational corporations and in the world economy.

79. Huntington, Samuel P. TRANSNATIONAL ORGANIZATIONS IN WORLD POLITICS. *World Pol. 1973 25(3): 333-368.* Analyzes the great expansion in transnational organizations, their structure, and relations with the nation-state. A transnational organization may be as diverse as the Chase Manhattan Bank and the World Bank, Air France and the Strategic Air Command, the Ford Foundation and the Catholic Church, but each 1) is large and centrally

organized, 2) performs specialized functions, and 3) performs these functions across international boundaries. The strong force of nationalism after 1945 became "identified with political fragmentation," while internationalism as expressed through international cooperation has not been a success. Instead a wholly unanticipated transnationalism—particularly US multinational corporations, disinterested in sovereignty and free of internal political restraints— emerged as a revolutionary force "apart from the existing structure of international relations." 37 notes.   C. W. Olson

80.   Ishikawa, Hirotomo.   THE HIDDEN HAND—MULTINATIONAL CORPORATIONS.   *Japan Q. [Japan] 1976 23(3): 247-254.* The "military-industrial complex" now finds expression in the burgeoning of the multinational corporations. Their "money power" is so great as to be able to influence the fate of nations. This can be seen in relation to US politics during the Richard M. Nixon regime, but also around the world. A major tool in the transfer of huge sums of money are the numerous "tax-havens" they use around the world, secrecy being an important factor in the process, thereby wielding immense power in times of currency crisis. They were strongly behind the movement toward detente, having much to gain. The Japanese "general trading companies" are essentially a Japanese version of the multinational corporation.   R. V. Ritter

81.   Ivanov, I.   KONGLOMERATY V SISTEME FINANSOGO KAPITALA   [Conglomerates within the system of finance capital]. *Mirovaia Ekonomika i Mezhdunarodnye Otnosheniia [USSR] 1977 (5): 46-57.* The rapid development of US and European conglomerates in the last two decades and their decline during 1969-71 and 1974-75 illustrate instability in modern capitalism.

82.   Ivanov, I.   VERKHUSHKA AMERIKANSKOGO CHASTNO-PROMYSHLENNOGO BIZNESA   [The elite of American private industrial enterprise]. *Mirovaia Ekonomika i Mezhdunarodnye Otnosheniia [USSR] 1974 (2): 13-27.* A statistical breakdown and comparative study of the top 100 industrial companies with primary attention to their productivity during 1971-72.

83.   James, Ariel.   LA UNITED FRUIT COMPANY Y LA PENETRA-CIÓN IMPERIALISTA EN EL ÁREA DEL CARIBE   [The United Fruit Company and the imperialist penetration of the Caribbean area]. *Santiago [Cuba] 1974 (15): 69-80.* Examines the origins of the large-scale banana commerce in the United States in the 1870's; the 1899 amalgamation of two groups, incorporated as the United Fruit Company, which monopolized the US market and the Caribbean producing areas; consolidation of the U.F.C. "empire" and expansion through economic and political strategies; neocolonial domination in Central America; and exploitation and development of Cuban markets and contrasts with the Central American experience. Secondary sources; 8 notes.
                                                                      P. J. Taylorson

84.   Johnson, H. Thomas.   MANAGEMENT ACCOUNTING IN AN EARLY INTEGRATED INDUSTRIAL: E. I. DUPONT DE NEMOURS POWDER COMPANY, 1903-1912. *Business Hist. R. 1975 49(2): 184-204.* Studies the development of a modern accounting system at one of the first integrated industrial corporations. Concludes that the system allowed management to better plan future directions and control operations within the main

departments of the company, and that large firms need not necessarily "topple from the weight of internal inefficiency." Based on corporate records and secondary sources; 59 notes.
C. J. Pusateri

85. Karaganov, S. THE SUBVERSIVE ACTIVITIES OF THE MULTINA-TIONALS. *Int. Affairs [USSR] 1976 (10): 50-58.* Examines the many ways in which US-based multinational corporations influence US foreign policy toward developing nations and influence their domestic policy.

86. Karjala, Dennis S. THE BOARD OF DIRECTORS IN ENGLISH AND AMERICAN COMPANIES THROUGH 1920. Horn, Norbert and Kocka, Jürgen, ed. *Recht und Entwicklung der Grossunternehmen im 19. und frühen 20. Jahrhundert* (Göttingen: Vandenhoeck & Ruprecht, 1979): 204-226. Focuses on three basic legal issues in English and US corporate development, 1860-1920: 1) the separation of managerial power between the board of directors and the shareholders; 2) the development of proxies by which management remained in control of the company; and 3) the legal duties of the directors to the corporation and the shareholders and their enforcement. 145 notes, biblio. German summary.
S

87. Karnes, Thomas L. LA STANDARD FRUIT Y LA STEAMSHIP COMPANY EN NICARAGUA (LOS PRIMEROS ANOS) [The Standard Fruit and Steamship Company in Nicaragua (the first years)]. *Anuario de Estudios Centroamericanos [Costa Rica] 1977 3: 175-213.* Standard Fruit started lumber and banana operations in Honduras in 1899. In 1921 it expanded operations into Nicaragua. Here the enterprise during the 1920's and 1930's proved to be unprofitable due to labor recruitment difficulties, inadequate supplies for workers, poor soil, banana diseases, economic instability, and civil wars, including destruction of property by Augusto César Sandino's forces. It was not until the 1970's that the firm, now called United Brands, showed signs of profitability. Based mainly on the archives of the Standard Fruit Co.; 31 notes.
H. J. Miller

88. Keegan, Warren J. MULTINATIONAL SCANNING: A STUDY OF INFORMATION SOURCES UTILIZED BY HEADQUARTERS EXECU-TIVES IN MULTINATIONAL COMPANIES. *Administrative Sci. Q. 1974 19(3): 411-421.* Finds that executives rely on external sources for information about their business environment and use unsystematic methods of information gathering.

89. Kendrick, John W. INCREASING PRODUCTIVITY. *Pro. of the Acad. of Pol. Sci. 1979 33(3): 190-202.* Analyzes the sources of economic growth in the US business economy with special reference to productivity increases, 1948-77. Table.
K. N. T. Crowther

90. Keohane, Robert O. NOT "INNOCENTS ABROAD": AMERICAN MULTINATIONAL CORPORATIONS AND THE UNITED STATES GOV-ERNMENT. *Comparative Pol. 1976 8(2): 307-320.* Reviews Richard J. Barnet and Ronald E. Müller's *Global Reach: The Power of the Multinational Corporations;* Charles T. Goodsell's *American Corporations and Peruvian Politics;* Theodore H. Moran's *Multinational Corporations and the Politics of Dependence: Copper in Chile;* and Mira Wilkins' *The Maturing of Multinational Enterprise:*

American Business Abroad from 1914 to 1970. Barnet and Müller analyze the ideologies of multinational managers, the host government-firm relationship in developing nations, and the problems connected with the takeover of the world productive system by these companies. Wilkins traces the foreign activities of American corporations since World War II, indicating that US businesses have contributed to the economic growth of the host country. Moran discusses the dependency thesis and Goodsell tests the accuracy of the thesis in Peru where American firms participated in national politics. Moran and Goodsell maintain multinational corporations are not taking over the world. Wilkins concludes American business and diplomacy have used each other to gain supremacy. 23 notes.   R. I. Vexler

91. Kindleberger, Charles P. ORIGINS OF UNITED STATES DIRECT INVESTMENT IN FRANCE. *Business Hist. R. 1974 48(3): 382-413.* Reviews the long history of American investments in France. Despite the postwar phenomenon of multinational corporations, US investment in France dates back to the time of Napoleon. Actual multinational concerns are almost as old. Economic penetration proceeded rapidly until 1929. The Great Depression and World War II slowed the movement considerably, and not until the postwar period did a new spurt begin. The present-day American multinational firm is but a natural and logical offspring of the 19th-century variety. Table, 109 notes, appendix.
                                                                        V. L. Human

92. Kirichenko, E. EVOLUTSIIA UPRAVLENIIA ZAGRANICHNOI DEIATEL'NOST'IU AMERIKANSKIKH KOMPANII [Evolution of the management of the foreign economic activity of American companies]. *Mirovaia Ekonomika i Mezhdunarodnye Otnosheniia [USSR] 1978 (12): 33-43.* Outlines the structure of the foreign branches of American companies: their import built-in and export built-in departments, their international divisions and general principles of organization.

93. Kochevrin, Iu. AKTSIONERNAIA SOBSTVENNOST' I KONTROL' V KRUPNOI KORPORATSII [Joint-stock ownership and control in large corporations]. *Mirovaia Ekonomika i Mezhdunarodnye Otnosheniia [USSR] 1978 (5): 42-52.* Analyzes the contemporary stage of development of joint-stock companies and financial capitalism and sees the increased role of managers as not a diminution but a refinement of capitalists' control.

94. Kochevrin, Iu. KORPORATSII, GOSUDARSTVO I RYNOK KAPITALA [Corporations, the state, and the capital market]. *Mirovaia Ekonomika i Mezhdunarodnye Otnosheniia [USSR] 1980 (5): 49-58.* Follows the growth and activities of speculative capital, chiefly in the United States, from the 1960's until the market crisis of 1974-75, when established capital came into its own again and the need to reinforce it became apparent. 2 graphs, 28 notes. English summary.

95. Koenig, Thomas; Gogel, Robert; and Sonquist, John. MODELS OF THE SIGNIFICANCE OF INTERLOCKING CORPORATE DIRECTORATES. *Am. J. of Econ. and Sociol. 1979 38(2): 173-186.* Four different models explaining the significance of the patterns of interlocking directorates in the American economy are delineated and examined to discover a few of the behavioral predic-

tions inherent in each. Empirical tests are employed to examine the general pattern of replacement of interlocking relationships between the largest American firms when ended through the death of an outside director. Another test employed is to examine the stability of interlock patterns over time. From the results it is concluded that interlocking directorates do not generally represent evidence of close interconnections between specific corporations but do connect some stable, city-based groups.

96. Kristol, Irving. CORPORATE CAPITALISM IN AMERICA. *Public Interest 1975 (41): 124-141.* Assesses capitalism and anti-capitalism, and the federal government particularly since 1945.   S

97. Krogh, Harold C. GUARANTEES AGAINST LOSS TO TRANSNA-TIONAL CORPORATIONS. *Ann. of the Am. Acad. of Pol. and Social Sci. 1979 (443): 117-128.* Guarantees and funding to cope with possible losses to transnational corporations, alternatively referred to as multinational corporations, encompass risk management principles, theory, and applications. The paper analyzes the risks faced by multinational corporations in their overseas operations, including credit and political risks; the latter treating of such risks as currency devaluation, expropriation of plants, kidnapping of key executives, and ransom demands. Risks to property valuation receives emphasis, but often risks to persons reflect an intertwine in risk management by transnational enterprises. Various private and public insurance mechanisms are available to meet these problems, and the effects of these approaches on society are examined.   J

98. Kumar, Krishna. MULTINATIONAL CORPORATIONS AND TRANSNATIONAL RELATIONS. *J. of Pol. & Military Sociol. 1979 7(2): 291-304.* Review article illustrating different intellectual contexts of eight social science works on multinational corporations. The liberal-diffusionist school believes that multinational corporations facilitate the development of the maximum use of scarce human and material resources. A second school treats the multinationals as imperialistic and undesirable while a third neo-mercantilist school argues that multinational corporations are best "understood with reference to the complex interplay of national interests on the world scene." The decline of US leadership has fostered economic nationalism and regionalism which will in turn affect the growth of the multinationals.   S

99. Lall, Sanjaya. TRANSFER-PRICING AND MULTINATIONAL CORPORATIONS. *Monthly R. 1974 26(7): 36-45.* Examines issues and data on transfer-pricing of commodity trade by multinational manufacturing corporations.

100. LaMont, Howard. MULTINATIONAL ENTERPRISE, TRANSFER PRICING, AND THE 482 MESS. *Columbia J. of Transnat. Law 1975 14(3): 383-433.* Discusses issues evolving from the application of Section 482 of the Internal Revenue Code to transfer price determinations of multinational corporations in the 1960's-70's, emphasizing tax administration.

101. Lawrie, Robert F. C. CORPORATE FREEZEOUTS: A COMPARI-SON OF CONTROLS IN THE UNITED STATES AND ENGLAND. *New York U. J. of Int. Law and Pol. 1982 14(3): 595-641.* Compares US and British approaches to corporate freezeouts, "the expropriation of a minority

shareholding by a majority in exchange for cash" or stocks to exclude the minority from further participation in reorganized corporations, and suggests that the United States might benefit from incorporating British methods.

102.   Leacock, Ruth.   JFK, BUSINESS, AND BRAZIL.   *Hispanic Am. Hist. Rev. 1979 59(4): 636-673.* President John F. Kennedy's Alliance for Progress was launched without business support on the assumption that the Communist threat would come from the poor in Latin America. When leftist João Goulart became president of Brazil, this policy began to change. The expropriation of an ITT subsidiary by the Brazilian state of Rio Grande do Sul, the suggested nationalization of AMFORP, which wished to sell to Brazil, and Brazil's attempts to control iron properties of Hanna Mining Corporation were regarded as Communistic, anti-United States moves. The Kennedy administration became more business-oriented in its dealings with Brazil. US businessmen and the CIA played a financial part in the 1962 elections in Brazil in an attempt to overthrow Goulart. The roles of US Ambassador Lincoln Gordon and ITT president Harold S. Geneen are discussed. 128 notes.   B. D. Johnson

103.   Leathers, Charles G. and Evans, John S.   VEBLEN'S IDEAL AND THE CONTEMPORARY U.S. ECONOMY: A CONTRAST.   *Am. J. of Econ. and Sociol. 1974 33(4): 409-415.* Refutes the assertion that the power structure of the modern corporate state is identical to Thorstein Veblen's "soviet of technicians" by examining differences in production practices and consumption goals. Two views of the modern corporate state are discussed: John Kenneth Galbraith's "technostructure" and Jay M. Gould's "technical elite." Based on secondary sources; 18 notes.   W. L. Marr

104.   Lekachman, Robert.   AMERICAN BUSINESS THEN AND NOW. Frese, Joseph R. and Judd, Jacob, ed. *An Emerging Independent American Economy 1815-1875* (Tarrytown, N.Y.: Sleepy Hollow Pr., 1980): 180-194. A comparative study of the role and nature of business and business leaders since 1850. In the 19th century, businessmen were more important than the government, faced no powerful opposition, and were looked upon as heroes and models to emulate. That all has passed; no recent list of great men includes a captain of industry. Yet the power remains, though it is definitely eroding. 6 notes.
                                                                    V. L. Human

105.   Leonard, H. Jeffrey.   MULTINATIONAL CORPORATIONS AND POLITICS IN DEVELOPING COUNTRIES.   *World Pol. 1980 32(3): 454-483.* Review article on the activities of multinational corporations (MNC's), focusing on the domestic political system, in individual host countries. Taken together, these studies indicate that MNC impact on politics in developing nations depends on the particular political circumstances in each country. Key domestic political actors often do not behave as predicted by either liberal or Marxist world models, but are of fundamental importance.   J/S

106.   Levitt, Theodore.   MANAGEMENT AND THE "POST-INDUS-TRIAL" SOCIETY.   *Public Interest 1976 (44): 69-103.* The post-industrial society is one that has shifted from a production to a service economy. Its main problem is that of becoming as productive as the manufacturing economy of the 19th century. The key to the solution is management, which was responsible for

the success of the industrial age by directing, organizing, and managing the use of scientific knowledge, inventions, and machines. So many service industries are sluggish today because of the absence of industrial modes of managerial thought. Businesses in the service sector that have made good use of management include McDonald's hamburger outlets, Transamerica Title Insurance Corporation, and the Building Controls and Components Group of Honeywell, Inc. Management is also crucial for efficient government operations.   S. Harrow

107.   Lipson, Charles H.   CORPORATE PREFERENCES AND PUBLIC POLICIES: FOREIGN AID SANCTIONS AND INVESTMENT PROTEC-TION.   *World Pol. 1976 28(3): 396-421.* Since 1959 Congress has tried to protect U.S. direct foreign investments from expropriation by quite explicit amendments to various foreign assistance acts. Probably the most important of these legislative efforts, the Hickenlooper amendment, the Gonzales amend-ments, and the effective repeal of the Hickenlooper amendment, are contradictory and have been applied only sporadically. By developing testable hypotheses that can accurately and parsimoniously predict these varied legislative and diplomatic policies, this article attempts to demonstrate the value of a radical analysis of American foreign policy. After those hypotheses are evaluated, they are com-pared with propositions derived from pluralist and bureaucratic analysis. Finally, the policy history is reconsidered to show that changes in the external environ-ment, particularly the rise of economically powerful nationalist regimes, have led to a significant evolution in the policy preferences of large multinational firms.
                                                                                                             J

108.   Little, Douglas J.   TWENTY YEARS OF TURMOIL: ITT, THE STATE DEPARTMENT, AND SPAIN, 1924-1944.   *Business Hist. Rev. 1979 53(4): 449-472.* Previous writers on American multinational corporations have underestimated the important role of the US government in protecting overseas business operations. The history of the International Telephone and Telegraph Corporation (ITT) in Spain illustrates this governmental role, because ITT's ability to survive the successive Spanish governmental upheavals in the 1930's depended in large part on the mediating efforts of the US State Department. Specifically, only threats of rejecting Spain's application for Export-Import Bank credit by the State Department forced Franco to renew ITT's franchise in 1939 rather than turn it over to Nazi interests. Based largely on State Department records in the National Archives; 65 notes.   C. J. Pusateri

109.   Loehr, William and Satish, Raichur.   A DECADE OF UNITED STATES INVESTMENT ACTIVITY IN AFRICA: IMPLICATIONS FOR ECONOMIC DEVELOPMENT.   *Africa Today 1973 20(1): 45-58.* American investment in Africa focuses on the extractive industries and receives high return relative to investment elsewhere, yet the result is little spillover into local markets and the creation of technocratic enclaves. American investment must be directed to indigenous infrastructure and local markets. Based on Department of Com-merce documents and secondary sources; 4 tables, 18 notes.   G. O. Gagnon

110.   Lovett, Robert W.   BUSINESS MANUSCRIPTS AT BAKER LI-BRARY, 1969-1979.   *Business Hist. Rev. 1979 53(3): 386-391.* In December 1978 the Manuscripts Division of the Harvard Business School's Baker Library published the fourth edition of its collection guide, *Manuscripts in Baker Library:*

A Guide to Sources for Business, Economic, and Social History. The volume lists the more than 1400 holdings, 100 added since the guide's third edition in 1969. The only generalization about the newest additions is that they deal mainly with New England business and businessmen. 2 notes.   C. J. Pusateri

111.   Magdoff, Harry and Sweezy, Paul, eds.   CAPITAL SHORTAGE: FACT AND FANCY. *Monthly Rev. 1976 27(11): 1-19.* Analyzes the failure of American capitalism to effectively develop capital expansion, and suggests that the underlying problem is capitalism itself. Though the productive capacity of the United States is enormous (and grossly underutilized), corporate spokesmen claim that capital expansion can occur only at the expense of consumer spending. Once again, monopoly capitalism is attempting to correct its inherent weaknesses at popular expense.   M. R. Yerburgh

112.   Malecki, Edward J.   LOCATIONAL TRENDS IN R&D BY LARGE U.S. CORPORATIONS, 1965-1977. *Econ. Geography 1979 55(4): 309-323.* Examines the locational trends of research and development firms during 1965-77 and finds that the firms tend to locate away from large city regions.

113.   Mansfield, Edwin and Wagner, Samuel.   ORGANIZATIONAL AND STRATEGIC FACTORS ASSOCIATED WITH PROBABILITIES OF SUCCESS IN INDUSTRIAL R & D. *J. of Business 1975 48(2): 179-198.* Intrafirm barriers retard technological change. The rates of technical completion, commercialization, and economic success for projects derived from research and development departments of 20 firms showed wide variation. Closer integration of research and development with the marketing department and quantitative project selection methods encouraged earlier study of profit potentials and higher commercialization rates. However, quantitative selection discouraged technologically ambitious projects and resulted in a smaller overall profit. Primary and secondary sources; 7 tables, 20 notes.   J. W. Williams

114.   Mansfield, Edwin and Romeo, Anthony.   TECHNOLOGY TRANSFER TO OVERSEAS SUBSIDIARIES BY U.S.-BASED FIRMS. *Q. J. of Econ. 1980 95(4): 737-750.* Sheds light on the controversy over the transfer of technology by US-based firms by studying the nature of the technology being transferred, its rate of leakage to non-US competitors, the extent to which it benefits non-US users and suppliers, and the characteristics of the non-US firms that are most affected by it.

115.   Marris, Robin and Mueller, Dennis C.   THE CORPORATION, COMPETITION, AND THE INVISIBLE HAND. *J. of Econ. Literature 1980 18(1): 32-63.* A vast body of new literature has emerged on the implications of the invisible hand in the United States which is more consistent with empirical evidence than neoclassical economic theory.

116.   Martins, Luciano.   LA POLÍTICA DE LAS CORPORACIONES MULTINACIONALES NORTEAMERICANOS EN AMÉRICA LATINA [The policy of American multinational corporations in Latin America]. *Rev. Mexicana de Ciencia Pol. [Mexico] 1973 19(72): 39-63.* If, as V. I. Lenin said, imperialism is the last step of capitalism, then the multinational expansion into Latin America is an expression of the imperialistic designs of the United States.

117. McAlmon, George. AMERICAN MANUFACTURERS ARE LOS-ING WORLD MARKETS. *Center Mag. 1979 12(6): 8-12.* Discusses the decline in the quantity and quality of US products in the face of increased competition from superior technology and engineering from West Germany and Japan; 1970's.

118. McCrea, Joan M. CAPITALISM AND THE BUSINESS WORLD TODAY. *Rocky Mountain Social Sci. J. 1974 11(2): 113-119.* Reviews seven books on multinational corporations in the 20th century.

119. McCurdy, Charles W. AMERICAN LAW AND THE MARKETING STRUCTURE OF THE LARGE CORPORATION, 1875-1890. *J. of Econ. Hist. 1978 38(3): 631-649.* This paper employs the techniques of legal history to explore the relationship between the rise of big business and the size of the American market. It emphasizes law as a determinant of market size, and it analyzes judicial construction of the Constitution's commerce clause over time to delineate the role of integrated corporations in generating legal change. Specifically, the paper suggests that if the American market is defined as a free-trade unit, enlargement of the market was a result of, rather than a prerequisite for, the post-Civil War revolution in business organization.   J

120. McQuaid, Kim. BIG BUSINESS AND PUBLIC POLICY IN CONTEMPORARY UNITED STATES. *Q. Rev. of Econ. and Business 1980 20(2): 57-68.* The Business Roundtable was an alliance composed of the chief executive officers of the largest US companies, corporate lawyers, and construction contractors who were originally interested in weakening labor unions. Under the leadership of the March Group—created by John Harper and Fred Borch, chairmen, respectively, of Alcoa and General Electric—their focus changed to one of improving the status of business with the public, Congress, and the civil service. This new quasipublic role on the part of business leadership indicated both the coming of political age of executives and the symbiosis of government and business. 14 notes, 28 ref.   S

121. McQuaid, Kim. CORPORATE LIBERALISM IN THE AMERICAN BUSINESS COMMUNITY, 1920-1940. *Business Hist. Rev. 1978 52(3): 342-368.* Traces the activities of "corporate liberals," businessmen who favored an enlightened partnership among themselves, government, and organized labor, from World War I through the Great Depression. Disappointed with the abrupt ending of Wilson's wartime economic planning agencies, they turned to programs of welfare capitalism, efficiency, and employee representation plans. The presentation of the Swope Plan, authored by General Electric's Gerard Swope, signalled a new impetus for corporate liberalism in the early 1930's, which then promptly went into decline in the latter half of the decade. The coming of World War II, however, provided a fresh opportunity for the corporate liberals who flocked into the new war production agencies and gained renewed influence. Archival materials and government records; 47 notes.   C. J. Pusateri

122. Miller, Arthur S. THE AMERICAN ECONOMIC CONSTITUTION. *Center Mag. 1982 15(4): 18-37.* Discusses the growth of corporate power as a natural extension of the Founding Fathers' ideal of governmental control by the propertied, powerful classes and the corporations' ability to control the lives of Americans in ways that are undemocratic.

123. Moberg, David. RETOOLING THE INDUSTRIAL DEBATE. *Working Papers for a New Soc. 1980 7(6): 32-39.* Discusses the reindustrialization approach to sagging industry in the United States, characterized by less government intervention, less influence by outsiders such as environmentalists, consumerists, and trade unions on business directions, and more tax breaks, and the corporatist approach which is another way of increasing corporate power, and considers the response by the Left to corporate control during 1945-80.

124. Moran, Theodore H. FOREIGN EXPANSION AS AN "INSTITUTIONAL NECESSITY" FOR U.S. CORPORATE CAPITALISM: THE SEARCH FOR A RADICAL MODEL. *World Pol. 1973 25(3): 369-386.* Examines the reasons US multinational corporations continue direct foreign capital investment and why this is considered vital to corporate strategies past, present, and future. The pressure for making and keeping foreign investments is much stronger than neoclassical or neo-Marxist economists believe or the models of surplus capital demonstrate. American capitalism with its "tightly held technology, uncertain information, large economies of scale, and unstable imperfect competition," creates these pressures which lead even the largest and most advanced corporations to defend themselves against competition by investing abroad. Based on a paper presented to the Harvard Faculty Seminar on International Inequality, March 1972; 4 tables, graph, 30 notes.   C. W. Olson

125. Moran, Theodore H. MULTINATIONAL CORPORATIONS AND THE POLITICAL ECONOMY OF U.S.-EUROPEAN RELATIONS. *J. of Int. Affairs 1976 30(1): 65-79.* As a prelude to moving out of US hegemony, the European Economic Community countries have tried to avoid economic and technological dependence on the United States, as reflected in the activities of the multinational corporations, but they do not suggest the growth of a cohesive, confident, self-reliant Europe. 37 notes.   V. Samaraweera

126. Morano, Louis. MULTINATIONALS AND NATION-STATES: THE CASE OF ARAMCO. *Orbis 1979 23(2): 447-470.* Examines the Arabian-American Oil Company (ARAMCO), until 1972 wholly owned by four giant American oil companies, and its relations with the Saudi Arabian state. Traces the development of the triangular relationships between ARAMCO, Saudi Arabia, and the United States and the changes in the structure of the world oil industry. After 1972, Saudi Arabia had a 25% ownership which was to gradually increase to control by 1983, but situations have already developed in which ARAMCO has been almost defenseless against Saudi demands. 29 notes.
R. V. Ritter

127. Mueller, Willard F. THE FOOD CONGLOMERATES. *Pro. of the Acad. of Pol. Sci. 1982 34(3): 54-67.* Discusses the role of mergers, the nature of conglomerate power, strategies of reciprocal selling, conglomerates and labor relations, and state and federal controls. When an industry is dominated by powerful conglomerates, the only sources of effective entry are conglomerates in other industries. 8 notes.   T. P. Richardson

128. Nader, Ralph; Green, Mark; and Seligman, Joel. THE MYTH OF CORPORATE DEMOCRACY. *Washington Monthly 1976 8(5-6): 54-61.* Corporations are not governed democratically by their shareholders, but are run by

bureaucratic managers who take advantage of and often violate lenient state corporate laws, compensate themselves with high salaries and pensions, and are often inefficient in their autocratic management.

129. Nash, Gerald D. KEEPING BUSINESS HONEST. *Rev. in Am. Hist. 1981 9(2): 201-205.* Review essay of Saul Engelbourg's *Power and Morality: American Business Ethics, 1840-1914* (1980).

130. Nelson, Daniel. FIFTH COLUMN AT CANANEA: A STOCK-HOLDER CIRCUMVENTS COLONEL W. C. GREENE. *J. of Arizona Hist. 1979 20(1): 47-64.* Describes economist-financier Frederick Winslow Taylor's efforts to penetrate the financial operations of Colonel William Cornell Greene's Greene Consolidated Copper, located in Cananea, Sonora, Mexico. Greene, in New York City, met with Taylor, a highly established financial consultant. From his investigation of the market, Taylor began buying large blocks of Greene Consolidated Copper stock, eventually placing Atherton B. Wadleigh, a mechanical engineer, in a financial position in the Cananea operations in Mexico. Wadleigh gave private reports to Taylor who used the information, which often differed from that released by Greene. The efforts of Taylor and Greene to operate the works independently of the rival Amalgamated Copper Company were relatively short-lived, because, in 1907, Thomas F. Cole from Amalgamated negotiated a merger which saw the demise of Greene's holdings. Greene fell from notoriety, but Taylor later became known as the promoter of scientific management. 4 photos, 35 notes. K. E. Gilmont

131. Nye, Joseph S., Jr. MULTINATIONAL CORPORATIONS IN WORLD POLITICS. *Foreign Affairs 1974 53(1): 153-175.* Multinational corporations have become important factors in world politics by carrying out three roles: 1) the direct role through private foreign policy, e.g. ITT in Chile and United Fruit in Guatemala, 2) an unintended direct role as instruments of influence e.g. Polaroid in South Africa and the one-third of Canadian companies that are foreign-owned, and 3) indirect roles by setting the agenda for interstate politics, e.g. International Petroleum Corporation and Peru, the "tail that wagged the dog of American policy there." The multinational and the nation-state will continue to exist in "uneasy tension." 15 notes. C. W. Olson

132. Olson, Richard Stuart. ECONOMIC COERCION IN INTERNATIONAL DISPUTES: THE UNITED STATES AND PERU IN THE IPC EXPROPRIATION DISPUTE OF 1968-1971. *J. of Developing Areas 1975 9(3): 395-413.* When President Belaúnde of Peru in 1968 agreed to compensate the American-owned International Petroleum Company (subsidiary of the Standard Oil Company of New Jersey), the military exiled him to Argentina, expropriated all IPC holdings, and declared that no compensation would be paid for seized oil fields. Controlling 80% of Peru's domestic petroleum market at the time of the seizure, IPC had previously been accused of tax evasion and intervention in internal politics. Under Belaúnde's compromise, IPC would have ceded its subsoil claims to the state in return for absolution of all past debts, taxes, and claims against the company. The 1962 Hickenlooper Amendment (under which the US President could cut off aid to a country that expropriated American-owned property without reaching a compensation agreement within six months) was applied to a limited extent, limited because US interests own most of Peru's

copper and there was fear that they would also be expropriated. Indirect sanctions were more effective since the perpetrator could not so easily be identified. Other expropriations were made by the military government of General Velasco but fair compensation was usually paid. Developing nations are vulnerable to several direct and indirect economic sanctions which encourage them to work within the Western capitalistic system. 3 tables, 3 figs., 44 notes.   O. W. Eads, Jr.

133.   Orr, Dale.   THE DETERMINANTS OF ENTRY: A STUDY OF THE CANADIAN MANUFACTURING INDUSTRIES.   *R. of Econ. and Statistics 1974 56(1): 58-66.* Examines economic factors affecting the expansion of US industries into Canada.   S

134.   Ovinnikov, R. S.   TRANSNATSIONAL'NYE MONOPOLII I ISTORI-CHESKII PROTSESS   [The transnational monopolies and historical process]. *Novaia i Noveishaia Istoriia [USSR] 1979 (5): 14-29.* Analyzes the peculiarities of the emergence and functioning of the most gigantic corporations ever known —the transnational monopolies. The author shows how the transnationals, outgrowing the boundaries of their own countries, have become the direct owners of enterprises abroad. At the same time, they are particularly national companies, for they are pumping out profits to the advantage of the mother group, which is controlled by the capital of only one country. Hence the policy aimed at strangling the economies of other countries, and, above all, of the developing ones.   J

135.   Priest, George L.   CARTELS AND PATENT LICENSE ARRANGE-MENTS.   *J. of Law and Econ. 1977 20(2): 309-377.* Patent license arrangements can be in violation of the Sherman Act. Proposes new methods for determining the competitive effect of unilateral patent licensing and cross-licensing. Provides examples of US cartels. Primary and secondary sources; 251 notes.
                                                        C. B. Fitzgerald

136.   Priest, T. B.   EDUCATION AND CAREER AMONG CORPORATE CHIEF EXECUTIVE OFFICERS: A HISTORICAL NOTE.   *Social Sci. Q. 1982 63(2): 342-349.* "Examines educational characteristics and career patterns" of the chief executives from approximately 100 American corporations during 1940, 1955, and 1970.

137.   Pursell, Carroll W., Jr.   TESTING A CARRIAGE: THE "AMERICAN INDUSTRY" SERIES OF SCIENTIFIC AMERICAN.   *Technology and Culture 1976 17(1): 82-92.* From January 1879 to March 1883 *Scientific American* ran a series of articles on "American Industry," with the intention of presenting "a concise and intelligent description of the leading industries of this continent." Because of their profuse illustrations, the articles are particularly useful to the study of the history of technology in the 19th century. Lists 87 of the illustrations with the name and location of the firm, the products, and the issue in which each appeared. Illus., table, 4 notes.   S

138.   Ray, Edward John.   FOREIGN DIRECT INVESTMENT IN MANU-FACTURING.   *J. of Pol. Econ. 1977 85(2): 283-297.* Presents a simple model, based on profit-maximizing behavior, that can be used to derive estimable equations for U.S. foreign direct investment in manufacturing. Estimation of foreign-investment equations requires estimates of production functions for U.S.

manufacturing subsidiaries abroad. Specifically, estimates the production function to be a constant-returns-to-scale homogeneous, transcendental logarithmic function. Also presents evidence in the form of an estimated foreign-direct-investment equation that domestic and foreign markets may be imperfectly competitive.   J

139. Riner, Reed D.   THE SUPRANATIONAL NETWORK OF BOARDS OF DIRECTORS.   *Current Anthrop. 1981 22(2): 167-172.* Discusses the interlocking effect when an individual serves simultaneously as a member on two or more governing boards of large corporations and other agencies, traces the evolution of this phenomenon since the 16th century, and notes its persistence, adaptivity, and integrative effects.

140. Ruben,   George.   INDUSTRIAL   RELATIONS   IN   1980   INFLUENCED BY INFLATION AND RECESSION.   *Monthly Labor Rev. 1981 104(1): 15-20.* Review of industrial relations in 1980, focusing on large losses by General Motors, Ford, Chrysler, and American Motors, and United States Steel, the companies' turn to the government and the United Auto Workers for help, collective bargaining, internal union affairs, the truce between J. P. Stevens & Co. and the Clothing and Textile Workers after a 17-year battle, and union wage increases.

141. Russett, Bruce M.   TESTING SOME THEORIES ABOUT AMERICAN FOREIGN POLICY.   *Bull. of Peace Proposals [Norway] 1975 6(1): 85-93.* Suggests the need to develop new kinds of evidence to support theories of American foreign policy. By studying the attitudes and preference of high-level executives of major corporations, evidence from the price of stocks, and finally the business and financial press, a better understanding of American foreign policy is possible. Secondary sources; 2 notes, references.   R. B. Orr

142. Schulz, Ann T.   THE MULTINATIONAL ILLUSION: THE FOREIGN POLICY ACTIVITIES OF US BUSINESS IN THE MIDDLE EAST.   *Studies in Comparative Int. Development 1979 14(3-4): 127-144.* Analyzes the activities of managers of US corporations in Egypt, Iran, and Saudi Arabia. In attempting to further their corporations' goals, managers function as diplomats without portfolio. This occurs because host governments rather than businessmen make key investment decisions. Both formal and informal information and communication networks are functioning. The importance of these corporate networks should not be overlooked, as they have a significant impact on diplomatic activity, with the input influencing the foreign policy of states. Suggested research should shed more light on corporate activities and influences. Secondary sources; 10 notes, 15 ref.   S. A. Farmerie

143. Seidman, Ann and Seidman, Neva.   UNITED STATES MULTINATIONALS IN SOUTH AFRICA.   *J. of Southern African Affairs 1976 1(special issue): 125-166.* A handful of the biggest firms in the United States have provided over three-fourths of US investments in South Africa. They are linked with each other, as well as with most of the nearly 400 other US companies which have invested in South Africa, through their boards of directors. Together, these firms comprised the growing economic interest which, even when it was smaller, apparently helped to convince the US National Security Council that in 1969 the US

government should maintain cordial relations with the South African government. It was these interests which Secretary of State Henry Kissinger was seeking to protect by his shuttle-diplomacy, designed to prevent major upheavals in South Africa. Secondary sources; 5 tables, 53 notes.   A. W. Howell

144. Selden, Mark. GLOBAL ENTERPRISE: THE AMERICAN RECORD IN ASIA. *Peace and Change 1976 4(1): 20-33.* Discusses the role of US multinational corporations in Asia, particularly Japan, the Philippines, and Indonesia, 1960's-70's.

145. Sharman, Ben. A TRADE UNIONIST VIEW OF MULTINATIONAL CORPORATIONS. *WorldView 1975 18(11): 31-35.* Discusses employee-employer relations and labor unions' views toward multinational corporations in the 1970's, including wages and job security.

146. Sklar, Richard L. POSTIMPERIALISM: A CLASS ANALYSIS OF MULTINATIONAL CORPORATE EXPANSION. *Comparative Pol. 1976 9(1): 75-92.* Examines the 20th-century development of corporate power in modern industrial society, considering the effect of economic oligarchy, managerial authority, and class formation on the rise of multinational corporations; examines recent works on economic development in nonindustrial societies.

147. Sonnichsen, C. L. PANCHO VILLA AND THE CANANEA COPPER COMPANY. *J. of Arizona Hist. 1979 20(1): 87-100.* An account of Pancho Villa's demands for money and supplies during November 1915 in Sonora, Mexico, from the Cananea Copper Co. Negotiations involved Cananea officials F. D. Hamilton, George Young, and Dr. L. D. Ricketts. Meetings were held concerning Villa's requests and the erroneous report that four individuals—Chief Surgeon Rembert H. Thigpen, Dr. Charles H. Miller, and two chauffeurs—were killed by Villa's men. Through various talks, the fate of the four was discussed, and their captivity was altered from murder to escape. Villa left the area after receiving $7500 in American money and bullion valued at $340,000. The Cananea Copper Company received partial claims from the Mexican government and Villa never threatened it again. 6 photos, notes.   K. E. Gilmont

148. Stevenson, Paul. THE MILITARY-INDUSTRIAL COMPLEX: AN EXAMINATION OF THE NATURE OF CORPORATE CAPITALISM IN AMERICA. *J. of Pol. and Military Sociol. 1973 1(2): 247-260.* "This article examines the role of military spending in the American economy. Such spending is viewed as being profitable for America's largest businesses and crucial to the maintenance of aggregate demand at home. Underlying this particular role of military spending the article notes that the American economy is a monopoly capitalist one with extensive economic interests abroad. Military spending is viewed as a defense of such foreign economic interests. Empirical evidence is offered to support the contention that contemporary capitalist economies depend upon military spending for their prosperity and viability. The arguments for conversion within a capitalist framework are critically examined."   J

149. Strauss, Norman. RISE OF AMERICAN GROWTH IN BRAZIL: DECADE OF THE 1870'S. *Americas: Q. Rev. of Inter-American Cultural Hist. 1976 32(3): 437-444.* During the 1870's US activities in streetcar and railway construction, scientific exploration, and commerce, as well as improve-

ment of direct steamship connections, all gave evidence of an increasing challenge to British economic predominance in Brazil. Based mainly on State Department dispatches; 37 notes. D. Bushnell

150. Sweezy, Paul M. MULTINATIONAL CORPORATIONS AND BANKS. *Monthly Rev. 1978 29(8): 1-9.* Although the capitalist system has always been global, multinational corporations have increased in size and number since the end of World War II, causing increased vulnerability to global economic problems, generating inflation and creating expanded debt which, in the event of default by a borrowing country, could precipitate an international economic crisis of enormous proportions.

151. Taira, Koji and Standing, Guy. MNCS: THE SIXTH SUPERPOWER. *Worldview 1974 17(2): 17-24.* Discusses the influence of US multinational corporations on the international economy, foreign relations, and domestic labor unions in the 1970's, including General Motors and International Telephone and Telegraph.

152. Tkachenko, A. MALYI BIZNES SSHA V MEZHDUNARODNYKH NAUCHNO-TEKHNICHESKIKH SVIAZIAKH [Small business in the United States and its international scientific and technical connections]. *Mirovaia Ekonomika i Mezhdunarodnye Otnosheniia [USSR] 1978 (11): 109-117.* Stresses the importance of technological innovation to small business in the United States in its struggle to compete with the big monopolies and examines the changes in the size and distribution of expenditure on industrial research during the 1960's-70's.

153. Tkachenko, A. SVIAZI MONOPOLISTICHESKOGO KAPITALA S MELKIM I SREDNIM BIZNESOM [Monopoly capital: its relation to small and medium businesses]. *Mirovaia Ekonomika i Mezhdunarodnye Otnosheniia [USSR] 1982 (8): 56-64.* Notes the increasing cooperation between large corporations and small businesses in the areas of research and development, the venture capital market, and business contracts during 1975-82. Russian.

154. Townshend, Harry. SIX STUDIES OF INDUSTRIAL ORGANISATION. *Scottish J. of Pol. Econ. [Great Britain] 1973 20(1): 75-79.* Reviews books by Lawrence J. White, C. K. Rowley, J. B. Heath, C. F. Pratten, Ajit Singh, and David Coombes. J. D. Neville

155. Unsigned. TOWARD A FULLY SELF-MANAGED INDUSTRIAL SECTOR IN THE UNITED STATES. *Administration and Soc. 1975 7(1): 85-106.* "The purpose of this study is to make a step in the direction of full implementation of self-management in this country." From a study by the Cornell Self-management Working Group. S

156. Vakhrushev, V. V. TRANSNATSIONAL'NYE KORPORATSII I BOR'BA RAZVIVAIUSHCHIKHSIA STRAN PROTIV IKH EKSPANSII [Transnational corporations and the struggle of developing nations against their expansion]. *Narody Azii i Afriki [USSR] 1979 (2): 3-15.* Studies effects of investments by multinational corporations in developing nations, quoting UN data. The corporations, especially the American-owned ones, became particularly powerful in the 1970's. Table, 51 notes. V. A. Packer

157. Väryrnen, Raimo. TRANSNATIONAL CORPORATIONS IN THE MILITARY SECTOR OF SOUTH AFRICA. *J. of Southern African Affairs 1980 5(2): 199-255.* A detailed survey of the involvement of multinational corporations in the military sector of South Africa's political economy since 1960. South Africa has long welcomed foreign investments and technical expertise in its production of military and strategic goods, with emphasis during the 1970's on indigenizing this production. This process has involved large numbers of major Western firms and their South African subsidiaries, including many not directly related to munitions production, such as mining and electronics companies and banks. Based on published company and official reports, newspapers, and secondary sources; 204 notes.   L. W. Truschel

158. Vernon, Raymond. COMPETITION POLICY TOWARD MULTINATIONAL CORPORATIONS. *Am. Econ. R. 1974 64(2): 276-282.* Describes the development of international oligopolies since 1945, and discusses the policies of various nations to promote economic competition.

159. Vernon, Raymond; Barnet, Richard J.; and Müller, Ronald. AN EXCHANGE ON MULTINATIONALS. *Foreign Policy 1974 (15): 83-92.* Discusses the international impact of multinational corporations.   S

160. Vernon, Raymond. THE MULTINATIONAL ENTERPRISE AS SYMBOL. *Worldview 1977 20(5): 37-43.* Multinational corporations grow as progress in technology promotes a more global perspective; mentions economic hegemony, economic dependency, and potential threats to the autonomy of the nation-state.

161. Vernon, Raymond. THE MULTINATIONALS: NO STRINGS ATTACHED. *Foreign Policy 1978-79 (33): 121-134.* Confusing and contradictory US policies toward multinational corporations are based on the desire of the United States, like other governments, to seize full advantage of such corporations' dual status. Overseas subsidiaries are expected to receive the rights of nationals in the host country while retaining the special privileges due them as foreign enterprises. Jurisdictional controversy over control of these businesses will plague international relations until a new set of institutions is created at the international level to deal with the entire range of government-business relationships.   T. L. Powers

162. Vernon, Raymond. STORM OVER THE MULTINATIONALS: PROBLEMS AND PROSPECTS. *Foreign Affairs 1977 55(2): 253-262.* Many of the so-called ills of multinational enterprise are actually the effects of a "shrinking world space" caused by technological advances. With the exception of some UN and European efforts, governments have reacted trivially. National jurisdictions must first be untangled; afterwards, cooperation seems more feasible among industrial countries than between industrial and developing nations. Nations have become more interdependent, but their bargaining power against multinational corporations also has increased. Adapted from the author's forthcoming *Storm over the Multinationals: the Real Issues* (Cambridge: Harvard U. Pr.); 6 notes.
                                                    W. R. Hively

163. Vogel, David. THE CORPORATION AS GOVERNMENT: CHALLENGES & DILEMMAS. *Polity 1975 8(1): 5-37.* Professor Vogel's article is an introduction to the literature of the business corporation as government and a valuable analysis of the problem itself—the publicness of the corporation and the legitimacy and accountability of its government. His essay indicates both the impact of the contemporary counter-corporate movement and its limits, inherent in working within populist ideas. When people think of the business corporation as a public institution rather than a private one, there are consequences, he suggests, but whether the effects have been or are likely to be really basic concerning who wields power and for what ends is more doubtful.   J

164. Vogel, David. THE RESPONSIBILITIES OF MULTINATIONAL CORPORATIONS. *Society 1979 16(3): 52-56.* Criticizes the activities of multinational corporations since the mid-1960's and discusses the need for corporations to accept responsibility for their behavior and effects in society.

165. Vojnović, Milan. TRANSNACIONALNE KOMPANIJE I KAPITALISTIČKE INDUSTRIJSKE ZEMLJE [The multinational corporations and the capitalist industrial countries]. *Medjunarodni Problemi [Yugoslavia] 1976 28(2): 69-91.* Considers how the Western industrial nations have attracted more foreign investment than the developing nations, ca. 1960-75, and discusses the way in which the multinational corporations have become the principal agents in the internationalization of the American economy.

166. Volkov, O. PERENAKOPLENIE KAPITALA I VNESHNEE'-KONOMICHESKAIA E'KSPANSIIA MONOPOLII SSHA [Excessive capital accumulation and the external economic expansion of the US monopolies]. *Mirovaia Ekonomika i Mezhdunarodnye Otnosheniia [USSR] 1978 (3): 37-48.* The export of capital instead of products and the growth of multinational corporations in the United States is a result of excessive concentration of capital and leads to a further intensification of the general crisis of capitalism.

167. Ward, Sally K. ECONOMIC OWNERSHIP IN U.S. COMMUNITIES: CORPORATE CHANGE, 1961-75. *Social Sci. Q. 1981 62(1): 139-150.* Absentee ownership of economic institutions in US communities has greater economic implications than presently understood. The author used the absentee ownership data from a 1961 survey by *Fortune* that presents specific ownership patterns for the 500 largest industrial corporations. Secondary sources; 2 tables, 37 notes.
                    M. Mtewa

168. Weidenbaum, Murray and Rockwood, Linda. CORPORATE PLANNING VERSUS GOVERNMENT PLANNING. *Public Interest 1977 (46): 59-72.* Corporate planning and government planning are fundamentally different. The former attempts to forecast and react to the future. The latter tries to regulate and control it. Further, the onus of failure in corporate planning falls on the company and its shareholders, while the taxpayer and the consumer bear the brunt of an error in government planning. It is difficult to find an unambiguous example of a successful business planning operation, but the government experience is more negative than that of the private sector. Major federal decisions at the peak of enthusiasm for the Planning-Programming-Budgeting System, established in 1965, were deeper involvement in Vietnam and the overpromotion of

the Great Society domestic programs. Government planning can be internally oriented toward the management of its own affairs, or it can be external, involving government powers over the private sectors of the economy. The former is entirely proper; the latter is a matter of debate. 2 notes.   S. Harrow

169. Wells, Gilbert M. and Wells, Allen. INTERNATIONAL HAR-VESTER AND YUCATAN'S HENEQUEN INDUSTRY: THE DYNAMICS OF CORPORATE CONTROL DURING THE PORFIRIATO. *Secolas Ann. 1981 12: 54-64.* Examines the mechanism of control which enabled the International Harvester Company to establish what has been referred to as an invisible or informal empire in the state of Yucatán, Mexico, 1902-15.

170. Werking, Richard Hume. BUREAUCRATS, BUSINESSMEN, AND FOREIGN TRADE: THE ORIGINS OF THE UNITED STATES CHAMBER OF COMMERCE. *Business Hist. Rev. 1978 52(3): 321-341.* The US Chamber of Commerce was formed in 1912, but its establishment was due primarily to the work of key government officials more than to the business community itself. The officials were concerned with expanding American efforts, and sought a mechanism which might bring a closer working relationship between merchants and manufacturers and public authorities. In particular these officials were located in the new Department of Commerce and Labor and its Bureau of Manufacturers, and were themselves engaged in a bureaucratic rivalry of their own with the State Department over control of the commercial attache service and other overseas economic activities. Government documents in the National Archives and private papers; 60 notes.   C. J. Pusateri

171. Wilkins, Mira. MULTINATIONAL CORPORATIONS. *Latin Am. Res. Rev. 1982 17(2): 185-198.* Reviews 11 books published since 1975 on multinational corporations. These works provide a wide-ranging, multidisciplinary examination of issues such as comparing US and non-US multinationals, transfer prices, transfer of technology, and business practices. 15 notes.
                                                                    J. K. Pfabe

172. Williams, Randall and Dent, Hilda. BILLION DOLLAR SHELL GAME. *Southern Exposure 1980 8(1): 86-91.* The Jim Walter Company began as a manufacturer of shell homes, to be completed by the purchaser. That was in 1946. Today the Jim Walter Corporation is a conglomerate with interests ranging from building materials to coal mining. Less than half of its 25,000 employees are union members. It is the nation's largest builder of single-family homes, and only a fifth are now sold as shells. The company evolved from humble beginnings to its present $2 billion financial status. Some growing pains are described. 4 photos.   H. M. Parker, Jr.

173. Williamson, Oliver E. THE MODERN CORPORATION: ORIGINS, EVOLUTION, ATTRIBUTES. *J. of Econ. Lit. 1981 19(4): 1537-1568.* Examines the current nature of the corporation and how this character evolved, emphasizing that the modern corporate entity must be seen as the product of the need to economize on transition costs.

174. Willrich, Mason and Marston, Philip M. PROSPECTS FOR A URANIUM CARTEL. *Orbis 1975 19(1): 166-184.* Discusses the possibilities for a uranium cartel among countries with nuclear power industries in the 1970's, emphasizing the implications for US trade and foreign policy.

175. Young, Lewis H. WHY U.S. COMPANIES CAN COMPETE. *J. of Internat. Affairs 1974 28(1): 81-90.* The commercial pessimism of 1971 has radically changed to optimism in 1974 due to US devaluations and a lower inflation rate relative to foreign rates. US productivity is superior due to technological edges in important areas, a function of extensive research and development efforts. To retain its competitive edge, the United States must revise its antitrust laws and halt inflation with sound fiscal and monetary policies.

R. D. Frederick

176. Zeitlin, Maurice. CORPORATE OWNERSHIP AND CONTROL: THE LARGE CORPORATION AND THE CAPITALIST CLASS. *Am. J. of Sociol. 1974 79(5): 1073-1119.* "An 'astonishing consensus' exists among academic social scientists concerning the impact of the alleged separation of ownership and control in large corporations on the class structures and political economies of the United States and similar countries. The question is whether this separation is a 'pseudofact,' which has, therefore, inspired incorrect 'explanations,' 'inferences,' and 'theories,' namely, that the presumed separation has either transformed or eliminated the former 'capitalist class' and therefore rendered inapplicable a class theory of the division of the social product, class conflict, social domination, political processes, and historical change. If the separation of ownership and control has not occurred, then 'managerial' theories are without foundation. The discrepant findings of numerous studies are reviewed and problems of method and measurement discussed, concluding that the empirical question is quite open. Critical questions are posed for research into the internal differentiation and integration of the dominant ('upper') class in the United States." J

177. —. BUILDING RESEARCH. *Southern Exposure 1980 8(1): 101-118.* Criticizes contemporary corporations involved in the diverse areas of heavy construction, housing, landscaping, and building materials. American contractors are losing out in overseas construction to other nations. Particular interest is focused on Brown & Root, Inc., a subsidiary of Halliburton, concentrating on the South. Very poor housing has been erected in recent years, and very little in the rural areas where serious housing shortages exist. The culprit in every instance seems to be the multicorporation conglomerate. 3 photos, 16 tables, graph.

H. M. Parker, Jr.

178. —. [GAINS AND LOSSES FROM INDUSTRIAL CONCENTRATION]. *J. of Law and Econ. 1979 22(1): 183-211.*
Lustgarten, Steven. GAINS AND LOSSES FROM CONCENTRATION: A COMMENT, *pp. 183-190.* Assesses Sam Peltzman's article *(J. of Law and Econ. 1977 20(2): 229-263.)* Presents an alternate model for analyzing the impact of changes in industrial concentration ratios on production costs and output prices; growth interaction effects are deleted and cost effects are included.
Scherer, F. M. THE CAUSES AND CONSEQUENCES OF RISING INDUSTRIAL CONCENTRATION: A COMMENT, *pp. 191-208.* Presents alternative analysis of Peltzman's study of industrial concentration 1947-67, focusing on the correlation of concentration and unit price reduction and offering insights into current antitrust policy.

Peltzman, Sam. THE CAUSES AND CONSEQUENCES OF RISING IN-
DUSTRIAL CONCENTRATION: A REPLY, *pp. 209-211.* Responds to
Scherer's criticisms focusing on economies of scale, effects of price reduction,
and process innovation; emphasizes the importance of the variety and complexity of industrial change, 1947-67.

179. —. [MICROECONOMIC STUDIES OF CORPORATE MERGERS].
Lev, Baruch and Mandelker, Gershon. THE MICROECONOMIC CONSE-
QUENCES OF CORPORATE MERGERS. *J. of Business 1972 45(1):
85-104.* The authors examine the economic effect of mergers with regard to
impact on the firms concerned and their stockholders.
Honeycutt, T. Crawford. THE MICROECONOMIC CONSEQUENCES OF
CORPORATE MERGERS: A COMMENT. *J. of Business 1975 48(2):
267-274.* Contends that Lev and Mandelker used an inappropriate methodology and a faulty sample, as the paired sample technique requires a perfect
match between merging and control firms that does not exist. A purified
sample's results contradicted their conclusions, as merging firms failed to
become relatively more profitable. Secondary sources; table, 9 notes.
Reid, Samuel Richardson. THE MICROECONOMIC CONSEQUENCES OF
CORPORATE MERGERS: COMMENT. *J. of Business 1975 48(2): 275-
280.* Lev and Mandelker failed to consider the historical pattern of mergers
since the 1920's which has involved sustained combination activity. It is
practically impossible to isolate a sample with "clean" before and after
merger periods. They also ignored the variations among types of mergers,
although these variations may differ in results from traditional horizontal
and conglomerate types. Secondary sources; 2 tables, 6 notes.
Lev, Baruch and Mandelker, Gershon. REJOINDER TO REID AND
HONEYCUTT. *J. of Business 1975 48(2): 281-282.* The merging and
control groups differed considerably for both size and number of merger
aspects. Nonmerging firms might be completely different from merging
firms and might create àn inappropriate control group. Definitions of merger
types are presently too vague to operationalize. Honeycutt's purification,
which used only 18 of 69 firms in the original sample, invited a biased
"average" resulting from the effects of a single extreme value. Secondary
sources; 2 notes.   J. W. Williams

180. —. MULTINATIONAL CORPORATIONS. *Foreign Policy 1973
(12): 79-112.*
Diebold, John. WHY BE SCARED OF THEM?, *pp. 79-95.*
Lodge, George C. MAKE PROGRESS THE PRODUCT, *pp. 96-107.*
Church, Frank. COMMENT, *pp. 98-103.*
Diebold, John and Lodge, George C. DEBATE: DIEBOLD VS. LODGE,
pp. 107-112.   S

181. —. [OPERATING IN MORE THAN ONE JURISDICTION: THE
CAPTAIN'S PARADISE? (A) BUSINESS; (B) LABOR]. *Am. Soc. of Int.
Law Pro. 1974 68: 250-265.*
Moorhead, Thomas B. REMARKS BY THE CHAIRMAN, *pp. 250-251.*
Vagts, Detlev. OPERATING IN MORE THAN ONE JURISDICTION—
BUSINESS, *pp. 251-254.*

Considers the international legal problems in North America created by the
divergent regulation of multinational corporations and international labor unions
in the United States, Canada, and Mexico since 1937.

2

BANKING, INVESTMENTS, AND SERVICE INDUSTRIES

182. Achkasov, A. MEZHDUNARODNAIA E'KSPANSIIA KOMMER-CHESKIKH BANKOV SSHA [The international expansion of the commercial banks of the United States]. *Mirovaia Ekonomika i Mezhdunarodnye Otno-sheniia [USSR] 1978 (6): 112-116.* Describes the system and expansion of the American commercial banks which facilitate the operations of major multinational corporations outside the United States.

183. Adams, Donald R., Jr. THE BEGINNING OF INVESTMENT BANKING IN THE UNITED STATES. *Pennsylvania Hist. 1978 45(2): 99-116.* On 18 March 1813, during the War of 1812, Secretary of the Treasury Albert Gallatin initiated the public bidding system that was to characterize subsequent government borrowings. A financial syndicate led by David Parish, Stephen Girard, and John Jacob Astor subscribed for 57% of that $16,000,000 loan. This effort can be considered the nation's first investment banking endeavor. Based on the David Parish Letter Books, Stephen Girard Papers, *American State Papers,* and other materials; 2 photos, 5 tables, 38 notes. D. C. Swift

184. Adams, Donald R., Jr. PORTFOLIO MANAGEMENT AND PROF-ITABILITY IN EARLY NINETEENTH-CENTURY BANKING. *Business Hist. Rev. 1978 52(1): 61-79.* Previous scholars have argued that early commercial bankers focused on soundness rather than profit maximization as their business objective. The recent availability of the records of Stephen Girard's Bank, one of the largest and most important from 1812-31, indicates that the reverse was the case in the instance of the Girard institution. Banking was a profitable enterprise, and Girard's was more profitable than most. Based on Girard records; 3 tables, 42 notes. C. J. Pusateri

185. Armour, Robert A. and Williams, J. Carol. IMAGE MAKING AND ADVERTISING IN THE FUNERAL INDUSTRY. *J. of Popular Culture 1981 14(4): 701-710.* Examines the changing forms and contents of American funeral business advertising since the early 19th century. Increasing consumer awareness is likely to further modify this type of advertising and its traditional rhetoric and variety of euphemisms. Based on funeral industry publications; 14 notes. D. G. Nielson

186. Asch, Peter. THE ROLE OF ADVERTISING IN CHANGING CON-CENTRATION, 1962-1972. *Southern Econ. J. 1979 46(1): 288-297.* Concludes that the contribution of advertising intensity to changes in industrial concentration was insignificant for the years studied.

187. Astapovich, A. GLAVNOE ORUDIE EKSPANSII MEZH-DUNARODNYKH KORPORATSII SSHA [The main weapon of expansion employed by US international corporations]. *Mirovaia Ekonomika i Mezhdunarydnye Otnosheniia [USSR] 1979 (1): 66-78.* Discusses the rapid increase in the export of American capital in the postwar period and the large profits made from foreign investments.

188. Barrett, Glen. RECLAMATION'S NEW DEAL FOR HEAVY CON-STRUCTION: M-K IN THE GREAT DEPRESSION. *Idaho Yesterdays 1978 22(3): 21-27.* Despite the poor economic climate, the 1930's were a period of growth for heavy construction companies involved in major irrigation, reclamation, flood control, and hydroelectric projects sponsored by federal and state agencies. The Morrison-Knudsen Company, also known as the M-K Company of Boise, Idaho, was one of these. M-K, founded in 1912 by H. W. Morrison and M. H. Knudsen, helped build 20 dams in the western states, 1933-40. 5 illus., 22 notes.   B. J. Paul

189. Becker, Theodore M. and Stern, Robert N. PROFESSIONALISM, PROFESSIONALIZATION, AND BIAS IN THE COMMERCIAL HUMAN RELATIONS CONSULTING OPERATION: A SURVEY ANALYSIS. *J. of Business 1973 46(2): 230-257.* A survey "to determine policies and practices of consulting firms that deal with human factor problems" indicates a bias in favor of management. A major cause is the failure of the human relations consulting operation to meet the accepted standards for professionalization. Secondary sources; 3 tables, 51 notes, appendix.   C. A. Gallacci

190. Bentley, Marvin. INCORPORATED BANKS AND THE ECO-NOMIC DEVELOPMENT OF MISSISSIPPI, 1829-1837. *J. of Mississippi Hist. 1973 35(4): 381-401.* Examines the role of incorporated banks in the development of Mississippi 1829-37, a period which "stands out as the most dynamic in the economic and political development of the state" and during which 15 such banks began operation. Although others criticize the banks, the author concludes that they "were an important factor in promoting economic development" and that they accomplished this in what could be called a "financially conservative manner . . . through a controlled growth of their loan and money-creating activities. The banks as a group were effective in aggregating funds and distributing loans." Based on primary sources, including bank manuscripts deposited in the Department of Archives, Louisiana State University, Baton Rouge; 3 tables, 9 notes.   J. W. Hillje

191. Bergan, Harold. INDUSTRY'S BONDAGE FETISH. *Washington Monthly 1981 12(11): 18-23.* Describes industrial development bonds (IDB's), which reward investors with untaxed interest, and can be borrowed more cheaply than bank loans because "the federal tax code permits state and local governments to use their tax-exempt borrowing privilege on behalf of private businesses," benefiting private industry at the taxpayer's expense, and gives examples of the use of IDB's in Bangor, Wisconsin, and Madison, Wisconsin; 1979-81.

192.   Berry, Daniel E.; Kunde, James E.; and Moore, Carl M.   THE NEGOTI-
ATED INVESTMENT STRATEGY: IMPROVING INTERGOVERNMEN-
TAL EFFECTIVENESS BY IMPROVING INTERGROUP RELATIONS.
J. of Intergroup Relations 1982 10(2): 42-57. Discusses the application of the
negotiated investment strategy procedures for investing public and private resources in Gary, Indiana, Columbus, Ohio, and St. Paul, Minnesota, to solve
social problems during 1979-80.

193.   Black, Harold; Schweitzer, Robert L.; and Mandell, Lewis.   DISCRIMI-
NATION IN MORTGAGE LENDING.   *Am. Econ. Rev. 1978 68(2): 186-191.*
From data provided by Comptroller of the Currency-Federal Deposit Insurance
Corporation's national survey of banks, the authors construct two models for
analysis. The first model indicates that when race is the only factor, blacks are
less likely to be granted loans than nonblacks. However, the second model, based
on other factors used by bankers, indicates that the racial variable is not statistically significant. Tables, ref.   D. K. Pickens

194.   Blackford, Mansel G.   BANKING AND BANK LEGISLATION IN
CALIFORNIA, 1890-1915.   *Business Hist. R. 1973 47(4): 482-507.* Discusses
how California bankers coped with the transformation of the American economy
in the late 19th and early 20th centuries. Bankers in California were concerned
with controlling the forces of economic change, a task exacerbated by banking
instability and the rapid growth and diversification of the state's economy. They
attempted to solve their problems by forming cooperative associations, lobbying
for needed and helpful legislation, and establishing professional standards for
themselves. Based on California Banking Commission and Banker's Association
reports, contemporary newspaper and journal reports, and secondary sources; 2
tables, 86 notes.   N. J. Street

195.   Blair, Roger D. and Vogel, Ronald J.   A SURVIVOR ANALYSIS OF
COMMERCIAL HEALTH INSURERS.   *J. of Business 1978 51(3): 521-529.*
Economies of scale in administering commercial health insurance have been
found using multiple-regression techniques. This suggests that over time the large
health insurers ought to increase in number and importance at the expense of the
smaller firms. The survivor technique was applied to the commercial health
insurance industry for the 1958-73 period. As we anticipated, the smallest size
class shrank continuously over the period in question. In contrast to a priori
expectations, all the other size classes appeared to be viable. This result is analyzed in the context of some health insurance industry peculiarities.   J

196.   Bordo, Michael David.   THE INCOME EFFECTS OF THE SOURCES
OF NEW MONEY: A COMPARISON OF THE UNITED STATES AND
THE UNITED KINGDOM, 1870-1913.   *Explorations in Econ. Hist. 1977
14(1): 20-43.* Except for one subperiod, 1879-96, the effects were generally similar
in both countries. Differences in the way in which money, high-powered money,
and bank money were introduced into the two economies explain variations in
nominal income between 1879 and 1896. Based on published statistics and secondary accounts.   P. J. Coleman

197. Brand, Horst. PRODUCTIVITY IN THE PHARMACEUTICAL INDUSTRY. *Monthly Labor Rev. 1974 97(3): 9-14.* Productivity in the pharmaceutical industry in the United States from 1963 to 1972 has risen consistently, reflecting growth in demand and changes in the technology of quality control.

198. Brockhaus, William L. PROSPECTS FOR MALPRACTICE SUITS IN THE BUSINESS CONSULTING PROFESSION. *J. of Business 1977 50(1): 70-75.* The jump in the number of malpractice suits against business and management consultants indicates their development as a legally recognized profession. During 1971-72 claims rose 75 percent for one liability insurer. The appearance and purchase of insurance show that a new phase of professional liability has begun. Primary and secondary sources; 11 tables, 2 notes.   J. W. Williams

199. Calvert, Jeff. GOLD BUG GUMBO. *Reason 1981 13(2): 33-36, 81-82.* Report on the five-day long convention of investment advisors, deflationists, and inflationists sponsored by Jim Blanchard's National Committee for Monetary Reform in November 1980 in New Orleans.

200. Campbell, Norman A. and Hammell, Robert W. DEVELOPMENT OF THE THIRD PARTY PAYMENT CONCEPT FOR MEDICAL AND PHARMACEUTICAL SERVICES. *Pharmacy in Hist. 1973 15(3): 117-123.* The increase in pharmacy prescriptions payment by private and government insurers has proven a major problem. The National Pharmacy Insurance Council, founded in 1969 to promote cordiality among pharmacies, underwriters, and beneficiaries, walks a delicate line between agreement among druggists on dispensing fees, antitrust violation, and a satisfactory claims processing system for druggists vis-à-vis insurance companies. Includes historical background on health and accident insurance. Based on primary sources; 19 notes.   N. Gamer

201. Canal, Carlos M. BUSINESS: AMERICAN BANKS IN BLACK AFRICA. *Africa Report 1975 20(5): 15-16.* Discusses US and European banks' lending of money to African countries during 1972-74, and why US banks wish to do business in Africa.

202. Candilis, Wray O. COMMERCIAL BANK FINANCING OF THE HOUSING INDUSTRY IN THE UNITED STATES DURING THE SIXTIES AND THE NEED FOR NEW APPROACHES. *Rev. Int. d'Hist. de la Banque [Italy] 1973 6: 47-66.* Stresses the necessity of establishing new national housing principles by the commercial banking industry and the public sector alike, in order to develop new ideas in the field of housing.

203. Carnes, Richard B. LAUNDRY AND CLEANING SERVICES PRESSED TO POST PRODUCTIVITY GAINS. *Monthly Labor Rev. 1978 101(2): 38-42.* Describes changes in the composition of and productivity in the cleaning industry in the United States from 1958 to 1976.

204. Carosso, Vincent P. THE WALL STREET MONEY TRUST FROM PUJO THROUGH MEDINA. *Business Hist. R. 1973 47(4): 421-437.* Traces the history of the "money trust" controversy through the first half of the 20th century. Begins with the congressional subcommittee report of Arséne Pujo, whose ideas were taken and incorporated by Louis M. Brandeis, forming the basis for future business legislation and investigations. During the 1930's-40's, govern-

ment investigation pointed to the financial concentration in New York and proposed compulsory competitive bidding for new securities. The culmination of the anti-money trust actions was the anti-trust case of *United States* v. *Henry S. Morgan* (US, 1947), which focused on traditional banker relationships, historical position, and reciprocity. The defense disproved the money trust theory and showed how competitive bidding helped only the big firms. Judge Harold R. Medina dismissed the case with prejudice. Concludes that these attacks on money power were unjustified on both economic and legal grounds. Based on US government documents, contemporary newspaper and journal reports, and secondary sources; 24 notes. N. J. Street

205. Chandler, Lester V. THE BANKING CRISIS OF 1933. *Rev. in Am. Hist. 1974 2(4): 558-563.* Review article prompted by Susan Estabrook Kennedy's *The Banking Crisis of 1933* (Lexington: U. Pr. of Kentucky, 1973) which outlines the book's contents, shows the significance of the February-March bank crisis, and assesses Kennedy's explication of the crisis.

206. Corn, Joseph. SELLING TECHNOLOGY: ADVERTISING FILMS AND THE AMERICAN CORPORATION, 1900-1920. *Film & Hist. 1981 11(3): 49-58.* Discusses the use of film by corporations like General Electric, Ford, Dupont, and International Harvester to either advertise their products in short films, or to present educational films "that promoted a company's products indirectly by treating its business in dramatic or historical fashion."

207. Daly, George and Moore, William J. EXTERNALITIES, PROPERTY RIGHTS AND THE ALLOCATION OF RESOURCES IN MAJOR LEAGUE BASEBALL. *Econ. Inquiry 1981 19(1): 77-95.* Discusses the distribution of wealth between players and owners in professional baseball in relationship to the reserve clause, the player draft, and the allocation of players among teams; data from 1955-76 indicate that the empirical generalizations of previous economists were unjustified.

208. Dreese, G. Richard. BANKS AND REGIONAL ECONOMIC DEVELOPMENT. *Southern Econ. J. 1974 40(4): 647-656.*

209. Ellis, L. Tuffly. THE NEW ORLEANS COTTON EXCHANGE: THE FORMATIVE YEARS, 1870-1880. *J. of Southern Hist. 1973 39(4): 545-564.* Describes the formation and development of the New Orleans Cotton Exchange during 1871-80, established as a means to revive and regulate the cotton market in that city. By 1880 the Exchange was the leading cotton market in the world and had set up a futures market. It was able to restore order to the local market, curb further decline of trade, and help improve communication and transport between the city and other areas, developing a "spirit of mutual cooperation among New Orleans traders." Based on reports of the New Orleans Cotton Exchange, US government documents, contemporary newspaper reports, and primary and secondary sources; 56 notes. N. J. Street

210. Epstein, Amy Kallman. MULTIFAMILY DWELLINGS AND THE SEARCH FOR RESPECTABILITY: ORIGINS OF THE NEW YORK APARTMENT HOUSE. *Urbanism Past & Present 1980 5(2): 29-39.* Families can be housed in single- or multiple-dwelling units. Before the 1860's, multiple units were tenements and housed the poor. With a decline in domestic servants

and narrow lots, which countered single-family homes, New York City builders tried four experimental living units, which were multifamily and intended for the upper classes: Stuyvesant House, Haight House, Stevens House, and 1267 Broadway. These buildings introduced apartment houses to New York. The buildings succeeded by extending multiple dwellings beyond its use for the poor; it failed by housing only the wealthy. 7 fig., 38 notes. B. P. Anderson

211. Falke, Josef. ANLEGERSCHUTZ UND UNTERNEHMENSPUB-LIZITÄT: DIE ZULASSUNG VON AKTIEN ZUM BÖRSENHANDEL BIS ZUR NEW DEAL-GESETZGEBUNG IN VERGLEICHENDER SICHT [Investor protection and corporate disclosure: A comparative view of stock exchange listing requirements before New Deal legislation]. Horn, Norbert and Kocka, Jürgen, ed. *Recht und Entwicklung der Grossunternehmen im 19. und frühen 20. Jahrhundert* (Göttingen: Vandenhoeck & Ruprecht, 1979): 619-646. Examines the development of stock exchange regulation in France, Germany, Great Britain, and the United States from the 19th century to 1934 and concludes that in all cases under review, regulations for quotations of shares preceded legislation for the protection of shareholders. Scandals, promoterism, and crashes were decisive factors in securities legislation and stock exchange regulations on corporate disclosure. 139 notes, 70 ref. English summary. S

212. Fonner, David Kent. THE FAILURE OF THE FARMERS AND DROVERS NATIONAL BANK OF WAYNESBURG, PENNSYLVANIA. *Pennsylvania Mag. of Hist. and Biog. 1980 104(2): 221-239.* Though a strong bank from its inception in 1835, the Farmers and Drovers National Bank was closed in 1906 because of its directors' (especially James B. F. Rinehart's) criminal malpractices and the rapid shift of the area from agriculture to industry. The closure by federal bank examiners had drastic regional effects on Greene County, possibly reaching almost to the present. Based on papers of the Comptroller of the Currency and others, National Archives, on newspapers, and on secondary works; 95 notes. T. H. Wendel

213. Forbes, Stephen W. CAPITAL AND SURPLUS FORMATION IN THE NONLIFE INSURANCE INDUSTRY, 1956-70. *Q. R. of Econ. and Business 1974 14(3): 15-34.* "Sources of 1956-70 capital and surplus change in the nonlife insurance industry involving underwriting and investment operations, dividend policies, and external financing are evaluated in relation to the behavior of randomly selected samples of stock and mutual insurers. Although the average capacity position of the insurers did not change markedly during the period, the adoption of generally accepted accounting principles and the relaxation of pricing regulations would have partly alleviated the heavy reliance upon capital gains and the significant reduction in the 1956-70 underwriting capabilities experienced by many of the insurers. Regulatory reform in this regard is badly needed." J

214. Fraas, Arthur. THE SECOND BANK OF THE UNITED STATES: AN INSTRUMENT FOR AN INTERREGIONAL MONETARY UNION. *J. of Econ. Hist. 1974 34(2): 447-467.* Establishment of a uniform national currency with a fixed rate of exchange by the Second Bank of the United States during the 1820's meant the end of the old monetary system of flexible exchange rates which had permitted regional price autonomy. Despite initial US Treasury support of the old system, the Second Bank of the United States finally succeeded

in creating a monetary union to regulate an interregional balance of payments system. Based on contemporary published accounts, official published documents, and secondary sources; 3 tables, graph, 37 notes, biblio.

O. H. Reichardt

215. Fraser, Donald R. and Richards, R. Malcolm. THE PERSISTENCE OF BANK PROFITABILITY: EVIDENCE AND EXPLANATION. *Q. Rev. of Econ. and Business 1978 18(4): 98-101.* Studies large banking organizations that persistently have above or below average profits, 1965-74.

216. Fugate, Robert. THE BANCOKENTUCKY STORY. *Filson Club Hist. Q. 1976 50(1): 29-46.* Unravels the complicated financial developments that led to the closing of the National Bank of Kentucky and the BancoKentucky Company in 1930. Both businesses were dominated by speculator James B. Brown of Louisville. As early as 1925 Federal officials warned the directors of the National Bank of Brown's unsafe policies. In an effort to buttress the weakened bank, Brown formed BancoKentucky Company in 1929 and gained control of several banks in the region. By 1930 a combination of speculative loans, the onset of the depression, and a disastrous merger with Caldwell and Company of Nashville, Tennessee, destroyed both the holding company and the bank. Documented from legal records and newspapers. 46 notes.   G. B. McKinney.

217. Gandolfi, Arthur E. STABILITY OF THE DEMAND FOR MONEY DURING THE GREAT CONTRACTION—1929-1933. *J. of Pol. Econ. 1974 82(5): 969-983.* "This paper uses cross-sectional state data to test the stability of the demand for money (total bank deposits) during the Great Contraction. The demand for deposits is defined as a function of state permanent income, the rate of interest paid on deposits, and the rate of state bank failures. Separate yearly demand functions are estimated for each year of the period, and these results strongly suggest that the demand for deposits was stable over this period and that the contraction had a negligible effect on the size and significance of the income and interest-rate elasticities."   J

218. Ginzberg, Eli and Brecher, Charles. THE ECONOMIC IMPACT OF JAPANESE INVESTMENT. *New York Affairs 1979 5(3): 97-110.* Examines the effects of foreign investments on the US economy, in particular, the enormous impact that Japanese investments have had on New York City since the mid-1960's.

219. Glasberg, Davita Silfen. CORPORATE POWER AND CONTROL: THE CASE OF LEASCO CORPORATION VERSUS CHEMICAL BANK. *Social Problems 1981 29(2): 104-116.* Focuses on the unsuccessful attempt of Leasco Data Processing Equipment Corporation to acquire Chemical Bank of New York; Chemical Bank devastated Leasco by dumping the corporation's stock in its possession to set an example, demonstrating that "fundamental power lies with those financial institutions which possess the control to dispose of massive blocks of stock in pension and trust funds."

220. Grunwald, Kurt. THREE CHAPTERS OF GERMAN-JEWISH BANKING HISTORY. *Leo Baeck Inst. Year Book [Great Britain] 1977 22: 191-208.* The combination of a relative lack of anti-Jewish prejudice and presence of material self-interest formed the basis of economic collaboration between the

many German rulers and the Jews after 1648. Jews' ability to procure goods and services, dispose of war booty advantageously, and provide necessary funds made them indispensable to their masters. The history of early 19th-century commercial banking in the United States shows the great contributions of immigrants, mostly from southwestern Germany. Summarizes the banking history of Abraham S. Joseph (1827-92) of Michelstadt and his descendants in Germany and England. 3 illus., 40 notes.   F. Rosenthal

221.   Guttman, Daniel and Willner, Barry.   FLIM-FLAM, DOUBLE-TALK, AND HUSTLE: THE CONSULTING INDUSTRY. *Washington Monthly 1976 7(11): 46-53.* Consulting and contracting firms administer as much as $100 billion annually of federal funds; adapted from the authors' book, *The Shadow Government* (New York: Pantheon, 1976).

222.   Haeger, John Denis.   EASTERN FINANCIERS AND INSTITU-TIONAL CHANGE: THE ORIGINS OF THE NEW YORK LIFE INSUR-ANCE AND TRUST COMPANY AND THE OHIO LIFE INSURANCE AND TRUST COMPANY. *J. of Econ. Hist. 1979 39(1): 259-273.* This article examines the establishment in the 1830's of the New York Life Insurance and Trust Company and the Ohio Life Insurance and Trust Company. Utilizing manuscript letters, company records, and government reports, the author contends that conservative financiers, exemplified by Isaac and Arthur Bronson of New York City, structured both firms in an effort to reform the speculative practices of commercial banks and to move capital into the agricultural sector, particularly in the West. The trust company's development also marked an important step in the financiers' search for more efficient methods of capital mobilization and formation.   J

223.   Hartzog, B. G., Jr.   THE IMPACT OF NOW ACCOUNTS ON SAV-INGS AND LOAN BEHAVIOR AND PERFORMANCE. *Q. Rev. of Econ. and Business 1979 19(3): 97-108.* Presents empirical evidence relating to the impact of NOW [Negotiable Order of Withdrawal] accounts on the behavior and performance of savings and loan associations. The key concerns of both the theoretical discussion and the empirical evidence are 1) will NOW accounts cause increased operating expenses for S & Ls which would be passed on in the form of higher mortgage rates? and 2) will NOW account funds be considered an inappropriate source of funds for mortgages due to the transactions nature of those accounts? The empirical evidence suggests a negative answer to these questions.   J

224.   Heimer, Carol A.   THE RACIAL AND ORGANIZATIONAL ORIGINS OF INSURANCE REDLINING. *J. of Intergroup Relations 1982 10(3): 42-60.* Discusses geographical and racial factors that insurance companies use in determining rates for various groups and the practice of redlining, the refusal to grant insurance coverage to property in certain geographical areas inhabited by minority groups.

225.   Henderson, Cary S.   LOS ANGELES AND THE DODGER WAR, 1957-1962. *Southern California Q. 1980 62(3): 261-289.* Describes how Los Angeles acquired the Dodger baseball franchise amid opposition, litigation, and controversy. Faced with poor attendance and an obsolete stadium, Brooklyn

Dodger owner Walter O'Malley decided to move to another city. At the same time, Los Angeles Mayor Norris Poulson determined that his city should acquire a major-league baseball team. Opposition to the move developed over Chavez Ravine, an ideal location for a stadium but set aside for public housing. Between 1957 and 1959 final approval of the new Dodger home was delayed by lawsuits, appeals, and bitter debate in the Los Angeles City Council. Despite the controversy, the city did well in its arrangements. Unlike other cities which must fill municipally owned stadiums, Los Angeles collects property taxes from privately owned Dodger Stadium. The Dodgers are thus more committed to Los Angeles than other teams which move from one city to another as lucrative opportunities arise. 132 notes.   A. Hoffman

226.   Henry, J. S.   FROM SOAP TO SOAPBOX: THE CORPORATE MERCHANDISING OF IDEAS.   *Working Papers for a New Society 1980 7(3): 55-57.* Analyzes corporation advertising from the early 1950's through 1980 and concludes that much of it has become perniciously ideological, posing a threat to fundamental freedoms by virtue of its solidarity and pervasiveness.

227.   Herman, Edward S.   DO BANKERS CONTROL CORPORATIONS? *Monthly R. 1973 25(2): 12-29.* Analyzes the control of corporations, focusing on the influence exerted by banks through their trust department operations.   S

228.   Hirschey, Mark.   THE EFFECT OF ADVERTISING ON INDUSTRIAL MOBILITY, 1947-72.   *J. of Business 1981 54(2): 329-339.* Uses as measures rates of entry and established firm growth. Empirical findings suggest that advertising upsets rather than reinforces the market share stability of established firms. Like some earlier findings, these results tend to support the advertising-as-procompetitive thesis.   J/S

229.   Hoffmeister, J. Ronald.   USE OF CONVERTIBLE DEBT IN THE EARLY 1970'S: A REEVALUATION OF CORPORATE MOTIVES.   *The Q. Rev. of Econ. and Business 1977 17(2): 23-31.* Utilizing responses of 53 corporations to a questionnaire, motives influencing use of the convertible feature in debt financing during the early 1970's were investigated. Found to be of major but equal importance were 1) a motivation eventually to shift the debt to common stock when stock prices rise (delayed equity financing) and 2) the need to reduce the interest cost of the debt issue. Next in importance was concern with enhancing an otherwise difficult issue to sell. Response patterns as a function of firm size and the type of firm (industrial versus finance) are compared.   J

230.   Holland, Donald R.   VOLNEY B. PALMER: THE NATION'S FIRST ADVERTISING AGENCY MAN.   *Pennsylvania Mag. of Hist. and Biog. 1974 98(3): 353-381.* Volney B. Palmer (1799-1864), the first advertising agent in the United States, pioneered and perfected the concept of systematic advertising in the nation's newspapers. By alerting businessmen and manufacturers to structural changes in the business market and to the existence of distant markets, systematic advertising was a catalyst of mid-19th-century industrial development. Primary and secondary sources; 61 notes.   E. W. Carp

231.   Horowitz, Daniel.   CONSUMPTION, CAPITALISM AND CULTURE.   *Rev. in Am. Hist. 1978 6(3): 388-393.* Review article prompted by Stuart Ewen's *Captains of Consciousness: Advertising and the Social Roots of the Consumer Culture* (New York: McGraw-Hill, 1976).

232. Horstman, Ronald. TRADE UNIONS IN THE BANKING FIELD: A FOOTNOTE ON THE HISTORY OF ST. LOUIS. *Missouri Hist. Soc. Bull.* *1978 34(2): 104-105.* Describes the Telegraphers National Bank in St. Louis during 1922-42. Owned by the Brotherhood of Railway Telegraphers, the bank flourished under the leadership of Edward J. Manion and Vernon O. Gardner. 2 photos.					H. T. Lovin

233. Jackson, W. Turrentine. STAGES, MAILS AND EXPRESS IN SOUTHERN CALIFORNIA: THE ROLE OF WELLS, FARGO & CO. IN THE PRE-RAILROAD PERIOD. *Southern California Q. 1974 56(3): 233-272.* A study of the operations of Wells, Fargo & Company in southern California from 1852 until the completion of the transcontinental railroad in 1869. The company pursued an aggressive business policy during a period of intense competition. Other stage companies provided similar services, but none matched Wells, Fargo in its comprehensive program of banking, express, and transportation. When necessary the company joined with other concerns in providing service to various areas, but the company's eventual plan was to buy out or otherwise absorb competing lines. By 1869 Wells, Fargo dominated transportation to and within California. Primary sources, including company records and newspapers, and secondary studies; illus., photos, 140 notes.					A. Hoffman

234. James, John A. COST FUNCTIONS OF POSTBELLUM NATIONAL BANKS. *Explorations in Econ. Hist. 1978 15(2): 184-195.* The general trend in the United States was for banking costs to decline, though the rate of decline varied from region to region. At the beginning of the 20th century many rural banks, especially in the South, were below the minimum efficient size. Low population density and high illiteracy rates help, but do not fully explain, the retardation in southern economic development. Based on published documents and secondary accounts; table, fig., 18 notes, biblio.					P. J. Coleman

235. James, John A. THE DEVELOPMENT OF THE NATIONAL MONEY MARKET, 1893-1911. *J. of Econ. Hist. 1976 36(4): 878-897.* In this article the convergence of U.S. interregional interest rates in the late nineteenth century is examined and two major hypotheses are tested in the framework of a bank portfolio selection model based on the capital-asset-pricing model. Both the spread of the commercial paper market and the lowering of entry barriers through the reduction of national bank minimum capital requirements are rejected as principal explanations. The erosion of local monopoly power is shown to have been of central importance, and this development was due to the growth of state rather than national banks.					J

236. Johnson, David M. DISNEY WORLD AS STRUCTURE AND SYMBOL: RE-CREATION OF THE AMERICAN EXPERIENCE. *J. of Popular Culture 1981 15(1): 157-165.* Both the organization of work and the physical structure of Disney World mirror the US economic and social order. Disney World itself, however, may be seen as a miniature state governed by the Disney Corporation which, as an all-pervasive monopoly, manipulates its tourist population. Note, biblio.					D. G. Nielson

237. Johnson, Lane J. NEW YORK'S PRIMACY WITHIN THE AMERICAN BANKING SYSTEM: MEGALOPOLIS AND THE ORGANIZATION OF AMERICAN SPACE. _Michigan Academician 1974 6(3): 281-289._ Considers the influence of the northeastern megalopolis on the American socioeconomic system, using banking as an index of spatial influence. S

238. Johnson, Rodney D. and Meinster, David R. THE PERFORMANCE OF BANK HOLDING COMPANY ACQUISITIONS: A MULTIVARIATE ANALYSIS. _J. of Business 1975 48(2): 204-212._ Deposits at banks affiliated with holding companies jumped from 20 percent to 50 percent of all commercial bank deposits following the 1970 amendment to the Holding Company Act of 1956. Earlier studies disclosed no performance effects but used only univariate methods and failed to control for intervals since acquisition. Multiple discriminant analysis showed differences in pricing behavior and a more aggressive investment policy that persisted at least four years, suggesting a "performance cycle." Primary and secondary sources; 6 tables, 9 notes. J. W. Williams

239. Keating, Barry P. and Keating, Maryann O. NONPROFIT FIRMS, DECISION-MAKING AND REGULATION. _R. of Social Econ. 1975 33(1): 26-42._ An economic study of nonprofit firms, specifically credit unions. S

240. Keehn, Richard H. MARKET POWER AND BANK LENDING: SOME EVIDENCE FROM WISCONSIN, 1870-1900. _J. of Econ. Hist. 1980 40(1): 45-52._ The pioneering work of Lance Davis on regional bank loan rates in the United States from 1870 to 1914 generated several attempts to explain the observed regional interest rate differentials and their subsequent narrowing by 1914. This article reports on a more direct test of the hypothesis that barriers to capital mobility were due to monopoly power on the part of local bankers. Tests using data on individual banks and local markets for one state, Wisconsin, suggest that local competitive conditions did not exert a significant influence on bank lending performance. This may be the result of relatively free entry into Wisconsin banking during the period. J

241. Kennedy, Susan Estabrook. THE MICHIGAN BANKING CRISIS OF 1933. _Michigan Hist. 1973 57(3): 237-264._ Weeks before the national banking moratorium in 1933, Michigan's banking structure collapsed. Needing substantial loans to survive the collapse of the economy, the two large holding companies that dominated the state's financial scene were unable to qualify for aid from the Reconstruction Finance Corporation because they lacked sufficient liquid assets. Michigan's crisis soon merged with the national collapse. 3 illus., 96 notes. D. L. Smith

242. Kessel, Reuben A. and Clark, Truman A. A STUDY OF EXPECTATIONAL ERRORS IN THE MONEY AND CAPITAL MARKETS, 1921-1970. _J. of Law and Econ. 1976 19(1): 1-15._ "Presents an analysis of government securities data to test the prediction . . . that the expected realized rate of return on long-term bonds exceeds that on short-term bonds." Treasury Department statistics and secondary sources; 4 tables, 28 notes. J. Reed

243. Khudyakova, L. NOVAYA ROL'AMERIKANSKIKH MEZHDUNARODNIKH BANKOV [The new role of American international banks]. _Mirovaia Ekonomika i Mezhdunarodnye Otnosheniia [USSR] 1979 (2):_

118-126. Studies the recent changes in the sphere of international credit and finance, and in the internationalization of capitalist production. Tables, biblio.

244. Klein, Maury. MAN OF MYSTERY. *Am. Hist. Illus. 1977 12(6): 10-18.* The public image of Jay Gould (1836-92) was at best exaggerated and misleading. Gould was vulnerable to adverse publicity because of his desire for privacy and his frail personal bearing. Nevertheless, he was a shrewd entrepreneur. "No other individual, except perhaps J. P. Morgan, exerted so great an influence upon the nation's rail system." His accomplishments, 1879-81, were "unprecedented in the business and financial life of the country." He died in 1892 and left an estate of $72 million. 11 illus. D. Dodd

245. Lawson, Ronald. THE POLITICAL FACE OF NEW YORK'S REAL ESTATE INDUSTRY. *New York Affairs 1980 6(2): 88-109.* Discusses the policies of the political segments of New York City's real estate owners, including the Real Estate Board of New York (founded in 1896), the Associated Builders and Owners (founded in 1910), the Association for a Better New York (founded in 1967-68), the three biggest and most influential, and the Community Housing Improvement Program (1967), the Bronx Realty Advisory Board (mid-1940's), other localized landlords, and issue-specific groups.

246. Lurie, Jonathan. THE CHICAGO BOARD OF TRADE, THE MERCHANTS' EXCHANGE OF ST. LOUIS, AND THE GREAT BUCKET SHOP WAR, 1882-1905. *Missouri Hist. Soc. Bull. 1973 29(4, Pt. 1): 243-259.* The two major midwestern commodity exchanges, the Chicago Board of Trade and the Merchants' Exchange of St. Louis, normally cooperated in providing "a rationalized market framework" beneficial to producers, sellers, distributors, and consumers. To circumvent the rules and disciplinary powers of the two exchanges, "bucket shops" developed in Chicago and St. Louis. Bucket shops provided a less expensive outlet for commodity speculative activities on a smaller scale than was permitted by the two legitimate exchanges. The Chicago Board of Trade attempted to curb the bucket shops and sought the cooperation of its St. Louis counterpart. The St. Louis group responded warily and never cooperated fully in the war against the bucket shops. The Chicago Board of Trade ultimately prevailed over the bucket shops. Based on the records of the Chicago and St. Louis commodity exchanges, on government documents, and on secondary sources; 47 notes. H. T. Lovin

247. Lynch, Joseph D. THE BANKER OF THE SOUTHLAND IN 1885. *Western States Jewish Hist. Q. 1977 9(3): 226-228.* The Farmers' and Merchants' Bank of Los Angeles was founded in 1868 with $200,000 in paid-up capital. Under Mr. Isaias W. Hellman, the president and major stockholder, it grew to be the sixth largest in the state in volume of business. By avoiding speculation and investing only where growth and natural development were certain, the bank gained the confidence and esteem of the business community. Reprint of article in the *Los Angeles Herald* "Annual" issue of January 1885; photo. B. S. Porter

248. MacCann, Richard Dyer. THE FIRST TYCOONS: SOME OBSERVATIONS ON THE HAMILTONIAN TRADITION IN EARLY FILM COMPANIES. *Indiana Social Studies Q. 1981 34(2): 5-9.* Discusses the Hamiltonian

tradition of trusting "private industry to work for the best interests of the nation" in the early American film industry, which, like other successful industries, was organized vertically, focusing on Adolph Zukor's Paramount Pictures, Metro-Goldwyn-Mayer, and United Artists.

249. MacKay, Malcolm. THE REGULATION OF HEALTH INSUR-ANCE. *Pro. of the Acad. of Pol. Sci. 1980 33(4): 81-91.* Traces the history of US health insurance and health insurance regulation since the 19th century. Considers health maintenance organizations (HMO's) and "second opinion programs as factors in controlling health costs." Attributes the failure of the insurance regulatory system in controlling costs to its inability to prevent escalating costs. Consumer deductible and uniform hospital reporting procedures offer some hope. Yet, the future of the health insurance industry is difficult to predict. It will survive only if the public perceives it as more capable than the government in the area of cost control, quality assurance, and prompt payment.   D. F. Ring

250. Madison, James H. THE EVOLUTION OF COMMERCIAL CREDIT REPORTING AGENCIES IN NINETEENTH-CENTURY AMERICA. *Business Hist. R. 1974 48(2): 164-186.* When the Mercantile Agency began operation in New York in 1841 it became the first organization to provide detailed credit information about businessmen over a large geographical area. Shows the evolution of this type of enterprise until it became, at the end of the century, a successful and essential service in the American business world. The field was finally dominated by the Bradstreet and Dun agencies. 72 notes.
R. V. Ritter

251. McConnell, John J. and Schlarbaum, Gary G. RETURNS, RISKS, AND PRICING OF INCOME BONDS, 1956-76: (DOES MONEY HAVE AN ODOR?). *J. of Business 1981 54(1): 33-63.* The authors explore two explanations for the infrequent use of income bonds by US corporations. The traditional explanation is that income bonds have the "smell of death," being persistently underpriced. The second is that there are some "deadweight" costs associated with income bonds. Neither of these explanations provides a satisfactory rationale for the reluctance of corporations to make widespread use of income bonds.
J/S

252. McKie, James W. ADVERTISING AND SOCIAL RESPONSIBIL-TIY. *Society 1979 16(3) 39-43.* Examines business advertising in the United States since the 1950's, particularly two issues; the effect of advertising on consumer behavior, and the possibility that advertising may give certain businesses a monopoly on their product over others. Discusses regulatory policy and the public's responsibility regarding advertising practices.

253. McNulty, James E. A REEXAMINATION OF THE PROBLEM OF STATE USURY CEILINGS: THE IMPACT IN THE MORTGAGE MAR-KET. *Q. Rev. of Econ. and Business 1980 20(1): 16-29.* This paper reviews the research on the impact of state usury ceilings. Existing econometric studies (with some exceptions) rely primarily on cross-sectional analysis, and also they appear to suggest that usury ceilings are restrictive only when the ceiling is below average market rates. However, other evidence of a fairly wide distribution of rates within urban mortgage markets suggests that, as interest rates are rising, a given ceiling

would begin to be restrictive even before the *average* rate prevailing in the market reaches the ceiling rate. This hypothesis was upheld in tests using data for savings and loan associations in Georgia. Because there were approximately 17 states with 10 percent usury ceilings in mid-1978, when average market rates were in the 9-1/2 percent-9-3/4 percent range, the restrictiveness of usury ceilings may be significantly greater than is generally considered to be the case. Furthermore, the evidence developed here suggests that the movement toward floating usury ceilings in many states in recent years may not be a welcome development since such ceilings would tend to discourage higher-risk loans, even when the general availability of mortgage credit is good.   J

254. Michelman, Irving S.   A BANKER IN THE NEW DEAL: JAMES P. WARBURG.   *Rev. Int. d'Hist. de la Banque [Italy] 1974 8: 35-59.* James P. Warburg, scion of one of the great German Jewish banking houses in the United States, was one of the few Wall Streeters to become part of the FDR administration. Drawn into the frantic preparations to reopen the banks in March 1933, Warburg became a delegate to the World Economic Conference in London, only to resign shortly after his appointment. Roosevelt made it clear that domestic monetary policy could not be compromised by international agreements. Roosevelt's decision to take the United States off the gold standard and to accept legislation which gave him far-reaching power to increase the money supply led Warburg to break with the administration. A successful polemicist and writer, Warburg became associated with the anti-New Deal faction and the Liberty League. Secondary sources; 24 notes.   D. McGinnis

255. Olmstead, Alan L.   MUTUAL SAVINGS BANK DEPOSITORS IN NEW YORK.   *Business Hist. R. 1975 49(3): 287-311.* Author describes the background of mutual savings bank customers in the first half of the 19th century, the distribution of deposits by amounts, and the attempts by bank operators to force wealthier depositors out of the clientele. Concludes that such banks attracted many middle and upper class depositors as well as laboring class customers. Based on bank records and other primary sources; 6 tables, 63 notes.
C. J. Pusateri

256. Olmstead, Alan L.   NEW YORK CITY MUTUAL SAVINGS BANK PORTFOLIO MANAGEMENT AND TRUSTEE OBJECTIVES.   *J. of Econ. Hist. 1974 34(4): 815-834.* Profiteering was an inconsequential motive among trustees of mutual savings banks. Types of investments in portfolios of four of New York City's oldest banks converged as legal restraints were removed. The trend suggested a similar purpose, to maximize profits, and rapid response to market forces. Continued observance of usury laws and balances between mortgage loans and government securities held reflected pursuit of depositors' welfare. Based on bank reports and secondary sources; table, 5 graphs, 36 notes.
J. W. Williams

257. Palley, Howard A.   POLICY FORMULATION IN HEALTH: SOME CONSIDERATIONS OF GOVERNMENTAL CONSTRAINTS ON PRICING IN THE HEALTH DELIVERY SYSTEM.   *Am. Behavioral Scientist 1974 17(4): 572-584.* Inflation of prices in the health services field has been modified but not stopped.   S

258. Paul, Allen B.; Gregory, Owen, (commentary). THE PAST AND FUTURE OF THE COMMODITIES EXCHANGES. *Agric. Hist. 1982 56(1): 287-305, 317-325.* Futures trading in commodities was stable during 1924-47 but grew at an average annual rate of 7% during the period of monetary stability, 1947-70, and 15% during 1970-80. The number of exchanges has declined despite the growing number of trades. Agricultural commodities were the first traded on futures exchanges, followed by metals and other nonagricultural commodities, foreign currencies, and debt instruments. Comments, pp. 317-325. Based largely on USDA futures statistics; 3 tables, 12 notes. D. E. Bowers

259. Paul, Eliza. CONNING CONGRESS—THE WILD CARD STORY. *Washington Monthly 1974 5(11): 47-50.* Legislation on an interest rate war between banks and savings and loan associations. S

260. Pauly, Mark V. OVERINSURANCE AND PUBLIC PROVISION OF INSURANCE: THE ROLE OF MORAL HAZARD AND ADVERSE SELECTION. *Q. J. of Econ. 1974 88(1): 44-62.*

261. Penn, William S., Jr. and Saunders, J. Edwin. COMMERCIAL BANK TRADING AREAS. *San José Studies 1977 3(3): 91-106.* Examines the impact which trade area has on commercial banking, 1976.

262. Poindexter, J. C. and Jones, C. P. THE EFFECT OF RECENT TAX POLICY CHANGES ON MANUFACTURING INVESTMENT. *Q. R. of Econ. and Business 1973 13(4): 79-88.* "The purpose of this article is to evaluate the impact on manufacturing investment of recent (1971) changes in tax policy. The neoclassical model of investment behavior is employed in a partial equilibrium analysis in which modifications of the cost of capital measure are made and newly published capital stock data are utilized. Estimates of the impact of recent tax policy changes are obtained by predicting gross investment under alternative tax policies. The results suggest that recent tax policy changes have provided a significant stimulus to manufacturing investment during the current expansion." J

263. Porter, Philip K. and Scully, Gerald W. MEASURING MANAGERIAL EFFICIENCY: THE CASE OF BASEBALL. *Southern Econ. J. 1982 48(3): 642-650.* Based on studies of major league baseball teams during 1961-1980, analyzes managerial efficiency by manager and by team, managerial marginal revenue product, rate of change in managerial efficiency over years of experience, and relative factor price efficiency.

264. Rappaport, George D. THE FIRST DESCRIPTION OF THE BANK OF NORTH AMERICA. *William and Mary Q. 1976 33(4): 661-667.* Reproduces the letter of John Wilson to Joseph Pendleton 1 April 1782—the earliest full account of American commercial banking. Wilson, accountant of the Bank of North America, reveals an understanding of principles of commercial banking and also the shortcomings of certain practices of the Bank. The Bank was primarily a service institution. Wilson comments on monetary and credit policies. The brief annotation relates to secondary sources; 19 notes. H. M. Ward

265. Redlich, Fritz. THE ROLE OF PRIVATE BANKS IN THE EARLY ECONOMY OF THE UNITED STATES. *Business Hist. Rev. 1977 51(1): 90-93.* Assesses private banking in early American history and describes the operations of unchartered financial agencies. Tasks for future research are set forward, including an investigation of the origins of deposit creation and the introduction of the check. 3 notes. C. J. Pusateri

266. Riesz, Peter C. SIZE VERSUS PRICE, OR ANOTHER VOTE FOR TONYPANDY. *J. of Business 1973 46(3): 396-403.* An "investigation of the relationship between network television advertising and acquisition activity in a major consumer packaged-goods industry," and a contribution to the controversy over whether there are advertising discounts and price concessions within network television. Both large and small firms budget for a single network with the amount of concentration remaining stable over a wide range of budget sizes. However, "this indirect test of the size-price relationship does not indicate the presence of network pricing structures that systematically favor large advertisers." Based on secondary sources; 2 figs., 2 tables, 14 notes.

C. A. Gallacci

267. Rose, Peter S. and Scott, William L. RISK IN COMMERCIAL BANKING: EVIDENCE FROM POSTWAR FAILURES. *Southern Econ. J. 1978 45(1): 90-106.* Profiles US commercial and savings banks, 1946-76, which have failed for financial and economic reasons.

268. Rosentraub, Mark S. and Nunn, Samuel R. SUBURBAN CITY INVESTMENT IN PROFESSIONAL SPORTS: ESTIMATING THE FISCAL RETURNS OF THE DALLAS COWBOYS AND TEXAS RANGERS TO INVESTOR COMMUNITIES. *Am. Behavioral Scientist 1978 21(3): 393-414.* Explores the extent to which suburbs (as compared with central cities) can hope to recapture original investments used to attract professional teams; uses Arlington and Irving, Texas, discussing history, economic activity, policymaking implications for local government; covers 1968-75.

269. Russell, Francis. BUBBLE, BUBBLE—NO TOIL, NO TROUBLE. *Am. Heritage 1973 24(2): 74-80, 86.* In late 1919, Italian-born Charles Ponzi (1882-1949) opened his Securities and Exchange Company in Boston, Massachusetts. He promised, and paid, 50 percent and higher interest rates for investments. His secret was to take advantage of varying currency exchange rates in different parts of the world. The Boston *Post* finally discovered that Ponzi was an ex-convict, Charles Bianchi, who had been involved in a similar scheme in Canada. His collapse in 1920 brought tangled legal situations, failure of several banks, and revelation of other criminal activities. It did not end his colorful career in other activities. 8 illus. D. L. Smith

270. Schultze, Quentin J. PROFESSIONALISM IN ADVERTISING: THE ORIGIN OF ETHICAL CODES. *J. of Communication 1981 31(2): 64-71.* Discusses professionalism in modern-day advertising as a movement by practitioners to sanction the business's social status and legitimize its economic advantages.

271. Schweikart, Larry. "YOU COUNT IT": THE BIRTH OF BANKING IN ARIZONA. *J. of Arizona Hist. 1981 22(3): 349-368.* Traces the vicissitudes of banking services from 1866 until 1896, when banks were firmly established and regulated. Outlines the role played by the banks in the development of Arizona. 6 photos, 43 notes.   G. O. Gagnon

272. Sfurua, Melor. THE METAMORPHOSES OF THE "BIG BOARD." *Int. Affairs [USSR] 1977 (9): 115-121.* Analyzes the declining condition of the stock market. Some critics argue that financial imperialism is giving way to something better, such as "little man" capitalism, but there is no evidence to support this assertion. In truth, Wall Street has sealed its own doom by scaring away the small investors and not providing enough profits for large investors. The press valiantly endeavors to suppress the growing numbers of suicides, but the fact remains that Wall Street is passing from existence in favor of other, more up-to-date and highly specialized investment structures.   V. L. Human

273. Shapiro, Walter and Kaufman, Aleta. CONFERENCES AND CONVENTIONS: THE $20-BILLION INDUSTRY THAT KEEPS AMERICA FROM WORKING. *Washington Monthly 1977 8(12): 4-11.* Corporate executives and government officials diversify and delegate their work so that conference and convention attendance takes up half of their work time.

274. Simon, Yves. BOURSES DE COMMERCE ET MARCHÉS À TERME DE MARCHANDISES [Produce exchanges and commodity markets]. *Défense Natl. [France] 1979 35(Apr): 121-136.* Studies the spectacular growth in the number and value of transactions dealt with by produce exchanges, 1968-78, with special reference to the newly created US exchanges.

275. Siwek, Andrzej. TOWARZYSTWA UBEZPIECZENIOWE NA RYNKU KAPITALISTYCZNYM [Insurance companies: institutions of finance capital]. *Ekonomista [Poland] 1974 (1): 137-153.* Examines the allocation of insurance companies' capital in the United States and Great Britain, 1945.

276. Slater, Michael. FLATBUSH: CITIBANK'S TEST FLIGHT. *New York Affairs 1982 7(2): 39-49.* Discusses Citibank's Community Banking Pilot program in Brooklyn's Flatbush neighborhood, a private program begun in 1978 to finance and staff a turnaround in Flatbush's housing and commercial decline, planned for three years but, because the project started slowly, expanded to five years.

277. Smiley, Gene. THE EXPANSION OF THE NEW YORK SECURITIES MARKET AT THE TURN OF THE CENTURY. *Business Hist. Rev. 1981 55(1): 75-85.* During 1895-1905 the New York Stock Exchange became the most important national market for industrial securities. At the same time, the first great wave of corporate mergers was taking place. There is evidence that the second event followed from the first. Statistical data indicates investors perceived increases in the expected returns on industrial securities as well as lowered risks for these stocks while bond returns were less satisfactory than before. The result was a shift toward industrial securities in the portfolios of financial institutions. Based principally on published statistical data of the period; 4 tables, 18 notes.

C. J. Pusateri

278. Smiley, Gene. REGIONAL VARIATION ON BANK LOAN RATES IN THE INTERWAR YEARS. *J. of Econ. Hist. 1981 41(4): 889-901.* Reports on estimated country national bank loan rates by state, and city national bank loan rates by city during 1916-40. Describes the variation in country and city bank loan rates. Primary sources; 2 tables, 6 fig., 13 notes. J. Powell

279. Spratt, John S. BANKING PHOBIA IN TEXAS. *Southwest R. 1975 60(4): 341-354.* Describes the history of banks and banking in Texas, from the chartering of the first Bank of Texas in 1835 by the Congress of the Republic, to the present. S

280. Spreng, Francis. THE BIRTH OF THE PITTSBURGH STOCK EXCHANGE. *Western Pennsylvania Hist. Mag. 1975 58(1): 69-80.* Traces the history of stocks, securities, and the oil trade in Pittsburgh which led eventually to the establishment of the Pittsburgh Stock Exchange, 1896. S

281. Stern, Robert N. and Becker, Theodore M. THE EFFECTS OF TASK ENVIRONMENTS ON STRATEGIES FOR CONTROLLING CLIENTS. *Pacific Sociol. R. 1973 16(4): 477-494.* Study of the standardization of task environments and its effect on customers in industrial consulting firms. S

282. Sweezy, Paul. INVESTMENT BANKING REVISITED. *Antioch Rev. 1981 39(2): 241-251.* Reviews the history of investment banking in the United States over the last century, from the financial activities of J. P. Morgan to the international conglomerate of Merrill Lynch in 1980, with special emphasis on the period between 1890 and the outbreak of World War II.

283. Sweezy, Paul M. INVESTMENT BANKING REVISITED. *Monthly Rev. 1982 33(10): 1-14.* Gives an overview of the financial history of the United States during the 19th and early 20th centuries, especially the role of the investment banker, which updates the author's "Decline of the Investment Banker," *Antioch Review* 1941 1(1).

284. Tatalovich, Raymond. A SYSTEMS ANALYSIS OF LEGISLATIVE POLITICS IN THE AMERICAN MEDICAL ASSOCIATION'S HOUSE OF DELEGATES. *Southern Q. 1974 12(3): 253-271.* Analyzes the role, scope, function, and responsibilities of the American Medical Association's House of Delegates. Makes special reference to legislative procedures and actions and assesses positive and negative aspects. 3 tables, 26 notes. R. W. Dubay

285. Tomaskovic-Devey, Donald and McKinlay, John. BAILING OUT THE BANKS: THE UNITED STATES AND PRIVATE INTERNATIONAL DEBT. *Social Policy 1981 11(4): 8-17.* Discusses the US bailout of financially troubled corporations, banks, and Third World nations in the context of the capitalist state's role to create social relations conducive to capital accumulation; and discusses the extent to which the interests of big business influences American economic policy.

286. Urquhart, Michael. THE SERVICES INDUSTRY: IS IT RECESSION-PROOF? *Monthly Labor Rev. 1981 104(10): 12-18.* The growth rate for the services producing sector of the economy (including banking, insurance, medicine, real estate, legal services) continues to grow and remains healthy while being relatively insensitive to cyclical recessions since 1945.

287. Vélez-I., Carlos G. SOCIAL DIVERSITY, COMMERCIALIZATION, AND ORGANIZATIONAL COMPLEXITY OF URBAN MEXICAN/-CHICANO ROTATING CREDIT ASSOCIATIONS: THEORETICAL AND EMPIRICAL ISSUES OF ADAPTATION. *Human Organization 1982 41(2): 107-120.* Analyzes the diversity of sectors in which rotating credit associations occur among Mexicans and Mexican Americans in urban areas of Mexico and the United States during the 1970's, focusing on commercial features relevant to such associations and the complex organizational structures which develop among them.

288. Volk, Stephen. THE ICE HARVEST: THE MEN AND MACHINERY OF A FORGOTTEN INDUSTRY. *Palimpsest 1981 62(3): 90-96.* Describes the big business of ice cutting in 19th-century Iowa, focusing on the machinery used and the men who dominated the industry in Cedar Falls; J. M. Overman, George Clark in the mid-19th century, John Riley by 1893, and Hugh Smith by 1917, whose business continued to serve Cedar Falls until 1934.

289. Wallace, Michael and Kalleberg, Arne L. INDUSTRIAL TRANSFORMATION AND THE DECLINE OF CRAFT: THE DECOMPOSITION OF SKILL IN THE PRINTING INDUSTRY, 1931-1978. *Am. Sociol. Rev. 1982 47(3): 307-324.* Printers have long been considered the epitome of the skilled blue-collar craftsmen. Recently, however, all this has been changing. The steady decline of industrial profit margins after World War II has led many large printing establishments to introduce more sophisticated printing technologies, particularly computerized typesetting processes, which have routinized work tasks and led to a decline of skill among printing craftsmen. Gives substantive and empirical evidence for these processes and supports the theory of industrial transformation. Skill levels in the industry have declined largely due to the shift to capital-intensive printing techniques. Social relations of production between employers and employees influence the nature of technology utilized in an industry.   J/S

290. Watkins, Alfred J. FELIX ROHATYN'S BIGGEST DEAL. *Working Papers Mag. 1981 8(5): 44-52.* Describes the economic program of investment banker Felix Rohatyn, traces his life and financial career, and lists works by and about him, 1940-81.

291. White, Eugene Nelson. THE MEMBERSHIP PROBLEM OF THE NATIONAL BANKING SYSTEM. *Explorations in Econ. Hist. 1982 19(2): 110-127.* In the two decades before 1914, several factors prevented the American national banking system from maintaining its dominance over state-chartered banks. These factors included innovative practices by state banks, such as deposit banking and the rise of trust companies, the reduction of state charter requirements, and the development of antibranch banking lobbies. Based on published documents and statistics and secondary accounts; table, 20 notes, ref.
                                                                                         P. J. Coleman

292. Wicker, Elmus. A RECONSIDERATION OF THE CAUSES OF THE BANKING PANIC OF 1930. *J. of Econ. Hist. 1980 40(3): 571-583.* The banking panic of 1930 has special significance for assessing the causal role of money during the Great Depression. A detailed examination of the panic-induced

bank closings in November reveals that poor loans and investments in the 1920's were the principal factor contributing to the accelerated rate of bank suspensions. These findings are consistent with the Friedman-Schwartz interpretation of the 1930 banking panic as a purely autonomous disturbance largely unrelated to the decline in economic activity. They are inconsistent with Peter Temin's conjecture that declining prices of lower-grade corporate bonds and the agricultural situation played an important causal role.   J

293. Wilkins, Mira. VENEZUELAN INVESTMENT IN FLORIDA: 1979. *Latin Am. Res. Rev. 1981 16(1): 156-165.* Venezuelan investment in Florida has skyrocketed since 1973. The $63 million-plus invested in Dade County land and Florida banks only scratches the surface of Venezuelan investment. Those investing are wealthy entrepreneurs. Among factors stimulating investment are new wealth from high oil prices, the search for new opportunities due to expansion of government ownership at home, and the desire for low-risk investments. Based on Agricultural Stabilization and Conservation Service, Federal Reserve, Comptroller of the Currency, and Securities and Exchange Commission records; table, 2 charts, 26 notes.   J. K. Pfabe

294. Winslow, John. THE BANKER'S ATTACK ON FREE ENTER-PRISE. *Washington Monthly 1976 8(4): 34-41.* The mid-1970's are witnessing new mergers in which banks are financing conglomerate expansion through corporate takeovers which are encouraging monopolies.

295. Yeats, Alexander J.; Irons, Edward D.; and Rhoades, Stephen A. AN ANALYSIS OF NEW BANK GROWTH. *J. of Business 1975 48(2): 199-203.* Using a projection of annual deposit growth based on similarities among 48 banks that opened during 1960-63, shows how costly delays in management decisions can be reduced. The number of years since a bank was established accounted for 48 percent of variation. The percentage change in disposable income in the county, the number of other banks entering the market, and the quarter in which the bank was established accounted for another 15%. Secondary sources; 5 notes.   J. W. Williams

296. Zakharova, V. AKTSIONERNYI KAPITAL I SDVIGI V KREDIT-NOI SISTEME S.SH.A [Share capital and progress in the credit system of the USA]. *Mirovaia Ekonomika i Mezhdunarodnye Otnosheniia [USSR] 1979 (6): 99-107.* Studies the accumulation of share capital by industrial corporations in the United States and the serious changes in credit-finance relations. Tables, biblio.

297. Zanot, Eric J. THE NATIONAL ADVERTISING REVIEW BOARD, 1971-1976. *Journalism Monographs 1979 (59): 1-46.* Modeled on Great Britain's Advertising Standards Agency, the National Advertising Division (NAD) of the Council of Better Business Bureaus (CBBB) and the National Advertising Review Board (NARB) are self-regulating commissions of the advertising industry designed to eradicate false and deceptive advertising.

298. Zelizer, Viviana A. HUMAN VALUES AND THE MARKET: THE CASE OF LIFE INSURANCE AND DEATH IN 19TH-CENTURY AMERICA. *Am. J. of Sociol. 1978 84(3): 591-610.* Discusses the legitimization of life insurance in the 19th century as a result of the establishment of monetary equiva-

lents of death, which previously had been a culturally defined aspect of the social order.

299. Zelizer, Viviana A. THE PRICE AND VALUE OF CHILDREN: THE CASE OF CHILDREN'S INSURANCE. *Am. J. of Sociol. 1981 86(5): 1036-1056.* Children's life insurance, which began in the United States in 1875, was viewed suspiciously because in Europe it had, since the 16th century, seemed an outright bet against a child's survival and, in the 19th century, it perpetuated the view of the lower class child as a mere financial asset. Insurance companies overcame the opposition of child savers, however, by claiming that children's insurance was a symbolic recognition of the sacred value of working class children's lives and a means of providing them with proper mourning rituals, a campaign so successful that in the 20th century children's insurance has become less a token of respect for dead working class children than a token of love for living middle class children.

300. —. [BANKING AND GROWTH IN NINETEENTH CENTURY AMERICA]. *Explorations in Econ. Hist. 1973 10(3): 305-318.*
Redlich, Fritz. AMERICAN BANKING AND GROWTH IN THE NINE-TEENTH CENTURY: EPISTEMOLOGICAL REFLECTIONS, *pp. 305-314.* The author of *The Molding of American Banking: Men and Ideas* (New York: 1968) discusses Richard E. Sylla's criticism of the book in a previous article in *Explorations in Economic History,* 1971-72, 9(2): 197-227.
Sylla, Richard E. ECONOMIC HISTORY "VON UNTEN NACH OBEN" AND "VON OBEN NACH UNTEN": A REPLY TO FRITZ REDLICH, *pp. 315-318.* P. J. Coleman

301. —. "A BIG, BIG, BUSINESS." *Southern Exposure 1980 8(3): 36-40.* Real estate developer Perry Mendel's day nursery company, Kinder-Care Learning Centers, Incorporated, started in Montgomery, Alabama, in 1969 and now has over 600 centers in 35 states and two Canadian provinces.

302. —. [EARLY PRIVATE BANKERS]. *J. of Econ. Hist. 1976 36(1): 173-197.*
Sylla, Richard. FORGOTTEN MEN OF MONEY: PRIVATE BANKERS IN EARLY U.S. HISTORY, *pp. 173-188.* Historical accounts of banking developments in the pre-1860 period of U.S. history focus almost exclusively on banking institutions chartered by state and federal governments. Private, unincorporated banks, although known to have existed, are generally ignored as either unimportant numerically or not truly commercial banks in terms of their functions. This paper draws on a variety of literary and quantitative evidence to infer that such views are perhaps in error. Some potential implications of the findings for antebellum banking and monetary history are essayed.
Davis, Lance E. and Cochran, Thomas C. DISCUSSION, *pp. 189-197.*
J

303. —. REVIEW OF THE MONTH: BANKS—SKATING ON THIN ICE. *Monthly R. 1975 26(9): 1-21.* Discusses the current economic crisis, including the social class implications, facing America's banks and the capitalist system in general.

3

TRANSPORTATION

304. Aldrich, Mark. A NOTE ON RAILROAD RATES AND THE POPULIST UPRISING. *Agric. Hist. 1980 54(3): 424-432.* Populism movement was related to changes in railroad rates on agricultural goods. Traditionally it has been believed that the Populists appeared because of long-term rising or steady railroad rates. But political science theory contends that protests occur when conditions deteriorate after a period of improvement. A look at railroad rates suggests that the political science model is correct. Railroad rates generally fell until about 1880, then began to rise into the 1890's at a time when water transportation rates were still falling. Uses railroad data and secondary sources; 3 tables, 18 notes.   D. E. Bowers

305. Altshuler, Constance Wynn. THE SOUTHERN PACIFIC CAPER. *J. of Arizona Hist. 1980 21(1): 1-10.* Traces the illegal opening of Arizona's first railroad line by the Southern Pacific Railroad. Ignoring prohibitions from Washington and the military, the company simply built the line and began operations; public opinion protected the company from any consequences. Covers 1875-78. Based on periodical, archival and secondary sources; 4 pictures, 8 notes.
G. O. Gagnon

306. Atack, Jeremy et al. THE PROFITABILITY OF STEAMBOATING ON WESTERN RIVERS: 1850. *Business Hist. R. 1975 49(3): 346-354.* Assesses rates of return in steamboating on western rivers in the mid-19th century. Concludes that the enterprise was not a losing investment after 1830, as previous writers have argued, and that the profit was "approximately the same as that earned in slave-based cotton farming." Based on government censuses of manufacturing; table, 34 notes.   C. J. Pusateri

307. Baerwald, Hans H. LOCKHEED AND JAPANESE POLITICS. *Asian Survey 1976 16(9): 817-829.* Japanese politicians accepted bribes from Lockheed Corporation officials in 1976; the disclosures affected Lockheed and Japanese national politics.

308. Bail, Eli. CALIFORNIA BY MOTOR STAGE. *California Hist. Q. 1976 55(4): 306-325.* Traces the growth of intercity bus transportation in California from the 1910's to the Great Depression. Early California stage operators were numerous and innovative, modifying truck chassis and heavier auto bodies to create unique motor stages well in advance of similar efforts back East. As natural opponents of the railroads, motor stage companies organized the Motor

Carriers Association of California in 1918. Three major companies emerged by the early 1920's: California Transit Company, Pickwick Stages, and Motor Transit Company. The companies built their own buses, provided transporation throughout California and as far east as El Paso, and competed successfully with railroads. By 1926 they consolidated to eliminate inefficiency through relentless competition. The Railroad Commission approved the Tri-Stage Merger, defining territories of service for the three leading companies. The Greyhound system soon absorbed the California Transit Company and Pickwick Stages. Motor Transit Company was bought by Pacific Electric in 1930. With the Great Depression, the companies no longer built their own buses. Photos.   A. Hoffman

309.   Baker, William A.   THE CLIPPERS.   *Mankind 1976 5(9): 60-65.* The golden age of clipper shipbuilding was from 1850 until 1857, when the construction of such vessels was curtailed by an economic depression in the United States. The clipper ships were developed to take advantage of trade offering high freight rates for speedy passage, with the China trade being an early example. The use of clipper ships was considerable in the trade network created between the east coast and California following the discovery of gold in the latter area, and between the United States, Great Britain, and Australia following gold strikes in Australia in 1851. The average sailing time for clipper ships from New York around Cape Horn to San Francisco was 130 days, with many ships cutting that time down to 100 days and, on occasion, even shorter periods. The "Down-Easter" clipper ships represented the highest development of the sailing merchant ship in the history of the world.   N. Lederer

310.   Baldwin, Deborah.   AMTRAK: THE WRECK WE HAVE TO FIX. *Washington Monthly 1979 11(3): 42-48.* Describes the positive aspects of riding Amtrak based on a train trip taken in 1979, but points out that the meals are poor and schedule confusion is typical.

311.   Barrett, Paul.   PUBLIC POLICY AND PRIVATE CHOICE: MASS TRANSIT AND THE AUTOMOBILE IN CHICAGO BETWEEN THE WARS.   *Business Hist. Rev. 1975 49(4): 473-497.* Traces the decline of mass transit riding and the growing reliance on automobile transportation during the first half of the 20th century. Attributes the alteration in riding habits to a number of factors including outmoded public policies that discouraged both new private investment in and also public ownership of transit systems. Based on primary and secondary sources; 68 notes.   C. J. Pusateri

312.   Barrett, Paul.   TRANSPORTATION: TECHNOLOGY AND POLICY.   *Social Sci. J. 1981 18(2): 105-109.* Reviews Charles Bright's *The Jet Makers: The Aerospace Industry from 1945 to 1972* (Lawrence: Regents Press of Kansas, 1978), and Mark H. Rose's *Interstate: Express Highway Politics 1941-1956* (Lawrence: Regents Press of Kansas, 1979), two works which expose an important source of confusion about transportation policy: its apparent purposefulness belies a reality of compromise and reaction to crisis.

313.   Barsness, Richard W.   MARITIME ACTIVITY AND PORT DEVELOPMENT IN THE UNITED STATES SINCE 1900: A SURVEY.   *J. of Transport Hist. [Great Britain] 1974 2(3): 167-184.* Port development in the United States, especially in the 20th century, has been a neglected area of historical

research. Surveys ports with particular reference to large scale growth in total commerce, fundamental technological changes in merchant vessels and cargo handling systems, the appearance of endemic industrial disputes since the 1930's, and the various factors which have led to increased port competition. Primary and secondary sources; fig., 51 notes. R. G. Neville

314. Bassett, Thomas Day Seymour. 500 MILES OF TROUBLE AND EX-CITEMENT: VERMONT RAILROADS, 1848-1861. *Vermont Hist. 1981 49(3): 133-153.* Railroads, collectively the largest 19th-century Vermont enterprise, affected every element in Vermont society, and changed the landscape and the human outlook. New village centers developed near depots. What Boston and local capitalists lost on railroad bankruptcies they sometimes regained in trade, real estate and other industry, while the managers and their lawyers profited. Farms rose in value and shipped more livestock and dairy products to Boston. Accidents claimed victims among workmen and passengers, with little compensation. Hillsides were stripped of woods to fuel the locomotives which substituted coal by the 1860's. 10 illus., map, 35 notes. A

315. Beene, Graham. WHERE ARE YOU NOW BENITO, NOW THAT WE NEED YOU? *Washington Monthly 1980 12(2): 51-58.* Discusses the failure of the Northeast Corridor Improvement Project (NECIP) to improve rail passenger service in the Boston-Washington area since its inception in 1976.

316. Bezilla, Michael. THE DEVELOPMENT OF ELECTRIC TRACTION ON THE PENNSYLVANIA RAILROAD, 1895-1968. *Pennsylvania Hist. 1979 46(3): 195-211.* By 1938, the Pennsylvania Railroad had electrified 600 route-miles of track. Almost all of this electrification was accomplished after 1928 at a cost in excess of $250,000,000. Financial factors, including the artificially lower cost of operating diesel engines, prevented further electrification. Suggests that electrification of heavily travelled lines may again become feasible if petroleum prices continue to climb. 3 photos, 28 notes. D. C. Swift

317. Bezilla, Michael. STEAM RAILROAD ELECTRIFICATION IN AMERICA, 1920-1950: THE UNREALIZED POTENTIAL. *Public Hist. 1982 4(1): 29-52.* Traces the use of electric traction for locomotive power, introduced in 1895 by the Baltimore and Ohio Railroad; other railroads did not convert to electric power from steam power, switching to diesel instead during the 1940's and early 50's.

318. Bias, Charles V. THE MERGER OF THE CHESAPEAKE AND OHIO RAILWAY AND THE BALTIMORE AND OHIO RAILROAD COMPANIES. *J. of the West Virginia Hist. Assoc. 1980 4(1): 24-34.* Chronicles the consolidation of the Chesapeake and Ohio Railway and the Baltimore and Ohio Railroad under the Transportation Act (US, 1940), emphasizing state and Interstate Commerce Commission participation in final decisions, 1958-62.

319. Black, Paul V. EMPLOYEE ALCOHOLISM ON THE BURLING-TON RAILROAD, 1876-1902. *J. of the West 1978 17(4): 5-11.* The management of the Chicago, Burlington & Quincy Railroad (CB&Q) tried several means to eliminate alcohol-related incidents. The initial policy, formed in the 1860's, was to prohibit liquor sales in company-owned facilities, and to discourage employees' patronage of saloons. The second major policy was enforced temperance, both on

and off duty, under threat of dismissal. A meeting of the CB&Q Superintendents' Association in 1883 established a policy that survived 20 years, but gave enforcement power to local authorities rather than to the board of directors. Based on Chicago, Burlington & Quincy Railroad Papers, Newberry Library, Chicago, Illinois; 3 photos, 37 notes.   B. S. Porter

320. Blair, Seabury. HOW WE HUSTLED SILK TO THE EAST. *Pacific Northwesterner 1981 25(4): 49-57.* Trains shipped raw silk imported from China and Japan from the docks at Vancouver, B.C., Seattle, Portland, and San Francisco; focuses on the northern and western railroads such as the Great Northern, the Union Pacific, Northern Pacific, and the CMStP&P.

321. Bohi, Charles W. and Grant, H. Roger. STANDARDIZED RAILROAD STATIONS IN KANSAS: THE CASE OF THE ATCHISON, TOPEKA & SANTA FE. *Kansas Hist. 1981 4(1): 39-52.* Railroad depots contained a waiting room, office, and freight-baggage areas. Competition and civic pressure drove many lines to build elaborate stations, but the Santa Fe relied mainly on standardized buildings. At first, its stations had only two minor structural features that distinguished them from other stations: a beveled bay and an overhanging roof. These features gave the agent a better view of the track and shielded him from the sun. Around 1890 the line added a gabled dormer over the office, a structural feature that made it even easier to identify its stations. Once the line was satisfied that a town was becoming an important center, it often rebuilt the station of brick or stone, but the gabled-dormer hallmark remained. Kansas Public Utilities Commission reports, Kansas State Board of Railroad Commissions reports, articles and books; illus., 3 drawings, 8 notes.
                                                                    W. F. Zornow

322. Brooks, Peter W. THE COMING OF JET TRANSPORTATION. *Aerospace Hist. 1981 28(4): 218-229.* Surveys the development of jet transportation and assesses the comparative launching costs and engineering and manufacturing effort required for each successive generation of aircraft. Beginning with the De Havilland Comet of the early 1950's, new types of airliners have been introduced every 12 or 13 years. By the 1970's the great bulk of the world's airline capacity consisted of wide-body subsonic jets massively supported by many smaller standard-body aircraft of broadly similar performance. The cost, in constant values, for each generation increased by a factor of four, while the aircraft's weight and the engineering and production man-hours required roughly doubled. Primary sources; 9 photos, 7 tables, 32 notes.   J. K. Ohl

323. Brown, A. E. THE LOUISIANA & ARKANSAS RAILWAY: STRUCTURE AND OPERATION IN THE AGE OF STEAM. *Railroad Hist. 1981 (144): 51-59.* Provides a history of the Louisiana & Arkansas Railway, one of the last major railroads formed in the United States, noting its chartering in 1898 near Springhill, Louisiana, and its assimilation of the Louisiana Railway & Navigation Co. in 1929.

324. Brown, Dee. THE TRANSCONTINENTAL RAILROAD. *Am. Heritage 1977 28(2): 14-25.* After 1869 it was possible to travel by train to the Pacific Ocean. The trip was long and nerve-racking. Indians, buffalo, prairie fires, blizzards, snow drifts, poor food and numerous stops combined to provide adventure for the passengers. 7 illus.   B. J. Paul

325. Burt, William D. THE PLOT TO TAKE OVER AMERICA'S RAIL-ROADS. *Reason 1981 12(11): 20-28.* Discusses the move toward nationalization of railroads in the United States, catalyzed by the Federal Railroad Administration (FRA), a part of the Department of Transportation since the mid-1960's.

326. Butler, Bruce. LAST CALL OF THE STEAM WHISTLE ON RAILS OF THE INLAND EMPIRE. *Pacific Northwesterner 1981 25(4): 58-64.* History of railroads in the Pacific Northwest from 1851, when F. A. Chenoweth built a portage line around the rapids of the Columbia River near The Dalles, Oregon, until the use of steampower ended and diesel power grew; the last steam engine ceased operation in 1958.

327. Butler, John L. THE SANDUSKY AUTOMOBILE COMPANY. *Northwest Ohio Q. 1980 52(4): 261-272.* Traces the history of the Sandusky Automobile Company, focusing on the conceptual contributions made by Sandusky president James J. Hinde to the production strategy of Henry Ford.

328. Butler, W. Daniel. THE NEZPERCE RAILROAD WAR. *J. of the West. 1978 17(4): 21-27.* The Union Pacific and the Northern Pacific railroads, rivals in the 1880's and 1890's for rights-of-way in north-central Idaho, compromised by agreeing to joint operations under the name Camas Prairie Railroad Company (CPRC). Their monopoly was soon threatened by T. A. Johnson of the Nezperce & Idaho Railroad line, who wanted to expand into the timber region of the Camas Prairie's service area. Through the 1910's, Johnson constructed short lines on limited capital until, in 1922, he was indebted and defeated by the more powerful CPRC. Based on records of the CPRC; 5 photos, 2 maps.
B. S. Porter

329. Canes, Douglas W.; Christensen, Laurits R.; and Swanson, Joseph A. PRODUCTIVITY GROWTH, SCALE ECONOMICS, AND CAPACITY UTILIZATION IN U.S. RAILROADS, 1955-74. *Am. Econ. Rev. 1981 71(5): 994-1002.* Given the change of trip and haul lengths, it is difficult to achieve a clear or constant estimate of productivity growth. The variable cost function and total cost function revealed different estimates of productivity growth. Apparently, behavioral assumptions have serious implications for measuring productivity growth. 7 tables, biblio.
D. K. Pickens

330. Carlson, Robert. IVAN D. CHRISTIANSON—GRANVILLE. *North Dakota Hist. 1977 44(4): 31-33.* Interviews longtime railroad employee Ivan D. Christianson. Granville, South Dakota, was a bustling railroad entrepot during the 1920's as farmers shipped large quantities of grain out of the area and received supplies in return. Rapid shipment of grain following harvest was essential, given the paucity of grain storage facilities. Station personnel had to be adept in many preautomation skills, including mail shipment and receipt, telegraphy, and train communication.
N. Lederer

331. Carlson, Rodney L. SEEMINGLY UNRELATED REGRESSION AND THE DEMAND FOR AUTOMOBILES OF DIFFERENT SIZES, 1965-75: A DISAGGREGATE APPROACH. *J. of Business 1978 51(2): 243-262.* Breaking the automobile market into segments—subcompact, compact, intermediate, full-size, and luxury—helps explain the demand for 1965-75. Per capita

disposable income had the greatest impact; auto stock, the least. Sale price influenced subcompacts and luxury demands least, partly because subcompacts became popular as second cars, reflecting rising living standards. Feelings that only subcompacts give real gas economy will enhance subcompact sales if either gasoline shortages or higher gasoline prices develop. Secondary sources; 3 tables, 2 graphs, 20 notes.   J. W. Williams

332. Carnes, Richard B. PRODUCTIVITY TRENDS IN INTERCITY TRUCKING. *Monthly Labor Rev. 1974 97(1): 53-57.* Surveys productivity trends in intercity trucking in the United States between 1954 and 1972; the fairly uniform increase reflected the gradual introduction of technological innovation, larger capacity trucks, and an improved interstate highway system.

333. Carnes, Richard B. PRODUCTIVITY TRENDS FOR INTERCITY BUS CARRIERS. *Monthly Labor Rev. 1981 104(5): 23-27.* Briefly profiles the Class I regulated bus industry since the early 1900's when it began, focusing on the 0.4% rise in productivity per employee-hour during 1954-79 due to "a small average annual increase in industry output of 0.1 percent combined with an average annual decline in employee hours of 0.3 percent."

335. Chandler, William W. ORIGIN AND GROWTH OF FAST FREIGHT LINES. *Railroad Hist. 1979 (141): 98-115.* Traces the need for and the development and merits of fast freight railroads, from the 1850's to 1889; reprinted from *The Station Agent,* December 1889.

336. Church, Roy. MYTHS, MEN, AND MOTOR CARS: A REVIEW ARTICLE. *J. of Transport Hist. [Great Britain] 1977 4(2): 102-112.* Review article prompted by David Lewis's *The Public Image of Henry Ford: An American Folk Hero and his Company* (Wayne State U. Pr., 1976) and R. J. Overy's *William Morris, Viscount Nuffield* (London: Europa Publications, 1976). Compares Henry Ford and William Morris, their respective approaches to their social origins, their apprenticeships, and their attitudes toward production methods, advertising, and free enterprise. The Ford organization consisted of a huge integrated plant as a single facility. Morris preferred to rely on the supply of assembly components from specialists. This meant that whereas Ford was soon immersed in the complex problems of large-scale internal management, Morris's managerial role before 1924 centered on coordination of component suppliers and control of a relatively small work force. Secondary sources; 8 notes.   C. Anstey

337. Cicarelli, James. WHATEVER HAPPENED TO THE TURBINE CAR? *Bull. of the Atomic Scientists 1974 30(10): 25-28.* Examines the turbine engine and its obvious advantages—low oil consumption, minimal maintenance, and low exhaust emissions—over internal combustion engines; assesses the attitudes of the automobile industry toward mass production of such cars, during 1953-73.

338. Clark, Christopher. THE RAILROAD SAFETY PROBLEM IN THE USA 1900-1930. *Transport Hist. [Great Britain] 1977 6(3)-7(1): 54-74.* Sees inadequacies in US railroads in the 1900's and considers whether these were removed in the 1920's sufficiently to account for the dramatic fall in the accident rate. Railroad safety was achieved primarily because of the threats of road competition and public ownership. 92 notes. See also abstract 15A:1220.
                                                                    C. A. McNeill

339. Clark, Christopher. THE RAILROAD SAFETY PROBLEM IN THE UNITED STATES 1900-1930. *Transport Hist. [Great Britain] 1974 7(2): 97-123.* Between 1890 and 1910 the rate of railroad accidents to passengers and employees in the United States rose sharply, but after 1914 this trend was reversed. Discounts the "traffic level" theory as an explanation and discusses other aspects of railroad safety including: 1) the introduction of safety devices, safety appliance laws, research projects, improved recruitment and training of labor procedures, better working conditions, and equipment maintenance standards, 2) the establishment of Employers' Liability legislation which ended the essentially laissez-faire attitude of railroad companies to accidents, 3) advances in permanent way and block signaling, 4) the rising cost of accidents and the emergence of the belief among employers that the prevention of accidents was financially advantageous, and 5) the inauguration by companies of safety departments and campaigns. Points to areas of study, such as the role of government and labor, where more thorough research is required. Primary and secondary sources; 2 graphs, 92 notes.   R. G. Neville

340. Cotroneo, Ross R. RESERVING THE SUBSURFACE: THE MINERAL LANDS POLICY OF THE NORTHERN PACIFIC RAILWAY. *North Dakota Hist. 1973 40(3): 16-25.* To secure adequate funds for construction and the stimulation of immigration and permanent settlements, the Northern Pacific Railway initiated a policy of selling land surrounding the railroad. The company insisted on reserving mineral rights on most of the property even though this resulted in loss of sales to purchasers who wanted clear title. However, hostile public reaction and state and local government taxation of mineral reservations altered company policy to allow for the release of some mineral rights. The author analyzes the evolution of company policy, focusing on the Montana and North Dakota situation. Based on letters and company reports; 7 illus., 54 notes.
S. Tomlinson-Brown

341. Cox, Thomas R. SINGLE DECKS AND FLAT BOTTOMS: BUILDING THE WEST COAST'S LUMBER FLEET, 1850-1929. *J. of the West 1981 20(3): 65-74.* In the 1850's any available vessel was used as a lumber carrier. During 1860-80 San Francisco was the center for construction of crafts designed specifically for the coast lumber trade. Shipbuilding in Oregon and Washington offered some competition, but steam schooners were produced more efficiently in the San Francisco Bay area, near sources of metal and machinery. By the 1920's several port cities made steel-hulled vessels for the cargo trade, but the industry ended in the Great Depression. During 1850-1929, ship design and materials were modified to meet the demands of a specialized trade on a dangerous coastline. Based on material in special collections in libraries of the universities of Oregon and Washington, and published works; 5 photos, illus., 40 notes.
B. S. Porter

342. Crafton, Steven M. and Hoffer, George E. ESTIMATING A TRANSACTION PRICE FOR NEW AUTOMOBILES. *J. of Business 1981 54(4): 611-621.* Researchers' assumptions have contradicted earlier findings that transaction prices and list prices differed significantly. This paper develops a model estimating the transaction prices of new automobiles. It is argued that transaction prices for new automobiles are market determined. Transaction prices are found to be a function of dealer inventories and several other variables. Dealer invento-

ries measured in terms of daily selling rates are used in the model as a proxy for market conditions.   J/S

343.   Crowther, Simeon J.   THE SHIPBUILDING OUTPUT OF THE DEL-AWARE VALLEY, 1722-1776.   *Pro. of the Am. Phil. Soc. 1973 117(2): 90-104.* Describes the quantitative output of colonial shipbuilding in the areas of south-eastern Pennsylvania, Delaware, and West Jersey for 1722-76, and "casts new light on the development of Atlantic commerce as a whole in the eighteenth century." Based on the Ship Register of Pennsylvania, Pennsylvania Land Grant Manuscripts, and secondary sources; 11 tables, 26 notes.   C. W. Olson

344.   Cull, George E.   THE LARK-95.   *Am. Aviation Hist. Soc. J. 1980 25(4): 277-280.* Discusses the early days of the California Aero Company, formed in 1958 by the author and Ronald R. Logan to build planes, the Lark-95 in particular, as it was officially designated in 1960; 1958-63.

345.   DeLorean, John Z. and Wright, J. Patrick.   BOTTOM-LINE FEVER AT GENERAL MOTORS.   *Washington Monthly 1980 11(11): 26-35.* Excerpt from former General Motors Corporation executive DeLorean's autobiographical *On a Clear Day You Can See General Motors,* originally scheduled to be published by Playboy Press, withdrawn, and finally published by coauthor Wright.

346.   Derrick, W. Edwin and Smallwood, James.   MILES OF TRACK: THE COMING OF RAILROADS TO OKLAHOMA.   *Red River Valley Hist. Rev. 1981 6(3): 87-93.* Covers most of the important rail developments in the state and the hardships of building such roads; by the time of statehood in 1907, the network of railroads in Oklahoma was virtually complete.

347.   de Vries, John A.   BILL MCMAHON, THE MOONEY "FLIVVER" AND THE GRAY GOOSE.   *Am. Aviation Hist. Soc. J. 1979 24(4): 288-290.* Bill McMahon, an airline electrician, combined forces with designers Al Mooney and his brother Art Mooney in Denver, Colorado, to produce a monoplane named the Mooney *Flivver* in 1930, and then he joined the Lewis-American Aircraft Co. in Denver to build the *Gray Goose* in 1933.

348.   Dew, Lee A.   OWENSBORO'S DREAM OF GLORY: A RAILROAD TO RUSSELLVILLE.   *Filson Club Hist. Q. 1978 52(1): 26-45.* Chronicles the many problems faced by the promoters of a railroad between Owensboro and Russellville, Kentucky. Supported primarily by local government bonds, the road was started in 1869 and not completed until 1883. By that time the road had been absorbed into the larger Louisville and Nashville Railroad system which provided the necessary capital to complete it. Based on local newspapers and Louisville and Nashville records at the Tennessee State Library and Archives; 70 notes.
                                                                G. B. McKinney

349.   Dickson, Paul.   THE GREAT RAILROAD WAR OF 1877.   *Am. Heritage 1978 29(2): 56-61.* The railroad strike of 1877 resulted from wage cuts made by the railroads during the Depression of 1873. Though most of the nation was affected, Pittsburgh was hit hardest. Before it ended, federal troops had been sent in and more than 100 persons had been killed. The strike failed primarily because of its lack of organization. 14 illus.   J. F. Paul

350. Doezema, William R. RAILROAD MANAGEMENT AND THE INTERPLAY OF FEDERAL AND STATE REGULATION, 1885-1916. *Business Hist. Rev. 1976 50(2): 153-178.* Seeks to answer whether railroad managers sought federal regulation of their lines in order to avoid the chaos of state rules. Uses content analysis of two railroad journals and their editorials over three decades. Concludes that the historical literature of the past has overestimated the radicalism of state regulation, and that many railroad executives found it profitable to exploit the inconsistencies in state laws. Based on periodical material; 3 tables, 58 notes.   C. J. Pusateri

351. Dole, Richard F. THE PORTLAND COMPANY. *Railroad Hist. 1978 (139): 5-38.* The Portland Company manufactured railroad machinery and locomotives in Portland, Maine, 1848-1906.

352. Dornfeld, A. A. STEAMSHIPS: A HUNDRED YEARS AGO. *Chicago Hist. 1975 4(3): 148-156.* Discusses the importance of steamship travel to the development of Chicago and some of the famous steamships in its history, 1821-1949.   S

353. Dornfield, A. A. STEAMSHIPS AFTER 1871. *Chicago Hist. 1977 6(1): 12-22.* Discusses the evolution of steamships, 1871-1976 and their importance in shipping on the Great Lakes as they virtually put schooners out of business.

354. Dortmund, E. K. AN AMERICAN TRINITY: RAILROADS, LAND GRANTS, AND CORRUPTION IN THE 1850'S. *Res. Studies 1974 42(3): 167-174.*

355. Drennan, Matthew P. NEW YORK'S AIRLINES INDUSTRY FLIES HIGH. *New York Affairs 1980 6(2): 80-84.* Briefly traces the airline industry in the United States since 1958 as background to that industry in New York City, where it is one of the biggest and brings in huge profits (in 1978 the airlines added more than $1.5 billion to the city).

356. Due, John F. A COMMENT ON RECENT CONTRIBUTIONS TO THE ECONOMICS OF THE RAILWAY INDUSTRY. *J. of Econ. Literature 1975 13(4): 1315-1320.* Bibliographical essay concerning the problems of railroads during the 1970's and the economic reforms needed by the industry.

357. Duggan, Edward P. MACHINES, MARKETS, AND LABOR: THE CARRIAGE AND WAGON INDUSTRY IN LATE-NINETEENTH-CENTURY CINCINNATI. *Business Hist. Rev. 1977 51(3): 308-325.* Tests H. J. Habakkuk's labor supply hypothesis which asserts that a labor shortage stimulated rapid technological change. Carriage and wagon producers in Cincinnati did not appear to suffer from such a shortage. They sought production techniques to increase output, not to save on labor costs. They also invested more capital in developing markets than in manufacturing, indicating a belief that there was more to gain from marketing innovations than from production. Based on governmental records and periodical sources; 30 notes.   C. J. Pusateri

358. Duke, John. NEW-CAR DEALERS EXPERIENCE LONG-TERM GAINS IN PRODUCTIVITY. *Monthly Labor Rev. 1977 100(3): 29-33.* Analyzes the output productivity, profits, and employment patterns involved in the operations of franchised new-car dealers during 1958-75.

359. Dunn, James A., Jr. PUBLIC OWNERSHIP OF U.S. RAILROADS IN COMPARATIVE PERSPECTIVE. *Policy Studies J. 1975 4(1): 49-53.* Reformulates the debate over nationalization of the railroads in light of other nations' experiences.

360. Edson, William D. THE ILLINOIS TERMINAL: CORPORATE STRUCTURE AND STEAM POWER. *Railroad Hist. 1981 (145): 106-109.* Presents a brief history of the expansion of the Illinois Terminal Railroad, from its charter in 1895 until its acquisition by the Norfolk & Western in 1981, including a roster of the railroad's steam powered engines from 1899 to 1924.

361. Eggert, Gerald G. GUNFIRE AND BRICKBATS: THE GREAT RAILWAY STRIKES OF 1877. *Am. Hist. Illus. 1981 16(2): 16-25.* Tells of the bloody railway strike that began in West Virginia in July 1877 and spread to rail centers in all parts of the country leading to disorders that "produced the first near-national emergency strike in the country's history, led to massive governmental intervention in a labor dispute, established important precedents for dealing with later strikes, and opened a new epoch in American labor history."

362. Fabar, Al. AUTO IN THE EIGHTIES: UNCARS AND UNWORKERS. *Radical Am. 1979 13(1): 30-37.* Discusses the "1973-74 oil embargo and price rise, government-imposed fuel economy standards, and the re-emergence of intense international auto market competition," their effects on the US automobile industry, and "possible ramifications of those changes for working class politics in the industrial sector."

363. Fisher, Barbara. MARITIME HISTORY OF THE READING, 1833-1905. *Pennsylvania Mag. of Hist. and Biog. 1962 86(2): 160-180.* Describes the role that the Reading Railroad played in Philadelphia's maritime progress and in the reshaping of the port of Philadelphia from 1833 to 1905, a period when America began to look westward for trade, rather than to Europe and the Atlantic markets.

364. Fleisig, Heywood. THE CENTRAL PACIFIC RAILROAD AND THE RAILROAD LAND GRANT CONTROVERSY. *J. of Econ. Hist. 1975 35(3): 552-566.* Questions whether promoters of the Central Pacific Railroad (now Southern Pacific) were oversubsidized. Confirms the traditional view that subsidies were not an economic necessity because they "influenced neither the decision to invest in the railroad nor the speed of its construction." Notes that estimates of rate of return for the railroad developers using government funds range from 71% to 200%, while estimates of private rates of return range from 15% to 25%. Based on primary and secondary sources; table, 42 notes.

D. J. Trickey

365. Fleisig, Heywood. THE UNION PACIFIC RAILROAD AND THE RAILROAD LAND GRANT CONTROVERSY. *Explorations in Econ. Hist. 1973/74 11(2): 155-172.* Confirms the traditional view that land grants affected

neither the decision to construct railroads nor the pace of construction. Both the projected and the actual rate of return on the investment was so adequate as to make subsidization a "giveaway." Based on primary and secondary sources; 2 tables, 46 notes.										P. J. Coleman

366.	Floyd, Fred.	THE STRUGGLE FOR RAILROADS IN THE OKLA-HOMA PANHANDLE.	*Chronicles of Oklahoma 1976/77 54(4): 489-518.* Examines difficulties of residents of the Oklahoma panhandle area in attaining adequate railroad systems due to confusing territorial status and poor economic conditions, 1880's-1930's.

367.	Foster, Mark Stewart.	DELIVERING THE MASSES: RECENT EX-CURSIONS IN TRANSPORTATION HISTORY.	*J. of Urban Hist. 1981 7(3): 381-389.* Reviews six books dealing with automobiles and urban transportation and finds that the authors agree on few points although there is a consensus that the politicization of transportation has hampered technological development and innovation. 6 notes.										T. W. Smith

368.	Frankel, Ernst G.	THE POTENTIAL FOR FOREIGN OWNERSHIP IN THE U.S. MARITIME INDUSTRY.	*US Naval Inst. Pro. 1980 106(2): 36-41.* Many foreign industrial firms are investing heavily in US shipyards and shipping companies. Foreign investments in and foreign ownership of US ship-yards and shipping may come about soon. It is quite possible that soon much of the US shipbuilding industry could be foreign-owned. This would not necessarily be bad, because foreign investment does offer some advantages. At the same time, however, the United States must make certain that certain major elements of the maritime industry in this country do not fall under foreign control. 2 photos.
										A. N. Garland

369.	Frew, James R.	THE EXISTENCE OF MONOPOLY PROFITS IN THE MOTOR CARRIER INDUSTRY.	*J. of Law & Econ. 1981 24(2): 289-315.* Presents a model of certificate valuation for motor carriers of general freight, which shows a consistent pattern of monopoly rents in the motor carrier industry.

370.	Frye, Harry A.	THE FITCHBURG RAILROAD: A CORPORATE GENEALOGY.	*Railroad Hist. 1982 (146): 60-63.* Traces the changing owner-ship and corporate consolidation of the Fitchburg Railroad, chartered in 1842, which was absorbed by the B & M Railroad in 1919; the last Fitchburg locomo-tive survived until 1939.

371.	Fuller, John W.	INFLATIONARY EFFECTS ON TRANSPORTA-TION.	*Ann. of the Am. Acad. of Pol. and Social Sci. 1981 (456): 112-122.* US transportation is faced with uncertainty, overextension, and bankruptcy, due less to energy price inflation or the high cost of replacement capital than to a long history of inappropriate government policies. Economic regulation and govern-ment promotion, in virtually every mode of transportation, have led to inflexibil-ity and technological stagnation. A complicating factor in this inflationary period, however, is the tie between energy consumption and public user-fee receipts, which has led to modal service declines or higher subsidies as energy prices have risen.										J/S

372. Gibb, Hugh R. MENDES COHEN: ENGINEER, SCHOLAR AND RAILROAD EXECUTIVE. *Maryland Hist. Mag. 1979 74(1): 1-10.* A testimonial to the life and career of Mendes Cohen (1831-1915) of Baltimore, whose engineering innovations were instrumental in the expansion of the early Baltimore & Ohio. As president of the Pittsburgh & Connellsville Railroad, he unsuccessfully fought the Pennsylvania Railroad for control of the Pittsburgh traffic in the 1870's. One of Baltimore's leading citizens, he served on commissions for everything from streetcar fenders to a sanitary sewage system, and was closely involved with the Maryland Historical Society—as secretary during 1882-1904 and as president during 1904-13. His home at 825 North Charles Street was a center of civic activity, philanthropy, and American railroad history. Primary sources; 27 notes. G. J. Bobango

373. Gordinier, Glenn S. MARITIME ENTERPRISE IN NEW JERSEY: GREAT EGG HARBOR DURING THE NINETEENTH CENTURY. *New Jersey Hist. 1979 97(2): 105-117.* Shipbuilding and coastal trade were the two most important aspects of maritime enterprise in Great Egg Harbor. At least 27 wharves in this area were involved in trading goods domestically. A customs port handled foreign vessels. The availability of lumber from nearby forests made the construction of ships profitable. The lack of local railroads, a decline in the use of wooden ships, and the closing of the customs district all contributed to the fall of Great Egg Harbor's stature in the early 20th century. Secondary sources; illus., map, 29 notes. E. R. McKinstry

374. Grant, H. Roger. CAPTIVE CORPORATIONS: THE FARMERS' GRAIN & SHIPPING COMPANY, 1896-1945. *North Dakota Hist. 1982 49(1): 4-10.* The Farmers' Grain & Shipping Company, founded as a farmers' railroad by Joseph M. Kelley during the peak years of Populist reform, soon became a captive corporation of the Great Northern. Because farmers in Ramsey and Towner counties, North Dakota, benefited, it existed until Great Northern chose to effect a dissolution in 1945. Based on F G & S Co. Papers in Great Northern Collection, Minnesota Historical Society; 25 notes, 6 illus. G. L. Olson

375. Grant, H. Roger. "INTERURBANS ARE THE WAVE OF THE FUTURE": ELECTRIC RAILWAY PROMOTION IN TEXAS. *Southwestern Hist. Q. 1980 84(1): 29-48.* During the 1890's, electric railway developers promised to bring affordable, clean, convenient transportation to Texas. Although the boom period lasted from 1909 until a little beyond World War I, the failure rate was high. Of the 22,500 miles of electric railway planned for Texas, only 500 miles of track were laid. Many lines failed because the companies had been founded by individuals or groups who had little money or railway experience. By the 1930's, automobiles and trucks provided cheap, efficient interurban transportation. The result was the demise of the electric railway system. Mainly secondary sources; 19 photos, map, 22 notes. R. D. Hurt

376. Grant, H. Roger. WYOMING'S ELECTRIC RAILWAY PROJECTS. *Ann. of Wyoming 1980 52(1): 16-21.* Beginning in 1887 with a technological breakthrough by Frank Julian Sprague, electric railroads quickly established themselves as an ideal means for interurban and intraurban transportation. By the early 1900's, even towns in sparsely populated Wyoming were excited by ideas

of electric railway projects. Both Cheyenne and Sheridan constructed electric trolley systems within their own city limits, but the broader vision of linked interurbans never materialized beyond the 17-mile Sheridan Railway and Light Company line. Based on *Street Railway Journal* and *Electric Railway Journal;* 4 photos, map, 20 notes. M. L. Tate

377. Grinde, Donald A., Jr. ERIE'S RAILROAD WAR: A CASE STUDY OF PURPOSIVE VIOLENCE FOR A COMMUNITY'S ECONOMIC AD-VANCEMENT. *Western Pennsylvania Hist. Mag. 1974 57(1): 15-23.*

378. Grinnell, George Bird. BUILDING THE NORTHERN PACIFIC. *Idaho Yesterdays 1972/73 16(4): 10-13.* Following the right-of-way of the Northern Pacific from Walla Walla to Missoula, tall stands of timber and fertile prairies were an invitation to settlers. Originally published in *Forest and Stream*, 9 February 1882. Illus. B. J. Paul

379. Haites, Erik F. and Mak, James. THE DECLINE OF STEAMBOAT-ING ON THE ANTE-BELLUM WESTERN RIVERS: SOME NEW EVIDENCE AND AN ALTERNATIVE HYPOTHESIS. *Explorations in Econ. Hist. 1973 11(1): 25-36.* Compares former estimates of construction and operating tonnage of steamboats with newly derived estimates for 1811-60. Argues that the generally accepted view that railroad expansion led to an absolute decline in steamboating is erroneous. Cites movements in general economic activity as the most important influence on western steamboat activity. Based on statistics and secondary sources; 3 tables, 25 notes, appendix. P. J. Coleman

380. Halpern, Paul J. THE CORVAIR, THE PINTO AND CORPORATE BEHAVIOR: IMPLICATIONS FOR REGULATORY REFORM. *Policy Studies Rev. 1982 1(3): 540-545.* Discusses the problems inherent in trying to direct actions in the automobile industry toward socially desirable results, demonstrating that some firms may stay with what is socially undesirable for a greater short-term profit; the General Motors Corporation's Corvair and the Ford Motor Company's Pinto exemplify such corporate short-sightedness.

381. Hamburg, James F. RAILROADS AND THE SETTLEMENT OF SOUTH DAKOTA DURING THE GREAT DAKOTA BOOM, 1878-1887. *South Dakota Hist. 1975 5(2): 165-178.* Lack of transportation was the most notable deterrent to white settlement in South Dakota by the late 1870's. When railroads began to push into eastern sections of the territory, their combination with free land and beneficial environmental conditions led to a boom in settlement. The railroad companies not only offered transportation, but also platted townsites, established by their subsidiary companies. Most of the towns platted from 1880 on were along rail lines. Several methods were used to attract immigrants and settlers from the east to settle in the southern part of the Dakotas. Rapid growth took place in those areas reached by rail lines. With the exception of the Black Hills region, settlement in western South Dakota was not begun during the boom. Population of South Dakota increased from 11,766 to 328,808 during the boom years. The rapid growth was partially halted by a widespread economic depression. Based on primary and secondary sources; map, 3 photos, 2 tables, 25 notes. A. J. Larson

382. Hamm, George A.   THE ATCHISON ASSOCIATES OF THE SANTA
FE RAILROAD.   *Kansas Hist. Q. 1976 42(4): 353-365.* The Atchison Associates, a group of speculators, politicians, and businessmen from Kansas and the
East, came to the rescue of the Atchison, Topeka and Santa Fe Railroad Company and set it on the way to becoming a multimillion dollar enterprise by
building the first 28 miles of the line from Topeka to Burlingame in 1868-69. The
Associates might have mastered the construction, administrative, and financial
problems associated with building the line; but legal troubles, unstable national
economic conditions, and uncertainties in the land grants forced them in 1869 to
return the work to the company. By this time the track was down, and one of
the numerous projected railroads could show it was more than a speculator's
dream. Primary and secondary sources; 2 charts, 35 notes, 2 appendixes.
                                                                    W. F. Zornow

383. Hammer, Kenneth M.   FREIGHTERS AND RAILROADS: THE
GROWTH OF THE BLACK HILLS FREIGHT AND STAGE LINES AND
THE ROLE OF THE RAILROADS.   *J. of the West 1981 20(2): 21-30.* By the
end of 1876, the Black Hills gold rush had brought 20,000 people to Deadwood
in Dakota Territory. Situated hundreds of miles from the nearest railhead, Deadwood was connected to towns east of the Missouri River or south of the Platte
by ungraded, and seasonally impassable, trails. Freight and passenger service was
provided by freight and stage lines terminating at distant rail stations. Several
competing railroads planned extensions to the Black Hills in the 1870's, but none
materialized. Only in the late 1880's did rail service link the eastern and western
regions of Dakota, forcing the freight and stage lines to shift their operations or
go out of business.   Map, 66 notes.   B. S. Porter

384. Handley, Lawrence R.   SETTLEMENT ACROSS NORTHERN AR-
KANSAS AS INFLUENCED BY THE MISSOURI AND NORTH ARKAN-
SAS RAILROAD.   *Arkansas Hist. Q. 1974 33(4): 273-292.* The railroad shaped
the pattern of settlement and economic growth of northern Arkansas towns
between 1880 and the 1920's. 33 new settlements arose, five disappeared and
several small towns and industries grew rapidly as the railroad passed along a
303-mile route between Seligman, Missouri, and Helena, Arkansas. Maps illustrate the alteration of village residence, road, and commercial growth patterns to
take advantage of the railroad. Based on newspaper accounts, interviews and
secondary sources; 7 maps, 62 notes.   T. L. Savitt

385. Hatch, Lorenzo Hill.   UTAH NORTHERN RAILROAD.   *Idaho Yesterdays 1978 22(1): 26-28.* In a letter to the editor, published in the *Idaho
Statesman* (Boise), 23 May 1874, Hatch described the extending of the Utah
Northern Railroad into Franklin, Idaho, and the accompanying upsurge in business. He encouraged the expeditious linking of Boise to a railroad line in order
to continue that city's growth. 3 illus., 8 notes.   B. J. Paul

386. Hayes, John D.   THE MARITIME WORLD IN 1973.   *US Naval Inst.
Pro. 1974 100(3): 242-252.* Merchant ships rather than warships have become the
tools of power upon the seas. Largely international in character, these ships carry
any cargo anywhere and "there is peace at sea because men seek profit from this
last area of free enterprise." Of notice during 1973 were the results of the July
1972 US-Soviet wheat agreement, the US subscription to flag discrimination,

thereby revising "a long time policy of freedom of ocean trade," the changes in living conditions for the merchant seaman, the changes in the world's merchant fleets, the developments in US shipping and shipbuilding, the Arab oil embargo, and talk of expanding the US Coast Guard into an international service "to bring order to the world ocean in all the categories where corrective action is needed: in pollution control, crew competence, vessel inspection, and traffic control." 7 photos, table, 5 notes.   A. N. Garland

387. Hayut, Yehuda. CONTAINERIZATION AND THE LOAD CENTER CONCEPT. *Econ. Geog. 1981 57(2): 160-176.* "This study examines technological changes in ocean transportation, with an emphasis on containerization, in light of their effects on seaport systems and on their closely related components: hinterlands, forelands, and ocean trades routes," focusing "on the dynamics of the container port system with a particular emphasis on the phenomenon of 'dominant container ports,'" based on a five-phase model covering the 1960's-81.

388. Hillman, Raymond W. SHIPBUILDING ON THE STOCKTON CHANNEL. *Pacific Hist. 1977 21(1, supplement): 36-40.* Shipbuilding has been an active industry in Stockton from 1850 to the present.   G. L. Olson

389. Hirschey, Mark John. RAILROAD FREIGHT SERVICE: A CHALLENGE FOR NEW PUBLIC POLICY. *Public Policy 1979 27(2): 49-68.* Analysis of the effects of federal legislation 1973-76 indicates that it has encouraged a promerger policy for the railroad freight industry and in light-density or branch line service.

390. Hirst, Eric. TRANSPORTATION ENERGY USE AND CONSERVATION POTENTIAL. *Sci. and Public Affairs 1973 29(9): 36-42.* Examines traffic and energy consumption for intercity freight and passenger traffic and intracity passenger traffic, 1950-70.

391. Hoffius, Steve. RAILROAD FEVER. *Southern Exposure 1977 5(1): 47-58.* Few subjects in southern history have generated as much mythology and nostalgia as the railroads. Railroads played an important role in southern popular music and literature as well as in the daily lives of southerners. Even though the railroads considered passenger service to be an inconvenience, they served as the primary southern mode of transportation from the 1830's until recent years. Southern railroad companies today, such as the Seaboard, Norfolk & Western and the Southern Railway, realize large profits from their freight service and investments.   N. Lederer

392. Hofsommer, Donovan L. BAWLING CATTLE AND BARKING BRAKEMEN: AN OKLAHOMA RAILROAD MEMORY. *Chronicles of Oklahoma 1976 54(3): 360-369.* Examines the role of the Missouri, Kansas, and Texas Railway in the Oklahoma cattle industry, 1865-1972.

393. Hofsommer, Donovan L. THE CONSTRUCTION STRATEGIES OF RAILROADS IN THE OKLAHOMA PANHANDLE. *Chronicles of Oklahoma 1980 58(1): 77-91.* By the 1890's people began to settle the Oklahoma Panhandle in sufficient numbers to warrant the construction of railroads to transport their agricultural products. Various proposals for construction misfired

until 1912 when the Wichita Falls and Northwestern Railway (WF&NW) extended its track westward to the townsite of Forgan. This compelled the leaders of Beaver City, 10 miles to the south, to build their own track to intercept the WF&NW line. Eventually this blossomed into the Beaver, Meade and Englewood railroad (BM&E) which by 1931 extended 105 miles westward to Keyes, Oklahoma, and served thousands of Panhandle citizens. Illus., 3 photos, map, 29 notes.   M. L. Tate

394.   Hofsommer, Donovan L.   "THE GRANDEST RAILROAD PROJECT OF THE AGE."   *Ann. of Iowa 1977 44(2): 118-136.* Organized in 1856, the Iowa Central Railroad planned to join St. Louis and St. Paul via several eastern Iowa communities. Some Iowans considered it "the grandest railroad project of the age." In a few years, however, a lack of support from St. Louis merchants, rivalries among several Iowa towns, and corporate mergers which created competing lines, doomed the Iowa Central and the "venture ended in a debacle." Based on secondary sources and newspaper; map, 3 photos, 32 notes.
                                                                    P. L. Petersen

395.   Hofsommer, Donovan L.   TOWNSITE DEVELOPMENT ON THE WICHITA FALLS AND NORTHWESTERN RAILWAY.   *Great Plains J. 1977 16(2): 107-122.* During 1900-20, businessmen Joseph A. Kemp and Frank Kell of Wichita Falls, Texas, built the Wichita Falls and Northwestern Railway some 305 miles into the panhandle of Oklahoma. The railroad and townsite developments "promoted the settlement of one of the country's last frontiers." 6 illus., map, 33 notes.   O. H. Zabel

396.   Hofsommer, Donovan L.   WHAT IS THE FUTURE FOR RAILROAD BRANCH LINES IN RURAL AREAS?   *Chronicles of Oklahoma 1978-79 56(4): 393-408.* During 1969 the Missouri-Kansas-Texas Railroad Company (M-K-T or Katy) requested permission from the Interstate Commerce Commission to abandon 331 miles of its track in western Oklahoma. Katy Railroad executives pointed out that freight hauling was on the decline in that area and that the cost of repair for old track would be prohibitive. Some grain elevator operators and wheat farmers argued that continued railroad service was necessary to their economic well-being, but the Interstate Commerce Commission ruled in the railroad's favor. Though western Oklahoma branch lines finally were abandoned on 31 January 1973, Congress plans to undertake a future study of branch lines throughout the nation. Primary sources; 6 photos, map, 25 notes.
                                                                    M. L. Tate

397.   Holmes, Oliver W.   STAGECOACH TRAVEL AND SOME ASPECTS OF THE STAGING BUSINESS IN NEW ENGLAND, 1800-1850.   *Massachusetts Hist. Soc. Pro. 1973 85: 36-57.* Discusses the many stagecoach lines serving New England and the relationship of the lines to the turnpikes and the steamboat. Details the financing of various companies and presents vignettes of the drivers, the central figures of the old staging business. Based on manuscripts, ledgers, newspapers and traveler's accounts; 27 notes.   J. B. Duff

398.   Holt, Glen E.   THE MAIN LINE AND SIDE TRACKS: URBAN TRANSPORTATION HISTORY.   *J. of Urban Hist. 1979 5(3): 397-406.* Review article prompted by Clay McShane's *Technology and Reform: Street Rail-*

ways and the Growth of Milwaukee, 1887-1900; John P. McKay's *Tramways and Trolleys: The Rise of Urban Mass Transport in Europe;* and Carl W. Condit's *The Railroad and the City: A Technological and Urbanistic History of Cincinnati.* Finds a need in the field of urban transportation to go beyond the nuts and bolts of technology and to investigate the social forces and institutions that shaped the technological developments and in turn to study the social consequences of those changes. 15 notes. T. W. Smith

399. Hopkins, George. MAYBE WE SHOULD HELP PAN AM. *Washington Monthly 1976 8(7): 53-61.* Discusses the financial difficulties of Pan American World Airways, which has been receiving assistance from its own employees and which is now requesting a government subsidy.

400. Hopkins, George. THE TEXAS AIRLINE WAR. *Washington Monthly 1976 8(1): 12-19.* Southwest Airlines, an unregulated carrier that began flying in Texas in 1971, launched a price war that reveals the dubious policies of the Civil Aeronautics Board and federal subsidies to airlines.

401. Huber, Leonard V. THE MISSISSIPPI LEVIATHANS. *Louisiana Hist. 1981 22(3): 239-251.* Describes the huge steamboats, from 1,000 to 2,500 tons, which plied the Mississippi River between the Civil War and the 1890's. Based in part on newspaper and other contemporary accounts; 8 illus. R. E. Noble

402. Hudson, John C. NORTH DAKOTA'S RAILWAY WAR OF 1905. *North Dakota Hist. 1981 48(1): 4-19.* The battle between James J. Hill's Great Northern Railway and Edward Pennington's *Soo Line Railroad* to control access across northern North Dakota resulted in nearly 500 miles of new track and more than 50 new towns in one year. Abandoned townsites "were the real casualties of a war between two railroads." Based on Great Northern Railway Collection and Soo Line Company records at Minnesota Historical Society; 13 illus., 81 notes. G. L. Olson

403. Hughes, James W. REALTORS, BANKERS AND POLITICIANS IN THE NEW YORK/NEW JERSEY PORT AUTHORITY. *Society 1974 11(4): 63-70.* Port Authority refuses to fund deficit-producing mass transit facilities, preferring profit-making enterprises which benefit realtors and bankers at the expense of urban commuters. One of five articles in this issue on state politics and public interests. S

404. Jacobson, D. S. THE POLITICAL ECONOMY OF INDUSTRIAL LOCATION: THE FORD MOTOR COMPANY AT CORK 1912-26. *Irish Econ. and Social Hist. [Ireland] 1977 4: 36-55.* After investigations of Ireland as early as 1912, Henry Ford in 1917 opened a subsidiary in Cork, Henry Ford & Son Ltd., to manufacture his Fordson tractors. Details factors in Ireland and in Great Britain that made it not only possible but also likely that Ford would decide to establish a plant in Ireland. Discusses the significance of the Ford Company's reliance not just on usual location determinants but also on bargaining with the Irish Free State and Great Britain for future gains, particularly in reference to the presence or absence of British tariffs on items imported from Ireland as the political situation in Ireland shifted, 1916-23. 94 notes. S

405. Jeansonne, Glen. THE AUTOMOBILE AND AMERICAN MORAL-
ITY. *J. of Popular Culture 1974 8(1): 125-131.* The automobile was viewed in
the 1920's as a threat to traditional morality. The car displaced the parlor in
courtship, and emancipated youth by allowing them to escape from parental
supervision. It also facilitated bank robberies and bootlegging. The automobile
industry fostered installment buying and this moderated traditional hostility to
indebtedness. Primary and secondary sources; 30 notes.   E. S. Shapiro

406. Johnson, Arthur L. THE BOSTON-HALIFAX STEAMSHIP LINES.
Am. Neptune 1977 37(4): 231-238. Presents a history of the steamship lines
(Cunard, the Yarmouth Steam Navigation Company, the Boston & Colonial
Steamship Company) which operated between Boston, Massachusetts, and Hali-
fax, Nova Scotia, 1840's-1917. Based on newspapers and monographs; 25 notes.
                                                                 G. H. Curtis

407. Johnson, Arthur L. FROM *EASTERN STATE* TO *EVANGELINE*: A
HISTORY OF THE BOSTON-YARMOUTH, NOVA SCOTIA, STEAMSHIP
SERVICES. *Am. Neptune 1974 34(3): 174-187.* Account of steamship transportation between two North American ports through four phases of development (1855-1955). Competition with the automobile and rising operating costs
led to its decline. Based on primary and secondary sources; 48 notes.
                                                                 G. H. Curtis

408. Johnson, Arthur L. THE INTERNATIONAL LINE: A HISTORY OF
THE BOSTON-SAINT JOHN STEAMSHIP SERVICE. *Am. Neptune 1973
33(2): 79-94.* A history of the coastal trade between Boston and New Brunswick.
The vessels used on the line were constructed solely to carry light cargo and
passengers. The company prospered until World War I, surviving the temporary
disruption of the Civil War and powerful railroad competition. It could not,
however, successfully compete with the automobile, and World War II brought
the International or the Eastern Steamship Company, as it had become, to a close.
Efforts to revive the service after the war were unsuccessful. 8 photos, 50 notes.
                                                                 V. L. Human

409. Johnson, H. Thomas. MANAGEMENT ACCOUNTING IN AN
EARLY MULTIDIVISIONAL ORGANIZATION: GENERAL MOTORS
IN THE 1920'S. *Business Hist. Rev. 1978 52(4): 490-517.* An advanced management accounting system was an indispensable component of the multidivisional structure introduced at General Motors Corporation in the 1920's by
Pierre Du Pont, Alfred Sloan, and Donaldson Brown. An application of the
techniques already in use in the Du Pont Company, the system provided an
annual operating forecast comparing divisional goals with those of central management, sales reports and flexible budgets that measured actual results against
expectations, and more effective resource allocation among the divisions. Based
primarily on published sources, especially contemporary trade and professional
journals; 2 tables, 40 notes.   C. J. Pusateri

410. Keeler, Theodore E. RAILROAD COSTS, RETURNS TO SCALE,
AND EXCESS CAPACITY. *R. of Econ. and Statistics 1974 56(2): 201-208.*

411. Keeran, Roger R. COMMUNIST INFLUENCE IN THE AUTOMO-BILE INDUSTRY, 1920-1933: PAVING THE WAY FOR AN INDUSTRIAL UNION. *Labor Hist. 1979 20(2): 189-225.* Although small in number, the Communists formed a nucleus in the auto industry in the 1920's which challenged "welfare capitalism." Through shop activity, newspapers, strike support, and fraternal society meetings, the Communists spread the idea of industrial unionism and established the base for success of unionism in the 1930's. Based on the records of the Auto Workers Union, newspapers, and oral history; 58 notes.

L. L. Athey

412. Keisling, Phil. THE GREAT TRAIN ROBBERY: HOW TO MAKE A BILLION FROM A BANKRUPT RAILROAD. *Washington Monthly 1982 14(5-6): 24-29, 32-35.* Discusses how the Penn Central Corporation, number 123 on the *Fortune* list of the largest American companies, rose to its strong financial position after the bankruptcy in 1970 of the Penn Central Transportation Company.

413. Kendall, Lane C. THE MODERN AMERICAN MERCHANT MARINE: A PICTORIAL. *US Naval Inst. Pro. 1979 105(12): 67-75.* On 1 August 1979, the US merchant fleet had 531 ships—245 dry cargo liners, 261 tankers, with an additional 9 tankers under construction, and 16 dry bulk ships. The country has much to be proud of in this fleet, but the merchant marine industry faces many serious problems. Hopefully, new ships, new management techniques, and new leaders will enable the merchant marine to solve its most serious problems, and, with national help and interest, will again prove itself to be a force in the eyes of the public. 28 photos.

A. N. Garland

414. Keyes, Norman C., Jr. and Middleton, Kenneth R., comp. THE GREAT NORTHERN RAILWAY COMPANY: ALL-TIME LOCOMOTIVE ROS-TER, 1861-1970. *Railroad Hist. 1980 (143): 20-162.* Lists "all motive power—steam, diesel, electric, and motor car—owned by the Great Northern Railway Company, its predecessor lines, and its fully-controlled subsidiaries."

415. Kirby, Frank E. and Rankin, A. P. THE BULK FREIGHTER OF THE GREAT LAKES. *Inland Seas 1978 34(3): 218-223.* Bulk cargoes on the Great Lakes initially travelled in schooners. In 1869 the pioneer bulk steamer, *R. J. Hackett,* appeared. Steel hulls arrived with the *Spokane* in 1886. The deepening of the channels between the Lakes permitted the building of ever larger vessels so that by 1896 more than half the bulk steamers exceeded 2,000 tons. Until Alex E. Brown introduced a cable and bucket unloading system in 1882 all vessels had to be emptied by hand. In 1899 the Hulett Unloader eliminated hand filling of the bucket but required specially designed holds. The *James H. Hoyt* of 1900 introduced hatches on 12-foot centers which permitted filling all holds simultaneously and four years later the *Augustus B. Wolvin* added a clear hold with slanting side which automatically concentrated the ore or grain for unloading. The result was "a most efficient, economical, and capacious carrying machine." Reprints from *The Marine Review* of August 1911 a paper presented at the Jubilee Meeting of the Institute of Naval Architects in London.

K. J. Bauer

416.   Klein, Maury.   IN SEARCH OF JAY GOULD.   *Business Hist. Rev. 1978 52(2): 166-199.* Jay Gould was regarded as the supreme business villain of his era. Examines the accuracy of that image and finds that Gould's record "defies easy generalization." Gould's principal achievement was his influence upon the development of western railroad systems and the attendant lowering of the cost of transportation. Based mainly on periodical and secondary sources; 93 notes.   C. J. Pusateri

417.   Kothe, Robert J.   DETROIT ELECTRIC.   *Chronicle 1981 17(3): 32-34.* Sketches the history of gasoline- versus electric-powered cars, discussing in particular the Detroit Electric produced by the Detroit Electric Car Company, founded by William A. Anderson, from the success of the early models of 1906-07 to the eventual closure of the company during World War II.

418.   Kothe, Robert J.   JACKSON CARS: "NO HILL TOO STEEP—NO SAND TOO DEEP."   *Chronicle 1981 17(1): 23-25.* Recounts the history of the Jackson Automobile Company, founded in 1902 by successful Michigan businessmen George Matthews and Charles Lewis, dwelling especially on the model types produced by the company and its advertising campaigns, neither of which were able to avert the firm's bankruptcy in 1923.

419.   Kothe, Robert J.   REO: THE CAR YOU WON'T FORGET.   *Chronicle 1982 18(1): 21-23.* Discusses the formation of the R. E. Olds Company in Lansing, Michigan, in 1904 and describes the REO automobile produced by the company until the mid-1930's and the REO trucks, which were produced until 1975.

420.   Ladenson, Mark L. and Stoga, Alan J.   RETURNS TO SCALE IN THE U.S. TRUCKING INDUSTRY.   *Southern Econ. J. 1974 40(3): 390-396.*

421.   Lane, Bruce M. and Lane, C. Gardner.   NEW INFORMATION ON SHIPS BUILT BY DONALD MCKAY.   *Am. Neptune 1982 42(2): 118-137.* In 1880 the Census Office employed Henry Hall to gather information on shipbuilding in the United States. In 1883 he and his brother copied documents concerning ships constructed by Donald McKay into a notebook labeled "Models and Measurements." Describes the information and drawings in that notebook and analyzes the relationship of this material to other documentation on McKay ships. Based on Hall's Census Reports in the National Archives; his notebook at the Penobscot Marine Museum, Searsport, Maine; documents in the Peabody Museum, Salem, Massachusetts, and secondary sources; 30 notes.
                                                                          J. C. Bradford

422.   Larcom, Paul S.   EASTWARD HO BY AIR: A HISTORY OF BOSTON-MAINE AND CENTRAL VERMONT AIRWAYS (WITH AN EARLY HISTORY OF THEIR SUCCESSOR NORTHEAST AIRLINES).   *Am. Aviation Hist. Soc. J. 1980 25(4): 242-250.* Covers 1927-72.

423.   Laws, Forrest.   THE RAILROAD COMES TO TENNESSEE: THE BUILDING OF THE LA GRANGE AND MEMPHIS.   *West Tennessee Hist. Soc. Papers 1976 (30): 24-42.* Delineates the financial vicissitudes of the attempts to build a railroad from LaGrange to Memphis in the early 1930's, the purpose of which would provide a cheap farm-to-market route for west Tennessee cotton

growers. In the past historians have attributed the failure of this venture to the Panic of 1837; the author points out that the rivalry between the towns of Memphis and Ft. Pickering together with the shortsightedness of some Memphis businessmen did as much to bring about the demise of the Memphis and La-Grange as did the panic. Much of the work done on the railroad was later absorbed by the larger enterprise, the Memphis and Charleston, which was completed in the 1850's, and was one of the most successful of the southern antebellum rail operations. Based largely on primary sources; 94 notes.

H. M. Parker, Jr.

424. Leary, William M., Jr. AT THE DAWN OF COMMERCIAL AVIA-TION: INGLIS M. UPPERCU AND AEROMARINE AIRWAYS. *Business Hist. Rev. 1979 53(2): 180-193.* American aircraft manufacturers fared poorly in the early 1920's because of a surplus of former military planes. The Aeromarine Plane and Motor Company was one of those that failed after an energetic attempt at operating America's first airline. The firm, established by Inglis Uppercu in 1914, despite its eventual failure, flew more than a million passenger-miles in less than four years. Its inability to survive proved the necessity for a federal subsidy finally provided by the Air Mail Act (US, 1925). Based on periodical literature of the era and federal governmental records; 38 notes.   C. J. Pusateri

425. LeShane, Albert A., Jr. AEROMARINE AIRWAYS, INC. *Am. Avia-tion Hist. Soc. J. 1980 25(3): 162-180.* Aeromarine Airways, Inc., provided seaplane mail and passenger service between Havana and the Florida Keys; it expanded to the eastern seaboard and to cities along the Mississippi River; 1920-24.

426. Leslie, Stuart W. CHARLES F. KETTERING AND THE COPPER-COOLED ENGINE. *Technology and Culture 1979 20(4): 752-776.* As a weapon in the sales war with Ford, General Motors began in 1919 to develop an air-cooled engine for a cheaper Chevrolet. In 1921 GM design engineers led by Charles F. Kettering finally succeeded in brazing copper cooling fins to the cylinders, thereby eliminating the costly tubing and radiator of the water-cooled engine, and the first models were featured at the New York Automobile Show in 1923. But only 100 cars were ever sold, and this most ambitious innovation of GM's short career had by 1925 become a costly failure. The main reason was conflict between Kettering's design engineers, who "grossly underestimated the difficulty of converting a prototype into a mass produced article," and the pro-duction engineers, who raised many practical objections to the innovation. Based on the Kettering Archives; 4 illus., 77 notes.   C. O. Smith

427. Leslie, Stuart W. THOMAS MIDGLEY AND THE POLITICS OF INDUSTRIAL RESEARCH. *Buiness Hist. Rev. 1980 54(4): 480-503.* Thomas Midgley was a distinguished industrial chemist employed by the General Motors Corp. for nearly three decades until his death in 1944. General Motors executives, notably Charles Kettering and Alfred Sloan, were skillful in suggesting research topics with commercial potential, yet also allowing Midgley some freedom to pursue the theoretical aspects of research. The scientist's enthusiasm and morale thus remained high. The case shows that the management of industrial research involves special personnel problems that must be deftly administered. Based largely on the Charles Kettering Papers and on industry publications; illus., 72 notes.   C. J. Pusateri

428.   Levin, Richard C. and Weinberg, Daniel H.   ALTERNATIVES FOR RESTRUCTURING THE RAILROADS: END-TO-END OR PARALLEL MERGERS?   *Econ. Inquiry 1979 17(3): 371-388.* Predicts a wave of railroad mergers and empirically shows that end-to-end mergers are socially preferable to parallel mergers, due to better service and lower costs; uses historical data from US railroad companies, 1957-75.

429.   Lewis, W. David and Newton, Wesley Phillips.   THE DELTA-C&S MERGER: A CASE STUDY IN AIRLINE CONSOLIDATION AND FEDERAL REGULATION.   *Business Hist. Rev. 1979 53(2): 161-179.* During the 1950's a wave of mergers swept the airline industry, and no company was more deeply involved than Delta Air Lines Inc., which had evolved into a relatively small but profitable regional carrier. After a number of abortive merger attempts with other lines, Delta successfully combined with Chicago and Southern Air Lines, Inc. in 1953 and was thereby transformed into a major national airline. This type of merger fitted in well with Civil Aeronautics Board policy. The CAB preferred combinations of existing airlines to the granting of new route awards. Based on company records; 3 maps, 23 notes.   C. J. Pusateri

430.   Lightfoot, Ralph B.   SIKORSKY FLYING BOATS.   *Am. Aviation Hist. Soc. J. 1979 24(4): 242-261.* Surveys the development, use, and design requirements of Sikorsky flying boats, airplanes capable of landing on and taking off from water, 1912-45.

431.   Love, Terry M.   THE AIRCRAFT OF NORTH CENTRAL AIRLINES.   *Am. Aviation Hist. Soc. J. 1977 22(4): 276-288.* Covers 1940-76, focusing on when North Central Airlines served only the northern Midwest.

432.   Luning Prak, N.   PULLMAN.   *Spiegel Historiael [Netherlands] 1977 12(4): 236-241.* George M. Pullman (1831-97) invented the famous sleeping car in 1858 and in 1880 established the city of Pullman near Chicago. Here his workers lived in company homes and sent their children to company schools. In 1885 and again in 1893 wages were reduced, but not rents. A strike in 1894 was supported by the American Railway Union. The strike was broken because President Cleveland called out federal troops, invoking the Sherman Anti-Trust act of 1890. Illus., biblio.   G. D. Homan

433.   Mahrer, Douglas L., ed.   THE DIARY OF WILSON HOWELL CARPENTER: AN ACCOUNT OF THE 1877 RAILROAD RIOTS.   *Western Pennsylvania Hist. Mag. 1977 60(3): 305-313.* Reprints excerpts from the diary of Wilson Howell Carpenter concerning railroad rioting which broke out in Pennsylvania in 1877 following a period during 1873-77 of hardship, lowering of freight prices, and intense competition between various railroads.

434.   Marple, David.   TECHNOLOGICAL INNOVATION AND ORGANIZATIONAL SURVIVAL: A POPULATION ECOLOGY STUDY OF NINETEENTH-CENTURY AMERICAN RAILROADS.   *Sociol. Q. 1982 23(1): 107-116.* Deals with technological innovation, particularly the introduction of the steel rail, and its impact on the survival rate of 214 railroads in 14 states, finding that the age of a railroad company and the size of its operation influenced the survival rate more than did the new technology.

435.   Martin, Albro.   RAILROADS AND THE EQUITY RECEIVERSHIP: AN ESSAY ON INSTITUTIONAL CHANGE.   *J. of Econ. Hist. 1974 34(3): 685-709.* During 1870-90 federal judges modified traditional railroad bankruptcy arrangements in order to maintain vital rail services. Legal modifications permitted expert railroad managers, who often initiated bankruptcy proceedings, to continue operation of the lines and to develop business reorganization plans which subordinated investor interests to efforts to cut high fixed charges, to attract additional capital, and to rationalize operations. Based on contemporary statistical sources, official government documents, and secondary sources; 2 tables, 43 notes.   O. H. Reichardt

436.   Marx, Thomas G.   TECHNOLOGICAL CHANGE AND THE THEORY OF THE FIRM: THE AMERICAN LOCOMOTIVE INDUSTRY, 1920-1955.   *Business Hist. Rev. 1976 50(1): 1-24.* Traces the technological changes faced by the locomotive building industry in the first half of the 20th century, principally the shift from steam to diesel power. Relates that experience to the economic theories of the firm offered by various scholars, especially pertaining to innovation and to profit-maximizing behavior. The author concludes that his results point to the need for a "richer theoretical framework" in which to place the process of technological change and accompanying management decision-making. Based on annual reports of companies and secondary sources; 40 notes.
                                                                C. J. Pusateri

437.   May, James W., Jr.   ATLANTA TRANSIT STRIKE, 1949-1950, PRELUDE TO SALE.   Fink, Gary M. and Reed, Merl E., eds. *Essays in Southern Labor History: Selected Papers, Southern Labor History Conference, 1976.* (Westport, Conn.; London, England: Greenwood Pr., 1977): 208-219. Studies the years of disagreements and negotiations between labor and management which preceded the Atlanta transit strike, longest in the city's history. Unable to break the deadlock with Division 732 of the Amalgamated Association of Street, Electric Railway and Motor Coach Employees of America, the Georgia Power Company sold its recently modernized Atlanta transit properties to the locally controlled Atlanta Transit Company. In forcing this sale Division 732 had "successfully challenged Atlanta's traditionally impervious power structure." 42 notes.   R. V. Ritter

438.   May, Martha.   THE HISTORICAL PROBLEM OF THE FAMILY WAGE: THE FORD MOTOR COMPANY AND THE FIVE DOLLAR DAY. *Feminist Studies 1982 8(2): 399-424.* Examination of a specific case of the institution of the family wage challenges previous interpretations. Neither nasty patriarchal attitudes desiring female subordination, nor working-class adaptation of the ideology of domesticity explains the five dollar day at Ford. The auto company used this wage rate, double the going rate, to combat high turnover, to forestall unionization and an imminent strike, and to reflect production changes. A more complex mediation between the productive and reproductive aspects of labor is suggested than has been previously offered.   73 notes.   S. Hildenbrand

439.   McCorkle, James L., Jr.   THE ILLINOIS CENTRAL RAILROAD AND THE MISSISSIPPI COMMERCIAL VEGETABLE INDUSTRY. *J. of Mississippi Hist. 1977 39(2): 155-172.* From the 1880's on, the Illinois Central Railroad led railroads operating in Mississippi in the promotion of an

increasingly extensive commercial vegetable industry. The railroad conducted demonstration work, established a special agriculture department, cooperated with state agencies, and participated in meetings. Producers often charged that railroad freight rates were excessive. Based on newspapers and Illinois Central Railroad records; 69 notes. J. W. Hillje

440. McGregor, Alexander C. THE ECONOMIC IMPACT OF THE MUL-LAN ROAD ON WALLA WALLA, 1860-1883. *Pacific Northwest Q. 1974 65(3): 118-129.* Examines two periods when the Mullan Road from Walla Walla, Washington to Fort Benton, Montana served a worthwhile purpose: 1) 1860-70, when it served as an access route for Walla Walla trade to the newly discovered mining areas, and 2) 1870-83, when it helped the city's merchants to develop trade with eastern Washington settlers. Although the original purposes of the road failed to become a reality, Walla Walla was well served as were the mining personnel and the eastern Washington agricultural areas which thereby found Walla Walla a useful supply center. 2 maps, 61 notes. R. V. Ritter

441. McLear, Patrick E. THE GALENA AND CHICAGO UNION RAIL-ROAD: A SYMBOL OF CHICAGO'S ECONOMIC MATURITY. *J. of the Illinois State Hist. Soc. 1980 73(1): 17-26.* Traces the history of the Galena and Chicago Union Railroad from 1836, when it was chartered, to 1853, when the railroad reached Freeport, a town northeast of Rockford, Illinois. Elijah K. Hubbard took control of the enterprise in 1837, while Elihu Townsend supplied the capital. Focuses on William B. Ogden, who became president of the railroad that conveyed Wisconsin goods to Lake Michigan ports. The railroad had a definite impact on the emergence of Chicago as the commercial and trade center of the Midwest. 52 notes, 5 illus., photo. G. V. Wasson

442. Mealor, W. Theodore, Jr. FUNCTIONAL AND SPATIAL PAT-TERNS OF GEORGIA SHORT LINE RAILROADS, 1915-1978. *West Georgia Coll. Studies in the Social Sci. 1979 18: 25-42.* Surveys the functional characteristics of the short line systems and relates them to the failure, survival, or incorporations of the short lines into statewide networks.

443. Mellor, R. E. H. A BASIC RAILWAY PASSENGER NETWORK IN THE UNITED STATES. *Geography [Great Britain] 1973 58(2): 163-166.* Discusses the decline in passenger service on US railroads since the 1930's, and the services of the National Railroad Passenger Corporation (AMTRAK) which was formed in 1971.

444. Melvin, Patricia Mooney. STEAMBOATS WEST: THE LEGACY OF A TRANSPORTATION REVOLUTION. *Old Northwest 1981-82 7(4): 339-357.* The steamboat was a major factor in the transformation of the trans-Appalachian west into the urban-industrial center of the United States during 1810-90. The steamboat not only stimulated trade and commerce in the Old Northwest, but it also created new industries, increased the population, and established new job opportunities. The photographs in the Inland Rivers Collection of the Public Library of Cincinnati and Hamilton County help document the impact of the steamboat on life in the Old Northwest. Based on the Inland Rivers Collection at the Public Library of Cincinnati and Hamilton County and other primary sources; 18 photos, map, 22 notes. P. L. McLaughlin

445. Mercer, Lloyd J. BUILDING AHEAD OF DEMAND: SOME EVIDENCE FOR THE LAND GRANT RAILROADS. *J. of Econ. Hist. 1974 34(2): 492-500.* Tests hypotheses that during 1864-1900, western railroads were built ahead of demand. Two hypotheses, that profit rates on western railroads were less than rates on alternative investments, and that a direct relation existed between a railroad's profit and its age, are both true. A third hypothesis, that railroads were privately unprofitable, is not true in all cases. Based on the author's unpublished manuscript, published statistics, and secondary sources; 4 tables, 12 notes. O. H. Reichardt

446. Merrill, Maurice H. THE OKLAHOMA CENTRAL RAILROAD. *Chronicles of Oklahoma 1981-82 59(4): 465-471.* Describes the towns along the Oklahoma Central Railroad which was built to carry coal from Lehigh to Chickasha, where cotton was loaded. Railroad promoters increased profits by selling lots at the new town sites and extracting "bonus" money from already existing towns. In 1913 the line was sold to the Santa Fe Railroad. Map. M. L. Tate

447. Meyer, Stephen. ADAPTING THE IMMIGRANT TO THE LINE: AMERICANIZING IN THE FORD FACTORY, 1914-1921. *J. of Social Hist. 1980 14(1): 67-82.* The Ford Motor Company's Americanization Program, carried on by the Ford Sociological Department and the Ford English School, was a paternalistic effort to insure that the workers were worthy of remaining Ford employees and receiving the benefits of the Ford Profit Sharing Plan and the Five Dollar Day initiated in 1914. The company sought to train diligent, clean, and thrifty workers. By 1920 the company's high profits had been undercut by changes in the industry and the Americanization programs were dropped, as was the financial incentive of offering the inflated equivalent of the 1914 five dollar a day wage. 38 notes. C. M. Hough

448. Micketti, Gerald F. THE BRADLEY TRANSPORTATION LINE. *Inland Seas 1979 35(1): 13-20.* Formed in 1912 to carry limestone from the quarries at Rodgers City, Michigan, the line grew to eight large freighters in 1960. In 1967 it was consolidated with the Pittsburgh Steamship Division of US Steel to form the Great Lakes Fleet of the steel company. The Michigan Limestone & Chemical Company's employee paper; 17 notes, illus. K. J. Bauer

449. Middleton, Kenneth R. and Keyes, Norman C., Jr. THE GREAT NORTHERN RAILWAY COMPANY: PREDECESSORS AND FULLY-CONTROLLED SUBSIDIARIES. *Railroad Hist. 1980 (143): 8-19.* Alphabetical listing of predecessor companies and subsidiaries of the Great Northern Railway Company in the United States and Canada from the 1850's to the early 1900's.

450. Miner, H. Craig. THE KANSAS AND NEOSHO VALLEY RAILROAD: KANSAS CITY'S DRIVE FOR THE GULF. *J. of the West 1978 17(4): 75-85.* The Kansas & Neosho Valley Railroad (K&NV) was incorporated in March 1865 with the object of connecting Kansas City (Kansas) with Galveston (Texas) and a Gulf harbor. With the backing of James F. Joy, president of the Chicago, Burlington & Quincy, the K&NV obtained congressional approval for a federal land grant. Joy delayed transferring needed funds for construction, and owing to financial difficulties, the railroad built only as far as the Kansas state

line. Based on Kansas City records in Native Sons Collection, Kansas City Public Library; documents of K&NV in St. Louis-San Francisco Railway, Frisco Building, St. Louis, Missouri; James F. Joy Papers, Detroit Public Library; 4 photos, 2 maps, 17 notes.   B. S. Porter

451. Mitchell, F. Stewart. THE CHICAGO, MILWAUKEE & ST. PAUL RAILWAY AND JAMES J. HILL IN NORTH DAKOTA TERRITORY, 1879-1885. *North Dakota Hist. 1980 47(4): 11-19.* Scholars have emphasized the Great Northern Railway and the Northern Pacific Railroad when discussing the period of railroad construction in Dakota Territory. They have overlooked James J. Hill's effort, using his concept of territorial imperative, expressed through force, to prevent the Milwaukee Road from consolidating its position in Dakota Territory. Based on material in the archives of the Chicago, Milwaukee & St. Paul and Fargo and Southern railroads; 3 photos, 4 maps, 37 notes.
G. L. Olson

452. Morris, Stuart. STALLED PROFESSIONALISM: THE RECRUIT-MENT OF RAILWAY OFFICIALS IN THE UNITED STATES, 1855-1940. *Business Hist. R. 1973 47(3): 317-334.* Studies American railway management recruitment, 1855-1940, examining professional status, promotion, and career structure. In the 19th century recruitment and promotion was bureaucratic and systematic, innovatively organized to put the railroads at the vanguard of the "managerial revolution." By the 1900's, however, the railroad bureaucracy had become rigid, and difficulties were encountered with recruitment of college-trained engineers and managers who were not attracted to a promotion system increasingly hindered by inflexibility, departmentalization, and a hegemony of seniority. This "stalled professionalism" contributed to the economic decline of railways. Based on contemporary journal reports, US government documents, primary and secondary sources; 2 tables, 60 notes.   N. J. Street

453. Morton, Alexander L. NORTHEAST RAILROADS: RESTRUC-TURED OR NATIONALIZED. *Am. Econ. R. 1975 65(2): 284-288.* While federal regulations have damaged the railroads, the author believes that the current solution—the United States Railway Association—is just the first step toward nationalization caused by transportation forces in the market place.
D. K. Pickens

454. Munski, Douglas C. THE FRISCO PERIOD OF THE CHICAGO AND EASTERN ILLINOIS RAILROAD: A STUDY IN EARLY TWEN-TIETH CENTURY RAILWAY GEOGRAPHY. *North Dakota Q. 1980 48(1): 69-80.* Discusses the geographical impact on the lower midwest of the acquisition of the Chicago and Eastern Illinois Railroad by the St. Louis-San Francisco Railroad in 1902, which Frisco controlled until 1913.

455. O'Bannon, Patrick W. RAILROAD CONSTRUCTION IN THE EARLY TWENTIETH CENTURY: THE SAN DIEGO AND ARIZONA RAILWAY. *Southern California Q. 1979 61(3): 255-290.* Describes the construction of the San Diego and Arizona Railway, the last major railroad constructed in the United States. Built during 1907-19 at a cost of more than $17 million, the railroad was promoted by John D. Spreckels to improve San Diego's connections with the east. Unknown to most San Diegans, the Southern Pacific

Railroad provided major financial backing and expert advice. Although there were problems in labor turnover, the Mexican Revolution (part of the route was through Baja California), and geographic obstacles, the project benefited from technological developments lacking in the dramatic era of 1860's construction. Suggests that the San Diego and Arizona illustrates the problems and accomplishments of early 20th-century railroad construction and contrasts with the better-known efforts of the 19th century. Illus., photos, 180 notes.   A. Hoffman

456. Overton, Richard C. ABANDONMENT IN THE CORN COUNTRY. *J. of the West 1978 17(4): 86-94.* On 3 December 1943, the Chicago, Burlington & Quincy Railroad (CB&Q) applied to the Interstate Commerce Commission (ICC) to abandon 21.8 miles of line between Mt. Ayr, Iowa, and Grant City, Missouri. The ICC authorized the abandonment, but chose this insignificant case as the vehicle for establishing the Burlington Formula, a statement of terms and conditions for the benefit of employees displaced by rail line abandonment. This precedent-making decision was the culmination of union attempts to have the ICC establish safeguards for employees adversely affected. Based on Chicago, Burlington & Quincy Law Department files and Interstate Commerce Commission, Finance Docket 14,426; 3 photos, map, 3 tables, 32 notes.

B. S. Porter

457. Patton, Edwin P. AMTRAK IN PERSPECTIVE: WHERE GOEST THE POINTLESS ARROW? *Am. Econ. R. 1974 64(2): 372-377.* Discusses the performance of the National Railroad Passenger Corporation (AMTRAK) from 1971 to 1973.

458. Peters, A. Gerald and Wood, Donald F. HELICOPTER AIRLINES IN THE UNITED STATES 1945-75. *J. of Transport Hist. [Great Britain] 1977 4(1): 1-16.* Examines four helicopter airlines operating in New York, Chicago, Los Angeles, and San Francisco during 1945-65, and during the 10 years after the ending of subsidies in 1965. The high cost of operating helicopters, given the limited consumer market, meant that Los Angeles Airways could only operate with subsidization. Once San Francisco-Oakland Helicopter Airlines demonstrated that it did not need government funds, Congress ceased in mid-1965 all subsidy payments to the Los Angeles, New York, and Chicago airlines. Two of the airlines ceased operations. The New York and San Francisco operations survived, largely because the areas they served contain many water barriers to conventional surface transport. Based on material from the annual reports of LAA, NYA, CHA and SFO. 4 illus., 31 notes.   C. Anstey

459. Phillips, Jerry. THE *WATERMAN ARROWBILE. Aviation Q. 1979 5(1): 4-13.* Describes the history of the *Waterman Arrowbile,* the world's first flying automobile, and its initial cross-country flight in 1938; author was the craft's pilot.

460. Pierce, William C. THE RISE AND FALL OF THE YORK AND CUMBERLAND RAIL ROAD. *Maine Hist. Soc. Q. 1976 15(3): 107-128.* Traces the financial and personnel problems of the York and Cumberland Rail Road from its beginnings in July 1848 until its accession by the Boston and Maine in 1900. Stresses its services to the farmers of York County, Maine, between Portland and South Berwick and its internal management disputes between Smith and McIntyre. Illus.   P. C. Marshall

461.   Pisarski, Alan E.   TRANSPORTATION.   *Ann. of the Am. Acad. of Pol. and Social Sci. 1981 (453): 70-95.* Given the large shares of national resources, time, and capital invested in transportation, it is surprising how little understood are the motivations and circumstances that stimulate travel and the scale and nature of the benefits that derive from transportation. The development of social indicators in the transport sector would improve understanding of transportation, and improve public decisions in the coming decade. The key element in the mobility of the US population will continue to be the automobile.
J/S

462.   Pisney, Raymond F.   JAMES S. MCDONNELL AND HIS COMPANY: A VISION OF FLIGHT AND SPACE.   *Gateway Heritage 1981 2(1): 2-17.* James S. McDonnell founded the McDonnell Aircraft Corporation in 1939, placing his corporation at St. Louis, Missouri, where ample skilled tradesmen were available. He also chose St. Louis because with his corporation distant from West Coast aircraft centers, he might have an advantage in securing government contracts. Since 1939, the corporation prospered from aircraft manufacturing; since the 1950's it prospered from producing data processing equipment. Through the McDonnell Foundation, the company founder has supported higher education and civic enterprises. 24 photos.   H. T. Lovin

463.   Preston, Howard L.   THE AUTOMOBILE BUSINESS IN ATLANTA, 1909-1920: A SYMBOL OF "NEW SOUTH" PROSPERITY.   *Georgia Hist. Q. 1974 58(2): 262-277.* Atlanta, Georgia, hosted the first automobile show outside of either New York or Chicago 6-13 November 1909. The South had not previously been considered a potential market for cars because of poor roads and low incomes. The automobile show was the beginning of a new era. Automobile sales agencies and related businesses sprang up in Atlanta, producing new jobs and housing. Robert W. Woodruff, later of Coca-Cola fame, left his father's ice plant to begin work with the automobile industry. Based on primary sources; 43 notes.   M. R. Gillam

464.   Prickett, James R.   COMMUNIST CONSPIRACY OR WAGE DISPUTE?: THE 1941 STRIKE AT NORTH AMERICAN AVIATION.   *Pacific Hist. Rev. 1981 50(2): 215-233.* The strike at the North American Aviation plant in Inglewood, California, in the summer of 1941 resulted from an attempt to bring aircraft workers into the United Automobile Workers of America (UAW) and to increase wages. The union's negotiating committee twice postponed the strike while trying to work out a settlement with the National Defense Mediation Board, but the union voted to strike when the board proved to be dilatory. US Army forces broke the strike, and the UAW organizer of aircraft workers, a Communist, advised the strikers to return to work. There is no evidence that the strike was Communist-inspired. Communist leaders in the UAW in southern California had tried to prevent the strike. Based on oral history interviews, labor union records and publications, and other primary sources; 76 notes.
R. N. Lokken

465.   Primack, Phil.   DEATH OF THE *HIAWATHA*.   *Washington Monthly 1979 11(10): 16-23.* Discusses the mismanagement of Amtrak and its unfair preemption of the North Coast *Hiawatha* line in 1979.

466.   Pugach, Noel H.   AMERICAN SHIPPING PROMOTERS AND THE SHIPPING CRISIS OF 1914-1916: THE PACIFIC & EASTERN STEAMSHIP COMPANY.   *Am. Neptune 1975 35(3): 166-182.* Because Sino-American trade experienced soaring shipping rates and a shortage of ships after the outbreak of World War I, US and Chinese officials supported efforts to launch a Chinese-American steamship line. Consequently, the Pacific & Eastern Steamship Company was formed in 1915. The venture proved unsuccessful, however, owing to speculators and opportunists jockeying for control of the company and failing to honor their obligations. Primary and secondary sources; 38 notes.

G. H. Curtis

467.   Ralston, Leonard F.   RAILROAD INTERESTS IN EARLY IOWA. *Ann. of Iowa 1973 41(7): 1129-1147.* Places traditionally maligned 19th-century railroad leaders in the perspective of local Iowa times and issues.   S

468.   Ratliff, Ophelia Wood.   THE TEXAS & PACIFIC IN WARD COUNTY, 1880-1910.   *Permian Hist. Ann. 1981 21: 97-109.* Provides detailed information about the purpose and construction of section houses along the rail route and discusses the railroad's impact on the development of the region.

469.   Ray, William W.   CRUSADE OR CIVIL WAR? THE PULLMAN STRIKE IN CALIFORNIA.   *California History 1979 58(1): 20-37.* Describes the effect of the 1894 Pullman strike in California. Historians have overlooked events in California which highlighted public disaffection with the Central Pacific-Southern Pacific's economic and political dominance, the regional variations in the strike, and the relative effectiveness of the American Railway Union. The ARU's boycott of Pullman cars and trains which used them was most effective in Sacramento, disappointing in the Bay area, and minimal in Los Angeles. However, the strike persisted in California after the dispute ended in Pullman, Illinois, where the strike had originated. The strike brought out longstanding grievances over wage reductions but it also indicated the degree to which Californians disliked the Southern Pacific. The impact of the strike in California included the calling out of federal and state troops for the first time to maintain order, electoral successes by Populist candidates, and violence and sabotage by desperate ARU members. Railroads viewed ARU agitation as civil war; ARU supporters considered it a crusade for the rights of unskilled workers. Primary and secondary sources; 7 photos, 44 notes.   A. Hoffman

470.   Rea, John C.   THE TENNESSEE MIDLAND RAILWAY.   *West Tennessee Hist. Soc. Papers 1981 35: 118-121.* A succinct history of the organization and growth of the line of the Tennessee Midland Railway from Memphis to Perryville, Tennessee—its greatest length. Organized in 1886, the line reached Perryville in 1890. However, the hopes for a profitable venture failed, and in 1895 the railroad was sold to cover its debts. It became part of other railroad lines. Based on newspaper accounts and secondary materials; 2 illus., map, 14 notes.

H. M. Parker, Jr.

471.   Reichardt, Otto H.   INDUSTRIAL CONCENTRATION AND WORLD WAR II: A NOTE ON THE AIRCRAFT INDUSTRY.   *Business Hist. Rev. 1975 49(4): 498-503.* A statistical case study of the aircraft industry in World War II. Concludes that a trend toward less rather than more concentra-

tion took place, thus revising some previous scholarly interpretations. Based on government data and published sources; 2 charts, table, 10 notes.

C. J. Pusateri

472.   Reid, June R.   THE TEXAS AND PACIFIC RAILROAD, MARTIN COUNTY. *Permian Hist. Ann. 1981 21: 79-83.* Traces the impact of the Texas & Pacific Railroad on the social and economic development of Martin County in west Texas from 1881 to 1976, focusing on the area's early settlers and on the construction of section houses along the route by the railroad company.

473.   Renaud, Vern and Wolff, Fred.   "HELL RIDER": THE GLENN CURTISS STORY. *Aviation Q. 1979 5(1): 30-71.* Traces the career of Glenn Curtiss, racer, developer, inventor of the "flying boat" and many other aircraft, and "Father of Naval Aviation," from his birth in 1878 to the merging of the Curtiss company with the Wright company in 1929.

474.   Rosenberg, Leon J. and Davis, Grant M.   DALLAS AND ITS FIRST RAILROAD. *Railroad Hist. 1976 (135): 34-42.* Offers a history of railroads in Dallas, Texas, the influence which they had on the exact placement of the city, and the political and economic events which affected the location of railroad connections, 1843-73. 40 notes.

475.   Rysavy, Don.   D. W. HINES AND THE FARMERS' RAILROAD: A CASE STUDY IN POPULIST BUSINESS ENTERPRISE, 1894-1898. *North Dakota Q. 1979 47(4): 20-34.* In 1894, David Willington Hines (1863-?) conceived a plan to build a Farmers' Railroad in North Dakota, constructed by the farmers without capital as an alternative to the exorbitant rates of the Great Northern and Northern Pacific railroads controlled by eastern capitalists; but poor financial planning and the farmers' inability to cooperate caused the plan to fail.

476.   Salsbury, Stephen M.   TWENTIETH CENTURY RAILROAD MANAGERIAL PRACTICES: THE CASE OF THE PENNSYLVANIA RAILROAD. *Res. in Econ. Hist. 1977 (supplement 1): 43-54.* Discusses the causes of the collapse of the Pennsylvania Railroad system. Railroads had been the first massive industries and quickly developed new methods of management. And at that point the system became frozen. David Bevan, financial officer of the Penn Central in 1951, determined to make some changes. He modernized the financial aspects of the railroad and introduced a computer data system. But merger with the New York Central in 1968 caused the system to come under the control of Alfred Perlman, who essentially scrapped the new methods; collapse came in 1970. 13 notes, ref.

V. L. Human

477.   Sawers, Larry.   AMERICAN GROUND TRANSPORTATION RECONSIDERED. *Rev. of Radical Pol. Econ. 1979 11(3): 66-69.* A review of Bradford Snell's *American Ground Transportation: A Proposal for Restructuring the Automobile, Truck, Bus, and Rail Industries* (Washington, D.C.: US Government Printing Office, 1974) and *The Truth About American Ground Transportation—A Reply by General Motors,* 1974. Snell argues that the General Motors Corporation has so increasingly dominated American land transportation that it is now a monopoly. Charges such as that GM built vehicles for Germany during World War II, forced railroads to switch to GM diesel locomo-

tives, and destroyed trolleys in favor of GM buses, are disputed by the company's traditional and expected reply. 2 notes.   V. L. Human

478.   Schmidt, William H., Jr.   THE SINGULAR MILWAUKEE: A PRO-FILE.   *Railroad Hist. 1977 (136): 5-21.* The Milwaukee Road railroad system began in Milwaukee, Wisconsin, in 1850 and branched out throughout the frontier in Iowa, Minnesota, and Illinois.

479.   Schreiner, Herm.   THE WACO STORY PART I: CLAYTON BRUKNER & THE FOUNDING YEARS.   *Am. Aviation Hist. Soc. J. 1980 25(4): 281-299.* Traces the early years of the Waco Aircraft Company, founded in 1923 as the Advance Aircraft Company, in Troy, Ohio, by Clayton J. Brukner (1896-1977) and Elwood "Sam" Junkin, focusing on the planes designed and built by Waco until 1930. Article to be continued.

480.   Schwantes, Carlos A.   THE MILWAUKEE ROAD'S PACIFIC EX-TENSION, 1909-1929: THE PHOTOGRAPHS OF ASAHEL CURTIS. *Pacific Northwest Q. 1981 72(1): 30-40.* In 1905 the Chicago, Milwaukee, St. Paul and Pacific Railroad—called the Milwaukee Road—began construction of an extension line from Minnesota to Tacoma, Washington. An expensive electrification project on part of the line and the lack of population centers along its western tracks forced the railroad into receivership in 1925. Even after a company reorganization, the Milwaukee Road remained financially weak and in 1980 ended all further service. Photographs taken during the early period by Asahel Curtis illustrate the railroad's heyday. Primary sources; 14 photos, map, 7 notes.
M. L. Tate

481.   Selby, Edward B., Jr. and Meadows, John C.   GEORGIA RAILROAD AND BANKING COMPANY: THE TAX CASES AND THE PLAN FOR CAPITAL READJUSTMENT.   *Georgia Hist. Q. 1981 65(3): 240-250.* When the Georgia Railroad and Banking Company was formed in 1833, its charter contained a tax exemption provision. Various court battles over taxation and conflicts over readjusting the company's capital in the 1950's are described. Based on company documents, court records and other sources; 36 notes.
G. R. Schroeder

482.   Shedd, Jeffrey.   AMTRAK: CONGRESS'S TOY TRAINS.   *Reason 1981 13(1): 20-28.* Examines the beleagured Amtrak railroad system and the role Congress has played in its modern history, from the $40 million first apportioned for it by Congress in 1970 to the present annual subsidy of $900 million.

483.   Sheehan, Michael F.   LAND SPECULATION IN SOUTHERN CALI-FORNIA: THE ROLES OF RAILROADS, TROLLEY LINES AND AUTOS. *Am. J. of Econ. and Sociol. 1982 41(2): 197-209.* Southern California's transportation system was subjected to speculative manipulation from the time of the railroads, through the period of the electric interurban trolleys and the rise of the automobile up until the energy crisis of the 1970's. The dominant underlying force in each period is shown to have been combinations of developer-speculators and local politicians. These groups, motivated by a desire for rapid development for speculative reasons, were able to exercise effective control over the provision of major infrastructural improvements. The argument is made that such control, and the developmental pattern resulting from it, can never be in the public interest.   J

484.   Shimokawa, Koichi.   AN ASPECT OF FORD MOTOR COMPANY: BUSINESS IDEOLOGY, MANAGEMENT ORGANIZATION AND MASS-PRODUCTION SYSTEM.   *Keieishigaku [Japan] 1973 7(3): 1-31.* Article in Japanese.   J

485.   Sidhu, Nancy D.; Charney, Alberta; and Due, John F.   COST FUNCTIONS OF CLASS II RAILROADS AND THE VIABILITY OF LIGHT TRAFFIC DENSITY RAILWAY LINES.   *Q. Rev. of Econ. and Business 1977 17(3): 7-24.* The purpose of this study was to determine the nature of the cost functions of Class II railroads and their significance for the viability of light traffic railway lines. Multiple regression analysis was used on samples of Class II railroads for 1968 and 1973 to determine the influence of distance and volume of traffic upon cost per ton mile. Substantial economies from heavier traffic were found, but most of these were exhausted at volumes of traffic relatively low compared with those of Class I railroads. Distance has influence upon some cost items but not upon the two major ones: maintenance of way and train operating costs. Length of line is shown to be an important determinant of the viability of light traffic lines, in an inverse fashion.   J

486.   Smalley, Jack.   BLOOD ON THE RAILS.   *Westways 1977 69(3): 18-23, 82.* Discusses the bloody fighting between the Atchison, Topeka & Santa Fe Railroad and the Denver & Rio Grande Railroad over the laying of track into the silver and iron mines of Oro City, Colorado, 1880.

487.   Smith, Philip C.   WILLIAM BENTLEY ON TRADE AND THE MARINE ARTIFICERS.   *Essex Inst. Hist. Collections 1977 113(3): 204-215.* Much of our knowledge regarding ships, shipyards, and the shipbuilding industry in Salem comes from the Reverend William Bentley's diary. Because Salem was a maritime town, its shipbuilding reflected the commercial and economic fortunes of Salem. The life of Elias Hasket Derby, as recorded by Bentley in his diary, exemplified these trends. Offshoots of the shipbuilding industry, such as the Salem Duck Manufactory (sailcloth), Salem Iron Factory, and the ropewalk industries, were also tied to the commercial fortunes of Salem. Based on the diary (1784-1819) of William Bentley; 2 notes.   R. S. Sliwoski

488.   Sprague, John S.   IT HAPPENED IN HAMMONDSPORT: HOW GLENN CURTISS BROUGHT THE AVIATION INDUSTRY TO THE NIAGARA FRONTIER.   *Niagara Frontier 1979 26(3): 53-61.* Brief history of heavier-than-air aviation and aviation pioneers, 1853-1929, focusing on Glenn Hammond Curtiss who won the Grande Semaine d'Aviation in Rheims, France in 1909, and started building planes in Hammondsport, New York, before moving to Buffalo, which became the home of the largest aviation industry in the world during 1910-14; follows the development of the Curtiss Aeroplane and Motor Corp. until 1929.

489.   Sprague, Stuart Seely.   THE CANAL AT THE FALLS OF THE OHIO AND THE THREE CORNERED RIVALRY.   *Register of the Kentucky Hist. Soc. 1974 72(1): 38-54.* Land speculation and urban rivalry complicated the struggle for development of a canal at the Falls of the Ohio River. When the Indiana Company was chartered in 1804, the Kentucky legislature chartered the Ohio Canal Company. The intense rivalry hindered stock selling and other devel-

opment, but the financial success of the Erie reawakened interest in 1823. The first vessel passed through on 21 December 1830, thanks to extensive federal aid. Based on primary and secondary sources; 56 notes. J. F. Paul

490. Stapleton, Darwin H. THE ORIGIN OF AMERICAN RAILROAD TECHNOLOGY, 1825-1840. *Railroad Hist. 1978 (139): 65-77.* A dozen US civil engineers visited and studied in Great Britain during 1825-40 and provided the technology transfer necessary to begin US railroads.

491. Stewart, Peter C. RAILROADS AND URBAN RIVALRIES IN AN-TEBELLUM EASTERN VIRGINIA. *Virginia Mag. of Hist. and Biog. 1973 81(1): 3-22.* Railroad construction provided a focus for the acceleration of economic rivalry between Richmond, Petersburg, and Norfolk from the 1830's through the 1850's. Richmond's place as a political center provided legislative leverage and attracted able promoters and sufficient capital. Richmond outdistanced its rivals handily, with Petersburg gaining little more than Norfolk. The rivalry left an enduring legacy. Based on railroad archives, manuscripts, and newspapers; 60 notes. C. A. Newton

492. Stoesen, Alexander R. ROAD FROM RECEIVERSHIP: CLAUDE PEPPER, THE DU PONT TRUST, AND THE FLORIDA EAST COAST RAILWAY. *Florida Hist. Q. 1973 52(2): 132-156.* Describes the battle between Senator Claude Pepper and Ed Ball, senior trustee of the Du Pont estate, over the future organization of the Florida East Coast Railroad. The railroad had passed into receivership in 1931 and by 1945 had built a surplus of 20 million. Pepper attempted to bring about a merger with the Atlantic Coast Line railroad, while Ball fought for independent management under du Pont control. Although no settlement was reached until 1958, the climax of the acrimonious battle came with Pepper's failure to win renomination in 1950. Primary and secondary sources; map, 102 notes. J. E. Findling

493. Talbott, Paul T., Jr. THE AIRCRAFT HISTORY OF DELTA AIR LINES, 1929-1979. *Am. Aviation Hist. Soc. J. 1979 24(3): 226-234.* Beginning as a crop dusting enterprise, Huff Daland Dusters, Inc., Delta Air Lines graduated to cargo shipping and eventually passenger transport, 1929-79.

494. Taylor, David G. THOMAS EWING, JR., AND THE ORIGINS OF THE KANSAS PACIFIC RAILWAY COMPANY. *Kansas Hist. Q. 1976 42(2): 155-179.* When Thomas Ewing, Jr., arrived in Kansas in 1856 the Leavenworth, Pawnee and Western Railroad Company was little more than a paper corporation dating to 1855. The road, which was to extend to the 100th meridian along the Smoky Hill River, would pass through lands held by the Delaware and Potawatomi Indians. Ewing was active in raising funds and lobbying in Washington, but his major contribution came in the form of land negotiations with the Indians. The L P & W was authorized to join the Union Pacific at the 100th meridian by the Pacific Railway Act of 1862. Ewing and his friends had transformed a nearly defunct corporation into a thriving enterprise destined to become the Kansas Pacific Railway Co. Primary and secondary sources; illus., 67 notes. W. F. Zornow

495. Thompson, George H.   ASA P. ROBINSON AND THE LITTLE ROCK AND FORT SMITH RAILROAD. *Arkansas Hist. Q. 1980 39(1): 3-20.* Details the problems and progress of the building of the Little Rock and Fort Smith Railroad ca. 1867-76. Josiah Caldwell of Boston capitalized much of it, Warren Fisher, Jr., was the contractor, and Asa P. Robinson, who founded the town of Conway, Arkansas, was in charge of construction. Finances were a major problem. James G. Blaine, Speaker of the House of Representatives and presidential candidate, was implicated in one scandal. Based mostly on primary sources; table, 60 notes.   G. R. Schroeder

496. Tillapaugh, J.   THE TEXAS & PACIFIC ON THE LLANO ESTACADO, 1881. *Permian Hist. Ann. 1981 21: 85-95.* Describes the struggles of the Texas & Pacific Railroad in 1881 to lay tracks in the Llano Estacado (Staked Plains) of Ector County in west Texas, and the impact of the railroad on the region's economic life.

497. Trainor, Linda L.   THE GREAT AMERICAN DREAM CAR. *Am. Hist. Illus. 1980 15(4): 18-21.* Preston Thomas Tucker manufactured 51 of his innovative and popular Tucker automobiles in 1948 before indictments from the federal government closed his operations; later, he was acquitted on all counts.

498. Tribe, Ivan M.   DREAM AND REALITY IN SOUTHERN OHIO: THE DEVELOPMENT OF THE COLUMBUS AND HOCKING VALLEY RAILROAD. *Old Northwest 1978 4(4): 337-351.* Relates the early failures and final success in bringing a railroad to the coal-rich Hocking District, Perry County, in southern Ohio. Organized in 1866 the Columbus and Hocking Valley Railroad Co. began construction in 1867. Progress was slow, but by August 1869 the line reached Nelsonville from which the first load of coal left for Columbus on 17 August. In the following year the line reached Athens, and spur lines were under construction. The C&HV was a prosperous railroad contributing to the industrialization of Columbus. Railroad archives, county histories, and secondary works; map, 34 notes.   J. N. Dickinson

499. Turner, Charles W.   THE LOUISA RAILROAD COMPANY: GENESIS OF CHESSIE'S SYSTEM. *Virginia Cavalcade 1980 29(3): 130-135.* Traces the early years of the Louisa Railroad Company of Virginia, which was chartered in 1836 by the General Assembly, destroyed during the Civil War, and rebuilt in 1866; it became the Chesapeake and Ohio Railroad in 1867, and is now the Chessie System, which extends from Newport News and Norfolk, Virginia to St. Louis, Missouri.

500. Vagts, Detlev F.   RAILROADS, PRIVATE ENTERPRISE AND PUBLIC POLICY: GERMANY AND THE UNITED STATES 1870-1920. Horn, Norbert and Kocka, Jürgen, ed. *Recht und Entwicklung der Grossunternehmen im 19. und frühen 20. Jahrhundert* (Göttingen: Vandenhoeck & Ruprecht, 1979): 604-618. Compares and contrasts the development of the railroads in the United States and Germany, concluding that Germany's willingness to administer and support its railways as public utilities was manifest at the outset, while in the United States public administration of the railways came only late and reluctantly, and there was enormous public resentment directed against the

railroad tycoons. Regulations meant to curb monopolistic practices were established and eventually the Interstate Commerce Commission was given great regulatory power over the railroad companies. 44 notes, 44 ref. German summary.   S

501. Villalon, L. J. Andrew and Laux, James M. STEAMING THROUGH NEW ENGLAND WITH LOCOMOBILE. *J. of Transport Hist. [Great Britain] 1979 5(2): 65-82.* The Stanley Steamer, first mass-produced, lightweight, inexpensive car in the United States, was built by the Locomobile Company, in 1899, and was a small steam car. It was put into production after two designers, the Stanley brothers, teamed up with two financiers, the magazine magnate John Brisben Walker and the asphalt paving king, Amzi Lorenzo Barber. The production rate of the company was very high, compared with most of its competitors, and it also exported many of its cars. By 1903 the steam car was no longer profitable. Later the company shifted its production to petrol cars. Based on private collections in US state libraries; table, 47 notes.   E. J. Adams

502. Walker, Henry P. PRE-RAILROAD TRANSPORTATION IN THE TRANS-MISSISSIPPI WEST: AN ANNOTATED BIBLIOGRAPHY. *Arizona and the West 1976 18(1): 53-80.* The coming of the railroads sharply divides the story of long-distance transportation in the Trans-Mississippi West. The 125 annotated items are divided into categories: nonscholarly classics, river and bay steamers, packtrains, stagecoaching, camels, wagon freighting, steam wagons, and multiple combinations. Studies on roads, bridges, and ferries, as well as reminiscences, are excluded.   D. L. Smith

503. Ward, James A. POWER AND ACCOUNTABILITY ON THE PENNSYLVANIA RAILROAD, 1846-1878. *Business Hist. R. 1975 49(1): 37-59.* In 1846 the Pennsylvania Railroad was chartered by the Pennsylvania state legislature in an attempt to diffuse power within the organization by giving executive authority to a committee responsible to stockholders. By 1878, however, power had been centralized in the hands of the officers led by John Edgar Thomson and Thomas A. Scott. Based on primary sources; 95 notes.
C. J. Pusateri

504. Wathen, Richard B. FROM JEFFERSONVILLE TO THE KLONDIKE: THE HOWARD SHIPYARD'S ALASKA CONTRACT. *Indiana Mag. of Hist. 1974 70(4): 283-295.* The Howard Company Shipyards built four woodburning sternwheelers for the Klondike Gold Rush traffic. Already too busy to handle any more work, Edmunds J. Howard submitted a bid for the four boats at three times the normal price and was awarded the contract. Traces the expedition of the Howard builders to Dutch Harbor on Unalaska Island. Primary and secondary sources; 2 illus., 3 photos, 25 notes.   N. E. Tutorow

505. Weinstein, Robert A. NORTH FROM PANAMA, WEST TO THE ORIENT: THE PACIFIC MAIL STEAMSHIP COMPANY, AS PHOTOGRAPHED BY CARLETON E. WATKINS. *California Hist. 1978 57(1): 46-57.* The Pacific Mail Steamship Company controlled passenger and cargo traffic from Panama north to Pacific Coast cities from its charter in 1848. In 1867, with government subsidy, the company began service to China and Japan from its home port, San Francisco. The last of the great wooden steamers were built

by the company: opulent ships with room for 250 first-class and 1,000 steerage passengers. The company mainly employed Chinese crews, which aroused the enmity of whites seeking work on the Pacific Coast. As a major corporation with numerous ships, the company decided to record its accomplishments. Carleton E. Watkins, a noted San Francisco photographer, was engaged to photograph company facilities and ships in 1871. Photos.   A. Hoffman

506.   Wheeler, Lawrence and Collins, Bernard M.   BUILDING A FLEET TO SUIT THE MARKET AND THE MILITARY.   *US Naval Inst. Pro. 1981 107(4): 58-63.* Reviews merchant marine policy since 1936 and the growth of the charter market, 1936-79.

507.   White, Bruce M.   WORKING FOR THE RAILROAD: LIFE IN THE GENERAL OFFICES OF THE GREAT NORTHERN AND NORTHERN PACIFIC, 1915-21.   *Minnesota Hist. 1978 46(1): 24-30.* The records of the Northern Pacific and Great Northern Railroads as preserved in the Minnesota Historical Society provide informative data on the daily work lives of the white collar employees in the railroads' St. Paul headquarters. Despite being located in the same building, the management of the companies kept their employees deliberately apart through physical and bureaucratic means, in an effort to prevent employee comparisons of working conditions, salaries, etc. The Great Northern set up a cafeteria in 1916 to which employees were lured by the staging of employee-rendered entertainments. Memoranda reproduced indicate that company officials were disturbed by employee neglect and/or damage of company property, excessive noise and boisterous behavior, and by the throwing of objects from company windows, endangering and even injuring passers-by. Primary sources.   N. Lederer

508.   White, John H.   RAILROAD CAR BUILDERS OF THE UNITED STATES.   *Railroad Hist. 1978 (138): 5-29.* Surveys railroad car building firms (private and railroad company associated), 1870's-1960's, broken down into major US geographical areas; includes a comprehensive list of shops which gives company name, location, operative years, and sponsor.

509.   White, John H., Jr.   THE STEAM RAILROAD COMES TO CINCINNATI.   *Cincinnati Hist. Soc. Bull. 1974 32(4): 177-183.* Discusses the advent of steam railroads in Cincinnati, Ohio, 1837-70, emphasizing the Little Miami Line and the construction specifications of the *Gov. Morrow* (locomotive).

510.   White, W. Thomas.   BOYCOTT: THE PULLMAN STRIKE IN MONTANA.   *Montana 1979 29(4): 2-13.* The Pullman Strike of 1894 had a significant impact on Northern Pacific Railroad employees in Montana. Great Northern and Union Pacific railroads experienced less disruption. American Railway Union members in Billings, Livingston, Butte, Helena, and Missoula participated. Troops from the 22d US Infantry patrolled Northern Pacific track and a major confrontation developed between the troops and citizens of Livingston. Unionized miners from western Montana communities supported A.R.U. efforts. After the strike ended, N.P. and U.P. officials blacklisted many Montana railroad employees. Six A.R.U. leaders were also convicted of violating an antistrike injunction. The Pullman Strike was a central event in the labor turbulence and political activism, which swept Montana during the 1890's, fostered by strong

antirailroad populism in the state. Based on contemporary newspapers, US Army materials in the National Archives, and secondary sources; 7 illus, 41 notes.

R. C. Myers

511. Williams, R. E. THE AIRCRAFT OF DONALD DOUGLAS. *Am. Aviation Hist. Soc. J. 1981 26(1): 72-79.* Pictorial essay of the achievements of Donald Douglas in the design and development of airplanes; 1932-38.

512. Wilson, William H. THE ALASKAN RAILROAD AND THE AGRI-CULTURAL FRONTIER. *Agric. Hist. 1978 52(2): 263-279.* In order to increase railroad revenues through the transportation of agricultural commodities, officials of the federally owned Alaskan railroad conceived a plan of colonizing the Matanuska Valley. Despite extensive railroad involvement, many of the attempts at colonization failed because of Alaska's arduous climate, poor soil, and the great distance from profitable markets. A few of the settlers did, however, remain to form the nucleus of Alaska's present agricultural community. Covers 1915-40. Primary and secondary sources; 37 notes. R. T. Fulton

513. Wilson, William H. RAILROAD AND REINDEER. *Alaska J. 1980 10(4): 56-61.* Describes the attempt by Otto F. Ohlson, appointed general manager of the Alaskan railroads in 1928, to connect the railroad with the reindeer industry. Discusses the reindeer operation of the Lomen family, the principals in the industry. 5 photos, 19 notes. E. E. Eminhizer

514. —. THE PIERCE-ARROW MOTOR CAR COMPANY. *Niagara Frontier 1978 25(3): 57-84.* Entire issue dedicated to the history of the Pierce-Arrow Motor Car Company of Buffalo, New York, and the businessmen who constituted the core of the company: Charles Clifton, George K. Birge, and Henry May, from 1873 to 1938.

515. —. PULLMAN-STANDARD. *Railroad Hist. 1978 (138): 52-70.* Reprints a January 1938 article from *Fortune* magazine which discusses the Pullman-Standard Car Manufacturing Co., the history of Pullman, Incorporated, 1860's-1936, and offers a short biography of its founder, George Mortimer Pullman (1831-97).

4

COMMUNICATIONS

516. Bagdikian, Ben H. CONGLOMERATION, CONCENTRATION, AND THE MEDIA. *J. of Communication 1980 30(2): 59-64.* Discusses the pattern of competition and corporate control over the American mass media, their influence on public opinion and government policy, and the entry of newspaper corporations into the stock exchange.

517. Barnett, Stephen R. NEWSPAPER MONOPOLY AND THE LAW. *J. of Communication 1980 30(2): 72-80.* Examines the effects of "anticompetitive economic practices" and "government intervention in the media marketplace through the Newspaper Preservation Act" passed in 1970, on monopoly in the newspaper industry in the United States since the Supreme Court decision, *Times-Picayune Publishing Co.* v. *United States* (US, 1953), which upheld the legality of combination rates for advertisers in newspapers.

518. Bean, Donald P. THE QUALITY OF AMERICAN SCHOLARLY PUBLISHING IN 1929. *Scholarly Publ. [Canada] 1981 12(3): 259-268.* Reprints a 1929 report from Donald P. Bean, manager of the University of Chicago Press, which was the first examination of American scholarly publishing, enumerating five reasons for inferior scholarship: lack of editorial rigor, overemphasis of quantity over quality, poor training of graduate students, pressures for abbreviation, and weakness in criticism.

519. Beck, Joe. PIONEERING IN TELEVISION IN THE TWIN CITIES. *Minnesota Hist. 1979 46(7): 274-285.* A personal account of the author's part in getting television started in Minneapolis-St. Paul, and promoting its development in the last half of the 1940's. Beginning as director of television for WTCN in Minneapolis when radio broadcasters had little enthusiasm for TV's potential, he soon formed his own company, Beck Studios, Inc. By 1947 the company opened its Twin City Television Lab to train people in the use of this new medium. Students came from all parts of the country, and eventually supplied a large percentage of the TV personnel over the whole nation. Several experiments in public service proved the worth of television despite the slowness with which funding was available for development. 15 photos, 26 notes. R. V. Ritter

520. Bellefeuille, Julie. PRINTING IN CALIFORNIA 1831-1930. *Pacific Historian 1975 19(3): 261-270.* Discusses the printing industry in California from the first recorded line of type in 1831 to international recognition for the work of John Henry Nash in 1930. Notes significant newspaper, book, and type developments. Secondary sources; 29 notes. G. L. Olson

521. Berlin, Barry. THE BUFFALO NEWSPAPER LEGAL BATTLE. *Journalism Q. 1981 58(4): 618-623.* In 1977 the Buffalo *Courier-Express* brought an antitrust suit, based on the Sherman Antitrust Act, (US,1891), against its competitor, the Buffalo *Evening News,* alleging that the tactics of the *News* in promoting a new Sunday edition were designed to ruin the *Courier-Express.* A preliminary injunction was issued against the *News* shortly thereafter but was reversed by a federal appellate court in 1979 on the grounds that no intent to ruin the *Courier-Express* had been proved. The case was still awaiting trial in 1980. Until a jury rules on the case, few conclusions can be drawn regarding the effectiveness of the Sherman Act in promoting diversity in this newspaper market. Based on judicial documents; 36 notes. J. S. Coleman

522. Besen, Stanley M. and Soligo, Ronald. THE ECONOMICS OF THE NETWORK-AFFILIATE RELATIONSHIP IN THE TELEVISION BROADCASTING INDUSTRY. *Am. Econ. R. 1973 63(3): 259-268.* Examines the manner in which advertising revenues are shared. "The use of uncompensated time and of option time, both contribute to the ability of television networks to extract the quasi rents which would otherwise accrue to local stations as a result of their network affiliation." An analysis of the impact of the ban on option time, the restriction on the maximum permissible sharing ratio, and the new Prime Time Access Rule demonstrates that "these rules in addition to the limitation on station ownership imposed by the Group Ownership Rule may be important barriers to the development of a fourth network." 25 notes, biblio. R. V. Ritter

523. Boyd, Marjorie. GETTING A HANDLE ON AT&T. *Washington Monthly 1979 10(10): 37-47.* The American Telephone & Telegraph Company's status as a regulated utility encourages its unnecessary and abusive spending, because expansion is the only permissible means for increasing profits.

524. Brotman, Stuart N. THE NEW ERA. *Wilson Q. 1981 5(1): 76-85.* Discusses cable television, subscription television, communication satellites, and videorecorders and their effects on the television industry and viewers.

525. Brunner, Ronald D. and Chen, Kan. IS CABLE THE ANSWER? *J. of Communication 1978 28(2): 81-84.* Traces the freedom in American communications since the Bill of Rights and examines the expectations of the communications industry for cable television until 1977 when these expectations were undermined by corporate dominance of the few large networks.

526. Cawelti, John G. CULTURAL PLURALISM AND THE MEDIA OF THE FUTURE: A VIEW FROM AMERICA. *Cultures [France] 1977 4(3): 56-82.* Suggests possible approaches for the development of new mass media to stimulate diverse subcultures and to diminish the restrictive control by commercial interests of major vehicles of communication, 1960's-70's.

527. Ciscel, David and Collins, Tom. THE MEMPHIS RUNAWAY BLUES. *Southern Exposure 1976 4(1/2): 143-149.* The shutdown of a Radio Company of America plant in Memphis, Tennessee, was due in part to union demands and the corporation's reluctance to satisfy them, 1965-70.

528. Dessauer, John P. PITY POOR PASCAL: SOME SOBERING RE-FLECTIONS ON THE AMERICAN BOOK SCENE. _Ann. of the Am. Acad. of Pol. and Social Sci. 1975 (421): 81-92._ Despite impressive sales gains in recent decades and substantial growth in the number of book buyers, book publishers are handicapped by serious weaknesses in the retail distribution system upon which the bulk of their marketing depends. The industry has largely itself to blame for these difficulties. Publishers are producing many more titles than the market can absorb. Retailers, though proliferating in number, often offer only very limited title selections to their clientele, thereby alienating the special interest customers that constitute the large majority of serious book buyers. The industry has failed, furthermore, to develop an effective fulfillment system by which specialized titles could be efficiently delivered on special order. The problem calls for industrywide cooperative action which has thus far failed to materialize. There are indications, however, that a new generation of publishing and retail managers is more receptive to new approaches, thus offering hope for an eventual solution. J

529. Dymmel, Michael D. TECHNOLOGY IN TELECOMMUNICA-TIONS: ITS EFFECT ON LABOR AND SKILLS. _Monthly Labor Rev. 1979 102(1): 13-19._ Discusses technological advances in the US telecommunications industry and future productivity in that industry.

530. Eberhard, Wallace B. CIRCULATION AND POPULATION: COM-PARISON OF 1940 AND 1970. _Journalism Q. 1974 51(3): 503-507._ US news-paper circulation has been maintained over the past 30 years. S

531. Filstrup, Jane. IN CELEBRATION OF SMALL PRESSES. _Wilson Lib. Bull. 1979 54(3): 165-169._ Discusses the proliferation of small presses in America since the 1960's, important because of the smallness of the operation and the unflagging spirit of the publishers.

532. Garofalo, Reebee and Chapple, Steve. THE PRE-HISTORY OF ROCK AND ROLL. _Radical Am. 1980 14(4): 61-71._ A variety of factors made possi-ble the ascent of rock and roll music by 1955. Chief among them were the 1941 battle for control of music rights between the American Society of Composers, Authors and Publishers (ASCAP) and Broadcast Music, Inc. (BMI), the collapse of the big bands after World War II, the scramble by the record companies for new markets including rhythm and blues (formerly "race music") in the late 1940's, the development of new recording technology (tapes and hi-fi records) that made production better and cheaper, and the importance of the local disc jockey. C. M. Hough

533. Globerman, Steven and Diodati, James. MARKET STRUCTURE, IN-TERNAL ORGANIZATION, AND R & D PERFORMANCE IN THE TELECOMMUNICATIONS INDUSTRY. _Q. Rev. of Econ. and Business 1980 20(4): 70-85._ Examines the empirical relationship between vertical and quasi-vertical integration and R & D (research and development) performance for a sample of US telecommunications equipment manufacturers. Holding other relevant factors constant, a firm's relative R & D performance is positively and significantly related to the concentration of its final sales to a single end-user, that is, to whether it is quasi-integrated. Integration by legal ownership does not affect a supplier's R & D performance, given that it is already quasi-integrated. J/S

534. Gomery, Douglas. RETHINKING U.S. FILM HISTORY: THE DE-PRESSION DECADE AND MONOPOLY CONTROL. *Film and Hist. 1980 10(2): 32-38.* Discusses the concept of finance capitalism which originated in Russia with Lenin's *Imperialism: The Highest State of Capitalism* (1916), and criticizes the common acceptance of the belief that financiers gained control of the American film industry in the 1930's, suggesting instead that monopolistic corporations, with the government's support, controlled the industry.

535. Henderson, Bill. INDEPENDENT PUBLISHING: TODAY AND YESTERDAY. *Ann. of the Am. Acad. of Pol. and Social Sci. 1975 (421): 93-105.* The independent press movement is flourishing in America. Most of these independent presses have organized into the Committee of Small Magazine Editors and Publishers (COSMEP). The large commercial publishers continue to refuse financial support to independent presses, although these same commercial publishers often reap financial dividends from the creativity and experimentation fostered by the small presses. Despite nonsupport from the commercial establishment, the independent movement in this country has always prospered. Authors in this tradition include Thomas Paine, Parson Weems, Washington Irving, John Bartlett, Walt Whitman, Mary Baker Eddy, General Henry Robert, Samuel Clemens (Mark Twain), Stephen Crane, Edwin Arlington Robinson, Upton Sinclair, Carl Sandburg, Ezra Pound and Anais Nin. The small press movement continues today with several advantages not enjoyed in the past: associations like COSMEP, new distributors, open-minded review media and large bookstore chains that simplify distribution problems once thought to be insoluble for the independent publisher.   J

536. Hoddeson, Lillian. THE EMERGENCE OF BASIC RESEARCH IN THE BELL TELEPHONE SYSTEM, 1875-1915. *Technology and Culture 1981 22(3): 512-544.* Basic research at the Bell Telephone System evolved slowly after 1880 when technical problems created by commercial objectives led to the founding of the engineering department. By 1910, technical problems, such as how to develop a repeater to amplify attenuated waves for transcontinental lines, had become so difficult that the company sought "deeper understanding of underlying physical phenomena" by officially organizing an in-house department of basic research in April 1911. Based on company records; 111 notes.
C. O. Smith, Jr.

537. Howard, Herbert H. OWNERSHIP TRENDS IN CABLE TELEVISION: 1972-1979. *Journalism Q. 1981 58(2): 288-291.* For the period under study, these trends emerge: 1) the industry continues to grow and expand, 2) multiple-system ownership dominates the industry, with over 60% of all subscribers being served by the 50 largest Multiple System Owners, and 3) large corporations are becoming the principal owners of the top cable organizations. 2 tables, 5 notes.
J. S. Coleman

538. Hurwitz, Sol. THE CORPORATE ROLE. *J. of Communication 1978 28(2): 73-76.* Examines the role and influence of large American corporations in television, specifically a possible fourth network sponsored by corporate interests; late 1970's.

539. Hynds, Ernest C. TRENDS IN DAILY NEWSPAPERS IN THE UNITED STATES. *Gazette [Netherlands] 1979 25(3): 135-149.* Surveys recent changes in the daily newspaper industry. Local monopolies, group ownership, cross-media ownership, and public ownership have the potential to threaten the free flow of information. The economic position of the industry appears good, although the future may be more uncertain. As newspapers have made changes in appearance and content in order to increase circulation, a number of surveys and research reports have been utilized in planning these changes. The production process has been greatly facilitated by the introduction of electronic aids including computer systems for use in type production, video display terminals, and optical character readers. Secondary sources; 48 notes. J. S. Coleman

540. Kay, Peg. POLICY ISSUES IN INTERACTIVE CABLE TELEVISION. *J. of Communication 1978 28(2): 202-208.* Discusses several questions dealt with by federal agencies regarding interactive cable television and its services, since interactive telecommunication systems have appeared, 1970's.

541. Kenyon, Robert E., Jr. U.S. PERIODICALS ARE HEALTHY, WEALTHY, AND WISE. *Gazette: Int. J. for Mass Communication Studies [Netherlands] 1977 23(1): 42-49.* The year 1976 was a record revenue year for American periodicals, especially because of advertising. Reasons for this increase in spending on magazine advertising are: 1) fewer TV sets in use; 2) a trend towards selective market selling; 3) anticipated increased cost effectiveness; and 4) the oversold condition of TV advertising. Most American magazines want to generate 50% of their operating revenue from circulation, and 50% from advertising. Currently the ratio is 45% circulation, 55% advertising. Some problems will continue to plague the magazine industry in the future, especially because of the tenuous US postal situation and the questionable paper supply. W. A. Wiegand

542. Langdale, John V. THE GROWTH OF LONG-DISTANCE TELEPHONING IN THE BELL SYSTEM, 1875-1907. *J. of Hist. Geography 1978 4(2): 145-159.* A desire to control long-distance telephone service in the United States eventually led to Bell's control of most telephone business. With Bell holding a monopoly during 1875-94, other companies found it difficult to compete with Bell's widespread interregional system. Nonetheless, competition during 1895-1907 spurred Bell (and its holding company after 1900, the American Telephone and Telegraph Company) to improve its service and seek innovations to ensure its dominance. By 1907, the company's technical advances and continued control of its ever-wider interregional network proved too difficult for other successful competition. A general agreement of the Bell case with models of technological innovation and industry structure is seen. Secondary sources; map, 2 tables, 2 diagrams, 44 notes. A. J. Larson

543. Lasky, Betty. LET'S MAKE A MOVIE. *Westways 1979 71(11): 22-25.* Discusses the beginnings of the Jesse L. Lasky Feature Play Company in Hollywood formed in 1914, with Lasky as president, Samuel Goldfish (later Goldwyn) as general manager, and Cecil B. De Mille as director-general, and the first movie the fledgling company made, *The Squaw Man,* Hollywood's first feature-length film, based on the play by Edwin Milton Royle; 1911-14.

544. Lee, Larry. THE PRIVATE REALITY OF PUBLIC TELEVISION. *Working Papers for a New Soc. 1981 8(2): 34-41.* Traces the rise and fall of Boston's WGBH and San Francisco's KQED, the most successful and innovative public television stations, and attributes their current plight to fiscal mismanagement and to the fact that stations intended as public institutions have "become mainly private playgrounds" with priorities increasingly destructive of the public service programming they purportedly support.

545. Leff, Leonard J. INSTANT MOVIES: THE SHORT UNHAPPY LIFE OF WILLIAM SARGENT'S ELECTRONOVISION (1964-65). *J. of Popular Film and Television 1981 9(1): 20-29.* Brief background history of electronic filmmaking from the late 1940's to the mid-1960's, focusing on the creation of electronovision in 1963 by Mark Armistead Television, Inc., a quick and inexpensive way to make movies using television technology; discusses William Sargent, Jr.'s ill-fated Electronovision, Inc., 1964-65.

546. Maisel, Richard. THE DECLINE OF MASS MEDIA. *Public Opinion Q. 1973 37(2): 159-170.* "An adequate perspective on our institutions tends to be possible only in retrospect. This article examines media growth trends over the past twenty years and finds the interpretation of them greatly distorted. Contrary to past expectations, mass media are shrinking in size relative to the total economy and the specialized media are becoming increasingly important." J

547. McVey, Sheila. NINETEENTH CENTURY AMERICA: PUBLISHING IN A DEVELOPING COUNTRY. *Ann. of the Am. Acad. of Pol. and Social Sci. 1975 (421): 67-80.* An examination of publishing in nineteenth century America pinpoints many of the problems faced by a country recently freed from colonial bonds and attempting to develop an indigenous culture. The problems faced are not only those of literacy rates, distribution of books and the nature of talented native authors. Cultural heritage, economic ties, political exigencies and legal traditions bind publishers in neo-colonial countries to the former mother country. A study of nineteenth century America illustrates the complexities and strength of the relation between developing and developed countries. An understanding of the difficulties faced by Americans trying to overcome intellectual dependence on British culture may help Third World countries cut to the heart of the problem more quickly than did the United States. J

548. Neavill, Gordon B. BOOK DISTRIBUTION AND MARKETING IN THE UNITED STATES: A REVIEW ARTICLE. *Lib. Q. 1977 47(1): 62-70.* Review article prompted by Benjamin M. Compaine's *Book Distribution and Marketing, 1976-1980* (White Plains, New York: Knowledge Industry Publications, 1976), dealing with growth trends in the book publishing industry and major commercial channels for the distribution of general books in the 1960's-70's.

549. Newlin, Lyman. THE RISE AND FALL OF RICHARD ABEL AND CO., INC. *Scholarly Publishing 1975 7(1): 55-61.* Describes the meteoric rise of Richard Abel and Co. in the 1960's, based on the personal chemistry of Richard Abel, and the service to academic libraries his firm supplied with books. It failed in 1974 because of tight money, heavy investment in computerization, and too many services that were unprofitable.

550.   Nichols, Bill.   WHATEVER HAPPENED TO SATURDAY NIGHT? THE RECENT CINEMA.   *Queen's Q. [Canada] 1979 86(3): 383-408.* Laments the demise of cinema during 1950-79. The changes in Hollywood in recent years are due to a large, complex shift in the economics of commercial film production over the last 10 years. It is not that films have lost their vitality, but that they have not remained what they were in years past. In the mid-1960's, the economic base of the film industry took on a new form. Several of the major studios succumbed to the march of monopoly. Studios were no longer in the motion picture business per se, but became economically linked with other divisions of the corporations that owned them. More businesslike management emerged. With this horizontal integration of studios in larger corporate structures, revenue from motion pictures did not necessarily flow back into further film production, but could be siphoned into another division. There has been a trend to produce fewer movies, but using larger budgets in both production and advertising. This is termed the Big Bang technique, and includes mass distribution of the film from the outset. Secondary sources; 45 notes.   J. Powell

551.   Oppenheim, Jerrold.   UHF TELEVISION: BREAKING THE MONO-LITH.   *Society 1975 12(6): 68-71.* Discusses how UHF television could be used to provide more local programming if the Federal Communications Commission (FCC) would protect local stations by removing restrictions (1960's-70's).   S

552.   Owen, Bruce M.   THE ECONOMIC VIEW OF PROGRAMMING. *J. of Communication 1978 28(2): 43-47.* Examines the structure of television programming in the United States in the 1970's from an economic point of view.

553.   Painter, Linda L.   THE RISE AND DECLINE OF STANDARD RA-DIO TRANSCRIPTION COMPANY.   *JEMF Q. 1981 17(64): 194-200.* Discusses the success of Standard Radio, a transcription company formed by Jerry King in 1934 in Los Angeles, the country and western music recording center, and focuses on the artists, such as the Sons of the Pioneers, Frankie Laine and Nat King Cole, who recorded there until Standard fell victim to television in 1954.

554.   Persky, Joel.   SELF REGULATION OF BROADCASTING—DOES IT EXIST?   *J. of Communication 1977 27(2): 202-210.* Examines the purportedly self-regulatory position of the National Association of Broadcasters from 1922 to the present, concluding that this argument is untenable.

555.   Powell, Walter.   THE BLOCKBUSTER DECADE: THE MEDIA AS BIG BUSINESS.   *Working Papers for a New Soc. 1979 7(2): 26-36.* Growing corporate control and related-company mergers in the information and entertainment industries, 1960's-70's, may result in less diversity and block opportunity for new, serious work to reach the national audience.

556.   Powell, Walter W.   COMPETITION VERSUS CONCENTRATION IN THE BOOK TRADE.   *J. of Communication 1980 30(2): 89-97.* Examines the factors that contribute to limiting the trend toward oligopoly in the American publishing industry, including foreign competition, small presses, and the numerous types of publishable books, focusing on corporate mergers of the 1960's and 1970's.

557.   Pusateri, C. Joseph.   RADIO BROADCASTERS AND THE CHAL-
LENGE OF TELEVISION: A NEW ORLEANS CASE.   *Business Hist. Rev.
1980 54(3): 303-329.* Radio station operators faced a difficult decision in the late
1940's, whether to seek television channel grants from the FCC or to confine their
activities to the proven profitability of AM broadcasting. New Orleans' WWL,
a major southern station and a CBS affiliate, internally debated the issue during
1947 and 1948. A relatively conservative ownership feared jeopardizing AM
profits by investing in the extremely costly and speculative venture of television.
Finally, under pressure from outside expertise and the fear of being frozen out
of the limited channel grants available, WWL filed for television. The WWL
experience demonstrates the risk-taking aspect of technological innovation. Based
mainly on WWL station records; 5 tables, 62 notes.   A

558.   Putnam, John B.   HIGHBROW TOBACCO: THE GENESIS OF
AAUP.   *Scholarly Publishing [Canada] 1974 5(4): 301-308.* "The oldest and
largest of university press associations was not born easily; good-humoured references to tobacco originally helped ease controversy and adversity. But from the
small, informal meetings of the 1920s has developed a large-scale, changing
program of service."   J

559.   Reich, Leonard S.   INDUSTRIAL RESEARCH AND THE PURSUIT
OF CORPORATE SECURITY: THE EARLY YEARS OF BELL LABS.
Business Hist. Rev. 1980 54(4): 504-529. Firms establish industrial research
laboratories not only to develop new products and processes but also as market
protection. The defensive strategy attempts to collect patents, forestalling competition. The American Telephone and Telegraph Co. (AT&T) research program,
for example, was created both to develop long-distance telephoning and to protect
AT&T against the new technology represented by radio. Both goals were realized.
AT&T's Bell Telephone System rapidly grew in size and importance. Government records and documents and some private papers; 3 illus., 78 notes.
                                                               C. J. Pusateri

560.   Reich, Leonard S.   RESEARCH, PATENTS, AND THE STRUGGLE
TO CONTROL RADIO: A STUDY OF BIG BUSINESS AND THE USES OF
INDUSTRIAL RESEARCH.   *Business Hist. Rev. 1977 51(2): 208-235.* Using
the early radio industry as a case study, discusses the use of corporate research
and the pursuit of patents to gain control of a market. Three methods of employing patents for purposes other than production are outlined: to prevent competition, to keep competitors from acquiring a strong patent position of their own,
and to use as trading devices. Concludes that science has been "compromised"
by the employment of research in the unproductive enterprise of seeking monopolies. Based on governmental documents and published sources; 53 notes.
                                                               C. J. Pusateri

561.   Robinson, Michael J. and Olszewski, Ray.   BOOKS IN THE MARKET-
PLACE OF IDEAS.   *J. of Communication 1980 30(2): 81-88.* Examines the
difficulty in entering the American publishing industry and the increase in market
concentration, using the mass market paperbook industry as an example, focusing
on Pocket Books which was founded in 1939.

562. Robinson, Walter.　GIMME SHELTER: ART AND THE IRS.　*Art in Am. 1980 68(6): 9, 11, 13, 152, (9): 9, 11, 13, 15, 17.* Part I. The entire fine print industry, including artists, distributors, print shops, and art magazines, benefits from print tax shelters in which wealthy investors get depreciation deductions and an investment tax credit while marketing prints through retail outlets. Part II. Tax shelter-financed prints are poor prints, and such investments are not based on sound economics.

563. Rosen, Philip T.　MARVEL OF RADIO.　*Am. Q. 1979 31(4): 572-581.* Reviews books on the history of broadcasting: Eric Barnouw's *A History of Broadcasting in the United States* (2 vols.; New York: Oxford U. Pr., 1966-68), Asa Briggs's *The History of Broadcasting in the United Kingdom* (3 vols.; New York: Oxford U. Pr., 1961-70), Robert Metz's *CBS: Reflections in a Bloodshot Eye* (New York: Playboy Pr., 1975), and David Holbrook Culbert's *News for Everyman: Radio and Foreign Affairs in Thirties America* (Westport, Conn.: Greenwood Pr., 1976). Though each of the studies makes an important contribution, there is much that remains to be explored in the history of broadcasting. Note.　　　　　　　　　　　　　　　　　　　　　　　　　D. K. Lambert

564. Schement, Jorge Reina and Singleton, Loy A.　THE ONUS OF MINORITY OWNERSHIP: FCC POLICY AND SPANISH-LANGUAGE RADIO. *J. of Communication 1981 31(2): 78-83.* Studies the structure and programming of the Spanish-language radio industry, especially ownership and time devoted to public service broadcasting.

565. Silver, Rollo G.　COPPER-FACING: AN INCIDENT IN THE HISTORY OF TYPEFOUNDING.　*Library [Great Britain] 1974 29(1): 103-110.* Though early power presses in the United States increased printers' productivity, they caused the rapid deterioration of printing type. Damage however was retarded by copper-facing the typeface. This technique was invented by Luke Vanderveer Newton (1809-1880) who patented the process in 1850, organized the Newton Copper Type Company in 1851 and saw the adoption of the technique by many US newspapers. The firm successfully opened offices in London by 1853 and survived until 20th-century printing developments rendered copper-facing obsolete. 42 notes.　　　　　　　　　　　　　　　　　　　　　D. H. Murdoch

566. Smart, James G.　INFORMATION CONTROL, THOUGHT CONTROL: WHITELAW REID AND THE NATION'S NEWS SERVICES. *Public Hist. 1981 3(2): 23-42.* Discusses monopolistic control of the nation's news services, exemplified through American editor Whitelaw Reid of the New York *Tribune* and his use of the media to present news from his own conservative viewpoint during the crucial period 1885-92.

567. Smith, Edward J. and Fowler, Gilbert L., Jr.　THE STATUS OF MAGAZINE GROUP OWNERSHIP.　*Journalism Q. 1979 56(3): 572-576.* In the United States, 102 companies publish two or more periodicals issued at least quarterly. The 480 magazines published by these companies collectively account for a circulation of 222,585,584—nearly 9% of the total magazine circulation nationwide. Of the companies, the four largest are CBS, Inc., Ziff-Davis Pub., Meredith Corp., and Hearst Corp.; most have headquarters in the Middle Atlantic states, especially in New York City. Based on data in publishing industry directories; 5 tables, 20 notes.　　　　　　　　　　　　R. P. Sindermann, Jr.

568. Snitow, Ann Barr. MASS MARKET ROMANCE: PORNOGRAPHY FOR WOMEN IS DIFFERENT. *Radical Hist. Rev. 1979 (20): 141-161.* Harlequin Enterprises' romance fiction stresses distinct differences (often unbridgeable) between the sexes, passive female roles, and lack of either irony or realism in catering to the romantic desires of its female audience; 1970's.

569. Spehr, Paul C. FILMMAKING AT THE AMERICAN MUTOSCOPE AND BIOGRAPH COMPANY, 1900-1906. *Q. J. of the Lib. of Congress 1980 37(3-4): 413-421.* Discusses the production of films between 1900 and 1906 by the American Mutoscope and Biograph Company in New York City. More venturesome than most other early film companies, this company helped lay the groundwork for later film creativity by producing films of a more sensational nature in the areas of sex, comedy, and drama. The company moved from short and primitive productions in 1900 to larger and more sophisticated films by 1906. The company's film production also moved from an outdoor rooftop studio to an indoor studio with artificial light which made longer and more complicated films possible. Based on company production logs in the library of the Museum of Modern Art in New York City and on films in the Library of Congress; illus., 4 photos, chart, 4 notes. P. L. McLaughlin

570. Sterling, Christopher H. TRENDS IN DAILY NEWSPAPER AND BROADCAST OWNERSHIP, 1922-1970. *Journalism Q. 1975 52(2): 247-256.* An examination of ownership trends in radio and newspapers within the top 100 markets during the last 50 years. With the growth of broadcasting the number of media outlets has grown tremendously. The total number of owners has grown also, while concentration of ownership has declined since 1950. This may be reversed by 1980: small independent owners are being squeezed by increasing costs, and conglomerate control is increasing. Based on research undertaken for the National Association of Broadcasters, and on primary sources; 6 tables, 18 notes. K. J. Puffer

571. Suber, Howard. POLITICS AND POPULAR CULTURE: HOLLYWOOD AT BAY, 1933-1953. *Am. Jewish Hist. 1979 68(4): 517-534.* The politics of hysteria and repression that overtook the United States found an easy scapegoat in Hollywood for the fearful, the demagogic, political adventurers, union busters, and latent anti-Semites, as much as fellow travelers and crypto-Communists. Makes clear that long-term labor union and political conflicts in the film industry contributed significantly to the second Red Scare of 1947 with its "Hollywood Ten" and its blacklist. Based on interviews, court depositions and other primary sources; photo, 32 notes. F. Rosenthal

572. Tebbel, John. FROM RAGS TO RICHES: THE MEDIA IN AMERICAN SOCIETY. *Q. J. of the Lib. of Congress 1981 38(1): 42-50.* Reviews the development of the mass media in American society, from early newspapers to the development of modern newspapers, paperback books, magazines, and radio and television, and how the various media have been viewed by the public and the government. Until recently, the media have been well protected by the First Amendment. However, as indicated by the 1978 Burger Supreme Court decisions, the media are becoming increasingly threatened by a hostile public, government, court system, and business community. Illus. A. R. Souby

573.   Tobier, Emanuel and Willis, Mark A.   HAS NEW YORK'S PRINTING INDUSTRY BOTTOMED OUT?   *New York Affairs 1980 6(2): 59-69.* Discusses the reasons for the decline in New York City's printing industry (letterpress, lithographic process, screen printing, engraving, and gravure) since 1950, the dramatic decline during the early 1970's, and the slow revival of the industry since the mid-1970's.

574.   Varis, Tapio.   THE MASS MEDIA TNCS: AN OVERALL REVIEW OF THEIR OPERATIONS AND OF CONTROL OPTIONS.   *Cooperation and Conflict [Denmark] 1978 13(4): 193-213.* Recent discussions on transnational corporations (TNCs), especially in the UN, have been extended to include global communications and the mass media. An effort is made here to approach a definition of the mass media TNCs, as well as to describe the actual operations of these enterprises. The main focus is on the information media, although some observations on the entertainment media are also made. The control options of these TNCs are discussed with particular attention to the problems connected with the introduction of an international code of conduct. The general conclusions are that a more systematic collection of data is needed, and that more preparatory research on the definitional aspects must be carried out. The paper suggests that institutions, unions, and other groupings active in international communication could give continuous input to the work of the code of conduct for the media, and should strengthen and use the existing alternative sources of information. A carefully planned national and international communication policy is of vital importance for progress in this field. 57 notes.   J

575.   Weaver, David H. and Mullins, L. E.   CONTENT AND FORMAT CHARACTERISTICS OF COMPETING DAILY NEWSPAPERS.   *Journalism Q. 1975 52(2): 257-264.* Examines the relationship among editorial content, format, and circulation of competing newspapers. Leading newspapers have more news of the home, human interest, and sports. Trailing newspapers were more likely to adopt a contemporary format. Most leaders published in the afternoon, and subscribed to more news services. Of the trailing newspapers, 57% were older. Based on a study commissioned by the News Research Center of the American Newspaper Publishers Association and on primary sources; 3 tables, 19 notes.   K. J. Puffer

576.   Wilbur, Susan K.   THE HISTORY OF TELEVISION IN LOS ANGELES, 1931-1952.
PART I: THE INFANT YEARS.   *Southern California Q. 1978 60(1): 59-76.* Television experimentation in Los Angeles was led by Don Lee, who began W6XAO-TV in 1931, and by the Paramount Picture Corporation, which started W6XYZ-TV in 1942. Both stations utilized technical experts who developed equipment to improve television transmissions. Operational expenses were carried by station owners, because there were no commercial programs. W6XAO-TV achieved a number of TV firsts in Los Angeles, including showing the first feature-length motion picture on TV in 1933 and the first broadcasting of the Rose Parade in 1940. By 1939 W6XAO-TV had a regular weekly schedule of programs. W6XYZ-TV commenced regular programing in 1943. World War II delayed TV program development but contributed to electronic innovations and development. After the war the Federal Communications Commission reserved Channel 1 as a national

emergency channel and in 1946 granted licenses to eight applicants for commercial operations. Whereas in the early years of Los Angeles television concentrated on technical experimentation, in the period after 1946 television focused on the social implications of TV broadcasting. Primary and secondary sources; 49 notes.

PART II: THE BOOM YEARS. *Southern California Q. 1978 60(2): 183-205.* In January 1947 W6XYZ-TV became KTLA-TV, the first commercial television station in Los Angeles and in fact in the western United States. KTLA-TV began its commercial life with sports coverage, especially wrestling, live coverage of news events, and commercially sponsored shows, of which musical variety programs were most popular. By 1948 some 16,000 television sets were in use in Los Angeles. Television set manufacturers sponsored programs to attract viewers at neighbors' homes and in public places to buy their own TV sets. Court test cases made it possible for television coverage of sports events. Local newspapers signed pacts with the new TV stations to share information on news and sports coverage. By 1948 KTLA-TV was joined by KTSL-TV (formerly Don Lee's W6XAO-TV); KLAC-TV, owned by Dorothy Schiff Thackrey; and KFI-TV, owned by Earle C. Anthony. Because the stations needed to fill air time, new companies entered the field to provide stations with programs. With KTLA-TV as the city's leader, the new TV stations continued to progress through 1948. Primary and secondary sources; photos, 40 notes.

PART III: TELEVISION DURING THE FREEZE. *Southern California Q. 1978 60(3): 255-285.* In 1949 three new Los Angeles TV stations were established: KTTV *(Times-Mirror),* KNBH (NBC), and KEGA (ABC). Events in 1949-52 included the F.C.C. freeze on construction of new TV stations, the beginning of the Emmy awards, several changes of ownership and call letters among the city's seven stations, and construction of new broadcasting facilities by the major networks. The number of TV sets in Los Angeles quadrupled in 1949. By October 1951 there were more than a million. Until development of the coaxial cable made instantaneous national programming possible, local stations relied on their own programming or on kinescopes. One notable achievement by KTLA was the live telecast of an atom bomb test in 1952. Questions surfaced over such issues as pay TV, an educational TV channel, and coverage of sports events. Introduction of the coaxial cable and the lifting of the F.C.C. freeze marked an end to the first phase of Los Angeles TV history, once new stations soon were started on the UHF channels and network programming achieved a nationwide audience. Based mainly on contemporary published sources; 72 notes. A. Hoffman

577. Williamson, Mary E. JUDITH CARY WALLER: CHICAGO BROADCASTING PIONEER. *Journalism Hist. 1976-77 3(4): 111-115.* Studies the broadcasting career of Judith Cary Waller with station WMAQ in Chicago, Illinois, from 1922 to 1957, and her contribution to the development of the radio industry.

578. Wolseley, Roland E. THE ROLE OF MAGAZINES IN THE U.S.A. *Gazette: Int. J. for Mass Communication Studies [Netherlands] 1977 23(1): 20-26.* American periodicals fall into two classes: the consumer or mass-oriented magazine, and the specialized magazine. The former fulfills commercial and

social functions. The commercial function, unfortunately, dictates that the magazine be profit-oriented, and this inhibits the magazine's willingness to speak out on any but the most localized issues for fear of losing advertising revenue. Although only the book performs its function of disseminating information better than the American magazine, magazine owners should work on becoming less profit-oriented. W. A. Wiegand

579. Yagoda, Ben. HOLLYWOOD CLEANS UP ITS ACT: THE CURIOUS CAREER OF THE HAYS OFFICE. *Am. Heritage 1980 31(2): 12-21.* The Motion Picture Producers and Distributors of America, popularly known as the Hays Office (after its first director, William Harrison Hays), was formed in 1922 to put a curb on the sexual content of Hollywood films by instigating a code of decency.

5

ENERGY

580. Ackerman, Frank and MacEwan, Arthur. ENERGY AND POWER. *Monthly R. 1974 25(8): 1-14.* Examines the political and corporate business aspects of America's "energy crisis" with particular emphasis on the Middle East oil cartel.   S

581. Ackermann, John A. THE IMPACT OF THE COAL STRIKE OF 1977-1978. *Industrial and Labor Relations Rev. 1979 32(2): 175-188.* In an effort to determine whether the 109-day-long coal strike of 1977-78 constituted a national emergency within the meaning of the Taft-Hartley Act, this study examines, among other sources, the results of weekly surveys by the BLS of both the actual and expected effects of the strike on large employers in 11 coal-dependent states. The study finds that employer predictions of strike effects proved to be consistently exaggerated; those effects probably never constituted an actual emergency; and in fact the strike's economic impact was diminishing when President Carter finally invoked Taft-Hartley in response to growing political pressures.   J

582. Armentano, D. T. THE PETROLEUM INDUSTRY: A HISTORICAL STUDY IN POWER. *Cato J. 1981 1(1): 53-85.* Discusses the history of the oil industry from 1846 to 1980, finding that monopoly power in petroleum has not been a product of the free market but of political interventionism.

583. Arriola, Enrique. LOS INTERESES PETROLEROS, CALLES Y LOS CONFLICTOS DE 1924 [The oil companies' interests, Calles, and the conflict of 1924]. *Bol. del Archivo General de la Nación [Mexico] 1977 1(1): 26-30.* Reprints four letters between American businessmen Vernon J. Rose and Arthur C. Rath on the attitude of US corporations toward the Mexican oil policies of President Plutarco Elías Calles, 1924-28. Based on documents in the Archivo General de la Nacion; illus.   J. A. Lewis

584. Banks, Alan. THE REPORT OF THE PRESIDENT'S COMMISSION ON COAL: A REVIEW ESSAY. *Appalachian J. 1982 9(4): 295-301.* Critical review of the federal coal mining study by the President's Commission on Coal, headed by John D. Rockefeller IV, which was instigated after the 110-day coal miner's strike that ended in March 1978 during Jimmy Carter's administration.

585. Barcia Trelles, Camilo. EL PETRÓLEO, GRAN PROTAGONISTA [Oil, the great protagonist]. *Rev. de Política Int. [Spain] 1973 (130): 11-28.* Examines the use of oil as a weapon in international politics in war and peace: relations between the United States and Mexico show that foreign control of such a valuable economic resource can prevent political peace and economic development.

586. Baughman, Martin L. ENERGY AND THE ELECTRIC UTILITIES. *Current Hist. 1978 74(437): 210-214, 228.* Describes the history and organization of the electric utilities industry and the problems it faces as consumer of one-third the nation's dwindling primary energy resources.

587. Bissell, Richard E. THE ROLE OF THE INTERNATIONAL OIL COMPANIES. *Current Hist. 1978 74(437): 202-205, 227.* Discusses the 100-year history of the multinational oil companies; recently they have lost the public's confidence, especially because of the 1973-74 Arab oil embargo.

588. Bond, Jon R. OILING THE TAX COMMITTEES IN CONGRESS, 1900-1974: SUBGOVERNMENT THEORY, THE OVERREPRESENTATION HYPOTHESIS, AND THE OIL DEPLETION ALLOWANCE. *Am. J. of Pol. Sci. 1979 23(4): 651-664.* This study tests an overrepresentation hypothesis derived from a subgovernment theory of policymaking in an effort to explain the adoption and maintenance of the oil depletion allowance over time. Oil states do not tend to be overrepresented on tax committees of Congress during expected periods. The condition of oil state representation on tax committees and/or in key leadership positions is not associated with variation in the oil depletion allowance over time. Therefore, when one moves beyond anecdotal and short run data to a systematic analysis over a long period of time, the conventional, overrepresentation explanation of why the oil depletion allowance became policy and persisted for so long is not supported. These null findings lead to alternative explanations, and suggest limitations on the subgovernment theory of policy making.   J

589. Bonnifield, Paul. ENERGY RESOURCES ON THE SOUTHERN GREAT PLAINS. *Chronicles of Oklahoma 1981 59(3): 345-359.* As the gold and silver mining frontier moved into the Denver area in 1859, the need for a cheap source of energy became critical for the first time on the Great Plains. Coal provided that source, and, with the coming of the railroads, coal mining expanded to all areas of the West. By World War I wildcatting for oil and natural gas turned the southern Plains into a boom area, especially in western Oklahoma and the Texas Panhandle. The petroleum industry grew alongside the agricultural frontier, and, in the case of the 1930's Dust Bowl, it helped maintain some prosperity for communities that otherwise would have been economically devastated. Based on newspapers and secondary sources; 35 notes.   M. L. Tate

590. Carnes, Richard B. PRODUCTIVITY AND TECHNOLOGY IN THE ELECTRIC LAMP INDUSTRY. *Monthly Labor Rev. 1978 101(8): 15-19.* Discusses the increase in lampmaking manufacture through 1977, specifically since 1954, and suggests ideas and alternatives for the continued growth and production of lampmaking in light of current fuel shortages.

591. Caudill, Harry M. THE STRANGE CAREER OF JOHN C. C. MAYO. *Filson Club Hist. Q. 1982 56(3): 258-289.* John Caldwell Calhoun Mayo was born and reared on a small country farm in Appalachia and died the richest man in Kentucky. He achieved this transformation by being the first person to recognize the commercial possibilities of the vast coal reserves of southeastern Kentucky. Mayo developed the broadform deed that allowed him and his partners to purchase mineral rights to large tracts of poor mountain farm land at greatly reduced prices. Joining with West Virginia Senator Clarence Wayland Watson, Virginia Congressman Campbell Bascom Slemp, and industrialists John Davison Rockefeller and John Newlon Camden, Mayo became a political and financial power in three states. He was able to maintain his empire by convincing the Kentucky Supreme Court to uphold a law liquidating Virginia Revolutionary War land claims in the coal mining counties of Kentucky. Based on contemporary newspapers and unpublished studies.   G. B. McKinney

592. Chandler, Geoffrey. THE INNOCENCE OF OIL COMPANIES. *Foreign Policy 1977 (27): 52-70.* Examines and defends the thesis that major world oil companies should not be faulted for the world oil crisis. Conditions of the 1950's and 1960's allowing cheaper oil drastically changed. The Arab oil boycott (1973-74) and the formation of the Organization of Petroleum Exporting Countries require oil importing countries to deal with a situation likely to continue into the 1980's.   H. R. Mahood

593. Chapman, Stephen. THE GAS LINES OF '79. *Public Interest 1980 (60): 40-49.* Many Americans believed the oil shortage of 1979 was really the result of a conspiracy by oil companies to make large profits. Actually, the Iranian revolution, panic buying and stockpiling by car owners, and Energy Department policies created the gasoline shortage. Rebuts arguments presented by holders of the oil company conspiracy theorists.   J. M. Herrick

594. Christensen, L. R. and Green, William H. AN ECONOMETRIC ASSESSMENT OF COST SAVINGS FROM COORDINATION IN U.S. ELECTRIC POWER GENERATION. *Land Econ. 1978 54(2): 139-155.* A statistical analysis of 138 electric utilities in 1970 to determine whether cost savings result from increased coordination of electricity production. Finds no statistical evidence of cost savings from increased coordination, but does find evidence that mergers of small electric companies could result in cost savings. 4 tables, fig., appendix (firms included in the analysis), 13 notes, 10 ref.
                          E. S. Johnson

595. Christensen, Laurits R. and Greene, William H. ECONOMIES OF SCALE IN U.S. ELECTRIC POWER GENERATION. *J. of Pol. Econ. 1976 84(4, Part 1): 655-676.* We estimate economies of scale for U.S. firms producing electric power. Cross-section data for 1955 and 1970 are analyzed using the translog cost function. We find that in 1955 there were significant scale economies available to nearly all firms. By 1970, however, the bulk of U.S. electricity generation was by firms operating in the essentially flat area of the average cost curve. We conclude that a small number of extremely large firms are not required for efficient production and that policies designed to promote competition in electric power generation cannot be faulted in terms of sacrificing economies of scale.   J

596.   Church, Frank.   THE IMPOTENCE OF OIL COMPANIES.   *Foreign Policy 1977 (27): 27-51.* US oil companies in the Middle East are subject to policy manipulation by the producing country, Saudi Arabia as an example. The Senator believes the Carter administration must correct this policy deficiency. Based on US Senate staff studies.   H. R. Mahood

597.   Cotkin, George B.   STRIKEBREAKERS, EVICTIONS AND VI-OLENCE: INDUSTRIAL CONFLICT IN THE HOCKING VALLEY, 1884-1885.   *Ohio Hist. 1978 87(2): 140-150.* Examines the absence of violence toward strikebreakers in the Hocking Valley coal strike of 1884-85 in Ohio. Immigrant strikebreakers were brought to the coal mines by the operators and armed guards were posted on the properties, but violence against the strikebreakers was rare. When violence did appear, it was directed against the coal companies' property. Lasting over nine months, the strike ended in defeat for the miners. The strikers clearly had imposed limitations on the forms and objects of their violence. Based on manuscripts, archives, newspapers, and secondary sources; 2 illus., 43 notes.
N. Summers

598.   Critchlow, Robert V.   TECHNOLOGY AND LABOR IN ELECTRIC POWER AND GAS INDUSTRY.   *Monthly Labor Rev. 1978 101(11): 18-22.* Discusses the effects of new technology on the occupational structure of the electric power and natural gas industry, 1960-77.

599.   Dangerfield, Linda A.; McCartney, Hunter P.; and Starcher, Ann T. HOW DID MASS COMMUNICATION, AS SENTRY, PERFORM IN THE GASOLINE "CRUNCH?"   *Journalism Q. 1975 52(2): 316-320.* Examines mass media performance prior to and during the 1973-74 gasoline shortage. The American Petroleum Institute and individual oil companies issued warnings before 1971. The media mentioned the possibility of future problems, with no consensus concerning the reasons for it, and in November 1973 informed the nation that there was a crisis. The media viewed the oil companies' pronouncements with suspicion. Based on primary sources; fig., 16 notes.
K. J. Puffer

600.   DiLorenzo, Thomas J. and Robinson, Ralph.   MANAGERIAL OBJEC-TIVES SUBJECT TO POLITICAL MARKET CONSTRAINTS: ELECTRIC UTILITIES IN THE US.   *Q. Rev. of Econ. and Business 1982 22(2): 113-125.* Compares the behavior of public and private firms in the electric utility industry with respect to the practice of price discrimination and to production efficiency. Political competition may partly alleviate the inherent inefficiencies of public firms in the electric power industry. Equivalent degrees of price discrimination by public and private firms also exist.   J/S

601.   Dorsey, George.   THE BAYONNE REFINERY STRIKE OF 1915-1916.   *Polish Am. Studies 1976 33(2): 19-30.* This strike started on 15 July 1915 at "Jersey Standard's great refinery in Bayonne" when about 100 still cleaners demanded a 15% pay increase justified by a work speedup and publicly announced anticipated company profits. When other workers joined in, the company answered by hiring armed guards from P. J. Berghoff, a New York City "industrial service." The strike, of unorganized workers, spread to other companies. In confrontations, one Pole was killed and four others were wounded. The

strike ended by the end of July after promises of pay increases, a change of a foreman, and an appeal to wartime patriotism. Fifteen months later, another strike erupted to improve upon the two dollars-per-day wages. Though not apparent in 1915 and 1916, a new industrialism, one of concern for the worker, was beginning to play a recognizable role in the American economic world. Based primarily on newspaper accounts; 27 notes. S. R. Pliska

602. Ervin, Osbin L. LOCAL FISCAL EFFECTS OF COAL RESOURCE DEVELOPMENT: A FRAMEWORK FOR ANALYSIS AND MANAGEMENT. *Policy Studies J. 1978 7(1): 9-16.* Examines economic growth and employment acceleration in coal mining communities in Illinois with increased coal production; emphasizes the need for responsible planning in order to guarantee integrity of community life, 1970's.

603. Fassina, Elia. UNA ANALISI DEL COMPORTAMENTO DELLE MAGGIORI IMPRESE PETROLIFERE MULTINAZIONALI NELL'ULTIMO TRENTENNIO [An analysis of the behavior of the largest multinational oil companies during the last 30 years]. *Riv. Int. di Sci. Sociali [Italy] 1981 89(2): 138-165.* Examines the behavior of the oil companies and attempts to determine the advantages and disadvantages they have experienced as a result of the world economic crisis. Italian.

604. Gandre, Donald A. RECENT CHANGES IN COAL TRAFFIC ON THE GREAT LAKES. *Inland Seas 1978 34(1): 51-58.* Because of the growing use of western low-sulphur coal and its overland shipment by unit train, the tonnage of coal carried by Great Lakes vessels dropped 45% during 1965-75. Most of the decline occurred in westward shipments from Lake Erie ports, notably Toledo. Based on Bureau of Mines and Army Corps of Engineers reports. K. J. Bauer

605. Giddens, Paul H. HISTORICAL ORIGINS OF THE ADOPTION OF THE EXXON NAME AND TRADEMARK. *Business Hist. R. 1973 47(3): 353-366.* Examines the adoption in 1972 of the EXXON name and trademark by Humble Oil and Refining Company and Standard Oil Company of New Jersey. Traces the history of the name change from US government anti-trust actions against Standard Oil in 1910, through competition and change in the oil industry, to the conflicts over name and marketing and the decision to drop other names in favor of EXXON. Based on Humble and Standard Oil Company of New Jersey (EXXON) documents and reports, US government documents, contemporary newspaper and journal reports and secondary sources; 35 notes. N. J. Street

606. Giddens, Paul H. THE NAVAL OIL RESERVE, TEAPOT DOME AND THE CONTINENTAL TRADING COMPANY. *Ann. of Wyoming 1981 53(1): 14-27.* Traces the Teapot Dome Scandal beginning in 1921 when Secretary of the Interior Albert Fall received control over the naval oil leases from the secretary of the navy. Despite immediate complaints from Senator Robert LaFollette, Congress was slow to investigate the questionable transfer, and President Calvin Coolidge offered little help when the question was again raised in 1923. Senator Thomas Walsh kept the issue before a congressional committee and in 1924 uncovered the financial connection between Fall and oil magnates Ed-

ward Doheny and Harry Sinclair. Amid the unraveling of the scandal, three cabinet officers resigned and Fall went to prison. Based on congressional studies of naval oil leases; 4 photos, 84 notes.   M. L. Tate

607. Giebelhaus, August W.   FARMING FOR FUEL: THE ALCOHOL MOTOR FUEL MOVEMENT OF THE 1930S. *Agric. Hist. 1980 54(1): 173-184.* A movement to use alcohol produced from food as a substitute for gasoline became important in the 1930's as a means of dealing with the problem of low farm prices and surplus crops. The petroleum industry defeated legislation to aid alcohol production but a privately sponsored plant at Atchison, Kansas, funded by the Chemical Foundation, went into production in 1936 and sold fuel at 2,000 service stations in the Midwest. The high cost of making alcohol led to its closing two years later. Many people objected to alcohol fuels because they clogged fuel lines, burned inefficiently, and tended to separate into their component parts. 41 notes.   D. E. Bowers

608. Gilderhus, Mark T.   SENATOR ALBERT B. FALL AND "THE PLOT AGAINST MEXICO."   *New Mexico Hist. R. 1973 48(4): 299-311.* There were allegations that Senator Albert Bacon Fall of New Mexico and American oil producers sought military intervention in 1919 against the government of Venustiano Carranza. Fall and the oil men denied the accusation, but most scholars have accepted the substance of the charge as valid.   J. H. Krenkel

609. Graebner, William.   GREAT EXPECTATIONS: THE SEARCH FOR ORDER IN BITUMINOUS COAL, 1890-1917.   *Business Hist. R. 1974 48(1): 49-72.* The US bituminous coal industry suffers from "excessive competition." Shows that the industry has repeatedly failed "to control output or prices, whether by various kinds of trade association, mergers, or by attempts to secure government sanctions for cooperation." The Department of Justice has, through its opposition to consolidation, contributed to the industry's condition. "The fundamental problem lies in the basic economic conditions in the industry." 74 notes.   R. V. Ritter

610. Greene, Richard.   EMPLOYMENT TRENDS IN ENERGY EXTRACTION.   *Monthly Labor Rev. 1981 104(5): 3-8.* Discusses the increase in exploration for and extraction of oil and natural gas in the United States since the 1973-74 Arab oil embargo, which has in turn increased employment in these industries.

611. Guccione, Eugene.   WHY COAL WON'T BE AMERICA'S ENERGY SALVATION.   *Reason 1977 9(6): 16-20.* Coal mining will not solve the energy crisis, because of the slowness in increasing mine production, denial of federal coal lands to mining enterprises, and the impossibility of reaching western coal mining land, 1970-85.

612. Gutman, Herbert G.   LA POLITIQUE OUVRIÈRE DE LA GRANDE ENTREPRISE AMÉRICAINE DE "L'ÂGE DU CLINQUANT": LE CAS DE LA STANDARD OIL COMPANY   [The labor policy of the American corporation in the Gilded Age: The case of the Standard Oil Company]. *Mouvement Social [France] 1978 (102): 67-99.* This article calls attention to the emergence of the "large factory" in the early 1870's and examines the labor policies of one of the largest and best known of these firms, the Standard Oil Company of Ohio. It raises the question: what was the impact of the large factory on the

recruitment and discipline of workers, on working conditions, methods of payment, the power of workers vis-à-vis their employers and the relations among workers? The ability of a firm like Standard Oil to adopt modern technology and machinery met with a serious obstacle: the Coopers' International Union, which was in many ways the model of a successful organization of skilled nineteenth century American craftsmen. The mechanization of the barrel industry was, on the other hand, a threat to the Coopers: it destroyed their craft and their life style. The union's strength was broken by the large oil refiners and the barrel manufacturers who sold to them. After militant struggles waged in New York, Cleveland and Pittsburgh, the coopers were crushed. Multi-plant organization, financial resources and command of the market, as well as the support Standard Oil got from the Cleveland authorities enabled Rockefeller to render the skilled and semi-skilled coopers powerless and their major weapon, the strike, ineffective.

J

613. Hannah, Leslie. PUBLIC POLICY AND THE ADVENT OF LARGE-SCALE TECHNOLOGY: THE CASE OF ELECTRICITY SUPPLY IN THE U.S.A., GERMANY AND BRITAIN. Horn, Norbert and Kocka, Jürgen, ed. *Recht und Entwicklung der Grossunternehmen im 19. und frühen 20. Jahrhundert* (Göttingen, Vandenhoeck & Ruprecht, 1979): 577-589. Electric power companies in the United States were economically efficient because of economic rather than legislative factors. Municipal and other smaller companies cooperated to produce electricity at a relatively low cost. Absence of competition and lack of cooperation between private capital and government-owned power suppliers caused inefficiency and inadequacies in Great Britain's electric power system. Large privately-financed companies and municipally- and state-owned companies cooperated smoothly to insure the supply of power in Germany. Indeed, the government companies often became shareholders in the investor-owned companies. Covers 1880's-1920's. 22 notes, 24 ref. German summary. S

614. Haycock, Obed C. ELECTRIC POWER COMES TO UTAH. *Utah Hist. Q. 1977 45(2): 173-187.* Lucien L. Nunn and Paul N. Nunn were key figures in the development of electricity in Utah and the West. Their Nunn (1898) and Olmstead (1903) plants were significant in the development of new ideas, equipment, and practices, and in providing technical training. Most power plants were poorly financed and equipped. Companies frequently merged to stop destructive competition such as duplicate lines and equipment. In 1912 Utah Power and Light Company formed to integrate power sources into one system. Primary and secondary sources; 11 illus., 45 notes. J. L. Hazelton

615. Hogan, Michael J. INFORMAL ENTENTE: PUBLIC POLICY AND PRIVATE MANAGEMENT IN ANGLO-AMERICAN PETROLEUM AFFAIRS, 1918-1924. *Business Hist. R. 1974 48(2): 187-205.* Studies the development of a *modus operandi* for handling oil rich areas in the post-World War I period. The US State Department abandoned unilateralism in favor of a policy that encouraged multinational, especially Anglo-American, management of petroleum resources by private business leaders. This policy was followed in Persia, Mesopotamia, and Latin America. Nationalism, neutrality, and the "open door," were redefined to accommodate the new vision of expert management and cooperative capitalism. "In practice, the dream of an 'all-British' system and the American vision of an open door world had come out as an informal Anglo-

American entente, institutionalized at the private level, surrounded with the mystique of enlightened capitalism and masked behind tortured concessions to competitive symbols." 64 notes.   R. V. Ritter

616. Horn, James J. MEXICAN OIL DIPLOMACY AND THE LEGACY OF TEAPOT DOME. *West Georgia Coll. Studies in the Social Sci. 1978 17: 99-112.* Threats of military intervention in Mexico over enactment of legal provisions forbidding foreign ownership of lands, particularly oil land, died when public disclosure of the Teapot Dome Scandal made headlines, 1926-27.

617. Hughes, Thomas P. THE ELECTRIFICATION OF AMERICA: THE SYSTEM BUILDERS. *Technology and Culture 1979 20(1): 124-161.* In 1880 Thomas Edison personified the inventive stage of electric light and power, but contrary to legend he was no tinkerer. His notebooks show that his inventive method synthesized the technical, economic and scientific. About 25 years later, a large scale management stage appeared in the work of Samuel Insull, who created "an all-embracing" Chicago system of electric power. A third stage of financial system building appeared in the 1920's with S. Z. Mitchell, who introduced holding companies "by which the growth of utility systems might continue on a regional and even a national scale." All three men were "strong holistic conceptualizers." 95 notes.   C. O. Smith

618. Johnson,Clyde. CIO OIL WORKERS' ORGANIZING CAMPAIGN IN TEXAS, 1942-1943. Fink, Gary M. and Reed, Merl E., eds. *Essays in Southern Labor History: Selected Papers, Southern Labor History Conference, 1976.* (Westport, Conn.; London, England: Greenwood Pr., 1977): 173-188. A narrative (by an ex-organizer) of strategies and results in the efforts of the Congress of Industrial Organizations to organize oil workers in Texas in the early years of World War II. Covers the campaigns in Port Arthur, the Pan American campaign in Texas City, the Southport campaign, the Ingleside Humble campaign, the Baytown Humble Oil campaign, and the Gulf oil campaign. Notable were the company's exploitation of race issues and its appeals to "patriotism."
                                                    R. V. Ritter

619. Jones, J. Marshall, Jr. THE HISTORY OF THE ARK-LA-TEX OIL INDUSTRY. *North Louisiana Hist. Assoc. J. 1981 12(2-3): 67-77.* A brief history of the oil and gas industry of eastern Texas, northern Louisiana, and southern Arkansas. The first successful well was drilled at Spindletop in southeast Texas in 1901. Quickly, other finds followed. In 1905, the Caddo Field had its beginning in Caddo Parish, Louisiana. This area was later the site of a conflict between independent producers and major oil companies. Still more discoveries were made in the 1920's and 30's. Secondary sources.   J. F. Paul

620. Kalisch, Philip A. DEATH DOWN BELOW: COAL MINE DISASTERS IN THREE ILLINOIS COUNTIES. *J. of the Illinois State Hist. Soc. 1972 65(1): 5-21.* Two dozen coal mine disasters in Franklin, Saline, and Williamson Counties between 1904 and 1962 helped to bring about federal and state legislation for mine safety regulations. The southern Illinois area, commonly called "Egypt," is an example of the development of wage concerns pertinent to modern safety concerns. Traces the changing attitudes of the coal miners and the mine owners in developing and improving the coal mining industry. Based on

government documents and contemporary newspaper accounts; 3 illus., 2 maps, 2 graphs, diagram, 57 notes.   A. C. Aimone

621.   Kane, N. Stephen.   CORPORATE POWER AND FOREIGN POLICY: EFFORTS OF AMERICAN OIL COMPANIES TO INFLUENCE UNITED STATES RELATIONS WITH MEXICO, 1921-1928. *Diplomatic Hist. 1977 1(2): 170-198.* Two case studies of the interaction between American oil companies and the US Department of State indicate that the companies "failed to exert effective influence on the foreign policy process" in their efforts to protect their foreign investments in Mexico. The State Department's position concerning Mexico's petroleum legislation was actually based on "the Department's long-standing commitment to the concept of fair treatment of United States citizens and their capital abroad in the fields of trade and investment within the framework of generally accepted principles of international law." Based on primary and secondary sources; 89 notes.   G. H. Curtis

622.   Kaufman, Burton I.   MIDEAST MULTINATIONAL OIL, U.S. FOREIGN POLICY, AND ANTITRUST: THE 1950'S. *J. of Am. Hist. 1976 63(4): 937-959.* The Truman and Eisenhower administrations sought, through American-controlled multinational oil companies, to assure America a reliable oil supply and to prevent the spread of Soviet influence in the Third World. This policy worked admirably well in the 1950's, but it has failed in the 1970's. To use these corporations as instruments of foreign policy, Truman and Eisenhower granted the oil companies certain immunities from antitrust laws. In the process, they undermined their own case against international cartels, and may have contributed to the formation of OPEC (the Organization of Petroleum Exporting Nations). Based on US Senate documents, hearings, and secondary sources; 49 notes.   W. R. Hively

623.   Kaufman, Burton I.   OIL AND ANTITRUST: THE OIL CARTEL CASE AND THE COLD WAR. *Business Hist. Rev. 1977 51(1): 35-56.* The Truman administration initiated antitrust prosecution of the five largest American oil companies in 1952, seeking to force divestment of their integrated operations. However, the governmental commitment to antitrust was eventually subordinated to foreign policy requirements—specifically, to countering a perceived Soviet threat in the Middle East and to assuring the nation a cheap and plentiful supply of energy during the Cold War. Based principally on Department of Justice files; 58 notes.   C. J. Pusateri

624.   Kerr, K. Austin.   LABOR-MANAGEMENT COOPERATION: AN 1897 CASE. *Pennsylvania Mag. of Hist. and Biog. 1975 99(1): 45-71.* A review of the 1897 strike of the United Mine Workers in western Pennsylvania and its consequences. The harsh depression of the 1890's hit the coal industry severely, and owners competed ruthlessly for markets. The workers struck without warning, hoping to catch the owners off guard. The ploy worked fairly well, with a convention of worker and management representatives producing a satisfactory settlement. The impetus of the time was toward resolving disputes harmoniously, but it failed to survive the severe challenges of the decades to come. 105 notes.   V. L. Human

625. Lewis, Ronald L. "THE DARKEST ABODE OF MAN": BLACK MINERS IN THE FIRST SOUTHERN COAL FIELD, 1780-1865. *Virginia Mag. of Hist. and Biog. 1979 87(2): 190-202.* Discusses eastern Virginia coal field development. Although free workers were employed in the mines, slave labor was essential to these enterprises, in high- and low-skill jobs. Relates the nature of and the response to mine safety problems, including insurance on the miners. The mines declined when capital investments shifted to the Appalachian area. 2 tables, 60 notes.   P. J. Woehrmann

626. Lilienthal, David E. LOST MEGAWATTS FLOW OVER NATION'S MYRIAD SPILLWAYS. *Smithsonian 1977 8(6): 82-89.* Our society, preoccupied with bigness, is neglecting a source of energy which need not harm the environment. The FPC found that if 10 percent of the nations' 50,000 small dams were even partially developed, the equivalent of 180 million barrels of oil could be saved annually. The greatest waste of hydroelectric potential in in New England where many abandoned 19th-century mills could be refurbished, such as at the Hagley Museum in Delaware, to supply community energy needs at lower costs. 7 illus.   S. R. Quéripel

627. Lockwood, Charles. IN THE LOS ANGELES OIL BOOM, DERRICKS SPROUTED LIKE TREES. *Smithsonian 1980 11(7): 187-206.* In 1900, Los Angeles bristled with oil derricks. During the 1920's, California produced a third of America's petroleum. Edward Laurence Doheny, later of Teapot Dome fame, started the boom in 1892 when he drilled the first well. Soon Los Angeles wells were oversupplying the somewhat limited market, but the boom continued. Many neighborhoods were blighted by the dirt, oil spills, noise, and worker shanty towns until city regulations became tougher. Several scandals arose in connection with the oil industry, including Teapot Dome. The Depression ended the boom, but 500 wells still pump today.   J. G. Packer

628. Mancke, Richard B. COMPETITION AND MONOPOLY IN WORLD OIL MARKETS: THE ROLE OF THE INTERNATIONAL OIL COMPANIES. *Cato J. 1981 1(1): 107-127.* Discusses the decline in large oil companies' power after World War II, which culminated in the formation of the Organization of Petroleum Exporting Countries; present concern about the companies' alleged abuses is misdirected, diverting oil-importing countries from coming to terms with their energy problems.

629. Mancke, Richard B. PETROLEUM CONSPIRACY: A COSTLY MYTH. *Public Policy 1974 22(1): 1-13.* The 1972 fuel shortage was not a conscious oil industry conspiracy.   S

630. Mann, Fred. THE MISSING LINK: WHY WE CAN'T STAND UP TO OPEC. *Washington Monthly 1979 11(3): 50-57.* Provides reasons why the United States is unable to reduce its dependence on foreign energy supplies and produce some fuel reserves of its own, 1974-79.

631. Mariger, Randall. PREDATORY PRICE CUTTING: THE STANDARD OIL OF NEW JERSEY CASE REVISITED. *Explorations in Econ. Hist. 1978 15(4): 341-367.* If the firm's pricing behavior is tested against a model reflecting its dominant position in the market, the traditional interpretation of predatory price cutting becomes questionable. Based on published court records

and other documents and secondary accounts; 4 tables, 3 fig., 40 notes, 14 ref., 2 appendixes,   P. J. Coleman

632. Maroney, James C.   THE TEXAS-LOUISIANA OIL FIELD STRIKE. Fink, Gary M. and Reed, Merl E., eds. *Essays in Southern Labor History: Selected Papers, Southern Labor History Conference, 1976.* (Westport, Conn.; London, England: Greenwood Pr., 1977): 161-172. Studies of the 1917 strike of Texas and Louisiana oil field workers as an illustration of some employers' inexorable opposition to organized labor and great resentment of all concessions made to labor by the Wilson administration. Producers gained a clear victory in opposition to the findings of the President's Mediation Commission. Union effectiveness was not to be regained before the 1930's. It all ended in employer unity, but continued division in the ranks of union members. 32 notes.

R. V. Ritter

633. Newcomb, Richard.   THE AMERICAN COAL INDUSTRY. *Current Hist. 1978 74(437): 206-209, 228.* Discusses the 50-year decline of the American coal industry, and its recent revival prospects since the mid-1970's, in spite of environmental problems, because of increased doubt that a workable nuclear technology could be developed soon.

634. Osipov, B.   PROBLEMY NEFTEKHIMII KAPITALISTICHES-KIKH STRAN   [Problems of petroleum industry in capitalist countries]. *Mirovaia Ekonomika i Mezhdunarodnye Otnosheniia [USSR] 1976 (3): 113-120.* Analyzes the growth, structure, technology, and prospects of the oil industry and trade in Western Europe, the United States and Japan.

635. Pratt, Joseph A.   THE PETROLEUM INDUSTRY IN TRANSITION: ANTITRUST AND THE DECLINE OF MONOPOLY CONTROL IN OIL. *J. of Econ. Hist. 1980 40(4): 815-837.* The discovery of vast oil fields in Texas after 1901 encouraged competition in an industry previously dominated by Standard Oil of New Jersey. The manner in which the state of Texas enforced its antitrust and corporation laws hastened the growth of several major new oil companies, most notably Gulf Oil and The Texas Company, by constraining the activities of Standard in the new fields. In so doing, these Texas laws shaped the transition from near monopoly to near oligopoly in the oil industry. Such beneficial results of state laws were, however, largely accidental, since weaknesses in the government's capacity to monitor changes in the burgeoning industry undermined its ability to define and implement systematic regulatory policies.   J

636. Primeaux, Walter J.   THE DECLINE IN ELECTRIC UTILITY COMPETITION. *Land Econ. 1975 51(2): 144-148.* Describes competition between electric utility companies in The Dalles, Oregon, and Hagerstown, Maryland. Notes the differing decisions by state utility commissions and how they affected the competitive situation. 27 notes, biblio.   E. S. Johnson

637. Prindle, David F.   THE TEXAS RAILROAD COMMISSION AND THE ELIMINATION OF THE FLARING OF NATURAL GAS, 1930-1949. *Southwestern Hist. Q. 1981 84(3): 293-308.* During the 1930's and 1940's, Texas oil producers flared natural gas from their wells, because it had minimal market value. The Texas Railroad Commission, which controlled the state's oil and gas industry, held that flaring destroyed a precious natural resource and that the

pressure from recycled gas would increase oil production. Although the state authorized the Railroad Commission to end strip-and-flaring operations in 1935, oil producers continued to burn casinghead gas. The Railroad Commission was unable to prevent that flaring until William J. Murray, a staunch advocate of natural gas conservation, was appointed to the Commission in 1947. Murray's leadership, together with rising natural gas prices and Federal Power Commission support, enabled the Commission to close oil fields until producers stopped the wasteful practice of flaring casinghead gas. By 1949, Texan natural gas was strictly regulated and conserved. Based on the records of the Texas Railroad Commission and oral interviews; 58 notes. R. D. Hurt

638. Pusateri, C. Joseph. THE "TURN ANOTHER SCREW" AFFAIR: OIL AND RAILROADS IN THE 1880'S. *Register of the Kentucky Hist. Soc. 1975 73(4): 346-355.* In the struggle between Standard Oil Company and numerous independent oil companies, much has been made of a letter from F. D. Carley, a jobber for Standard, to the Louisville and Nashville Railroad, urging them to tighten their billing system and suggesting that one independent, George Rice, had paid less than the required per-barrel rate. Although foes of Standard have cited this as proof of Standard's attempt to suppress competitors, the author feels the letter has been misread and exaggerated. Primary and secondary sources; 28 notes. J. F. Paul

639. Rand, Christopher T. U.S. TAX LAW AND THE PRICE OF OIL. *Worldview 1974 17(12): 15-18.* Discusses how US tax laws benefit Arab states and the Organization of Petroleum Exporting Countries (OPEC) at the expense of the United States in the 1970's.

640. Riddick, Winston W. THE NATURE OF THE PETROLEUM INDUSTRY. *Pro. of the Acad. of Pol. Sci. 1973 31(2): 148-156.* Examines exploration, production, and distribution components of the oil and natural gas industry in the United States, with references to the Middle East, 1967-73. S

641. Rigin, Y. THE USA: OIL DIPLOMACY AND THE MONOPOLIES. *Int. Affairs [USSR] 1978 (8): 74-81.* The American energy crisis which began in 1973 is mainly due to the unjustifiably wide gap between domestic production and consumption of energy. This suits the American oil monopolies, for they have manipulated the world refining and distribution market so that it is more profitable for them to exploit foreign petroleum sources than domestic ones.

642. Ritchie, Stark. THOSE INTEGRATED OIL COMPANIES: IS A BREAKUP DESIRABLE? *Am. Bar Assoc. J. 1974 60(7): 826-830.* "The Federal Trade Commission staff report on the oil industry repeated the myth that the large, integrated oil companies are not competitive and should be broken up. The myth was repeddled by the article in [the December 1973 issue of *Am. Bar. Assoc. J.].* The truth is that the industry is competitive. Shortages of petroleum and price increases have resulted from government policies and the actions of the O.P.E.C. cartel." J

643. Rogers, George. OFF-SHORE OIL AND GAS DEVELOPMENTS IN ALASKA: IMPACTS AND CONFLICTS. *Polar Record [Great Britain] 1974 17(108): 255-275.* Discusses off-shore drilling for oil and gas in the construction of the Alaska pipeline from Prudhoe Bay on Alaska's Arctic coast to Valdez on

the Gulf of Alaska in 1974, emphasizing economic and environmental factors.

644. Roth, Stephen. OIL AND ALASKA: THE FIGHT FOR NAVAL PE-
TROLEUM RESERVE NO. 4, 1959-62. *J. of the West 1972 11(3): 531-541.*
In January 1959 Alaska Senator E. L. Bartlett and Representative Ralph J. Rivers
introduced legislation to open up Naval Petroleum Reserve No. 4 for mineral
leasing and private development. Despite several attempts to get the bills passed,
they were defeated by the personal opposition of House Armed Services Committee Chairman Carl Vinson. The aging Vinson, a Navy advocate since his first
election to the House in 1914, reacted as if the reserve were his own and refused
to recognize the needs and problems of Alaska. Based on government records and
secondary works; 47 notes, appendix.   B. S. Porter

645. Rundell, Walter, Jr. PHOTOGRAPHS AS HISTORICAL EVI-
DENCE: EARLY TEXAS OIL. *Am. Archivist. 1978 41(4): 373-398.* While
historians generally employ photographs in the same manner as written documents, there are special concerns related to the preparation of photographic
histories, including: historical quality of the photograph, pictorial quality of both
original and reproduction, optical distortion and bias on the part of the photographer, repositories' unsystematic collection practices, and accurate identification
of subjects. Based on the author's experience preparing the book *Early Texas Oil:
A Photographic History, 1866-1936;* 14 photos, 15 notes.   G.-A. Patzwald

646. Rustow, Dankwart A. PETROLEUM POLITICS 1951-1974: A FIVE-
ACT DRAMA RECONSTRUCTED. *Dissent 1974 21(2): 144-153.*

647. Rycroft, Robert W. THE UNITED STATES OIL INDUSTRY.
Current Hist. 1978 74(437): 193-197, 225-226. Discusses the increasing conflict
between the need for development of new technology and sources for domestic
energy, and the pressures for federal regulation of the oil industries since the 1973
energy crisis.

648. Sabate, Robert W. BIG, BAD OIL: NOT SO BAD AFTER ALL.
Am. Bar Assoc. J. 1974 60(6): 716-717. "Those accusing the oil industry of
monopoly and tax favoritism should recognize that oil is a high risk, stiffly
competitive business."   J

649. Sheitoyan, Robert G. LA CRISE ÉNERGÉTIQUE AMÉRICAINE:
UNE ANALYSE DE L'INDUSTRIE ÉNERGÉTIQUE AMÉRICAINE ET
LA BALANCE DES PAIEMENTS [The American energy crisis: An analysis
of the American energy industry and the balance of payments]. *Études Interna-
tionales [Canada] 1974 5(3): 542-553.* Examines the problems involved in the
balance of payments and energy costs and projects them through 1985. The
American deficit will continue, but in diminishing amounts. Reviews the implication of America's energy crisis in the Middle East and Europe. Primary and
secondary sources; 6 tables, 17 notes.   J. F. Harrington

650. Sheridan, David. A SECOND COAL AGE PROMISES TO SLOW
OUR DEPENDENCE ON IMPORTED OIL. *Smithsonian 1977 9(5): 30-37.*
Beginning in wood-poor England and Scotland in the late 18th century, the first
coal age spread to the Continent and the United States, fueling the Industrial
Revolution. Unable to compete with oil and gas, dirty coal began to decline in

1910. Today coal represents 90 percent of the nation's remaining fossil fuel reserve. "Burning coal in the quantities envisaged in the Carter plan would add as much nitrogen oxides . . . to the air as do all the cars." New jobs may be one of the second coal age's most positive impacts. Discusses other problems involved. Illus.   E. P. Stickney

651. Simmons, James C.   THE GREAT SPINDLETOP OIL RUSH. *Am. West 1980 17(1): 10-13, 61-62.* The single most important oil find in the United States was made 10 January 1901, on a knob of land near Spindletop Springs near Beaumont, Texas, thanks to the persistence of landowner Pattillo Higgins and mining engineer Anthony F. Lucas. It shifted the center for the American oil industry from the Ohio-West Virginia-Pennsylvania region, broke Standard Oil's longstanding production and distribution monopoly, and inspired the invention of a technology that brought the birth of the modern oil industry, including such giants as Gulf and Texaco. Production of Spindletop's oil continues, but the importance of the field as a producing pool lasted only into the 1930's. 2 illus., note, biblio.   D. L. Smith

652. Smith, Rodney T.   AN ECONOMIC ANALYSIS OF INCOME GROWTH BY U.S. OIL FIRMS: THE ROLES OF U.S. OIL REGULATION AND OPEC.   *J. of Business 1982 55(4): 427-478.* Ascertains how US oil firms were affected by US petroleum price regulation and the Organization of Petroleum Exporting Countries' pricing policies during the 1970's. Two major economic interpretations are supported by the results: US oil price regulation transferred income from US crude oil producing to US refining interests, without any benefit provided to US consumers; and foreign crude oil production subsidiaries of US firms were not beneficiaries of increased world prices for crude oil.
                                                                                        J/S

653. Stobaugh, Robert B.   THE OIL COMPANIES IN THE CRISIS. *Daedalus 1975 104(4): 179-202.* Allocation of oil during the oil crisis of 1973-74 became the responsibility of the multinational oil companies. Harried by both host and home governments, the companies attempted to distribute the oil in a manner that would equalize the shortages. Although distribution was relatively efficient and generally fair, the experience led oil companies to view future allocations as a government responsibility. Based on government documents and secondary sources; 8 tables, 74 notes, appendix.   E. McCarthy

654. Stradley, Scott A.   A DESCRIPTION OF THE DETERMINANTS OF THE AVERAGE PHYSICAL PRODUCT OF LABOR IN UNDERGROUND COAL MINING.   *North Dakota Q. 1977 45(4): 128-141.* Geological conditions and federal regulations determine the yield of underground coal mines; covers 1969-77.

655. Swomley, John, Jr.   ACCUSED: THE OIL COMPANIES.   *Focus/- Midwest 1974 9(61): 50-52.*

656. Turner, Louis.   THE OIL MAJORS IN WORLD POLITICS.   *Int. Affairs [Great Britain] 1976 52(3): 368-380.* Examines the influence of the eight major multinational oil companies upon world affairs in the light of their changing relationships with governments. Stresses the increased need for the companies to deal with pressure from governments in both consumer and producer countries. Secondary sources; 28 notes.   P. J. Beck

657. Vernon, Raymond. AN INTERPRETATION. *Daedalus 1975 104(4): 1-14.* The rise of independent oil companies was the key factor in the oil crisis of 1973-74. Their vulnerability generally broke deadlocks in conflicts with the oil-exporting countries. Internal political and economic problems, moreover, prevented the oil-importing countries from rational response. International oil companies were left to define the problems in terms of their own interests and to seek their own solutions. E. McCarthy

658. Volkov, O. "EKSSON" ["Exxon"]. *Mirovaia Ekonomika i Mezhdunarodnye Otnosheniia [USSR] 1976 (8): 119-123.* Analyzes the development and activity of the leading industrial corporation Exxon, its connections with the Rockefeller family, and particularly its foreign expansion since the mid-1960's.

659. Wallach, Bret. THE WEST SIDE OIL FIELDS OF CALIFORNIA. *Geographical Rev. 1980 70(1): 50-59.* After many years of decline, the oil fields of the southwestern San Joaquin Valley are more productive than ever. The area is a museum of antiquated equipment, revived by secondary recovery technology and by the decision to open the Elk Hills Naval Petroleum Reserve. The reserve is operated by the Department of Energy and Chevron, but the older, oil-producing territory, held by a dozen companies, is divided into thousands of small parcels formed under land laws antedating the Minerals Leasing Act. Area payrolls are large again, but workers increasingly commute from Bakersfield, as the West Side towns are steadily losing population. J

660. Willrich, Mason. THE MULTINATIONAL OIL INDUSTRY'S FUTURE ROLE. *Virginia Q. Rev. 1976 52(4): 560-578.* Analyzes the world oil situation by examining the interests of low-cost producers (OPEC), high-cost producers with self-sufficiency potential (United States, Great Britain, etc.), and importers without self-sufficient potential (France, Germany, Japan, etc.). Concludes that "the private multinational corporation offers a vehicle for centralized economic management in a decentralized international political system." O. H. Zabel

661. Wilson, David A. PRINCIPLES AND PROFITS: STANDARD OIL RESPONDS TO CHINESE NATIONALISM, 1925-1927. *Pacific Hist. Rev. 1977 46(4): 625-647.* In March 1925 the Kuomintang (Nationalist) government in Kwangtung Province sought to solve its financial problems by imposing a tax on imported kerosene. The tax was resisted by the two major suppliers, Standard Oil Company of New York and the Asiatic Petroleum Company, Ltd., as contrary to treaty provisions. The oil companies imposed an embargo, to which the Nationalists responded by threatening to create a government monopoly to control kerosene prices. Support from workers in Kwangtung and Hong Kong and oil from the Soviet Union enabled the Kuomintang to resist the embargo. In March 1926, the companies agreed to accept a tax in return for dissolution of the government monopoly. The American government reluctantly accepted the agreement despite the encroachment on treaty rights. The foreign companies and governments had recognized the strength of the Nationalist government in South China, but had also strengthened the conservative elements in the Nationalist coalition, which were willing to compromise with foreign powers. Based on documents in the National Archives and Hoover Library and on published primary sources; 70 notes. W. K. Hobson

662.   Wool, Harold.   COAL INDUSTRY RESURGENCE ATTRACTS VA-
RIETY OF NEW WORKERS.   *Monthly Labor Rev. 1981 104(1): 3-8.* Reports
on recent trends in employment in the coal industry characterized by an influx
of younger men, higher educational levels among laborers and an increase in
women employees both underground and on the surface since 1970 despite dangerous working conditions.

663.   —.   PRIVATE UTILITIES: THE CORE OF THE PROBLEM: TAC-
TICAL INFORMATION ON YOUR LOCAL UTILITY.   *Southern Exposure
1979 7(4): 67, 77-97.* A series of charts on each of the 16 major utilities operating
in the South, who owns and runs it, where it spends its money, what influence
it exercises on whom. Especially important are lines of influence showing relationships of directors to other corporations, boards, and executives, also the top
stockholders of each. The introduction discusses the various public relations
emphases, viz., educational programs in public schools, public lectures, general
advertising, lobbying, industry development, and picking law firms with the
"proper" connections. Illus., map.   R. V. Ritter

664.   —.   TEXAS BECAME TEXAS.   *Am. Heritage 1977 28(3): 48-55.*
Traces the development and impact of the Texas oil industry, with 13 captioned
photographs. Most of the photographs are from *Early Texas Oil: A Photographic
History* by Walter Rundell, Jr. (Texas A & M Pr., 1977). 13 illus.
                                                                          B. J. Paul

6

FOOD AND FIBER

665. Abel, Ernest L. WHEN TOBACCO WAS KING. *Am. Hist. Illus.* *1977 11(10): 10-19.* Discusses the history of the cultivation of tobacco in Virginia, 1613-1732, and the important role which it played in the economy of that colony.

666. Aiken, Charles S. THE EVOLUTION OF COTTON GINNING IN THE SOUTHEASTERN UNITED STATES. *Geographical R. 1973 63(2): 196-224.* "Cotton ginning in the southeastern United States can be structured in terms of three 'revolutions' or periods of rapid technological change. The Eli Whitney gin was the principal contribution during the revolution that closed the eighteenth century and began the nineteenth. As a result of the second revolution, which followed the Civil War, building morphology changed, the number of gins decreased, and new business allied with ginning developed. In the 1940's mechanical harvesting of cotton initiated the third revolution. This revolution also caused building alterations, accelerated declines in the number of gins, and produced changes in the sizes of service areas. The present ginning industry is a product of continuing evolutionary processes that are influenced primarily by economic, technological, and political factors." J

667. Anderson, Harry H. THE WOMEN WHO HELPED MAKE MIL-WAUKEE BREWERIES FAMOUS. *Milwaukee Hist. 1981 4(3-4): 66-78.* Traces the history of the brewing industry during 1840-1900 in Milwaukee and focuses on the influence of women and the son-in-law syndrome on the continuance of breweries such as Pabst, Blatz, and Schlitz as family businesses.

668. Anderson, James E. AGRICULTURAL MARKETING ORDERS AND THE PROCESS AND POLITICS OF SELF-REGULATION. *Policy Studies Rev. 1982 2(1): 97-111.* Discusses marketing orders, their administration, and their political context, with special attention to their impact on commodity prices and the process of self-regulation in marketing order policy.

669. Applen, Allen G. LABOR CASUALIZATION IN GREAT PLAINS WHEAT PRODUCTION: 1865-1902. *J. of the West 1977 16(1): 5-9.* Examines the mechanization of wheat farming in the midwest and its effect on the labor force. It necessitated a migratory work force and demanded fewer skills among the farm workers than before. A labor vacuum existed in the Plains states but the labor was needed only about 15 weeks a year. This casualization of labor, and the lower skill level required, lowered the worker's status. R. Alvis

670. Aronowitz, Stanley. "BUTTER FROM BOEING, HAM FROM ITT." *Social Policy 1974 5(3): 12-22.* Discusses the impact of large corporations in agriculture and the food industry on US food prices and trade, 1930-74.

671. Arthur, Bill. THE DARLINGTON MILLS CASE: OR 17 YEARS BEFORE THE COURTS. *New South 1973 28(3): 40-47.* A textile company's resistance to unionization. S

672. Bachus, Edward J. WHO TOOK THE ORANGES OUT OF ORANGE COUNTY? THE SOUTHERN CALIFORNIA CITRUS INDUSTRY IN TRANSITION. *Southern California Q. 1981 63(2): 157-173.* Analyzes changes in the southern California citrus fruit industry since its commercial origins in the 1870's. Irrigation, railroad access to eastern markets, and creation of the California Fruit Growers Exchange (now Sunkist) made southern California dominant in production of oranges and lemons. Until 1950, Los Angeles and Orange counties led in acreage and citrus production. Since then, the industry has shifted geographically. Florida's frozen orange juice has outstripped California production of eating oranges. Southern California's amazing population growth and urbanization came at the expense of the region's agricultural land and economy. Los Angeles and Orange counties are now almost completely urban; smog, taxes, and high land prices contributed to agricultural decline. Southern California counties are still major fruit producers, however, utilizing new laws, farming methods, and markets. 4 tables; 86 notes. A. Hoffman

673. Bahr, Betsy. THE ANTIETAM WOOLEN MANUFACTURING COMPANY: A CASE STUDY IN AMERICAN INDUSTRIAL BEGIN-NINGS. *Working Papers from the Regional Econ. Hist. Res. Center 1981 4(4): 27-46.* Traces the two year long operation of the Antietam Woolen Manufacturing Company in Funkstown, Maryland, from June 1814 to 1816 as an example of one of the numerous textile mills that formed to meet a higher demand for cloth during the Napoleonic Wars but was squeezed out of business shortly after because of English competition after the wars.

674. Ballew, Stephen; Brooks, Joan; Brotz, Dona; and Ives, Edward. "SU-THIN": (IT'S THE OPPOSITE OF NOTHIN"). *Northeast Folklore 1977 18: 5-117.* An oral history of lumber operations near the Little Musquash Lake, Washington County, Maine, during 1945-47. St. Regis Company, which owned the land, sold the stumpage rights to the Dead River Company, which in turn hired George Morrison to cut the lumber. Text includes the poem, "Suthin," by James McKinnon, an exegesis, and an oral history of Maine lumber operations. Includes information on contracts and subcontracts, crew and camp construction, equipment, the actual logging work, camp administration and maintenance, and the food operation. 30 illus., 14 notes, biblio. D. R. Jamieson

675. Bardan, Benyamin. THE COTTON TEXTILE AGREEMENT 1962-1972. *J. of World Trade Law [Switzerland] 1973 7(1): 8-35.* "The Long-Term Arrangement Regarding International Trade in Cotton Textiles has been in operation for ten years. It is proposed that it should be extended in 1973 to cover other textile products. This article offers a timely evaluation of the Arrangement and discusses whether it constitutes a precedent for the future organization of trade in products other than textiles." J

676.   Bateman, Fred.   THE "MARKETABLE SURPLUS" IN NORTHERN DAIRY FARMING: NEW EVIDENCE BY SIZE OF FARM IN 1860. *Agric. Hist. 1978 52(3): 345-363.* Although few specialized commercial dairy farms existed in 1860, dairying was already an important part of the agricultural economy. Most farms produced at least a small surplus of dairy products which could be sold off the farm. In the Northeast even small farms had marketable surpluses of butter and cheese. In the Northwest only larger farms had the potential for commercial production. Based on a sample of agricultural census data; 5 tables, 27 notes.   D. E. Bowers

677.   Bergquist, H. E., Jr.   THE BOSTON MANUFACTURING COMPANY AND ANGLO-AMERICAN RELATIONS 1807-1820.   *Business Hist. [Great Britain] 1973 15(1): 45-55.* Founded in 1812, the Boston Manufacturing Company exemplifies the state of American industrial development during the period when war cut off English competition. Francis Cabot Lowell (1775-1817) went to England to learn the design of new machinery which, with improvements, was manufactured in Massachussetts. The firm's heavy durable cotton sheeting survived the postwar reopening of international trade. Lowell was active in the movement leading to the mildly protectionist tariff of 1816. Based on unpublished dissertation.   B. L. Crapster

678.   Berner, Richard C.   SOURCE MATERIALS FOR PACIFIC NORTHWEST HISTORY: THE PORT BLAKELY MILL COMPANY RECORDS. *Pacific Northwest Q. 1958 49(2): 82-83.* A description of the papers of the Port Blakely Mill Company, a firm with widespread interests in the West and the Pacific, for the period 1876-1923, bestowed to the University of Washington Library.

679.   Blackburn, George M. and Racards, Sherman L.   THE TIMBER INDUSTRY IN MANISTEE COUNTY, MICHIGAN.   *J. of Forest Hist. 1974 18(1/2): 14-21.* Local ownership dominated the timber industry in Manistee County from 1841 to the early 1870's. "This study focuses primarily on land and sawmill ownership in order to show the extent of local versus outside ownership." Based on secondary sources; 2 photos, map, 6 tables, 22 notes.
                                          D. R. Verardo

680.   Boles, Donald E. and Rupnow, Gary L.   LOCAL GOVERNMENTAL FUNCTIONS AFFECTED BY THE GROWTH OF CORPORATE AGRICULTURAL LAND OWNERSHIP: A BIBLIOGRAPHIC REVIEW. *Western Pol. Q. 1979 32(4): 467-478.* The roles that corporations will play in the agricultural system and land ownership patterns are complicated by a paucity of research on that subject and upon the extent of its present influence upon the rural community and local governmental units. Empirical information is frequently inadequate in part because data on corporations in farm related areas were not collected by the US Agriculture Census until 1969. Many earlier studies fail to emphasize that corporate farms vary substantially in size and in their goals. They run the gamut from the large industrial type to a small family farm corporation, which may have sought its charter for purposes of estate planning advantages. One problem in accurately assessing the impact upon rural communities of changes in corporate farm and land ownership patterns is traceable to the lack of an agreed upon definition of what a farm corporation is, or should be. This

may account for the lack of a formal national policy concerning the growth of corporate ownership of agricultural lands. 66 notes.   J

681. Breimyer, Harold F. THE CHANGING AMERICAN FARM. *Ann. of the Am. Acad. of Pol. and Social Sci. 1977 (429): 12-22.* The American farm has never been as homogeneous or as stable as it appears in nostalgic recollection. Its historic emphasis on fee simple ownership by operating proprietors was nevertheless a marked departure from its feudal antecedent and remains relevant today. Farmers' desires for status and for managerial independence have not mitigated. They are subject to 1) changes, such as increase in size, that have no deep significance; and 2) other changes, such as increased dependence on nonfarm inputs, that bring more specialization of enterprise, including growing detachment of livestock (and poultry) farming from crop farming, and that make farming more sensitive to the terms of relationship with input-supplying as well as market industries. Encroachment of those industries via vertical integration (ownership or contract) along with internal growth of some farms to larger than family size gradually shrink the dominance of the traditional family farm. Even so, the most viable unit may be the part-time or retirement farm, which does not depend heavily on farm income. The ultimate question relates to what national policy is to be. Past policy has been ambivalent, and no clear direction for the future is to be seen.   J

682. Brown, S. G. SOME DEVELOPMENTS IN WHALING, 1975-81. *Polar Record [Great Britain] 1982 21(131): 165-170.* Presents a brief outline of developments since 1975 in the whaling industry, including general industrial decline and the International Whaling Commission's actions to reduce some catch limits and to increase the number of species under protection.

683. Browne, William P. FARM ORGANIZATION AND AGRIBUSINESS. *Pro. of the Acad. of Pol. Sci. 1982 34(3): 198-211.* Not all of the influential economic interests of agriculture are on the farm. Specialized agricultural business had to develop, and now they are larger in scale than farming. Agribusiness lobbying has brought to agricultural policy uncertainty and complexity. The political emergence of agribusiness does more than numerically complicate coalitions. The economic interests of these lobbies on support issues are not easily defined by an input or output role in servicing agriculture. Based on primary and secondary sources; 4 notes.   T. P. Richardson

684. Burns, Malcom R. OUTSIDE INTERVENTION IN MONOPOLISTIC PRICE WARFARE: THE CASE OF THE "PLUG WAR" AND THE UNION TOBACCO COMPANY. *Business Hist. Rev. 1982 56(1): 33-53.* John S. McGee and L. G. Telser hypothesized that a predatory assault on a significant competitor had the unanticipated effect of creating a profitable business opportunity for outside interests who might side with the threatened firm, bolster it with new funds, and then, finally, sell out on favorable terms offered by the aggressor. The experience of the American Tobacco Company in its attempt at extending its cigarette monopoly into chewing tobacco tends to support the hypothesis. Liggett & Myers was the threatened firm and the Union Tobacco Company was the vehicle employed by the outside interests. After the purchase of Union Tobacco in 1899, American Tobacco and its subsidiaries controlled over 75% of the cigarette, chewing, and smoking tobacco markets in the United States. Based on

a US Bureau of Corporations Report and other governmental documents as well as periodicals of the era; 3 illus., 2 tables, 36 notes. C. J. Pusateri

685. Burroughs, Jean M. NEW MEXICO PEANUT BUTTER: THE REAL STORY. *Palacio 1978 84(1): 39-41.* Chronicles the history of Deaf Smith brand peanut butter and the peanut industry in Roosevelt County, New Mexico, 1914-78.

686. Candee, Richard. THE "GREAT FACTORY" AT DOVER, NEW HAMPSHIRE: THE DOVER MANUFACTURING CO. PRINT WORKS, 1825. *Old-Time New England 1975 66(1-2): 39-51.* Gives the history and describes the architecture and construction of the cotton mills built by the Taunton Manufacturing Company, the Merrimack Manufacturing Company, and the Dover Manufacturing Company between 1820 and 1825 to introduce and increase mechanical calico printing in New England; focuses on the Dover Manufacturing Co. Print Works built at Dover, New Hampshire in 1825.

687. Caves, Richard E. and Rosen, Joel B. UNCERTAINTY, TRANSACTIONS COSTS, AND THE SIZE DISTRIBUTION OF RIVAL FIRMS: THEORY AND EVIDENCE FROM THE WOMEN'S OUTERWEAR INDUSTRY. *Q. Rev. of Econ. and Business 1982 22(3): 6-22.* Covers 1954-77.

688. Chang, Hui S. A STUDY OF INDUSTRY LOCATION FROM POOLED TIME-SERIES AND CROSS-SECTION DATA: THE CASE OF COTTON TEXTILE MILLS. *Q. Rev. of Econ. and Business 1979 19(3): 75-88.* Pooled time-series and cross-section data across states from 1951 to 1960 are used to study the shift of cotton textile mills from New England to southern states. Ordinary-least-squares, the dummy variable technique, and the error component model are used to analyze the data. Results show that, contrary to the conclusions of previous studies, only about 30 percent of the location of the cotton textile industry is explained by the local wage rate, the level of industrialization, and supply availability of raw cotton. Results also indicate that, if incorrect statistical procedures were used, conclusions reached could be seriously erroneous. J

689. Cipolla, Carlo M. EUROPEAN CONNOISSEURS AND CALIFORNIA WINES, 1875-1895. *Agricultural Hist. 1975 49(1): 294-310.* The California wine industry grew rapidly during the 1870's-80's while European grapes were suffering from phylloxera. Prices in America were depressed due to overproduction but exports rose as Europeans turned more to American wine as a well produced *vin ordinaire* in preference to the often adulterated, cheap European wines. 3 tables, 59 notes. D. E. Bowers

690. Clive, Alan. THE MICHIGAN FARMER IN WORLD WAR II. *Michigan Hist. 1976 60(4): 291-314.* Michigan farmers' contribution to the World War II effort, obscured by the preeminent position of the automobile industry, has been largely ignored and forgotten. Although total land under production and acres harvested increased only modestly during the war, agricultural production during 1942 broke all records; and it remained substantial thereafter. The war's impact seemed to augur well for the future of the family farm in Michigan, but proved, in the end, to be nothing more than a momentary postponement of agriculture's gradual decline. Primary sources; 10 photos, 99 notes. D. W. Johnson

691. Cochrane, Willard W. THE PRICE OF FARM PRODUCTS IN THE FUTURE. *Ann. of the Am. Acad. of Pol. and Social Sci. 1977 (429): 23-35.* Focuses on the behavior of U.S. grain prices in the context of prospective world developments over the next several decades. First looks at the process of farm price determination. Next looks at the dramatic movements in farm prices, particularly grain prices, in the period 1970-75. Given this background, we explore in some depth what is likely to be the trend in world grain prices over the next 25 years and the bases of that trend development. The conclusion is reached that world grain prices are likely to trend upward over the period 1975-2000. It is argued, however, that grain prices are not likely to move along a smooth trend; to the contrary, grain prices are likely to fluctuate widely, sharply, and unpredictably around trend. Finally, the policy implications of future grain price behavior are explored and some tentative policy suggestions presented. J

692. Conrat, Maisie and Conrat, Richard. HOW U.S. FARMERS BECAME SPECIALISTS—IN CASH AND DEBTS. *Smithsonian 1977 7(12): 48-55.* Increasing industrialization and urbanization broadened markets for farmers, and technological innovation and invention of steampowered equipment allowed for larger farm plots, 1860's-1900; yet specialization of crop growth often led to indebtedness, so that while many large operations gained notoriety, small farmers continued to suffer hardship.

693. Cozine, James J. and Warlick, Karen. A QUARTER CENTURY OF AGRICULTURAL ARTICLES: A SURVEY OF THE PERIODICAL LITERATURE CONCERNING THE RED RIVER VALLEY, 1950-1976. *Red River Valley Hist. Rev. 1978 3(1): 126-136.* Bibliography of articles from historical and agricultural journals pertaining to agriculture in the Red River Valley states of Arkansas, Colorado, Texas, Kansas, Louisiana, Missouri, Oklahoma, and New Mexico, 1950-76.

694. Crook, Morgan R. and O'Grady, Patricia D. SPALDING'S SUGAR WORKS SITE, SAPELO ISLAND, GEORGIA. *Industrial Archaeol. [Great Britain] 1977 12(4): 318-350.* Reports the results of the 1976 archaeological investigations of the Thomas Spalding sugar works, provides an economic background for the development of sugar operations, and examines 19th-century sugar production.

695. Danhof, Clarence H. THE FARM ENTERPRISE: THE NORTHERN UNITED STATES, 1820-1860'S. *Res. in Econ. Hist. 1979 4: 127-191.* Because of the well-known inadequacies of the Federal Censuses of Agriculture, our knowledge of the economic and financial characteristics of agricultural enterprises in the northern United States prior to 1870 is very sparse. However, farm financial accounts, frequently including interpretative commentary, exist in substantial numbers. Summaries of some 190 such accounts are presented in substantially comparable form. Other contemporary information presented permits evaluation of these accounts. Some of these enterprises were "average," but most classify in the upper third of all farms measured by net value of product, integration with the market, and profitability. The data have many other potential applications. Further exploration of these sources of information is highly desirable. Based on 19th-century US farm journals and agricultural society reports; 19 notes, ref., appendix. J

696. Decanio, Stephen. COTTON "OVERPRODUCTION" IN LATE NINETEENTH-CENTURY SOUTHERN AGRICULTURE. *J. of Econ. Hist. 1973 33(3): 608-633.* Quantitative analysis of supply functions suggests that "southern cotton farmers were as flexible and as price-responsive as wheat farmers in the rest of the United States during the late nineteenth and early twentieth centuries." Southern growers were economically astute in rejecting the proposed panacea of diversification. "No evidence of alleged traditionalism, or of merchants' insistence on cotton" leading to overspecialization or overproduction can be found. The frequently expressed idea that cotton overproduction fueled the Populist movement of the 1890's must therefore be reexamined. Primary and secondary sources; 5 tables, 2 graphs, 29 notes. W. R. Hively

697. Dennen, R. Taylor. CATTLEMEN'S ASSOCIATIONS AND PROPERTY RIGHTS IN LAND IN THE AMERICAN WEST. *Explorations in Econ. Hist. 1976 13(4): 423-436.* Tests two hypotheses about the impact of property rights formation on the cattle industry and shows that claims to the open range reflected an effort to maximize income by competing cattlemen. Based on manuscripts in the Montana State Historical Society Library, Helena, and at the University of Montana Library, Missoula, and on published documents and secondary sources. P. J. Coleman

698. Dick, Trevor J. O.; with commentary by Rasmussen, Wayne D. MECHANIZATION AND NORTH AMERICAN PRAIRIE FARM COSTS 1896-1930. *J. of Econ. Hist. 1982 42(1): 199-206, 216-217.* Attempts to document and account for cost savings on North American small-grain prairie farms in the early 20th century. Costs of production are analyzed using the price and yield data abundantly available. Cost conjectures are developed and compared with scattered farm data that itemize inputs and reveal some aspects of farming technique. Total costs per acre, despite year to year fluctuations, appear to have fallen gradually over the entire period consistent with a comprehensive and continuous learning process, rather than only suddenly in the late 1920's when there was a marked increase in the sales of gasoline-powered farm machinery. Comments pp. 216-217. J

699. Dobson, Jeffrey R. and Doyon, Roy. EXPANSION OF THE PINE OLEORESIN INDUSTRY IN GEORGIA: 1842 TO CA. 1900. *West Georgia Coll. Studies in the Social Sci. 1979 18: 43-57.* Discusses the pine oleoresin industry in Georgia, analyzing its economic and cultural significance, the extent of its exploitation, and the primary factors determining location.

700. Drache, Hiram M. MIDWEST AGRICULTURE: CHANGING WITH TECHNOLOGY. *Agric. Hist. 1976 50(1): 290-302.* The trend toward large, individually owned farms will continue into the future because of their inherent efficiency, and the effect of government programs. Machinery, modern management techniques, and the availability of skilled labor have enabled farms to expand almost without limit, regardless of crop grown. Based on interviews 1971-73 with owners of large farms across the country; 10 notes. D. E. Bowers

701. Dublin, Thomas. WOMEN, WORK, AND THE FAMILY: FEMALE OPERATIVES IN THE LOWELL MILLS, 1830-1860. *Feminist Studies 1975 3(1/2): 30-39.* Between 1830 and 1860 Lowell, Massachusetts, was a leading center of textile manufacture in the United States. From 1830 to 1845 women operatives formed a majority of the mill workforce. They were native-born and lived in company-owned boarding houses, which became centers of community life, and which provided the organizational base for the Lowell labor movement. After 1845 Irish immigrant men and women became a significant portion of the mill population. Immigrant women tended to live with their families (usually parents) rather than in boarding houses. Family dependence on the income of these female children meant greater caution in strike action and discouraged labor activity in Lowell during the 1850's. Primary and secondary sources; 33 notes.

S. R. Herstein

702. Duke, John and Huffstutler, Clyde. PRODUCTIVITY IN SAWMILLS INCREASES AS LABOR INPUT DECLINES. *Monthly Labor Rev. 1977 100(4): 33-37.* Analyzes relations among sawmill productivity, technological change, and labor input during 1958-75.

703. Eisterhold, John A. MOBILE: LUMBER CENTER OF THE GULF COAST. *Alabama R. 1973 26(2): 83-104.* Discusses the antebellum lumber industry and export market at Mobile. Large tracts of pine, cypress, and hardwoods in Alabama gave Mobile major importance by the 1820's, when steam sawmills were introduced along nearby rivers and streams. Production and exports rose steadily in the 1830's and 1840's; peak production came in 1854-55. Economic preferences for cotton, increased local and regional demand for lumber, and the mounting cost of shipping space later caused the export market to decline. The West Indies, France, and Spain were chief markets. Problems included a chronic shortage of skilled workers, racial tensions, and early attempts at unionization. Based on primary and secondary sources; 128 notes.

J. F. Vivian

704. Evans, Priscilla Ann. MERCHANT GRISTMILLS AND COMMUNITIES, 1820-1880: AN ECONOMIC RELATIONSHIP. *Missouri Hist. R. 1974 68(3): 317-326.* Discusses the economic relationships between gristmills, operators, and pioneer communities by examining 52 Missouri mills. Mills attracted settlers and were considered a public utility, encouraging a community's economic development by providing a grain market and cash or credit for purchase power for the farming community. The mills also extended the geographical boundaries of trade patterns and encouraged the development of associated industries. Based on Missouri and US government documents, interviews, primary and secondary sources; 2 illus., 5 photos, 28 notes.   N. J. Street

705. Fairbanks, F. A. IN SEARCH OF THE ABALONE. *Pacific Hist. 1976 20(4): 461-474.* Discusses the abalone industry in California and depicts a day aboard an abalone diving vessel. Abalone meat was known to Indians and used by early Chinese immigrants. The industry grew during the 20th century. Modern fishermen dive in deep waters and are under rigid governmental controls. 3 illus.   G. L. Olson

706. Feller, Irwin. THE DIFFUSION AND LOCATION OF TECHNO-LOGICAL CHANGE IN THE AMERICAN COTTON-TEXTILE INDUSTRY, 1890-1970. *Technology and Culture 1974 15(4): 569-593.* New England cotton-textile manufacturers lost the competitive struggle with new plants opening in the South, not because they failed to invest in innovations like the Draper automatic loom, but because of labor costs and other disadvantages. By contrast, the textile-machine industry remained in the North until the 1950's, when enough skilled labor became available in the South. Based on secondary sources; 56 notes.
C. O. Smith

707. Ficken, Robert E. GIFFORD PINCHOT MEN: PACIFIC NORTH-WEST LUMBERMEN AND THE CONSERVATION MOVEMENT, 1902-1910. *Western Hist. Q. 1982 13(2): 165-178.* The 1902 disastrous forest fires in Washington and Oregon and the accompanying human casualties precipitated intense public interest in the prevention of future disasters. Large timber owners headed a conservation movement to secure government protection of their threatened holdings from disaster, mismanagement, and the more radical forms of environmental preservation. The lumbermen found themselves allies of the nation's chief forester, Gifford Pinchot. This era came to a close in 1910, when Pinchot was dismissed by the William Howard Taft administration and when the anti-Taft dominated national conservation congress of that year called for increased federal regulation. These initiated a period of intense enmity between lumbermen and regulation-oriented conservationists. 64 notes. D. L. Smith

708. Ficken, Robert E. and Sherrard, William R. THE PORT BLAKELY MILL COMPANY, 1888-1903. *J. of Forest Hist. 1977 21(4): 202-217.* Port Blakely, on the tip of Bainbridge Island across Puget Sound from Seattle, was the site of the largest sawmill in the world in the 1890's. Sailing vessels carried its wood to South America, Hawaii, Japan, Australia, and China. Nova Scotian William Renton (1818-91) had founded the mill in 1864 and rebuilt it when it burned in 1888. The company was sold in 1903 for about $3 million to John W. Eddy and David E. Skinner. Based on records of the PBM Company and on secondary sources; 11 illus., 52 notes. F. N. Egerton

709. Ficken, Robert E. WEYERHAEUSER AND THE PACIFIC NORTH-WEST TIMBER INDUSTRY, 1899-1903. *Pacific Northwest Q. 1979 70(4): 146-154.* Wealthy financier Frederick Weyerhaeuser's 1899 entry into the logging industry of Washington transformed the timber industry of the Pacific Northwest. The old San Francisco-based companies gradually sold out to Weyerhaeuser or other midwestern investors and only the big companies which bought large tracts of timber lands were able to match the competition. Soon Weyerhaeuser Timber Company towered above the rest and it became the crucial unifying factor in the region's most chaotic industry. 3 photos, 37 notes. M. L. Tate

710. Finger, Bill. TEXTILE MEN: LOOMS, LOANS AND LOCKOUTS. *Southern Exposure 1976 3(4): 54-65.* Presents biographies of southern textile industry figures, 1918-40: J. Spencer Love, a mill owner, Lacy Wright, a mill hand, and Joe Pedigo, a labor organizer.

711. Fogelson, Nancy. THEY PAVED THE STREETS WITH SILK: PAT-ERSON, NEW JERSEY SILK WORKERS, 1913-1924. *New Jersey Hist. 1979 97(3): 133-148.* In 1913, Paterson silk workers staged one of a long series of strikes that culminated in 1924 with a violent outbreak that received extensive coverage in New York newspapers. During this decade, laborers in the silk industry were unable to secure beneficial changes for themselves because so many of their number left to form their own businesses and because mill owners deserted the city in search of cheap labor available elsewhere in abundance. In addition, management did not modernize machinery or production systems, but relied on antiquated business practices that eventually led to the death of the industry in Paterson. Based on interviews, contemporary newspaper accounts, ACLU papers, and secondary sources; 3 illus., 46 notes.   E. R. McKinstry

712. Fornari, Harry D. THE BIG CHANGE: COTTON TO SOYBEANS. *Agric. Hist. 1979 53(1): 245-253.* Soybean cultivation in the United States is comparatively recent, coming ultimately from China where soybean history goes back to 3000 B.C. After World War I they became a major source of feed and oil, the big boom coming during World War II. When the surplus of cotton became a major problem at the beginning of the Great Depression however, there was a push by the Agriculture Department to substitute beans in southern agriculture. Diversified uses for soybean products greatly spurred their replacement of cotton as the major staple crop. Table, 16 notes.   R. V. Ritter

713. Fornari, Harry D. RECENT DEVELOPMENTS IN THE AMERICAN GRAIN STORAGE INDUSTRY. *Agric. Hist. 1982 56(1): 264-271.* Grain storage remained much like it had in Biblical times until the adoption of mechanical bucket elevators in the 1840's. Improvements in elevators since then, such as concrete and steel construction, mechanical aeration, faster loading and unloading, various safety devices, and an increase in storage capacity have enabled the United States to become the world's leading grain exporter. 13 notes.
D. E. Bowers

714. Frame, Robert M., III. MILLS, MACHINES AND MILLERS: MINNESOTA SOURCES FOR FLOUR-MILLING RESEARCH. *Minnesota Hist. 1978 46(4): 152-162.* Between the 1880's and the 1930's Minneapolis was the flour-milling capital of the world. Very few operating mills remain today in the city, although a few survive in other parts of the State. The history of the flour-milling industry in Minnesota has been largely unrecorded by the historian. Valuable sources for the compilation of this history exist in the files of the *Northwestern Miller,* a publication designed for the major elements in the industry, and in the records of tis longtime business manager, William C. Edgar. The *American Miller* magazine concentrated on the interests of the smaller, largely rural millers. The technological side of the industry is worth investigation; sources exist for this research, although most of the early machinery of the industry has not been preserved.   N. Lederer

715. Francis, David W. ANTEBELLUM AGRICULTURAL REFORM IN DEBOW'S REVIEW. *Louisiana Hist. 1973 14(2): 165-177. Debow's Review,* published in New Orleans beginning in 1846, published many articles promoting scientific methods and reform in agriculture. These articles reveal the active mind of James D. B. DeBow and show that the technical mind of the Old South was

more developed than has generally been suggested. These articles discussed the uses of chemistry and fertilizers, rotation of crops, seed selection, diversification of crops and products, insect pests and pesticides, improvement of implements and processes in cotton and sugar production, fences, drainage, weather and climate, and agricultural goals and policies. DeBow's personal views dominated these pages. He believed that the South produced most of the nation's wealth while the North absorbed most of the profits. He called for an end to this colonial status through diversification of crops and related agricultural reforms, with agriculture remaining the foundation of southern economic and political power. 72 notes.   R. L. Woodward, Jr.

716. Gibson, Charles Dana.   HISTORY OF THE SWORDFISHERY OF THE NORTHWESTERN ATLANTIC.   *Am. Neptune 1981 41(1): 36-65.* Traces the development of the swordfishery from its establishment as a regular, if secondary, fishery by the 1870's to the present. The evolution of methods (from harpooning under sail to longlining from trawlers), grounds (from an inshore to an outer bank fishery) and participants (Canadians entered the fishery in 1909) are described. Based on newspaper articles; 12 notes.   J. C. Bradford

717. Gordon, Laurie and Salkin, John.   "EAT ME AND GROW YOUNG!": ORANGE CRATE ART IN THE GOLDEN STATE.   *California Hist. Q. 1977 56(1): 52-72.* Uses the lithographed labels from orange crates to trace the development of advertising in California's citrus industry. From the 1890's to World War II orange growers purchased a wide range of label designs as lithographers elevated their work to an art form. Up to 60 separate colors were used. Each grower used three separate brand names in a secret coding of quality. Designs reflected the idea of selling California as well as selling the oranges. Labels included scenes of ships, trains, planes, beautiful buildings, lush groves, athletics, gold themes, attractive women, and the Wild West. Eventually the brand name rather than the picture became the most important part of the illustration. Orange crate art abruptly ended and was replaced by a two-color stamp during World War II when material shortages caused wooden crates to be superseded by cardboard boxes. Today the labels are collected as art items. Photos.
                                                                                                         A. Hoffman

718. Greer, Douglas F.   THE CAUSES OF CONCENTRATION IN THE US BREWING INDUSTRY.   *Q. Rev. of Econ. and Business 1981 21(4): 87-106.* Concentration in the brewing industry has soared during the past three decades due, in part, to mergers and vigorous price combat and, largely, to economies of scale and product differentiation, the most recent outbreak of which was triggered by Miller Beer after its acquisition by Philip Morris; concentration is likely to increase, but once shares stabilize at a high level, advertising should subside.

719. Gregor, Howard F.   THE LARGE FARM AS A STEREOTYPE: A LOOK AT THE PACIFIC SOUTHWEST.   *Econ. Geography 1979 55(1): 71-87.* Examination of farming in California, Nevada, Hawaii, Arizona, and Utah indicates that, contrary to popular opinion, large agricultural units are exceptions, that they do not threaten small agricultural units, and that urbanization tends to stimulate rather than discourage agricultural production.

720. Guice, John D. W. CATTLE RAISERS OF THE OLD SOUTHWEST: A REINTERPRETATION. *Western Hist. Q. 1977 8(2): 167-187.* Corrects the general impression that the cattle industry on the American frontier leaped from the Appalachians to the Great Plains. Argues that the cattle raisers of the Old Southwest must be rescued from historiographic obscurity. The cis-Mississippi, non-Iberian antecedents of the Texas cattle frontier cannot be ignored. 88 notes.
                                                                    D. L. Smith

721. Haggberg, Marie. CHANGING PATTERNS IN THE GARMENT INDUSTRY. *New York Affairs 1980 6(2): 85-87.* Reprints interviews with representatives from government, management, and labor in the garment industry in New York City, 1979.

722. Hammer, Kenneth M. BONANZA FARMING: FORERUNNER OF MODERN LARGE SCALE AGRICULTURE. *J. of the West 1979 18(4): 52-61.* In the 1870's, railroads began to bring homesteaders to the Red River Valley near the Dakota-Minnesota border. The Northern Pacific Railroad (NPRR), which had large grants of government land, established a demonstration farm as part of its campaign to encourage settlement. Oliver Dalrymple, who managed the NPRR's Cass-Cheney farm, produced the first big wheat crop in 1876. News of this success raised land prices and led to more bonanza farms owned by eastern investors. The factory system of production required efficient farm machinery operated by many temporary employees and draft animals. The extension of rail lines and high demand in Europe for American wheat promoted rapid settlement, but a decline in wheat prices in the 1890's made large-scale farming less advantageous, and the bonanza farms were subdivided into small farms. Based on collections in the State Historical Societies of North Dakota and Minnesota; 2 illus., 4 photos, 2 tables, 37 notes.   B. S. Porter

723. Hareven, Tamara K. THE LABORERS OF MANCHESTER, NEW HAMPSHIRE, 1912-1922: THE ROLE OF FAMILY AND ETHNICITY IN ADJUSTMENT TO INDUSTRIAL LIFE. *Labor Hist. 1975 16(2): 249-265.* A case study of the Amoskeag Mills in Manchester, New Hampshire, which demonstrates the effect of ethnocentrism and family ties upon the modernization process. When the corporation introduced an efficiency and welfare system, the workers responded with attempts to control job mobility and hiring through their own ethnic and family affiliations. This was largely successful until the nine-month strike of 1922. Based on statistical family research, government reports and the *Amoskeag Bulletin*. Table; 25 notes.   L. L. Athey

724. Hart, John Fraser. THE DEMISE OF KING COTTON. *Ann. of the Assoc. of Am. Geographers 1977 67(3): 307-322.* Cotton fields were associated closely with rolling plains and black people in the traditional South. Cotton acreage within the region has declined sharply from its peak in 1929, and the crop has become increasingly concentrated in favored areas. The demise of cotton is best described by a mini-atlas of comparable maps of cotton and its correlatives. The once close relationship between cotton and black people has weakened steadily since World War I. The long term effect of the boll weevil on cotton acreage may have been exaggerated.   J

725. Hearden, Patrick J. AGRICULTURAL BUSINESSMEN IN THE NEW SOUTH. *Louisiana Studies 1975 14(2): 145-159.* Argues that, contrary to other studies, in the last three decades of the 19th century southern agricultural businessmen allied with urban entrepreneurs in calling for southern economic independence which would be based primarily on large scale textile manufacturing. This was especially the case in South Carolina, North Carolina, Georgia, Alabama, and Mississippi. Such agrarian support for the New South of industrialization and manufacturing also came from major farm groups such as the Grange and the Farmers Alliance. Primary and secondary sources; 67 notes.

B. A. Glasrud

726. Herndon, G. Melvin. THE IMPACT OF THE AMERICAN REVOLUTION ON AGRICULTURE AND AGRARIAN LEADERSHIP IN THE SOUTH: AN INTERPRETATION. *Louisiana Studies 1976 15(3): 279-286.* In 1794 the English Board of Agriculture sent William Strickland (1787-1854) to the United States to observe farm practices and production, probably in response to an increase in emigration from England. Strickland visited parts of New England, New York, and Virginia and reported on land conditions, land prices, slavery, and agricultural techniques. He concluded that productivity of the soil in the southern states had been much greater before the Revolution; the decline was due to the demise of the landed aristocracy and to the growth of democracy. The author refutes Strickland's observations, claiming bias to discourage emigration. In reality production was increasing, as a result of new crops and expanding farm lands west of the mountains. Based essentially on secondary sources; 26 notes.

J. Buschen

727. Hurt, R. Douglas. THE SHEEP INDUSTRY IN OHIO, 1807-1900. *Old Northwest 1981 7(3): 237-254.* Discusses the boom and bust cycles that characterized the sheep industry in Ohio. Vacillating tariff policies, fluctuating wool prices, changing demand, periodic overexpansion of the industry, and roaming dogs made sheep raising an uncertain endeavor. The best years of the sheep industry were over by the turn of the century, but it had played a major role in developing the state's agricultural industry in the 1900's. Primary sources; 37 notes.

P. L. McLaughlin

728. Hutchinson, W. H. THE SIERRA FLUME AND LUMBER COMPANY OF CALIFORNIA, 1875-1878. *Forest Hist. 1973 17(3): 14-20.* The short-lived Sierra Flume and Lumber Company of California (11 November 1875 to 8 July 1878) was "one of the largest, most complex lumber operations in the land." Located in Butte, Tehama, and Shasta Counties, it had an investment exceeding $1,500,000 and owned 200,000 acres of timber. It failed in 1878 when a financial panic hit San Francisco during a drought in the central valleys of California. Based on newspapers and company records; 7 illus.

D. R. Verardo

729. Jacobs, Julius L. CALIFORNIA'S PIONEER WINE FAMILIES. *California Hist. Q. 1975 54(2): 139-174.* A survey of viticulture and enology in California. Of the more than 240 bonded wineries in the state, only four which trace their origins back to the 19th century—Biane, Mirassou, Wente, and Concannon—are still under family operation. The history of these four and other pioneering wine families are described. California proved ideal for the production

of fine red and white wines. Although the industry received a setback during Prohibition, it has expanded greatly since its repeal, with more than 325 million gallons being produced. Both tiny producers and giant companies have contributed to making wine production a major California industry. Primary sources, including oral history interviews and secondary studies; 5 illus., 19 photos, 37 notes.   A. Hoffman

730. Jeremy, David J.   INNOVATION IN AMERICAN TEXTILE TECH-NOLOGY DURING THE EARLY 19TH CENTURY.   *Technology and Culture 1973 14(1): 40-76.* Nine major innovations came to characterize the New England textile industry during 1815-40: 1) large-scale production, 2) production of standardized low- or medium-quality goods, 3) vertically integrated manufacturing, 4) flow production, 5) maximum use of inanimate power, 6) high operating speeds, 7) mechanical vertical integration, 8) maximum mechanical control and work, and 9) automatic fault detection. They were developed "in response to the pressures of crowded product markets and the structures of industrial organizations interacting with the shortage of unskilled labor." 5 illus., table, 97 notes.   C. O. Smith

731. Jeremy, David J.   INVENTION IN AMERICAN TEXTILE TECH-NOLOGY DURING THE EARLY NINETEENTH CENTURY, 1790-1830. *Working Papers from the Regional Econ. Hist. Res. Center 1982 5(4): 1-45.* Compares British and American patent registrations, showing that more patents for mechanical improvements in cotton and woolen manufacturing were registered in the eastern United States than in Britain: 433 against 276.

732. Johnson, Keach.   STRUGGLE IN THE STOCKYARDS: THE RISE AND FALL OF THE COOPERATIVE LIVESTOCK COMMISSION CO. *Arizona and the West 1976 18(4): 315-332.* The Cooperative Livestock Commission Company was organized in 1906 by cattle, sheep, and hog raisers. They hoped to bypass the livestock exchanges that were increasing their commissions for handling animals and deal directly with buyers and sellers. The established stock exchanges undermined the efforts of the company which folded in 1909. It was premature and too ambitious for its time. Stockgrowers in the Trans-Mississippi West were not yet sufficiently aware of their common interests to make a sustained common stand. 5 illus., 44 notes.   D. L. Smith

733. Jordan, Terry G.   EARLY NORTHEAST TEXAS AND THE EVOLU-TION OF WESTERN RANCHING.   *Ann. of the Assoc. of Am. Geographers 1977 67(1): 66-87.* Chronicles the development of the western American cattle ranching complex which was derived from an offshoot transplanted from the Carolinas 1820-50 in northeast Texas and later carried westward to be blended with Spanish, Acadian, and lower southern Anglo traditions of cattle-herding, 1870.

734. Kaups, Matti.   NORTH SHORE COMMERCIAL FISHING, 1849-1870. *Minnesota Hist. 1978 46(2): 43-58.* Key developments 1849-70 facilitated the creation of the economically important fishing industry along the Minnesota North Shore of Lake Superior. The population became aware of the commercial possibilities of fishing. The completion of a winter road in 1856 and the opening of the Lake Superior and Mississippi Railroad between Duluth and St. Paul in

1870 made large-scale fish harvesting profitable. The development of the fishing industry was characterized by geographically diverse, minimally capitalized individual and partnership firms which used simple fishing techniques and equipment. Many residents participated part-time in commercial fishing. Periodic overfishing occurred. N. Lederer

735. Keuchel, Edward F. THE POLISH AMERICAN MIGRANT WORKER: THE NEW YORK CANNING INDUSTRY 1900-1935. *Polish Am. Studies 1976 33(2): 43-51.* In New York state the early canning industry was primarily rural. By 1900, when local sources could no longer meet the expanding labor demands, migrant workers, including many Polish Americans, were introduced. An investigation by the New York State Factory Investigating Commission in 1912 described jobs, wages, and living conditions. Polish Americans continued in canning through World War II, but by then in the canneries; blacks and Puerto Ricans succeeded them in the field. Based chiefly on the 1912 report and on other secondary sources, all in English; 21 notes. S. R. Pliska

736. Killick, J. R. THE TRANSFORMATION OF COTTON MARKETING IN THE LATE NINETEENTH CENTURY: ALEXANDER SPRUNT AND SON OF WILMINGTON, N.C., 1866-1956. *Business Hist. Rev. 1981 55(2): 143-169.* Major improvements took place in the system for marketing southern cotton internationally during 1880-1920. Alexander Sprunt and Son was probably the largest cotton exporting firm in the United States in that period and its history reflected those changes. Improvements included the installation of efficient cotton compresses to reduce the size of bales, a more sophisticated attitude toward futures trading, successful negotiation of special volume transportation rates, and the establishment of overseas branches. After World War I, the firm experienced a decline in part because of an aging management, family friction, and a failure to effectively expand activities into the trans-Mississippi cotton region. Based on company records; 4 tables, 50 notes. C. J. Pusateri

737. Killick, John R. THE COTTON OPERATIONS OF ALEXANDER BROWN AND SONS IN THE DEEP SOUTH, 1820-1860. *J. of Southern Hist. 1977 43(2): 169-194.* Southern historiography has focused on the slave plantation system of the interior rather than on the commercial trader of the ports. This neglect of the interregional and international cotton trade organization is unfortunate, considering the importance of the Atlantic commerce to the cotton system. A study of the British-American firm of Alexander Brown and Sons reveals that, contrary to general belief, cotton trading firms were so competitive that they did not normally accumulate great profits. Furthermore the Civil War era saw the beginning of the end of British firms in this business on a major scale; in the postwar years they were replaced by domestic, often southern, firms. Based on mss. and printed primary and secondary sources; 4 tables, 38 notes. T. D. Schoonover

738. Kulik, Gary B. PATTERNS OF RESISTANCE TO INDUSTRIAL CAPITALISM: PAWTUCKET VILLAGE AND THE STRIKE OF 1824. Cantor, Milton, ed. *American Workingclass Culture: Explorations in American Labor and Social History* (Westport, Conn.: Greenwood, 1979): 209-240. Focuses on the 1824 strike among textile workers at the Pawtucket, Rhode Island,

weaving and spinning mills to demonstrate local resistance to industrialization in the textile industry and working-class opposition to the mill owners.

739. LaFerney, Preston E. FIBER PRODUCTION AND TRADE IN THE DEVELOPMENT OF THE FAR WEST. *Agric. Hist. 1975 49(1): 251-257.* Western agriculture began to develop rapidly after 1850, with the emphasis changing from cattle to diversified farming. Wool production became important after 1860, peaked in 1930, and is still a leading crop. Cotton became important in the first three decades of the 20th century. The West's favorable climate and innovative people made agriculture a leading industry. 12 notes.

D. E. Bowers

740. Langenbach, Randolph. AMOSKEAG MILLYARD REMEM-BERED. *Historic Preservation 1975 27(3): 26-29.* Begun in Manchester, New Hampshire, in 1838 by the Amoskeag Manufacturing Co., the Amoskeag Mill-yard (mills and related structures) "achieved an extraordinary unity of design" and "was the world's largest textile plant" before corporate liquidation in 1936. Urban renewal has destroyed much since 1968. 6 photos. R. M. Frame III

741. Lea, Arden J. COTTON TEXTILES AND THE FEDERAL CHILD LABOR ACT OF 1916. *Labor Hist. 1975 16(4): 485-494.* Cotton textile indus-trialists shifted their position on federal regulation of child labor during 1907-16 as a result of increased competition and a desire for uniformity and stability. The Keating-Owen Act, conservative in nature, served the interests of large industrial-ists who promoted use of the Federal government to stabilize the economy, although the Act was levied against business interests in a particular section of the country. Child labor and voting tables presented on pp. 492-493. Based on census reports and the *Congressional Record*; 20 notes. L. L. Athey

742. Levine, Susan. "HONOR EACH NOBLE MAID": WOMEN WORK-ERS AND THE YONKERS CARPET WEAVERS' STRIKE OF 1885. *New York Hist. 1981 62(2): 153-176.* A prolonged strike at the Alexander Smith and Sons Carpet Company in Yonkers, New York, in 1885 revealed sources of conflict between a new, mostly female work force and an expanding industrial management. Wage cuts, the firing of Knights of Labor union members, and management interference with work rhythms and social behavior in the mills brought on the strike. Management did not recognize the union and considered strikers former employees. The strikers, however, had community support. The arrest of women strikers outraged the town. The strike ended when the company made concessions to the workers. However, the company resumed antiunion activity in 1886. Based on contemporary newspapers and other primary sources; 8 illus., table, 36 notes. R. N. Lokken

743. Lewis, Richard. TREE FARMING: A VOLUNTARY CONSERVA-TION PROGRAM. *J. of Forest Hist. 1981 25(3): 166-169.* Examines the history of the American Tree Farm System and the emerging notion of trees as a renewable resource. Although tree farms date from the early 20th century, the tree farm system was founded in 1941 in the Douglas-fir region of western Oregon and Washington. It has spread nationwide. Discussion includes early criticisms of the movement and later adaptations to the rapid changes in the forest products industry in the 1960's and 70's. Secondary sources; 3 photos. R. W. Judd

744. Lillard, Charles. LOGGING FACTS AND FICTION: A BIBLIOG-RAPHY. *Sound Heritage [Canada] 1977 6(3): 73-77.* Alphabetical listing of books (both fiction and nonfiction) on the logging industry in the Pacific Northwest and British Columbia, 1890's-1960's.

745. Lohof, Bruce A. HAMBURGER STAND: INDUSTRIALIZATION AND THE AMERICAN FAST FOOD PHENOMENON. *Industrial Archaeol. Rev. [Great Britain] 1978 2(3): 265-276.* Discusses the advent of fast food, namely the machine-made hamburger, asserting that it was a part and a consequence of the American industrial revolution, and examines the changes which industrial imperatives have made in American culture.

746. Lozier, J. W. THE FORGOTTEN INDUSTRY: SMALL AND ME-DIUM SIZED COTTON MILLS SOUTH OF BOSTON. *Working Papers from the Regional Econ. Hist. Res. Center 1979 2(4): 101-124.* Describes the small and medium sized cotton mills in southern New England and New York, 1810-40.

747. Lydon, James G. FISH FOR GOLD: THE MASSACHUSETTS FISH TRADE WITH IBERIA, 1700-1773. *New England Q. 1981 54(4): 539-582.* Previous studies on the fishing trade of 18th-century New England mistakenly concentrated upon the Boston fish trade even though Boston was not a major fish exporting center. The result of this bias has been to emphasize the significance of West Indian outlets for fish and undervalue the importance of the Iberian market. This quantitative study shows that the West Indies and Southern Europe were of nearly equal importance as market areas, and, as the colonists recognized, complemented each other. It is clear that the commercial expansion of Salem and the other north shore towns in the third quarter of the 18th century were due in large part to the fish trade with Southern Europe. Based on English diplomatic and mercantile correspondence, Massachusetts trade statistics, and data from Iberian port records; 8 tables, 94 notes. R. S. Sliwoski

748. Madden, John L. AN EMERGING AGRICULTURAL ECONOMY: KANSAS, 1860-1880. *Kansas Hist. Q. 1973 39(1): 101-114.* Between 1860 and 1880 Kansas changed from a region possessing an underdeveloped farming society, little capital and industry, inadequate educational facilities, unstable political climate, and insufficient labor to a region with an agricultural economy approaching production levels equal to or greater than the national average. The transition was accomplished by using the agricultural resources base to greater capacity and by the influx of innovations, people, and capital from other regions. 8 tables, 11 notes. W. F. Zornow

749. Mandle, Jay R. THE PLANTATION ECONOMY AND ITS AFTER-MATH. *R. of Radical Pol. Econ. 1974 6(1): 32-48.* A plantation economy based upon share-cropping continued in the South after the Civil War, but from 1910 the labor demands of a dynamic northern capitalist society, intensified by the decrease in immigrants, opened industrial employment to Negroes. Although generally confined to low-income occupations, a substantial degree of upward mobility has occurred recently. The economic differences within the black population and occupational convergence of black and white laborers in the future may create a biracial working-class movement. Based on published official statistics and secondary works; 2 tables, fig., 20 notes. P. R. Shergold

750.   Markoff, Dena S.   THE SUGAR INDUSTRY IN THE ARKANSAS RIVER VALLEY: NATIONAL BEET SUGAR COMPANY.   *Colorado Mag. 1978 55(1): 69-92.* The initial phase of experimentation for the American beet sugar industry occurred from 1888 to 1897 as beet technology was developed and irrigation ditches and railroads were built. "The decade from 1897-1906 witnessed rapid expansion of beet sugar factories in the United States. Seventy-one were erected during these years." An example is the National Beet Sugar Company plant at Sugar City, Colorado, in the Arkansas River Valley. The company and associated corporations built irrigation systems, the community, and the factory, and sold land to beet farmers. Opening in 1900, the plant operated for 68 years, after 1902 as the National Sugar Manufacturing Company, "the smallest independent, sugar company in the United States." Primary sources; 11 illus., 51 notes.

751.   Masson, Jack K. and Guimary, Donald L.   PILIPINOS AND UNIONIZATION OF THE ALASKAN CANNED SALMON INDUSTRY.   *Amerasia J. 1981 8(2): 1-30.* Describes the working conditions in the Alaskan salmon industry in the early 1900's and the entrance of Filipino labor into the canneries. First efforts to unionize the Filipinos occurred in 1933 and continued with both inter- and intraunion disputes until 1938 when the industry finally recognized the Congress of Industrial Organizations' United Cannery, Agricultural, Packing and Allied Workers of America as the bargaining agent for the laborers.   Secondary sources; 71 notes.   E. S. Johnson

752.   Matheny, Robert L.   LUMBERING IN THE WHITE MOUNTAINS OF ARIZONA, 1919-1942.   *Arizona and the West 1976 18(3): 237-256.* Promotion to establish large-scale commercial lumbering in eastern Arizona's White Mountains began as early as 1910. Encouraged by several federal agencies and war needs, companies went into operation in 1919. The efforts proved frustrating and unprofitable in the postwar recession. New investors took over but met financial ruin during the Great Depression. Recapitalized in 1935, the operations limped along until World War II made the White Mountain lumber industry profitable. 7 illus., map, 46 notes.   D. L. Smith

753.   Maxwell, Robert S.   THE FIRST BIG MILL: THE BEGINNINGS OF COMMERCIAL LUMBERING IN TEXAS.   *Southwestern Hist. Q. 1982 86(1): 1-30.* Although Spanish priests and monks were the first loggers in east Texas, the lumbering industry did not begin to flourish until after the Civil War. Northerners, such as Henry J. Lutcher and G. Bedell Moore, provided the necessary capital and organizational ability for the development of large, commercial sawmills and for the expansion of the railroad network. In 1877, Lutcher and Moore built the first large-scale sawmill in East Texas at Orange. That mill provided the basis for a comprehensive lumbering industry, and it marked the beginning of a bonanza lumbering era that did not end until the Great Depression of the 1930's.   Based on the Lutcher and Moore Diary, Stephen F. Austin University, and secondary sources; 10 photos, map, 47 notes.   R. D. Hurt

754.   Maxwell, Robert S.   THE IMPACT OF FORESTRY ON THE GULF SOUTH.   *Forest Hist. 1973 17(1): 30-35.* "Not until the great white pine forests of the Lake States neared exhaustion did the [lumber] industry turn to the yellow pine stands of the South." Early conservationists instituted scientific forestry

practices in the Gulf South, preventing despoliation and paving the way for today's southern forest products industry. Illus., 2 photos, 26 notes.

D. R. Verardo

755. May, William J., Jr. THE COLORADO SUGAR MANUFACTUR-ING COMPANY: GRAND JUNCTION PLANT. *Colorado Mag. 1978 55(1): 15-45.* There had been some interest in sugar beet culture in Colorado as early as 1841, but 1899 saw the opening of the pioneer beet sugar factory by the Colorado Sugar Manufacturing Company at Grand Junction. Traces the development of capital in Denver, the building of the huge factory, the search for labor, especially in production of beets, the gradual mechanization of growing beets and the "host of obstacles" faced. Both 1899 and 1900 were disastrous seasons for the Grand Junction factory. Subsequently the plant was sold several times before it closed in 1931. In spite of this initial failure the beet sugar industry presently is an important factor in the Colorado economy. Based mainly on primary sources; 28 illus., 89 notes.

O. H. Zabel

756. McCorkle, James L., Jr. PROBLEMS OF A SOUTHERN AGRARIAN INDUSTRY: COOPERATION AND SELF-INTEREST. *Southern Studies 1978 17(3): 241-254.* During 1925-40 Mississippi and Texas commercial tomato and cabbage growers were unable to maintain satisfactory prices by voluntary controls through regional cooperative markets. Individual self-interest overrode general prosperity. Appeals were made to the federal government for tariff agreements with Mexico and Canada, and the Federal Surplus Commodities Corporation bought excess production to maintain price stability. Only a regulated economy preserved these agricultural industries. Based on newspaper accounts; 51 notes.

J. Buschen

757. McGaw, Judith A. TECHNOLOGICAL CHANGE AND WOMEN'S WORK: MECHANIZATION IN THE BERKSHIRE PAPER INDUSTRY, 1820-1855. Trescott, Martha Moore, ed. *Dynamos and Virgins Revisited: Women and Technological Change in History* (Metuchen, N.J.:Scarecrow Pr., 1979): 77-99. Mechanization in the Massachusetts paper industry in the 19th century did not greatly affect sex segregation on the job. Women essentially continued doing the same jobs before and after the introduction of various machines which were typically tended by men. Women's work continued to be unskilled, but, because it was not generally involved with machines, the working conditions of women improved relative to the men's. 16 fig., 20 notes.

J. Powell

758. McGrain, John W. "GOOD BYE OLD BURR": THE ROLLER MILL REVOLUTION IN MARYLAND, 1882. *Maryland Hist. Mag. 1982 77(2): 154-171.* The country millers of Maryland and other eastern and southern states passed through one mechanical revolution in the 1870's and another in the 1880's. By the end of the century many a fortune had been sunk into buying an array of highly specialized apparatus that in numerous instances generated insufficient revenue to pay for itself. From the centuries-old use of the common millstone to the "middlings purifier" to the "roller mill" of chilled steel patented in 1880, American millers witnessed a veritable stampede to install each new and more elaborate system, as flour milling expanded immensely. Along with this came a great debate over the food value of the pure white versus stone-ground brown

flour. Based on the *American Miller,* 1879-99, contemporary press; 70 notes.
G. J. Bobango

759. McGregor, Alex. FROM SHEEP RANGE TO AGRIBUSINESS: A CASE HISTORY OF AGRICULTURAL TRANSFORMATION OF THE COLUMBIA PLATEAU. *Agric. Hist. 1980 54(1): 11-27.* Traces the evolution of farming techniques in eastern Washington and northeastern Oregon (called the Palouse region), through the activities of the McGregor family who arrived as sheepherders in 1882, from Scotland. Today, the McGregor Land and Livestock Company, through adherence to good farming practices, grosses in excess of 90 million dollars annually. Based on primary sources, including material in the McGregor family as well as secondary sources; 28 notes. R. T. Fulton

760. McGregor, Alexander C. INDUSTRY ON THE FARM: MCGREGOR LAND AND LIVESTOCK AND THE TRANFORMATION OF THE CO-LUMBIA PLATEAU WHEAT BELT SINCE 1930. *Pacific Northwest Q. 1982 73(1): 31-38.* Livestock and grain prices collapsed throughout Washington's Columbia Plateau during the early 1930's because of overproduction. The road to recovery was symbolized by highly efficient operations such as the McGregor Land and Livestock Company which by experimentation and diversification rebounded from the depression. It pioneered in the use of mechanized equipment, chemical fertilizers, insecticides, and cattle feed lots. Sheep production remained more tenuous for the company and it sold the last herds in 1979. Based on government documents and interviews; 4 photos, 30 notes. M. L. Tate

761. McKelvey, Blake. LUMBER AND WOOD PROCESSING IN ROCH-ESTER'S HISTORY. *Rochester Hist. 1978 40(1): 1-24.* Chronicles lumbering and wood processing in Rochester, New York, 1788-1880.

762. McMenamin, Michael and Connelly, Diane. HOW SUNKIST PUT THE SQUEEZE ON THE FTC. *Reason 1981 13(7): 45-50.* In light of its dumping of millions of naval oranges to keep prices artificially high, this article examines Sunkist Growers, Inc.'s monopoly power over the western citrus fruit industry, explaining how and why the giant agricultural cooperative during 1977-80 cowed the FTC (Federal Trade Commission) into allowing the monopoly to continue intact.

763. McWhiney, Grady. THE REVOLUTION IN NINETEENTH-CEN-TURY ALABAMA AGRICULTURE. *Alabama Rev. 1978 31(1): 3-32.* The Civil War and Reconstruction devastated the Alabama livestock industry. Thieving freedmen, northern dumping of commodities and its effect on prices and quality, pellagra, and the abandonment of antebellum husbandry practices, among other reasons, inhibited recovery. The Yankee work ethic was not an integral part of antebellum livestock raising, but the southern system was sufficient to meet population needs. Primary and secondary sources; 50 notes.
J. F. Vivian

764. Meiners, Fredericka. THE TEXAS BORDER COTTON TRADE, 1862-1863. *Civil War Hist. 1977 23(4): 293-306.* Confederate General Hamilton Prioleau Bee, commanding Brownsville and the Rio Grande, had to implement confusing economic regulations to control cotton exports. Corruption riddled the business. Inequitable exemptions fed public dissatisfaction. Nothing worked until

Bee's forced "loan" idea threatened total confiscation in 1863. The plan foreshadowed Cotton Bureau policy, but all this was too late. Based on OR, Series I and archival and secondary sources; 42 notes. R. E. Stack

765. Menard, Russell R. SECULAR TRENDS IN THE CHESAPEAKE TOBACCO INDUSTRY, 1617-1710. *Working Papers from the Regional Econ. Hist. Res. Center 1978 1(3): 1-34.* Discusses secular trends in the tobacco growing industry in Virginia and Maryland, 1617-1710, describing long-term movements in price, production, and income; effects of population; and social consequences of expansion; commentary by Jackson Turner Main appears in the same issue, pages 119-123.

766. Miller, J. Scott; Heindl, Fred; Dixon, D. Andrew, Jr.; Conner, J. Richard; and Waldrop, John E., Jr. AN OVERVIEW OF THE CATFISH FARMING INDUSTRY IN MISSISSIPPI. *J. of NAL Assoc. 1981 6(1-4): 20-24.* Traces the development, growth, marketing, research, and agency support of the catfish farming industry in Mississippi from its beginnings in 1965 to 1980, in the Delta of Mississippi, which is known as the "Catfish Capital of the World."

767. Mochizuki, Kiyondo. AMERIKA NO APARERU SANGYŌ—1972 NEN KŌGYŌ SENSASU NO ICHIKENKYŪ [The clothing industry in the United States: a study of the 1972 Census on Manufactures]. *Matsuyama Shōdai Ronshū [Japan] 1977 28(4): 159-177.* The structure of the US clothing industry consists largely of highly competitive small businesses. The labor-intensive nature of the industry hinders the development of modern, large-scale enterprises, although these are more advanced in the spheres of menswear and underwear. Since the 1960's there has been a tendency for production to stagnate or to decline and for imports from developing nations to increase. Radical changes in the structure of demand are characterized by trends toward the increasing use of man-made fibres and toward clothing of a practical and casual nature. 1972 Census on Manufactures; 4 tables. J. E. Hunter

768. Morgan, George T., Jr. CONFLAGRATION AS CATALYST: WESTERN LUMBERMEN AND AMERICAN FOREST POLICY. *Pacific Hist. Rev. 1978 47(2): 167-187.* Destructive forest fires in 1902 and 1910 in Oregon, Washington, Idaho, and Montana challenged the myth of forest inexhaustibility and ended apathy concerning the need for public fire control measures in the woods. Lumbermen played a more important and more forward-looking role in constructing the new policy than historians have recognized. George S. Long, western manager of the Weyerhauser Timber Company, was especially prominent in the movement to obtain state and federal fire protection. Based on unpublished lumber company records, published government documents, and newspapers; 57 notes. W. K. Hobson

769. Morrissey, Charles T. ORAL HISTORY AND THE CALIFORNIA WINE INDUSTRY: AN ESSAY REVIEW. *Agric. Hist. 1977 51(3): 590-596.* Ruth Teiser, Director of the California Wine Industry Oral History Project, has recorded 24 interviews bound in 20 volumes (19 of which are open to research). The interviewees include Martini (both father and son), Petri, Wente, Gallo, Perelli-Minette, Rossi, and Brother Timothy of Christian Brothers. The other 15 interviews are with viticulturalists and enologists at the University of California as well as two bankers, a wine merchant, an attorney, and a publicist. R. T. Fulton

770. Moses, Vincent. MACHINES IN THE GARDEN: A CITRUS MO-NOPOLY IN RIVERSIDE, 1900-1936. *California History 1982 61(1): 26-35.* Describes the monopoly on equipment used to process citrus production. Fred Stebler founded the California Iron Works (C.I.W.) in 1909 and George Parker organized the Parker Machine Works in the same year. The two competitors, both based in Riverside County, California, fought for control of the market until they merged in 1921. Stebler patented numerous inventions used in the processing of citrus, including washers, dryers, conveyors, and labelers. Of special note were the C.I.W.'s fruit sizer, fruit distributor, and fruit separator machines. In 1929 Stebler and Parker sold out to the Food Machinery Corporation which long maintained control over citrus machinery production. Primary and secondary sources; 5 photos, 20 notes.   A. Hoffman

771. Moyer, Curt. THE FRANK A. HUBBELL COMPANY, SHEEP AND CATTLE. *New Mexico Hist. Rev. 1979 54(1): 64-72.* Discusses the establishment and operation of one of the largest sheep ranches in New Mexico. Frank A. Hubbell (1862-1929) began his ranch with 200 sheep in the early 1880's near Salt Lake in New Mexico. Hubbell purchased and leased large amounts of land to greatly expand the ranch. Hubbell became an influential leader of the Republican Party in New Mexico and turned the ranching business over to his three sons in 1910. Hubbell's sons had transformed the ranch into a mechanized system by the 1960's. In 1968, when all the sheep were sold due to coyote problems, the ranch converted entirely to cattle production. 22 notes.   P. L. McLaughlin

772. Muller, Edward K. and Groves, Paul A. THE CHANGING LOCA-TION OF THE CLOTHING INDUSTRY: A LINK TO THE SOCIAL GEOGRAPHY OF BALTIMORE IN THE NINETEENTH CENTURY. *Maryland Hist. Mag. 1976 71(3): 403-420.* Examines the nature, growth, location, ownership, and industrial organization of Baltimore's post-civil war clothing industry. Unskilled women predominated in the putting out (outside shop) system of the new ready-to-wear warehouses and factory enterprises. The wholesale manufacturer "became the central organizing force" in expanding the industry, and the contracting system not only met the expanding demands for ready-to-wear garments, but spawned the infamous "sweatshop" networks. The pedestrian nature of the employment linkage meant that residential patterning of workers as the industry expanded depended more on business organization and availability of intraurban transit networks allowing middlemen to move raw materials to the sweatshops than on ethnic groupings or the availability of housing. Urban historians need to consider the location of employment more than they have, even though essential sources of data such as census enumerations are problematic. 3 illus., 6 figs., 5 tables, 51 notes.   G. J. Bobango

773. Musoke, Moses S. MECHANIZING COTTON PRODUCTION IN THE AMERICAN SOUTH: THE TRACTOR, 1915-1960. *Explorations in Econ. Hist. 1981 18(4): 347-375.* The introduction of the tractor into the cotton industry in the American South resulted in modernization of agricultural processes and replaced sharecropping, the foundation of postbellum cotton production. In 1920 there were 36,500 tractors in the South. In 1940 there were 271,000; and during the next two decades the number rose to more than 1.4 million. This was accompanied by a decline of 90% in the number of sharecroppers' farms during 1930-59. Primary sources; 7 tables, ref., appendix.   J. Powell

774. Musoke, Moses S. and Olmstead, Alan L.   THE RISE OF THE COT-
TON INDUSTRY IN CALIFORNIA: A COMPARATIVE PERSPECTIVE.
J. of Econ. Hist. 1982 42(2): 385-412. By 1950 cotton had emerged as one of
California's leading crops, and California had become an important cotton producing state. The institutional and environmental settings associated with cotton
cultivation in California differed markedly from those found in the Cotton South.
Both institutional conditions, such as the size of farms, and environmental factors, such as the region's dry weather during the harvest season, help explain the
more rapid mechanization of picking in California.   J

775. Myers, J. Walter, Jr.   FOREST FARMERS ASSOCIATION: A VOICE
FOR SOUTHERN TIMBER RESOURCES.   *J. of NAL Assoc. 1978 3(3-4):
89-91.* Discusses the interests and activities of the Forest Farmers Association,
founded in 1940; its members in the 15 southern states represent 70% of the total
commercial forest lands in the South, particularly motivating forest owners to
grow trees and teaching them to do it better.

776. Nickless, Pamela J.   A NEW LOOK AT PRODUCTIVITY IN THE
NEW ENGLAND COTTON TEXTILE INDUSTRY, 1830-1860.   *J. of Econ.
Hist. 1979 39(4): 889-910.* The antebellum cotton textile industry has been characterized as experiencing rising labor productivity despite technological stagnation. Explanations of this phenomenon often emphasize the role of changes in
labor quality. New data on skilled workers make it possible to construct a labor
input index that accounts for changes in skill mix. Labor productivity is then
analyzed in the context of changes in total-factor productivity. A very different
picture of productivity change in the textile mills emerges, casting doubt on the
hypothesis of technological stagnation and emphasizing the importance of an
increasing capital-labor ratio in maintaining productivity advance. 6 tables, 35
notes, appendix.   J

777. Nolan, Dennis R. and Jonas, Donald E.   TEXTILE UNIONISM IN
THE PIEDMONT, 1901-1932.   Fink, Gary M. and Reed, Merl E., eds. *Essays
in Southern Labor History: Selected Papers, Southern Labor History Conference,
1976.* (Westport, Conn.; London, England: Greenwood Pr., 1977): 48-79. A
study designed to round out the argument previously developed which attributes
to outside forces the failure of the textile unions to form stable local organizations
and negotiate improvements in wages and working conditions. The workers and
unions also brought on problems themselves, by "rash and poorly planned strikes,
internal feuds, poor leadership, and the failure of interested groups to provide
financial aid." The textile industry in the Piedmont Plateau is the locale for the
study. Whatever the strength of outside forces, the workers and their organizations often were their own worst enemies. 75 notes.   R. V. Ritter

778. O'Connell, Lucille.   THE LAWRENCE TEXTILE STRIKE OF 1912:
THE TESTIMONY OF TWO POLISH WOMEN.   *Polish Am. Studies 1979
36(2): 44-62.* A personal account of two participants in the textile strike against
the Everett Mill in Lawrence, Massachusetts, as revealed in testimony before the
Committee on Rules of the House of Representatives on 2-7 March 1912. In their
testimony, 14-year-old Victoria Winiarczyk and the older, more experienced
Josephine Liss describe the hardships, deprivations, and dire poverty of their
fellow immigrant workers. The strike radicalized many of the mill women and

led them to militancy, collective action, and even membership in the Industrial Workers of the World. This strike was the first victory in the United States by unskilled, immigrant wage earners. Documented sources in English; 14 notes.

S. R. Pliska

779. Oden, Jack P. CHARLES HOLMES HERTY AND THE BIRTH OF THE SOUTHERN NEWSPRINT PAPER INDUSTRY, 1927-1940. *J. of Forest Hist. 1977 21(2): 76-89.* Early sources of newsprint for American newspapers were forests of northeastern United States and Canada. Paper mills in those regions could produce enough newsprint for both countries. Pine trees of southeastern United States were considered unsuitable for newsprint because they were presumed to have a high resin content. Charles Holmes Herty (d. 1938) was a prominent Georgia chemist who discovered that the presumption about the unsuitability of pines for newsprint was erroneous. He organized and ran a research laboratory that worked out a process for making newsprint from pines. Primary and secondary sources; 11 photos, 64 notes.

F. N. Egerton

780. Olmstead, Alan L. THE MECHANIZATION OF REAPING AND MOWING IN AMERICAN AGRICULTURE, 1833-1870. *J. of Econ. Hist. 1975 35(2): 327-352.* Reexamination of evidence undermines Paul A. David's threshold theory of technological diffusion ("The Mechanization of Reaping in the Ante-Bellum Middle West" pp. 3-39 in Henry Rosovsky, ed., *Industrialization in Two Systems,* New York: 1966). Technological changes that drastically increased machines' productivity did occur between 1833 and the 1870's. Sharing and contracting of reapers was practiced widely, especially in newly developing regions. These factors operated mainly at the critical points for diffusion studies —the economic margins. Based on primary and secondary sources; table, graph, 55 notes.

J. W. Williams

781. Overton, Jim; Arnold, Bob; and Hall, Bob. THE MEN AT THE TOP: THE STORY OF J. P. STEVENS. *Southern Exposure 1978 6(1): 52-63.* The textile firm J. P. Stevens & Co., Inc., was founded in New England by Nathaniel Stevens in 1813. It was almost exclusively controlled until recent years by members of the Stevens family, including Robert Stevens, Secretary of the Army during the first Eisenhower administration. During the Depression the firm expanded into the South, relying on its extensive trade relations with the region through its commission house. Actual physical expansion into the South began following World War II, fueled by union organizing pressure on Stevens' northern plants. By the middle 1960's, Wall Street financiers and bankers joined southern capitalists on the firm's Board of Directors as Stevens traded exclusive family control in favor of financial backing for diversification of product lines.

N. Lederer

782. Palmer, William R. and Palmer, Eugene, comp. THE EARLY SHEEP INDUSTRY IN SOUTHERN UTAH. *Utah Hist. Q. 1974 42(2): 178-188.* Discusses sheep raising and wool shearing and handling in southern Utah 1862-81.

783. Pate, J'Nell. THE FORT WORTH STOCKYARDS COMPANY AS A BIG BUSINESS ENTERPRISE. *Panhandle-Plains Hist. Rev. 1979 52: 63-74.* Fort Worth, Texas, owed much of its late 19th-century economic growth to the

cattle industry and especially to the "Big Five" meat packers—led by Swift and Armour—who controlled the Fort Worth Stockyards Co. Beginning in the 1920's, legalistic efforts to break the monopoly of the Big Five gradually accomplished that goal, but by the 1950's, the major packers faced a declining business and subsequently trimmed their operations. Recent efforts to renovate the stockyards and restore the Exchange Building have proven successful as numerous small businesses have opened in the area. 27 notes. M. L. Tate

784. Persigehl, Elmer S. and York, James D. SUBSTANTIAL PRODUCTIVITY GAINS IN THE FLUID MILK INDUSTRY. *Monthly Labor Rev. 1979 102(7): 22-27.* Covers 1958-77.

785. Powers, William M. SAN DIEGO'S TUNA FLEET: A PICTORIAL. *US Naval Inst. Pro. 1979 105(1): 66-77.* Most of the US high seas tuna fishing fleet, 100 of 140 oceangoing ships, call San Diego their home port. But the tuna business, one area of the US maritime industry that is an outstanding example of successful free enterprise, is seriously threatened today by the government's insistence that tuna fishermen must reduce the number of porpoises they kill to zero, a goal the fishermen feel they will not be able to meet. Another important problem for the fishermen has been the territorial waters question, and the question of buying fishing permits from certain Latin American countries. If these problems are not solved, the tuna ships may be forced to change their national registration and they may go to other fishing grounds. 28 photos.
A. N. Garland

786. Quinlan, Maria. LUMBERING IN MICHIGAN. *Michigan Hist. 1978 62(4): 37-41.* Michigan started its lumber industry ca. 1840 and was America's major producer of lumber during 1869-99; focuses on innovations to increase production, the lives of the lumbermen, and changes in Michigan's economy and environment.

787. Quinn, Carin C. THE JEANING OF AMERICA—AND THE WORLD. *Am. Heritage 1978 29(3): 14-21.* A German immigrant, Levi Strauss (1829-1902), came to New York in 1848 and went to San Francisco in 1850, intent on selling canvas for tents. Finding a need for a sturdy material for men's pants, Strauss made a pair from some of his canvas. From then on, he was in business. Spreading to the eastern United States during the 1930's, today the market for jeans is worldwide. 16 illus. J. F. Paul

788. Raup, Philip M. CORPORATE FARMING IN THE UNITED STATES. *J. of Econ. Hist. 1973 33(1): 274-290.* Studies the development of corporate farming in the United States, especially since the 1930's. Analyzes the factors that made such farming more possible and desirable after 1950 and estimates the impact of this mode of agriculture on labor, capital, and the economy as a whole. The peak of recent large-scale corporation farming was attained during 1965-70. Comments by Lloyd J. Mercer and Peter Passell, pp. 291-299. 36 notes. S

789. Raynor, Bruce. UNIONISM IN THE SOUTHERN TEXTILE INDUSTRY: AN OVERVIEW. Fink, Gary M. and Reed, Merl E., eds. *Essays in Southern Labor History: Selected Papers, Southern Labor History Conference, 1976.* (Westport, Conn.; London, England: Greenwood Pr., 1977): 80-99. Textile

unionization in the South has come on hard times; total disorganization and discouragement after losing ground for 25 years, is the order of the day. Studies some of the sources of past frustration in textile organizing, assesses the current state of labor relations in the industry, and projects future trends in textile unionism. The failures may be attributed to: 1) the effective (if illegal) antiunion tactics employed by mill owners, 2) a hostile political climate, and 3) the nature of the southern labor force. There have been, however, a sufficient number of significant changes in the labor situation and personnel to justify some optimism for the future. 31 notes. R. V. Ritter

790. Reynolds, Bruce J.; Lowitt, Richard, (commentary). TELCOT: A CASE STUDY OF ELECTRONIC MARKETING. *Agric. Hist. 1982 56(1): 83-98, 117-121.* Traditionally cotton selling was handled at individual cotton gins where local buyers competed. As market news became more available, farmers looked for ways to achieve better prices through cooperative marketing. The Plains Cotton Cooperative Association of Lubbock, Texas, pioneered in the use of computer information networks to aid in selling cotton. TELCOT, which it established in 1975, permits merchants and farmers to join together via an on-line computer to auction cotton. It gives farmers local access to buyers, allows rapid interior assembly of cotton, and promotes efficiency in the complicated pricing of cotton through different quality levels. Comments, pp. 117-121. Based on interviews and other primary and secondary sources; 36 notes. D. E. Bowers

791. Robbins, William G. THE GREAT EXPERIMENT IN INDUSTRIAL SELF-GOVERNMENT: THE LUMBER INDUSTRY AND THE NA-TIONAL RECOVERY ADMINISTRATION. *J. of Forest Hist. 1981 25(3): 128-143.* Unable to control competition in the rapidly contracting economy of the 1930's, lumber industry leaders experimented with industrial self-regulation under the auspices of the New Deal's National Recovery Administration. Minimum price regulations of the Lumber Code Authority were mainly the work of large operators. Despite industry receptiveness at the outset, the code proved disappointing. Regional rivalries, differences over the code's role in conserving forest resources, dissatisfaction among small operators, and the competitive nature of the industry plagued the relatively weak Lumber Code Authority. Noncompliance became critical in 1934, and the experiment had lost its credibility by April 1935. Based on records of various trade associations as well as personal papers, federal documents, and secondary sources; 7 photos, 58 notes. R. W. Judd

792. Rogerson, William T., Jr. NEW ENGLAND FISHERMEN—IMPER-ILED SPECIES. *US Naval Inst. Pro. 1973 99(12): 44-49.* Confronted with severe competition from well organized, subsidized foreign fleets, the New England fishing industry faces ruin. To salvage the industry the American government should provide federal aid to increase fishing capacity, institute a government insurance program for vessels and men, compensate fishermen for gear lost to foreign trawlers, and regulate foreign catches off Georges Banks. 3 illus. J. K. Ohl

793. Rome, Adam Ward. AMERICAN FARMERS AS ENTRE-PRENEURS, 1870-1900. *Agric. Hist. 1982 56(1): 37-49.* Late 19th-century American farmers adopted many of the methods of businessmen. Responding to an increasingly uncertain market, farmers turned to economic forecasting and careful planning in order to anticipate future markets. Despite their efforts, farmers were in a severe depression by the 1890's. Still clinging to the ideal of an independent yeomanry, they were not prepared to advocate such 20th-century solutions as pressure politics, trade organizations, and government subsidies. 51 notes.   D. E. Bowers

794. Roppel, Patricia. LORING. *Alaska J. 1975 5(3): 168-178.* Discusses the history of the salmon packing industry in Loring, Alaska, 1883-1936. 11 photos, reproduction, 54 notes.

795. Roth, Dennis. TECHNOLOGY AND PRODUCTIVITY IN THE PACIFIC NORTHWEST LUMBER INDUSTRY. *J. of NAL Assoc. 1979 4(3-4): 64-68.* Provides data on technological change, productivity gains, and employment in the Pacific Northwest lumber industry from 1899 to the early 1970's.

796. Rothstein, Morton. THE BIG FARM: ABUNDANCE AND SCALE IN AMERICAN AGRICULTURE. *Agric. Hist. 1975 49(4): 583-597.* American agriculture is unique in the large average size of farms that has existed from the beginning, the widespread ownership of land, and the absence of demographic pressures to divide land into smaller and smaller units. The first very large farms did not appear until the early 19th century when southern cotton planters aggressively extended their holdings, and the use of machinery in the North allowed farmers to put a much greater acreage under cultivation. The Civil War and diminishing returns, however, put a check on the growth of large farms. By the 1920's American agriculture was a composite of large and small farms. Rapid technological change following World War II has brought a renewed movement to consolidate small farms into large ones, which may bring painful social and economic adjustments. 28 notes.   D. E. Bowers

797. Rothstein, Morton. WEST COAST FARMERS AND THE TYR-ANNY OF DISTANCE: AGRICULTURE ON THE FRINGES OF THE WORLD MARKET. *Agric. Hist. 1975 49(1): 272-280.* Changing demand for western products has had a major impact on Pacific Coast farmers. The importance of wheat exports after 1860 meant that grain production in the West differed from that elsewhere—larger farms, fewer middlemen, and more powerful merchant firms. These developments put Pacific agriculture in a good position to adapt to new types of farming when dietary habits changed after the turn of the century. 19 notes.   D. E. Bowers

798. Sande, Theodore Anton. THE TEXTILE FACTORY IN PRE-CIVIL WAR RHODE ISLAND. *Old-Time New England 1975 66(1-2): 13-31.* Describes the volume, style, configuration, and decorative style of textile factories built in Rhode Island, where textile factories originated in the United States, from the early 1790's until the Civil War; they were copied from factories built in England in 1702.

799. Savage, William W., Jr. COWS AND ENGLISHMEN: OBSERVA-
TIONS ON INVESTMENT BY BRITISH IMMIGRANTS IN THE WEST-
ERN RANGE CATTLE INDUSTRY. *Red River Valley Hist. R. 1974 1(1):*
37-45.

800. Savoie, Ronald. THE SILK INDUSTRY IN NORTHAMPTON.
Hist. J. of Western Massachusetts 1977 5(2): 21-32. Traces the history of the silk
industry in Northampton, Massachusetts, during 1830-1930. Discusses the contributions of Samuel Whitmarsh, who began silk cultivation and weaving in the
area in 1835. Focuses on the Corticelli Company, founded as Nonotuck Company, which absorbed many small firms and continued in business until 1930
when Northampton's silk industry ended. 101 notes.   W. H. Mulligan, Jr.

801. Sayre, Charles R. COTTON MECHANIZATION SINCE WORLD
WAR II. *Agric. Hist. 1979 53(1): 105-124.* Studies of the development of
mechanization for cotton farming indicate rapid progress. This can be seen in
each stage of cotton growing and harvesting, and in the spread and utilization of
available technology throughout southern and southwestern cotton growing
areas. Improvement and development in efficiency can also be demonstrated. The
use of this technology also demands the development of work skills and a degree
of labor sophistication that has not always kept pace. The newer "farming systems" have affected farm size and have resulted in regional shifts. There are still
many improvement needs demanding further research and development. 3 tables,
3 charts, 2 notes.   R. V. Ritter

802. Schaeffer, Donald. YEOMEN FARMERS AND ECONOMIC DEMO-
CRACY: A STUDY OF WEALTH AND ECONOMIC MOBILITY IN THE
WESTERN TOBACCO REGION, 1850-1860. *Explorations in Econ. Hist.*
1978 15(4): 421-437. Tentative results for Kentucky and Tennessee suggest that
yeoman farmers were not being forced out, though the gap in wealth between
them and planters widened. As a consequence, some yeoman farmers may have
chosen to migrate to the developing cotton region to the south and west. Based
on manuscript census records and published accounts; 9 tables, fig., 14 notes,
appendix, 19 ref.   P. J. Coleman

803. Schmitz, Mark. THE TRANSFORMATION OF THE SOUTHERN
CANE SUGAR SECTOR, 1860-1930. *Agric. Hist. 1979 53(1): 270-285.* Any
description and analysis of the cane sugar sector must consider legal and economic developments elsewhere, particularly the whims of Congress. Following
the Civil War there came a "new organizational hierarchy based on large manufacturing units and independent cane growers." There was also a shift in non-
southern supply and demand while there were reduced subsidies to cane
producers, diminishing their role in supplying US consumption. Most of the study
centers in Louisiana. 5 tables, 42 notes.   -   R. V. Ritter

804. Schulman, Michael D. OWNERSHIP AND CONTROL IN
AGRIBUSINESS CORPORATIONS. *Rural Sociol. 1981 46(4): 652-668.* An
empirical investigation of stock ownership and control among US agribusiness
corporations; data on stock ownership patterns from a sample of 153 public
corporations and 25 private corporations engaged in agribusiness (farm inputs,
processing, distribution), shows that family or proprietary control is substantial,
over 60%.

805. Scott, Roy V. AMERICAN RAILROADS AND THE PROMOTION OF FORESTRY. *J. of Forest Hist. 1979 23(2): 72-81.* Railroads have always had a vital stake in the nation's forest resources, as users and carriers of wood products. Railroad forestry programs fall into three clearly defined historical stages. The first involved promotion of tree planting on the western plains as part of railroad colonization work in the late 19th century. The second, stimulated by fear of timber famine early in the 20th century, emphasized conservation (especially wood-preservation programs) and large-scale tree planting to meet future needs. Companies hired foresters and pushed educational campaigns to combat forest fires and other problems. The third stage evolved out of the earlier ones, emphasizing railway development work—the generation of more freight traffic through promotion of better forest management practices. Cooperation with industrial and other private landowners was seen in the railroads' technical assistance programs, demonstration forests, and tree farms. Public agencies and forest industry firms took over these duties in the 1960's and 1970's, thus bringing the third stage to an end. Secondary sources; 6 illus., map, 40 notes.

R. J. Fahl

806. Searle, Newell. MINNESOTA STATE FORESTRY ASSOCIATION: SEEDBED OF FOREST CONSERVATION. *Minnesota Hist. 1974 44(1): 16-29.* Details the history of the Minnesota State Forestry Association, 1876-1925. Relates its growth and programs to those of similar state and national organizations. Its program was "strong and comprehensive." 5 illus., map, 58 notes.

D. L. Smith

807. Seghesio, Susanne R. FOUR GENERATIONS OF THE SEGHESIO FAMILY IN THE WINE BUSINESS. *Pacific Hist. 1977 21(3): 248-261.* Eduardo Seghesio's family has been involved in the California winemaking industry's Chianti area since 1886, owning vineyards since 1895. Originally supplying wine to other vineyards, the business is still family-run, and recently has developed its own label. 5 photos.

G. L. Olson

808. Sharrer, G. Terry. FLOUR MILLING IN THE GROWTH OF BALTIMORE, 1750-1830. *Maryland Hist. Mag. 1976 71(3): 322-333.* Discusses the American flour and grain trade to Europe and the West Indies as affected by famines, crop failures, and the Napoleonic Wars abroad, and the Jeffersonian embargo at home. Waterloo and the British Corn Laws greatly diminished these markets and US consumption and the trade with South America replaced them. Baltimore dominated the flour trade in both periods due to the milling technology of Oliver Evans, the introduction of steam power in processing, and the merchant-millers' development of drying processes which greatly retarded spoilage. Still, by 1830 New York's competition was felt keenly, and Baltimoreans were hard-pressed to match the merchantability standards despite more rigorous inspection controls than earlier, nor could they match the greater financial resources of their northern rivals. Primary and secondary sources; 30 notes. G. J. Bobango

809. Sharrer, G. Terry. FOOD TECHNOLOGY IN THE 20TH CENTURY. *J. of NAL Assoc. 1980 5(1-2): 21-26.* Traces developments in food technology in the United States during the 20th century such as railroads, the trucking industry, electricity, a number of new foods, forced air drying, freezing and irradiation, chemical additives and vitamin fortification, packaging, and

supermarkets involving men such as Clarence Birdseye (1886-1956) and C. W. Post, and companies such as Pillsbury, Campbell Soup, and H. J. Heinz.

810. Sharrer, G. Terry; Schmitz, Mark, (commentary). THE MERCHANT-MILLERS: BALTIMORE'S FLOUR MILLING INDUSTRY, 1783-1860. *Agric. Hist. 1982 56(1): 138-150, 167-171.* In the years before 1815 the export of flour to the West Indies and South America became a major business for Baltimore merchants. The introduction of automated machinery and steam power encouraged merchants to specialize in flour, including a number of millers who also traded in flour. The growth of these domestic markets advanced Baltimore's importance as a milling center. Comments, pp. 167-171; 35 notes.
D. E. Bowers

811. Sheets, Hal. BIG MONEY IN HUNGER. *Worldview 1975 18(3): 10-16.* Discusses the shortage in the 1972 world food supply that increased demands for US grains and the response of the US government's Commodities Exchange Authority and foreign aid policies, controlled as they are by the food industry, which is geared to profit and oblivious to human need.

812. Shelton, Cynthia J. TEXTILE PRODUCTION AND THE URBAN LABORER: THE PROTO-INDUSTRIALIZATION EXPERIENCE OF PHILADELPHIA, 1787-1820. *Working Papers from the Regional Econ. Hist. Res. Center 1982 5(4): 46-89.* Shows that urban textile manufacturing was based on the labor of the poor and that manufactories were modelled on English and colonial workhouses.

813. Silvia, Philip T., Jr. THE POSITION OF WORKERS IN A TEXTILE COMMUNITY: FALL RIVER IN THE EARLY 1800S. *Labor Hist. 1975 16(2): 230-248.* Examines employer-dominance in the textile industry of Fall River, Massachusetts. Although a critique of labor conditions was led by Robert Howard, a muleskinner, the policies of the employers regarding grievances, wages, work conditions and company housing were maintained as a part of a laissez-faire philosophy hostile to organized labor in the 1880's. Based upon reports of the Massachusetts Bureau of Labor Statistics and Senate committees, newspapers and secondary sources; 32 notes.
L. L. Athey

814. Smith, David C. THE LOGGING FRONTIER. *J. of Forest Hist. 1974 18(4): 96-106.* Discusses the impact of logging, especially East Coast loggers, tools, and techniques, on the American frontier. Biblio.
L. F. Johnson

815. Smith, David C. THE PAPER INDUSTRY IN CALIFORNIA TO 1900. *Southern California Q. 1975 57(2): 129-146.* Describes the early attempts to establish a paper-making industry in California, focusing on the fortunes of the California Paper Company, founded at Stockton in 1873. Problems included lack of capital and the need to import machinery, chemicals, wood pulp, rags, and other supplies from distant locations. Stockton also lacked a supply of wood pulp, which had to be brought from Oregon. After decades of effort and the expenditure of hundreds of thousands of dollars, the industry caught on, assisted by the expansion of metropolitan newspapers. The operation moved later to Oregon, avoiding the expense of shipping wood pulp to Stockton, and eventually evolved through several reorganization changes into the Crown-Zellerbach Corporation. Based on primary sources, company minute books, correspondence, and published studies; 38 notes.
A. Hoffman

816. Smith, David C. PULP, PAPER, AND ALASKA. *Pacific Northwest Q. 1975 66(2): 61-70.* Discusses attempts since 1914 to establish a profitable wood pulp and paper industry in the Pacific Northwest based on lumber from Alaska.

817. Sprague, Stuart Seely. THE WHALING PORTS: A STUDY OF NINETY YEARS OF RIVALRY, 1784-1875. *Am. Neptune 1973 33(2): 120-130.* A consideration of economic competition between port cities during the whaling era. Cities rose and fell in importance as vessels, technology, and whaling grounds changed. The gold rush in California resulted in San Francisco being the dominant port for a time, a role traditionally played by New England cities. The whaling industry declined sharply after 1850, the result of a financial panic, the Crimean War, rising costs, and the introduction of kerosene and petroleum products. By 1875 the whaling industry was dead, and many formerly famous ports became inconspicuous hamlets. 16 photos, 10 tables, 18 notes.
V. L. Human

818. Stephens, Lester D. FARISH FURMAN'S FORMULA: SCIENTIFIC FARMING AND THE "NEW SOUTH." *Agric. Hist. 1976 50(2): 377-390.* Farish Furman began experimenting with fertilizers in 1878 on his Georgia cotton farm. By studying the cotton plant he devised a formula for compost involving manure, acid phosphate, kainit, and cottonseed which restored his depleted lands to fertility. His fertilizer quickly became popular, and was probably a factor in raising cotton yields throughout the South. 28 notes.
D. E. Bowers

819. Stokesbury, James L. SAGA OF THE YANKEE WHALERS. *Am. Hist. Illus. 1974 9(7): 4-11, 43-50.* "In the 17th century the whaling industry was in decline in Europe, but it was just getting started in the New World. Colonists from the eastern end of Long Island out to Cape Cod took up systematic whale hunting, first setting up lookout posts and then going out in their small boats for whale hunting offshore. . . . By the first decade of the 19th century New Bedford men were scanning the high latitudes of the South Atlantic, and Indian harpooners from Gay Head were striking whales off the coast of Australia. . . . The years 1820 to 1860 saw the whaling industry at the peak of its enterprise and prosperity." By the beginning of the 20th century, the whalers began to disappear, and by 1906 there were only 42 American whalers left afloat. 7 illus., 2 photos, 6 reproductions.
D. D. Cameron

820. Street, Richard S. MARKETING CALIFORNIA CROPS AT THE TURN OF THE CENTURY. *Southern California Q. 1979 61(3): 239-253.* Describes how California agriculturists developed professional marketing techniques to make their products available to eastern consumers. The typical 19th-century diet lacked fruit and vegetables. As California agricultural production increased, and methods of preserving produce improved, growers faced the problems of distribution and consumer education. The problems were met by forming agricultural cooperatives and intensive advertising campaigns. Among the most successful were the California Fruit Growers Exchange which sold 75% of California's citrus crop under its Sunkist label, and the California Associated Raisin Company of Fresno, with the Sun Maid brand. Even the avocado, which met initial consumer resistance because of its odd taste, received advertising attention. The industry also developed packaging for its defective products in such forms

as marmalade, orange juice, and even vinegar. By the 1920's, with assistance from government certification of standards, fruit and vegetables had become a basic part of the American diet. 13 notes.   A. Hoffman

821.   Strite, Daniel D.   HURRAH FOR GARIBALDI!   *Oregon Hist. Q. 1976 77(3): 213-237, (4): 341-368.* Part I. Describes the establishment and workings of the Garibaldi lumber mill on Tillamook Bay, Oregon. The mill was constructed to serve the shipbuilding needs of World War I, but the conflict ended before the plant was in operation. The Garibaldi mill was large, but not the largest in the state. Emphasizes the operation of the mill and the equipment used in converting a raw log into finished lumber. The mill was quite modern, featuring the bandsaw, the latest method in cutting efficiency. 14 photos, note. Part II. Describes procedures and equipment used to handle finished lumber. Discusses shipping methods, the decline of unlimited forests, reforestation, and efforts to utilize all parts of the tree. Explores wages and hours, housing conditions, and the nature of the town spawned by the mill. The Garibaldi mill collapsed in 1935, a victim of the Great Depression and a disastrous forest fire. It was revived in 1943 but died in 1974. 8 photos.   V. L. Human

822.   Suerth, Jeff.   GERBER'S: A COMPANY FOUNDED THROUGH A FRUSTRATING EXPERIENCE.   *Chronicle 1979 15(3): 4-9.* Frustrated over the difficulty of straining peas for her infant daughter, Dorothy Gerber suggested that her husband, Daniel F. Gerber, use the pureeing machinery in his canning manufactory, the Fremont Canning Company of Fremont, Michigan, to prepare baby food, which led to the growth of commercial baby food canning and distributorship and other products, 1927-79.

823.   Taylor, Morris F.   THE MAXWELL CATTLE COMPANY, 1881-1888.   *New Mexico Hist. R. 1974 49(4): 289-324.* The Maxwell land grant (1.7 million acres in Colfax County) was the subject of much legal action. Farming took precedence over cattle raising on the land. Poor financial condition forced the land grant company to sell the land to the Maxwell Cattle Company in mid-March 1884, but the violent winter of 1885-86 caused big losses for the new owners. Notes.   J. H. Krenkel and S

824.   Thomas, Elizabeth H.   FOREST PROTECTION AND THE FOUNDING OF PENNSYLVANIA'S FIRST FORESTRY SCHOOL, 1901-1903. *Pennsylvania Hist. 1977 44(4): 291-315.* In the late 1870's, Joseph Trimble Rothrock, M.D., began a crusade for scientific forest management in Pennsylvania which led to his becoming the commonwealth's first Commissioner of Forestry in 1895. His most notable achievement was founding the Pennsylvania State Forest Academy at Mont Alto in 1903. His able collaborator in this effort was State Forester George H. Wirt. Based on the Wirt Papers, Pennsylvania Forestry Department documents, and other materials; illus., 71 notes.   D. C. Swift

825.   Tucker, Barbara M.   THE MERCHANT, THE MANUFACTURER, AND THE FACTORY MANAGER: THE CASE OF SAMUEL SLATER. *Business Hist. Rev. 1981 55(3): 297-313.* Samuel Slater and the New England textile mills he operated represented the first stage of the Industrial Revolution in America. In the management of the mills, he at first preferred direct, personal supervision and was suspicious of salaried managers. When his various enter-

prises became more numerous, he eventually found it necessary to employ salaried factory agents, thus creating a separation between entrepreneurial and operational functions. Slater's early managerial ideas reflected traditional mercantile thinking, but beginning in the 1830's he abandoned them in order to meet the new demands of an expanding factory system. Based on archival records of Slater enterprises and personal papers; 56 notes. C. J. Pusateri

826. Urisko, James A. PRODUCTIVITY IN GRAIN MILL PRODUCTS: OUTPUT UP, EMPLOYMENT STABLE. *Monthly Labor Rev. 1977 100(4): 38-43.* Discusses grain mill productivity, employment rates, technology, capital investment, distribution methods, and raw material extraction during 1963-74.

827. Usselman, Steven W. SCIENTIFIC MANAGEMENT WITHOUT TAYLOR: MANAGEMENT INNOVATIONS AT BANCROFT. *Working Papers from the Regional Econ. Hist. Res. Center 1981 4(4): 47-77.* Briefly discusses the scientific management innovations set forth by Frederick Winslow Taylor for American businesses, focusing on the scientific management techniques of management consultants Miller, Franklin, and Stevenson, an industrial engineering company from New York, which was hired in 1911 by the cotton textile finishing company, Joseph Bancroft and Sons Company of Wilmington, Delaware, after a Taylor associate was unsuccessful in streamlining the work load in several departments; reorganization was completed in 1927.

828. Vogt, Kathryn A. THE MISSOURI SHORTHORN INDUSTRY: THE LEONARD FAMILY LEGACY. *Gateway Heritage 1982 2(4): 16-23.* In 1825, Nathaniel Leonard created Ravenswood, which later became a showplace farm in Cooper County, Missouri. There he and his descendants created great wealth and enjoyed opulent lifestyles. Their economic successes derived primarily after 1839 from astute herdsmanship of English shorthorn cattle. Based on printed histories and archival sources; 16 photos, biblio. H. T. Lovin

829. Wade, Louise Carroll. "SOMETHING MORE THAN PACKERS." *Chicago Hist. 1973 2(4): 224-231.* Chicago's meatpackers created a large industry by utilizing all parts of the animals and by controlling all aspects of the business, especially their employees. They created a dynasty by having their sons continue the family business. Establishment of the Union Stock Yards in 1865-66 and introduction of refrigerated railroad cars aided the rapid growth. In two short decades the Armours, Swifts, and Nelson Morris (d. 1907) became meat barons. 6 photos. N. A. Kuntz

830. Wallace, Anthony F. C. A COTTON MANUFACTURING VILLAGE: ROCKDALE, PA., 1825-1865. *Working Papers from the Regional Econ. Hist. Res. Center 1977 1(1): 57-78.* Examines the economic conditions and industrialization of the cotton industry of Rockdale, Pennsylvania, and applies the findings to other manufacturing and production towns located in the Delaware Valley, 1825-65. With comments by Merritt Roe Smith, pp. 79-85.

831. Walsh, Margaret; Schmitz, Mark, (commentary). FROM PORK MERCHANT TO MEAT PACKER: THE MIDWESTERN MEAT INDUSTRY IN THE MID NINETEENTH CENTURY. *Agric. Hist. 1982 56(1): 127-137, 167-171.* Before the Civil War, midwestern meat packing was handled primarily by storekeepers on a part-time, seasonal basis. Even big city packers were primar-

ily merchants. During the 1860's-70's a change occurred as regional packers who were clearly manufacturers rather than merchants became important. Because of improved ice packing, which allowed year-round operation, and the availability of large amounts of capital, a small group of large packers suddenly acquired a large part of the market in the 1870's. Comments, pp. 167-171; 2 tables, 25 notes.

D. E. Bowers

832. Walsh, Margaret. INDUSTRIAL OPPORTUNITY OF THE URBAN FRONTIER: "RAGS TO RICHES" AND MILWAUKEE CLOTHING MANUFACTURERS, 1840-1880. *Wisconsin Mag. of Hist. 1974 57(3): 174-194.* Challenges the persistence of the "rags to riches" idea in American culture by looking at the business careers of Milwaukee's leading clothing manufacturers for a 40 year period. Emphasizes that, rather than any single factor, Jewish connections, German origins, technological innovation, previous business experience, substantial capital and credit, and good local market conditions, when combined in varying degrees, were the ingredients of a successful company. Instead of a spectacular leap from rags to riches, the Milwaukee clothing manufacturers' experience suggests that vertical mobility was possible, but "it was generally modest in both its claims and its end results." 12 illus., 5 tables, 51 notes.

N. C. Burckel

833. Walsh, Margaret. PORK PACKING AS A LEADING EDGE OF MIDWESTERN INDUSTRY, 1835-1875. *Agric. Hist. 1977 51(4): 702-717.* Small pork-packing factories in the Midwest, during 1835-75, represented the beginnings of industry in what had been a frontier, rural society. Specialized goods and services, needed by these small entrepreneurships, could only be supplied in those areas that were beginning to experience rapid population growth, improved communications, and increasing urbanization. Based on primary and secondary sources; 2 tables, graph.

R. T. Fulton

834. Walsh, Margaret. THE SPATIAL EVOLUTION OF THE MID-WESTERN PORK INDUSTRY, 1835-75. *J. of Hist. Geography 1978 4(1): 1-22.* Processing of raw materials was the major industry in the Midwest. Pork processing illustrates the general pattern of development. The volume of pork packing in the Midwest rose steadily during 1835-75, but the major centers of this industry shifted as the dependence on river transportation declined and the railroads developed. Primary and secondary sources; 6 tables, 5 graphs, 29 notes.

F. N. Egerton

835. Weiher, Kenneth. THE COTTON INDUSTRY AND SOUTHERN URBANIZATION, 1880-1930. *Explorations in Econ. Hist. 1977 14(2): 120-140.* Using central place theory, shows that the hierarchy of central services associated with the cultivation and marketing of cotton and cotton byproducts shaped the pace and pattern of urbanization and were fundamentally responsible for the location, size, and growth of most southern cities through the 1920's. Published documents and secondary accounts; 2 figs., 5 tables, 27 notes, 14 refs.

P. J. Coleman

836. Weiler, N. Sue. WALKOUT: THE CHICAGO MEN'S GARMENT WORKERS' STRIKE, 1910-1911. *Chicago Hist. 1979-80 8(4): 238-249.* Examines the men's garment industry in Chicago which began growing rapidly after

the Chicago Fire of 1871, particularly the division of the manufacturing process into operations performed at sweatshops for the large Chicago clothing firms such as Hart, Schaffner & Marx, The House of Kuppenheimer, the Scotch Wollen Mills, Royal Tailors, and Society Brand; focuses on the 1910-1911 men's garment workers' strikes which started when 18 year old Hannah Shapiro walked out on her sewing job.

837. Welsh, Carol Holderby. CATTLE MARKET FOR THE WORLD: THE OKLAHOMA NATIONAL STOCKYARDS. *Chronicles of Oklahoma 1982 60(1): 42-55.* When Edward Morris and Company opened a packing plant in October 1910, Oklahoma City began a remarkable economic growth through stockyards and slaughterhouses. City fathers offered tax incentives, land, and even cash bonuses to entice other meat-packing firms. By the 1940's feeder-yard operations were beginning to replace the original packinghouses as the main enterprise. A 1980 fire at the Livestock Exchange Building not only destroyed one of Oklahoma City's most historic buildings, it also symbolized the end of an era. Based on Oklahoma City newspapers and interviews; 5 photos, 40 notes.

M. L. Tate

838. Wessman, James W. THE SUGAR CANE HACIENDA IN THE AGRARIAN STRUCTURE OF SOUTHWESTERN PUERTO RICO IN 1902. *Rev. Interamericana [Puerto Rico] 1978 8(1): 99-115.* At the beginning of the 20th century, the agrarian structure of southwestern Puerto Rico was changing from the family-style hacienda system to that of the corporate sugar mills. This was a change from one form of capitalism to another, not a transition from feudalism or semifeudalism to capitalism as often suggested. Based primarily on information from José Ferreras Pagán's *Biografía de las riquezas de Puerto Rico: riqueza azucarera* (San Juan, 1902); map, 7 tables, 18 notes.

J. A. Lewis

839. Wheeler, David L. THE BEEF CATTLE INDUSTRY IN THE OLD NORTHWEST, 1803-1860. *Panhandle-Plains Hist. R. 1974 47: 28-45.* The Old Northwest Territory comprised an area known as the Interior Lowlands which offered soils and climate conducive to pioneer agriculture and livestock production. The Ohio Valley developed a livestock business by the 1820's. Utilizing cheap feed, surplus corn, and improved breeds to maximize output at minimal expense, Ohio farmers captured the eastern market by driving cattle across the mountains. By the 1840's Illinois had become the main livestock-producer, and the Ohio Valley was transformed into an intermediate feeder region. Two decades later Iowa, Missouri, and Texas supplied most of the nation's beef, and in turn Illinois became both a feeder area and center of the packing industry. Based on secondary sources; map, 82 notes.

M. L. Tate

840. Wheeler, David L. THE ORIGIN AND DEVELOPMENT OF THE CATTLE FEEDING INDUSTRY IN THE SOUTHERN HIGH PLAINS. *Panhandle-Plains Hist. Rev. 1976 49(1): 81-90.* The Texas Panhandle has become a major beef producing region since the 1930's when irrigation was introduced to create a surplus of feed grains. Good profits and high demand encouraged major cattle raising programs by the 1950's and large feedyards were constructed to handle the increased population. However, substantial amounts of water must soon be discovered and new markets must be opened or the Panhandle's cattle

industry will have to retrench by the 1980's. Based on secondary sources; 55 notes.   M. L. Tate

841. Wik, Reynold M. SOME INTERPRETATIONS OF THE MECHANI-ZATION OF AGRICULTURE IN THE FAR WEST. *Agric. Hist. 1975 49(1): 73-83.* American farmers have shown relatively little technical ingenuity, but they have been successful in adapting to different environments. In the Central Valley of California, dry climate and flat land permitted the early use of the combine for harvesting wheat and encouraged the development of unusually large machines. The Caterpillar tractor was invented specifically to farm the soft delta soil. 39 notes.   D. E. Bowers

842. Williams, Anne S. INDUSTRIALIZED AGRICULTURE AND THE SMALL-SCALE FARMER. *Human Organization 1981 40(4): 306-312.* Studies small-scale farming in three western Montana counties, and examines how such enterprises survive against large-scale competitors and other economic obstacles.

843. Wilson, James A. CATTLEMEN, PACKERS, AND GOVERNMENT: RETREATING INDIVIDUALISM ON THE TEXAS RANGE. *Southwestern Hist. Q. 1971 74(4): 525-534.* Analyzes the maneuvers of cattlemen (ca. 1890-1910) to break the stranglehold of the "Big Five" Chicago meat packers on livestock prices. At first the producers' efforts to combat the packer combines were disjointed and weakened by extreme individualism. The cattlemen's eventual realization of the need for congressional legislation to combat price fixing demanded that they organize for cooperative endeavor. "Rawhide individualism withered in the face of monopoly, yet it retreated slowly." 36 notes.
                                                                     R. V. Ritter

844. Wood, Charles L. CATTLEMEN, RAILROADS, AND THE ORIGIN OF THE KANSAS LIVESTOCK ASSOCIATION: THE 1890'S. *Kansas Hist. Q. 1977 43(2): 121-139.* Marketing forced cattlemen into association with railroads, stockyards, packing plants, and other industries whose rapid consolidation often convinced cattlemen that they were falling under the control of hostile economic powers. Cattlemen met this consolidation by forming groups to protect their interests. The Kansas Livestock Association was the outgrowth of strong dissatisfaction with railroad rates and the methods employed to weigh cattle cars. Primary and secondary sources; illus., 27 notes.   W. F. Zornow

845. Wood, Eleanor N. THE STORY OF STEEL. *Mankind 1975 5(1): 17-21, 60-65.* Iron and steel have played a major role in world affairs since the days of the New Stone Age. The use of iron for weapons and tools was important to the cultures of the Palestinians, Assyrians, Greeks, Romans and Macedonians. In modern times important techniques for the making of steel were devised by Abraham Darby, Benjamin Huntsman, Alfred Krupp and Henry Bessemer. The career of Andrew Carnegie epitomized the rise to power and wealth of the modern steel magnate.   N. Lederer

846. Woods, W. N. SIXTY-FIVE YEARS WITH FARM CO-OPERA-TIVES. *Northwest Ohio Q. 1978 50(1): 29-40, (2): 64-76.* Part I. Recounts experience since 1907 with the social, legislative, and business functions of such farm organizations as the Grange, mutual insurance organizations, bargaining

associations, farmers' elevators, and seed improvement associations. Part II. Discusses the Ohio Farm Bureau Federation and agricultural cooperatives, 1913-78. Article to be continued.

847. York, James D. NONWOOL YARN MILLS EXPERIENCE SLOW GAINS IN PRODUCTIVITY. *Monthly Labor Rev. 1982 105(3): 30-33.* Traces the increase in productivity in the nonwool yarn industry during 1958-80, particularly 1973-80, focusing on statistics of employment, plant size, technology, capital spending, and markets.

848. Zeisel, Rose N. MODERNIZATION AND MANPOWER IN TEXTILE MILLS. *Monthly Labor R. 1973 96(6): 18-25.* Discusses the influence of technological change in the production level of skilled labor in textile mill industries in the 1960's and 70's.

849. —. [AMERICAN AGRICULTURAL PRODUCTION AND ITS EFFECT ON GREAT BRITAIN]. *Agric. Hist. 1976 50(1): 125-155.*
Jewell, C. Andrew. THE IMPACT OF AMERICA ON ENGLISH AGRICULTURE, *pp. 125-136.* Because Great Britain's implement manufacturers of the 19th century desired to produce many different versions of the same implement, they faced massive imports of standardized American equipment. Shortages of labor, especially during the Civil War, turned America to mechanized farm machinery. The USA soon outstripped world competition in its production. England was one of many countries which succumbed to the importation of agricultural machinery—her own manufacturers suffering accordingly. Based on primary and secondary sources; 22 notes.
Fornari, Harry D. U.S. GRAIN EXPORTS: A BICENTENNIAL OVERVIEW, *pp. 137-150.* The United States throughout its history has interacted in world affairs because of its massive grain exports. Even before the Civil War, US grain exports to Europe amounted to a considerable percentage of total exports. US surplus grain production has given rise to an extremely efficient system for the handling, storage, and distribution of grains in America. Based on primary and secondary sources; 37 notes.
Rothstein, Morton. AGRICULTURAL EXCHANGES: COMMENT, *pp. 151-155.* Comments on Jewell's and Fornari's hypotheses. Discusses the interaction of farmers, both in America and Great Britain. Assesses the impact of American agricultural exports on the world economy. Based on primary and secondary sources; 5 notes.   R. T. Fulton

850. —. CAPITAL'S FLIGHT: THE APPAREL INDUSTRY MOVES SOUTH. Mora, Magdalena and DelCastillo, Adelaida R., ed. *Mexican Women in the United States: Struggles Past and Present* (Los Angeles: U. of California Chicano Studies Res. Center, 1980): 95-104. The garment industry provides a clear illustration of capital's mobility and its effect on the working class. Since World War II, thousands of jobs in the apparel sector were exported. Domestic production has dramatically shifted its geographic locus, as the firms have abandoned their birthplaces in the large industrial cities of the Northeast and Midwest in favor of the rural South. The reasons for this exodus and its effects on the working class, particularly in the Northeast and the South, are discussed. Reprinted from *NACLA Report on the Americas* formerly *NACLA's Latin America and Empire Report* 1977, 11(3): 2-9; 2 tables, 32 notes.   J. Powell

851. —. CLARK KINSEY'S LOGGING PHOTOGRAPHS. *Pacific Northwest Q. 1975 66(2): 71-75.* Reprints eight photographs taken 1914-45 by photographer Clark Kinsey which portray daily life and labor in the lumber industry in Washington and Oregon.

852. —. [DISCUSSION FORUM ON WORLD FISHERIES CATCH STATISTICS, 1938-1979]. *Social Sci. Q. 1982 63(2): 381-387.*
Simon, Julian L. PAUL EHRLICH SAYING IT IS SO DOESN'T MAKE IT SO, *pp. 381-385.* Criticizes Ehrlich's response to Simon regarding his comments on an article by Ehrlich *(Social Sci. Q.* 1981 62(1): 7-49), particularly Ehrlich's use of rhetoric, his assertions not based on scientific fact, and his inaccurate predictions about catch statistics during 1938-79.
Ehrlich, Paul R. THAT'S RIGHT—YOU SHOULD CHECK IT FOR YOURSELF, *pp. 385-387.* Response to Simon's criticisms.

853. —. [FARMING THE GREAT PLAINS AND THE CANADIAN PRAIRIES]. *Agric. Hist. 1977 51(1): 78-108.*
Drache, Hiram. THOMAS D. CAMPBELL—THE PLOWER OF THE PLAINS, *pp. 78-91.* Thomas D. Campbell was one of the first successful large-scale farmers. With capital from Eastern bankers he established a huge wheat farm in Montana using big machines. Assuming ownership of the farm in 1921, Campbell proved the economies of scale in large, mechanized farming by succeeding in a decade of low wheat prices. Campbell pioneered in the use of windrow harvesting, motorized wagon trains, soil conservation, and enlightened labor practices. 18 notes.
Ankli, Robert E. FARM INCOME ON THE GREAT PLAINS AND CANADIAN PRAIRIES, 1920-1940, *pp. 92-103.* Farm income in the American Great Plains and Canadian Prairie Provinces fell after World War I, recovered some in the mid-1920's, and dropped sharply during the 1930's. Declining yields from drought were at least as responsible for this as falling prices. Large farms and those in areas less affected by drought suffered least. Diversifying from wheat to cattle would have had little effect on income. Table, 40 notes.
Anderson, Terry L. BONANZA FARMERS AND SUBSISTENCE: A RESPONSE, *pp. 104-108.* Campbell's improved technology, as discussed by Drache, did little to help small farmers. As one of the first users of this technology, Campbell benefited from the lack of competition, but he was also fortunate in acquiring his capital at a low cost. Ankli presents useful new data on wheat production and farm income but draws few conclusions and doesn't make allowance for the changing exchange rate between US and Canadian dollars. Both papers have overlooked the effect of government policies. D. E. Bowers

854. —. [LABOR SUPPLY, THE ACQUISITION OF SKILLS, AND THE LOCATION OF SOUTHERN TEXTILE MILLS, 1880-1900]. *J. of Econ. Hist. 1981 41(1): 65-73.*
Carlson, Leonard A. LABOR SUPPLY, THE ACQUISITION OF SKILLS, AND THE LOCATION OF SOUTHERN TEXTILE MILLS, 1880-1900, *pp. 65-71.* The development of the textile industry in the South was shaped by the fact that by 1870 most experienced workers lived in the Piedmont. Thus, a firm which wished to hire experienced workers would have been led

to choose the Piedmont Plateau, similarly, mills producing more difficult finer count cloth would have chosen the Piedmont in order to hire experienced workers. Finally, the persistence of a virtually all white work force may be explained by the fact that most experienced workers were white and would have resisted working in integrated mills.

Oates, Mary J. DISCUSSION, *pp. 72-73.* J

855. —. [LIMITATIONS OF ENTRY IN THE UNITED STATES FISHING INDUSTRY: COMMENT AND REPLY]. *Land Econ. 1975 51(2): 177-185.*

Owens, James. LIMITATIONS OF ENTRY IN THE UNITED STATES FISHING INDUSTRY: A COMMENT, *pp. 177-178.* Comments on R. C. Bishop's article of the same title *(Land Econ.* 1973 49(4): 381-390), arguing that a large percentage of fishermen are job mobile and that advocates of not limiting the number of fishermen do not consider the need for conservation. Biblio.

Wilson, James and Olson, Fred. LIMITATIONS OF ENTRY IN THE UNITED STATES FISHING INDUSTRY: A SECOND COMMENT, *pp. 179-181.* The authors disagree with Bishop's contentions that limitations of entry into the fishing industry should not occur because the industry is too unimportant to warrant regulation, and that it would result in a reduction of food output. 2 notes, biblio.

Bishop, R. C. LIMITATION OF ENTRY IN THE UNITED STATES FISHING INDUSTRY: A REPLY, *pp. 182-185.* Acknowledges that there may be some other benefit from limiting the entry into commercial fishing than economic efficiency and that such a policy might be advisable in certain situations. 2 notes, biblio. E. S. Johnson

856. —. TEXTILE RESOURCES. *Southern Exposure 1976 3(4): 80-85.* The Institute for Southern Studies here provides a bibliography of books on the Southern textile industry and two famous strikes, 1929 and 1934; includes three diagrams on corporate interconnections.

7

MINING

857. Armstrong, Dee A. and Coghill, W. W. THE OZARK-MAHONING COMPANY IN THE PERMIAN BASIN. *Permian Hist. Ann. 1980 20: 105-109.* Traces the history of the Ozark Chemical Company, predecessor of the Ozark-Mahoning Company, during the period 1925-80, focusing on its search for sources of sodium sulfate and means of extracting it in the Permian Basin in Ward County, Texas.

858. Beistline, Earl H. ALASKA'S MINERAL BONANZAS OF YESTER-YEAR. *J. of the West 1981 20(2): 68-81.* Alaska's major mining areas included Sitka, Juneau, Nome, Fairbanks, Kennecott, and Goodnews Bay. Canada's Klondike gold rush contributed to the Alaskan mining industry. Miners learned how to make a profit even on low-grade ores, such as those from the Treadwell and Alaska Juneau gold mines. Permafrost and a subarctic climate were overcome by technological improvements in mining equipment to develop profitable, large-scale mining operations for gold, silver, copper, and platinum. Map, 3 illus., 11 photos, 16 notes.											B. S. Porter

859. Berry, Thomas S. GOLD! BUT HOW MUCH? *California Hist. Q. 1976 55(3): 246-255.* Estimates the amount and value of gold production in the 1848-61 period. Economic problems in the gold rush included smuggling gold out of California to avoid insurance and freight charges, lack of a consistent system of measurement, and unofficial methods of purchasing and marketing gold. Private assayers, refiners, and coiners minted coins and bars which often circulated at a discount. In 1854 the San Francisco Mint began operations. However, coin shortages periodically occurred, especially in the autumn when production was down and bills were due. Methods of estimating the value of California gold vary, but total gold output from 1848-1900 probably reached $1.4 billion, with a modern value of $8.5 billion. Based on contemporary and secondary published works; photos, 2 tables, illus., 14 notes.											A. Hoffman

860. Bollinger, Donna Stiffler. THE IRON RICHES OF MICHIGAN'S UPPER PENINSULA. *Michigan Hist. 1978 62(4): 9-13.* Traces the history of iron mining at Michigan's three iron ranges (Marquette, Menominee, and Gogebic) since the early 1840's; during the 19th century, all three ranges were major ore producers, but during the 20th century, operations have been reduced.

861. Brett, Jeanne M. and Goldberg, Stephen B. WILDCAT STRIKES IN BITUMINOUS COAL MINING. *Industrial and Labor Relations Rev. 1979 32(4): 465-483.* Investigates wildcat strikes in bituminous coal mines, finding that high-strike mines resemble low-strike mines in working conditions, age of work force, and area standard of living. In low-strike mines, however, management is more accessible to labor and they have a problem-solving relationship.　J/S

862. Bucco, Edith E. FOUNDED ON ROCK: COLORADO'S STOUT STONE INDUSTRY. *Colorado Mag. 1974 5(4): 317-335.* Traces the expansion of William H. B. Stout's stone quarries at Fort Collins, Colorado, and the concomitant growth of civil, educational, and railroad facilities, 1880-1900.

863. Bundtzen, Thomas K. A HISTORY OF MINING IN THE KANTISHNA HILLS. *Alaska J. 1978 8(2): 150-161.* The mining history of the Kantishna Hills region, northeast of McKinley National Park beginning with the discovery of gold in 1903. A gold rush began in 1905. Mining camps lived off the land, largely on wild game. A major problem was the transportation of the ore. The area produced gold, silver, antimony, lead, and zinc in considerable quantity. Improved prices of metals, and improved machinery for recovery of ore, processing, and transportation have kept the operations going until recently when the area was withdrawn from further activity by legislation with a view to possible inclusion in the National Park system. 14 photos, map, 39 notes.
R. V. Ritter

864. Chadwick, Robert A. MONTANA'S SILVER MINING ERA: GREAT BOOM AND GREAT BUST. *Montana 1982 32(2): 16-31.* Silver mining began in Montana and boomed in the 1880's because of a combination of factors: geographic concentration of silver in shallow vein systems, maintenance of a subsidized silver market by the federal government, infusion of outside capital, evolution of mining and smelting technology, and railroad construction. Between 1883 and 1891, silver production in Montana ranked first or second nationwide, with the mines at Butte, Alta, and Granite as primary producers. The boom collapsed in 1893 because of depletion of the state's resources and the collapse of silver prices. Silver mining did continue, but at a reduced level. The Montana silver mining era exemplifies the common tendency for booms to develop, become overblown, and finally collapse into extended slumps and depressions. Based on US Geological Survey publications, contemporary newspapers, and secondary sources; 5 illus., map, 3 graphs, 53 notes.
R. C. Myers

865. Cieply, Michael. THE LODED HEARST. *Westways 1981 73(6): 32-35, 76-77.* Details the career of George Hearst, father of William Randolph Hearst, during his successful attempts of 1876-79 to consolidate various mining claims in the Deadwood district of South Dakota, which provided the foundation of the Hearst family fortune.

866. Clark, William B. and Fuller, Williard F., Jr. MINING FOR GOLD IN CALIFORNIA: THE ORIGINAL SIXTEEN-TO-ONE MINE. *J. of the West 1981 20(2): 53-59.* The original Sixteen-to-One Mine at Alleghey in Sierra County, California, was the last sustained, commercial lode gold mining operation in the state. A number of claims from the 1890's were consolidated in the Sixteen-to-One, incorporated in October 1911. Discoveries of extremely rich ore

bodies in the 1920's, and an increase of the official price of gold in 1934, led to boom times up to World War II, when operation was restricted. In 1954 operation was resumed on a smaller scale than before the war. Rising costs and declining productivity forced closure of the mine in 1965. Condensed from an article in *Mineral Information Service,* May 1968, published by California Division of Mines and Geology; 3 maps, 2 photos.   B. S. Porter

867.   Davies, Christopher S.   POLICY IMPLICATIONS FOR THE BANK-ING OF LIGNITE LEASES, BASTROP COUNTY, TEXAS: 1954-1979. *Econ. Geography 1981 57(3): 238-256.* Presents "an analysis of the long-term banking of lignite [a soft coal] leases, estimated contributions to company profits, and prospective reclamations expenditures [which] can help clarify the lines along which leasing continues to develop in the U.S., where national policy is to actively pursue coal and lignite extraction on resource bearing lands," focusing on Bastrop County, Texas.

868.   Dersch, Virginia Jonas.   COPPER MINING IN NORTHERN MICHI-GAN: A SOCIAL HISTORY.   *Michigan Hist. 1977 61(4): 290-321.* The auto-mobile industry image associated with Michigan has obscured the fact that the first US mining boom occurred in the remote Keweenaw Peninsula during the early 1840's. Primitive conditions, lack of experience, the region's remoteness, and transportation problems spelled failure for virtually every entrepreneur until 1866. In that year, the Calumet and Hecla Mining Company pioneered a new approach to locating and mining copper, and the social and economic develop-ment of the area accelerated markedly. Soon the company possessed monopoly control, and despite efforts by organized labor, prevented unionization until 1943. But a 1913 miners' strike dealt the industry a blow from which it never recovered. Secondary sources; 16 photos, table, glossary, 53 notes.   D. W. Johnson

869.   Eggleston, William S.   MINING FOR GOLD IN CALIFORNIA: REMINISCENCES OF AN OLD TIMER.   *J. of the West 1981 20(2): 48-52.* During his college years, 1921-26, the author had temporary jobs as a miner in California's Mother Lode. The Central Hill Mine, near San Andreas, was an underground placer mine, where all drilling was done by hand. The Virginia-Belmont and the Oriental were lode mines. Experiences with the day-labor em-ployment agency, co-workers, high-grading, equipment, and the dangers of working in the mines are described.   B. S. Porter

870.   Eller, Ronald D.   THE COAL BARONS OF THE APPALACHIAN SOUTH, 1880-1930.   *Appalachian J. 1977 4(3/4): 195-207.* The remarkably homogeneous social group of coal barons in the Appalachian South began as isolated mine operators employing a small number of miners, and then, as the industry matured and expanded, were forced to accept, at least to some degree, their social responsibilities and to manage their labor force.   M. T. Wilson

871.   Fell, James E., Jr.   ROCKEFELLER'S RIGHT-HAND MAN: FRED-ERICK T. GATES AND THE NORTHWESTERN MINING INVEST-MENTS.   *Business Hist. Rev. 1978 52(4): 537-561.* Gates, a Baptist minister turned businessman, was given oversight of many of John D. Rockefeller's non-oil industry investments, including those in mining in the states of Washington and Idaho. The Washington investments, because of a sharp drop in the market price

of silver in the 1890's and low ore value, proved especially unprofitable. Through patience and skillful manipulation, Gates was finally able to negotiate a sale of the properties to the American Smelting and Refining Company in 1905, thereby turning an apparent loss into a substantial profit. Based principally on private papers in the Rockefeller Archives; 59 notes.   C. J. Pusateri

872. Fleming, Jack. COPPER TOWN KING. *Nevada Hist. Soc. Q. 1982 25(1): 28-45.* Traces the Nevada mining career of John C. Kinnear (1885-1975) but focuses on 1928-45, when he directed the Nevada Mines Division of the Kennecott Copper Corporation. In those years, Kinnear kept the mines and smelters prosperous. Regarded as a benevolent despot at McGill and surrounding company towns, his humanism won him great respect and caused Kinnear to shoulder many civic responsibilities. Based on Kinnear's autobiography, interviews with his contemporaries, and secondary sources; photo, 54 notes.
                                                                              H. T. Lovin

873. Foley, Patricia T. and Clark, Joel P. THE EFFECTS OF STATE TAX-ATION ON UNITED STATES COPPER SUPPLY. *Land Econ. 1982 58(2): 153-180.* Uses data for 47 copper operations in the United States to construct a supply model for copper. This model is then used to investigate the results of various state tax strategies. Finds state tax rates would affect long-term copper output depending on their level and the states involved. Uses interviews with individual mine operators; 8 tables, 6 fig., biblio.   E. S. Johnson

874. Gowaskie, Joseph M. FROM CONFLICT TO COOPERATION: JOHN MITCHELL AND BITUMINOUS COAL OPERATORS. *Historian 1976 38(4): 669-688.* During 1898-1907 bituminous coal fields consisted of thousands of individually owned mines competing for profit and new markets. Relations between operators and unions were turbulent. After profits plunged in 1897 many operators agreed that recognition of the United Mine Workers of America, led by John Mitchell, would provide order. Employers overcame their resistance to unionization because further conflict in the soft coal industry would lead to their economic destruction. Notes.   M. J. Wentworth

875. Gracy, David B., II. MOSES AUSTIN ... AND THE DEVELOP-MENT OF THE MISSOURI LEAD INDUSTRY. *Gateway Heritage 1981 1(4): 42-48.* In present-day Washington County, Missouri, Moses Austin (1761-1821) mined lead and in a crude smelter extracted 8,960,000 pounds of metal from 1797 to 1817. A colonizer also, he encouraged emigration to Missouri and struggled for better transportation. He tried his hand at banking where he was less successful and was bankrupted in the Panic of 1819. Based on printed collections of Austin Papers and archival documents in the Barker Texas History Center, University of Texas; 9 photos, 23 notes.   H. T. Lovin

876. Grauman, Melody Webb. KENNECOTT: ALASKAN ORIGINS OF A COPPER EMPIRE, 1900-1938. *Western Hist. Q. 1978 9(2): 197-211.* An outcropping of immensely rich copper ore in south central Alaska, discovered in 1900, led to exploitation of an ore body "unequaled anywhere" in this century. Its development fell to two powerful organizations, the Alaska Syndicate, 1906-15, and the Kennecott Copper Corporation, beginning in 1915. The Syndicate remained constricted by the business philosophy of the previous century. Ken-

necott applied the tenets of scientific management to developing business technology. Although the Alaskan Kennecott mines closed in 1938, the corporation is today's largest copper conglomerate in the world. It includes mines, railroad networks, concentrators, power plants, smelters, refineries, fabricators, and interests in other minerals in two continents. Kennecott's broadest significance, however, arises from its role in the business and economic world. 47 notes.

D. L. Smith.

877. Green, Jim. HOLDING THE LINE: MINERS' MILITANCY AND THE STRIKE OF 1978. *Radical Am. 1978 12(3): 3-27.* Although commonly viewed as a defeat for the mine workers, the long strike of 1977-78 actually represents a partly successful rank and file struggle to minimize the defeats which the coal operators, with the acquiescence of the United Mine Workers of America leadership, sought to impose on the union members. The miners were desperately endeavoring to preserve as many of their earlier hard-won gains as possible, including health and medical benefits, with a special emphasis on free clinical care. Increase in miners' pensions also was a major issue. The strikers also upheld the tradition of waging local wildcat strikes to gain safety and other improvements. Left-wing political groups, most notably the Miners Right to Strike Committee, sought to politicize the struggle. N. Lederer

878. Haase, Carl L. GOTHIC, COLORADO: CITY OF SILVER WIRES. *Colorado Mag. 1974 51(4): 294-316.* Describes the development of the Copper Creek silver wire mines, 1878-79, and the resultant growth of the settlement at Gothic.

879. Huth, Tom. MINING THE WEST: WILL OUR HERITAGE SURVIVE? *Hist. Preservation 1981 33(3): 10-19.* Discusses realized and potential problems from the impact of energy and precious metals mining in the western states, focusing on the threat to historical and cultural resources and preservation.

880. Levitt, James H.; Notarianni, Philip F.; and Bannon, Barbara. MINING AT ALTA: A FURTHER LOOK. *Utah Hist. Q. 1977 45(2): 158-162.* Alta, Utah, was an important lead and silver mining area during the mid-19th century; small operations continued into the 1960's. An interview with Page Blakemore, a mining engineer, covers methods of remining old tailings or dumps, and future prospects. Alta has large amounts of zinc, lead, and silver. Screening dumps for these was profitable until the Tooele smelter closed, leaving no market. Mining could start again if technological changes made it profitable or a smelter began in Alta. Based primarily on an interview with Page Blakemore; illus., 3 notes.

J. L. Hazelton

881. Mansfield, Edwin. BASIC RESEARCH AND PRODUCTIVITY INCREASE IN MANUFACTURING. *Am. Econ. Rev. 1980 70(5): 863-873.* A statistically significant relationship exists between the level of research and development expenditures and productivity, based on a study of 119 firms. Unfortunately, in the last 10 years all of the studied industries have cut research and development expenditures. 2 tables, 25 notes, biblio. D. K. Pickens

882. Marshall, Philip C. POLYCHROMATIC ROOFING SLATE OF VERMONT AND NEW YORK. *APT Bulletin [Canada] 1979 11(3): 77-87.* Traces the rise of slate quarrying in Vermont and eastern New York and describes the processing in mills there, 1850's-1970's.

883. Miles, P. and Wright, N. J. R. AN OUTLINE OF MINERAL EX-
TRACTION IN THE ARCTIC. *Polar Record [Great Britain] 1978 19(118):
11-38.* Discusses mining in the Arctic Circle in the USSR, Scandinavia, Canada,
and Alaska, 1917-78.

884. Munn, Robert F. THE DEVELOPMENT OF STRIP MINING IN
SOUTHERN APPALACHIA. *Appalachian J. 1975 3(1): 87-92.*

885. Paul, Rodman W. A TENDERFOOT DISCOVERS THERE ONCE
WAS A MINING WEST. *Western Hist. Q. 1979 10(1): 4-20.* Analyzes the
evolution of the historiography of the mining West over the last 40 years. The
new mining history has shifted its emphasis from the romanticism of the mid-19th
century gold rushes to a social and technological examination of the era during
1870's-20th century. The recent literature is concerned with social mobility,
urbanization, labor relations, the role of women and the family, politics, and
quantitative methods. Illus., 45 notes. D. L. Smith

886. Pitcaithley, Dwight. ZINC AND LEAD MINING ALONG THE
BUFFALO RIVER. *Arkansas Hist. Q. 1978 37(4): 293-305.* Traces the history
of the rise and decline of lead and zinc mining in the Buffalo River area of
Arkansas from the first discovery of the minerals in the 1700's through the boom
of 1916-17 and subsequent decline in production. Poor transportation was always
the greatest obstacle to the productivity of the region. Primary and secondary
sources; illus., 46 notes. G. R. Schroeder

887. Poss, John R. THE GRAND CANYON'S HIDDEN HOARD.
Westways 1982 74(6): 37-39, 73-74. Surveys prospecting and mining activities in
the Grand Canyon of Arizona since the 16th century, focusing on uranium
mining; prospector Daniel Hogan discovered a uranium deposit in 1891 but its
utility and value were unknown until the 1950's, and $50 million worth of
uranium was mined by 1969.

888. Powell, H. Benjamin. THE PENNSYLVANIA ANTHRACITE IN-
DUSTRY, 1769-1976. *Pennsylvania Hist. 1980 47(1): 3-28.* Focuses on the
agrarian-mercantile age, 1769-1850; the age of industrialism, 1850-1914, which
has received the most scholarly attention; and the age of managerial economy,
which is characterized by the interaction of big government, big labor, and big
business as mutually countervailing powers. Primary sources and other materials;
photo, 67 notes. D. C. Swift

889. Powell, William E. THE CHEROKEE-CRAWFORD COAL FIELD
OF SOUTHEASTERN KANSAS: A STUDY IN SEQUENT OCCUPANCE.
Midwest Q. 1981 22(2): 113-125. Analyzes the development and effects of coal
mining in two counties of southeastern Kansas from the mid-19th century to the
present. Rudimentary mining (1840's-1860's) enhanced early settlement and was
the forerunner of commercial mining. Shaft mining (1870's-1950's) attracted
numerous immigrants of diverse origins and stimulated economic growth and
diversification. Mechanized strip mining (1870's to the present) developed con-
currently with the shaft mining, which it gradually replaced. 2 tables, fig., 15
notes. M. E. Quinlivan

890. Riell, Robert B. THE 1917 COPPER STRIKE AT GLOBE, ARIZONA. *J. of Arizona Hist. 1977 18(2): 185-196.* The Western Federation of Miners and the Industrial Workers of the World were receptive to membership that was militant socialist. On 2 July 1917, all copper mines in the country were struck, precipitating crises all over the West. Describes the strike in Globe, Arizona from the viewpoint of a company man, the paymaster. 3 illus.

D. L. Smith

891. Rubenstein, Harry R. THE GREAT GALLUP COAL STRIKE OF 1933. *New Mexico Hist. Rev. 1977 52(3): 173-192.* As a result of the depression, union membership in New Mexico declined. AFL craft unions began to reorganize and the mine workers became the most active in regard to strikes. The Gallup mining community was involved in the most serious strikes. The coal miners were affected most by the depression. The National Guard was used against the strikers. The eastern mining districts had more serious strikes than those in New Mexico. The Gallup strike was not isolated, but a part of the turmoil of the 1930's. 65 notes.

J. H. Krenkel

892. Skinner, Brian J. CYCLES IN MINING AND THE MAGNITUDE OF MINERAL PRODUCTION. *Tr. of the Royal Soc. of Can. [Canada] 1977 15: 13-27.* Notes that in the history of discovery and exploitation of metallic mineral resources in industrial countries there is a consistent pattern of growth followed by decline. Similar patterns also exist in the amount of mineral smelting and processing in a country, in the exportation of metals, in the development of the industries making use of the metals, and eventually in the importation of supplies as production falls below demand. Suggests that we rely on ore minerals for our metal supplies. A finite quantity of these minerals are recoverable; thus, the aforementioned cycles are inevitable. Concludes that the United States and Canada are well into their productive cycles. Table, 12 fig., biblio.

J. D. Neville

893. Spence, Clark C. THE GOLDEN AGE OF DREDGING: THE DEVELOPMENT OF AN INDUSTRY AND ITS ENVIRONMENTAL IMPACT. *Western Hist. Q. 1980 11(4): 401-414.* The introduction of gold dredging revolutionized mineral technology, applying mass production techniques to placer deposits and enabling profitable working of ground that was untouchable before. The highly sophisticated dredge technology, developed especially in California, spread throughout the world. The height of American gold dredging, especially in California and Alaska, lasted from 1905 to 1920. Dredges wreaked havoc upon the environment, raising some charges of aesthetic offenses, polluted streams, and despoiled farm land: the environmental damage. Even so, westerners were seldom much bothered as long as arable land was abundant. Environmental impact activism is a post-World War II development. 46 notes.

D. L. Smith

894. Spier, William. A SOCIAL HISTORY OF MANGANESE MINING IN THE BATESVILLE DISTRICT OF INDEPENDENCE COUNTY. *Arkansas Hist. Q. 1977 36(2): 130-157.* Cushing, Arkansas, was a manganese mining center which was developed in the late 1840's and reached its peak production during the 1890's-1930's. Most workers were either local farmers wishing to earn extra money during slack seasons or migrants from nearby states.

Pay was only $1.50 per day or $4.00 per ton of coal mined and delivered to Batesville, the nearest railroad terminus. Workers enjoyed simple, but often rowdy, lives. There was little food, clothing, or shelter for their families, and only the hope for a big strike tomorrow kept them going. Based on interviews with former miners; 4 illus., 94 notes.   T. L. Savitt

895.   Sprague, Stuart Seely.   THE GREAT APPALACHIAN IRON AND COAL BOOM OF 1889-1893.   *Appalachian J. 1977 4(3,4): 216-223.* An increased demand for iron and coal in 1889 sparked a frenzy of land speculation throughout Appalachia until the panic of 1893 caused iron and coal prices to plummet; yet, despite the region's quick return to isolation, the Appalachians learned from the experience.   M. T. Wilson

896.   Spude, Robert L.   MINERAL FRONTIER IN TRANSITION: COPPER MINING IN ARIZONA, 1880-85.   *New Mexico Hist. R. 1976 51(1): 19-34.* Lewis Williams' new copper smelting operation at Bisbee in 1880 helped create a copper boom, as did extension of railroads across Arizona and New Mexico 1878-83. By 1886 New York-based corporations had gained control of the mines, the mining camps had tamed down, and hostility toward Indians had abated.   S

897.   Stall, Sid and Stall, Marge.   RELICS OF A WILDERNESS INTERLUDE.   *Am. West 1976 13(5): 26-33.* The prospecting and mining heyday of south-central Colorado, in a 500-square-mile area of the eastern San Juan Mountains, lasted from the 1870's until the end of the century. There remains little reminder of the activity in what is now virtually a wilderness area, except for the remnants of an occasional building or abandoned machinery. 6 illus.
                                                                   D. L. Smith

898.   Stearns, Robert A.   ALASKA'S KENNECOTT COPPER AND THE KENNECOTT COPPER CORPORATION.   *Alaska J. 1975 5(3): 130-139.* Discusses the establishment of the Kennecott Copper Corporation, 1900-15, and the prime movers behind the operation, Stephen Birch and Charles G. Hubbard. 12 photos, map, 25 notes.

899.   Stern, Mark.   BLACK STRIKEBREAKERS IN THE COAL FIELDS: KING COUNTY, WASHINGTON: 1891.   *J. of Ethnic Studies 1977 5(3): 60-70.* Relates the activities of the Oregon Improvement Company's recruitment and use of Negroes from Iowa and Illinois at its Newcastle and Franklin mines during the Knights of Labor-inspired strike of 1891. Contrary to the white miners' stereotypes, the blacks involved were not "collected from the slums" or "unconscious tools of the company," but were for the most part experienced coal miners who had gone through industrial conflicts before, were conscious of their role, and had some ideological justification for their actions. Local black leaders preached a philosophy of self-help and racial pride, and saw the managers of the corporation as allies against the Knights and the white workers. Events in King County contradict the dominant interpretation of the phenomenon of the black strikebreaker, and show that Booker T. Washington's creed was less a rationalization of racism than a stress on cultural pride and separateness. Primary and secondary sources; 29 notes.   G. J. Bobango

900.   Stout, Steve.   TRAGEDY IN NOVEMBER: THE CHERRY MINE DISASTER.   *J. of the Illinois State Hist. Soc. 1979 72(1): 57-69.* Reviews antecedents of the fire disaster in the coal mine at Cherry, Illinois, in 1909. The disaster could easily have been prevented had anyone taken it seriously soon enough. An electrical failure had caused kerosene torches to be used for light; they ignited some bales of hay used to feed the mine mules. Miners passed the fire when it could easily have been extinguished, thinking it was under control. When finally the fire was fought, the effort was so incompetent that it actually spread the blaze. Rescue efforts were not ideal, either. Altogether, 259 miners lost their lives. 8 photos, 45 notes.   V. L. Human

901.   Todd, Cecil.   METAL MINING AND ITS ASSOCIATED INDUS-TRIES IN TUCSON.   *J. of Arizona Hist. 1981 22(1): 99-128.* Summarizes the complex history of Tucson's struggle to capitalize on its location to profit from mining. Mining, though never immensely profitable, stimulated the growth of all facets of Tucson economy. Secondary sources, 10 photos, 43 notes.
                                                                   G. O. Gagnon

902.   Walker, Billy D.   COPPER GENESIS: THE EARLY YEARS OF SANTA RITA DEL COBRE.   *New Mexico Hist. Rev. 1979 54(1): 5-20.* De-scribes the discovery and development of the Santa Rita copper mines in south-western New Mexico. Francisco Manuel de Elguea (d. 1809), a wealthy merchant from Chihuahua, was the first to develop the mines into a profitable venture. Spanish and Mexican mining methods and problems at Santa Rita are discussed, emphasizing the years 1800-25. Includes reports concerning the mines from Zebulon M. Pike (1779-1813) and James O. Pattie (1804-1850?). Photo, 51 notes.
                                                                   P. L. McLaughlin

903.   Wheeler, Hoyt N.   MOUNTAINEER MINE WARS: AN ANALYSIS OF THE WEST VIRGINIA MINE WARS OF 1912-1913 AND 1920-1921. *Business Hist. Rev. 1976 50(1): 68-91.* Analyzes causes of the violence occurring in the West Virginia mine wars of the first quarter of the 20th century. Tests various social science theories. Concludes that there was a belief on the part of both forces that they were "locked in a struggle to the death" against the other side. The fear that the enemy represented a conspiracy of outside forces and the general familiarity of the mountaineers with weapons and with violence were also contributing factors. Based especially on governmental findings; 83 notes.
                                                                   C. J. Pusateri

904.   Wildman, Perry.   GREAT DAYS AT SILVER KING.   *J. of Arizona Hist. 1977 18(4): 387-404.* The Silver King mine, near present Superior, Arizona, produced millions of dollars in rich silver ore in 20 years. The author, a leading merchant and postmaster of the mining town, presents his recollections of the bustling life in Silver King, 1879-89. 2 illus.   D. L. Smith

905.   Wilson, Marjorie Haines.   GOVERNOR HUNT, THE "BEAST" AND THE MINERS.   *J. of Arizona Hist. 1974 15(2): 119-138.* Arizona governor George W. P. Hunt championed the laboring man. Personally incorruptible, he was attacked publicly and privately by corporations in the 1915-17 war years for his prolabor stance. Hunt and the corporations cooperated amicably when their goals coincided; otherwise, the governor and "The Beast," as Hunt called the

outside-the-state financed corporations, ably fought in politics, economics, and public opinion. 4 illus., 66 notes. D. L. Smith

906. Wold, Frances. THE WASHBURN LIGNITE COAL COMPANY: A HISTORY OF MINING AT WILTON, NORTH DAKOTA. *North Dakota Hist. 1976 43(4): 4-20.* W. D. Washburn, Minnesota politician and railroad entrepreneur, founded the Washburn Lignite Coal Company in 1900 to exploit lignite coal found in large quantities on the extensive land acreage owned by the Washburn Land Co. in North Dakota. The company prospered during the early 20th century. It drew upon the part-time labor of local farmers. Gradually it increasingly depended on imported fulltime miners, many of them immigrants. The company's paternalistic attitudes toward its employees were seriously shaken by the advent of the United Mine Workers of America during and after World War I and by the long strike of 1924. By 1930 the successor owners of the Washburn interests converted the operation to strip mining and threw hundreds of miners out of work. Based on oral interviews and on newspaper and secondary sources. N. Lederer

8

MANUFACTURING AND MERCHANDISING

907. Allen, Robert C. THE PECULIAR PRODUCTIVITY HISTORY OF AMERICAN BLAST FURNACES, 1840-1913. *J. of Econ. Hist. 1977 37(3): 605-633.* Develops "partial and total factor productivity indices to measure the growth and relative levels of efficiency [of blast furnaces] in the United States, Britain, France, Belgium, and Germany. . . . These measures establish the existence of the mid-century American-European productivity gap and demonstrate the extraordinary speed with which it was closed in the 1870s and 1880s. . . . The most important new technique was the reduction in the amount of limestone charged in the blast furnace." Based on US Census Bureau, US Bureau of Labor Statistics and secondary sources; 2 fig., 7 tables, 46 notes. D. J. Trickey

908. Amato, Louis; Ryan, J. Michael; and Wilder, Ronald P. MARKET STRUCTURE AND DYNAMIC PERFORMANCE IN U.S. MANUFACTURING. *Southern Econ. J. 1981 47(4): 1105-1110.* Examines the relation between the size of firms and changes in technology; 1958-72.

909. Anderson, Charles. THE GREAT AMERICAN SOFT DRINK. *Mankind 1977 5(11): 8-13.* The process of carbonating drinks became a commercial reality with the emergence of the soft drink industry in the 1880's. In 1886 Coca-Cola came on the market, later reaching fame and fortune through the merchandising genius of Asa G. Candler. Pepsi-Cola became a competitor in the late 1890's, later seriously challenging Coke through offering a 12-ounce bottle for the same price as the latter's 6-1/2-ounce bottle. At the same time that the two cola drinks waged economic warfare, Seven-Up was created and eventually dominated the lime-lemon drink market. N. Lederer

910. Andrews, E. G. TELEPHONE SWITCHING AND THE EARLY BELL LABORATORIES COMPUTERS. *Ann. of the Hist. of Computing 1982 4(1): 13-19.* Presents the history of the Bell Telephone Laboratories's research on both automated data processing for machine switching and digital computation, which advanced telephone technology. These improved "machine accuracy and dependability and ease of programming, operation and maintenance." Pioneers in this research were G. R. Stobiz, who drafted the initial Complex Computer design in 1937, Samuel B. Williams, who developed the pushbutton feature and a simplified circuitry in 1938, C. E. Boman, who designed

the external equipment in 1939, and A. J. Bendernagel, who oversaw Complex Computer construction in 1939. Bell continued to redesign and modify the computer through Model VI in 1950. Primary sources; 2 photos, table, 3 notes, ref.

N. A. Newhouse

911. Arbuckle, Robert D. JOHN NICHOLSON AND THE ATTEMPT TO PROMOTE INDUSTRY IN THE 1790S. *Pennsylvania Hist. 1975 42(2): 99-114.* A prominent Philadelphia merchant and state comptroller general, John Nicholson played a major role in efforts to promote manufacturing in Pennsylvania in the 1790's. His chief project was the development of a manufacturing complex at the Falls of the Schuylkill. Attempting to benefit from mistakes made in establishing a similar and unsuccessful project at Paterson, New Jersey, Nicholson endeavored to promote a variety of enterprises at his complex. Nevertheless, the effort failed and Nicholson died in debtors' prison in 1800. Based on Nicholson papers and other materials; illus., 92 notes.   D. C. Swift

912. Asher, Robert. PAINFUL MEMORIES: THE HISTORICAL CONSCIOUSNESS OF STEELWORKERS AND THE STEEL STRIKE OF 1919. *Pennsylvania Hist. 1978 45(1): 61-86.* Most skilled steelworkers in the Pittsburgh district remained at work during the Steel Strike of 1919. Many factors influenced their defection, but none was more important than their recollection of earlier unsuccessful confrontations with the companies. Many of the skilled steelworkers had participated in those strikes, and others had been told of the events by "old timers" in the steel towns. The skilled steelworkers who did not support the 1919 strike doubted the ability of the union leadership, respected the power and wealth of the companies, and understood the relationship between paternalism and repression. Based on interviews undertaken by David Saposs and others in 1920, US Senate hearings, recent oral history interviews, and other materials; 3 tables, 56 notes.   D. C. Swift

913. Barrett, Nancy S.; Gerardi, Geraldine; and Hart, Thomas P. A FACTOR ANALYSIS OF QUARTERLY PRICE AND WAGE BEHAVIOR FOR U.S. MANUFACTURING. *Q. J. of Econ. 1974 88(3): 385-408.* Identifies the main economic variables associated with movements of quarterly price and wage statistics for US manufacturing.   S

914. Bateman, Fred and Weiss, Thomas. MARKET STRUCTURE BEFORE THE AGE OF BIG BUSINESS: CONCENTRATION AND PROFIT IN EARLY SOUTHERN MANUFACTURING. *Business Hist. R. 1975 49(3): 312-336.* Concludes that pure competitive conditions did not exist in pre-Civil War America but that, instead, "imperfectly competitive markets, producer concentration, and the power to control price by individual sellers clearly were possible theoretically" prior to the rise of big business in the United States. Statistics indicate that the average degree of concentration in Southern industry was already high by 1860. Based primarily on US Census of Manufacturing records; 4 tables, 19 notes, 4 appendixes.   C. J. Pusateri

915. Baughman, James L. CLASSES AND COMPANY TOWNS: LEGENDS OF THE 1937 LITTLE STEEL STRIKE. *Ohio Hist. 1978 87(2): 175-192.* Examines events in Canton, Youngstown, and Warren (Ohio) during the 1937 "Little Steel" strike, the first major strike since 1919. Discusses the relation-

ship of the communities to the month-long labor-management conflict. After the strike of the Youngstown Sheet and Tube, Inland Steel, and Republic Steel, not solidarity but demoralization and internal division characterized the employees. The union never came close to victory—after four weeks the laborers began filing back into the mills and the managers had halted the impressive advance for CIO organization in the nation's basic industries. Through examination of the communities involved, discusses why the union lost. Based on primary and secondary sources; 3 illus., 48 notes.   N. Summers

916. Becker, William H. AMERICAN MANUFACTURERS AND FOREIGN MARKETS, 1870-1900: BUSINESS HISTORIANS AND THE "NEW ECONOMIC DETERMINISTS." *Business Hist. R. 1973 47(4): 466-481.* Discusses theories of recent diplomatic historians, especially those of William Appleman Williams, on American expansionism at the end of the 19th century. They explain it as a result of industrial overcapacity and a need for foreign markets. Modifies this interpretation through a reexamination of 19th-century American industry and the export market. Concludes that manufacturers did not turn to foreign markets to solve their excess problem, but rather sought domestic means to control prices and production, often by agreement among themselves. The motives behind expansion into overseas markets during this period need to be researched before a new interpretation of American expansionism can be accurately assessed. Based on US government documents and secondary sources; table, 19 notes.   N. J. Street

917. Beeten, Neil. POLISH AMERICAN STEELWORKERS: AMERICANIZATION THROUGH INDUSTRY AND LABOR. *Polish Am. Studies 1976 33(2): 31-42.* The United States Steel Corporation in Gary, Indiana, manipulated immigrant workers under the guise of Americanization. In a final analysis, both immigrants and the employers profited from the corporation programs. Unplanned and unnoticed during the process, however, was a steady exposure of the immigrant workers to the merits of unionization, the potential benefits of organized strikes, and the necessary techniques of survival in a hard economic world. Covers ca. 1906-20. Based primarily on English newspaper accounts; 21 notes.   S. R. Pliska

919. Benson, Susan Porter. THE CINDERELLA OF OCCUPATIONS: MANAGING THE WORK OF DEPARTMENT STORE SALESWOMEN, 1900-1940. *Business Hist. Rev. 1981 55(1): 1-25.* By 1900 department store managers, recognizing a need to increase sales volumes in order to cover high fixed costs, attempted to develop a more effective salesforce of the working class shopgirls employed as clerks. In the following decades management emphasized training in skilled selling and later the resocialization of the saleswomen themselves. The program failed because of an inherent contradiction in managerial philosophy; the saleswomen were expected to behave as skilled professionals in dealing with customers, but they were treated as low-paid and unskilled employees in all other ways by store owners. Based primarily on industry and trade association periodicals; 73 notes.   C. J. Pusateri

920. Benson, Susan Porter. PALACE OF CONSUMPTION AND MACHINE FOR SELLING: THE AMERICAN DEPARTMENT STORE, 1880-1940. *Radical Hist. Rev. 1979 (21): 199-221.* Displays, layouts, including

bargain basements, and merchandise itself in department stores reveal merchandisers' assumptions about social classes: clientele and personnel; 1880-1940.

921. Berck, Peter. HARD DRIVING AND EFFICIENCY: IRON PRODUCTION IN 1890. *J. of Econ Hist. 1978 38(4): 879-900.* The best practice of American methods for producing iron in 1890 was slightly better than the methods employed in Great Britain. The difference in industrial technology was not of sufficient magnitude to have any bearing on Britain's decline as an industrial power. Profits in America were quite large; profits rose because Americans did not anticipate the growth in the demand for pig iron.   J/S

922. Betheil, Richard. THE ENA IN PERSPECTIVE: THE TRANSFORMATION OF COLLECTIVE BARGAINING IN THE BASIC STEEL INDUSTRY. *Rev. of Radical Pol. Econ. 1978 10(2): 1-24.* An account of the attempt by management to impose a "wages productivity deal" on unions in the steel industry during 1946-73 and the manner in which collective bargaining led to the Experimental Negotiating Agreement of 1973.

923. Blackford, Mansel G. SCIENTIFIC MANAGEMENT AND WELFARE WORK IN EARLY TWENTIETH CENTURY AMERICAN BUSINESS: THE BUCKEYE STEEL CASTINGS COMPANY. *Ohio Hist. 1981 9(3): 238-258.* Discusses the Buckeye Steel Castings Company and the underlying progressive vision of President (1908-27) S. P. Bush. This small to medium-size corporation in Columbus had a strong impact on the surrounding social and economic environment and was able to develop an efficient, low-cost foundry operation and avoid labor unrest during the early 1900's by combining the scientific management of its steel foundry and the adoption of welfare work practices for its laborers and local community. Based on the company records, the collections of the Ohio Historical society, interviews, and other primary sources; 2 photos, 3 tables, 74 notes.   L. A. Russell

924. Blatt, Martin. FROM BENCH LABORER TO MANUFACTURER: THE RISE OF JEWISH OWNERS IN THE DECLINING SHOE INDUSTRY IN LYNN. *Essex Inst. Hist. Collections 1979 115(4): 256-269.* In the early 20th century, many Jewish immigrants from Poland and Russia settled in Lynn to work in the shoe factories. Oral interviews with seven immigrants involved in the shoe industry present a composite picture of the characteristics of Jewish manufacturers in Lynn, Massachusetts. Traces the course by which these enterprising shoe workers, in particular, Cecil Weinstein (b. 1913), became factory owners. Based on oral interviews; 35 notes.   R. S. Sliwoski

925. Boorstin, Daniel J. A. MONTGOMERY WARD'S MAIL-ORDER BUSINESS. *Chicago Hist. 1973 2(3): 142-152.* Aaron Montgomery Ward (1843-1913) started his first mail-order house in 1872. By an ingenious use of the railroads and by tying his company to the Patrons of Husbandry (the Grangers), Ward could offer rural America the largest number of goods at extremely low prices. His catalog, printed by the most modern methods, allowed the customer to see pictures of articles for sale. Later, the company took advantage of Rural Free Delivery and helped work for a parcel post system. The early 20th century was the heyday of mail orders. By World War I, Ward's had become an American tradition. 10 illus.   N. A. Kuntz

926. Boulding, Kenneth E.   THE WAR INDUSTRY.   *Pro. of the Acad. of Pol. Sci. 1979 33(3): 91-100.* Reviews the many elements of inflationary increases in the economy, 1930-79; examines in particular, the correlation of defense spending to these increases. No unequivocal cause-and-effect relationship has yet been clearly defined. 2 tables.   K. N. T. Crowther

927. Brand, Horst and Huffstutler, Clyde.   THE PAPER AND PLASTIC BAG INDUSTRY: TWO DISTINCT PRODUCTIVITY PHASES.   *Monthly Labor Rev. 1980 103(5): 26-30.* Analyzes the sluggish increase in the industry during 1954-66 and the notable increase during 1967-77, concluding that improved technology, rapid growth in output, and marked consumer demand were the primary factors in this change.

928. Burch, Philip H., Jr.   THE NAM AS AN INTEREST GROUP. *Pol. and Soc. 1973 4(1): 97-130.* Points to a dearth of research about the National Association of Manufacturers since the 1940's and its role as spokesman for major manufacturers. Observes that smaller concerns were again in the majority on the governing boards of the NAM by the late 1940's, as they had been prior to the Depression, that this trend did not begin to reverse itself again until the 1960's, and that since the early 1970's a "blend of business representation" has been achieved. Also notes concomitant shifts in the strength of the conservative voice of the NAM and its influence. Primary and secondary sources; 69 notes.
                                                                         D. G. Nielson

929. Busch, Jane.   AN INTRODUCTION TO THE TIN CAN.   *Hist. Archaeol. 1981 15(1): 95-104.* The tin can has played a significant role in American history and can play a significant role in archaeology. Beginning with the food can, the author traces developments in canning and can manufacturing, and briefly discusses can shape and labeling. The narrative continues with the beer can, the center of can manufacturing innovation after 1935. There are obstacles facing archaeologists interested in tin cans. One is corrosion; another is the lack of archaeological and documentary research on this artifact.   J

930. Carey, John L.   PRODUCTIVITY IN THE STEEL FOUNDRIES INDUSTRY.   *Monthly Labor R. 1973 96(5): 8-11.* Discusses productivity in the steel foundries industry 1954-71, showing slower long run growth as a result of increased emphasis on quality control and giving data on capital expenditures and technological changes in the industry.

931. Coerver, Don M. and Hall, Linda B.   NEIMAN-MARCUS: INNOVATORS IN FASHION AND MERCHANDISING.   *Am. Jewish Hist. Q. 1976 66(1): 123-136.* As innovative merchants and merchandizers Neiman-Marcus of Dallas, Texas, revolutionized the Southwestern approach to fashion. Relates the story of the store, its founders, and its progress until the present. 44 notes.
                                                                         F. Rosenthal

932. Cohen, Steven R.   STEELWORKERS RETHINK THE HOMESTEAD STRIKE OF 1892.   *Pennsylvania Hist. 1981 48(2): 155-177.* John A. Fitch's study of steelworkers in Pittsburgh was part of the famous *Pittsburgh Survey* of 1909. This article is based on Fitch's field notes on 145 interviews; 45 of those interviewed participated in the Homestead Strike. In addition to illuminating the union's internal problems during the strike, these notes demonstrate how the

Carnegie Steel Company reduced workers' security and compensation while destroying the Amalgamated Association of Iron and Steel Workers movement in its mills and extracting more work from its employees. Based on the Fitch notes and other materials; 33 notes. D. C. Swift

933. Cooke, Edward S., Jr. THE BOSTON FURNITURE INDUSTRY IN 1880. *Old-Time New England 1980 70(257): 82-98.* Essay in two sections consisting of "a quantitative analysis of the craftsmen and the overall industry [relying] upon the United States Census records of 1880," and draws "upon the descriptions of individual firms contained in the ledgers of the Mercantile Agency, the credit reference agency that was a predecessor of Dun and Bradstreet."

934. Cooling, B. Franklin. THE FORMATIVE YEARS OF THE NAVAL-INDUSTRIAL COMPLEX: THEIR MEANING FOR STUDIES OF INSTITUTIONS TODAY. *Naval War Coll. R. 1975 27(5): 53-62.* The heritage of the much discussed "military-industrial complex" can be traced directly to the first of the truly modern weapons systems on which it now thrives—the large and expensive, steelplated, steam-propelled battleship of the late 19th century. Faced with the demands of building a new steel navy, men like Secretary of the Navy B. F. Tracy forged the basic links between industry and Government which proved beneficial to both, but which also led to the practices and expansive military budget with which we are all familiar. J

935. Cooling, Benjamin Franklin. THE MILITARY-INDUSTRIAL COMPLEX: UPDATE ON AN OLD AMERICAN ISSUE. Karsten, Peter, ed. *The Military in America: From the Colonial Era to the Present* (New York: Free Pr., 1980): 317-329. Discusses the military-industrial complex (MIC) which began during the Civil War and burgeoned in the Gilded and Progressive eras. Examines the power that the MIC holds on American society in the remotest areas; 1861-1970's.

936. Duggal, Ved P. INDUSTRIALIZATION OF PUERTO RICO TILL 1970. *Horizontes [Puerto Rico] 1975 19(37): 93-113.* Traces the development of industrialization in Puerto Rico during 1940-70. Comments on the US interest in the process, the effects of industrialization on employment and income, dependence on US capital, and the quality of industrialization. Stresses the need for the encouragement of local enterprise so that the country does not continue to be subject to the vagaries of foreign trade and investment patterns. Primary and secondary sources; 3 tables, 54 notes, appendix. P. J. Taylorson

937. Duke, John. CONSTRUCTION MACHINERY INDUSTRY POSTS SLOW RISE IN PRODUCTIVITY. *Monthly Labor Rev. 1980 103(7): 33-36.* Compares economic growth and productivity in the construction machinery industry in the United States for each year between 1958 and 1978, including data on employment, investments, technology, and future developments, and concludes that 1977-78 showed strong gains.

938. Eastman, Joel W. ENTREPRENEURSHIP AND OBSOLESCENCE: OWEN W. DAVIS, JR. AND THE KATAHDIN CHARCOAL IRON COMPANY, 1876-1890. *Maine Hist. Soc. Q. 1977 17(2): 69-84.* Describes the efforts of Owen W. Davis, Jr., a representative of the new managerial class, to save the

Katahdin Charcoal Iron Company in northern Maine from going out of business during 1876-88. New turbine water wheels, higher furnace stacks, new charcoal kilns, housing improvements for workers and new roasting techniques for high sulphide iron ore were used to no avail. Plant operations were stopped in 1890. 42 notes.   P. C. Marshall

939.   Ettema, Michael J.   TECHNOLOGICAL INNOVATION AND DE-SIGN ECONOMICS IN FURNITURE MANUFACTURE.   *Winterthur Port-folio 1981 16(2-3): 197-223.* Technological improvements were accepted slowly by furniture manufacturers, who could not afford to invest or manufacture indiscriminately during 1850-1920. Scholars must consider technoeconomic conditions when examining the decorative arts. Some aesthetic choices are linked to economic compromises. Based on personal interviews, oral recollections, trade publications, and other sources; 26 fig., 55 notes.   N. A. Kuntz

940.   Friedman, Brian L.   PRODUCTIVITY GAINS IN THE DRUGSTORE INDUSTRY, 1958-79.   *Monthly Labor Rev. 1980 103(11): 18-22.* A rise in output per hour of people in the drug and proprietary store industry from 1958 until 1973 was followed by a slowdown in productivity from 1973 to 1979 due to a decline in spending in the retail trade and in prescriptions filled and refilled, to competition from other retail stores, and to a decrease in small independent drugstores coupled with an increase in chain stores.

941.   Glaser, William A.   CROSS-NATIONAL COMPARISONS OF THE FACTORY.   *J. of Comparative Administration 1974 3(1): 83-118.*

942.   Hekman, John S.   AN ANALYSIS OF THE CHANGING LOCATION OF IRON AND STEEL PRODUCTION IN THE TWENTIETH CENTURY. *Am. Econ. Rev. 1978 68(1): 123-133.* Compares alternative explanations of the westward movement of steel production in the United States from Pennsylvania to Chicago, Cleveland, and Detroit between 1910 and 1972, using the results of an econometric model. Previous explanations have associated the change with geographical differences in the cost of production, but the econometric evidence indicates that cost differences had little or nothing to do with this movement. The crucial variable explaining the relatively greater growth of the western producers have been the differential growth of demand by steel-using industries. Based on official statistics and secondary works; 10 tables, 6 notes.   D. J. Nicholls

943.   Hessen, Robert.   THE BETHLEHEM STEEL STRIKE OF 1910. *Labor Hist. 1974 15(1): 3-18.* Details the protracted struggle between labor and management in the Bethlehem Steel strike of 1910. Triggered by the intransigence of Charles M. Schwab, the president, the strike was led by the skilled machinists. Although the company managed to maintain local support and break the strike within a three-month period, it signalled the beginning of increased federal regulation of the American steel industry. Movement of the strikers to other cities and lack of union financial resources also contributed to its failure. Based on the Bethlehem *Globe,* other newspapers and periodicals. 43 notes.   L. L. Athey

944.   Hill, Charles.   FIGHTING THE TWELVE-HOUR DAY IN THE AMERICAN STEEL INDUSTRY.   *Labor Hist. 1974 15(1): 19-35.* Reviews the movement against the twelve-hour day in the steel industry and details the intricate maneuvering of a diverse group of opponents and supporters ranging

from John A. Fitch, President Harding, Secretary of Commerce Herbert Hoover, Paul Kellogg, and others during 1923. The reform was achieved, and the steel companies had little difficulty in making the changeover to the eight-hour day. Based on the files of the War Labor Policies Board, the Samuel McCune Lindsay papers, the Herbert Hoover papers, and *The Survey*. 96 notes.   L. L. Athey

945. Hounshell, David A. PUBLIC RELATIONS OR PUBLIC UNDER-STANDING?: THE AMERICAN INDUSTRIES SERIES IN *SCIENTIFIC AMERICAN*. *Technology and Culture 1980 21(4): 589-593.* If the rest of the American Industries series from Munn & Company's *Scientific American* newspaper (1879-82) are like number 73 on the McCormick Harvesting Machine Company, 14 May 1881, then the historian must use them with caution. That article was written and paid for as an advertisement by Cyrus McCormick, Jr. It was a highly idealized description of what he intended the McCormick Reaper Works to become, not of what it was. Based on McCormick manuscripts; illus., 13 notes.   C. O. Smith, Jr.

946. Howard, Robert A. INTERCHANGEABLE PARTS REEXAMINED: THE PRIVATE SECTOR OF THE AMERICAN ARMS INDUSTRY ON THE EVE OF THE CIVIL WAR. *Technology and Culture 1978 19(4): 633-649.* By contrast with the military sector, which enjoyed unlimited resources, arms makers in the private sector found interchangeability a prohibitively expensive and "quite unnecessary" goal; they continued to practice fitting, which required greater skill in one operation but resulted in lower overall costs. Table, illus., 21 notes.   C. O. Smith

947. Hudson, Samuel. THE MAN WHO FOUNDED THE J. L. HUDSON COMPANY. *Chronicle 1981 17(1): 4-9.* Studies the life of J. L. Hudson (1846-1912) whose success as a merchandiser stemmed from nonconformity—in politics, in civic activities, and especially in business policies and philosophy—a maverick attitude evident in the radically new concepts in sales and customer relations he introduced in Detroit, Michigan, which opened up a new era in the city's business life.

948. Humphrey, David Burras and Moroney, J. R. SUBSTITUTION AMONG CAPITAL, LABOR, AND NATURAL RESOURCE PRODUCTS IN AMERICAN MANUFACTURING. *J. of Pol. Econ. 1975 83(1): 57-82.* This paper presents estimates of partial elasticities of substitution among reproducible capital, labor, and an input aggregate of natural resource products. We are specifically interested in two hypotheses: i) Are natural resource products strictly complementary in production with either capital or labor? ii) Are resource products typically less substitutable with capital than with labor? To both questions the answer is, generally, no. Two modes of investigation are used, one based on a translog production function and the other making use of a translog cost function. For most industry groups, the estimated substitution elasticities obtained from the cost function are somewhat lower than those based on the translog production function.   J

949. Ignatius, David. WHO KILLED THE STEEL INDUSTRY? *Washington Monthly 1979 11(1): 8-21.* Discusses the steel industry, 1870's-1970's, assessing the impact of federal regulation, tariffs, labor unions, and cheap foreign steel (primarily Japanese) on the present state of the industry.

950. Kawahito, Kiyoshi. THE STEEL DUMPING ISSUE IN RECENT U.S.-JAPANESE RELATIONS. *Asian Survey 1980 20(10): 1038-1047.* By December 1977 the allegation that Japanese producers had engaged in massive steel dumping in the US market, particularly in 1976, had become widely accepted in the United States. But Japanese producers generally did not dump steel in the US market. Both general economic conditions and the steel industry's anti-import campaigns caused the misunderstanding. Japanese steel producers contributed to US misconceptions by responding ineffectively to the charges. 20 notes. M. A. Eide

951. Kittell, Robert S. THE OMAHA ICE TRUST, 1899-1900: AN URBAN MONOPOLY. *Nebraska Hist. 1973 54(4): 633-646.* Delineates the brief history of the monopoly, how it operated, and how it was broken by legal action on the part of an aroused community. R. Lowitt

952. Klaw, Spencer. "ALL SAFE, GENTLEMEN, ALL SAFE!" *Am. Heritage 1978 29(5): 40-47.* After Elisha Otis demonstrated the crash-proof elevator in 1853, the popularity of passenger elevators changed the skylines of cities. Improvements continued and most elevators now have electrically powered traction. 22 illus. B. J. Paul

953. Kondrat'ev, V. "FLUOR" [Fluor]. *Mirovaia Ekonomika i Mezhdunarodnye Otnosheniia [USSR] 1980 (10): 144-147.* Examines the structure and economic development of Fluor Corporation, an engineering company, during 1972-78. Russian.

954. Lauderbaugh, Richard A. BUSINESS, LABOR, AND FOREIGN POLICY: U.S. STEEL, THE INTERNATIONAL STEEL CARTEL, AND RECOGNITION OF THE STEEL WORKERS ORGANIZING COMMITTEE. *Pol. and Soc. 1976 6(4): 433-457.* "Private" foreign diplomacy led to the US Steel Corp.'s collective bargaining agreement with the Steel Workers Organizing Committee (SWOC) in early 1937. The agreement with the SWOC depended upon a verbal commitment to join the Entente Internationale de L'Acier (International Steel Cartel). In contravention of New Deal policies and US antitrust laws, the agreement included import restrictions, thereby controlling competition in the international steel market, and in turn protecting the US market. The agreement with SWOC served to camouflage the international aspects of the "invisible tariff" protecting the US steel market from the eyes of Roosevelt's New Dealers. 48 notes. D. G. Nielson

955. Lutey, Kent. LUTEY BROTHERS MARKETERIA: AMERICA'S FIRST SELF-SERVICE GROCERS. *Montana 1978 28(2): 50-57.* Lutey grocery stores began in Butte, Montana, under Joseph Lutey, Sr., in 1897, and quickly became one of the largest retail, wholesale, and mail order groceries in the state. After Joseph Lutey's death in 1911, his sons Joseph, Jr., and William J., operated the firm as Lutey Brothers. In 1912, William applied the idea of cafeteria-style self-service to the grocery business and opened the "Marketeria" in Butte. He secured a trademark for this term and for "Groceteria" in 1913, and operated the nation's first self-service grocery store until business conditions in Butte forced an end to the operation in 1924. In 1916, Clarence Saunders of Memphis, Tennessee, modeled his Piggly Wiggly grocery chain after the Lutey

operation. During World War I, William Lutey served as Federal Food Administrator for the Retail Food Industry in Montana, and contributed many Lutey products to aid European war victims. Based on material in the Montana Historical Society, Helena, and author's reminiscence; 9 illus.   R. C. Myers

956. Lynn, Catherine. DECKING COLUMBIA'S WALLS. *Am. Heritage 1981 33(1): 81-89.* From their beginnings in the United States in 1756, wallpaper printers urged protection for their industry. Although their appeals for protectionism were only part of a general campaign, wallpaper makers could use scenes of war, patriotism, and heroics to sell their product and their ideas. As times and interests changed, so did the patterns they created. Foreign competitors continued, but by the late 19th century, Americans had captured most of the trade. 14 illus.   J. F. Paul

957. Margolin, Ia. DZHENERAL ELEKTRIK [General Electric]. *Mirovaia Ekonomika i Mezhdunarodnye Otnosheniia [USSR] 1980 (5): 126-132.* Traces the expansion of the General Electric Company from the founding of the Edison Electric Light Company in 1878, and, using the company's own publications, documents the spread of its worldwide monopoly, which has vigorously resisted all attempts at control. 2 tables, 6 notes.

958. Massouh, Michael. TECHNOLOGICAL AND MANAGERIAL INNOVATION: THE JOHNSON COMPANY 1883-1898. *Business Hist. Rev. 1976 50(1): 47-68.* Describes a manufacturing company established by Tom L. Johnson, the Progressive mayor of Cleveland, Ohio, in 1883. Established to meet the needs of the expanding street railway business, it was a pioneer in making a number of industrial innovations, including one of the earliest national marketing systems staffed by its own trained salesmen. Management ideas generated by the Johnson Company were later copied by such industrial giants as DuPont and General Motors. Based largely on periodical materials of the period and on private papers; 56 notes.   C. J. Pusateri

959. McFadden, Joseph M. MONOPOLY IN BARBED WIRE: THE FORMATION OF THE AMERICAN STEEL AND WIRE COMPANY. *Business Hist. Rev. 1978 52(4): 465-489.* The production of barbed wire, which began in the 1870's, saw a growing movement toward monopolization, culminating in the formation of the American Steel and Wire Company of New Jersey in Trenton in 1899. It controlled at the time of its establishment some 96% of all barbed wire manufacturing facilities in the United States. Early attempts at pooling agreements in the 1880's had proved unsuccessful, and instead the trust device eventually was employed. The result was economics of scale and enhanced profit possibilities. Based on corporate records, contemporary trade journals, and government documents; 2 tables, 54 notes.   C. J. Pusateri

960. McGuire, Phillip. TECHNOLOGY AND COMMERCE: THE GAS LIGHT INDUSTRY'S RESPONSE TO EDISON'S ELECTRIC BULB. *Potomac Rev. 1973 6(2): 70-75.* Illustrates tactics used by the gas light industry to maintain its monopoly in lighting after Thomas Edison's invention of the electric bulb in 1879 caused the electric light industry to gain control of the market.

961. McQuaid, Kim. AN AMERICAN OWENITE: EDWARD A. FILENE AND THE PARAMETERS OF INDUSTRIAL REFORM, 1890-1937. *Am. J. of Econ. and Sociol. 1976 35(1): 77-94.* Edward A. Filene introduced industrial democracy in his Boston department store in 1891. He was deposed from the presidency of the store in 1928. His experiment ceased and thereafter he was denied any effective authority. He also directed his liberal energies to local, state, and national affairs such as his ambitious plan of urban reform, "Boston 1915." Such efforts were equally unsuccessful. He was a spokesman for the New Capitalism and a supporter of the New Deal, but in both movements his integrity isolated him from his peers. His enduring contributions were the cooperative and credit union movements.   P. Travis

962. McQuaid, Kim. COMPETITION, CARTELLIZATION AND THE CORPORATE ETHIC: GENERAL ELECTRIC'S LEADERSHIP DURING THE NEW DEAL ERA, 1933-1940. *Am. J. of Econ. and Sociol. 1977 36(4): 417-428.* Relations between General Electric Co. leaders and New Deal economic advisors and agencies resulted in sincere attempts at humanizing the managerial-capitalist order, an ideal which did not last long within the corporate structure.

963. Meyerhuber, Carl I., Jr. BLACK VALLEY: PENNSYLVANIA'S ALLE-KISKI AND THE GREAT STRIKE OF 1919. *Western Pennsylvania Hist. Mag. 1979 62(3): 251-265.* Analyzes the antiunion activities and violence in the Allegheny-Kiskiminetas Valley during the Great Steel Strike of 1919.

964. Mizuno, Goro. E. I. DYUPON-SHA NI OKERU KEIEI NO TENKAI [Growth of E. I. du Pont de Nemours & Co. and its administrative organization]. *Shakaikeizaishigaku (Socio-Economic Hist.) [Japan] 1966 32(1): 68-88.* Traces the growth of E. I. du Pont de Nemours & Co., a family organization in the US explosives industry, from 1802 to 1921.

965. Mohl, Raymond A. THE GREAT STEEL STRIKE OF 1919 IN GARY, INDIANA: WORKING-CLASS RADICALISM OR TRADE UNION MILITANCY? *Mid-America 1981 63(1): 36-52.* The 1919 Gary, Indiana, steel strike was notable for the absence of widespread radicalism, the lack of violence, and the moderation of the steel workers in the face of antiunion propaganda and martial law. The workers wanted better wages, shorter hours, and improved working conditions. Steel industry leaders successfully portrayed the strikers as bolshevists which alarmed the civic leaders and the local press. The US Army, led by General Leonard Wood, was called in to impose martial law on Gary. Notes.   M. J. Wentworth

966. Moye, William T. THE END OF THE 12-HOUR DAY IN THE STEEL INDUSTRY. *Monthly Labor Rev. 1977 100(9): 21-26.* Discusses attempts 1890's-1923 to reduce the work day in the steel industry from 12-hour shifts; examines the American Iron and Steel Institute's 1923 concession in light of the Harding Administration and groups which lobbied for the reduction in work hours.

967. Murray, Lawrence L. REVIEW ESSAY: THE MELLON FAMILY, MAKING AND SHAPING HISTORY: A SURVEY OF THE LITERATURE. *Western Pennsylvania Hist. Mag. 1979 62(1): 61-66.* Covers 1885-1978.

968. Nelson, Daniel. THE NEW FACTORY SYSTEM AND THE UNIONS: THE NATIONAL CASH REGISTER COMPANY DISPUTE OF 1901. *Labor Hist. 1974 15(2): 163-178.* Assesses the impact of the new factory system, based on "welfare work," on the workers and the unions in the National Cash Register Company. "Welfare work" did not prevent the maintenance of the old autocratic foreman methods. The latter caused the dispute of 1901 which provoked criticism of "welfare work" practices, set back the attempt to organize mass production industries, and began a new phase in the emerging "new factory system." The N.C.R. Labor Department became the first modern personnel department in American industry. Based upon the McCormick Papers, the Gompers Letterbooks, unpublished correspondence, and the Dayton Daily Journal; 55 notes.   L. L. Athey

969. Nelson, Daniel. TAYLORISM AND THE WORKERS AT BETHLE-HEM STEEL, 1898-1901. *Pennsylvania Mag. of Hist. and Biog. 1977 101(4): 487-505.* Introducing time study and the differential piece rate, Frederick W. Taylor's scientific management and supposed labor force reorganization was a modest affair. It nevertheless yielded impressive results, showing how aggressive executives forced marginal employees to work harder. Based on Taylor Papers, Stevens Institute of Technology, published sources and secondary works; 56 notes.   T. H. Wendel

970. Norris, James D. and Livingston, James. JOY MORTON AND THE CONDUCT OF MODERN BUSINESS ENTERPRISE. *Chicago Hist. 1981 10(1): 13-25.* Biography of the founder of the Morton Salt Company and the Morton Arboretum, Joy Morton (b. 1855), an entrepreneur exemplifying the corporation man who organized bureaucratic, national corporations into institutions that dominated the American business scene.

971. Ognibene, Peter J. THE AIR FORCE'S SECRET WAR ON UNEM-PLOYMENT. *Washington Monthly 1975 7(5/6): 58-61.* The lobbyists for the Rockwell International corporation, makers of the B-1 nuclear bomber, portray the B-1 as "the $50-billion solution to the unemployment problem" rather than as a weapon of mass destruction.

972. Ohta, Makoto. PRODUCTION TECHNOLOGIES OF THE U.S. BOILER AND TURBOGENERATOR INDUSTRIES AND HEDONIC PRICE INDEXES FOR THEIR PRODUCTS: A COST-FUNCTION AP-PROACH. *J. of Pol. Econ. 1975 83(1): 1-26.* The hedonic approach has been proposed and used as a method to obtain quality-adjusted (hedonic) price indexes for the durable goods. The previous hedonic studies did not seem to pay careful attention to the economic factors which determine the functional forms of hedonic regression equations. This paper tries to analyze those factors for the US boilers and the turbogenerators purchased by the US steam electric power industry. This goal amounts to analyzing the production technologies of the industries producing these products under the maintained hypothesis of markup pricing. After analyzing them, we obtain the hedonic price indexes.   J

973. Otto, Phyllis Flohr. PRODUCTIVITY GROWTH BELOW AVER-AGE IN FABRICATED STRUCTURAL METALS. *Monthly Labor Rev. 1980 103(6): 27-31.* Reports that the fabricated structural metals industry, which

shapes metal parts for buildings, bridges, and overpasses, experienced a drop in productivity in 1973-78, and suggests reasons for this ongoing (1958-78) decline.

974. Otto, Phyllis Flohr. TRANSFORMER INDUSTRY PRODUCTIV-ITY SLOWS. *Monthly Labor Rev. 1981 104(11): 35-39.* Traces growth in the transformer industry during 1963-79.

975. Parry, Thomas G. TRADE AND NON-TRADE PERFORMANCE OF U.S. MANUFACTURING INDUSTRY: "REVEALED" COMPARA-TIVE ADVANTAGE. *Manchester School of Econ. and Social Studies [Great Britain] 1975 43(2): 158-172.* Discusses problems of measuring an industry's international competitiveness, suggesting a preliminary method of assessing the relationship between trade and nontrade forms of international commerce based on data on the "revealed" comparative advantage of trade and nontrade commerce in the present-day United States.

976. Parsons, Donald O. and Ray, Edward John. THE UNITED STATES STEEL CONSOLIDATION: THE CREATION OF MARKET CONTROL. *J. of Law & Econ. 1975 18(1): 181-219.* Analyzes the impact of the formation of the US Steel Corporation in 1901 on market structure and competition in the iron and steel industry through 1929.

977. Paskoff, Paul F. LABOR PRODUCTIVITY AND MANAGERIAL EFFICIENCY AGAINST A STATIC TECHNOLOGY: THE PENNSYLVA-NIA IRON INDUSTRY, 1750-1800. *J. of Econ. Hist. 1980 40(1): 129-135.* An increase in labor productivity and a reduction of fuel consumption rates were two notable and closely related achievements of the management of Hopewell Forge, an ironworks in 18th-century Pennsylvania. Significantly, these economies were realized in the face of technological stasis through learning by doing. The analysis of this accomplishment is cast in the larger context of the performance of the iron industry before and after 1800.   J

978. Patry, Bill. RETAIL: A WORKER'S OBSERVATIONS. *Monthly Rev. 1978 29(11): 23-31.* During the 1970's, chain retailers introduced merchandising methods and electronic equipment which reduced labor needs, provided constant checks and surveillance on workers, made workers interchangeable, and kept workers docile and poorly paid by employing part-time labor who frequently requested more hours.

979. Phelps, Byron E. EARLY ELECTRONIC COMPUTER DEVELOP-MENTS AT IBM. *Ann. of the Hist. of Computing 1980 2(3): 253-267.* This article deals primarily with the early beginnings of electronic computer development within IBM. It starts with the 603 prototype (first operational in 1942) and goes on to cover the major IBM electronic developments up through the 701, including the 603, SSEC, 604, CPC, and tape processing machine. It also briefly outlines early work at RCA and at NCR, based on patents on file in the US Patent Office and on the limited reports publicly available.   J

980. Qualls, P. David. MARKET STRUCTURE AND PRICE BEHAVIOR IN US MANUFACTURING, 1967-72. *Q. Rev. of Econ. and Business 1978 18(4): 35-58.* Tests various sorts of "administered pricing" hypotheses for the period 1967 to 1972, and addresses the question as to whether the industrial price

inflation during this period was of the market power "administered" type that, in the view of some, characterized the slower inflations of the late 1950's and early 1960's.   J

981.   Reichardt, Otto H.   INDUSTRIAL CONCENTRATION IN WORLD WAR II: THE CASE OF THE AIRCRAFT INDUSTRY.   *Aerospace Hist. 1975 22(3): 129-134.* Presents part of a larger study dealing with the economic impact of government procurement policies during World War II. Scholars are divided over the effects of government allocation and contracting policies on business concentration during the war. This study attempts to assess the problem through a multidimensional statistical survey of the aircraft industry. After conducting this survey, the author concludes that more research is needed before the data on the aircraft industry can be fully explained. Based on secondary sources; 5 tables, 31 notes.   C. W. Ohrvall

982.   Robinowitz, Robert S. and Riche, Martha Farnsworth.   PRODUCTIVITY IN THE READY-MIXED CONCRETE INDUSTRY.   *Monthly Labor R. 1973 96(5): 12-15.* Cites a moderate increase in productivity in the ready-mixed concrete industry 1958-71, giving data on changes in demand, employment, and technology.

983.   Roth, Winfried.   ZUR ENTWICKLUNG DER EISEN-UND STAHL-INDUSTRIE DER USA NACH 1945   [The development of the iron and steel industries in the United States after 1945]. *Jahrbuch für Wirtschaftsgeschichte [East Germany] 1979 (1): 71-92.* The US iron and steel industries grew as a result of concentration until the 1950's. Subsequently centralization occurred either through absorption by a conglomerate or by vertical integration of resources or marketing subsidies. Research and modernization lagged behind that in Europe and Japan, which assumed the leadership in production. By 1959 the United States was importing more finished steel than it exported. The government nevertheless protected the industries with favorable pricing and import policies, but has failed to help halt the decline. Based on US government statistics, congressional hearings' reports, and secondary sources from the United States and Europe; 2 tables, 113 notes.   E. L. Turk

984.   Samson, Peter.   THE DEPARTMENT STORE, ITS PAST AND FUTURE: A REVIEW ARTICLE.   *Business Hist. Rev. 1981 55(1): 26-34.* Reviews Leon Harris's *Merchant Princes: An Intimate History of Jewish Families Who Built Great Department Stores* (1979), Robert Hendrickson's *The Grand Emporiums: The Illustrated History of America's Great Department Stores* (1979), Gordon L. Weil's *The Great American Catalog Store and How It Grew* (1977) and Alison Adburgham's *Shopping in Style: London from the Restoration to Edwardian Elegance* (1979). The first three works are popular narratives meant for a nonscholarly audience, while the last is superior to the others in that it examines retailing's connection to the broader subject of urban history.   C. J. Pusateri

985.   Schallenberg, Richard H.   EVOLUTION, ADAPTATION AND SURVIVAL: THE VERY SLOW DEATH OF THE AMERICAN CHARCOAL IRON INDUSTRY.   *Ann. of Sci. [Great Britain] 1975 32(4): 341-358.* The last charcoal iron blast furnace in the United States shut down in 1945. The most

obvious reason for the extraordinary longevity of this industry was the almost unlimited supply of virgin timber in the United States. Although an obvious explanation, it is deceptive. The much more crucial reason for the longevity of the American charcoal iron industry was the technical difficulties involved in adapting coke- and coal-smelted iron to existing industrial processes. Until these technological problems could be overcome, charcoal iron was able to preserve a place for itself in the industrial environment of the late 19th and early 20th centuries. By concentrating their attention on the rapid advance of coke-smelted iron from 1870 onward, historians of the American iron industry have neglected this ability of the older iron technology to adapt to the new industrial conditions.

J

986. Schatz, Ronald. THE END OF CORPORATE LIBERALISM: CLASS STRUGGLE IN THE ELECTRICAL MANUFACTURING INDUSTRY, 1933-1950. *Radical Am. 1975 9(4-5): 187-205.* Considers the decline in union membership in the late 1940's after the corporations abandoned their liberal labor policies.

S

987. Scheuerman, William. ECONOMIC POWER IN THE UNITED STATES: THE CASE OF STEEL. *Pol. and Soc. 1975 5(3): 337-366.* Through a case study of the steel industry, disputes the arguments of the 1960's that declining market proportions indicate less corporate concentration and economic power. Examination of such factors as product specialization, mergers, takeovers by conglomerates, joint intraindustry subsidiaries, joint interindustry subsidiaries (which provide backward vertical integration and diversification), interlocking directorates, internationalization of production facilities, and relationships with major financial institutions, indicates that viewing each steel company independently produces a distorted picture, and shows that concentration (and thus economic power) in this primary industry is greater than generally acknowledged. Based on primary and secondary sources; 11 tables, 38 notes.

D. G. Nielson

988. Schoeplein, Robert N. SECULAR CHANGES IN THE SKILL DIF- FERENTIAL IN MANUFACTURING, 1952-1973. *Industrial and Labor Relations Rev. 1977 30(3): 314-324.* Shows that the skill differential in manufacturing, when measured on the national level, has remained surprisingly stable over the 1952-73 period, in spite of its history of narrowing throughout the first half of the century and the severe pressures of inflation during the years since 1965. At the level of individual cities, however, this skill differential is shown to be moving toward convergence at one of two points, with differentials tending to be considerably wider in less unionized cities than in more unionized cities.

J

989. Schultz, Robert G. THE MONROE DRUG COMPANY 1876-1976: A CENTURY OF CHEMICAL ENTERPRISE. *Missouri Hist. Rev. 1981 76(1): 1-21.* Edward N. Monroe opened a drug store in Unionville in 1876. J. Hugh Elson joined him, and by 1891 the Monroe Drug Company was formed to market a variety of dyes. Monroe, the organizer and sales promoter, and Elson, the scientist, built an industry that was not only a good example of small town enterprise, but also was an early example of vertical integration, the combination of all aspects of production from raw materials to consumer distribution. After

moving to Quincy, Illinois, in 1907, the company enjoyed further prosperity as German patents became available after World War I, and the name was changed in 1927 to the Monroe Chemical Company. Based on Putnam County, Missouri records, US Patent Office records, newspapers, interviews, letters to the author; illus., 85 notes. W. F. Zornow

990. Simon, Roger. LOOKING BACKWARD AT STEEL. *Antioch Rev. 1978 36(4): 441-462.* Two interviews with retired workers from the Bethlehem Steel Corporation reflect a wide range of responses about life histories, working conditions, life during the Depression, and union activity, 1910's-50's.

991. Skaggs, Julian C. and Ehrlich, Richard L. PROFITS, PATERNALISM, AND REBELLION: A CASE STUDY IN INDUSTRIAL STRIFE. *Working Papers from the Regional Econ. Hist. Res. Center 1978 1(4): 1-30.* Analysis of labor unrest and an 1886 strike at the Lukens Iron Works in Coatesville, Pennsylvania, indicates that management objected not to increased wages and benefits but to the potential for worker independence and the ensuing threat to paternalism and rights of ownership.

992. Skaggs, Julian C. and Ehrlich, Richard L. PROFITS, PATERNALISM, AND REBELLION: A CASE STUDY IN INDUSTRIAL STRIFE. *Business Hist. Rev. 1980 54(2): 155-174.* In the strike against the Lukens Iron Works in Coatesville, Pennsylvania, in 1886, the management's intransigence was due more to a desire to reaffirm a traditional paternalism than to the dollar cost of the workers' demands. The cause of many such confrontations of the period was a conflict over control of the firm; management saw labor's demands as threatening its own legitimate authority. Based on the Lukens Collection in the Eleutherian Mills Library; 6 graphs, 36 notes. C. J. Pusateri

993. Stapleton, Darwin H. THE DIFFUSION OF ANTHRACITE IRON TECHNOLOGY: THE CASE OF LANCASTER COUNTY. *Pennsylvania Hist. 1978 45(2): 147-157.* The technology for the use of anthracite coal in iron production, developed in Wales in 1826, was brought to Pennsylvania's Lehigh Valley in 1840. From there it was carried to other areas, among them Lancaster County, Pennsylvania. Details the design of the Chikiswalungo Furnace, located near Marietta in Lancaster County. 2 illus., 34 notes. D. C. Swift

994. Sternberg, Irma O. MEMPHIS MERCHANT FOR MORE THAN SIXTY YEARS: MY FATHER, "UNCLE" IKE OTTENHEIMER. *West Tennessee Hist. Soc. Papers 1981 35: 122-127.* Orphaned at the age of two, Ike Ottenheimer (1871-1963) grew up in the home of Jacob Goldsmith, who became one of Memphis's leading merchants. Ottenheimer, however, was the catalyst for the phenomenal growth of Goldsmith's, one of the leading department stores in the South. Among his merchandising innovations was a full-page ad in the first section of every edition of *The Commercial Appeal,* buying all the foreign-made merchandise he could when World War I began, conceiving the Goldsmith's Christmas Parade—a decade before Macy's, and insisting on good customer service based on the high quality of the merchandise. Secondary materials; 12 notes. H. M. Parker, Jr.

995.   Stone, Katherine.   THE ORIGINS OF JOB STRUCTURES IN THE STEEL INDUSTRY.   *R. of Radical Pol. Econ. 1974 6(2): 113-173.* Analyzes the transition by which, from the late 19th century, skilled workers lost control of the production process in the American steel industry. Union organization, the labor contract system, and the sliding scale for wages were destroyed: instead emerged an internal labor market in which a mass of semiskilled operatives were divided by wage incentive schemes, promotional hierarchies, and company welfare programs; and in which physical and mental work were artificially separated. Based on primary and secondary sources; 141 notes.   P. R. Shergold

996.   Thomas, Morgan D. and LeHeron, Richard B.   PERSPECTIVES ON TECHNOLOGICAL CHANGE AND THE PROCESS OF DIFFUSION IN THE MANUFACTURING SECTOR.   *Econ. Geography 1975 51(3): 231-251.* Examines the reasons for current establishment and growth patterns of manufacturing industries.   S

997.   Tomash, Erwin and Cohen, Arnold A.   THE BIRTH OF AN ERA: ENGINEERING RESEARCH ASSOCIATES, INC. 1946-1955.   *Ann. of the Hist. of Computing 1979 1(2): 83-97.* An account is presented of the early years of a pioneering computer company, Engineering Research Associates, Inc. (ERA), which was formed in 1946 at St. Paul, Minnesota, with Navy encouragement. This company was merged into Remington Rand Inc. in 1952, as was Eckert-Mauchly Computer Corporation two years earlier. These mergers created the basis for what later became the Univac division of Sperry Rand Corporation, or Sperry Univac. ERA's technological contributions are discussed, along with the company's pre-merger growth and financing problems. There were post-merger problems, primarily of organizational integration, but solid groundwork was being laid for Sperry Rand's eventual success in the data processing industry.
                                                                                    J

998.   Tsygichko, L.   STAL'NOI   GIGANT   [Steel   giant].   *Mirovaia Ekonomika i Mezhdunarodnye Otnosheniia [USSR] 1975 (11): 110-114.* Details the activity, production records, and operations of the Western world's largest steel producer, United States Steel Corporation, in relation to its rivals in other Western nations, 1950's-70's.

999.   Ubinger, John D.   ERNEST TENER WEIR: LAST OF THE GREAT STEELMASTERS.   *Western Pennsylvania Hist. Mag. 1975 58(3): 287-306, (4): 486-507.* Part I. Discusses the transitional role played by Ernest Tener Weir, a steelmaster turned entrepreneur in Pittsburgh's steel industry, 1900-29. Part II. Presents the role of the steel industry in the federal government and foreign affairs, 1930's-50's.   S

1000.   Uselding, Paul and Juba, Bruce.   BIASED TECHNICAL PROGRESS IN AMERICAN MANUFACTURING, 1839-1899.   *Explorations in Econ. Hist. 1973 11(1): 55-72.* Provides estimates of the factor-saving bias in manufacturing. Suggests that over the long run technical progress was labor-saving, though in certain decades it was capital-saving, indicating a cyclically induced response. Based on statistics and secondary sources; 3 figs., 12 notes, appendix.
                                                                          P. J. Coleman

1001. Vasilevski, E. MASHINOSTROENIE SSHA: PROBLEMY I PER-SPEKTIVY [Machine-building USA: Problems and prospects]. *Mirovaia Ekonomika i Mezhdunarodnye Otnosheniia [USSR] 1977 (2): 88-97.* Analyzes metal fabricating and machine-building industries during 1960-73 and concludes that they show low growth and need far more effectiveness.

1002. Vinci, John. CARSON PIRIE SCOTT: 125 YEARS IN BUSINESS. *Chicago Hist. 1979 8(2): 92-97.* The 125-year-old Carson Pirie Scott and Company of Chicago was founded in 1854 by John T. Pirie and Samuel Carson, two Scotsmen who were joined in 1856 by two Scottish brothers, George and Robert Scott; presents photographs of the store's locations in Chicago during 1880's-1904.

1003. Walker, Joseph E. THE END OF COLONIALISM IN THE MIDDLE ATLANTIC IRON INDUSTRY. *Pennsylvania Hist. 1974 41(1): 5-26.* Chronicle of the US iron industry and trade, and of its relationship with Great Britain during 1750-1850. S

1004. Wik, Reynold M. BENJAMIN HOLT AND THE INVENTION OF THE TRACK-TYPE TRACTOR. *Technology and Culture 1979 20(1): 90-107.* Alvin Lombard was the first to build a steam tractor that ran on its own tracks, but it was appropriate only to the lumber industry. Benjamin Holt, responding to the needs of large-scale agriculture in California first (1904-19) manufactured crawler-tractors to meet "wide commercial needs." Holt was the Henry Ford of Caterpillar tractors. Illus., 57 notes. C. O. Smith

1005. Wilder, Patricia S. THE PRODUCTIVITY TREND IN THE SOAPS AND DETERGENTS INDUSTRY. *Monthly Labor Rev. 1980 103(2): 26-30.* Productivity in the soap and detergent industry increased during 1958-77 due to such technological changes as high-speed bar production, but during the 1960's productivity was hindered as detergents were reformulated to meet environmental concerns.

1006. Williams, Mike and Menzer, Mitch. SOUTHERN STEEL. *Southern Exposure 1981 9(3): 74-79.* Discusses the history of the steel industry in Birmingham, Alabama, 1880-1981.

1007. Wise, George. A NEW ROLE FOR PROFESSIONAL SCIENTISTS IN INDUSTRY: INDUSTRIAL RESEARCH AT GENERAL ELECTRIC, 1900-1916. *Technology and Culture 1980 21(3): 408-429.* During the early years of GE's research lab the careers of Willie R. Whitney, William D. Coolidge, and Irving Langmuir showed that the new "industrial scientist was not molded into a worker on the intellectual assembly line, nor was he shielded from the hard facts of business." The role created for professional scientists at GE was instead a "blend of research freedom and practical usefulness" that produced scientific papers as well as innovations such as the tungsten filament. Based on GE archives; 58 notes. C. O. Smith

1008. Woodford, Arthur M. BEFORE THE HORSELESS CARRIAGE: DETROIT'S EARLY INDUSTRIAL AGE. *Chronicle 1979 15(1): 4-13.* Describes the growth of industry in Detroit, Michigan, 1840's-90's, including the manufacture of railway equipment, ships, sawmills, and stoves.

1009.   York, James and Brand, Horst.   PRODUCTIVITY AND TECHNOL-
OGY IN THE ELECTRIC MOTOR INDUSTRY.   *Monthly Labor Rev. 1978
101(8): 20-25.* Discusses the increase in productivity in the electric motor and
generator industry during 1954-76 including productivity trends, employment
trends, technological change, capital expenditures, and the future of the industry.

1010.   York, James D.   FOLDING PAPERBOARD BOX INDUSTRY
SHOWS SLOW RISE IN PRODUCTIVITY.   *Monthly Labor Rev. 1980
103(3): 25-28.* US productivity in the manufacture of folding paperboard boxes
has risen at nearly the same rate as for manufacturing generally in recent years.

1011.   York, James D. and Persigehl, Elmer S.   PRODUCTIVITY TRENDS
IN THE BALL AND ROLLER BEARING INDUSTRY.   *Monthly Labor
Rev. 1981 104(1): 40-43.* Productivity trends in the ball and roller bearing industry from 1958 to 1979 were characterized by rapid growth from 1958 to 1966,
followed by slow growth from 1966 to 1979, and a decline during 1979, focusing
on the market for bearings, employment patterns in the industry, and improved
technology.

1012.   —.   FOREIGN MARKETS FOR IRON AND STEEL, 1893-1913:
AN EXCHANGE OF OPINION ON THE WILLIAMS SCHOOL OF DIPLO-
MATIC HISTORY.   *Pacific Hist. R. 1975 44(2): 233-262.*
Becker, William H.   FOREIGN MARKETS FOR IRON AND STEEL, 1893-
     1913: A NEW PERSPECTIVE ON THE WILLIAMS SCHOOL OF DIP-
     LOMATIC HISTORY,   *pp. 233-248, 255-261.* The iron and steel industry
     did not conform to the Williams' school interpretation during the 1890's.
     The industry sought domestic solutions to its problems during the depression
     and only actively searched for foreign markets after the 1890's. The typical
     domestic solutions were vertical integration and horizontal association.
     These solutions created firms which were able to both cut costs and to raise
     the venture capital which made entry into foreign markets feasible. Based
     on published government documents, Andrew Carnegie Papers, and other
     published primary and secondary sources; table, 54 notes.
Schonberger, Howard.   WILLIAM H. BECKER AND THE NEW LEFT
     REVISIONISTS: A REBUTTAL,   *pp. 249-255, 262.* Statements by steel
     industry spokesmen in the 1890's and after show they believed foreign mar-
     kets were needed to solve the overproduction problem and that increased
     exports during the depression did help recovery. In any case, New Left
     revisionists do not argue economic determinism, but rather that American
     society is pervaded by an ideology which has led to expansion. Primary and
     secondary sources; 20 notes.   W. K. Hobson

1013.   —.   STEEL AND STAGNATION.   *Monthly Rev. 1977 29(6): 1-9.*
Describes the current crisis in the US steel industry, concluding that the economic
problems are inherent in capitalism and not simply a question of reduced demand
and foreign competition.

1014.   —.   [TRAILERS: THE FACTORY, THE BUSINESS, THE OWN-
ERS].   *Southern Exposure 1980 8(1): 14-25.*
Schlesinger, Tom.   TRAILERS: THE FACTORY,   *pp. 14-19.* Describes the
     mass production of trailers by Taylor Homes in North Carolina, and inter-

views factory employees critical of mechanization throughout the Southeast; 1972-79. 2 photos.

—.   TRAILERS: THE BUSINESS,   *pp. 19-23.* The financial profile of the trailer industry constantly shifts. Prices for mobile homes have increased since the general recession of 1974, while production has decreased. 2 charts.

Beaver, Pat and Putzel, Mary Jane.   TRAILERS: THE OWNERS, *pp. 23-25.* Interviews mobile home owners in Watauga County, North Carolina. 2 photos.   H. M. Parker, Jr./S

9

SOCIAL EFFECTS
AND ENVIRONMENTAL IMPACTS

1015. Abbott, Carl. "NECESSARY ADJUNCTS TO ITS GROWTH": THE RAILROAD SUBURBS OF CHICAGO, 1854-1875. *J. of the Illinois State Hist. Soc. 1980 73(2): 117-131.* Discusses the trend toward suburbanization around Chicago from the founding of Evanston in 1854 along the Chicago and Milwaukee Railroad, focusing on the role of railroad expansion and railroad companies' propaganda in the development of close to 100 suburban residential areas by the 1870's. Suburbanization slowed by 1875. Common Chicagoan attitudes toward the suburbs were evident in the period's advertising. Based on booster literature from that era and other forms of advertising; 4 drawings, photo, 3 tables, 53 notes. G. V. Wasson

1016. Adams, David Wallace and Edmonds, Victor. MAKING YOUR MOVE: THE EDUCATIONAL SIGNIFICANCE OF THE AMERICAN BOARD GAME, 1832 TO 1904. *Hist. of Educ. Q. 1977 17(4): 359-383.* The board game, an American mania, has reflected the changes in values that have occurred in American society. Early board games, such as *Mansion of Happiness* (1832), invented by Anne Abbott, a clergyman's daughter, stressed Christian values as the path to happiness. Later games, the forerunners of Parker Brothers' *Monopoly,* emphasized wealth and economic power as life's goal at a time when the growth of industrial capitalism and increasingly secular outlook made money the *summum bonum* in American society. 48 notes. J. C. Billigmeier

1017. Aho, C. M. and Orr, J. A. TRADE-SENSITIVE EMPLOYMENT: WHO ARE THE AFFECTED WORKERS? *Monthly Labor Rev. 1981 104(2): 29-35.* While the one in eight manufacturing jobs now related to exports have created openings for workers with above-average skills, imports have displaced job prospects in industries with less-skilled labor and more women and minorities.

1018. Alanen, Arnold R. DOCUMENTING THE PHYSICAL AND SOCIAL CHARACTERISTICS OF MINING AND RESOURCE-BASED COMMUNITIES. *APT Bull. [Canada] 1979 11(4): 49-68.* Resources used in devising a history of company towns in copper and iron ore mining regions of Minnesota, Michigan, and Wisconsin, 1845-1930, include community plats, maps, photographs, company records, social service workers' records, professional and technical journals, consultants' reports, government publications, newspapers, census records, and city directories.

1019.   Alanen, Arnold R.   THE "LOCATIONS": COMPANY COMMUNI-
TIES ON MINNESOTA'S IRON RANGES.   *Minnesota Hist. 1982 48(3):
94-107.* Residential clusters adjacent to mines, founded by a company when there
was no other townsite nearby or as a way of maintaining social control, were
numerous and were often the dominant form of housing in the Lake Superior
mining region. There were 175 of these founded on the Mesabi Range alone.
There were also squatters locations and model locations as companies moved into
a form of welfare capitalism around the turn of the century. Some towns, founded
by other capitalists as residential and commercial communities, reverted in public
identification to "locations." Based on primary sources, including the William
J. Bell Papers, government studies, and corporate archives; 15 illus., 37 notes.
C. M. Hough

1020.   Alanen, Arnold R.   THE PLANNING OF COMPANY COMMUNI-
TIES IN THE LAKE SUPERIOR MINING REGION.   *J. of the Am. Planning Assoc. 1979 45(3): 256-278.* In Michigan, Wisconsin, and Minnesota
community and social welfare plans did provide housing and services to employees and residents, however, the intent of these company towns was to increase
labor productivity and thus the profits of enterprise. The evolution of the region,
therefore, has been characterized by conflicts between the interests of corporations and those of the community.   J/S

1021.   Ayers, Edward L.   NORTHERN BUSINESS AND THE SHAPE OF
SOUTHERN PROGRESS: THE CASE OF TENNESSEE'S "MODEL CITY."
Tennessee Hist. Q. 1980 39(2): 208-222. Kingsport, Tennessee, was by most
material standards one of the more attractive small towns in the South in the early
part of this century. But the progress had its price. Southern towns such as
Kingsport traded their autonomy for paternalistic development. Their futures
depended upon the needs and desires of companies owned and controlled in the
North. Kingsport became the Model City because those needs and desires were
thoroughly planned and coordinated. Other southern communities became traditional hard-luck company towns because their northern creators did not plan
their domination so thoroughly. Newspapers and secondary studies; 50 notes.
H. M. Parker, Jr.

1022.   Barrera, Mario.   COLONIAL LABOR AND THEORIES OF IN-
EQUALITY: THE CASE OF INTERNATIONAL HARVESTER.   *Rev. of
Radical Pol. Econ. 1976 8(2): 1-19.* At International Harvester Company, 1831-
1976, attitudes toward minorities have been consistently oppressive; treatment of
minorities as subordinates is due to a basic belief in racial inequality fostered by
a colonial concept in race relations.

1023.   Barsky, C. B. and Personick, M. E.   MEASURING WAGE DISPER-
SION: PAY RANGES REFLECT INDUSTRY TRAITS.   *Monthly Labor
Rev. 1981 104(4): 35-41.* Attributes differences in wage dispersions among industries to characteristics such as degree of unionization, geographic location, occupational mix, and methods of wage payment: greatest wage dispersion occurs in
industries with broad occupational staffing or with much incentive pay; high-
paying industries, often heavily unionized, show less variation in earnings and a
penchant for single job rates.

1024.   Belz, Herman.   THE AMERICAN RESPONSE TO INDUSTRI-
ALISM: A CONSERVATIVE INTERPRETATION.   *Rev. in Am. Hist. 1977
5(4): 537-543.* Review article prompted by Morton Keller's *Affairs of State:
Public Life in Late Nineteenth Century America* (Cambridge, Mass.: The Belk-
nap Press of Harvard U. Pr., 1977).

1025.   Bennett, Dianne and Graebner, William.   SAFETY FIRST: SLOGAN
AND SYMBOL OF THE INDUSTRIAL SAFETY MOVEMENT.   *J. of the
Illinois State Hist. Soc. 1975 68(3): 243-256.* The industrial safety movement was
a Progressive Era reform dedicated to efficiency and conservation of men and
equipment, and directed and developed by businessmen. Robert J. Young of
Illinois Steel is credited with having been the first to use "Safety First" as a slogan
to spark a national safety campaign and to create national safety organizations.
The movement placed a special emphasis on safety regulations within the mining,
iron and steel, railroading, and agricultural machinery industries. By the 1930's
the slogan became so overused that it had lost most of its effectiveness.
N. Lederer

1026.   Bernstein, Alan et al.   SILICON VALLEY: PARADISE OR PARA-
DOX?   Mora, Magdalena and DelCastillo, Adelaida R., ed. *Mexican Women in
the United States: Struggles Past and Present* (Los Angeles: U. of California
Chicano Studies Res. Center, 1980): 105-112. Santa Clara County, California, in
the 1970's has developed into one of the most affluent counties in the nation
because of its strong economic base in the electronics industry. High technology
products such as satellites, computer memory disks, light emitting diodes, etc.,
are produced by over 120,000 workers in the 175 major electronics companies
alone. While the products are impressive, the working conditions and wages of
assemblers and technicians, most of whom are women, leave much to be desired.
Often workers are exposed to hazardous chemicals while on the job. Despite these
difficulties very few companies have union organizations. The same conditions
prevail in the Latin American and Asian branches of these companies. Based on
surveys of five electronics plants in Santa Clara County, California; table, 2
charts.   J. Powell

1027.   Bishop, Elva and Fulton, Katherine.   SHOOTING STARS: THE HEY-
DAY OF INDUSTRIAL WOMEN'S BASKETBALL.   *Southern Exposure
1979 7(3): 50-56.* The Hanes Hosiery women's basketball team of Winston-Salem,
North Carolina, dominated women's industrial basketball during the late 1940's
and early 1950's. The women on the team were employed by Hanes; their work
shifts were designed to allow them to participate in the basketball season. The
management of Hanes, led by company president J. N. Weeks, enthusiastically
supported the team as a promotional venture. Such players as Eunies Futch and
Evelyn Jordan were mainstays of a team which enjoyed extraordinary success
against its rivals (owing in no small part to the coaching efforts of Virgil Yow).
The team was disbanded in 1954 because of declining support from management
and employees. Based mainly on interviews.   N. Lederer

1028.   Black, Paul V.   EXPERIMENT IN BUREAUCRATIC CENTRALI-
ZATION: EMPLOYEE BLACKLISTING ON THE BURLINGTON RAIL-
ROAD, 1877-1892.   *Business Hist. Rev. 1977 51(4): 444-459.* On the Chicago,
Burlington & Quincy Railroad the use of a blacklist to screen future employees

was "a significant feature of the institutional experimentation" that developed with the rise of bureaucratic organization. Traces the origins of the blacklist, the types of discharge causes cited, and the reasons for its abolition. The abandonment of blacklisting reflected legislative pressure and the internal and external costs of the use of artitrary power. Based on corporate records; 3 tables, 29 notes.
C. J. Pusateri

1029.   Blake, David H.   LABOR'S MULTINATIONAL OPPORTUNITIES. *Foreign Policy 1973 (12): 132-143.* Points to trends toward a new sense of internationalism in labor movements in response to effects of multinational corporations.   S

1030.   Bloch, Ed.   PCB, UE, AND GE.   *Monthly Rev. 1981 33(5): 17-24.* Discusses how General Electric Company in 1975 was forced to clean up its use of polychlorinated biphenyl at the Fort Edward and Hudson Falls plants in New York, and the role of the United Electrical, Radio, and Machine Workers of America Local 332 in backing up General Electric in order to protect jobs.

1031.   Bolling, Landrum R.   WHAT DOES HIGHER EDUCATION EXPECT OF BUSINESS AND INDUSTRY?   *Liberal Educ. 1974 60(1): 15-26.* Discusses the concerns and expectations of higher education regarding business and industry in the United States in the 1970's.

1032.   Booth, Heather and Max, Steve.   CITIZEN VS. CORPORATION. *Social Policy 1980 11(1): 26-28.* Discusses corporations' efforts in the late 1970's to influence legislation, to shift the burden of America's declining economy to the middle class and the poor, and to eliminate whole areas from government regulation; and studies the response of popular forces to this encroachment.

1033.   Brook, Anthony.   GARY, INDIANA: STEELTOWN EXTRAORDINARY.   *J. of Am. Studies [Great Britain] 1975 9(1): 35-53.* Traces the development of Gary, Indiana during the 25-year period since the United States Steel Corporation chose it as the site for a steel-making complex in 1905. Corporation leaders preferred a "regulated and well-ordered community" at Gary but limited the corporation to minimal involvement in the city's affairs. Effective city planning and orderly development, therefore, were absent. Gary was beset by the same housing, environmental, and ethnic problems that other industrial cities encountered and avoided only the serious racial violence which afflicted other American cities during the 1910's. Secondary sources; 3 maps.   H. T. Lovin

1034.   Chernow, Ron.   GREY FLANNEL GOONS: THE LATEST IN UNION BUSTING.   *Working Papers for a New Soc. 1981 8(1): 18-25.* Professional union-busters, including industrial psychologists, personnel managers, and labor lawyers, beginning in the late 1970's, have used tactics unlike the violence of Pinkerton detectives; focuses on professional antiunionism at IBM, Polaroid, Texas Instruments, McDonald's, Procter & Gamble, Dupont, Delta, and Eastman Kodak, etc.

1035.   Cochran, Thomas Childs.   HISTORY AND CULTURAL CRISIS. *Am. Hist. R. 1973 78(1): 1-10.* History can be a valuable method of analysis for current problems that have long-term antecedents. What is currently regarded as a cultural crisis, involving a breakdown of law, order, and traditional beliefs, is obviously such a problem. Proposes that bureaucratic hierarchies have increased greatly in size and impersonality while the beliefs that justify them have weakened and demands for nonhierarchical equality have grown. While worldwide in its application, the hypothesis is illustrated from the institutions of American business. Business hierarchies large or small are authoritarian and were originally justified in a democratic society by the widely accepted need for developing the nation. Now, more general affluence and pollution of the environment from increased production are ending this major justification. In addition, in the 20th century, new psychological views divorced business success from moral virtue. In no other institution has the conflict between authority and democracy been more severe than in business, but similar difficulties are present in the other major social institutions. Mitigation of this confusion in, or absence of, values must apparently come from some new philosophy or ideology that can win general and deeply felt acceptance.   A

1036.   Colt, Cristine.   SEX DISCRIMINATION: CRISTINE COLT, AD-VERTISING SALESPERSON.   *Civil Liberties Rev. 1978 5(3): 28-37.* Cristine Colt, advertising salesperson for Dow Jones Co., publishers of *Barron's* and the *Wall Street Journal,* describes her 1975-77 protest against her employer's refusal to promote her to a deserved sales management position.

1037.   Comanor, William S.   RACIAL DISCRIMINATION IN AMERI-CAN INDUSTRY.   *Economica [Great Britain] 1973 40(160): 363-378.* Ana-lyzes statistically the pattern of racial discrimination in employment in US metropolitan areas and investigates the relationship between discrimination and industry profit rates.

1038.   Conway, Mimi.   COTTON DUST KILLS, AND IT'S KILLING ME. *Southern Exposure 1978 6(2): 29-39.* Byssinosis, "brown lung disease," is a prevalent problem among long term employees of Southern cotton mills. The mill owners, including Burlington Industries, Inc. which enjoys an excellent reputa-tion in the safety field, have strenuously endeavored to avoid payment of compen-sation for workers' claims of disability caused by byssinosis. The Carolina Brown Lung Association has been organized to forward workers' claims for compensa-tion. Burlington's insurance agent, Liberty Mutual Insurance Co., has by and large to date successfully thwarted payments for byssinosis-caused illnesses through the workmen's compensation system. Liberty Mutual is probably liable to third party suits resulting from possible negligence in serving as safety inspec-tors for the mills. Based on personal interviews.   N. Lederer

1039.   Davidson, Leonard.   SPONSORSHIP IN A MINORITY EMPLOY-MENT PROGRAM.   *Human Organization 1976 35(1): 21-32.* Discusses the influence of social environment on economically disadvantaged minority em-ployees in the 1960's and 70's, emphasizing the benefits of employee sponsorship in corporation training programs.

1040.   Davis, Donald F.   THE CITY REMODELLED: THE LIMITS OF AUTOMOTIVE INDUSTRY LEADERSHIP IN DETROIT, 1910-1929. *Social Hist. [Canada] 1980 13(26): 451-486.* Until recently, many authorities believed that leading business groups and professional men closely allied with them initiated and dominated efforts to organize municipal governments as if they were large, science-based corporations, with the integration and centralization of decisionmaking at the expense of popular control. In Detroit, automobile executives responded to social disorder by becoming interested in municipal reform, around 1910. Their interest waned after 1918. Rejection of an industry-backed subway in a 1929 referendum showed the limited nature of the industry's power. 2 illus., 87 notes.   D. F. Chard

1041. Davis, Harry E.   MULTIEMPLOYER PENSION PLAN PROVI-SIONS IN 1973. *Monthly Labor Rev. 1974 97(10): 10-16.* Multiemployer pension plan coverage in the United States increased sevenfold between 1950 and 1973, primarily due to the development of jointly administered negotiated plans in industries with multiemployer collective bargaining agreements.

1042. Davis, James C.   GROWING UP IN AN IRON TOWN AT THE TURN OF THE CENTURY: A MEMOIR BY JOHN GRIFFEN PEN-NYPACKER. *Pennsylvania Hist. 1977 44(3): 233-248.* Presents an edited portion of the memoirs of John G. Pennypacker, a civil engineer who spent most of his adult life on Wall Street in the investment business. Concludes in 1908, and deals with his childhood and youth in Phoenixville, Pennsylvania, a typical company town. Illus., map, 6 notes.   D. C. Swift

1043. Dawley, Alan.   DEATH AND REBIRTH OF THE AMERICAN MILL TOWN. *Labour [Canada] 1981-82 8-9(Aut-Spr): 137-152.* The problem of power in 19th-century mill towns rests on a conflict between employer absolutism and the democratic rights of the employees. The treatment of power has been inadequate; particularly in works influenced by symbolic anthropology, where the problem is seen to have been resolved in a consensual value system. However, the persistence of conflict in strikes and disorder compels an examination of the mechanisms of domination, as well as legitimacy. To this end, the ideas of Marx and Weber offer more valuable guidance than those of Durkheim.   J

1044. Dittmer, Richard W.   CORPORATE SOCIAL RESPONSIBILITY: AN OVERVIEW. *Crisis 1975 82(6): 215-218.* In response to the transfer of attention from a sense of accomplishment to a sense of shortcoming during the 1960's-70's, corporations have undertaken important social activities. Business leaders have come to grips with pervasive social problems because of society's expectations, the fear of government regulations, and enlightened self-interest. Action has been taken in education, training and employment, civil rights, and equal opportunity. Public opinion has increased the pressure on companies to solve some of the nation's major social problems.   A. G. Belles

1045. Doherty, William T., Jr.   THE INTERACTION OF AMERICAN BUSINESS AND AMERICAN RELIGION IN THE 19TH AND EARLY 20TH CENTURIES: A SAMPLING OF SCHOLARLY AND POPULAR INTERPRETATIONS. *North Dakota Q. 1982 50(1): 91-97.*

1046. Eberle, William D.   WHAT BUSINESS EXPECTS OF HIGHER ED-UCATION. *Liberal Educ. 1974 60(1): 5-14.* Discusses the expectations of the Committee for Economic Development for US higher education, focusing on educational policy, management, and finance, 1971-74.

1047. Ellinghaus, William M. BUSINESS INVOLVEMENT HELPS CITIES WORK. *Natl. Civic Rev. 1981 70(1): 17-21.* Cities solicit the help of business people who are no less obliged and are better equipped by training than most to help. J/S

1048. Epstein, Edwin M. CORPORATIONS AND LABOR UNIONS IN ELECTORAL POLITICS. *Ann. of the Am. Acad. of Pol. and Social Sci. 1976 425: 33-58.* Federal prohibitions of corporate and union contributions have been motivated by two objectives: to reduce or eliminate domination of the electoral process by business and labor through their aggregated wealth; and to protect stockholders and union members from having their organizations' funds used for political purposes of which they do not approve. Federal regulations have been largely ineffective in preventing corporate and union monies from reaching political candidates and parties both legally and illegally. Recent developments, including passage of the Federal Election Campaign Act of 1971 as amended in 1974, important decisions by the Supreme Court since 1972, and rulings by the Federal Election Commission, have widened the area of legal campaign-related activities in which corporations and labor organizations can engage, particularly through political action committees. The liberalization of previous restrictions, together with more rigorous and effective electoral disclosure requirements, and widespread public suspicion concerning the political activities of "special interests" make it likely that business corporations and labor unions will be quite circumspect in their election involvements during 1976. However, several legal and political issues which could affect corporate and union campaign activities in 1976 and beyond remain unresolved. J

1049. Eremenko, V. AGRARNYE OTNOSHENIIA V USLOVIIAKH SOVREMENNOGO KAPITALIZMA [Agrarian relationships in modern capitalism]. *Mirovaia Ekonomika i Mezhdunarodnye Otnosheniia [USSR] 1980 (2): 60-71.* The development of agrarian-industrial complexes in the capitalist world has led to the domination of individual farmers by large-scale industrial-agrarian entrepreneurship, with a consequent intensification of class antagonisms in the rural areas.

1050. Ermann, M. David. THE OPERATIVE GOALS OF CORPORATE PHILANTHROPY: CONTRIBUTIONS TO THE PUBLIC BROADCASTING SERVICE, 1972-1976. *Social Problems 1978 25(5): 504-514.* Reviews corporate contributions to the Public Broadcasting Service (PBS), studying operative goals during 1972-76 to determine what the organizations actually are doing. There is no emphasis on greater social responsibility by corporations, but they contribute in a public relations effort to influence the opinions of their critics. Philanthropy is one way that profit is transformed into social influence, and those corporations in a more hostile or unpredictable environment will be more generous with their money. Primary and secondary sources; 4 tables; 9 notes; refs.
A. M. Osur

1051. Ewing, David W. THE EMPLOYEE'S RIGHT TO SPEAK OUT: THE MANAGEMENT PERSPECTIVE. *Civil Liberties Rev. 1978 5(3): 10-15.* Discusses nine instances from the late 1960's-77 where the reluctance of corporate executives to use dissidents protesting practices or products dangerous to society as a useful resource in decisionmaking, resulted in disaster for their company.

1052. Feder, Donald A. NADERIZING THE GIANT CORPORATION. *Reason 1980 12(4): 24-28.* Analyzes the arguments of the anti-big business movement led by Ralph Nader, finding them simplistic and socialistic.

1053. Ferrar, Terry A. A RATIONALE FOR A CORPORATE AIR POLLUTION ABATEMENT POLICY. *Am. J. of Econ. and Sociol. 1974 33(3): 233-236.* Businessmen may find that pollution drives labor from the region in which the firms operate. These businessmen then have an economic incentive to spend money on pollution control. Secondary sources; 6 notes.   W. L. Marr

1054. Fickett, Laura J. WOODDALE: AN INDUSTRIAL COMMUNITY. *Delaware Hist. 1981 19(4): 229-242.* Describes the history of Wooddale on Red Clay Creek, Delaware, an industrial town that rose and fell with the fortunes of the Delaware Iron Works, the town's principal industry. Alan and James Wood built the company through good community relations and good marketing; they also invested in railroads and ancillary industries to develop the whole region. The life histories of several workers and a description of labor-management relations demonstrates the inclusive, humane character of the company and the Quaker beliefs of the Wood family. 50 notes.   R. M. Miller

1055. Folsom, Burton W. LIKE FATHERS, UNLIKE SONS: THE FALL OF THE BUSINESS ELITE IN SCRANTON, PENNSYLVANIA, 1880-1920. *Pennsylvania Hist. 1980 47(4): 291-309.* This examination of intergenerational mobility in Scranton between 1880 and 1920 focuses on 40 economic leaders who were corporate board members or officers in 1880. Only nine of the 40 had a son, son-in-law, or grandson who was a corporate officer in Scranton 40 years later. Six families had no male heirs; the children of other families moved elsewhere, and some showed no interest in corporate enterprise. A few heirs were dissolute. When national corporations expanded into Scranton, some outsiders received leadership positions. By 1920, a few immigrant families managed to achieve prominence. Based on city directories and other material; 2 photos, 30 notes.
     D. C. Swift

1056. Folsom, Burton W. A REGIONAL ANALYSIS OF URBAN HISTORY: CITY-BUILDING IN THE LACKAWANNA VALLEY DURING EARLY INDUSTRIALIZATION. *Working Papers from the Regional Econ. Hist. Res. Center 1979 2(4): 71-100.* Traces urban development in the anthracite coal-producing Lackawanna Valley in Pennsylvania from 1820 to 1880 as an example of a system of cities for business entrepreneurs, and the growth of industry and transportation to outside markets.

1057. Freitag, Peter J. THE CABINET AND BIG BUSINESS: A STUDY OF INTERLOCKS. *Social Problems 1975 23(2): 137-152.* A study of US Cabinet Secretaries during 1897-1973 supports C. Wright Mills's contention that there is a high degree of interchange of personnel between the elites of corporate and political institutions. In the executive branch elite businessmen are the rule rather than the exception. The exchange of positions of leadership provides a mechanism of communication between government and business, and able administrators in government will have to be businessmen. 6 tables, ref.
     A. M. Osur

1058.   Friedland,   Roger.   CORPORATE   POWER   AND   URBAN
GROWTH: THE CASE OF URBAN RENEWAL.   *Pol. & Soc. 1980 10(2): 203-224.*   Contrary to the accepted impression that urban renewal policies were
a response to urban decline, analysis suggests that they were instead a response
to national corporate interests in growing urban downtown economies. Examination of 100 cases shows that national corporate power played a significant role
in the formation of urban renewal policies, and that corporations thereby obtained subsidized land use changes in downtown areas. Covers 1960-75. 2 tables,
2 fig., 27 notes, appendix.   D. G. Nielson

1059.   Fuller, Justin.   BOOM TOWNS AND BLAST FURNACES: TOWN
PROMOTION IN ALABAMA, 1885-1893.   *Alabama R. 1976 29(1): 37-48.*
Describes the methods and devices typically employed to promote Alabama's
more than 23 boom towns when mining, industry, and rising prices were ascend-
ant. No boom-town experience equalled the growth of Birmingham; however the
steady decline in pig iron prices after 1890 undercut promoters' efforts. Peak
activity was reached during 1888-89. Primary and secondary sources; 23 notes.
                                                                J. F. Vivian

1060.   Gellert, Dan.   WHISTLE BLOWER: DAN GELLERT, AIRLINE
PILOT.   *Civil Liberties Rev. 1978 5(3): 15-19.*   Dan Gellert, a pilot for Eastern
Airlines, describes his 1972-78 struggle with the airline protesting a safety hazard
in their Lockheed 1011 aircraft.

1061.   Gersuny, Carl.   "A DEVIL IN PETTICOATS" AND JUST CAUSE:
PATTERNS OF PUNISHMENT IN TWO NEW ENGLAND TEXTILE
FACTORIES.   *Business Hist. Rev. 1976 50(2): 131-152.*   Compares and contrasts disciplinary methods in two New England textile mills, one in the early 19th
century, and the other in the 1970's. The author finds the similarities are greater
than the differences, and "the tension between the natural proclivities of the
human animal and the constraints of machine technology" are much the same
in any generation. Based on company records; 30 notes.   C. J. Pusateri

1062.   Gersuny, Carl.   INDUSTRIAL CASUALTIES IN LOWELL, 1890-
1905.   *Labor Hist. 1979 20(3): 435-442.*   Documents industrial accidents in
Lowell, Massachusetts. Safety was not a major concern, and workers were held
responsible. Based on Hamilton Co. records, Lowell Manufacturing Co. records,
and the Lowell Hospital Register; 2 tables, 14 notes.   L. L. Athey

1063.   Gersuny, Carl.   NEW ENGLAND MILL CASUALTIES: 1890-1910.
New England Q. 1979 52(4): 467-482.   Factory owners and insurance companies
did everything possible to limit what they had to pay to injured workmen. When
possible, they invoked the common law principles of contributory negligence,
assumption of risk, and the fellow-servant rule to deny obligation. Delaying
tactics were employed until victims settled for minimal amounts, and the judicial
process was undermined by influencing judicial appointments and conspiring
with attorneys behind their clients' backs. Based on Dwight Manufacturing Company, Lyman Mills, and Hamilton Manufacturing Company papers in Baker
Library, Harvard; 45 notes.   J. C. Bradford

1064. Gersuny, Carl. WORK INJURIES AND ADVERSARY PRO-
CESSES IN TWO NEW ENGLAND TEXTILE MILLS. *Business Hist. Rev.
1977 51(3): 326-340.* Describes work injuries in New England mills during 1895-
1916 and "the patterns of imputing contributory negligence." Concludes that
after the no-fault workmen's compensation law went into effect, the number of
injuries changed little but there was a sharp reduction in injuries blamed on
employee carelessness. Negligence charges before the law's enactment were often
economic expediency for the mill owner. Based on company records; 38 notes.
C. J. Pusateri

1065. Gilbert, James B. COLLECTIVISM AND CHARLES STEINMETZ.
Business Hist. R. 1974 48(4): 520-540. Charles Proteus Steinmetz "sketched a
version of socialism that would combine the economic structures and organizational patterns of the modern corporation with the broader social goals of economic democracy." Traces the impact of the corporate form of organization on
the utopian thought of American intellectuals prior to World War I, and shows
the practical outcome as illustrated in the activities of Steinmetz, especially his
relation to the National Association of Corporation Schools. 33 notes.
R. V. Ritter

1066. Gottlieb, Lois C. THE ANTIBUSINESS THEME IN LATE NINE-
TEENTH CENTURY AMERICAN DRAMA. *Q. J. of Speech 1978 64(4):
415-426.* The plays of Bronson Howard (1842-1908) and Augustus Thomas
(1857-1934) are among the few distinctly American dramas of their time. Both
playwrights were antibusiness. Howard, believing the capitalist system inherently
corrupt, concentrated on the deleterious effects of business on the individual.
Thomas, although criticizing the inhumanity of business on a large scale, believed
that the system itself was ultimately redeemable. Focuses on 1870's-90's. Based
on unpublished manuscripts and secondary sources; 30 notes. E. Bailey

1067. Greenwald, Maureen. WOMEN WORKERS AND WORLD WAR I:
THE AMERICAN RAILROAD INDUSTRY, A CASE STUDY. *J. of Social
Hist. 1975 9(2): 154-177.* World War I records of the railroad industry shows
women moved into jobs already identified as women's jobs. During 1917-30 the
number of women workers increased 42%. 55 notes. M. Hough

1068. Greer, Edward. RACISM AND U.S. STEEL, 1906-1974. *Radical
Am. 1976 10(5): 45-66.* Discrimination against Negroes in the Gary works of the
US Steel Corporation was initiated and controlled by the company rather than
as the result of the racist attitudes of white workers. Before the CIO, prejudice
against blacks was engendered by company officials to keep the working force
disunited and to maintain a marginal labor force at inferior pay for the worst jobs
in the plant. This discriminatory policy is still partially in being, owing to depart-
mental seniority regulations and to company control over the hiring of supervi-
sory personnel. Based on primary and secondary sources. N. Lederer

1069. Gyllenhammar, Pehr G. THE IMPACT OF AMERICAN CULTURE
ON MANAGEMENT ORGANIZATION AND THE TRANSPORTATION
INDUSTRY. Davis, Allen F., ed. *For Better or Worse: The American Influence in the World* (Westport, Conn.: Greenwood Pr., 1981): 105-110. Discusses
the influence of American cultural values on modern production technology,

especially the assembly line concept, which spread to the automotive industry in Germany and Sweden in the 1950's along with American ideas of management organization; tells of the European backlash against the dehumanizing aspects of the assembly line; and suggests that in the 1980's the direction of influence could be from Europe to the United States, as the latter begins to undergo a transition in corporate organization and production practices.

1070. Hacker, Sally L. SEX STRATIFICATION, TECHNOLOGY AND ORGANIZATIONAL CHANGE: A LONGITUDINAL CASE STUDY OF AT&T. *Social Problems 1979 26(5): 539-557.* Discusses the impact of technological displacement or job loss to machines, in terms of gender, race, and class during 1972-75 at the American Telephone and Telegraph Company (AT&T), when the federal government ordered that corporation to provide affirmative action plans to increase the number of women and minorities in management positions; although the plans went into effect, the number of women working anywhere in the system declined; and argues that civil rights and feminist groups should become aware of the pitfalls of legal measures to insure equal opportunity.

1071. Hagan, John. THE CORPORATE ADVANTAGE: A STUDY OF THE INVOLVEMENT OF CORPORATE AND INDIVIDUAL VICTIMS IN A CRIMINAL JUSTICE SYSTEM. *Social Forces 1982 60(4): 993-1022.* The legal conceptualization of corporate entities as juristic persons has both obscured and enhanced their influence in the criminal justice process. Consequences of this influence include greater success of corporate than individual actors in getting individual offenders convicted, greater formal equality in the treatment of individuals prosecuted for crimes against corporate than individual victims, and greater satisfaction of corporate than individual victims with their experiences in the criminal justice system. An increase in formal equality may accompany higher rates of conviction for individuals accused of crimes against "juristic persons," and may emphasize the important advantages a formal rational system of criminal law can provide these corporate entities.   J/S

1072. Hareven, Tamara K. FAMILY TIME AND INDUSTRIAL TIME: FAMILY AND WORK IN A PLANNED CORPORATION TOWN 1900-1924. *J. of Urban Hist. 1975 1(3): 365-389.* Cumulative individual employee files 1910-36 of the Amoskeag Manufacturing Company of Manchester, New Hampshire, coupled with marriage and insurance records and oral histories, reveal a pervasive family influence in working. Vacancies were discovered via word-of-mouth, family members substituted for each other, family finances postponed marriages and caused babies to be dropped off so women could return to work. Young children found summer jobs in the mills, and many met their future spouses there. 45 notes.   S. S. Sprague

1073. Harris, Ray K. LIFE IN POTLATCH WAS DIFFERENT. *Record 1976 37: 39-82.* Provides a historical account (ca. 1905-30) of the founding and growth of Potlatch, Idaho, a small company town which based its economy on the lumber industry. Focuses on the community's socioeconomic structure and the role of the Potlatch Lumber Company in its development. Based on MS., interviews, printed sources, and the author's reminiscences; 59 photos.
G. H. Curtis

1074.   Henderson, Alexa B.   FEPC AND THE SOUTHERN RAILWAY CASE: AN INVESTIGATION INTO DISCRIMINATORY PRACTICES DURING WORLD WAR II.   *J. of Negro Hist. 1976 61(2): 173-187.* For the first time, hearings into discrimination by railroad employers, all members of the Southeastern Carriers Conference, were held by the Fair Employment Practice Committee during World War II. Hundreds of black rail workers cooperated with the field investigators in building the FEPC's case against the railroads and all-white unions. However, the resolve of the FEPC was undermined by presidential vacillation. Based on the records of the FEPC; 45 notes.   N. G. Sapper

1075.   Hill, Richard Child.   TRANSNATIONAL CAPITALISM AND THE CRISIS OF INDUSTRIAL CITIES.   *J. of Intergroup Relations 1982 10(3): 30-41.* The decline of large Western cities is due to corporate flight—first to the suburban fringe and then to outlying areas and abroad—and to the internationalization of production.

1076.   Hoffmann, Carl and Reed, John Shelton.   SEX DISCRIMINATION? THE XYZ AFFAIR.   *Public Interest 1981 (62): 21-39.* Reviews theories held by proponents of affirmative action to support their efforts. The law should promote equality of opportunity and freedom from discrimination rather than attempt to mandate equality of result. Analyzes how an unnamed company, the XYZ Corporation, attempted to defend itself against charges it discriminated against female employees in promotions. A study conducted by the authors among XYZ employees showed more men than women asked to be promoted. Women held lower career aspirations than did males and were less likely than males to be willing to assume greater responsibilities, to "give up more." Marriage seemed to increase the likelihood of promotion-seeking behavior among men and decrease it among women employees. Parenthood had the same differential effect between the sexes. The relatively low proportion of women promoted at the XYZ Corporation did not result from discrimination but from behaviors and attitudes which precluded self-selection for promotions. Primary sources; 8 tables.
J. M. Herrick

1077.   Holland, Susan S.   EXCHANGE OF PEOPLE AMONG INTERNATIONAL COMPANIES: PROBLEMS AND BENEFITS.   *Ann. of the Am. Acad. of Pol. and Social Sci. 1976 (424): 52-66.* Discusses how the exchange of people throughout the world since 1948 by international companies has led to improved understanding and forging links of friendship and cooperation, or, conversely, to increased suspicion, resentment, and distrust. Adequate training has not been provided to personnel involved in exchanges. Other factors affecting the outcome of such exchanges include the willingness of the people involved to integrate into and become active members of the host community and the companies' policies concerning the hiring, training, compensation, and promotion of the host country nationals on the same basis as parent company managers. Benefits resulting from these exchanges include training of host country employees and transfer to them of productive management, marketing, and financial knowledge, creation of new jobs, and increased productive capabilities of the host countries.
J/S

1078.   Howard, Robert.   SECOND CLASS IN SILICON VALLEY.   *Working Papers Mag. 1981 8(5): 20-31.* Describes the "holistic" workplace concept of the electronics industry in Santa Clara County called Silicon Valley, and what it has provided for the engineers and computer scientists who are 25% of the workforce, and then compares those conditions with those of unskilled production workers.

1079.   Huddleston, Eugene L.   "THE GENERALS UP IN WALL STREET": RAY STANNARD BAKER AND THE RAILROADS.   *Railroad Hist. 1981 (145): 68-86.* Reexamines the reputation as a leading muckraker of Ray Stannard Baker (1870-1946) who wrote six articles on the "runaway corporate power" of the railroads for *McClure's* in 1905-06; Baker oversimplified issues, hardly addressed technical data on "railroad rates, operation, and regulation," and was not as great as Progressives then and since have thought.

1080.   Huerta, Faye C. and Lane, Thomas A.   PARTICIPATION OF WOMEN IN CENTERS OF POWER.   *Social Sci. J. 1981 18(2): 71-86.* Examines the degree of participation of women at the institutional level of the power structure vis-à-vis occupational and board positions, 1958-78.

1081.   Kalba, Kas.   POSTINDUSTRIAL PLANNING: A REVIEW FORWARD.   *J. of the Am. Inst. of Planners 1974 40(3): 147-155.* Reviews Daniel Bell's *The Coming of Post-Industrial Society* (New York: Basic Books, 1973).
                                                                              S

1082.   Kruse, John A.; Kleinfeld, Judith; and Travis, Robert.   ENERGY DEVELOPMENT ON ALASKA'S NORTH SLOPE: EFFECTS ON THE INUPIAT POPULATION.   *Human Organization 1982 41(2): 97-106.* Examines the positive effects of oil development at Prudhoe Bay on the Inupiat population of Alaska's North Slope during the 1970's, discusses its impact on employment and income, and describes the continuing importance of traditional subsistence activities among the Inupiat.

1083.   Larson, Calvin J.   PUBLIC SERVICE FOR PROFIT: THE CORPORATE RESPONSE TO THE URBAN CRISIS.   *Int. J. of Contemporary Sociol. 1978 15(3-4): 354-374.* Considers how successful the National Alliance of Businessmen and other business-sponsored ventures have been in alleviating urban poverty and unemployment among intercity minorities in the United States.

1084.   Laurie, Bruce; Hershberg, Theodore; and Alter, George.   IMMIGRANTS AND INDUSTRY: THE PHILADELPHIA EXPERIENCE, 1850-1880.   *J. of Social Hist. 1975 9(2): 219-248.* Attempts to provide more secure categories of occupational status for 19th-century activities beyond the ahistorical reach of sociological studies in this century. Examines 14 manufacturing industries in Philadelphia, 1850-80, and attempts to explain changes in the job status, and how the changes affected the distribution to different ethnic groups. Little change is seen in the ethnic distribution because of disadvantages different groups brought with them, and because industrialization did not necessarily equal mechanization. 11 tables, 5 figs., 30 notes.   M. Hough

1085. Leary, T. E. INDUSTRIAL ARCHEOLOGY AND INDUSTRIAL ECOLOGY. *Radical Hist. Rev. 1979 (21): 171-182.* Industrial archaeology yields much information about daily life, working conditions, and social conflicts along with material about technology, business, and engineering; 1799-1979.

1086. Lo, Clarence Y. H. THEORIES OF THE STATE AND BUSINESS OPPOSITION TO INCREASED MILITARY SPENDING. *Social Problems 1982 29(4): 424-438.* Examines several theories of the state, with a focus on the business community's opposition to governmental policy, particularly the opposition of US businessmen to increased military spending during 1948-53, which ultimately resulted in reduced military spending.

1087. Loustau, Nicolie Roscoe. CORPORATE PHILANTHROPY AND ART MUSEUMS. *Curator 1977 20(3): 215-226.* Discusses corporate support of the arts, especially art museums, 1965-77.

1088. Lynd, Robert S. DONE IN OIL. *J. of the Hist. of Sociol. 1979-80 2(1): 23-40.* First-person narrative of unsatisfactory living and working conditions in Elk Basin, a Rockefeller oil town in northern Wyoming, 1921.

1089. Mabry, Michael. THE IMPACT OF OIL IN WOOD COUNTY. *Northwest Ohio Q. 1978 50(2): 56-63.* Chronicles the discovery of oil in Wood County, Ohio, and the effect it had on areal social change and economic development, 1883-1917.

1090. Marchetti, Peter E. RUNAWAYS AND TAKEOVERS: THEIR EFFECT ON MILWAUKEE'S ECONOMY. *Urbanism Past & Present 1980 5(2): 1-11.* Denies Milwaukee's industrial character—that of family-run, medium-sized businesses, whose entrepreneurs preserve the good life. Rather, Milwaukee's, and many other northern cities', economy has been eroded by the runaway shop and the out-of-state takeover; that is, corporations that move south and takeovers by multinational corporations. The new economy is due to efficiency becoming more important than size, and small firms being unable to finance a large growth rate. Losing local control erodes a city's economy, services, and community involvement. Strategies to counter runaways and takeovers must be on a national level and involve alliances between trade unions and small entrepreneurs in northern cities. Based on statements before and testimonies to the Senate Select Committee on Small Business; 2 tables, biblio.
B. P. Anderson

1091. Matthews, Linda M. KEEPING DOWN JIM CROW: THE RAILROADS AND THE SEPARATE COACH BILLS IN SOUTH CAROLINA. *South Atlantic Q. 1974 73(1): 117-129.* Segregation existed in the South before, during, and after Reconstruction, though legally strict racial segregation began with the first Jim Crow railroad car bill in 1898 (passed after a decade of attempted legislation). There arose a dread that the younger generation of Negroes might not know their place. There also arose a feeling of insecurity among lower-class whites that Negroes were obtaining equality with them in the labor force and the factories, thus forcing them out of jobs. The long opposition to the bill had come largely from businessmen and pro-railroad men; these economic considerations were forced into the background by the fear of competition with blacks. 34 notes.
E. P. Stickney

1092. Matz, Deborah. CENTRAL CITY BUSINESS. *Society 1981 18(4): 51-54.* Uses the results of a survey taken of central city business in a select number of US cities to show that the private sector is vital both in providing employment opportunities and generating the tax revenues necessary to provide local public services.

1093. McClymer, John F. THE PITTSBURGH SURVEY, 1907-1914: FORGING AN IDEOLOGY IN THE STEEL DISTRICT. *Pennsylvania Hist. 1974 41(2): 169-186.* The *Pittsburgh Survey*, first published in 1909 in three issues of *Charities and the Commons*, was undertaken in 1907 by professors, social workers, charitable societies, and ethnic associations. It reflects the essentially moderate attitudes of a new class of social engineers who thought it possible to accurately measure the social effects of industrialization and to suggest viable remedies. Surveys of other industrial cities were modelled on this effort. Illus., 52 notes. D. C. Swift

1094. McCormick, Richard L. THE DISCOVERY THAT BUSINESS CORRUPTS POLITICS: A REAPPRAISAL OF THE ORIGINS OF PROGRESSIVISM. *Am. Hist. Rev. 1981 86(2): 247-274.* Early in the 20th century, the United States experienced a decisive and rapid political transformation affecting both the patterns of political participation and the nature and tasks of government. Interest groups took over many of the functions parties had once performed, and governmental regulation and administration became increasingly important. These and related political changes have often been associated with Progressivism, a reform movement that swept the country after 1900. Yet recent interpretations of Progressivism have tended to ignore the actual political circumstances from which reform emerged. This article argues that a key element of those circumstances was a series of developments reawakening and refashioning the historic US fear that business interests were corrupting politics and government. That discovery catalyzed the rapid political changes of the early 20th century. During 1905 and 1906 numerous states and cities experienced wrenching moments as citizens became aware of systematic politico-business alliances; and in the aftermath laws were passed curtailing the most common forms of business influence on politics—laws that helped create the modern bureaucratic state. Based on numerous contemporary documents and secondary literature; table, 60 notes. A

1095. McGouldrick, Paul F. and Tannen, Michael B. DID AMERICAN MANUFACTURERS DISCRIMINATE AGAINST IMMIGRANTS BEFORE 1914? *J. of Econ. Hist. 1977 37(3): 723-746.* Fits wage functions to two distinct data sources: US Immigration Commission surveys of 1908-10, supplemented by the 1909 Census of Manufactures, and a Department of Labor survey of production costs in nine protected industries, directed by the US Commissioner of Labor, Carroll D. Wright. Regression analysis applied to both sets of data concludes that there was moderate discrimination against southern and eastern European immigrants. Based on census data, Department of Labor statistics, and secondary sources; 3 tables, 34 notes. D. J. Trickey

1096. Ment, David. CORPORATIONS, UNIONS, AND BLACKS: THE STRUGGLE FOR POWER IN AMERICAN INDUSTRIAL CITIES. *J. of Urban Hist. 1981 7(2): 247-254.* This review essay examines three books

dealing with the three-sided struggle between unions, blacks, and corporations in large 20th-century cities: Linda Ann Ewen's *Corporate Power and Urban Crisis in Detroit,* Edward Greer's *Big Steel,* and August Meier and Elliott Rudwick's *Black Detroit and the Rise of the UAW.* One important question considered by each group is why the problems faced by the working class in general and black workers in particular did not lead to more militant action or even revolt. Note.
T. W. Smith

1097. Miller, Arthur S. THE MULTINATIONAL CORPORATION AND THE NATION-STATE. *J. of World Trade Law [Switzerland] 1973 7(3): 267-292.* "This article contributes to the current debate on the legal and political impact of the multinational corporation on the existing constitutional order in the United States. From his analysis, the author concludes that federalism in the United States will become moribund, Congress and the courts will suffer a marked decline in importance, and more power will flow to the executive branch." J

1098. Mills, Nicolaus. BROWN-LUNG COTTON-MILL BLUES. *Dissent 1978 25(1): 8-11.* Discusses the suppression of information on brown-lung, the occupational disease of cotton-mill workers, throughout the history of the American textile industry, and the progress in the late 1970's by the Carolina Brown Lung Association to eradicate the disease and bring the industry under control.

1099. Moberg, David. DETROIT: I DO MIND MOVING. *J. of Intergroup Relations 1981 9(1): 24-36* Discusses the impact of a General Motors Corp. decision to build a new assembly plant on the displaced residents of the neighborhood selected; assesses employment opportunities, taxes, housing and other labor concerns and examines the validity of the location choice in terms of public versus corporate interest.

1100. Mochizuki, Kiyohito. KUKAN SANGYŌ RON: NIJISSEIKISHO NO AMERIKA IFUKU KŌGYŌ [Sweatshops: the garment industry in early 20th-century America]. *Matsuyama Shōdai Ronshū [Japan] 1969 20(4): 29-48.* Covers working conditions and women and child labor.

1101. Munn, Robert F. THE DEVELOPMENT OF MODEL TOWNS IN THE BITUMINOUS COAL FIELDS. *West Virginia Hist. 1979 40(3): 243-253.* After 1880 coal companies began improving facilities in company towns; after 1900 some even built model towns located in Ohio, Kentucky, Pennsylvania, and mainly West Virginia. These emphasized recreation facilities, organized activities, better housing, and the elimination of saloons. Companies spent money on model towns to increase productivity, reduce labor turnover, forestall unionization, and improve their public relations. When prices fell after 1920 such welfare programs were cut. Based on government documents, mine journals, and other primary sources; 7 photos, 27 notes. J. H. Broussard

1102. Nadel, Mark V. BUSINESS AND POLITICS: THE POPULAR LITERATURE. *Am. Pol. Q. 1973 1(4): 529-537.* Reviews recent writings about the relationship between business and politics, corporate power and shortcomings in the profit system, 1970-73.

1103. Nash, Gerald D. GROSS NATIONAL PRODUCT OR PRODUCT OF NATIONAL GROSSNESS. *Rev. in Am. Hist. 1976 4(2): 237-243.* Review article prompted by Louis Galambos and Barbara Barrow Snow's *The Public Image of Big Business in America, 1880-1940: A Quantitative Study in Social Change* (Baltimore, Maryland: Johns Hopkins U. Pr., 1975); discusses the author's historiography based on an organizational approach to economic history.

1104. Northrup, Herbert R.; Wilson, James T.; and Rose, Karen M. THE TWELVE-HOUR SHIFT IN THE PETROLEUM AND CHEMICAL IN-DUSTRIES. *Industrial and Labor Relations Rev. 1979 32(3): 312-336.* This article reports the results of a 1977 field survey of managers in fifty plants in the United States and Canada that have recently instituted twelve-hour shifts in continuous operation situations in the chemical and petroleum industries. The authors reports that in all the plants studied the shift change has significantly improved morale without impairing efficiency, job safety, or workers' health. The drawbacks of this work schedule include the difficulty that some older workers have in adjusting to it; the possibility that it might not be feasible in industries in which the work is more arduous; and the general opposition of unions—which were present in only three of the fifty plants—to any lengthening of the workday.
J

1105. Parfit, Michael. A GATHERING STORM OVER SYNFUELS ON THE BIG SKY RANGE. *Smithsonian 1980 10(12): 70-79.* A report on the rise of opposition to a coal liquefaction plant slated to be constructed in McCone County, Montana, a sparsely settled farm community. Although the residents are philosophically a mixed bag, they have united remarkably well to oppose the plant. They are people who thrive on isolation, who argue that the government undervalues agriculture. Not influential in their own right, they have given the fuel company cause to pause, and their impetus has been picked up by neighboring coal-rich counties. 11 photos.
V. L. Human

1106. Parker, Russell D. ALCOA, TENNESSEE: THE EARLY YEARS, 1919-1939. *East Tennessee Hist. Soc. Publ. 1976 48: 84-103.* During its first 20 years, Alcoa, Tennessee, was a typical company town relatively free of social tensions with few efforts at unionization run by paternalistic officials, Victor J. Hultquist and Arthur B. Smith, who retired before the economic boom and altered the community situation brought about by World War II. Based on the Alcoa Company archives and oral interviews; 108 notes.
D. A. Yanchisin

1107. Parrish, John B. BUSINESS AND ACADEMIA: A NEW ERA? *J. of Social and Pol. Studies 1978 3(1): 75-84.* Changes since the late 1960's in business and academia (which have been alienated since 1933) include loss of faith in Keynesian economics, inflation, distrust of Big Government, and the emergence of a new wave of conservative intellectuals, which may indicate a future positive relationship between the two spheres.

1108. Peake, Charles F. RACIAL POLICIES OF AMERICAN INDUS-TRY. *New Scholar 1978 5(2): 351-364.* Review article prompted by William E. Fulmer's *The Negro in the Furniture Industry* (Philadelphia: U. of Pennsylvania Pr., 1973), Lester Rubin, *The Negro in the Longshore Industry* (Philadelphia: U. of Pennsylvania Pr., 1973), and Elaine Gale Wrong *The Negro in the Apparel*

Industry (Philadelphia: U. of Pennsylvania Pr., 1973). These are three additions to 30 volumes published in the Racial Policies of American Industry Series by the University of Pennsylvania Press. The result is a brief and clear picture of the series' achievement. Good statistical analysis illustrates the traditional discriminatory employment but it also shows the potential for reform that the 1960's promised if the economy continues in a pattern of growth. 34 notes.

D. K. Pickens

1109. Piott, Steven L.   MISSOURI AND THE BEEF TRUST: CONSUMER ACTION AND INVESTIGATION.   *Missouri Hist. Rev. 1981 76(1): 31-52.* Real wages rose slightly during 1891-97 and accelerated a little during 1898-1902, but they did not keep pace with the cost of living. Since prices did not decline even though large cattle supplies existed, the butchers and the public blamed the beef trust. Popular outcry in Missouri increased in 1902, convinced that after taking over the egg business in 1901, the trust hoped to corner all food products. As the legislature launched an investigation, the attorney general asked the state supreme court to compel the trust to pay fines or be ousted from Missouri. Consumers began a meat boycott, and the trust relaxed its grip for a time. Based on newspapers; illus., 53 notes.   W. F. Zornow

1110. Posadas, Barbara M.   THE HIERARCHY OF COLOR AND PSYCHOLOGICAL ADJUSTMENT IN AN INDUSTRIAL ENVIRONMENT: FILIPINOS, THE PULLMAN COMPANY, AND THE BROTHERHOOD OF SLEEPING CAR PORTERS.   *Labor Hist. 1982 23(3): 349-373.* The Pullman Company began hiring Filipino dining car attendants in 1925 to frighten black porters from supporting the recently organized Brotherhood of Sleeping Car Porters. Pullman established a "hierarchy of color" by paying its dining car attendants more than its porters. The brotherhood maintained a policy of welcoming Filipinos into the union; in 1933, however, the brotherhood supported proposed legislation to prohibit the employment of aliens in railroad service positions. Filipino dining car attendants supported the brotherhood in percentages equal to black porters, but did so for economic self-interest and not social assimilation. Based on interviews with Filipinos formerly employed by the Pullman Company, the papers of the Brotherhood of Sleeping Car Porters (Chicago and New York Divisions), and Pullman Company records; 74 notes.

L. F. Velicer

1111. Powell, H. Benjamin.   ESTABLISHING THE ANTHRACITE BOOMTOWN OF MAUCH CHUNK, 1814-1825.   *Pennsylvania Hist. 1974 3(41): 249-262.* Discusses 10 manuscripts and two newspaper articles related to the establishment of Mauch Chunk, an early Pennsylvania coal boomtown. The materials were drawn from the Jacob Cist collections at the Wyoming Historical and Geological Society (W.H.G.S.), the Academy of Natural Science of Philadelphia (A.N.S.P.), the Isaac A. Chapman Collection at the W.H.G.S., and the Charles Fisher Wells Collection at the A.N.S.P.; illus., 26 notes.

D. C. Swift

1112. Pratt, Joseph A.   GROWTH OR A CLEAN ENVIRONMENT? RESPONSES TO PETROLEUM-RELATED POLLUTION IN THE GULF COAST REFINING REGION.   *Business Hist. Rev. 1978 52(1): 1-29.* Traces the environmental impact of the growth of petroleum refining along the Gulf

Coast of Texas from the early 1900's-60's. Petroleum-related pollution was substantial throughout the period. Prior to World War I, no serious attempts were made to control pollution. Later the companies themselves and the American Petroleum Institute implemented unsuccessful voluntary efforts that were followed after 1940 by governmental action. Based on governmental and industry records and publications; 51 notes.   C. J. Pusateri

1113. Preston, Lee E. CORPORATION AND SOCIETY: THE SEARCH FOR A PARADIGM. *J. of Econ. Lit. 1975 13(2): 434-453.* Surveys literature on the relationship between corporations and society.   S

1114. Rae, John B. COLEMAN DU PONT AND HIS ROAD. *Delaware Hist. 1975 16(3): 171-183.* Thomas Coleman Du Pont (1863-1930) early recognized the need for new highway technology to handle the increasing automobile traffic. Du Pont proposed the establishment of a unified highway building program, and in 1911 convinced the Delaware assembly to incorporate a private company, the Coleman Du Pont Road, Inc., more commonly known as the Boulevard Corporation. The company would build a road connecting the state from north to south, acquiring a 200 foot right of way which would include a divided highway for automobiles, trolley tracks, roadways for horsedrawn vehicles, and separate roadways for heavy motor traffic. Political opposition and litigation over the company's right to condemn land retarded the roadbuilding progress, and by 1916 Du Pont, as a member of the newly created state highway department, turned over the company to the state which abandoned the multiple roadway system in favor of the conventional two-lane concrete highway. The highway was later incorporated into the national primary road network as segments of US Routes 13 and 113. 33 notes.   R. M. Miller

1115. Robbins, Albert and Krieger, Lois. RETALIATORY FIRING UNDER OSHA: ROBERT ELLIOT, PILE DRIVER. *Civil Liberties Rev. 1978 5(3): 37-41.* Robert Elliot, pile driver foreman for the P & Z Company in California, was fired in 1975 because of his complaint to the Metro Insurance Administration about unsafe working conditions, resulting in a successful Occupational Safety and Health Administration suit against the company.

1116. Robinson, Randall. GULF OIL'S STRATEGY TO APPEASE AND OPPRESS. *Black Scholar 1973/74 5(4): 51-55.* The Gulf Oil Company's public relations campaign to appease the black community conceals its oppressive policies in African countries such as Angola.   S

1117. Rotella, Elyce J. THE TRANSFORMATION OF THE AMERICAN OFFICE: CHANGES IN EMPLOYMENT AND TECHNOLOGY. *J. of Econ. Hist. 1981 41(1): 51-57.* Between 1870 and 1930 production methods in American offices changed substantially as mechanical devices were introduced and work was subdivided and routinized. A close correspondence is found between the timing of changes in the sex composition of clerical employment and the adoption of new techniques. The new technology led to increased hiring of female clerical workers by reducing the firm-specific skill requirements for clerical jobs.   J

1118. Roth, Leland M. THREE INDUSTRIAL TOWNS BY MCKIM, MEADE & WHITE. *J. of the Soc. of Architectural Hist. 1979 38(4): 317-347.* Assesses contributions to city planning by the architectural firm of McKim, Meade & White in the model company towns of Echota at Niagara Falls (New York), Roanoke Rapids (North Carolina), and Naugatuck (Connecticut). Attention is paid to total land usage with concern not only for dwellings, but also for such buildings as churches and libraries. Discusses anticapitalist bias against industrialists. Concludes that many industrialists believed "that it was both prudent and just to return to the people of the community a significant part of the wealth they had helped generate." Covers 1880's-1910's. 33 fig., 119 notes.

R. J. Jirran

1119. Rothstein, Morton. FRANK NORRIS AND POPULAR PERCEPTIONS OF THE MARKET. *Agric. Hist. 1982 56(1): 50-66.* Norris's unfinished trilogy, *The Epic of Wheat,* was among the first works to deal with the social consequences of economic change. Though not a muckraker, his attacks on railroad monopolies in *The Octopus* and futures trading in *The Pit* were embraced by reformers. Much of Norris's indictment was overdrawn. He exaggerated the problems caused by high railroad rates and land-grant policies and the extent to which speculators manipulated the futures market for their personal gain while other parts of the world were starving. Yet the picture he drew of farmers struggling with an increasingly impersonal economy and an ever more organized and expensive marketing and distribution system still applies today. 37 notes.

D. E. Bowers

1120. Sande, Theodore A.; Candee, Richard M.; DeLony, Eric N.; Eaton, Leonard K.; and Hildebrand, Grant. AMERICAN INDUSTRIAL ARCHITECTURE FROM THE LATE EIGHTEENTH TO THE MID-TWENTIETH CENTURY. *J. of the Soc. of Architectural Hist. 1976 35(4): 265-271.* Discuss the characteristics of industrial buildings which reflect the preoccupation with "commodity" and "firmness." This is evident in the American textile factory where the influence of technology, economy, and culture contributed to the architectural style and created two types of industrial towns, the mill village and the single-company town. Linking these towns together were the railroads whose trussed roof shed typified the spirit and confidence of 19th-century technology. Also discusses the work of Oscar A. Eckerman, architect to the John Deere Co. in the 19th century, and Albert Kahn. 5 illus.

M. Zolota

1121. Saxenian, AnnaLee. OUTGROWING THE VALLEY. *Working Papers Mag. 1981 8(5): 24-27.* Discusses the environmental, economic, and social problems that resulted from the concentration of highly trained professionals and poorly educated minority workers in the Silicon Valley electronics industry of Santa Clara County, California, during the 1950's-70's.

1122. Schleppi, John R. "IT PAYS": JOHN H. PATTERSON AND INDUSTRIAL RECREATION AT THE NATIONAL CASH REGISTER COMPANY. *J. of Sport Hist. 1979 6(3): 20-28.* During the industrial decline of the 1890's, John H. Patterson came to realize that skilled workers were needed to build cash registers, and he initiated programs affecting the welfare of his workers. He built a factory that was lighted and that could be easily ventilated in summer; it became a model for future factories. He brought John C. Olmsted to his National Cash Register Company in Dayton, Ohio, to landscape the grounds. Physical fitness and health programs became part of the workers' lives. In 1897, an athletic club and a bicycle club were formed. In 1905, a company baseball team was formed. Patterson's work improved working and living conditions in Dayton. Based on company publications; 24 notes.   M. Kaufman

1123. Schochet, Gordon J. SOCIAL RESPONSIBILITY, PROFITS, AND THE PUBLIC INTEREST. *Society 1979 16(3): 20-26.* Discusses the responsibilities of the business and technology communities in the United States in light of changing American values, attitudes, and demands since the 1950's.

1124. Schultze, Quentin J. "AN HONORABLE PLACE": THE QUEST FOR PROFESSIONAL ADVERTISING EDUCATION, 1900-1917. *Business Hist. Rev. 1982 56(1): 16-32.* The movement to establish advertising instruction as a part of the business education curricula at the college level was pushed by a variety of occupational groups. They saw such an objective as a means of generally elevating the status and prestige of the advertising field. The business groups endorsing the goal, however, never appreciated the difficulties involved in working with independent higher education institutions and never firmly committed themselves to hiring the products of the education they were advocating. Based principally on business periodicals of the era; 2 illus., 53 notes.
C. J. Pusateri

1125. Schwartz, Charles. THE CORPORATE CONNECTION. *Bull. of the Atomic Scientists 1975 31(8): 15-19.* After researching the corporate connections of academics on the President's Science Advisory Committee, the author found that over two-thirds of academic scientists on this prestigious committee were either on the board of directors of large (over $100 million) or medium-large ($10 to $100 million) corporations or were consultants of large corporations. A similar situation exists regarding the National Science Board. Concludes that capitalist interests own society. Based primarily on Dun & Bradstreet's *Million Dollar Directory*; table, 12 notes.   D. J. Trickey

1126. Seiler, Lauren H. and Summers, Gene F. CORPORATE INVOLVEMENT IN COMMUNITY AFFAIRS. *Sociol. Q. 1979 20(3): 375-386.* An extensive monitoring of the Jones and Laughlin (J&L) steel mill in Hennepin, Illinois suggests that absentee-owned corporations have the ability to involve themselves in local community affairs while maintaining an illusion of non-involvement. Three techniques J&L employed to exert influence are described: unilateral actions, cooptation, and intervention. The failure of reputational leadership data to identify corporate influentials is used to suggest both the success J&L had in concealing corporate influence and the inadequacy of the reputational technique for fully identifying power structures in verticalized communities.
J

1127. Servos, John W. THE INDUSTRIAL RELATIONS OF SCIENCE: CHEMICAL ENGINEERING AT MIT, 1900-1939. *Isis 1980 71(259): 531-549.* Should chemical research at the Massachusetts Institute of Technology (MIT) emphasize "pure" science or its industrial applications? The answer depended on the policy of the leader. Until 1919 the emphasis was on fundamental research; during the 1920's industrial contracts and applied science were dominant; and after 1930 the institute stressed "the increase in fundamental knowledge." In *America by Design* (1977), David Noble used the example of MIT to show that since World War I academic science has been dominated by corporate interests, but did not recognize that this industrial influence was sharply reduced after 1930. Based on MIT archives and related secondary sources; 3 tables, 70 notes. M. M. Vance

1128. Siddall, William R. NO NOOK SECURE: TRANSPORTATION AND ENVIRONMENTAL QUALITY. *Comparative Studies in Soc. and Hist. [Great Britain] 1974 16(1): 2-23.* Discusses the problems created for the environment by modern transportation in the United States and Great Britain from the 19th century to 1974.

1129. Slavin, Stephen L. BIAS IN US BIG BUSINESS RECRUITMENT. *Patterns of Prejudice [Great Britain] 1976 10(5): 22-26.* Examines the low incidence of Jews holding high-paying positions as executives in banks, insurance companies, and public utilities, 1972-74.

1130. Stewart, Peter C. THE SHINGLE AND LUMBER INDUSTRIES IN THE GREAT DISMAL. *J. of Forest Hist. 1981 25(2): 98-107.* The Great Dismal Swamp, an ecologically unique swampland on the Virginia-North Carolina border near the Atlantic coast, has a long history of forest exploitation. Since colonial times, entrepreneurs have devised means to extract the timber and convert it to shingles, lumber, and other products at mills located on the swamp's periphery. The principal operations are described. Despite generations of use—including construction of canals and conversion to agricultural land—many of the swamp's natural qualities remained intact. Recent awareness of the swamp's ecological importance led the Union Camp Corporation and other timber companies to donate large tracts to the Nature Conservancy, which in turn passed them to the federal government for creation of a national wildlife refuge. 4 illus., map, 54 notes. R. J. Fahl

1131. Szafran, Robert F. WHAT KINDS OF FIRMS HIRE AND PROMOTE WOMEN AND BLACKS? A REVIEW OF THE LITERATURE. *Sociol. Q. 1982 23(2): 171-190.* Covers 1967-80.

1132. Tarr, Joel A. CHANGING FUEL USE BEHAVIOR AND ENERGY TRANSITIONS: THE PITTSBURGH SMOKE CONTROL MOVEMENT, 1940-1950: A CASE STUDY IN HISTORICAL ANALOGY. *J. of Social Hist. 1981 14(4): 561-588.* In the 1940's Pittsburgh, Pennsylvania, succeeded in eliminating dense smoke by generating a new policy that required domestic consumers as well as industries and transportation companies to change their fuel type and/or combustion equipment. The case of Pittsburgh offers an example of energy transition accelerated by environmental policy based on control of fuel use and combustion equipment. An analysis of this case contains insights on organizational and individual roles in policy development and implementation; means of individual behavior modification; and the quality and diffusion of information regarding fuel supply, technological capabilities, and policy impacts on consumers. These are important areas to consider in the current transition from oil and natural gas to other fuels. 3 fig., 77 notes, appendix. J. Powell

1133. Tarr, Joel A. and DiPasquale, Denise. THE MILL TOWN IN THE INDUSTRIAL CITY: PITTSBURGH'S HAZELWOOD. *Urbanism Past & Present 1982 7(1): 1-14.* Examines the relationship between mill town environments within the industrial city section and the larger city itself. Focuses on development and change in the Hazelwood area, a ward of Pittsburgh. During the 1870's, the area became dominated by two employers: the Jones and Laughlin Steel Company and the Baltimore & Ohio Railroad. During 1870-1920, Hazelwood advanced independently of Pittsburgh. However, stagnation set in during 1920-50 and this led to the decline of the two major employers and transformed Hazelwood from an autonomous city to a neighborhood of Pittsburgh. Based on US census records, Pittsburgh city directories, and Pittsburgh Building Permit Records; map, 52 notes, appendix.   B. Anderson

1134. Thomas, Richard W. INDUSTRIAL CAPITALISM, INTRA-CLASS RACIAL CONFLICT AND THE FORMATION OF BLACK WORKING CLASS POLITICAL CULTURE. *J. of African-Afro-American Affairs 1979 3(1): 11-45.* Traces the rise of industrial capitalism during the 19th century, emphasizing the fostering of racial tension and provides a survey of the development of black labor unions during the 20th century.

1135. Thoreen, Peter W. ON THE PROFITABLE PROVISION OF PUBLIC GOODS AND SERVICES. *Am. Behavioral Scientist 1981 24(4): 573-598.* Examines the potential for, and the issues and alternatives associated with, the option of allowing more for-profit participation in the provision of public goods and services; traces the development of attitudes toward this option in the United States from 1900 to 1981; and discusses the role of William Norris of Control Data Corporation in formulating the posture of for-profit organizations toward the public goods/services sector.

1136. Thurow, Lester C. POPULAR MECHANICS: THE REDISTRIBUTION OF WEALTH. *Working Papers for a New Soc. 1976 3(4): 23-27, 69-77.* Discusses economic theory, taxes, and wealth redistribution in the 1970's, emphasizing the responsibility of corporations.

1137. Tyler, Gus. ON LIMITS OF "CORPORATE RESPONSIBILITY." *Dissent 1974 21(3): 431-439.* Discusses income, wealth, and corporate responsibility since 1945.   S

1138. Underhill, David. YUKKING IT UP AT CBS. *Southern Exposure 1975 2(4): 68-71.* Alleges discrimination toward southerners and other groups in the Columbia Broadcasting System in the 1970's.

1139. Vernon, Raymond. DOES SOCIETY ALSO PROFIT? *Foreign Policy 1973/74 (13): 103-118.* Assesses the social effects of multinational corporations.   S

1140. Virtanen, Keijo. THE INFLUENCE OF THE AUTOMOTIVE INDUSTRY ON THE ETHNIC PICTURE OF DETROIT, MICHIGAN, 1900-1940. *U. of Turku. Inst. of General Hist. Publ. [Finland] 1977 9: 71-88.* During 1910-30 the automotive industry drew the labor it needed largely from outside areas rather than from the immigrant communities already established in Detroit. The foreign-born population underwent its most vigorous increase at this time.

Social activity among the Finns living in Detroit, despite its late start, developed fairly vigorously; its inception was clearly bound up with the progress of the automotive industry. Statistics show that half of the Finns who had arrived in the United States after 1916 and resided in Detroit had made the journey from Finland straight to Detroit, the others having first lived in some other locality in the United States. Map, fig., 5 tables, 36 notes. E. P. Stickney

1141. Vogel, David. THE INADEQUACY OF CONTEMPORARY OPPO-SITION TO BUSINESS. *Daedalus 1980 109(3): 47-58.* Neither federal regulation of the American business sector as prescribed by the Left, nor deregulation of the same sector, as prescribed by the Right, provides an adequate response to present economic difficulties; at least a decade of political paralysis will elapse until realistic and practical analysis occurs.

1142. Vogel, David. THE POLITICIZATION OF THE CORPORATION. *Social Policy 1974 5(1): 57-62.* Discusses the widespread distrust of business corporations in the United States during the 1960's and 70's.

1143. Vogel, David. WHY BUSINESSMEN DISTRUST THEIR STATE: THE POLITICAL CONSCIOUSNESS OF AMERICAN CORPORATE EX-ECUTIVES. *British J. of Pol. Sci. [Great Britain] 1978 8(1): 45-78.* Discusses the historical context of antistatism among US businessmen; argues that most businessmen have proven incapable of understanding clearly the economic and political requirements of the socioeconomic system on the stability of which their own social existence rests.

1144. Wackman, Daniel B.; Gillmor, Donald M.; Gaziano, Cecilie; and Dennis, Everette E. CHAIN NEWSPAPER AUTONOMY AS REFLECTED IN PRESIDENTIAL CAMPAIGN ENDORSEMENTS. *Journalism Q. 1975 52(3): 411-420.* An examination of the nature of economic concentration in newpapers and its influence on endorsements. New chains were founded during 1960-68; 1969-72 saw the increase in the size of existing chains. Nonchain papers were more likely to endorse in every election. Chain papers were more likely to support the favored candidate of the press. In most chains the individual papers endorsed the same candidate; this suggests that informal controls are in operation. Based on an examination of data from *Editor and Publisher* for the presidential elections of 1960, 1964, 1968, and 1972. Based on primary and secondary sources; 6 tables, 2 figs., 29 notes. K. J. Puffer

1145. Wang, Chao Ling and Hilaski, Harvey J. THE SAFETY AND HEALTH RECORD IN THE CONSTRUCTION INDUSTRY. *Monthly Labor Rev. 1978 101(3): 3-9.* Statistics collected under the Occupational Safety and Health Act (1970) indicate that injuries and fatalities have dropped, 1972-75, in construction, the most dangerous major industry.

1146. Watkins, Alfred J. "GOOD BUSINESS CLIMATES": THE SECOND WAR BETWEEN THE STATES. *Dissent 1980 27(4): 476-484.* Moves made to the Sunbelt by corporations are part of a "war" waged against unions, welfare recipients, the unemployed, and publicly financed social service agencies in the hope of restoring a good business climate to the Northeast; corporations wishing to relocate should be assessed financial penalties to help ease the burdens on the communities they leave.

1147. White, Rudolph A. HAS BLS UNDERESTIMATED BUSINESS PH.D. DEMAND? *Monthly Labor Rev. 1979 102(9): 42-46.* Available statistics (1975-78) clearly disprove the conclusion in Bureau of Labor Statistics studies that business is the field with the greatest relative oversupply of PhD's; there is no clear signal that the market is near a balance.

1148. Whyte, William Foote. IN SUPPORT OF VOLUNTARY EMPLOYEE OWNERSHIP. *Society 1978 15(6): 73-82.* Discusses the advantages, conditions for success, and means of achieving employee-community ownership of plants that would otherwise be shut down, and gives a history of cooperatively owned plants in the United States and Mondragon, Spain, during 1943-77, in a presentation in support of the Voluntary Job Preservation and Community Stabilization bill introduced to the House of Representatives in 1978.

1149. Woodman, Harold D. BUSINESS HISTORY AS SOCIAL HISTORY. *Rev. in Am. Hist. 1978 6(1): 36-42.* Review article prompted by Mansel G. Blackford's *The Politics of Business in California, 1890-1920* (Columbus: Ohio State U. Pr., 1977) and Thomas C. Cochran's *200 Years of American Business* (New York: Basic Books, 1977).

1150. Woodworth, Warner. WORKERS AS BOSSES. *Social Policy 1981 11(4): 40-45.* Discusses the rise of worker-owned industries in America between 1970 and 1981 as a response to the industrial decline in the Northeast and Midwest of the nation; and illustrates this trend with the experience of the Rath Packing Company in Waterloo, Iowa, which in 1979 became worker-owned.

1151. Zuesse, Eric. LOVE CANAL: THE TRUTH SEEPS OUT. *Reason 1981 12(10): 16-33.* The Hooker Chemicals and Plastics Corporation, which in 1942 began dumping toxic waste in the Love Canal region in Niagara Falls, New York, warned the Niagara Board of Education of the site's dangers, but the board, which acquired it in 1953, and other governmental agencies repeatedly ignored Hooker's warnings; it is they, then, who bear primary responsibility for the Love Canal disaster despite the Justice Department's suit against Hooker (1979) and the accusations of Michael Brown's *Laying Waste* (1980).

1152. Zwerdling, Daniel. SAVING JOBS BY BUYING THE PLANT: EMPLOYEE OWNERSHIP: HOW WELL IS IT WORKING? *Working Papers for a New Soc. 1979 7(1): 14-27.* Discusses recent accomplishments and mistakes in worker and community takeovers of factories dumped by corporations, beginning in 1977, in order to save jobs; uses the efforts of the Mahoning Valley community in Ohio to purchase the Campbell plant of the Youngstown Sheet and Tube Co. steel mill as a primary example.

1153. —. HUMANIZING THE WORKPLACE: THEN AND NOW. *Society 1977 15(1): 112-115.* Discusses experiments, 1924-33, by the Western Electric Co. in collaboration with Harvard University, Graduate School of Business, to determine the ideal environment for maximum production and worker satisfaction; includes photos of work areas.

1154. —. [THE LOCATION OF THE HEADQUARTERS OF INDUSTRIAL COMPANIES].
Evans, Alan W. THE LOCATION OF THE HEADQUARTERS OF INDUS-

TRIAL COMPANIES.   *Urban Studies [Great Britain] 1973 10(3): 387-395.* Focuses on London, but makes comparisons with New York City. Finds no evidence of increased centralization of head offices in London, 1965-72; the same holds true for New York City, and over a longer period. Based mainly on lists of leading British industrial companies from *The Times* of London, and on US data; 8 tables, fig., biblio.

Burns, Leland S.   THE LOCATION OF THE HEADQUARTERS OF IN-DUSTRIAL COMPANIES: A COMMENT.   *Urban Studies [Great Britain] 1977 14(2): 211-214.* Statistics are based on data from *Fortune Magazine* Directory of the Largest US Corporations. During 1960-70 about 10 percent of the largest retail companies and five percent of the industrial firms relocated from central cities to those having no manufacturing-based economies. "Suburbanizing firms were attracted by . . . lower . . . rents and taxes." Moves from one central city to another involved such factors as access to consultants, laboratories, capital sources, and cultural facilities. The pattern of changing locations is different in the United States and Great Britain. 5 tables, biblio.   E. P. Stickney/S

10

GOVERNMENT REGULATION
AND INTERVENTION

1155.   Alperovitz, Gar and Faux, Jeff.   THE ECONOMY: WHAT KIND OF PLANNING?   *Working Papers for a New Soc. 1975 3(3): 67-73.* Discusses the inevitability of economic planning in the 1970's and proposes alternative planning systems to those favored by large, private corporations.

1156.   Anderson, Charles E.   HOSPITAL PRODUCTION: CAN COSTS BE CONTAINED?   *Am. Econ. Rev. 1979 69(2): 293-297.* Two types of regulatory structures are possible: the limited competition hospital industry, or, a fully planned hospital industry. Supports the latter, but does recognize that, in its ignoring market forces, several critical problems exist. 7 ref.   D. K. Pickens

1157.   Anderson, James E.   THE PUBLIC UTILITY COMMISSION OF TEXAS: A CASE OF CAPTURE OR RAPTURE?   *Policy Studies Rev. 1982 1(3): 484-490.* Although economic regulatory agencies are often captured by those whom they were established to regulate, in some instances the regulatory agencies themselves have decided to be overly responsive to the concerns of those they regulate, working for their interests ostensibly as a part of the overall public interest; the Texas Public Utility Commission, which began operating in 1976, exemplifies the corporate capture of a regulatory agency.

1158.   Annable, James E., Jr.   THE ICC, THE IBT, AND THE CARTELI-ZATION OF THE AMERICAN TRUCKING INDUSTRY.   *Q. R. of Econ. and Business 1973 13(2): 33-48.* "It has been frequently argued that the Interstate Commerce Commission has cartelized the commercial trucking industry. Friends of the ICC contend that this argument is refuted by the prevailing low profit levels in motor freight. The article examines this debate via the application of a model of collective bargaining to the industry. Two primary conclusions are drawn from the analysis: (1) The excess profits which accrue to the cartel have been expropri-ated by the Teamsters' Union and (2) The fact that some 60 percent of motor carriage is free of federal regulation has not impaired the union's ability to expropriate such profits. The analysis also suggests that the simple abolition of the ICC would not quickly disestablish the cartel."   J

1159.   Archibald, Robert R.   PRICE REGULATION IN HISPANIC CALI-FORNIA.   *Americas (Acad. of Am. Franciscan Hist.) 1977 33(4): 613-629.* In the late 18th century, prices were regulated in Spanish California both for goods brought from Mexico and for those produced locally. The regulatory process aroused numerous conflicts among contradictory goals of the Spanish government and between rival interests in California, notably the missions and the military. Based on archival sources; 55 notes. D. Bushnell

1160. Ardoin, Birthney. A COMPARISON OF NEWSPAPERS UNDER JOINT PRINTING CONTRACTS. *Journalism Q. 1973 50(2): 340-347.* Examines pairs of newspapers under joint printing contracts in 1964 and 1968, before and after the Justice Department sued Tucson papers for violating antitrust laws with such an agreement. S

1161. Astapovich, A. GOSUDARSTVO I KORPORATSII SSHA V US-LOVIIAKH NTR: VNESHNEEKONOMICHESKII ASPEKT [The state and corporations of the United States in the scientific and technological revolution: an external economic aspect]. *Mirovaia Ekonomika i Mezhdunarodnye Otnosheniia [USSR] 1982 (4): 64-76.* The scientific and technological revolution has resulted in increased competition in research and development for the United States from Japan and other developed and developing countries, forcing the United States as a sovereign state to become increasingly involved in supporting private corporations in their competitive efforts in the world market through devices such as tax relief, government subsidies, protectionist policies, and relaxation of laws regarding monopolies and free competition. Russian.

1162. Auddell, Robert M. and Cain, Louis P. [PUBLIC POLICY, THE CONSENT DECREE AND THE MEATPACKING INDUSTRY]. *Business Hist. Rev. 1981 55(2): 217-242, (3): 359-378.* Part 1. PUBLIC POLICY TOWARD "THE GREATEST TRUST IN THE WORLD." In 1919 the Federal Trade Commission (FTC) charged that the five major meat packers in the United States had achieved domination of the purchase of livestock and consequently had been able to force competitors out of the industry. While the packers later admitted they had established pools, the evidence does not prove the full extent of the FTC charges. Not only did competition from local and regional packers actually increase, but the latter had higher profit rates than the national firms. A consent decree was negotiated between the packers and the Justice Department in 1920, and this was followed in 1921 by the Packers and Stockyards Act. Neither policy response to the 1919 FTC report had much real effect on the wholesale meat industry, however. Part 2. THE CONSENT DECREE IN THE MEATPACKING INDUSTRY, 1920-1956. Examines the economic effects of the consent decree signed by the five major meatpacking firms in 1920. Arguing that conditions had substantially changed since the decree was fashioned to end monopoly power and to prevent the extension of that power to other areas of the food industry, the three remaining firms sought federal release from its terms in 1956. The courts showed poor economic judgement in denying that relief. Based on records of the FTC and other government documents; 3 tables, appendix, 50 notes. C. J. Pusateri

1163. Baack, Bennett D. and Ray, Edward John. TARIFF POLICY AND COMPARATIVE ADVANTAGE IN THE IRON AND STEEL INDUSTRY: 1870-1929. *Explorations in Econ. Hist. 1973 11(1): 3-23.* Summarizes previous studies of the relationship between the tariff and US economic growth, analyzing overall movements in tariffs, production, and imports. Criticizes the methodology of recent studies and concludes that the tariff had a significant and positive impact on the production of pig iron. Based on statistical data and secondary sources; 3 tables, 33 notes. P. J. Coleman

1164. Bagdikian, Ben H. MAXIMIZING PROFITS AT *THE WASHING-TON POST*. *Washington Monthly 1976 7(11): 26-35*. Discusses the pressmen's strike at the *Washington Post* (1975) as an example of the effects of emerging conglomerate control of American newspapers.

1165. Baxter, William F. REGULATION AND DIVERSITY IN COMMU-NICATIONS MEDIA. *Am. Econ. R. 1974 64(2): 392-399*. Discusses federal regulation of the press and electronic media since 1912.

1166. Baysinger, Barry D. and Meiners, Roger E. POLITICAL CONTROL OF THE CORPORATION: AN ATTACK ON NATURAL LIBERTY. *J. of Social and Pol. Studies 1980 5(1-2): 83-105*. Argues that the logical founda-tion used to support federal regulation of the corporate form in the United States is weak; continued reliance on market forces to temper the powers of large corporations is historically justified.

1167. Bess, David. "AN ACT OF FAITH AND HOPE" REVISITED. *US Naval Inst. Pro. 1981 107(10): 70-77*. The Merchant Marine Act (US, 1970) seemed to the author in the March 1975 *Proceedings* to mark a major change in the maritime policy of the United States, but a current survey of US shipbuild-ing efforts and the US merchant marine indicates that "the act's success has been limited." Secondary sources; 7 photos, 11 notes. A. N. Garland

1168. Bierce, William B. A NEW ERA IN INTERNATIONAL AVIA-TION: CAB REGULATION, RATIONALIZATION AND RESTRICTIONS ON THE NORTH ATLANTIC. *New York U. J. of Internat. Law and Pol. 1974 7(2): 317-360*. After analyzing the recent attempts of the Civil Aeronautics Board to regulate transatlantic air transportation, concludes that these policies "reflect a retreat from the American tradition of unbridled expansionism." "The defensive policies of the CAB and the Ford administration raise new hope for a rationalization of the economic chaos resulting from route saturation, foreign subsidies, and the scheduled carriers' suicidal attempts to compete with charter carriers at unprofitable rates." Primary and secondary sources; 222 notes.
M. L. Frey

1169. Blair, John M. DECENTRALIZING OIL CARTELS. *Society 1977 14(3): 57-62*. Evaluates the potential effectiveness of price and regulatory provi-sions of the Energy Policy and Conservation Act (1975) in dealing with antitrust violations of international oil cartels, 1950-70's.

1170. Brickman, Ronald and Jasonoff, Sheila. CONCEPTS OF RISK AND SAFETY IN TOXIC SUBSTANCES REGULATION: A COMPARISON OF FRANCE AND THE U.S. *Policy Studies J. 1980 9(3): 394-403*. The notions of risk and safety which play a conspicuous role in the regulation of toxic substances have shown a markedly different evolution in France and the United States; France has consistently avoided a substantive elaboration of safety con-cepts through legal texts, while the United States has moved toward the develop-ment of statutory criteria of risk assessment, balancing both the costs and benefits of regulation; 1899-1980.

1171. Burckel, Nicholas C. WILLIAM GOEBEL AND THE CAMPAIGN FOR RAILROAD REGULATION IN KENTUCKY, 1888-1900. *Filson Club Hist. Q. 1974 48(1): 43-60.* Uses the career of William Goebel to show that political ambition and reform ideas combined to form the basis of Progressivism. Goebel had built his career on a record of favoring state regulation of railroads and induced a state constitutional convention to include a railroad commission in the Kentucky constitution of 1891. In 1898, he supported a partisan election law which centralized election administration in the Democratically controlled state legislature. After Goebel received the 1899 Democratic gubernatorial nomination, the Republican candidate William S. Taylor stated that Goebel would use the election law to have himself counted into office, a charge that Goebel ignored. Taylor won the election by a small plurality, and Goebel was assassinated in the midst of his contest to overturn the results. Documentation from contemporary newspapers; 57 notes. G. B. McKinney

1172. Burns, Malcolm R. THE COMPETITIVE EFFECTS OF TRUST BUSTING: A PORTFOLIO ANALYSIS. *J. of Pol. Econ. 1977 85(4): 717-739.* Monthly stock prices are used to analyze the competitive effects of the Sherman Act dissolutions carried out against Standard Oil, American Tobacco, and American Snuff on December 1, 1911. Statistical tests of the price changes accompanying important developments in the litigation show rather strongly that investors did not expect dissolution to alter the performance of the snuff, tobacco, and petroleum industries. This conclusion is similar to the findings of previous studies of these cases, and the results indicate that applications of stock prices and finance theory can significantly augment the empirical research methods of industrial organization. J

1173. Caplan, Lincoln. THE RAILROADS' LAST STOP? *Working Papers for a New Soc. 1976 4(3): 46-52.* Evaluates the economic effectiveness and freight volume of the federally sponsored Consolidated Rail Corporation (Conrail) as an alternative to private railroads in the Northeast in the 1970's.

1174. Carnell, Richard S. FRANCIS G. NEWLANDS AND THE NATIONAL INCORPORATION OF THE RAILROADS. *Nevada Hist. Soc. Q. 1976 19(1): 2-25.* Traces the evolution of the philosophies of Senator Francis G. Newlands (1848-1917) from political conservatism to progressivism. Following the passage of the Reclamation Act of 1902, he saw it as a model for nationalization in other areas. He applied these principles to the problems of national railroad regulation. Eventually Congress accepted several of his principles and incorporated them into the Esch-Cummins Act (1920). Based on archival and newspaper sources and United States government documents; photo, 47 notes. H. T. Lovin

1175. Christansen, Gregory B. and Haveman, Robert H. PUBLIC REGULATIONS AND THE SLOWDOWN IN PRODUCTIVITY GROWTH. *Am. Econ. Rev. 1981 71(2): 320-325.* As compared to 1958-65, federal regulations decreased labor productivity from 12% to 21% from 1973 to 1977. Apparently government regulation has a depressing effect on the marketplace. 2 tables, biblio. D. K. Pickens

1176. Clark, Blue. THE BEGINNING OF OIL AND GAS CONSERVA-TION IN OKLAHOMA, 1907-1931. *Chronicles of Oklahoma 1977-78 55(4): 375-391.* Traces the gradual development of Oklahoma's oil and gas conservation policies which other petroleum states later copied. At first the enforcement was lax due to small investigatory staffs and laws filled with loopholes, but by the 1920's the Oklahoma Corporation Commission was able to enforce stricter regulations. A decreasing demand for petroleum during the Depression helped cut production and eliminate some waste. Based on government reports and newspapers; 3 photos, map, 45 notes.   M. L. Tate

1177. Clements, Donald W. RECENT TRENDS IN THE GEOGRAPHY OF COAL. *Ann. of the Assoc. of Am. Geographers 1977 67(1): 109-125.* Examines federal regulation influencing the coal industry, including the Clean Air Act Amendment (1970) which caused decline in Appalachian coal mining and increase in western coal mining; examines transportation methods and environmental impact of mining methods, 1969-77.

1178. Coase, R. H. THE MARKET FOR GOODS AND THE MARKET FOR IDEAS. *Am. Econ. R. 1974 64(2): 384-391.* Discusses the differences between federal regulation of ideas and the media, and federal regulation of the economy.

1179. Cochrane, James L. and Griepentrog, Gary L. COTTON TEXTILE PRICES 1965-66: THE MICROECONOMICS OF MORAL SUASION. *Southern Econ. J. 1977 44(1): 74-84.* Examines the effect which the Johnson administration's attempt to limit increases in wage and price levels had on the South and the price of cotton textiles, 1965-66.

1180. Cochrane, James L. and Griepentrog, Gary L. SULPHUR AND THE U.S. GOVERNMENT: PRICE FIGHTING IN THE 1960S. *Econ. Inquiry 1978 16(3): 360-384.* Narrates the interaction between the Johnson administration and the domestic sulphur industry regarding the successful federal regulation of sulphur prices as a wage-price control during the early commitment of US forces in Vietnam.

1181. Collins, Robert M. POSITIVE BUSINESS RESPONSES TO THE NEW DEAL: THE ROOTS OF THE COMMITTEE FOR ECONOMIC DE-VELOPMENT, 1933-1942. *Business Hist. Rev. 1978 52(3): 369-391.* Argues that previous scholars have not sufficiently noted the efforts of business elements that attempted to arrange a detente with the Roosevelt administration during the 1930's. One expression of this effort was the government's Business Advisory Council, a second was those businessmen who came to embrace the Keynesian solution of deficit spending, and a third spawned from academic-business dialogues initiated at the University of Chicago in 1936. All three of these sources played a role in the eventual formation of the Committee for Economic Development in 1942. The establishment of the CED was essentially the product of long-developing trend toward business-government collaboration begun years before. Based on private papers and published business periodicals; 90 notes.

                                                                C. J. Pusateri

1182. Cooke, Jacob E. TENCH COXE, ALEXANDER HAMILTON, AND THE ENCOURAGEMENT OF AMERICAN MANUFACTURES. *William and Mary Q. 1975 32(3): 369-382.* Examines the contributions of Tench Coxe, Assistant Secretary of the Treasury, to Alexander Hamilton's "Report on Manufactures" of December 1791. Compares Coxe's hastily prepared single draft with Hamilton's several drafts. Most of Coxe's proposals were adopted. Coxe showed more interest in cooperation between industry and agriculture, whereas Hamilton was more inclined to favor the dominance of industry. Notes Coxe's role in the formation of the Society for Establishing Useful Manufactures, its problems in operation, and reasons for failure. Based on the Coxe manuscript collection and Hamilton papers; 81 notes. H. M. Ward

1183. Cornish, William R. LEGAL CONTROL OVER CARTELS AND MONOPOLIZATION 1880-1914: A COMPARISON. Horn, Norbert and Kocka, Jürgen, ed. *Recht und Entwicklung der Grossunternehmen im 19. und frühen 20. Jahrhundert* (Göttingen: Vandenhoeck & Ruprecht, 1979): 280-305. Examines the development in France, Germany, Great Britain and the United States of laws to deal with cartels, monopolies, and other types of business combinations. Although the four countries displayed different attitudes toward the legality of various kinds of business practices (e.g., American courts were generally less reluctant than British courts to rule against the activities of business combinations during this period), they shared in the ad hoc nature of their laws in this area. Rulings by judges on a case by case basis rather than a broad approach attempting to cover the entire field of business law characterized the era's legal history. 28 ref. German summary. S

1184. Coulson, David C. ANTITRUST LAW AND THE MEDIA: MAKING THE NEWSPAPERS SAFE FOR DEMOCRACY. *Journalism Q. 1980 57(1): 79-85.* Ownership concentration in the news media poses a threat to the public's right to the free flow of information as much as does an attack on reporters' First Amendment rights. A 1946 Supreme Court ruling affirmed the government's right to enforce antitrust laws to prevent ownership combinations that create monopolies. However, the Justice Department has not been vigorous in asserting its enforcement powers. Based on court rulings and secondary sources; 42 notes. J. S. Coleman

1185. Covell, Ruth M. THE IMPACT OF REGULATION ON HEALTH CARE QUALITY. *Pro. of the Acad. of Pol. Sci. 1980 33(4): 111-125.* Surveys federal regulation of health care quality in cost control, utilization control, access control, and funding control. In each area, regulation has had unintended and often negative effects. Emphasizes the Professional Standards Review Organization Program (PSRO), a plan established by the 1972 Amendments to the Social Security Act to review medical care. Composed of physicians, the PSRO's evaluate all levels of care in hospitals and nursing homes. PSRO's can improve the quality of health care, but a number of factors have hindered their effectiveness. The author details how PSRO's can be better utilized and how other federal regulatory programs can be improved. Based on HEW Reports. D. F. Ring

1186. Cuff, Robert D. THE DILEMMAS OF VOLUNTARISM: HOOVER AND THE PORK-PACKING AGREEMENT OF 1917-1919. *Agric. Hist. 1979 53(4): 727-747.* Herbert C. Hoover's appointment as Food Administrator during World War I tested his belief in voluntary restraint of business. Recalcitrant pork packers who wanted to extract the maximum profit from wartime business made it difficult to control prices. But in order to justify his philosophy, Hoover was forced to defend the packers against the Federal Trade Commission and others in the administration who wanted sweeping reform of the industry and greater government control. The short wartime crisis and its accompanying prosperity made his voluntary approach look more successful than it would be during the Great Depression. 53 notes.   D. E. Bowers

1187. Cummings, F. Jay and Ruhter, Wayne E.   THE NORTHERN PACIFIC CASE.   *J. of Law and Econ. 1979 22(2): 329-350.* Investigates the records of two antitrust cases against Northern Pacific Railway in 1956 and 1958 in order to evaluate the Supreme Court's decision and contends that it was based on an incorrect view of the firm's tying contracts.

1188.   Curry, Robert L., Jr.   U.S.—DEVELOPING COUNTRY TRADE AND RESTRICTIVE BUSINESS PRACTICE POLICIES.   *J. of Internat. Affairs 1974 28(1): 67-79.* Trade patterns and production cycles in American trade with developing nations are maintained by cartels, multinational corporations, and other restrictive practices. To effectively protect developing nations' exports, the United States must expand its antitrust laws, most notably by repealing the Webb-Pomerene Act (1918), and take the initiative in multinational efforts to liberalize trade, most notably through the United Nations Conference on Trade and Development.   R. D. Frederick

1189.   Detzer, David W.   BUSINESSMEN, REFORMERS, AND TARIFF REVISION: THE PAYNE-ALDRICH TARIFF OF 1909.   *Historian 1973 35(2): 196-204.* In the early 20th century, reformers maintained that monopolies and protective tariffs enabled big business to raise prices and rob "the little man." Reduction of duties was considered part of progressivism, and reformers claimed credit when some rates were lowered in 1909. Actually, key businessmen,— manufacturers, shippers, publishers—not the reformers, were the most effective in bringing about this revision. Most progressive reforms, moreover, require the support of businessmen. "Without such patronage, reform laws die and are laid to rest in the congressional graveyard of unrequited dreams." Based on committee hearings, Commerce Department statistical abstracts, and the press; 28 notes.
                              N. W. Moen

1190.   Dobesh, Larry J.   PROFIT STANDARDS FOR REGULATED MOTOR CARRIERS.   *North Dakota Q. 1977 45(4): 52-73.* Evaluates the Interstate Commerce Commission's regulations on shipping prices for motor carriers; discusses alternative control measures, and asserts that true rate-of-return profit standards can not be devised until risk factors are incorporated into actual costs.

1191.   Douglas, Steven A.   POLICY ISSUES IN SPORTS AND ATHLETICS.   *Policy Studies J. 1978 7(1): 137-150.* Examines federal government attention to amateur and professional athletics and sports policymaking, 1974-77, including discussion of participation, equal opportunity, athletes' rights, safety, consumers' rights, television, drugs and gambling, litigation, and governance.

1192. Dunn, James A. RAILROAD POLICIES IN EUROPE AND THE UNITED STATES: THE IMPACT OF IDEOLOGY, INSTITUTIONS, AND SOCIAL CONDITIONS. *Public Policy 1977 25(2): 205-240.* Analyzes the bases for the American public policy process by conducting a cross-national study of public policymaking in Great Britain, France, and Germany. Focusing on rail transportation policy in these European nations, the author finds that ideology as well as social and economic conditions made governments contemplate public ownership of railroads. Analyzes economic effects of rail transportation policies in Europe. Discusses why rail transportation in the United States remained private. The Railroad Revitalization and Regulatory Reform Act (1975) and other recent railway policies greatly benefited American corporate interests. In the United States the European preconditions for nationalization of the rail system are not yet present. Based on government documents and secondary sources; 5 tables, 46 notes. J. M. Herrick

1193. Dunne, Gerald T. JUSTICE STORY AND THE MODERN CORPORATION—A CLOSING CIRCLE? *Am. J. of Legal Hist. 1973 17(3): 262-270.* Describes the role of justice Joseph Story in the making of corporation law during the 1830's.

1194. Duram, James C. THE FARM JOURNALS AND THE CONSTITUTIONAL ISSUES OF THE NEW DEAL. *Agric. Hist. 1973 47(4): 319-328.* Assesses the significance of the editorial response of nine major commercial agricultural and six major official farm organization publications to two crucial Supreme Court decisions, the invalidations of the National Industrial Recovery Act in May 1935 and the Agricultural Adjustment Act in January 1936. The constitutional positions of the farm journal editors were largely predetermined by their attitudes toward the New Deal. The position taken by the editors of the major farm organization journals was ambiguous, and thus Franklin Delano Roosevelt probably overestimated the support he would have received from farm organizations if a showdown with the Supreme Court could have been avoided. Based on farm journals; 30 notes. R. T. Fulton

1195. Eads, George. AIRLINE CAPACITY LIMITATION CONTROLS: PUBLIC VICE OR PUBLIC VIRTUE? *Am. Econ. R. 1974 64(2): 365-371.* Discusses the costs of capacity limitations which regulate competition on several air routes.

1196. Easterbrook, Gregg. STUCK ON BALTIC PLACE: WHY THE GOVERNMENT LOSES AT MONOPOLY. *Washington Monthly 1979 11(10): 40-48.* Criticizes the federal government's failure to effectively regulate large corporate trusts during the 1970's.

1197. Eckert, Ross D. EXPLOITATION OF DEEP SEA MINERALS: REGULATORY MECHANISMS AND US POLICY. *J. of Law and Econ. 1974 17(1): 143-178.* In the face of impending mining of mineral rich manganese nodules in seabeds, examines the impact which federal regulation of mining has on efficient exploitation and speculates on the powers with which regulatory agencies should be endowed.

1198. Eckert, Ross D. THE LIFE CYCLE OF REGULATORY COMMIS-
SIONERS. *J. of Law & Econ. 1981 24(1): 113-120.* Examines the propensity
of former federal regulatory commission members of the Interstate Commerce
Commission (ICC), the Federal Communications Commission (FCC), and the
Civil Aeronautics Board (CAB) to accept related private sector employment at
their term of office expiration and speculates on the possible conflict of interest;
1977-80.

1199. Felton, John Richard. THE COSTS AND BENEFITS OF MOTOR
TRUCK REGULATION. *Q. Rev. of Econ. and Business 1978 18(2): 7-20.*
Hypothesizing that entry controls, rate regulation, and limitations on the operations of exempt agricultural and private carriers have reduced the efficiency of
truck transportation in the United States, this study endeavors to quantify the
social costs of economic regulation. Even though the analysis is confined to
ICC-regulated Class I and Class II common carriers of general freight and private
carriers utilizing ordinary vans, it is estimated that added social costs of at least
$5.3 billion per year are being incurred. Meager benefits in the form of reduced
inventories might offset about 1 percent of this cost.   J

1200. Finegold, Kenneth. FROM AGRARIANISM TO ADJUSTMENT:
THE POLITICAL ORIGINS OF NEW DEAL AGRICULTURAL POLICY.
Pol. & Soc. 1982 11(1): 1-27. Examines the four major interrelated factors in the
government's failure to intervene in the prolonged agricultural depression that
followed World War I. Government intervention in the form of the Agricultural
Adjustment Administration (AAA), brought into being early in 1933, was possible only after the shift in business opinion following the Great Crash, after the
Democratic Party's victory in 1932, which in turn insured the effective use of the
existing academic-governmental agricultural-economic complex, and after farm
organizations provided the support necessary to win over acceptance of production controls by American farmers. 2 tables, 50 notes.   D. G. Nielson

1201. FitzSimons, Ann B. ANTITRUST AND THE SHIPPING INDUS-
TRY: INTERPRETATION OF THE SHIPPING ACT OF 1916. *New York
U. J. of Int. Law and Pol. 1979 12(1): 115-134.* "The administrative application
of antitrust principles in the liner shipping industry, in apparent disregard of the
precepts of the Shipping Act, might well be a major cause of the increased
uncertainty and heightened instability in the industry today."

1202. Foust, James D. U.S. BANKERS VS. THE DEPARTMENT OF JUS-
TICE: THE 1966 AMENDMENT TO THE BANK MERGER ACT, BANK-
ING STRUCTURE, AND REGULATION. *Rev. Int. d'Hist. de la Banque
[Italy] 1974 9: 80-106.* The Sherman and Clayton anti-trust laws were deficient
with respect to bank mergers. Prior to 1960 most banking legislation neglected
mergers and consolidation. This lack of legislation led to numerous clashes in the
early 1960's between the Comptroller of the Currency and the Board of Governors of the Federal Reserve System, who tended to look favorably on mergers,
and the Justice Department which viewed mergers in the light of antimonopoly
legislation. Although the Bank Merger Act of 1966 provided additional guidelines
regarding mergers, it left the banking authorities and the Justice Department in
adversary positions. Based on federal court cases, government documents, and
secondary sources; 4 tables, 105 notes.   D. McGinnis

1203. Fox, Eleanor M.   ANTITRUST AND FOREIGN EXPORT CAR-
TELS: THE NATIONAL COMMISSION'S REVIEW OF THE WEBB-
POMERENE EXEMPTION.   *New York U. J. of Int. Law and Pol. 1979 12(1):
59-111.* Presents Chapter 14 of the January 1979 report of the National Commission for the Review of Antitrust Laws and Procedures, relating to the antitrust
exemption allowed to export associations under the Webb-Pomerene Act (US,
1918).

1204. Frieden, Bernard J.   THE NEW REGULATION COMES TO SUBUR-
BIA.   *Public Interest 1979 55: 15-27.* New environmental and growth controls
on the homebuilding industry in northern California have financially burdened
homebuyers, especially young families trying to buy their first home. These
regulations have inflated the prices of individual projects and have eliminated the
construction of many housing units developers originally intended to build. The
new regulation has not benefited the public at large. Instead, it has given such
influential groups as environmental ideologues, and established suburbanites,
who are seeking to maintain the status quo, what they want.   S. Harrow

1205. Giglio, James N.   ATTORNEY GENERAL HARRY M. DAUGH-
ERTY AND THE UNITED GAS IMPROVEMENT COMPANY CASE,
1914-1924.   *Pennsylvania Hist. 1979 46(4): 346-367.* In 1922 and 1923, Attorney
General Harry M. Daugherty terminated antitrust actions against the Philadel-
phia-based United Gas Improvement Company, a street lighting trust. Although
indictments had been obtained, there were weaknesses in the government's case.
Yet, Daugherty's decision was based largely upon political considerations and his
friendship for the trust's attorneys. Based on the Wheeler Committee Investigation of Daugherty; photo, 58 notes.   D. C. Swift

1206. Glazer, Nathan.   REGULATING BUSINESS AND THE UNIVER-
SITIES: ONE PROBLEM OR TWO?   *Public Interest 1979 (56): 43-65.* In its
inception, the government regulation of business was punitive and that of higher
education, benign. After the middle 1960's government regulators came to view
higher education with the same "distance, suspicion, and hostility" as they did
business. Today there is a fully developed antagonism between regulators and
higher education, and the latter, along with business, suffer from excessive regulation. Differences in the mission and character of business and higher education
have inhibited a "great sense of communality." Yet, both should argue that "all
institutions should be freed from the illegitimate expansion of governmental
power, and its intrusion unnecessarily into the workings of autonomous institutions . . . And both should use their considerable influence and resources to
restrict regulation to its legitimate objectives."   S. Harrow

1207. Goff, David H. and Goff, Linda Dysart.   REGULATION OF TELEVI-
SION ADVERTISING TO CHILDREN: THE POLICY DISPUTE IN ITS
SECOND DECADE.   *Southern Speech Communication J. 1982 48(1): 38-50.*
Traces the dispute over television advertising aimed at children during 1970-81
as heard by the Federal Trade Commission (FTC); notes the ineffectiveness of
regulating agencies and a rapidly evolving regulatory atmosphere in the Reagan
administration.

1208. Golladay, V. Dennis. THE UNITED STATES AND BRITISH NORTH AMERICAN FISHERIES, 1815-1818. *Am. Neptune 1973 33(4): 246-257.* A study of the diplomatic struggle between the United States and Great Britain over American rights to fish off the coast of British America and the Newfoundland banks. The American case was handled largely by James Monroe, Secretary of State (and President, 1817-25), and John Quincy Adams, one of the Ghent commissioners (1814) and shortly to be minister to Britain. Both nations compromised their positions, with the United States the largest beneficiary. Knowing that Britain was anxious for settlement, the United States had a main tactic of delay. 49 notes.   R. V. Ritter

1209. Gottlieb, Amy Zahl. THE INFLUENCE OF BRITISH TRADE UNIONISTS ON THE REGULATION OF THE MINING INDUSTRY IN ILLINOIS, 1872. *Labor Hist. 1978 19(3): 397-415.* English and Scots immigrant miners settling in Illinois brought with them experience in political action and mining legislation. Their organizations supported legislation based on experience in Great Britain, and succeeded in 1872. Based on newspapers, periodicals, and legislative records; 36 notes.   L. L. Athey

1210. Griffin, Kenyon N. and Shelton, Robert B. COAL SEVERANCE TAX IN THE ROCKY MOUNTAIN STATES. *Policy Studies J. 1978 7(1): 29-39.* Examines severance tax policies affecting coal mining in Colorado, Montana, New Mexico, Utah, Arizona, and Wyoming, 1976-78.

1211. Guth, James L.; Lowitt, Richard, (commentary). FARMER MONOPOLIES, COOPERATIVES, AND THE INTENT OF CONGRESS: ORIGINS OF THE CAPPER-VOLSTEAD ACT. *Agric. Hist. 1982 56(1): 67-82.* The Justice Department has recently claimed that the Capper-Volstead Act (US, 1922), which legalized the marketing activities of agricultural cooperatives, never contemplated that cooperatives would dominate markets. Research shows that legislators were fully aware of the power of cooperatives and that milk marketing monopolies had been an issue since before World War I. The act was clearly intended to exempt farmer cooperatives from most of the antimonopoly restrictions of the Sherman and Clayton acts, to put the sympathetic Agriculture Department in charge of monitoring cooperatives, to base monopoly decisions on pricing behavior rather than market share, and to greatly expand the field in which cooperatives could act. Comments, pp. 117-121. Based on manuscripts and newspapers; 36 notes.   D. E. Bowers

1212. Guth, James L. HERBERT HOOVER, THE U.S. FOOD ADMINISTRATION, AND THE DAIRY INDUSTRY, 1917-1918. *Business Hist. Rev. 1981 55(2): 170-187.* The "milk question" during World War I offers a good case study in business and government relations. Herbert C. Hoover as administrator of the Food Administration mediated a three-cornered struggle between producers, distributors, and consumers. At first reluctant to intervene and treating the matter as a problem for local government, Hoover finally settled on limited intervention in selected urban markets in 1918 initially through public fact-finding commissions and then by quiet negotiations between producers and dealers. While Hoover's policy was marked by its ambiguous and inchoate qualities, it did serve the symbolic purpose of both convincing consumers something was being done about high milk prices and fostering more stable producer-distributor relations in the postwar years. Based mainly on federal records and other archival materials; 44 notes. C. J. Pusateri

1213. Hah, Chong-do and Lindquist, Robert M. THE 1952 STEEL SEIZURE REVISITED: A SYSTEMATIC STUDY IN PRESIDENTIAL DECISION MAKING. *Administrative Sci. Q. 1975 20(4): 587-605.* Formulates a coherent framework for analyzing presidential decisionmaking, specifically studying the 1952 seizure of the steel mills by President Harry S. Truman.

1214. Hall, Tom G. WILSON AND THE FOOD CRISIS: AGRICULTURAL PRICE CONTROL DURING WORLD WAR I. *Agric. Hist. 1973 47(1): 25-46.* Political pressures led the Wilson administration to impose controls on wheat prices in 1917. This policy held prices low enough to keep workers from striking and high enough to provide incentives to farmers. It also showed farmers that government intervention could work in their favor without altering the structure of American agriculture. Based on archival material, Congressional records, and newspapers and magazines; 53 notes. D. E. Brewster

1215. Halverson, James T. ARBITRATION AND ANTITRUST REMEDIES. *Arbitration J. 1975 30(1): 25-33.* "Under antitrust laws, it is illegal for an oil company to terminate the lease of an independent service station operator on the ground that he is selling tires, batteries, and auto accessories of a competing company. On the other hand, independent dealers often engage in business practices and commit managerial faults which do constitute 'just cause' for termination of their leases. Thus, when the Federal Trade Commission receives a complaint from the small businessman that he has been unfairly dealt with, the case involves questions of fact not unlike those commonly dealt with by labor arbitrators. It was therefore logical for the Commission to have evolved a policy of encouraging arbitration of dealership termination disputes. The most recent application of FTC policy was a consent decree settling a complaint against the Phillips Petroleum Company. By the terms of this decree, questions of just cause for termination will be resolved by AAA [American Arbitration Association] panelists. The FTC's Director of the Bureau of Competition describes the background and purpose of the Commission's policy with respect to arbitration."

J

1216. Harbeson, Robert W. RECENT TRENDS IN THE REGULATION OF INTERMODAL RATE COMPETITION IN TRANSPORTATION. *Land Econ. 1966 42(3): 315-326.*

1217. Hartman, Chester W.; Kessler, Robert P.; and LeGates, Richard T. MUNICIPAL HOUSING CODE ENFORCEMENT AND LOW-INCOME TENANTS. *J. of the Am. Inst. of Planners 1974 40(2): 90-104.* "Municipal housing code enforcement often leads to rent increases, tenant moves to lower cost housing, evictions, and reduction in the low-rent housing stock, and thus may harm low-income tenants more than it helps them. A tenant-oriented approach to code enforcement would acknowledge these defects and not permit "market realities" (that is, the owner's economic capabilities and motivations) to dictate enforcement practices and policies. Subsidies and controls that help low-income families afford decent housing must complement the state's legal requirement that all housing units meet code standards. A proposal is put forth for rehabilitation and rent subsidies, controls on rents, and changes in ownership and control of rental property to be used in coordination with housing code enforcement. The importance of full participation of tenants and tenant organizations is stressed in all phases of this new approach to code enforcement." J

1218. Hartman, Eric and Hopper, Jack. WHO'S TAMING WHOM IN TEXAS: CASE STUDY: REGULATORS COWER BEFORE UTILITIES. *Southern Exposure 1979 7(4): 72-76.* Studies how the Texas Public Utility Commission (PUC) has functioned as a regulatory agency. It began in 1975, with high hopes for furtherance of consumer interests, but now the utilities support it and the public is increasingly critical of its operations. When one traces the history of its regulatory policy and practice it becomes abundantly clear why this reversal has come about. There is growing public impatience with PUC operation, suggesting the very real possibility of another confrontation. Illus., table.
R. V. Ritter

1219. Hawke, G. R. THE UNITED STATES TARIFF AND INDUS-TRIAL PROTECTION IN THE LATE NINETEENTH CENTURY. *Econ. Hist. R. [Great Britain] 1975 28(1): 84-99.* Constructs tables showing effective protection (percentage additions to free trade levels) for categories of goods for 1879, 1889, and 1904. The increase in protection given US industries was less than is usually supposed. The most rapid industrial growth was not in the industries that were accorded the highest effective tariffs.
B. L. Crapster

1220. Hawley, Ellis W. ANTITRUST ON THE DEFENSIVE: THE AMERICAN MOVEMENT FOR A CARTELIZED ECONOMY, 1918-33. *Rev. in Am. Hist. 1976 4(4): 582-587.* Review article prompted by Robert F. Himmelberg's *The Origins of the National Recovery Administration: Business, Government, and the Trade Association Issue, 1921-1933* (New York: Fordham U. Pr., 1976); examines the NRA as a pivotal point in federal economic policy.

1221. Hawley, Ellis W. HERBERT HOOVER, THE COMMERCE SECRE-TARIAT, AND THE VISION OF AN "ASSOCIATIVE STATE," 1921-1928. *J. of Am. Hist. 1974 61(1): 116-140.* In the 1920's Hoover sought to expand the Commerce Department as the directing agency of economic development. He believed that efficient government agencies staffed by experts and connected with a multitude of trade associations and volunteer agencies could provide for a flexible response to social problems such as housing and child care and stimulate economic productivity without the coercion of a swollen bureaucracy. The department dealt with informational and promotional activities, sought to stabilize industry, encouraged cooperation with labor in areas such as unemployment and hours, and urged industrial "self-government" to stave off government intervention. The vision was dimmed by the depression but has relevance for those exploring solutions to current problems. 88 notes.
K. B. West

1222. Hazlett, Tom. THE VIEWER IS THE LOSER! *Reason 1982 14(3): 25-35.* Discusses the regulation of cable television by the Federal Communications Commission and the advantages and disadvantages of cable deregulation; focuses on the fight in Scottsdale, Arizona, over a cable franchise.

1223. Hendricks, Wallace; Feuille, Peter; and *Szerszen, Carol.* REGULA-
TION, DEREGULATION, AND COLLECTIVE BARGAINING IN AIR-
LINES. *Industrial and Labor Relations Rev. 1980 34(1): 67-81.* To test the
hypothesis that government regulation of an industry's product market increases
union power in that industry, this study first compares earning and the "scores"
of union contracts in airlines and manufacturing, and then compares negotiated
wage rates and union contract scores in the more regulated and the less regulated
segments of air transportation. The results, while not definitive because of data
limitations, consistently support the hypothesis for the period prior to the recent
deregulation of airlines. The authors nevertheless predict that deregulation will
have little effect on union power in this industry, arguing that the industry and
union characteristics that have developed over the 40 years of regulation have
created a bargaining environment that will not change significantly in the near
future.   J

1224. Henle, Peter and Schmitt, Raymond. PENSION REFORM: THE
LONG, HARD ROAD TO ENACTMENT. *Monthly Labor Rev. 1974 97(11):
3-12.* Examines the genesis of the Employment Retirement Income Security Act
(US, 1974), and some of its implications for workers and companies.

1225. Hewins, Dana C. REGULATION WITHOUT HISTORICAL JUS-
TIFICATION: THE CASE OF HOUSEHOLD MOVING. *Res. in Econ. Hist.
1982 (Supplement 2): 71-92.* During the depression of the 1930's, the moving
industry experienced intense competition, both among truckers, and with railroads. The Motor Carrier Act (US, 1935) was established in order to minimize
that competition between the railroads and the interstate truckers and to promote
financial responsibility and stability within the industry. The industry did not
need to be regulated, however, and was simply the victim of an attempt by
government to gather all motor carriers into a single industry. Primary sources;
13 notes, ref.   J. Powell

1226. Hirschey, Mark John. RAIL SERVICE SUBSIDIES: A CRITICAL
ANALYSIS OF THE PROGRAM. *Q. Rev. of Econ. and Business 1978 18(2):
39-54.* In 1974 Congress passed the Regional Rail Reorganization (3-R) Act and
adopted a program of rail service continuation subsidies to maintain service on
privately unprofitable, but socially desirable, light density or "branch" lines in
the northeastern United States. This program was expanded nationwide and
combined with an ambitious program of regulatory reform when Congress enacted the Railroad Revitalization and Regulatory Reform (4-R) Act of 1976. This
legislation has important implications for the efficiency of the industry and its
future role in a revitalized transportation sector. In this study, the local rail
service subsidy program which was created in this legislation is reviewed, and its
implications are critically analyzed.   J

1227. Hitchman, James H. THE BELLINGHAM PORT COMMISSION,
1920-1970. *J. of the West 1981 20(3): 57-64.* Bellingham, Washington, developed a large shipping industry based on timber, coal, fishing, ship supplies, and
passenger service during 1850-1920. To stimulate a lagging economy after World
War I, the Chamber of Commerce instituted the Bellingham Port Commission,
which improved and expanded port facilities. Both waterfront industry and shipping have increased. The port commission shows how the cooperation of govern-

ment and private enterprise is beneficial to the regional economy. Based on port commission documents and Army Corps of Engineers reports; map, 2 photos, 3 tables, 28 notes.   B. S. Porter

1228. Hochheiser, Sheldon. THE EVOLUTION OF U.S. FOOD COLOR STANDARDS, 1913-1919. *Agric. Hist. 1981 55(4): 385-391.* Federal regulation of synthetic food colors began after passage of the Food and Drug Act (US, 1906) when the Agriculture Department drew up a short list of dyes known to be safe. This list omitted oil soluble dyes, making it difficult for butter and margarine manufacturers to color their products. After years of tests by the Agriculture Department, four dyes were approved in 1918; but two of them were soon found unsafe and subsequently were withdrawn. Based on government records; 28 notes.   D. E. Bowers

1229. Hoover, Roy O. PUBLIC LAW 273 COMES TO SHELTON: IMPLE-MENTATION OF THE SUSTAINED-YIELD FOREST MANAGEMENT ACT OF 1944. *J. of Forest Hist. 1978 22(2): 86-101.* The brainchild of consulting forester David T. Mason and Senator Charles L. McNary of Oregon, Public Law 273 brought to life a unique experiment in forest management. The Sustained-Yield Forest Management Act (US, 1944) (P.L. 273) aimed to conserve resources in the traditional sense, but it was also intended to stabilize declining forest industries and dependent communities by combining federal and private lands into cooperative management units from which would flow continuous supplies of timber. Lengthy and complex negotiations between the Forest Service and the Simpson Logging Company of Shelton, Washington (occasionally involving other government agencies and interest groups) led to implementation of the law in 1946. Widely heralded as a success, the Shelton Cooperative Sustained-Yield Unit remains today the only one of its kind under P.L. 273. Based on Forest Service and company records; 8 photos, map, 78 notes.   R. J. Fahl

1230. Horn, Norbert. AKTIENRECHTLICHE UNTERNEHMENSOR-GANISATION IN DER HOCHINDUSTRIALISIERUNG (1860-1920): DEUTSCHLAND, ENGLAND, FRANKREICH UND DIE USA IM VER-GLEICH [Company law and the organization of large enterprises, 1860-1920: Germany, Great Britain, France and the United States in comparative perspective]. Horn, Norbert and Kocka, Jürgen, ed. *Recht und Entwicklung der Grossunternehmen im 19. und frühen 20. Jahrhundert* (Göttingen: Vandenhoeck & Ruprecht, 1979): 123-189. The joint-stock company became the most important legal form of large-scale business organization. Corporation law related to business organization in "1) the institutionalization of legally autonomous enterprise-units; 2) the division of the decision-making authority and its control within the enterprise; 3) the two-fold and changing role of shareholders as entrepreneurs and investors; [and] 4) legal instruments for external growth and concentration of enterprises." While the similarities between company laws were obvious, the connections between them and economic growth were less so and best understood by a precise definition of "the economic advantages of companies as a legal tool." This included large capital accumulation for large and risky investments, access to public capital markets, and autonomous legal existence. 336 notes, biblio. English summary.   S

1231. Hornbrook, Mark C. MEDICINAL DRUGS: RISKS AND REGU-LATIONS. *Current Hist. 1980 78(457): 201-205, 223-226.* Describes the role of the Food and Drug Administration in approving drugs for consumption, the approval process, and the effects of government regulation, 1960-78.

1232. Horowitz, Ira. MARKET ENTRENCHMENT AND THE SPORTS BROADCASTING ACT. *Am. Behavioral Scientist 1978 21(3): 415-430.* Discusses advertising industry effects of the Sports Broadcasting Act (1961) (which allows antitrust immunity to professional sports teams contracting their broadcasting rights to sponsored telecasts): namely the exclusion of open advertisement on precontracted air time; covers 1961-78.

1233. Hughes, Chip and Stanley, Len. OSHA: DYNAMITE FOR WORK-ERS. *Southern Exposure 1976 4(1-2): 75-82.* The Occupational Safety and Health Act (1970) meant that health safety requirements had to be met by manufacturers for workers in plants using toxic chemicals; chronicles reforms forced by workers in the Olin Corporation's Film Division in Brevard, North Carolina, concerning the inhalation of carbon disulfide (CS_2).

1234. Hughes, Jonathan R. T. TRANSFERENCE AND DEVELOPMENT OF INSTITUTIONAL CONSTRAINTS UPON ECONOMIC ACTIVITY. *Res. in Econ. Hist. 1976 1: 45-68.* A review of economic regulation in the United States, and reasons for it. The concept of the free economy has always been a fallacy; not only has the American economy always been regulated, but the very system of regulation has been borrowed from abroad, especially from Great Britain. Regulation soon became control, and control for social reasons followed. The remarkable aspect of the American system is its antiquity: reasoning and methods are ancient and have proved remarkably resistant to change. Regulation has always been designed to solve specific problems, with no overall economic objective in mind. 66 notes, ref.   V. L. Human

1235. Humphrey, Thomas F. THE STATES' ROLE IN POLICY IMPLE-MENTATION: TRANSPORTATION POLICY. *Policy Studies Rev. 1981 1(2): 323-334.* Describes the increased responsibilities assumed by state governments in implementing transportation policy during the last two decades; assesses the influence of the federal government on state transportation programs.

1236. Ippolito, Richard A. THE EFFECTS OF PRICE REGULATION IN THE AUTOMOBILE INSURANCE INDUSTRY. *J. of Law and Econ. 1979 22(1): 55-90.* Examines data pertaining to interstate differences in automobile insurance, 1971-73, refutes a hypothesis suggested by George J. Stigler that regulation is a tool benefiting producers at the cost of consumers.

1237. Ippolito, Richard A. and Masson, Robert T. THE SOCIAL COST OF GOVERNMENT REGULATION OF MILK. *J. of Law and Econ. 1978 21(1): 33-65.* Producers favor rigid government regulation of milk production and distribution, although technical advances, such as reconstituted milk, would permit lighter regulations. The gradual phaseout of some regulations would allow a fairer production-distribution pattern. Based on primary and secondary sources; 5 tables, 5 fig., 50 notes.   C. B. Fitzgerald

1238.   Jacobsen, Sally.   THE GREAT MONTANA COAL RUSH: A SPE-
CIAL REPORT.   *Sci. and Public Affairs 1973 29(4): 37-42.* Examines state
government efforts to maintain environmental quality through strict regulation
of strip mining allowed because of the energy crisis, 1970-72.

1239.   Jarrell, Gregg A.   THE DEMAND FOR STATE REGULATION OF
THE ELECTRIC UTILITY INDUSTRY.   *J. of Law and Econ. 1978 21(2):
269-295.* Discusses the establishment of a state-created, state-protected public
utility monopoly during 1907-38, and the effects of this form of state government
regulation on the price of electricity and the profits of the electricity producers.

1240.   Jarrell, Gregg A. and Bradley, Michael.   THE ECONOMIC EFFECTS
OF FEDERAL AND STATE REGULATIONS OF CASH TENDER OF-
FERS.   *J. of Law & Econ. 1980 23(2): 371-408.* The Williams Act (US, 1968),
designed to protect target shareholders in the tender offer process, increased
significantly the purchase price of target firms, decreased the returns to acquiring
firms, and reduced the volume and productivity of cash takeovers—in short had
negative effects with large social costs.

1241.   Jeffress, Philip W.   THE POLITICAL ECONOMY OF THE UNITED
STATES ENERGY POLICY.   *J. of Social and Pol. Studies 1979 4(1): 53-66.*
In consideration of a future national energy policy, discusses public policy from
1930 to 1970 and federal legislation since 1970, both of which have been affected
by relationships among an international oil cartel, unequal distribution of energy
costs, pollution, effects of escalating energy prices on the consumer and economy,
potential transfer of wealth from consumer to producers, and special interest
groups.

1242.   Johnson, Arthur T.   CONGRESS AND PROFESSIONAL SPORTS:
1951-1978.   *Ann. of the Am. Acad. of Pol. and Social. Sci. 1979 (445): 102-115.*
The relationship between government and professional sports is analyzed by
reviewing Congressional activity relative to professional sports during the period
1951-1978. During this time, nearly 300 pieces of sports legislation have been
proposed. Congressional concern with sports is explained by the impact of sports
events, such as franchise moves, upon specific constituencies, and league-initiated
requests for assistance. Conflicting perceptions in Congress of professional sports
as pure sport and big business help explain a change in Congress' posture toward
the sports leagues. The politics of professional sports is explored, and a Congres-
sionally defined right to access is identified and explained. The article concludes
that due to Congress' changing perception of professional sports, it has, on
occasion, enacted legislation opposed by the leagues. Nevertheless, the political
influence of club owners combined with the persistence of an idyllic image of
sports within Congress make such instances rare.   J

1243.   Jones, Ethel B.   STATE LEGISLATION AND HOURS OF WORK
IN MANUFACTURING.   *Southern Econ. J. 1975 41(4): 602-612.* Analyzes
the impact state legislation had on the decline in manufacturing hours worked
by labor during 1900-30.   S

1244.   Jonish, James E.   RECENT DEVELOPMENTS IN U.S. ANTIDUMP-
ING POLICY.   *J. of World Trade Law [Switzerland] 1973 7(3): 316-327.* "This
article examines the issues raised by antidumping duties imposed as a legitimate

form of protection against international dumping, both in general and in specific terms as relating to recent U.S. practice. The author's analysis reveals a renewal of activity under the U.S. Antidumping Act during the Nixon administration."

J

1245. Joskow, Paul L. and MacAvoy, Paul W. REGULATION AND THE FINANCIAL CONDITION OF THE ELECTRIC POWER COMPANIES IN THE 1970'S. *Am. Econ. R. 1975 65(2): 295-301.* Power companies must have rates of return at 14% to attract investment; but, on balance, existing regulatory procedures may be disastrous for the electric utility industry. 3 tables.

D. K. Pickens

1246. Kaus, Robert M. THE DARK SIDE OF DEREGULATION. *Washington Monthly 1979 11(3): 33-40.* Offers a negative evaluation of deregulation of American industry, beginning with the deregulation of baseball in 1976, discussing specifically the deregulation of the airlines industry.

1247. Kaus, Robert M. HOW THE PEOPLE LOST CONTROL: THE DE-CLINE AND FALL OF THE AMERICAN WAY OF REGULATION, PART I. *Washington Monthly 1979 11(5-6): 34-41.* Government regulation since the US Supreme Court struck down Franklin Roosevelt's National Recovery Administration in 1935 has been a total failure. To be continued.

1248. Keehn, Richard H. FEDERAL BANK POLICY, BANK MARKET STRUCTURE, AND BANK PERFORMANCE: WISCONSIN, 1863-1914. *Business Hist. R. 1974 48(1): 1-27.* A statistical analysis utilizing data from Wisconsin to examine banking history and banks' role in the economic development of the United States from the Civil War to the creation of the Federal Reserve System. Hypotheses examined are: 1) National banking laws slowed entry of new banks until the laws were changed in 1900, 2) National bank regulation affected profits until a change in regulations after 1900, 3) Substantial interregional and intrastate interest rate differentials existed in the 1870's, but declined, 4) Large scale banking brought reduced costs per unit of earning assets. 17 tables, 57 notes.

R. V. Ritter

1249. Kerr, K. Austin. THE MOVEMENT FOR COAL-MINE SAFETY IN NINETEENTH-CENTURY OHIO. *Ohio Hist. 1977 86(1): 3-18.* A survey of coal mine health and safety regulations from their conception. Discusses the organization of the Mining Commission in 1871, and its investigative work and early leaders, the creation of the post of State Inspector of Mines in 1874, and the attempts to have the state and federal governments assume responsibility for improving mining conditions and the political controversies involved. Based on contemporary comments and on manuscript, archival, and secondary sources; 3 illus., 44 notes.

J

1250. Konareva, L. ORGANIZATSIYA UPRAVLENIYA KACHEST-VOM PRODUKTSII V PROMYSHLENNOSTI SSHA [Organization of quality control in US industry]. *Voprosy Ekonomiki [USSR] 1980 (8): 111-120.* Detailed analysis of the mechanisms of quality control in contemporary US industry, viewed as a central concern in the capitalist economy.

1251. Kraft, Michael E. THE USE OF RISK ANALYSIS IN FEDERAL REGULATORY AGENCIES: AN EXPLORATION. *Policy Studies Rev. 1982 1(4): 666-675.* Explores how risk analysis, the combination of risk assessment and risk evaluation, is employed in federal regulatory agencies to shed some light on the problems and constraints that affect its use in public regulation of technological risks.

1252. LeBaron, Allen. THE NEW HAVEN DECISIONS AND INTERSTATE COMMERCE COMMISSION RATE PRESCRIPTIONS. *Land Econ. 1964 40(3): 324-331.*

1253. Lewis-Beck, Michael S. and Alford, John R. CAN GOVERNMENT REGULATE SAFETY? THE COAL MINE EXAMPLE. *Am. Pol. Sci. Rev. 1980 74(3): 745-756.* The federal government has been directly involved in coal mining safety for over 35 years, operating under three major pieces of legislation, enacted in 1941, 1952, and 1969. Opposing opinions regarding the effect of this legislation can be grouped into three categories: radical, reactionary, and reformer. A multiple interrupted time-series analysis indicates that, in fact, the 1941 and 1969 regulations significantly reduced the fatality rate in coal mining. Certain conditions seem related to the effectiveness of this safety legislation: birth order, provisions, enforcement, target population, and goals.   J/S

1254. Lewis-Beck, Michael S. MAINTAINING ECONOMIC COMPETITION: THE CAUSES AND CONSEQUENCES OF ANTITRUST. *J. of Pol. 1979 41(1): 169-191.* Major antitrust legislation includes the Sherman Antitrust Act (US, 1890), the Clayton Act (US, 1914), and the Celler-Kefauver Antimerger Act (US, 1950). Both the Antitrust Division of the Justice Department and the Federal Trade Commission are responsible for the enforcement of these laws. Enforcement activity appears to be determined neither by merger activity nor by presidential partisan politics. Congressional influence is extensive, especially in limiting the agencies' budgets. Neither Democrats nor Republicans are firmly committed to maintaining economic competition. "Antitrust endorsement, not antitrust enforcement, is part of the ritual behavior of American politicians . . . Government normally aims to help corporations rather than constrain them." 82 notes.   A. W. Novitsky

1255. Libecap, Gary D. ECONOMIC VARIABLES AND THE DEVELOPMENT OF THE LAW: THE CASE OF WESTERN MINERAL RIGHTS . *J. of Econ. Hist. 1978 38(2): 338-362.* The paper analyzes the development of private mineral rights law in the American West during the last half of the nineteenth century using a model of institutional change developed by Lance Davis and Douglass North. The study centers on one of the West's premiere mining regions, the Comstock Lode of Nevada, and it points out that the law progressed during the period from general, unwritten rules to highly specific statutes and court verdicts. The governmental units changed from the mining camp government to the territorial government and finally to the state government. The paper examines that progression by focusing on the desire of mine owners to use legal means to reduce ownership uncertainty, as both property values and competition increased rapidly while new ore discoveries were made. Quantitative measures of legal change are developed, and while the study primarily examines efficiency gains, equity effects are also considered. The paper concludes that those effects were likely small and that refinement in property rights law can be viewed as an adjustment process to reduce uncertainty.   J

1256. Long, William F.; Schramm, Richard; and Tollison, Robert. THE ECONOMIC DETERMINANTS OF ANTITRUST ACTIVITY. *J. of Law and Econ. 1973 16(2): 351-364.* Studies to what extent "industry welfare losses . . . explain the historical distribution of antitrust cases across different manufacturing industries" over the last 25 years. Economic variables may influence antitrust decisions, but much explanation of this activity lies outside the tested determinants. The Antitrust Division of the Justice Department needs to develop better statistical information on its activities. 5 tables, 10 notes, appendix.
C. A. Gallacci

1257. Longin, Thomas C. COAL, CONGRESS, AND THE COURTS: THE BITUMINOUS COAL INDUSTRY AND THE NEW DEAL. *West Virginia Hist. 1974 35(2): 101-130.* The depressed coal industry became a case study of New Deal economic policy. The National Recovery Administration Bituminous Coal Code temporarily boosted wages and prices. The Guffey Act (1935), supported by labor and small operators against the large companies, imposed wage price controls and collective bargaining. Struck down by the Supreme Court, it was replaced by a milder Coal Act (1937). Although these measures raised wages and reduced hours, they never solved the basic long-term problem of overcapacity; only World War II did that. Based on newspapers, congressional debates, and court cases; 47 notes.
J. H. Broussard

1258. Lucoff, Manny. THE RISE AND FALL OF THE THIRD RE-WRITE. *J. of Communication 1980 30(3): 47-53.* Discusses the role of the broadcasting industry in the 1979 House of Representatives defeat of Representative Lionel Van Deerlin's (D-Calif.) proposed Communications Act of 1979, a rewrite of the Federal Communications Act (US, 1934); the original act is seen here as a "cumbersome but necessary 'security blanket.'"

1259. Luksetich, William A. A STUDY OF REGULATION: THE MINNE-SOTA LIQUOR CASE. *Southern Econ. J. 1975 41(3): 457-465.* Describes the system of price controls on alcohol in Minnesota from 1951 to 1969, when it was repealed by the State Legislature, and compares the Minnesota case with a similar one in New York which was in effect from 1947 to 1964; also includes data on wholesale liquor prices from 1968 to 1971.

1260. Lurie, Jonathan. THE COMMODITIES EXCHANGE AND FED-ERAL REGULATION, 1922-1974: THE DECLINE OF SELF-GOVERN-MENT? *Policy Studies J. 1978 6(4): 488-492.* Discusses private commodities exchanges and their development into regulatory agencies of the federal government, 1922-74. One of 16 articles in this issue on agricultural policy.

1261. MacLaury, Judson. THE JOB SAFETY LAW OF 1970: ITS PAS-SAGE WAS PERILOUS. *Monthly Labor Rev. 1981 104(3): 18-24.* Traces the history of governmental legislation concerning workplace hazards from the first factory inspection law (Massachusetts, 1877) down to the Occupational Safety and Health Act (US, 1970) and then describes the three-year battle before Congress passed the 1970 act.

1262. Mahar, Franklyn D. THE POLITICS OF POWER: THE OREGON TEST FOR PARTNERSHIP. *Pacific Northwest Q. 1974 65(1): 29-37.* Studies the strategies started during the Eisenhower administration to establish an era of cooperation between private and public power resource groups in the Pacific Northwest. The Bonneville Power Administration came in for strong criticism under Eisenhower, and there was a concerted effort to subvert the development of the Columbia Valley Authority. The Eugene Water and Electric Board in Oregon and the Grant County Public Utility District in Washington served as "trial balloon" partnership ventures, but reelection of Senator Wayne Morse and several other Republican defeats insured the demise of the partnership concept. By the late 1960's, however, it had become evident that cooperation between the federal government and local agencies, both public and private, would be essential in the financing of power plants. 49 notes.   R. V. Ritter

1263. Manne, Henry G. FEDERAL CHARTERING: THE NEW AT-TACK ON CORPORATIONS. *Reason 1977 9(1): 16-21.* On 17 June 1976, before the Senate Commerce Committee, the author discussed corporations, defending their basic structure and offering opinion on corporation law.

1264. Margolis, Howard. THE POLITICS OF AUTO EMISSIONS. *Public Interest 1977 (49): 3-21.* Enforcement of tough automobile emissions standards enacted by Congress in the Clean Air Act (1970) has been regularly delayed through 1976. Despite talk of the bill's forcefulness and clarity, it is ambiguous enough to be acceptable to all parties—the automobile industry, environmentalists, and the government—while there is no solid scientific evidence to prove that the total elimination of auto emissions would detectably affect the nation's health. Although the failure to fully apply the 1970 legislation was greatly influenced by the oil embargo of 1973, flaws in the bill guaranteed protracted controversy over its implementation. These flaws can be traced to "political internalities," which pitted environmentalist interest against those of the producer, without directly involving the consumer.   S. Harrow

1265. Martin, Albro. THE TROUBLED SUBJECT OF RAILROAD REG-ULATION IN THE GILDED AGE—A REAPPRAISAL. *J. of Am. Hist. 1974 61(2): 339-371.* The Interstate Commerce Act of 1887 was primarily the result of a strong feeling against concentrations of economic power. The animus of the Hepburn Committee against pooling arrangements was directed by New York wholesalers who were alarmed at rate concessions given other eastern cities to maintain their westbound traffic over various trunk lines. Opposition to the long haul-short haul discrimination was not primarily based in the West, but in the older east coast areas near great eastern termini of trunk lines. In both cases the opposition was shortsighted and contributed to the long term problems of railroads in the United States. 74 notes.   K. B. West

1266. Marturano, Janice. U.S. LEGISLATIVE IMPORT RELIEF OP-TIONS: A COMPARISON OF PROCEDURES. *New York U. J. of Int. Law and Pol. 1981 13(4): 1049-1073.* Discusses the confusing array of federal statutory and regulatory provisions which present remedies to businesses seeking relief from import injury, and attempts to aid in selecting from among these options by detailing the procedures of the three most important: antidumping duties and countervailing duties under 1979 amendments to the Tariff Act of 1930 and sanctions under sections 201 and 406 of the 1979 amendments to the Trade Act of 1974.

1267. Marvel, Mary K. IMPLEMENTATION AND SAFETY REGULA-TION: VARIATIONS IN FEDERAL AND STATE ADMINISTRATION UNDER OSHA. *Administration & Soc. 1982 14(1): 15-33.* Concludes that the only way to avoid ineffective implementation of the Occupational Safety and Health Act (US, 1970) is "to forge links between policy formulation and imple-mentation," and to provide "a more prominent role for the policy analyst in program formulation."

1268. McCurdy, Charles W. THE KNIGHT SUGAR DECISION OF 1895 AND THE MODERNIZATION OF AMERICAN CORPORATION LAW, 1869-1903. *Business Hist. Rev. 1979 53(3): 304-343.* The conventional histori-cal wisdom that the 1896 Knight Sugar Trust decision of the Supreme Court was a manifestation of a judicial commitment to laissez faire is in error. The Fuller court believed state governments were competent to proceed against business combinations through *quo warranto* prosecutions, and it believed Pennsylvania would do so in this instance. To decide the case in favor of the Justice Department would have, in the court's view, interfered with state control of foreign corpora-tions. In state after state, however, authorities declined to use those powers for fear of local economic consequences. Based on judicial decisions and other public documents; 122 notes.   C. J. Pusateri

1269. McDonald, Rita and Dunbar, Robert G. THE INITIATION OF THE MCNARY-HAUGEN MOVEMENT IN MONTANA AND THE PACIFIC NORTHWEST. *Pacific Northwest Q. 1980 71(2): 63-71.* Declining crop prices and rising costs of production during the early 1920's hit Pacific Northwest wheat farmers especially hard and they began organizing to discuss marketing remedies. A plan suggested by George N. Peek and Hugh S. Johnson of the Moline Plow Company called for new tariffs to protect farmers from foreign producers and a federal program for price supports. Secretary of Agriculture Henry C. Wallace and Henry C. Taylor, head of the Bureau of Agricultural Economics, rallied behind the plan which formed the basis for the McNary-Haugen bill. Although the McNary-Haugen bill failed passage during the Republican administrations of the 1920's, it became the basis for subsequent New Deal legislation. Based on newspapers and archival sources; 5 photos, 37 notes.   M. L. Tate

1270. McFadyen, Richard E. THE FDA'S REGULATION AND CON-TROL OF ANTIBIOTICS IN THE 1950S: THE HENRY WELCH SCAN-DAL, FÉLIX MARTÍ-IBÁÑEZ, AND CHARLES PFIZER & CO. *Bull. of the Hist. of Medicine 1979 53(2): 159-169.* In late 1959, Dr. Henry Welch, a high official of the Food and Drug Administration, was charged with conflict of interest involving the federal regulation of antibiotics. The scandal indicated that it was dangerous for the agency to be closely intertwined with the industry it was supposed to regulate. Welch, who was chief regulator of the antibiotics industry, was chief editor of scientific papers sponsored by drug companies and which appeared in periodicals supported by the drug companies' own advertising and purchases of reprints. This went on from 1953 to 1960. The Kefauver investiga-tion revealed the degree to which Welch was indebted to the drug industry, and Welch resigned and received a federal disability pension. In 1962, amendments to the Food and Drug law revised the status of the agency and revitalized its regulation of drugs. 44 notes.   M. Kaufman

1271. McQuaid, Kim.   THE BUSINESS ADVISORY COUNCIL OF THE DEPARTMENT OF COMMERCE, 1933-1961: A STUDY IN CORPORATE/GOVERNMENT RELATIONS. *Res. in Econ. Hist. 1976 1: 171-197.* Discusses the Business Advisory Council and analyzes its power and influence. The council was early packed with powerful figures from the business, and especially the industrial world. Relationships with the federal government were stormy from the outset, as various reformers, powerful political personages, and organizations sought to shape the council to serve their own interests. In 1961, the council was in effect severed from its advisory role in the federal government. Public records were not maintained, but there is no evidence to suggest that the council really ran the country, or even served as a focus for a unified corporate ideal. 34 notes, ref.   V. L. Human

1272. McQuaid, Kim.   THE FRUSTRATION OF CORPORATE REVIVAL DURING THE EARLY NEW DEAL. *Historian 1979 41(4): 682-704.* Recent years have witnessed a shift in New Deal historiography, emphasizing continuities between the 1920's and 1930's. The concept of "corporate liberalism" has emerged from studies investigating the relationship between big business and the state. Examines two quasigovernmental agencies that enjoyed impressive measures of advisory influence during the early years of the New Deal—the Business Advisory Council of the Department of Commerce and the Industrial Advisory Board of the National Recovery Administration. Details the creation, early history, and membership of these agencies, and concludes that, while continuity between the New Era and the New Deal is overdrawn, corporate liberalism did weather the storm. Primary sources; 42 notes.   R. S. Sliwoski

1273. Mead, Walter J.   THE PERFORMANCE OF GOVERNMENT IN ENERGY REGULATIONS. *Am. Econ. Rev. 1979 69(2): 352-356.* Government regulation has been harmful to resource conservation; the reason is political economy. The government regulates energy with contradictory objectives in mind. Fifty years of governmental policy contributed to the current disaster in American energy programs. 12 ref.   D. K. Pickens

1274. Menzel, Donald C. and Edgmon, Terry D.   THE STRUGGLE TO IMPLEMENT A NATIONAL SURFACE MINING POLICY. *Publius 1980 10(1): 81-91.* The passage of the Surface Mining Control and Reclamation Act (US, 1977), known as the Coal Act, set the stage for an implementation struggle that pitted federal administrative rule-making against state mine regulatory practices, raising long-term questions about federal legislation mandating intergovernmental relations. The Office of Surface Mining, directed by Walter Heine, faced different problems in the arid West where much land being mined has been federally controlled, and in the East, where deep mining and ongoing state reclamation projects have complicated federal implementation. The 1979 Rockefeller Amendment extends implementation time and increases state autonomy. Based on US government documents and press reports; table, 27 notes.
C. B. Schulz

1275. Mochizuki, Kiyohito. NIJISSEIKI SHOTŌ AMERIKA NO KŌJŌ KANTOKUKAN SEIDO [The factory inspector systems in the United States in the early 20th century]. *Matsuyama Shōdai Ronshū [Japan] 1970 21(5): 19-37.* Discusses factory management, labor laws and their enforcement, factory inspection, and industrial and public policy in the United States in the early 20th century. E. Okuizumi/S

1276. Monkkonen, Eric. CAN NEBRASKA OR ANY STATE REGULATE RAILROADS? SMYTH V. AMES, 1898. *Nebraska Hist. 1973 54(3): 365-382.* Analyzes *Smith vs. Ames* from its inception in 1893 as a result of the Nebraska legislature's passage of the Newberry Bill regulating railroad rates. Examines the case within three distinct yet interrelated contexts: economic, social-political, and legal. Discusses the historiography of railroad regulation. R. Lowitt

1277. Moore, Thomas Gale. THE BENEFICIARIES OF TRUCKING REGULATION. *J. of Law and Econ. 1978 21(2): 327-343.* Discusses the benefits to labor and the holders of public convenience and necessity "carrying commodity" certificates deriving from the Interstate Commerce Commission (ICC)'s regulation of the trucking industry, 1938-76.

1278. Morash, Edward A. REGULATORY POLICY AND INDUSTRY STRUCTURE: THE CASE OF INTERSTATE HOUSEHOLD GOODS CARRIERS. *Land Econ. 1981 57(4): 544-557.* Finds an inverse relationship between carrier service and financial performance. Regulations inhibit the introduction of new systems of service delivery that might change carrier operating practices. Based on ICC and survey data; 3 tables, fig., 24 notes, biblio. E. S. Johnson

1279. Nadel, Mark V. THE HIDDEN DIMENSION OF PUBLIC POLICY: PRIVATE GOVERNMENTS AND THE POLICY-MAKING PROCESS. *J. of Pol. 1975 37(1): 2-34.* Challenges the widespread assumption of political scientists that public policy is limited to government policy. The prevailing definitions present a paradox that leads to confusion in such areas as the "nondecision" controversy: public policy is equated with government policy but it is frequently not clear whether particular organizations are governmental or non-governmental. Suggests that a preferable strategy would be to analyze the nature of public policy and then to determine who makes it. Public policy is defined as an allocation of values that is authoritative, binding, and intentional. Using large corporations as an example, a three-fold typology of public policy is presented: resource transfer, regulatory, and constituent policies. It is argued that in all three categories corporations implement policies that fulfill the criteria of public policy. J

1280. Nichols, Albert L. and Zeckhauser, Richard. GOVERNMENT COMES TO THE WORKPLACE: AN ASSESSMENT OF OSHA. *Public Interest 1977 (49): 39-69.* Congress passed the Occupational Safety and Health Act (1970) "to assure so far as possible . . . safe and healthful working conditions" for all workers. While imposing significant economic costs, the act has accomplished little. OSHA has failed because it has focused on job safety rather than on occupational health, and has employed direct regulation rather than an incentive approach. 9 notes. S. Harrow

1281. Nolan-Haley, Jacqueline M. THE TRIGGER PRICE MECHANISM: PROTECTING COMPETITION OR COMPETITORS? *New York U. J. of Int. Law and Pol. 1980 13(1): 1-25.* Discusses the degree to which foreign imports have been responsible for the decline of the US Steel Industry and government efforts to reduce these imports, most recently by means of the antidumping Trigger Price Mechanism, criticized as contrary to antitrust aims.

1282. Norval, Morgan. KEPT CRITICS. *Reason 1981 13(3): 37-42.* Traces the history of the Federal Trade Commission (FTC) from its founding in 1914 to its present role since the 1975 Federal Trade Commission Improvements Act (the Magnuson-Moss Act) which granted the FTC sweeping powers to issue industry-wide regulations; and comments on FTC abuses of its intervenor funding program, which result in higher costs for the consumer and increased bureaucracy.

1283. O'Day, Carol H. THE ROLE OF THE INTERVENTIONIST STATE IN FOOD AND AGRICULTURAL POLICY. *Social Sci. J. 1979 16(1): 1-16.* Discusses agricultural policy during 1800-1975 from a political viewpoint and offers insights for future evaluations of agricultural policy.

1284. Olson, C. Vincent and Trapani, John M., III. WHO HAS BENEFITED FROM REGULATION OF THE AIRLINE INDUSTRY? *J. of Law & Econ. 1981 24(1): 75-93.* Evaluates the policies of the Civil Aeronautics Board and shows that federal regulations have benefited the airlines at consumers' expense; 1971-80.

1285. Palmer, Bryan. CLASS, CONCEPTION AND CONFLICT: THE THRUST FOR EFFICIENCY, MANAGERIAL VIEWS OF LABOR AND THE WORKING CLASS REBELLION, 1903-1922. *R. of Pol. Econ. 1975 7(2): 31-49.* Considers managerial efforts to implement scientific management techniques, and to maximize efficiency at the expense of the workers, and the workers' response, such as the Illinois Central and Harriman lines Railroad Carmen's Strike (1911-15).

1286. Panzar, John C. REGULATION, DEREGULATION, AND ECONOMIC EFFICIENCY: THE CASE OF THE C.A.B. *Am. Econ. Rev. 1980 70(2): 311-315.* Discussing the Civil Aeronautics Board and the governmental sham of competitive contracting and other elements of regulation, cites three changes since the 1930's: 1) a renewed public interest in competition, 2) market growth due to competition within past regulation, and 3) airline markets are basically contestable in actuality. Michael E. Levine's discussion (pp. 318-319) questions the author's lack of distinction among perfect regulation, imperfect competition, and socially optimal prices. Accordingly, basic assumptions should be reexamined. 11 ref. D. K. Pickens

1287. Parker, Francis H. and Gilbert, Gorman. RAIL PLANNING—CRISIS AND OPPORTUNITY. *J. of The Am. Inst. of Planners 1977 43(1): 13-23.* The role of the federal and state governments with respect to railroads has been dramatically changed by the establishment of ConRail and Amtrak. No longer does the "railroad problem" mean passenger service only, and no longer does the problem rest only in the private sector. With the planning of ConRail, federal and state governments have moved solidly into rail planning and operations. Planners in the public sector will increasingly be concerned with a wide range of problems facing railroads. Currently, the impact of these problems is focused primarily on the state level where the responsibility lies for determining the feasibility of subsidizing unprofitable branch lines. However, other problems, such as urban rail relocation, are emerging as areas of public concern. This article outlines these problems as well as recent efforts to solve them.   J

1288. Peltzman, Sam. THE EFFECTS OF AUTOMOBILE SAFETY REG-
ULATION. *J. of Pol. Econ. 1975 83(4): 677-725.* Technological studies imply that annual highway deaths would be 20 percent greater without legally mandated installation of various safety devices on automobiles. However, this literature ignores offsetting effects of nonregulatory demand for safety and driver response to the devices. This article indicates that these offsets are virtually complete, so that regulation has not decreased highway deaths. Time-series (but not cross-section) data imply some saving of auto occupants' lives at the expense of more pedestrian deaths and more nonfatal accidents, a pattern consistent with optimal driver response to regulation.   J

1289. Perry, Charles S. GOVERNMENT REGULATION OF COAL
MINE SAFETY: EFFECTS OF SPENDING UNDER STRONG AND
WEAK LAW. *Am. Pol. Q. 1982 10(3): 303-314.* Federal government spending on mine health and safety has strongly reduced bituminous coal mine fatalities when safety law has been strong but not when law has been weak.   J

1290. Peterman, John L. THE INTERNATIONAL SALT CASE. *J. of
Law and Econ. 1979 22(2): 351-364.* Investigates the Supreme Court's decision that International Salt Co. was illegally tying the sale of their salt to the lease of the Lixator machine, positing that the deal in no way hurt the customers in the 1940's.

1291. Peterson, William H. THE PUBLIC INTEREST OF PRIVATE EN-
TERPRISE—AND THE PRIVATE INTEREST OF PUBLIC POLICY.
Freeman 1974 24(2): 82-87. "An attempt to define the limits of government which are consistent with private enterprise and consumer choice."   S

1292. Petkas, Peter J. THE U.S. REGULATORY SYSTEM: PARTNER-
SHIP OR MAZE? *Natl. Civic Rev. 1981 70(6): 297-301.* The US Regulatory Council was created in 1978 to coordinate the regulatory system of more than 90 agencies producing more than 2,000 rules per year. The system grew piecemeal, with little thought given over time to the cumulative impact. Working through the federal regional councils, and with state and local governments, major steps have been taken to bring better management to the process.   J

1293. Pettus, Beryl E. OSHA INSPECTION COSTS, COMPLIANCE
COSTS, AND OTHER OUTCOMES: THE FIRST DECADE. *Policy Studies
Rev. 1982 1(3): 596-614.* Despite the common criticism of the Occupational Safety and Health Act (US, 1970) that it has greatly increased the cost of operation of the regulated industries while providing few benefits, the program still has the potential to change working conditions and practices, particularly in industrial technology and innovation, labor-management relations, preventive industrial medicine, and other important areas.

1294.	Phillips, Almarin.	PUBLIC REGULATION AND CORPORATE SOCIAL BEHAVIOR: AN APPLICATION OF MANAGERIAL DISCRETION MODELS.	*R. of Social Econ. 1974 32(1): 49-61.*

1295.	Piott, Steven L.	MISSOURI AND MONOPOLY: THE 1890S AS AN EXPERIMENT IN LAW ENFORCEMENT.	*Missouri Hist. Rev. 1979 74(1): 21-49.* Early antitrust movements centered at the local and state levels where an aroused public and journalistic exposure impelled policymakers toward legislative solutions. Missouri's antitrust law did not work effectively until after 1898. Public anger and newspaper revelations about excessive fire insurance rates led the attorney general to go to court to argue the unconstitutionality of a provision exempting insurance companies in St. Louis and Kansas City under the law and to claim that the Kansas City Board of Fire Underwriters regulated rates throughout the state. The test case provided a model for other state antitrust movements. 7 illus., 9 photos, 64 notes.					W. F. Zornow

1296.	Pittman, Walter.	CHEMICAL REGULATION IN MISSISSIPPI: THE STATE LABORATORY (1882-).	*J. of Mississippi Hist. 1979 41(2): 133-153.* Discusses the regulatory services of the Mississippi State Chemical Laboratory, located on the Mississippi State University campus, and its key leaders during the organization's 97 years. Traces the laboratory's close association with Mississippi agriculture as well as its expanded jurisdiction into pure food and drug regulation, petroleum and chemical analysis, and research. Important figures in the laboratory's history include: John A. Myers, W. L. Hutchinson, William Flowers Hand, M. P. Etheredge, and Doctor James P. Minyard, Jr. The evolution of the laboratory's administrative structure into its present four divisions is discussed. Several dramatic incidents, such as the discovery of the contamination of millions of Mississippi chickens by the pesticide Dieldrin in 1974, illustrate the invaluable service which the State Laboratory has long rendered.					M. S. Legan

1297.	Platt, Rutherford H.	THE LOSS OF FARMLAND: EVOLUTION OF PUBLIC RESPONSE.	*Geographical Rev. 1977 67(1): 93-101.* State land use regulation and local land policy along Massachusetts' Connecticut River are responding to an ever-decreasing amount of land being used for farming, 1969-74.

1298.	Polley, Richard W.; Zaichkowsky, Judy; and Fryer, Christina.	REGULATION HASN'T CHANGED TV ADS MUCH.	*Journalism Q. 1980 57(3): 438-446.* Reports on a study of television commercials presented on three Canadian stations and one American station over a six-day period in 1977. The results, when compared with an earlier study, reveal that efforts to more effectively regulate television advertising have been largely unsuccessful in terms of increasing the amount of information available to the consumer in such ads. However, it appears that outright deception in television commercials has been reduced. 5 tables, chart, 10 notes.					J. S. Coleman

1299.	Ponko, Vincent W., Jr.	THE ALASKAN COAL COMMISSION. *Alaska J. 1978 8(2): 118-129.* An account of the appointment, duties and work of the Alaskan Coal Commission made responsible for mining, transporting and setting up storage and loading facilities at Portage Bay and Seward. It was intended that this would provide cheaper but satisfactory fuel for the Pacific fleet of the US Navy. The operation centered in the Chickaloon Coal Mine in the Matanuska Valley. The land was under the supervision of the Department of the Navy operating under a $1,000,000 appropriation from Congress. In 1922 the supervision reverted to the Alaskan Engineering Commission under the Department of the Interior. Much attention had been given to comfortable living conditions and recreation for the employees and their families. 8 photos, 34 notes.

R. V. Ritter

1300. Pool, Ithiel de Sola. GOVERNMENT REGULATION IN THE COMMUNICATION SYSTEM. *Pro. of the Acad. of Pol. Sci. 1982 34(4): 121-130.* Government has an interest in the universality and efficiency of communications, but it is not a simple item to legislate. However, by research and development expenditures, its own procurement policies, and standards for enfranchised common causes, the government can play an important role in promoting proficiency and progress. Primary sources; fig., 6 notes.

T. P. Richardson

1301. Porter, David. SENATOR PAT HARRISON OF MISSISSIPPI AND THE RECIPROCAL TRADE ACT OF 1940. *J. of Mississippi Hist. 1974 36(4): 363-376.* Shows how Mississippi Senator Pat Harrison, chairman of the Senate Finance Committee and a strong supporter of low tariff and reciprocal trade policies, worked closely with the executive branch in 1940 to extend the reciprocal trade program for three years. His actions saved a key administration program "from probable defeat." Harrison "shrewdly had exerted impressive influence at both the committee and floor levels" to win a series of close votes. Based on primary and secondary sources; 18 notes. J. W. Hillje

1302. Priebe, Paul M. and Kauffman, George B. MAKING GOVERNMENTAL POLICY UNDER CONDITIONS OF SCIENTIFIC UNCERTAINTY: A CENTURY OF CONTROVERSY ABOUT SACCHARIN IN CONGRESS AND THE LABORATORY. *Minerva [Great Britain] 1980 18(4): 556-574.* Discusses the medical and pharmacological debate concerning saccharin since its discovery in 1878, focuses on attempts at federal regulation since 1907, the role of the National Academy of Sciences, and the role of the Food and Drug Administration.

1303. Pucher, John. EQUITY IN TRANSIT FINANCE: DISTRIBUTION OF TRANSIT SUBSIDY BENEFITS AND COSTS AMONG INCOME CLASSES. *J. of the Am. Planning Assoc. 1981 47(4): 387-407.* Transit subsidies in the United States increased 11-fold between 1970 and 1979. One of the key justifications of this growth was the belief that the poor would be the primary beneficiaries. Overall, transit subsidization through taxation has redistributed income from high income to low income classes, but it has not been very effective in targeting benefits to the poor. The current transit program is therefore not primarily justifiable on the ground of progressive redistribution. J/S

1304. Rakowski, James P. and Johnson, James C. AIRLINE DEREGULATION: PROBLEMS AND PROSPECTS. *Q. Rev. of Econ. and Business 1979 19(4): 65-78.* Airline deregulation is now a fact of life. This article traces the turbulent history of the Air Transport Deregulation Act of 1978. Arguments for and against its enactment are noted, along with a brief regulatory history of the airlines. It is concluded that deregulation will prove beneficial to the traveling public, airline employees, and airlines. Biblio.   J

1305. Redburn, Thomas. OPEN FILES: LETTING EXXON IN. *Washington Monthly 1975 7(5/6): 18-21.* Examines the Freedom of Information Act (1966) and its 1974 amendments, noting that the chief beneficiaries have been large law firms and the corporations that can hire them to obtain information from government agencies concerning their rivals' trade secrets.

1306. Reid, Frank. THE RESPONSE OF WAGES TO THE REMOVAL OF CONTROLS: THE AMERICAN EXPERIENCE. *Industrial Relations [Canada] 1977 32(4): 621-627.* Assesses the format of wage and price controls, 1971-74, developing a model to explain the rate of wage change and the effect of the controls.

1307. Reingold, Lester. THE CRASHES OF '79: THE FAA STALLS OUT. *Washington Monthly 1979 11(10): 50-58.* Discusses the Federal Aviation Administration's failure to effectively promote flight safety in commercial airplanes during the 1970's.

1308. Reynolds, Alan. DOLLARS AND SENSE. *Reason 1982 14(1): 41-43, 49.* Asserts that government regulation of finance has failed to keep pace with the realities of modern banking, creating more problems than it solves.

1309. Rosapepe, James. CORPORATIONS AND STATE TAXES: THE BIG ONES GET AWAY. *Washington Monthly 1975 6(11): 14-19.* Advocates state auditing of corporations to insure voluntary compliance with state income tax regulations.   S

1310. Rosen, Corey. HOW THE GOVERNMENT DROVE THE SMALL AIRLINES OUT OF BUSINESS. *Washington Monthly 1977 9(4): 26-30.* Since World War II, the history of small airlines shows how the federal government harasses and discourages small businesses while protecting large corporations.

1311. Rosen, Philip T. BROADCASTING: THE POLITICS OF INNOVATION. *Continuity 1981 (3): 51-61.* Examines the government's struggle to regulate a budding radio industry and discusses the actions taken by the Navy Department, the Post Office Department, and the Commerce Department to impose controls on radio broadcasting. Ultimately Secretary of Commerce Herbert C. Hoover was successful in wresting control of radio broadcasting from the navy and post office by exercising licensing power.   W. A. Wiegand

1312. Rosenthal, Albert J. EMPLOYMENT DISCRIMINATION AND THE LAW. *Ann. of the Am. Acad. of Pol. and Social Sci. 1973 (407): 91-101.* "While there have been prohibitions, by the federal, state, and local governments, against racial discrimination in employment since the 1940s, the major legal weapon against such discrimination has been Title VII of the Civil Rights Act of 1964. The largest part of the burden of enforcing this statute has not been borne by the federal government, but rather by civil rights organizations, whose resources have been limited. A remarkable record of favorable judicial decisions has been achieved in cases brought under this statue. Nevertheless, the disparities between blacks and whites in average income and in proportionate unemployment have not been markedly reduced. Stronger legislation and a greater commitment on the part of all branches of government as well as the public seem necessary if there is to be more significant progress toward truly fair employment practices." J

1313. Rudzitis, Gundars. RESOLUTION OF AN OIL-SHRIMP ENVIRONMENTAL CONFLICT. *Geog. Rev. 1982 72(2): 190-199.* In response to the oil embargo, the United States established a Strategic Petroleum Reserve Program to store one billion barrels of oil in salt domes along the Texas and Louisiana coast. Because the program required the disposal of brine in the gulf, a controversy arose over the effects of the brine disposal on the shrimp industry. On one side was the US Department of Energy, on the other the US Environmental Protection Agency. A cost-benefit analysis resolved the dispute in favor of the latter. J

1314. Ruttenberg, Ruth. REGULATION IS THE MOTHER OF INVENTION. *Working Papers for a New Soc. 1981 8(3): 42-47.* Suggests, on the basis of the annual reports of several large American corporations, that arguments against pollution control and other forms of industry regulation by the federal government are largely misplaced, since regulatory practices have encouraged new inventions, generally increased productivity and efficiency, and have given rise to a new industry, pollution control, which by 1974 employed 677,900 workers.

1315. Saloutos, Theodore. NEW DEAL AGRICULTURAL POLICY: AN EVALUATION. *J. of Am. Hist. 1974 61(2): 394-416.* An analysis of the manifold aspects of New Deal farm policy demonstrates that efforts of the first Agricultural Adjustment Administration to raise prices to parity were not very successful, that acreage reduction was countered by expansion of yield per acre, that relatively few acres of crop land subject to erosion were in fact covered by plans of the Soil Conservation Service, and that the concept of the second AAA's "ever normal granary" did develop reserves and seemed to operate successfully. In spite of the "agricultural establishment," more was done for tenant farmers, sharecroppers, and farm laborers than is commonly supposed. On the whole, the New Deal constituted "the greatest innovative epoch in the history of American agriculture." 72 notes. K. B. West

1316. Sansone, Wallace T. DOMESTIC SHIPPING AND AMERICAN MARITIME POLICY. *US Naval Inst. Pro. 1974 100(5): 162-177.* An impending crisis in the rail and motor freight transportation industries has necessitated an expansion of the United States' waterborne carrying capacity to meet future needs. In October 1971, the Maritime Administration established the Office of Domestic Shipping to promote all segments of the domestic shipping industry, a move which recognized domestic shipping as an essential part of the US Merchant Marine "and a vital element of the national transportation system." 7 photos, chart, 12 notes. A. N. Garland

1317. Schaffer, Ronald. WORLD WAR I: BUSINESS. *Mankind 1977 5(11): 30-32.* The actions on the part of the federal government in World War I directed toward managing the war economy brought about a basic change in the structure of the American economy. It made palatable to businessmen the movement toward centralized governmental control that they had always previously opposed. The New Deal capitalized on these changed attitudes and in fact used many of the same methods that had originated during the conflict.

N. Lederer

1318. Schechter, Stephen L. THE CONCORDE AND PORT NOISE COMPLAINTS: THE COMMERCE AND SUPREMACY CLAUSES ENTER THE SUPERSONIC AGE. *Publius 1978 8(1): 135-158.* The four federal court decisions in *British Airways Bd.* v. *Port Authority of New York* (US, 1977) add little to existing law in this area. *City of Burbank* v. *Lockheed Air Terminal* (US, 1973) established the principle that Congress, through the Federal Aviation Act (US, 1958), "preempts the field of noise regulation insofar as it involves controlling the flight of aircraft," but a 1976 district court decision on a Hayward (California) city ordinance upholds the right of local bodies to regulate airport noise in their capacity as airport proprietors. *Air Transport Association* v. *Crotti* (US, 1975) upheld the right of states to order airport proprietors to set noise standards—but only for noise levels averaged over several hours. The last-minute noise requirements set by the Port Authority, after its bid to flatly ban SST's was ruled "discriminatory," were in fact met by the Concorde, and the fizzle may become deafening as the SST proves increasingly a white elephant. Table, 20 notes.

L. W. Van Wyk

1319. Schmidt, Benno C., Jr. ACCESS TO THE BROADCAST MEDIA: THE LEGISLATIVE PRECEDENTS. *J. of Communication 1978 28(2): 60-68.* Traces broadcast regulations since 1927 in the United States, and discusses the changing attitudes of the Federal Communications Commission and the Supreme Court from the Radio Act of 1927 until 1974.

1320. Seavoy, Ronald E. THE PUBLIC SERVICE ORIGINS OF THE AMERICAN BUSINESS CORPORATION. *Business Hist. Rev. 1978 52(1): 30-60.* In the colonial era, most corporations chartered by the Massachusetts and New York legislatures were created for charitable, religious, or educational purposes. Yet, the formation of these entities served as a "major training ground" for individuals who would later be principals in profit-making ventures. These public service organizations also "conditioned" society to the acceptance of the corporation as a permanent feature of economic life. Based on colonial records and published sources; 65 notes.

C. J. Pusateri

1321. Seltzer, Alan L. WOODROW WILSON AS "CORPORATE LIBERAL": TOWARD A RECONSIDERATION OF LEFT REVISIONIST HISTORIOGRAPHY. *Western Pol. Q. 1977 30(2): 183-212.* Examination of Woodrow Wilson's opposition to artificial combination, the Justice Department's antitrust prosecutions, Wilson's foreign trade policies, and his speeches on foreign trade reveals that Wilson supported vigorous antitrust policy, contrary to left revisionist interpretations.

1322. Semmens, John. REGULATION OF THE TRUCKERS, BY THE TRUCKERS, FOR THE TRUCKERS. *Reason 1979 10(11): 26-29.* Assesses the impact of federal regulation on the private trucking industry, especially in terms of costs to consumers, 1970's.

1323. Shearer, Derek. DREAMS AND SCHEMES: A CATALOGUE OF PROPOSALS. *Working Papers for a New Soc. 1975 3(3): 38-46.* Explores current legislative ideas for tax reform, full employment, controlling corporations and economic planning.

1324. Shultz, George P. and Dam, Kenneth W. REFLECTIONS ON WAGE AND PRICE CONTROLS. *Industrial and Labor Relations Rev. 1977 30(2): 139-151.* This article appraises the controls program of 1971-74 in the context of a general analysis of all such programs. The authors suggest, among other ideas, that wage and price control programs have a "life cycle" that is both inevitable and remarkably short in duration, that the tendency of such programs to concentrate on the largest firms and unions is based on a faulty analysis of how the economy operates, and that one of the most difficult problems faced by control programs is dealing with the unending interaction of controls with other public programs as well as with private actions. The authors conclude that the principal lesson of the 1971-74 experience is that wage and price controls are not an effective method for dealing with inflation. J

1325. Siedel, George J. CORPORATE GOVERNANCE UNDER THE FOREIGN CORRUPT PRACTICES ACT. *Q. Rev. of Econ. and Business 1981 21(3): 43-48.* A section of the Foreign Corrupt Practices Act (US, 1977) deals with accounting standards that apply to both foreign and domestic activities of companies. One of these standards requires a system of internal accounting controls. An examination of legislative history, administrative releases, and judicial opinions reveals that the meaning of internal accounting controls is unclear and subject to interpretation. Primary sources; 5 notes. A. Drysdale

1326. Skocpol, Theda and Finegold, Kenneth. STATE CAPACITY AND ECONOMIC INTERVENTION IN THE EARLY NEW DEAL. *Pol. Sci. Q. 1982 97(2): 255-278.* Discusses the failure of the National Recovery Administration and the relative success of the Agricultural Adjustment Administration (AAA) in the 1930's, to underline the greater capacity of the US government to intervene in the agricultural, rather than in the industrial, economy. Both administrations promised much during the early New Deal, but only the goals of the AAA were attainable. 75 notes. J. Powell

1327. Smith, Rodney T. and Phelps, Charles E. THE SUBTLE IMPACT OF PRICE CONTROLS ON DOMESTIC OIL PRODUCTION. *Am. Econ. Rev. 1968 68(2): 428-436.* The preliminary implication of this statistical study is that price controls did not significantly reduce production but that such controls did create a subtle curse: a future increase in real world oil prices which will mean more US income to OPEC than occurred in past price increases. In a comment, Stephen Breyer agrees with this finding but believes that the study addresses the wrong issue. Table, fig., ref. D. K. Pickens

1328. Steen, Harold K., ed. CAPITAL GAINS FOR FOREST LANDS: ORIGINS OF THE 1944 TAX LEGISLATION. *J. of Forest Hist. 1978 22(3): 146-153.* The Bailey Amendment of 1944 (to the Revenue Act of 1942) provided, following a congressional override of President Franklin D. Roosevelt's veto, capital gains tax treatment for forest lands. Capital gains are often linked to the postwar upsurge in the practice of industrial forestry, symbolized in the popular tree farm movement. Origins of this legislation are examined from several perspectives: 1) discussion and comment from Senators Walter F. George, Robert A. Taft, and Alben W. Barkley in the *Congressional Record* of 23 February 1944; 2) a 1965 interview with Wilson M. Compton, former secretary-manager of the National Lumber Manufacturers Association, who recalls the critical influence of lumbermen John Philip Weyerhaeuser, Jr., and Frederick K. Weyerhaeuser; 3) a 1967 interview with R. Clifford Hall, formerly a forest taxation specialist with the Internal Revenue Service, who remained skeptical of the validity and impact of capital gains; and 4) excerpts from the published diaries of David T. Mason, an eminent consulting forester who lobbied during 1943-44 for passage of the legislation. 3 illus. 					R. J. Fahl

1329. Stone, Alan. THE F.T.C. AND ADVERTISING REGULATION: AN EXAMINATION OF AGENCY FAILURE. *Public Policy 1973 21(2): 203-234.*

1330. Sumner, David. WILDERNESS AND THE MINING LAW. *Living Wilderness 1973 37(121): 8-18.*

1331. Swigert, Victoria Lynn and Farrell, Ronald A. CORPORATE HOMICIDE: DEFINITIONAL PROCESSES IN THE CREATION OF DEVIANCE. *Law & Soc. Rev. 1980-81 15(1): 161-182.* Focuses on the history of events surrounding the indictment of Ford Motor Company on the charge of reckless homicide. Using information from media accounts, suggests that the expansion of legal parameters to include formerly exempt behavior was preceded by the development of a vocabulary of deviance, personalization of harm, and attributions of nonrepentance to the offender. 					J/S

1332. Tedlow, Richard S. FROM COMPETITOR TO CONSUMER: THE CHANGING FOCUS OF FEDERAL REGULATION OF ADVERTISING, 1914-1938. *Business Hist. Rev. 1981 55(1): 35-58.* The Federal Trade Commission (FTC), as envisioned at its inception in 1914, was concerned with the prevention of anticompetitive behavior in industry and not the regulation of advertising or consumer protection. However, by the 1920's federal court decisions had circumscribed FTC flexibility in antitrust areas, and advertising industry spokesmen were themselves openly calling for federal action to supplant inefficient state efforts. The passage of the Wagner-Lea amendments in 1938 gave needed support to this FTC activity by attempting a definition of false advertising and by imposing new penalties for violations of commission orders. Based principally on governmental records and contemporary periodical literature; 68 notes. 					C. J. Pusateri

1333. Temin, Peter. THE ORIGIN OF COMPULSORY DRUG PRESCRIPTIONS. *J. of Law and Econ. 1979 22(1): 91-106.* Traces events 1906-38 leading to passage of the Federal Food, Drug, and Cosmetic Act (US, 1938), traces regulation by the Federal Drug Administration which differentiated between non-prescription and prescription drugs, and describes subsequent regulation by the Congress and the Supreme Court, 1938-50's.

1334. Tobin, Richard J. SAFETY-RELATED DEFECTS IN MOTOR VEHICLES AND THE EVALUATION OF SELF-REGULATION. *Policy Studies Rev. 1982 1(3): 532-539.* Reviews the National Highway Traffic Safety

Administration's self-regulating program including recall of vehicles, the ever-changing definition of defects, frequency of defect reports, and the notification of vehicle owners, concluding that self-regulation has serious defects of its own.

1335. Ulen, Thomas S. THE MARKET FOR REGULATION: THE ICC FROM 1887 TO 1920. *Am. Econ. Rev. 1980 70(2): 306-310.* The demand for regulation came from within the Interstate Commerce Commission from 1903 to 1920. Over the years, interest groups changed until the ICC became the greatest interest group of all. In his discussion (pp. 317-318), Ellis W. Hawley cites the bibliographical inadequacies of this article's thesis. Covers 1887-1920. 15 ref.

D. K. Pickens

1336. Ulen, Thomas S.; Lurie, Jonathan, (commentary). THE REGULA-TION OF GRAIN WAREHOUSING AND ITS ECONOMIC EFFECTS: THE COMPETITIVE POSITION OF CHICAGO IN THE 1870'S AND 1880'S. *Agric. Hist. 1982 56(1): 194-214.* The regulation of grain warehouses by Illinois had little effect on their operation. Regulatory laws carried few penal-ties, and most companies did not even bother to purchase the required licenses for operating. The industry ignored provisions against fraudulent warehouse receipts until a fire in 1872 revealed the extent of the practice and forced the industry to police itself. It was not regulation that reduced storage rates or slowed the increase in elevator capacity but rather the rise of the all rail route east, which reduced the need to unload grain in Chicago. Comments, pp. 211-214. Based on Chicago Board of Trade and regulatory documents; 2 tables, 63 notes.

D. E. Bowers

1337. Ullman, Robert. GM AND THE AUTO WORKERS: OSHA RE-SHUFFLES THE DECK. *Working Papers for a New Soc. 1978 6(3): 50-54.* Regulations of the Occupational Safety and Health Administration, 1971-78, have reduced health and safety hazards in General Motors' Pontiac (Michigan) automobile plant and have strengthened union-management relations by allowing unprecedented control over working conditions by the United Automobile Work-ers of America.

1338. Urofsky, Melvin I. PROPOSED FEDERAL INCORPORATION IN THE PROGRESSIVE ERA. *Am. J. of Legal Hist. 1982 26(2): 160-183.* The necessity of a federal incorporation law was debated throughout the Progressive era. Gaining adherents from business, government, labor, and the law, the social and economic backgrounds of the principal movers of such a law are assessed in light of their failure to have it enacted. The liberal New Jersey Holding Company Act of 1891 bypassed nearly all common law restrictions on corporations. Thus various interests gathered under William Jennings Bryan in 1896 to promote a tight and coordinated system of national legislation on company incorporations during 1900-11, but these interests broke up with the collapse of Theodore Roosevelt's Progressive coalition in the election of 1912. Based on government documents, correspondence of political and business leaders, and secondary sources; 68 notes.

L. A. Knafla

1339. Vietor, Richard H. K. BUSINESSMEN AND THE POLITICAL ECONOMY: THE RAILROAD RATE CONTROVERSY OF 1905. *J. of Am. Hist. 1977 64(1): 47-66.* Examines the controversy preceding the enactment of railroad legislation, specifically the Hepburn Act (US, 1906), which gave the Interstate Commerce Commission the power to fix rates. Identifies the business interests that opposed and supported the Hepburn Act, including the fruit, grain, lumber, livestock, and coal mining concerns. Shippers who suffered under contemporary conditions favored the act, while shippers and railroads that profited from existing rates resisted the change. 39 notes.   J. B. Reed

1340. Vogel, David. BUSINESS DISTRUST OF GOVERNMENT. *Center Mag. 1977 10(6): 69-78.* Discusses enmity existing between the business community and the federal government; offers explanations for this 20th-century development and touches on business attitudes toward democracy.

1341. Welborn, David M. and Brown, Anthony E. POWER AND POLITICS IN FEDERAL REGULATORY COMMISSIONS. *Administration and Soc. 1980 12(1): 37-68.* Studies seven federal regulatory commissions from 1961 to 1974 and concludes that, contrary to common perceptions, the structures of powers are notably stable, and that there is substantial integration in the position of chairman.

1342. West, Robert Craig. REAL BILLS, THE GOLD STANDARD, AND CENTRAL BANK POLICY. *Business Hist. Rev. 1976 50(4): 503-513.* The Federal Reserve Act was formulated to meet the economic circumstances of the late 19th and early 20th centuries and even before the Act went into operation, those circumstances had changed. As a result, the Federal Reserve System had to develop new policies and abandon such obsolete ones as the "real bills doctrine" and the gold standard. 19 notes.   C. J. Pusateri

1343. Whisenhunt, Donald W. HUEY LONG AND THE TEXAS COTTON ACREAGE CONTROL LAW OF 1931. *Louisiana Studies 1974 13(2): 142-153.* Studies the reaction to Governor Huey P. Long's proposal that all cotton-producing states forbid the planting of cotton in 1932 as a means of bolstering the sagging price of cotton. Getting Texas' approval and cooperation was crucial to its success; hence great pressure, not only from Long but also from other states. Texas finally passed its own less stringent regulatory bill, but that law was declared unconstitutional. The debate, however, did have value for the future in preparing the thinking of southern agriculture for the later New Deal crop limitation measures. 69 notes.   R. V. Ritter

1344. White, Roger S. STATE REGULATION OF COMMERCIAL BANKING IN U.S.A., 1781-1843. *Rev. Int. d'Hist. de la Banque [Italy] 1974 8: 1-21.* State governments inherited the implied power to grant charters of incorporation. By 1820 states had the power to set out conditions of incorporation, revise these conditions, and revoke charters, giving them the means to regulate the development of commercial banking. During the next 20 years, however, state regulation was ineffective, either because regulatory powers were not applied or not enforced. One possible exception to this was requirements regarding note redemption. Based on state legal codes, court cases, and secondary sources; 2 tables, 86 notes.   D. McGinnis

1345. Williams, Robert J. POLITICS AND REGULATORY REFORM: SOME ASPECTS OF THE AMERICAN EXPERIENCE. *Public Administration [Great Britain] 1979 57(Spr): 55-69.* Reviews attempts to reform the US independent regulatory agencies, 1937-79, and concludes that such executive proposals often represent frustrations at the constraints on executive power, although a recent change of emphasis reflecting a widespread view that there is excessive regulation has appeared in the Ash Council report of 1971.

1346. Williams, Robert J. THE POLITICS OF AMERICAN BROADCASTING: PUBLIC PURPOSES AND PRIVATE INTERESTS. *J. of Am. Studies [Great Britain] 1976 10(3): 329-340.* Reviews regulation by federal agencies of the American broadcasting industry since 1912. Since 1926 the Federal Radio Commission and the Federal Communications Commission, in turn, assumed the main regulatory responsibilities. Although accused of subservience to the vested interests regulated by the agencies, the latter generally performed ineffectively as a result of improper legislative guidance from Congress and political intimidation. The agencies became inordinately cautious and vacillating. Based on secondary sources; 20 notes. H. T. Lovin

1347. Witthans, Fred. ESTIMATES OF EFFECTIVE RATES OF PROTECTION FOR UNITED STATES INDUSTRIES IN 1967. *R. of Econ. and Statistics 1973 55(3): 362-364.*

1348. Wollert, James A. PROGRAMMING EVIDENCE RELATIVE TO THE ISSUES OF THE NCCB DECISION. *Journalism Q. 1978 55(2): 319-324.* Interprets television industry statistics for 1975 regarding programming practices and the "cross-ownership" of television stations by newspapers. The US Circuit Court of Appeals for the District of Columbia, in *National Citizens Committee for Broadcasting* v. *Federal Communications Commission* (1977), ordered the Federal Communications Commission (FCC) to work to abolish newspaper-broadcaster combinations in the interest of diversity in the media. This decision ignores evidence presented in 1975 to the court and the FCC that cross-owned television stations generally featured a higher percentage of news, public affairs, and other nonentertainment programming than did their local competitors. 28 notes. R. P. Sindermann, Jr.

1349. Wyche, Billy H. SOUTHERN INDUSTRIALISTS VIEW ORGANIZED LABOR IN THE NEW DEAL YEARS, 1933-1941. *Southern Studies 1980 19(20): 151-171.* Although the NIRA, or National Industrial Recovery Act (US, 1933), was at first greeted with enthusiasm by southern industrialists, they soon came to attack Section 7(a), which provided for collective bargaining. The general textile strike of 1934 and the emergence of the CIO (Congress of Industrial Organizations) aroused great fear and anger among the industrialists, who opposed the NLRA, or National Labor Relations Act (US, 1935), from the beginning. Economic rather than ideological factors played the leading role in shaping these views. Textiles, the leading industry of the South, had overexpanded and overproduced for many years, and costs had to be reduced. Union and management journals and other primary sources; 88 notes.
J. J. Buschen

1350. Wyman, Mark. MINING LAW IN IDAHO. *Idaho Yesterdays 1981 25(1): 14-22.* Idaho mining law had its antecedents in the laws worked out for the California mines. Hard-rock, deep-shaft mining demanded new laws, and the issue of mine safety became more important in the 20th century. Based on Idaho legal records, newspapers; illus., 2 photos, 33 notes. B. J. Paul

1351. Yandle, Bruce. A SOCIAL REGULATION CONTROVERSY: THE COTTON DUST STANDARD. *Social Sci. Q. 1982 63(1): 58-69.* Documents the evolution of the Occupational Health and Safety Administration's 1978 cotton dust standard, a prime example of social regulation in the 1970's designed to protect workers from the incidence of byssinosis, summarizes evidence presented by parties to the regulatory proceedings, and identifies the possible economic impacts of this controversial standard on the cotton textile industry and on cotton products.

1352. Yonce, Frederick J. LUMBERING AND THE PUBLIC TIMBER-LANDS IN WASHINGTON: THE ERA OF DISPOSAL. *J. of Forest Hist. 1978 22(1): 4-17.* Describes and analyzes the application of general land laws to the disposal of public timberland in Washington Territory and State. Public auction and private entry permitted unlimited purchases of surveyed land only during 1863-70, and US District Attorneys John J. McGilvra and Leander Holmes collected stumpage fees on government timber cut illegally rather than prosecute timber trespass. Thereafter the absence of legislation permitting acquisition of timber in quantities sizeable enough for commercial lumbering operations encouraged more trespass and subterfuge. The Timber and Stone Act (US, 1878), for example, diffused ownership into small, uneconomic units, thus forcing lumbermen to assemble larger units by fraudulent means. Though denounced by moralists, these deceits often represented practical accommodations to the irrelevancies and rigidities of the law. Actual concentration of timberland ownership was more a consequence of the Northern Pacific land grant than of the general land laws. Based on federal archival and published sources; map, table, 4 illus., 71 notes.   R. J. Fahl

1353. Zapadinskaia, S. GOSUDARSTVENNOE REGULIROVANIE SYR-'EVYKH OTRASLEI SSHA [The state regulation of raw material industries in the United States]. *Mirovaia Ekonomika i Mezhdunarodnye Otnosheniia [USSR] 1981 (10): 120-126.* Examines the introduction of government regulations for the raw materials industries during 1976-80. Russian.

1354. Zerbe, Richard O., Jr.; Lurie, Jonathan, (commentary). THE ORIGIN AND EFFECT OF GRAIN TRADE REGULATIONS IN THE LATE NINE-TEENTH CENTURY. *Agric. Hist. 1982 56(1): 172-193, 211-214.* By the 1870's the earlier American tradition of close regulation of business was beginning to reassert itself in the face of a dominant laissez faire philosophy. In the grain trade this change was spurred by technology, which centralized grain handling in places like Chicago and helped promote monopoly. Most of the regulatory laws of the late 19th century had the effect of making markets more efficient, as developments in Illinois indicate. Some of this effect was unintentional: the Act to Regulate Public Warehouses (Illinois, 1871) caused many warehouses to become private, and the Interstate Commerce Act (US, 1887) encouraged railroads to acquire warehouses as a way of avoiding rate regulation. The result was the development of grain merchandising elevators. Comments, pp. 211-214. Based on legal documents and trade statistics; 5 tables, 58 notes.
                                                                                  D. E. Bowers

1355. —. [MODERATE RENT CONTROL]. *Urban Affairs Q. 1981 17(2): 123-148.*
Gilderbloom, John Ingram. MODERATE RENT CONTROL: ITS IMPACT ON THE QUALITY AND QUANTITY OF THE HOUSING STOCK, *pp. 123-142.* The studies of George Sternlieb and others notwithstanding, short-term moderate rent control, instituted in the 1970's, had little or no impact on the amount of construction, maintenance, or taxable valuation of rental properties, primarily because moderate controls exempt all newly constructed housing, guarantee a fair and reasonable return on investment, and allow increases in operating expenses to be passed on to the tenant.
Sternlieb, George. COMMENT, *pp. 143-145.* The term "moderate rent control" is a slippery one; housing starts are not reliable data as most are government subsidized; and the adverse consequences of rent control are not always immediately apparent.
Gilderbloom, John Ingram. REPLY, *pp. 147-148.* Sternlieb's rebuttal suffers from inconsistencies and faulty methodological and statistical procedures. Primary sources; 7 notes, ref.   E. L. Keyser

1356. —. [THE POLITICAL ECONOMY OF BANKING REGULA-TION, 1864-1933]. *J. of Econ. Hist. 1982 42(1): 33-42.*
White, Eugene Nelson. THE POLITICAL ECONOMY OF BANKING REG-ULATION, 1864-1933, *pp. 33-40.* The laws and regulations that shaped the structure of the banking industry from the Civil War to the Great Depression were strongly influenced by the banking community. Legal constraints on banks were weakened by competition between state and federal regulators trying to increase membership in their banking systems. The elimination of regulation was not completed, however, because the politically most powerful group in the industry, the unit banks, had an interest in preserving some regulations.
Keehn, Richard H. DISCUSSION, *pp. 41-42.*   J

1357. —. SOVEREIGN COMPULSION DEFENSE IN ANTITRUST LIT-IGATION: NEW LIFE FOR THE ACT OF STATE DOCTRINE? *Am. Soc. of Int. Law. Pro. 1978 72: 97-118.*
—. SOVEREIGN COMPULSION DEFENSE IN ANTITRUST LITIGA-TION: NEW LIFE FOR THE ACT OF STATE DOCTRINE?, *pp. 97-98.* Lists and defines the parameters of the three basic doctrines of antitrust litigation: sovereign immunity, act of state, and foreign compulsion.
Fox, Eleanor M. REMARKS, *pp. 98-100.* Examines how the defense of sovereign compulsion fits into contemporary antitrust litigation.
Joelson, Mark R. REMARKS, *pp. 100-101.* Addresses the difficulties in separating a foreign government's commercial activities from its sovereign activities in each area of antitrust litigation.
Schwartz, Richard. REMARKS, *pp. 102-104.* The federal government should discourage restrictions that inhibit competition and human rights; cites antitrust decisions followed in European countries; 1965-77.
Williams, John S. REMARKS, *105-107.* Addresses blocking statutes (which prevent discovery of documents within territorial jurisdiction) as a basis for foreign compulsion pleas in antitrust litigation, as they have been used in contract litigation; 1977-78.

Rosenthal, Douglas E.   REMARKS,   *pp. 107-110.* Outlines proposed legislation aimed at setting up regimes of cooperation among foreign countries with blocking statutes (and who deny the Federal Maritime Commission access to foreign shipping conference operations documents).

—.   DISCUSSION,   *pp. 110-111.* Panel comments on the definition of compulsion, the nature of competition, and antitrust laws as a statement of national values.

Baer, Vicki E.   QUESTIONS FROM THE FLOOR,   *pp. 111-118.*

1358.   —.   [TRADE PROTECTION AS AN INTERNATIONAL COMMODITY: THE CASE OF STEEL].   *J. of Econ. Hist. 1980 40(1): 33-44.*

Yeager, Mary A.   TRADE PROTECTION AS AN INTERNATIONAL COMMODITY: THE CASE OF STEEL,   *pp. 33-42.* Trade protection commonly is viewed as a support—external and perhaps occasional—granted to an industry by government policymakers. Focusing on the steel industry, this study argues that protection is better viewed as a commodity, an input into the production of steel. The development of the market for the protection commodity during the past century is related to the history of regional, national, and international markets for steel.

Herbst, Lawrence A.   DISCUSSION,   *pp. 43-44.*   J

SUBJECT INDEX

Subject Profile Index (ABC-SPIndex) carries both generic and specific index terms. Begin a search at the general term but also look under more specific or related terms.

Each string of index descriptors is intended to present a profile of a given article; however, no particular relationship between any two terms in the profile is implied. Terms within the profile are listed alphabetically after the leading term. The variety of punctuation and capitalization reflects production methods and has no intrinsic meaning; e.g., there is no difference in meaning between "History, study of" and "History (study of)."

Cities, towns, and counties are listed following their respective states or provinces; e.g., "Ohio (Columbus)." Terms beginning with an arabic numeral are listed after the letter Z. The chronology of the bibliographic entry follows the subject index descriptors. In the chronology, "c" stands for "century"; e.g., "19c" means "19th century."

Note that "United States" is not used as a leading index term; if no country is mentioned, the index entry refers to the United States alone. When an entry refers to both Canada and the United States, both "Canada" and "USA" appear in the string of index descriptors, but "USA" is not a leading term. When an entry refers to any other country and the United States, only the other country is indexed.

The last number in the index string, in italics, refers to the bibliographic entry number.

A

Abalone industry. California. 19c-1970's. *705*

Abel, Richard. Booksellers. Libraries, academic. 1954-74. *549*

Accident Insurance. Judicial process. Labor. Management. New England. 1890-1910. *1063*

Accidents. Industry. Legislation. Occupational Safety and Health Act (US, 1970). 1877-1970. *1261*

Accounting. Business. Foreign Corrupt Practices Act (US, 1977). 1977-81. *1325*

—. General Motors Corporation. Management. 1920's. *409*

Accounting (systems development). Corporations. DuPont de Nemours, E. I. (Powder Company). Management. 1903-12. *84*

Act of state doctrine. Antitrust. Foreign Policy. International Trade. Sovereign compulsion. Trials. 1965-78. *1357*

Act to Regulate Public Warehouses (Illinois, 1871). Government regulation. Grain. Illinois. Interstate Commerce Act (US, 1887). Trade. 1870-1900. *1354*

Adams, John Quincy. Diplomacy. Fishing. Great Britain. Monroe, James. Newfoundland banks. USA. 1815-18. *1208*

Adburgham, Alison. Department stores (review article). Harris, Leon. Hendrickson, Robert. Weil, Gordon L. 1850-1975. *984*

Advertising. Agricultural cooperatives. California. Fruit and Fruit Crops. Nutrition. Vegetables. 1880's-1920's. *820*

—. American Industries series. Manufactures. McCormick, Cyrus, Jr. McCormick Reaper Works. Munn & Company. *Scientific American* (periodical). 1879-82. *945*

—. Antitrust. Broadcasting. Sports Broadcasting Act (US, 1961). 1961-78. *1232*

—. Automobiles. Bankruptcy. Jackson Automobile Company. Lewis, Charles. Matthews, George. Michigan. 1902-23. *418*

—. Breweries. Economic Conditions. Industry. Mergers. 1947-78. *718*

—. Business education. Colleges and Universities. Curricula. 1900-17. *1124*

—. California. Citrus industry. Lithographs. Orange crate art. 1877-1950. *717*

—. Canada. Federal Regulation. Television. USA. 1970-77. *1298*

—. Children. Federal Regulation. Television. 1970-81. *1207*

—. Colt, Cristine C. (account). Dow Jones Co. Sex discrimination. 1975-78. *1036*

—. Competition. Economic Growth. Industrial mobility. 1947-72. *228*

—. Consumers. Ewen, Stuart (review article). Social Customs. 19c-1976. *231*

—. Consumers. Government Regulation. Social responsibiltiy. 1950's-70's. *252*

—. Corporations. Films. 1900-20. *206*

—. Corporations. Human Rights. 1950's-80. *226*

—. Council of Better Business Bureaus (National Advertising Division). National Advertising Review Board. 1971-76. *297*

—. Death and Dying. Funeral industry. Public Relations. 1830-1980. *185*

—. Ethics. Professionalism. Social status. 20c. *270*

—. Federal Trade Commission. 1914-38. *1332*

—. Industrial concentration. 1963-72. *186*

—. Monopolies. Newspaper Preservation Act (US, 1970). Supreme Court. *Times-Picayune Publishing Co.* v. *United States* (US, 1953). 1953-78. *517*

—. Periodicals. 1976-77. *541*

—. Periodicals. 1977. *578*

Advertising discounts. Pricing structures. Television, network. -1973. *266*

Advertising regulation. Federal Trade Commission. Whealer-Lea Act (1938). 1914-71. *1329*

Advertising revenues. Business. Television. 1973. *522*

Advertising, systematic. Business History. Industrial development. Newspapers. Palmer, Volney B. 1794-1864. *230*

Aeromarine Airways, Inc. Air Lines. Seaplanes. South. 1920-24. *425*

Aeromarine Plane and Motor Co. Air Mail Act (US, 1925). Airplane Industry and Trade. Subsidies. Uppercu, Inglis. 1914-25. *424*

255

Aeronautics. Automobiles. Phillips, Jerry (account). *Waterman Arrowbile* (aircraft). 1920's-38. *459*

—. Eastern Airlines. Gellert, Dan (accounts). L-1011 (aircraft). Safety. Working Conditions. 1972-78. *1060*

Affirmative action. American Telephone and Telegraph Company. Employment. Management. Technology. Women. 1972-75. *1070*

—. Attitudes. Corporations. Men. Sex discrimination. Women. 1975-80. *1076*

AFL-CIO. Economic expansionism. Employment. Foreign policy. Multinational corporations. 1880's-1970's. *9*

Africa. Banks. Business. Europe. USA. 1972-74. *201*

—. Foreign Investments. USA. ca 1960-73. *109*

Age. Coal Mines and Mining. Management. Standard of living. Strikes, wildcat. Working conditions. 1970's. *861*

Agricultural Adjustment Administration. Agricultural policy. Attitudes. New Deal. 1920-33. *1200*

—. Federal Government. National Recovery Administration. 1933-39. *1326*

—. New Deal. Soil Conservation Service. 1933-41. *1315*

Agricultural businessmen. Industrialization. South, New. Textile industry. Urban entrepreneurs. 1870-1900. *725*

Agricultural commodities. Alaska (Matanuska Valley). Colonization. Railroads. 1915-40. *512*

—. Commodity exchanges. Stock Exchange. 1968-78. *274*

—. Freight and Freightage. Populism. Prices. Railroads. 1870-97. *304*

—. Grain production. Pacific Coast. 1846-1900. *797*

—. Marketing. Prices. Self-regulation. 1930-81. *668*

Agricultural cooperatives. Advertising. California. Fruit and Fruit Crops. Nutrition. Vegetables. 1880's-1920's. *820*

—. Agriculture Department. Capper-Volstead Act (US, 1922). Congress. Monopolies. 1914-22. *1211*

—. Business. Legislation. Ohio. Social Organization. Woods, W. N. (reminiscences). 1907-78. *846*

—. Citrus industry. Federal Trade Commission. Monopolies. Prices. Sunkist Growers. 1974-81. *762*

—. Computers. Cotton. Marketing. Plains Cotton Cooperative Association. Telecommunication. Texas (Lubbock). 1920's-70's. *790*

Agricultural Industry. California. Wine. ca 1830-1975. *729*

—. Corporations. 1930's-73. *788*

—. Corporations. Ownership. 1970's. *804*

—. Economic Regulations. Federal government. Mississippi. Prices. Texas. Voluntarism. 1925-40. *756*

Agricultural policy. Agricultural Adjustment Administration. Attitudes. New Deal. 1920-33. *1200*

—. Capitalism. Food. Government. 1800-1979. *1283*

Agricultural Production. Congress. Economic Conditions. Louisiana. Subsidies. Sugar industry. 1860-1930. *803*

—. Cotton. Economic Conditions. South. Soybeans. 1920's-75. *712*

—. Cotton. Far Western States. Wool. 19c-20c. *739*

—. Europe. Grain exports. Great Britain. International Trade. USA. 1770-1976. *849*

—. Farmers. Michigan. World War II. 1939-45. *690*

—. Farms. North. North Central States. Profit. 1820's-60's. *695*

—. Grain. Prices. 1970's. *691*

—. Haciendas. Mills. Puerto Rico, southwestern. Sugar industry. 1902. *838*

Agricultural reform. *Debow's Review*. South. 1846-61. *715*

Agricultural Technology and Research. California (Central Valley). Harvesting. Tractors. 1850's-1920. *841*

—. California (Riverside County). Citrus industry. Inventions. Mergers. Parker, George. Stebler, Fred. 1900-36. *770*

—. Cotton. Mechanization. South. Southwest. 1946-79. *801*

—. Cotton. Sharecroppers. South. Tractors. 1915-60. *773*

Agriculture. Alcohol. Business. Fuel. Motors. Prices. Surpluses. 1930's. *607*

—. American Revolution (impact). Great Britain. South. Strickland, William. 1794-95. *726*

—. Bibliographies. Periodicals. Red River Valley. 1950-76. *693*

—. Business. Lobbying. 1940-80. *683*

—. Caterpillar tractors. Holt, Benjamin. Tractors, track-type. 1904-19. *1004*

—. Cattle Raising. Old Northwest. 1803-60. *839*

—. Chemical Industry. Food Adulteration and Inspection. Government regulation. Mississippi State Chemical Laboratory. 1882-1979. *1296*

—. Competition. Montana, western. 1946-80. *842*

—. Corporations. Food industry. Prices. Trade. 1930-74. *670*

—. David, Paul A. Mechanization. Reaping. Technological diffusion. 1833-70. 1966. *780*

—. Economic Growth. Kansas. 1860-80. *748*

—. Great Plains. Labor casualization. Mechanization. Wheat. 1865-1902. *669*

Agriculture and Government. Constitutional issues. Farm journals. New Deal. 1935-36. *1194*

—. Farms, large. Modernization. Technology. 1970's. *700*

Agriculture Department. Agricultural cooperatives. Capper-Volstead Act (US, 1922). Congress. Monopolies. 1914-22. *1211*

—. Dyes. Federal regulation. Food. Public Health. 1913-19. *1228*

Air line war. Civil Aeronautics Board. Federal subsidies. Southwest Airlines. Texas. 1970's. *400*

Air Lines. Aeromarine Airways, Inc. Seaplanes. South. 1920-24. *425*

—. California (Los Angeles, San Francisco). Federal Government. Helicopters. Illinois (Chicago). New York City. Subsidies. 1945-75. *458*

—. Capacity limitation controls. Economic Regulations. 1973. *1195*

—. Chicago and Southern Air Lines, Inc. Civil Aeronautics Board. Delta Air Lines Inc. Federal regulation. Mergers. 1948-53. *429*

—. Civil Aeronautics Board. Competition. Contracts. Economic Regulations. Prices. 1930's-80. *1286*

—. Civil Aeronautics Board. Consumers. Federal regulation. 1971-80. *1284*

—. Collective bargaining. Deregulation. Federal Regulation. 1958-78. *1223*

—. Corporations. Federal Regulation. Small business. 1945-70's. *1310*

—. Deregulation. Federal Policy. Industry. 1976-79. *1246*

—. New York City. 1958-79. *355*

—. Illinois (Chicago). Mass transit. Public policy. 1900-50. *311*

—. Locomobile Company. New England. Stanley Steamer (automobile). 1899-1903. *501*

—. Models. Prices. 1956-81. *342*

B

Bag industry. Demand. Paper Industry. Plastics. Productivity. Technology. 1954-77. *927*

Baker, Ray Stannard. Muckraking. Railroads. 1905-06. *1079*

Balance of payments. Energy crisis. Foreign Relations. 1968-85. *649*

Ball bearing industry. Productivity. 1958-79. *1011*

Ball, Ed. Du Pont estate. Florida East Coast Railroad. Pepper, Claude. Railroad. 1926-58. *492*

Baltimore & Ohio Railroad. Chesapeake and Ohio Railway. Interstate Commerce Commission. Mergers. Railroads. Transportation Act (US, 1940). 1958-62. *318*

—. Economic Conditions. Jones and Laughlin Steel Company. Pennsylvania (Pittsburgh; Hazelwood). 1870-1975. *1133*

Bananas. Business. Caribbean Region. Foreign Relations. United Fruit Company. 1870's-1950's. *83*

—. Nicaragua. Standard Fruit Co. 1921-30's. *87*

BancoKentucky Company. Banking. Brown, James B. Kentucky (Louisville). National Bank of Kentucky. 1925-30. *216*

Bancroft, Joseph and Sons Company. Delaware (Wilmington). Miller, Franklin, and Stevenson (firm). Scientific management. Textile Industry. 1911-27. *827*

Bank deposits. Depressions. Economic Conditions. Great Contraction. Money (demand). 1929-33. *217*

Bank of North America. Banking, commercial. Pendleton, Joseph. Wilson, John (letter). 1782-84. *264*

Bank of Stephen Girard. Girard, Stephen. Profit. 1812-31. *184*

Bank of the United States, Second. Federal Government. Monetary system. 1815-30. *214*

Bank robberies. Automobiles. Bootlegging. Morality. ca 1920's. *405*

Banking. 1880-1980. *282*

—. Arizona. 1866-96. *271*

—. BancoKentucky Company. Brown, James B. Kentucky (Louisville). National Bank of Kentucky. 1925-30. *216*

—. Brotherhood of Railway Telegraphers. Gardner, Vernon O. Manion, Edward J. Missouri (St. Louis). Telegraphers National Bank. 1922-42. *232*

—. California. Economic Development. Legislation. 1890-1915. *194*

—. California (Los Angeles). Farmers' and Merchants' Bank. Hellman, Isaias W. Jews. 1868-85. *247*

—. California, southern. Transportation. Wells, Fargo & Company. ca 1852-69. *233*

—. Capital. Georgia Railroad and Banking Company. Railroads. Taxation. 1833-1980. *481*

—. Cities. Loans. Rural areas. 1916-40. *278*

—. Cities. Mexican Americans. Mexico. Rotating credit associations. 1970's. *287*

—. Competition. Loans. Wisconsin. 1870-1900. *240*

—. Comptroller of the Currency. Federal Reserve System (Board of Governors). Justice Department. Mergers. 1950-66. *1202*

—. Cost functions. Economic development. South. 1870-1976. *234*

—. Crime and Criminals. Farmers and Drovers National Bank (failure). Pennsylvania (Greene County; Waynesburg). Politics. Rinehart, James B. F. 1835-1906. *212*

—. Debt, public. Federal Government. Gallatin, Albert. Securities. War of 1812. 1813. *183*

—. Depressions. Money. Panic of 1930. 1920-30. *292*

—. Discrimination. Mortgages. Negroes. 1970-77. *193*

—. Economic Growth. Redlich, Fritz (review article). 19c. *300*

—. Economic Regulations. Political economy. 1864-1933. *1356*

—. Economic Structure. Megalopolis. New York City. Spatial influence. 1971. *237*

—. Federal Policy. Housing. 1960's-70's. *202*

—. Germany. Jews. 17c-19c. *220*

—. Government regulation. 1894-1914. *291*

—. Government regulation. 1933-82. *1308*

—. Investments. 19c-20c. *283*

—. Monetary policy. New Deal. Roosevelt, Franklin D. (administration). Warburg, James P. 1932-41. *254*

—. Mutual savings bank depositors. New York. Social Classes. 1819-61. *255*

—. Profit. 1965-74. *215*

—. Trade area. 1976. *261*

Banking (central). Federal Reserve System. Gold standard. Real bills. 1870-1930. *1342*

Banking, commercial. Bank of North America. Pendleton, Joseph. Wilson, John (letter). 1782-84. *264*

—. Corporation Charters. Law. State Government. 1781-1843. *1344*

Banking crisis. Depressions. Kennedy, Susan Estabook (review article). 1933. 1973. *205*

—. Michigan. Reconstruction Finance Corporation. 1933. *241*

Banking (failures). Economic Conditions. Finance. 1946-76. *267*

Banking history. Economic development. Federal Regulation. Federal Reserve System. Wisconsin. 1863-1914. *1248*

Banking, investment. Corporations. Law. 1865-1914. *18*

Banking (multivariate analysis). Business. Economic Development. Holding Company Act of 1956. 1970-74. *238*

Banking, private. Economic History. Financial agencies, unchartered. 1750-1860. *265*

—. Monetary history. 1800-60. *302*

Banking (trust accounts). Corporations, control of. Investments. 1973. *227*

Bankruptcy. Advertising. Automobiles. Jackson Automobile Company. Lewis, Charles. Matthews, George. Michigan. 1902-23. *418*

Bankruptcy arrangements. Business reorganization. Judges, federal. Railroads. ca 1870-90. *435*

Banks. Africa. Business. Europe. USA. 1972-74. *201*

—. Business. Capitalism. Developing Nations. Economic policy. 1981. *285*

—. Business. Deposit growth. Economic Conditions. 1960-71. *295*

—. Capitalism. Economic crisis. Social Classes. 1974-75. *303*

—. Conglomerate expansion. Corporations. Mergers. Monopolies. 1970's. *294*

—. Congress. Interest rate war. Legislation. Savings and loan associations. 1966-74. *259*

—. Economic Conditions. Multinational corporations. 1945-77. *150*

Bradley Transportation Company. Great Lakes. Limestone Quarrying. Michigan (Rogers City). Shipping. US Steel Corporation. 1912-67. *448*

Brazil. Alliance for Progress. Kennedy, John F. (administration). Multinational Corporations. Nationalization. 1961-63. *102*

—. Foreign Investments. Great Britain. USA. 1870's. *149*

Brazil (Amazonia). Ford, Henry. Plantations. Rubber. 1923-45. *52*

Breweries. Advertising. Economic Conditions. Industry. Mergers. 1947-78. *718*

—. Wisconsin (Milwaukee). Women. 1840-1900. *667*

Briggs, Asa. Barnouw, Eric. Culbert, David Holbrook. Metz, Robert. Radio (review article). 1920-76. *563*

Bright, Charles. Politics. Public Policy. Rose, Mark H. Transportation (review article). 1941-72. *312*

British Columbia. Bibliographies. Lumber and Lumbering. Pacific Northwest. 1890's-1960's. *744*

Broadcasting. Advertising. Antitrust. Sports Broadcasting Act (US, 1961). 1961-78. *1232*

—. Federal Regulation. 1912-70. *1346*

Brotherhood of Railway Telegraphers. Banking. Gardner, Vernon O. Manion, Edward J. Missouri (St. Louis). Telegraphers National Bank. 1922-42. *232*

Brotherhood of Sleeping Car Porters. Aliens. Filipinos. Labor. Negroes. Pullman Company. Railroads. 1925-55. *1110*

Brown & Root, Inc. Construction industry. Corporations. Housing. Rural areas. South. ca 1977-79. *177*

Brown, Alex E. Great Lakes. Shipping. Steamboats. Technological innovations. 1852-1910. *415*

Brown, James B. BancoKentucky Company. Banking. Kentucky (Louisville). National Bank of Kentucky. 1925-30. *216*

Brown lung disease. Burlington Industries, Inc. Carolina Brown Lung Association. Cotton. Liberty Mutual Insurance Co. South. 1970's. *1038*

—. Carolina Brown Lung Association. South. Textile industry. Workmen's Compensation. 1970's. *1098*

Brukner, Clayton J. Airplane Industry and Trade. Ohio (Troy). 1923-30. *479*

Bucket shops. Chicago Board of Trade. Commodity exchanges. Merchants' Exchange of St. Louis. Trade. 1882-1905. *246*

Buckeye Steel Castings Company. Bush, S. P. Management, scientific. Ohio (Columbus). Social Work. Steel Industry. 1890-1920. *923*

Budgets. Industry. Scientific Experiments and Research. Small Business. Technological innovations. 1946-75. *152*

Buffalo *Courier-Express.* Antitrust. Buffalo *Evening News.* Courts. New York. Newspapers. 1977-80. *521*

Buffalo *Evening News.* Antitrust. Buffalo *Courier-Express.* Courts. New York. Newspapers. 1977-80. *521*

Buildings. Carson Pirie Scott and Co. Illinois (Chicago). Retail Trade. 1854-1979. *1002*

—. Cities. Elevators. 1853-1979. *952*

Bureau of Labor Statistics. Business. Degrees, Academic. 1975-79. *1147*

Bureaucracies. Blacklisting. Chicago, Burlington & Quincy Railroad. Employment. North Central States. Railroads. 1877-92. *1028*

—. Chambers of Commerce. Commerce and Labor Department (Bureau of Manufactures). Economic Policy. Exports. State Department. 1890's-1913. *170*

Bureaucratic hierarchies. Authority. Business. Cultural crises. History. -1973. *1035*

Bureaucratic managers. Corporate democracy. Executive Behavior. 1970's. *128*

Burlington Industries, Inc. Brown lung disease. Carolina Brown Lung Association. Cotton. Liberty Mutual Insurance Co. South. 1970's. *1038*

Buses. California. Railroads. Transportation. 1910's-30's. *308*

—. Industry. Productivity. 1954-79. *333*

Bush, S. P. Buckeye Steel Castings Company. Management, scientific. Ohio (Columbus). Social Work. Steel Industry. 1890-1920. *923*

Business. Accounting. Foreign Corrupt Practices Act (US, 1977). 1977-81. *1325*

—. Advertising revenues. Television. 1973. *522*

—. Africa. Banks. Europe. USA. 1972-74. *201*

—. Agricultural cooperatives. Legislation. Ohio. Social Organization. Woods, W. N. (reminiscences). 1907-78. *846*

—. Agriculture. Alcohol. Fuel. Motors. Prices. Surpluses. 1930's. *607*

—. Agriculture. Lobbying. 1940-80. *683*

—. Alaska Syndicate. Copper Mines and Mining. Kennecott Copper Corporation. 1900-38. *876*

—. Antibusiness groups. Capitalism. Socialism. 1974. *60*

—. Archival Catalogs and Inventories. Harvard Business School (Baker Library). Manuscripts. New England. 1978. *110*

—. Attitudes. Federal Regulation. World War I. 1914-18. *1317*

—. Attitudes. Social responsibility. Technology. 1950's-70's. *1123*

—. Authority. Bureaucratic hierarchies. Cultural crises. History. -1973. *1035*

—. Bananas. Caribbean Region. Foreign Relations. United Fruit Company. 1870's-1950's. *83*

—. Banking (multivariate analysis). Economic Development. Holding Company Act of 1956. 1970-74. *238*

—. Banks. Capitalism. Developing Nations. Economic policy. 1981. *285*

—. Banks. Deposit growth. Economic Conditions. 1960-71. *295*

—. Bureau of Labor Statistics. Degrees, Academic. 1975-79. *1147*

—. Cabinet. Elites. Government. Mills, C. Wright. 1897-1973. *1057*

—. Capital and surplus change. Economic Policy. Insurance, nonlife. 1956-70. *213*

—. Cash tender offers. Economic Regulations. Williams Act (US, 1968). 1968-80. *1240*

—. City Government. 1975-80. *1047*

—. City Planning. Development. Indiana (Kingsport). North. Towns. 1880-1950. *1021*

—. Colleges and Universities. 1960's-77. *1107*

—. Columbia Plateau. Farming. McGregor family. Oregon, northeastern. Sheep. Washington, eastern. 1882-1980. *759*

—. Conferences. Conventions. Executives. Government. 1970's. *273*

—. Conservation of Natural Resources. Employment. Fishing industry. 1970's. *855*

—. Construction. Railroads (cars). 1870's-1960's. *508*

—. Consumers. Government. Public policy. 1974. *1291*

—. Corporate power. Politics. Profit system. 1970-73. *1102*

—. Corporate responsibility. Income. 1945-73. *1137*

—. American Railway Union. Illinois (Pullman). Strikes. 1893-94. *469*

—. Banking. Economic Development. Legislation. 1890-1915. *194*

—. Baseball. Dodger Stadium. Los Angeles Dodgers (team). 1956-62. *225*

—. Buses. Railroads. Transportation. 1910's-30's. *308*

—. Construction. San Diego and Arizona Railway. Southern Pacific Railroad. Spreckels, John D. 1907-19. *455*

—. Cotton industry. 1906-78. *774*

—. Economic Conditions. Gold production, value of. 1848-1900. *859*

—. Economic Regulations. Prices. Spain. 1768-1810. *1159*

—. Elliot, Robert. Lawsuits. Occupational Safety and Health Administration. P & Z Company. Working conditions. 1975-77. *1115*

—. Europe. Wine industry. 1875-95. *689*

—. Nash, John Henry. Printing. 1831-1930. *520*

—. Oral history. Teiser, Ruth (interviews). Wine industry. 1890's-1977. *769*

—. Seghesio family. Wine industry. 1886-1977. *807*

California Aero Company. Airplane Industry and Trade. Cull, George E. Lark-95 (aircraft). Logan, Ronald R. Personal narratives. 1958-63. *344*

California (Butte, Tehama, Shasta Counties). Lumber and Lumbering. Sierra Flume and Lumber Company. 1875-78. *728*

California (Central Valley). Agricultural Technology and Research. Harvesting. Tractors. 1850's-1920. *841*

California (Hollywood). Films. Hays, William Harrison. Motion Picture Producers and Distributors of America. Sex. 1922-56. *579*

—. Films. Jesse L. Lasky Feature Play Company. *Squaw Man* (film). 1911-14. *543*

California (Inglewood). Communist Party. North American Aviation. Strikes. United Automobile Workers of America. 1941. *464*

California (Los Angeles). Banking. Farmers' and Merchants' Bank. Hellman, Isaias W. Jews. 1868-85. *247*

—. Doheny, Edward Laurence. Oil Industry and Trade. 1892-1930. *627*

—. Recording Industry. Standard Radio. 1934-54. *553*

—. Television. 1931-52. *576*

California (Los Angeles, San Francisco). Air Lines. Federal Government. Helicopters. Illinois (Chicago). New York City. Subsidies. 1945-75. *458*

California (Mother Lode). Eggleston, William S. Gold Mines and Mining. Personal narratives. 1921-26. *869*

California, northern. Construction industry. Government regulation. Housing. Prices. Suburbs. 1970's. *1204*

California (Riverside County). Agricultural Technology and Research. Citrus industry. Inventions. Mergers. Parker, George. Stebler, Fred. 1900-36. *770*

California (San Diego). Federal Regulation. Fishing. Latin America. Territorial waters. Tuna. 1970's. *785*

California (San Francisco). Clothing industry. German Americans. Strauss, Levi. 1850-1970's. *787*

—. Economic Conditions. KQED (station). Massachusetts (Boston). Television, public. WGBH (station). 1945-81. *544*

—. Pacific Mail Steamship Company. Photography. Shipping. Watkins, Carleton E. 1867-71. *505*

California (San Francisco area). Lumber and Lumbering. Oregon. Shipbuilding. Washington. 1850-1929. *341*

California (San Joaquin Valley). Oil Industry and Trade. 1904-70's. *659*

California (Santa Clara County). Economic Conditions. Electronics industry. Environment. Social problems. 1950's-70's. *1121*

—. Electronics industry. Women. Working conditions. 1970-79. *1026*

—. Electronics industry. Working Conditions. 1972-81. *1078*

California (Sierra County; Allegheny). Gold Mines and Mining. Sixteen-to-One Mine. 1890-1965. *866*

California, southern. Automobiles. Land. Politics. Railroads. Speculation. Streetcars. 1880's-1970's. *483*

—. Banking. Transportation. Wells, Fargo & Company. ca 1852-69. *233*

—. Citrus industry. Urbanization. 1870-1980. *672*

California (Stockton). Business History. Crown-Zellerbach Corporation. Paper industry. ca 1856-1900. *815*

—. Shipbuilding. 1850-1970's. *388*

Calles, Plutarco Elías. Letters. Mexico. Multinational Corporations. Oil Industry and Trade. Rath, Arthur C. Rose, Vernon J. 1923-24. *583*

Calumet and Hecla Mining Company. Copper Mines and Mining. Labor Unions and Organizations. Michigan (Keweenaw Peninsula). Social Change. 1840-1968. *868*

Camas Prairie Railroad. Idaho, north-central. Johnson, T. A. Nezperce & Idaho Railroad. Railroads. 1910-22. *328*

Campaign Finance. Corporations. Electoral politics. Federal regulation. Labor Unions and Organizations. 1971-76. *1048*

Campbell, Thomas D. Drought. Farm income. Great Plains. Prairie Provinces. Wheat farming. 1915-1940. *853*

Canada. Advertising. Federal Regulation. Television. USA. 1970-77. *1298*

—. Alaska. Arctic. Mining. Scandinavia. USSR. 1917-78. *883*

—. Atlantic Ocean. Fishing. Swordfish. USA. 1870-1980. *716*

—. Chemical Industry. Oil Industry and Trade. USA. Working Conditions. 12-hour shifts. 1977. *1104*

—. Economic growth. Foreign investments. Nationalism. USA. 1961-74. *51*

—. Great Northern Railway. Locomotives. Railroads. USA. 1861-1970. *414*

—. Great Northern Railway. Railroads. USA. ca 1850-1910. *449*

—. Industrialization. Mineral Resources. Mining. USA. 1700-1977. *892*

—. Industry (expansion factors). USA. 1965. *133*

Canal. Indiana Company. Kentucky. Ohio River, Falls of the. 1804-30. *489*

Cananea Copper Co. Extortion. Mexico (Sonora). Villa, Pancho. 1915. *147*

Canneries. Alaska. Filipino Americans. Labor Unions and Organizations. Salmon. 1902-38. *751*

Canning industry. Archaeology. Tin. 1809-1980. *929*

—. Migrant Labor. New York State Factory Investigating Commission. Polish Americans. 1900-35. *735*

Capacity limitation controls. Air Lines. Economic Regulations. 1973. *1195*

Chemical Industry. Agriculture. Food Adulteration and Inspection. Government regulation. Mississippi State Chemical Laboratory. 1882-1979. *1296*

—. Canada. Oil Industry and Trade. USA. Working Conditions. 12-hour shifts. 1977. *1104*

—. Monopolies. Synthetic fibers. Textile Industry. 1970-79. *32*

—. Ozark-Mahoning Company. Texas (Ward County). 1925-80. *857*

Chemicals, toxic. Health safety requirements. North Carolina (Brevard). Occupational Safety and Health Act (US, 1970). Olin Corporation. 1970-74. *1233*

Chesapeake and Ohio Railway. Baltimore & Ohio Railroad. Interstate Commerce Commission. Mergers. Railroads. Transportation Act (US, 1940). 1958-62. *318*

Chesapeake Bay area. Economic Conditions. Maryland. Tobacco industry. Virginia. 1617-1710. *765*

Chicago and Eastern Illinois Railroad. North Central States. Railroads. Real Estate. St. Louis-San Francisco Railroad. South Central and Gulf States. 1902-13. *454*

Chicago and Southern Air Lines, Inc. Air Lines. Civil Aeronautics Board. Delta Air Lines Inc. Federal regulation. Mergers. 1948-53. *429*

Chicago Board of Trade. Bucket shops. Commodity exchanges. Merchants' Exchange of St. Louis. Trade. 1882-1905. *246*

Chicago, Burlington & Quincy Railroad. Alcoholism. Employees. Law Enforcement. Management. Railroads. 1876-1967. *319*

—. Blacklisting. Bureaucracies. Employment. North Central States. Railroads. 1877-92. *1028*

—. Interstate Commerce Commission. Iowa (Mt. Ayr). Labor Unions and Organizations. Missouri (Grant City). Railroads (abandonment). 1943-44. *456*

Chicago, Milwaukee, St. Paul and Pacific Railroad. Curtis, Asahel. Photography. Railroads. Western States. 1909-29. *480*

Chikiswalungo Furnace. Coal, anthracite. Iron Industry. Pennsylvania (Lancaster County; Marietta). Technology. 1840's. *993*

Child labor. Garment industry. Women. Working conditions. ca 1900-20. *1100*

Child Labor Act (1916). Cotton. Federal regulation. Textile Industry. 1907-16. *741*

Children. Advertising. Federal Regulation. Television. 1970-81. *1207*

—. Life insurance. Social Classes. 1875-1980. *299*

Chile. Foreign policy, private. International Telephone and Telegraph. Multinational Corporations. USA. 1960-74. *12*

China. International trade. Pacific & Eastern Steamship Company. Ships, shortage of. USA. World War I. 1914-16. *466*

—. Kerosene. Nationalism. Oil and Petroleum Products. Standard Oil Company of New York. Taxation. 1925-27. *661*

Christianson, Ivan D. (interview). Grain. Railroads. South Dakota (Granville). 1920's. *330*

Citibank. Community Banking Pilot program. Economic Conditions. Finance. New York City (Brooklyn; Flatbush). 1978-82. *276*

Cities. Automobiles. Politics. 1900-56. 1977-79. *367*

—. Banking. Loans. Rural areas. 1916-40. *278*

—. Banking. Mexican Americans. Mexico. Rotating credit associations. 1970's. *287*

—. Buildings. Elevators. 1853-1979. *952*

—. Condit, Carl W. Mass Transit (review article). McKay, John P. McShane, Clay. Railroads. 1880-1940. 1974-77. *398*

—. Corporations. Minorities. National Alliance of Businessmen. Poverty. Unemployment. 1960-78. *1083*

—. Economic Conditions. Industry. 1981. *1075*

—. Employment. Private sector. Public services. Taxation. 1980. *1092*

—. Ewen, Linda Ann. Greer, Edward. Industrial Relations (review article). Meier, August. Negroes. Rudwick, Elliott. 1900-81. *1096*

—. Great Britain (London). Industry. New York City. Office location. 1960-72. *1154*

—. Labor Unions and Organizations. Manufactures. Skill differential. 1952-73. *988*

—. Migration, Internal. Multinational Corporations (takeover). Wisconsin (Milwaukee). 1968-79. *1090*

Cities (promotion of). Alabama (Birmingham). Boomtowns. Iron Industry. Mining. 1871-96. *1059*

Citizen Lobbies. Coal liquefaction. Farmers. Industry. Montana (McCone County). Synthetic fuel. 1980. *1105*

—. Corporations. Courts. Government. Legislation. 1980. *49*

—. Corporations. Economic Conditions. Government regulation. Legislation. 1975-80. *1032*

Citrus industry. Advertising. California. Lithographs. Orange crate art. 1877-1950. *717*

—. Agricultural Cooperatives. Federal Trade Commission. Monopolies. Prices. Sunkist Growers. 1974-81. *762*

—. Agricultural Technology and Research. California (Riverside County). Inventions. Mergers. Parker, George. Stebler, Fred. 1900-36. *770*

—. California, southern. Urbanization. 1870-1980. *672*

City Government. Automobile Industry and Trade. Michigan (Detroit). Political Leadership. 1910-29. *1040*

—. Business. 1975-80. *1047*

—. Teaford, Jon C. (review article). Urbanization. 1650-1825. 1975. *10*

City Planning. Business. Development. Indiana (Kingsport). North. Towns. 1880-1950. *1021*

—. Company towns. Corporations. Mining. North Central States. 19c-20c. *1020*

—. Indiana (Gary). Social Problems. Steel Industry. US Steel Corporation. 1905-30. *1033*

Civil Aeronautics Board. Air line war. Federal subsidies. Southwest Airlines. Texas. 1970's. *400*

—. Air Lines. Chicago and Southern Air Lines, Inc. Delta Air Lines Inc. Federal regulation. Mergers. 1948-53. *429*

—. Air Lines. Competition. Contracts. Economic Regulations. Prices. 1930's-80. *1286*

—. Air lines. Consumers. Federal regulation. 1971-80. *1284*

—. Economic Regulations. Federal Policy. Transportation (air, transatlantic). 1960's-74. *1168*

—. Employment. Federal Communications Commission. Interstate Commerce Commission. Private sector. 1977-80. *1198*

Civil Engineering. Great Britain. Railroads. Technology. 1825-40. *490*

Civil War. Alabama. Livestock. Reconstruction. 1850-1970. *763*

Clark, George. Ice industry. Iowa (Cedar Falls). Overman, J. M. Riley, John. Smith, Hugh. 19c-1934. *288*

Class struggle. Corporations. Electrical manufacturing industry. Labor Unions and Organizations. 1933-50. *986*
—. Entrepreneurs. Farmers. Industry. 1945-80. *1049*
Clean Air Act (US, 1970). Automobile industry and Trade. Congress. Emissions standards. Environmentalists. Federal Regulation. 1970-76. *1264*
Cleaning industry. Productivity. 1958-76. *203*
Clerks. Employment. Technology. Women. 1870-1930. *1117*
Clifton, Charles. Automobiles. Birge, George K. May, Henry. New York (Buffalo). Pierce-Arrow Motor Car Company. 1873-1938. *514*
Clipper ships. Gold Rushes. International Trade. Shipbuilding. 1850-57. *309*
Clothing industry. California (San Francisco). German Americans. Strauss, Levi. 1850-1970's. *787*
—. Developing nations. Imports. Labor. Small business. 1972. *767*
—. Employment, location of. Maryland (Baltimore). Social geography. 1860-1900. *772*
Clothing manufacturers. Social Mobility. Wisconsin (Milwaukee). 1840-80. *832*
Coal. Appalachia. Economic Conditions. Iron. Land speculation. 1889-93. *895*
—. Environment. Montana. State government. Strip mining. 1970-72. *1238*
—. Fuel. Power Resources. 18c-1977. *650*
—. Great Lakes. Shipping. 1965-75. *604*
Coal, anthracite. Chikiswalungo Furnace. Iron Industry. Pennsylvania (Lancaster County; Marietta). Technology. 1840's. *993*
—. Industrialization. Pennsylvania (Lackawanna Valley). Urbanization. 1820-80. *1056*
Coal barons. Appalachia. Labor. Social responsibility. 1880-1930. *870*
Coal industry. Appalachia. Federal regulation. Western States. 1969-77. *1177*
—. Congress. New Deal. Supreme Court. 1932-40. *1257*
—. Environment. Nuclear Science and Technology. 1860's-1970's. *633*
—. Pennsylvania. Strikes. United Mine Workers of America. ca 1895-1925. *624*
Coal industry, bituminous. Competition, excessive. Economic conditions. Justice Department. 1890-1917. *609*
Coal liquefaction. Citizen Lobbies. Farmers. Industry. Montana (McCone County). Synthetic fuel. 1980. *1105*
Coal mine disasters. Illinois. Working Conditions. 1900-65. *620*
Coal Mines and Mining. Age. Management. Standard of living. Strikes, wildcat. Working conditions. 1970's. *861*
—. Alaskan Coal Commission. Navies. 1920-22. *1299*
—. American Federation of Labor. Depressions. New Mexico (Gallup). Strikes. 1933. *891*
—. Boomtowns. Pennsylvania (Mauch Chunk). 1814-25. *1111*
—. Carter, Jimmy (administration). President's Commission on Coal (report; review article). 1978. *584*
—. Columbus and Hocking Valley Railroad Co. Industrialization. Ohio, southern. 1866-81. *498*
—. Disasters. Fire. Illinois (Cherry). 1909. *900*
—. Economic Conditions. Strikes. 1977-78. *581*
—. Economic growth. Employment. Illinois. Planning. 1970's. *602*
—. Employers. Mitchell, John. United Mine Workers of America. 1897-1907. *874*
—. Energy crisis. Federal Government. Land. 1970's. *611*

—. Federal regulation. Geology. 1969-77. *654*
—. Federal Regulation. Industrial safety. 1942-79. *1289*
—. Federal Regulation. Legislation. Safety. 1941-70. *1253*
—. Government. Health and safety regulations. Ohio. 1869-81. *1249*
—. Great Britain. Illinois. Labor Unions and Organizations. Legislation. Lobbying. 1861-72. *1209*
—. Insurance. Investments. Safety. Slavery. Virginia, eastern. 1780-1865. *625*
—. Kansas (Cherokee, Crawford counties). 1840-1980. *889*
—. Kentucky. Mayo, John Caldwell Calhoun. 1864-1914. *591*
—. Labor. 1970-78. *662*
—. Labor. North Dakota (Wilton). United Mine Workers of America. Washburn Lignite Coal Company. 1900-30's. *906*
—. Leases. Texas (Bastrop County). 1954-79. *867*
—. Negroes. Oregon Improvement Company. Strikebreakers, black. Washington (King County). 1891. *899*
—. Ohio (Hocking Valley). Strikebreakers. Violence, absence of. 1884-85. *597*
—. Public Policy. Severance tax. Western States. 1976-78. *1210*
—. Strikes. 1977-78. *877*
Coal Mines and Mining (anthracite). Pennsylvania. 1769-1976. *888*
Coal Mines and Mining (bituminous). Kentucky. Model towns. Ohio. Pennsylvania. West Virginia. 1880-1930. *1101*
Coca-Cola. Pepsi-Cola. Seven-Up. Soft drink industry. 1880-1977. *909*
Cochran, Thomas C. Blackford, Mansel G. Business History (review article). 18c-1977. *1149*
Code of conduct. Labor Unions and Organizations. Multinational corporations. Organization for Economic Cooperation and Development. 1966-76. *65*
Cohen, Mendes. Engineering. Maryland (Baltimore). Railroads. 1847-1915. *372*
Cold War. Antitrust prosecution. Foreign policy. Middle East. Oil cartel case. 1950-65. *623*
Collective bargaining. Air Lines. Deregulation. Federal Regulation. 1958-78. *1223*
—. Experimental Negotiating Agreement. Steel industry. 1946-73. *922*
—. Labor unions and Organizations. Litton Industries. Multinational corporations. Royal Typewriter, shutdown of. 1960's-70's. *37*
—. Pensions (multiemployer). 1950-73. *1041*
Collectivism. Intellectuals. National Association of Corporation Schools. Steinmetz, Charles Proteus. Utopian thought. 1910-17. *1065*
Colleges and Universities. Advertising. Business education. Curricula. 1900-17. *1124*
—. Business. 1960's-77. *1107*
—. Developing nations. Education. Methodology. 1972-81. *918*
Colonization. Agricultural commodities. Alaska (Matanuska Valley). Railroads. 1915-40. *512*
Colorado (Denver). Design. *Flivver* (aircraft). *Gray Goose* (aircraft). Lewis-American Aircraft Co. McMahon, Bill. Mooney brothers. 1930-33. *347*
Colorado (Fort Collins). Quarrying. Stone industry. Stout, William H. B. 1880-1900. *862*
Colorado (Gothic). Settlement. Silver Mining. 1878-80. *878*
Colorado (Oro City). Atchison, Topeka & Santa Fe Railroad. Denver & Rio Grande Railroad. Railroads. 1880. *486*
Colorado (San Juan Mountains). Gold Mines and Mining. 1870's-1900. *897*

Colorado (Sugar City). Beets. National Beet Sugar Company. Sugar industry. 1888-1968. *750*

Colorado Sugar Manufacturing Company. Beets. Sugar industry. 1841-1978. *755*

Colorado (Uncompahgre Primitive Area). Mining Law (1872). Nature Conservation. Wilderness Act (1964). 1973. *1330*

Colt, Cristine C. (account). Advertising. Dow Jones Co. Sex discrimination. 1975-78. *1036*

Columbia Broadcasting System. Discrimination. Journalism. Southerners. 1970's. *1138*

Columbia Plateau. Business. Farming. McGregor family. Oregon, northeastern. Sheep. Washington, eastern. 1882-1980. *759*

Columbus and Hocking Valley Railroad Co. Coal Mines and Mining. Industrialization. Ohio, southern. 1866-81. *498*

Commerce. Economic History. Port development. Technology. 1900-70's. *313*

Commerce and Labor Department (Bureau of Manufactures). Bureaucracies. Chambers of Commerce. Economic Policy. Exports. State Department. 1890's-1913. *170*

Commerce, Atlantic. Business History. Delaware Valley. Pennsylvania, southeastern. Shipbuilding. West Jersey. 1722-76. *343*

Commerce Department. Business Advisory Council. Federal government. 1933-61. *179*

—. Federal Regulation. Hoover, Herbert C. Licensing. Radio. 1918-22. *1311*

—. Government intervention (avoidance). Hoover, Herbert C. Industry. Labor. 1921-28. *1221*

Commerce Department (Business Advisory Council). Corporate liberalism (concept). Historiography. National Recovery Administration (Industrial Advisory Board). New Deal. 1933-35. 1970's. *1272*

Commercial Law. Constitutions. Corporations. Marketing. 1875-90. *119*

Committee for Economic Development. Business Advisory Council. Keynesianism. New Deal. Roosevelt, Franklin D. (administration). Scholars. 1933-42. *1181*

—. Corporatism. 1942-64. *35*

—. Education, Finance. Educational policy. Higher education. Management. 1971-74. *1046*

Committee of Small Magazine Editors and Publishers. Authors. Business History. Publishing, independent. 1772-1975. *535*

Commodities. Multinational corporations. Transfer pricing. 1966-74. *99*

Commodities Exchange Authority. Food industry. Foreign aid policies. World food supply. 1972. *811*

Commodity exchanges. Agricultural Commodities. Stock Exchange. 1968-78. *274*

—. Bucket shops. Chicago Board of Trade. Merchants' Exchange of St. Louis. Trade. 1882-1905. *246*

—. Econometrics. 1927-80. *258*

—. Federal regulation. 1922-74. *1260*

Communication satellites. Television (cable, subscription). Videorecorders. 1980. *524*

Communications. Corporations. Diplomacy. Foreign policy. Middle East. 1979. *142*

—. Government regulation. 1927-80. *1300*

Communications Behavior. Chandler, Alfred D., Jr. (review article). Corporations. Management. Technology. 1960-79. *39*

Communications Bill. Federal Communications Act (US, 1934). House of Representatives. Lobbying. Radio. Television. VanDeerlin, Lionel. 1934-79. *1258*

Communications Technology. American Telephone and Telegraph Company. Bell Telephone System. Competition. Industry. Laboratories. 1900-25. *559*

—. American Telephone and Telegraph Company. Bell Telephone System. Competition. Monopolies. 1875-1907. *542*

—. Louisiana (New Orleans). Radio. Television. WWL (station). 1940-50. *557*

Communications (trends). Mass media. 1953-73. *546*

Communism. Capitalism. Ideological struggle. Multinational corporations. 1973. *75*

—. Government Regulation. Public Utilities. Texas Public Utility Commission. 1975-79. *1218*

Communist Party. Auto Workers Union. 1920-33. *411*

—. California (Inglewood). North American Aviation. Strikes. United Automobile Workers of America. 1941. *464*

Community Banking Pilot program. Citibank. Economic Conditions. Finance. New York City (Brooklyn; Flatbush). 1978-82. *276*

Compaine, Benjamin M. (review article). Books, distribution of. Marketing. Publishers and Publishing. 1960's-70's. *548*

Company towns. Anticapitalist sentiments. Architecture. Industry. McKim, Meade & White (firm). 1880's-1910's. *1118*

—. City Planning. Corporations. Mining. North Central States. 19c-20c. *1020*

—. Copper Mines and Mining. Documents. Iron mining. Michigan. Minnesota. Wisconsin. 1845-1930. *1018*

—. Iron mining. Minnesota (Lake Superior area). 1840's-1940's. *1019*

—. Ohio. Social Classes. Steel Industry. Strikes. 1937. *915*

Comparative analysis. Business History. Enterprises, large-scale. Europe, Western. Japan. USA. 19c-20c. *26*

Competition. Advertising. Economic Growth. Industrial mobility. 1947-72. *228*

—. Agriculture. Montana, western. 1946-80. *842*

—. Air Lines. Civil Aeronautics Board. Contracts. Economic Regulations. Prices. 1930's-80. *1286*

—. American Telephone and Telegraph Company. Bell Telephone System. Communications Technology. Industry. Laboratories. 1900-25. *559*

—. American Telephone and Telegraph Company. Bell Telephone System. Communications Technology. Monopolies. 1875-1907. *542*

—. Antitrust. Law Enforcement. Trade Regulations. 1890-1978. *1254*

—. Antitrust. Prices. Stocks and Bonds. 1910's. *1172*

—. Automobile Industry and Trade. Federal Regulation. Fuel. International Trade. Politics. Working class. 1973-79. *362*

—. Banking. Loans. Wisconsin. 1870-1900. *240*

—. Conglomerate mergers. Mergers. -1973. *59*

—. Corporations. Economic theory. Empiricism. Invisible hand (concept). Literature. 20c. *115*

—. Corporations. Mass media. Newspapers. Public opinion. Public Policy. Stock exchange. 1970's. *516*

—. Corporations. Mergers. Publishers and Publishing. 1960's-70's. *556*

—. Federal Trade Commission. Meat industry. 1900-21. *1162*

—. Germany, West. International Trade. Japan. Manufactures. 1970's. *117*

—. Great Northern Railway. North Dakota, northern. Railroads. Townsites. 1905. *402*

—. Paperback Books. Pocket Books (company). Publishers and Publishing. 1958-78. *561*

—. Automobile insurance. Federal Regulation. Prices. Stigler, George J. (thesis). 1971-73. *1236*

—. Business. Government. Public policy. 1974. *1291*

—. Energy Department. Gasoline shortage. Iran. Oil Industry and Trade. 1979. *593*

—. Federal regulation. Trucks and Trucking. 1970's. *1322*

—. Meat packing industry. Missouri. Trusts, Industrial. 1891-1902. *1109*

Containerization. Ports. Technology. Transportation. 1960's-81. *387*

Continental Trading Company. Congress. Fall, Albert Bacon. Oil Industry and Trade. Teapot Dome Scandal. 1921-29. *606*

Contracting policies. Airplane Industry and Trade. Industrial concentration. World War II. 1938-46. *981*

Contracts. Air Lines. Civil Aeronautics Board. Competition. Economic Regulations. Prices. 1930's. *1286*

—. Antitrust. Northern Pacific Railroad. Supreme Court. 1950's. *1187*

—. Baseball. Economic Theory. Property rights. 1955-76. *207*

Conventions. Blanchard, Jim. Economic Reform. Louisiana (New Orleans). National Committee for Monetary Reform. 1971-80. *199*

—. Business. Conferences. Executives. Government. 1970's. *273*

Coolidge, William D. General Electric Company. Industry. Langmuir, Irving. Scientific Experiments and Research. Whitney, Willie R. 1900-16. *1007*

Cooperative Livestock Commission Company. Livestock exchanges. Trans-Mississippi West. 1906-09. *732*

Coopers' International Union. Industrial Relations. Mechanization. Standard Oil Company of Ohio. 1870's. *612*

Copper Mines and Mining. Alaska. Birch, Stephen. Hubbard, Charles G. Kennecott Copper Corporation. 1900-15. *898*

—. Alaska Syndicate. Business. Kennecott Copper Corporation. 1900-38. *876*

—. Arizona. Boomtowns. Railroads. 1880-86. *896*

—. Arizona (Globe). Strikes. Western Federation of Miners. 1917. *890*

—. Calumet and Hecla Mining Company. Labor Unions and Organizations. Michigan (Keweenaw Peninsula). Social Change. 1840-1968. *868*

—. Company towns. Documents. Iron mining. Michigan. Minnesota. Wisconsin. 1845-1930. *1018*

—. Greene, William Cornell. Mexico (Sonora; Cananea). Multinational Corporations. Stock manipulations. Taylor, Frederick Winslow. Wadleigh, Atherton B. 1901-07. *130*

—. Kennecott Copper Corporation. Kinnear, John C. Nevada (McGill). 1928-45. *872*

—. New Mexico (Santa Rita del Cobre). 1800-25. *902*

—. State Government. Taxation. 1970-81. *873*

Copper-facing. Newton, Luke Vanderveer. Printing. Typefounding. 1850-1907. *565*

Corporate concentration. Economic power. Market proportions, declining. Steel industry. 1960's-70's. *987*

Corporate democracy. Bureaucratic managers. Executive Behavior. 1970's. *128*

Corporate liberalism (concept). Commerce Department (Business Advisory Council). Historiography. National Recovery Administration (Industrial Advisory Board). New Deal. 1933-35. 1970's. *1272*

Corporate ownership and control. Capitalist class. Social Classes (structure, theory). -1974. *176*

Corporate power. Business. Politics. Profit system. 1970-73. *1102*

Corporate responsibility. Business. Income. 1945-73. *1137*

Corporate state. Economic Structure. Galbraith, John Kenneth. Gould, Jay. Soviet of technicians. Veblen, Thorstein. 1954-72. *103*

Corporate strategies. Foreign investments. Multinational corporations. 1890's-1973. *124*

Corporate structure. General Electric Company. New Deal. 1933-40. *962*

Corporation as government. Counter-corporate movement. Populism. 1895-1975. *163*

Corporation Charters. Banking, commercial. Law. State Government. 1781-1843. *1344*

Corporation law. Antitrust. Judicial Administration. State government. Supreme Court. *United States* v. *E. C. Knight Company* (US, 1895). 1869-1903. *1268*

—. Cartels. Europe. Mergers. 1880-1914. *64*

—. Cartels. France. Germany. Great Britain. Monopolies. 1880-1914. *1183*

—. Economic growth. France. Germany. Great Britain. Stock Companies. 1860-1920. *1230*

—. Great Britain. Management. Stock Companies. 1860-1920. *86*

—. Story, Joseph. 1830's. *1193*

Corporation training programs. Employee sponsorship. Minorities. Social environment. 1960's-70's. *1039*

Corporations *See also* names of individual corporations, e.g. Exxon, Carnegie Steel Co., etc.

—. Accounting (systems development). DuPont de Nemours, E. I. (Powder Company). Management. 1903-12. *84*

—. Advertising. Films. 1900-20. *206*

—. Advertising. Human Rights. 1950's-80. *226*

—. Affirmative action. Attitudes. Men. Sex discrimination. Women. 1975-80. *1076*

—. Agricultural Industry. 1930's-73. *788*

—. Agricultural Industry. Ownership. 1970's. *804*

—. Agriculture. Food industry. Prices. Trade. 1930-74. *670*

—. Air Lines. Federal Regulation. Small business. 1945-70's. *1310*

—. Arizona. Hunt, George W. P. Miners. State Politics. 1915-17. *905*

—. Art Galleries and Museums. Philanthropy. 1965-77. *1087*

—. Auditing. Income tax regulations, state. 1967-74. *1309*

—. Automobile Industry and Trade. Corvair (automobile). Ford Motor Company. General Motors Corporation. Pinto (automobile). 1959-70's. *380*

—. Banking, investment. Law. 1865-1914. *18*

—. Banks. Conglomerate expansion. Mergers. Monopolies. 1970's. *294*

—. Behavior. Interlocking directorates. Models. 1965-70. *95*

—. Bibliographies. Farms. Land ownership. Local government. 1969-70's. *680*

—. Boards of directors. Organizational structure. 16c-20c. *139*

—. Brown & Root, Inc. Construction industry. Housing. Rural areas. South. ca 1977-79. *177*

—. Business. Economic Theory. Mergers. 1948-74. *179*

—. Business strategies. Depressions. 1900-75. *56*

—. Cable broadcasting systems. Ownership. Television. 1972-79. *537*

Costs. Capital. Corporations. Profit. 1945-78. *74*
—. Federal Regulation. Industry. Occupational Safety and Health Act (US, 1970). Working conditions. 1971-81. *1293*
Cotton. Agricultural Cooperatives. Computers. Marketing. Plains Cotton Cooperative Association. Telecommunication. Texas (Lubbock). 1920's-70's. *790*
—. Agricultural Production. Economic Conditions. South. Soybeans. 1920's-75. *712*
—. Agricultural Production. Far Western States. Wool. 19c-20c. *739*
—. Agricultural Technology and Research. Mechanization. South. Southwest. 1946-79. *801*
—. Agricultural Technology and Research. Sharecroppers. South. Tractors. 1915-60. *773*
—. Alexander Brown and Sons. Great Britain. International Trade. South. 1820-60. *737*
—. Bee, Hamilton Prioleau. Confederate Army. Economic regulations. International Trade. Texas border. 1862-63. *764*
—. Brown lung disease. Burlington Industries, Inc. Carolina Brown Lung Association. Liberty Mutual Insurance Co. South. 1970's. *1038*
—. Child Labor Act (1916). Federal regulation. Textile Industry. 1907-16. *741*
—. Exports. North Carolina (Wilmington). Sprunt, Alexander and Son. 1866-1956. *736*
—. Farming, scientific. Fertilizers. Furman, Farish. South. 1878-83. *818*
—. Mills. New England, southern. New York. 1810-40. *746*
—. New England. South. Textile industry. 1951-60. *688*
Cotton Acreage Control Law (Texas, 1931). Crop limitation. Long, Huey P. New Deal. South. 1931-33. *1343*
Cotton (decline). Boll weevil. Negroes. South. 1929-77. *724*
Cotton dust. Federal regulation. Occupational Safety and Health Administration. Textile industry. 1970's. *1351*
Cotton Exchange. Economic Development. Louisiana (New Orleans). 1870-81. *209*
Cotton ginning, evolution of. Southeastern States. 18c-1973. *666*
Cotton industry. California. 1906-78. *774*
—. Central place theory. Marketing. South. Urbanization. 1880-1930. *835*
—. Economic conditions. Industrialization. Manufacturing. Pennsylvania (Rockdale). Social change. 1825-65. *830*
Cotton mills. Architecture. Dover Manufacturing Co. Print Works. New Hampshire (Dover). Printing, calico. 1820-25. *686*
Cotton "overproduction". Farmers. South. ca 1880-1915. *696*
Cotton planters. Farms, large. Machinery, use of. Technological change. 19c-1975. *796*
Cotton Textiles. International Cotton Textile Agreement (1962). Trade. 1962-72. *675*
Cotton textiles, price of. Economic Conditions. Johnson, Lyndon B. (administration). Price controls. South. 1965-66. *1179*
Cotton-textile manufacturers. New England. South. Technological change. 1890-1970. *706*
Council of Better Business Bureaus (National Advertising Division). Advertising. National Advertising Review Board. 1971-76. *297*
Counter-corporate movement. Corporation as government. Populism. 1895-1975. *640*
Courts. Airports. Federal Regulation. Local Government. Noise complaints. 1958-77. *1318*

—. Antitrust. Buffalo *Courier-Express.* Buffalo *Evening News.* New York. Newspapers. 1977-80. *521*
—. Antitrust movements. Fire insurance. Kansas City Board of Fire Underwriters. Law enforcement. Missouri. 1889-99. *1295*
—. Citizen Lobbies. Corporations. Government. Legislation. 1980. *49*
Coxe, Tench. Hamilton, Alexander. Manufactures. Society for Establishing Useful Manufactures. 1790-92. *1182*
Credit. Capital. Corporations. 1970's. *296*
Credit reporting agencies. Business History. Mercantile Agency. New York. ca 1841-1900. *250*
Credit unions. Decisionmaking. Economics. Nonprofit firms. 1968-69. *239*
Crime and Criminals. Banking. Farmers and Drovers National Bank (failure). Pennsylvania (Greene County; Waynesburg). Politics. Rinehart, James B. F. 1835-1906. *212*
—. Corporations. Ford Motor Company. Law. 1976-80. *1331*
Criminal law. Corporations. Judicial Process. 20c. *1071*
Crop limitation. Cotton Acreage Control Law (Texas, 1931). Long, Huey P. New Deal. South. 1931-33. *1343*
Crown-Zellerbach Corporation. Business History. California (Stockton). Paper industry. ca 1856-1900. *815*
Cuba. Foreign Policy. Mexico. Multinational Corporations. 1880-1915. *73*
—. Law. Monopolies. Railroads. 1920-25. *53*
Culbert, David Holbrook. Barnouw, Eric. Briggs, Asa. Metz, Robert. Radio (review article). 1920-76. *563*
Cull, George E. Airplane Industry and Trade. California Aero Company. Lark-95 (aircraft). Logan, Ronald R. Personal narratives. 1958-63. *344*
Cultural crises. Authority. Bureaucratic hierarchies. Business. History. -1973. *1035*
Curricula. Advertising. Business education. Colleges and Universities. 1900-17. *1124*
Curtis, Asahel. Chicago, Milwaukee, St. Paul and Pacific Railroad. Photography. Railroads. Western States. 1909-29. *480*
Curtiss Aeroplane and Motor Corp. Airplane Industry and Trade. Curtiss, Glenn H. France (Rheims). New York (Buffalo, Hammondsport). 1853-1929. *488*
Curtiss, Glenn H. Airplane Industry and Trade. Curtiss Aeroplane and Motor Corp. France (Rheims). New York (Buffalo, Hammondsport). 1853-1929. *488*
—. Airplane Industry and Trade. Naval Air Forces. 1878-1929. *473*
Customers. Industrial consulting firms. Organizational Theory. Task environments, standardization of. 1972. *281*
Customs district. Lumber and Lumbering. New Jersey (Great Egg Harbor). Ports. Shipbuilding. Trade. 19c. *373*

D

Daily Life. Bethlehem Steel Company. Depressions. Labor Unions and Organizations. Pennsylvania. Working conditions. 1910-50's. *990*
—. Pennsylvania (Phoenixville). Pennypacker, John G. (memoirs). Youth. 1900-08. *1042*
Dairy industry. Federal Regulation. Food Administration. Hoover, Herbert C. 1917-18. *1212*
Dairying. Marketing. 1860. *676*

Dallas Cowboys (team). Investments. Sports (professional). Suburbs. Texas (Arlington, Irving). Texas Rangers (team). 1968-75. 268

Dams. Construction, heavy. Government. Idaho (Boise). Morrison-Knudsen Company. Western states. 1933-40. 188

—. Hydroelectric potential. New England. Power Resources. 1977. 626

Darlington Manufacturing Company. Labor Disputes (unionization). South Carolina (Darlington). Textile Workers Union of America. 1956-73. 671

Daugherty, Harry M. Antitrust. Federal Government. Pennsylvania (Philadelphia). Political Corruption. United Gas Improvement Company. 1914-24. 1205

David, Paul A. Agriculture. Mechanization. Reaping. Technological diffusion. 1833-70. 1966. 780

Davis, Owen W., Jr. Katahdin Charcoal Iron Company. Maine. 1876-90. 938

Day nurseries. Business. Kinder-Care Learning Centers. Mendel, Perry. 1969-80. 301

Deaf Smith brand. Food Industry. New Mexico (Roosevelt County). Peanut butter. 1914-78. 685

Dealers, franchised. Automobiles. Employment patterns. Productivity. Profit. 1958-75. 358

Death and Dying. Advertising. Funeral industry. Public Relations. 1830-1980. 185

—. Free market. Life insurance. Social Change. Values. 19c. 298

Debow's Review. Agricultural reform. South. 1846-61. 715

Debt. Corporations. Financing. 1970-72. 229

—. Farmers. Specialization. 1860's-90's. 692

Debt, public. Banking. Federal Government. Gallatin, Albert. Securities. War of 1812. 1813. 183

Decisionmaking. Business History. Institutional change. 1850-1970's. 29

—. Corporations. Dissent. Executives. 1960's-77. 1051

—. Credit unions. Economics. Nonprofit firms. 1968-69. 239

—. Executive Power. Steel seizure. Truman, Harry S. 1952-75. 1213

Defense spending. Economic Structure. Inflation. 1930-79. 926

Degrees, Academic. Bureau of Labor Statistics. Business. 1975-79. 1147

Delaware. Du Pont, Thomas Coleman. Highway Engineering. 1900-35. 1114

Delaware (Red Clay Creek; Wooddale). Friends, Society of. Industrial Relations. Iron Industry. Wood, Alan. Wood, James. 1814-73. 1054

Delaware Valley. Business History. Commerce, Atlantic. Pennsylvania, southeastern. Shipbuilding. West Jersey. 1722-76. 343

Delaware (Wilmington). Bancroft, Joseph and Sons Company. Miller, Franklin, and Stevenson (firm). Scientific management. Textile Industry. 1911-27. 827

DeLorean, John Z. (account). Executive Behavior. General Motors Corporation. 1970's. 345

Delta Air Lines. 1924-79. 493

Delta Air Lines Inc. Air Lines. Chicago and Southern Air Lines, Inc. Civil Aeronautics Board. Federal regulation. Mergers. 1948-53. 429

Demand. Automobile Industry and Trade. Economic Conditions. Income. Prices. 1965-75. 331

—. Bag industry. Paper Industry. Plastics. Productivity. Technology. 1954-77. 927

—. North Central States. Pennsylvania. Production. Steel Industry (location). 1910-72. 942

Democracy. Attitudes. Business community. Federal government. 20c. 1340

Denver & Rio Grande Railroad. Atchison, Topeka & Santa Fe Railroad. Colorado (Oro City). Railroads. 1880. 486

Department stores. Industrial Relations. Salesmen and Salesmanship. Women. 1900-40. 919

—. Marketing. Social classes. 1880-1940. 920

Department stores (review article). Adburgham, Alison. Harris, Leon. Hendrickson, Robert. Weil, Gordon L. 1850-1975. 984

Depletion allowance. Congress (committees). Oil Industry and Trade. Public Policy. Subgovernment theory. Taxation. 1900-74. 588

Deposit growth. Banks. Business. Economic Conditions. 1960-71. 295

Depressions. American Federation of Labor. Coal Mines and Mining. New Mexico (Gallup). Strikes. 1933. 891

—. Bank deposits. Economic Conditions. Great Contraction. Money (demand). 1929-33. 217

—. Banking. Money. Panic of 1930. 1920-30. 292

—. Banking crisis. Kennedy, Susan Estabook (review article). 1933. 1973. 205

—. Bethlehem Steel Company. Daily Life. Labor Unions and Organizations. Pennsylvania. Working conditions. 1910-50's. 990

—. Business strategies. Corporations. 1900-75. 56

—. Diplomatic history. Foreign markets. Steel industry. Williams school. 1893-1913. 1012

—. Grain. Livestock. McGregor Land and Livestock Company. Prices. Washington (Columbia Plateau). 1930's-82. 760

Derby, Elias Hasket. Bentley, William. Diaries. Economic Conditions. Massachusetts (Salem). Shipbuilding. 1784-1819. 487

Deregulation. Air Lines. Collective bargaining. Federal Regulation. 1958-78. 1223

—. Air lines. Federal Policy. Industry. 1976-79. 1246

—. Air Transport Deregulation Act (US, 1978). 1975-78. 1304

Design. Automobile Industry and Trade. Engines (copper-cooled). General Motors Corporation. Kettering, Charles. 1919-26. 426

—. Colorado (Denver). Flivver (aircraft). Gray Goose (aircraft). Lewis-American Aircraft Co. McMahon, Bill. Mooney brothers. 1930-33. 347

—. Furniture and Furnishings. Manufactures. Technological innovations. 1850-1920. 939

—. Seaplanes. Sikorsky Aircraft. 1912-45. 430

Detroit Electric Car Company. Automobiles. Michigan. 1906-41. 417

Developing Nations. Banks. Business. Capitalism. Economic policy. 1981. 285

—. Books, distribution of. Business History. Literacy. Publishing. USA. 1900's. 547

—. Clothing industry. Imports. Labor. Small business. 1972. 767

—. Colleges and Universities. Education. Methodology. 1972-81. 918

—. Economic development. Multinational corporations. 20c. 146

—. Economic growth. Government. Multinational Corporations (review article). Politics. USA. 1945-70's. 90

—. Economic Growth. Multinational Corporations. USA. 1945-74. 43

—. Food industry. Infant formula. Marketing. Protest movements. 1970-79. 55

—. Foreign investments. Multinational corporations. Western Nations. ca 1960-75. 165

—. Foreign policy. Multinational corporations. 1960's-70's. 85

—. Foreign Policy. Multinational corporations. 1960's-70's. *180*
—. International Trade. Labor. Multinational corporations. Political attitudes. 1966-75. *69*
—. International Trade. Law. USA. 1964-73. *1188*
—. Marketing. Milk substitutes. Multinational corporations. 1970's. *71*
—. Multinational corporations. 1971-79. *156*
—. Multinational corporations. Technology. 1960-76. *30*
—. Multinational Corporations (review article). Politics. ca 1950-80. *105*
Development. Alaska (Prudhoe Bay). Eskimos. Oil Industry and Trade. 1970's. *1082*
—. Business. City Planning. Indiana (Kingsport). North. Towns. 1880-1950. *1021*
—. Railroads. Texas & Pacific Railroad. Texas (Martin County). 1881-1976. *472*
—. Railroads. Texas & Pacific Railroad. Texas (Ward County). 1880-1910. *468*
Diaries. Bentley, William. Derby, Elias Hasket. Economic Conditions. Massachusetts (Salem). Shipbuilding. 1784-1819. *487*
Diesel power. Electric power. Railroads. Steam power. 1920-50. *317*
Diplomacy. Adams, John Quincy. Fishing. Great Britain. Monroe, James. Newfoundland banks. USA. 1815-18. *1208*
—. Communications. Corporations. Foreign policy. Middle East. 1979. *142*
—. Foreign Investments. Kissinger, Henry A. Multinational Corporations. South Africa. 1969-76. *143*
—. Foreign Investments. Mexico. Oil and Petroleum Products. Teapot Dome Scandal. 1926-27. *616*
Diplomatic history. Depressions. Foreign markets. Steel industry. Williams school. 1893-1913. *1012*
Disasters. Coal Mines and Mining. Fire. Illinois (Cherry). 1909. *900*
Disciplinary methods. Behavior. Labor. New England. Textile mills. 1828-38. 1970-72. *1061*
Discrimination. Banking. Mortgages. Negroes. 1970-77. *193*
—. Columbia Broadcasting System. Journalism. Southerners. 1970's. *1138*
—. Fair Employment Practices Committee. Negroes. Railroads. Southeastern Carriers Conference. World War II. 1941-45. *1074*
—. Immigrants. Manufacturers. 1880-1914. *1095*
—. Indiana (Gary). Negroes. US Steel Corporation. 1906-74. *1068*
—. Insurance. 1981. *224*
Discrimination, Employment. Business recruitment. Executives. Jews. 1972-74. *1129*
—. Industry. Metropolitan areas. Profit. Racism. 1973. *1037*
Discrimination, Employment (review article). Fulmer, William E. Negroes. Rubin, Lester. Wrong, Elaine Gale. 1865-1973. *1108*
Dismal Swamp. Lumber and Lumbering. North Carolina. Virginia. 1760's-1970's. *1130*
Disney World. Corporations. Monopolies. Social Organization. 1971-81. *236*
Dissent. Corporations. Decisionmaking. Executives. 1960's-77. *1051*
Documents. Company towns. Copper Mines and Mining. Iron mining. Michigan. Minnesota. Wisconsin. 1845-1930. *1018*
—. Lumber and Lumbering. Port Blakely Mill Company. Washington, University of (Library). 1876-1923. *678*
Dodger Stadium. Baseball. California. Los Angeles Dodgers (team). 1956-62. *225*

Doheny, Edward Laurence. California (Los Angeles). Oil Industry and Trade. 1892-1930. *627*
Domestic Policy. Maritime Administration (Office of Domestic Shipping). Merchant Marine. Shipping. 1971. *1316*
Douglas, Donald. Airplanes. Photographs. 1932-38. *511*
Dover Manufacturing Co. Print Works. Architecture. Cotton mills. New Hampshire (Dover). Printing, calico. 1820-25. *686*
Dow Jones Co. Advertising. Colt, Cristine C. (account). Sex discrimination. 1975-78. *1036*
Downtown areas. Corporations. Urban renewal. 1960-75. *1058*
Drama. Antibusiness sentiments. Howard, Bronson. Thomas, Augustus. 1878-95. *1066*
Dredging. Alaska. California. Environmental damage. Gold Mines and Mining. 1905-20. *893*
Driver response. Automobile safety regulation. Highway deaths, annual. 1947-80's. *1288*
Drought. Campbell, Thomas D. Farm income. Great Plains. Prairie Provinces. Wheat farming. 1915-1940. *853*
Drug trade. Productivity. Quality control. Technology. 1963-72. *197*
Drugs. Food and Drug Administration. Government regulation. 1960-78. *1231*
Drugstores. Productivity. Retail trade. 1958-79. *940*
Du Pont estate. Ball, Ed. Florida East Coast Railroad. Pepper, Claude. Railroad. 1926-58. *492*
Du Pont, Thomas Coleman. Delaware. Highway Engineering. 1900-35. *1114*
Dumping. Antidumping Act (1921). International Trade. 1968-73. *1244*
—. International Trade. Japan. Public Opinion. Steel Industry. 1974-78. *950*
DuPont and Co. Explosives. 1802-1921. *964*
DuPont de Nemours, E. I. (Powder Company). Accounting (systems development). Corporations. Management. 1903-12. *84*
Dyes. Agriculture Department. Federal regulation. Food. Public Health. 1913-19. *1228*
—. Elson, J. Hugh. Illinois (Quincy). Missouri (Unionville). Monroe Chemical Company. Monroe, Edward N. 1876-1976. *989*

E

Eastern Airlines. Aeronautics. Gellert, Dan (accounts). L-1011 (aircraft). Safety. Working Conditions. 1972-78. *1060*
Eckert-Mauchly Computer Corp. Computers. Mergers. Remington Rand Inc. Sperry Rand Corp. (Univac division). 1946-55. *997*
Ecology. Alaska pipeline. Off-shore drilling. Oil Industry and Trade. 1974. *643*
Econometrics. Commodity exchanges. 1927-80. *258*
—. Cost functions. Electric power industry. Price indexes (hedonic). Production technologies. 1971. *972*
Econometrics (Cobb-Douglas production function). Returns to scale. Trucks and Trucking. 1970. *420*
Economic competition. Industry. International Trade. Manufactures. 1970's. *975*
—. Manufacturing. Market structure. South. 1850-60. *914*
—. Market control. Steel Industry. US Steel Corporation. 1898-1929. *976*
—. Multinational corporations. Oligopolies. 1945-73. *158*

—. Ports. Whaling Industry and Trade. 1784-1875. *817*

Economic concentration. Newspaper chains (endorsements). Political Campaigns (presidential). 1960-72. *1144*

Economic Conditions. Advertising. Breweries. Industry. Mergers. 1947-78. *718*

—. Agricultural Production. Congress. Louisiana. Subsidies. Sugar industry. 1860-1930. *803*

—. Agricultural Production. Cotton. South. Soybeans. 1920's-75. *712*

—. Appalachia. Coal. Iron. Land speculation. 1889-93. *895*

—. Arizona (White Mountains). Lumber and Lumbering. 1919-42. *752*

—. Automobile Industry and Trade. Demand. Income. Prices. 1965-75. *331*

—. Automobiles. Transportation. 1960-80. *461*

—. Baltimore & Ohio Railroad. Jones and Laughlin Steel Company. Pennsylvania (Pittsburgh; Hazelwood). 1870-1975. *1133*

—. Bank deposits. Depressions. Great Contraction. Money (demand). 1929-33. *217*

—. Banking (failures). Finance. 1946-76. *267*

—. Banks. Business. Deposit growth. 1960-71. *295*

—. Banks. Multinational corporations. 1945-77. *150*

—. Bentley, William. Derby, Elias Hasket. Diaries. Massachusetts (Salem). Shipbuilding. 1784-1819. *487*

—. Border industry program. Mexico. Multinational corporations. USA. 1940-70. *48*

—. Business. Electric power. Germany. Great Britain. Public policy. 1880-1929. *613*

—. California. Gold production, value of. 1848-1900. *859*

—. California (San Francisco). KQED (station). Massachusetts (Boston). Television, public. WGBH (station). 1945-81. *544*

—. California (Santa Clara County). Electronics industry. Environment. Social problems. 1950's-70's. *1121*

—. Cattle Raising. Kansas Livestock Association. Marketing. Railroads. 1890's. *844*

—. Chesapeake Bay area. Maryland. Tobacco industry. Virginia. 1617-1710. *765*

—. Citibank. Community Banking Pilot program. Finance. New York City (Brooklyn; Flatbush). 1978-82. *276*

—. Cities. Industry. 1981. *1075*

—. Citizen Lobbies. Corporations. Government regulation. Legislation. 1975-80. *1032*

—. Coal industry, bituminous. Competition, excessive. Justice Department. 1890-1917. *609*

—. Coal Mines and Mining. Strikes. 1977-78. *581*

—. Corporations. 1950-80. *173*

—. Corporations. 1970's. *21*

—. Corporations. Federal regulation. 20c. *1166*

—. Corporations. Government. Research and development. 1950-79. *1161*

—. Corporations. Great Britain. Inflation. Stocks and Bonds. USA. 1934-56. *41*

—. Corporations. Ownership, absentee. 1961-75. *167*

—. Cotton industry. Industrialization. Manufacturing. Pennsylvania (Rockdale). Social change. 1825-65. *830*

—. Cotton textiles, price of. Johnson, Lyndon B. (administration). Price controls. South. 1965-66. *1179*

—. Electronics. Information. Newspapers, daily. 1970-78. *539*

—. General Motors Corporation. Labor. Local Politics. Location. Michigan (Detroit). Public Policy. 1970-80. *1099*

—. Grain mills. 1963-74. *826*

—. Hepburn Committee. Interstate Commerce Act (US, 1887). Northeastern or North Atlantic States. Railroad regulation. ca 1870-1910. *1265*

—. Industry. Midwest. Pork-packing. Urbanization. 1835-75. *833*

—. Inflation. Price controls. Wages. 1971-74. *1324*

—. LaGrange and Memphis Railroad (proposed). Panic of 1837. Railroads. Tennessee. 1830-50. *423*

—. Manufacturing. Natural resource products. Substitution, partial elasticities of. 1960's-70's. *948*

—. Manufacturing. Prices. Wage statistics. 1953-70. *913*

—. Marketing. Multinational corporations. 1970. *76*

—. Multinational corporations. Production, internationalization of. 1941-76. *50*

—. New York City. Stock Exchange. 1895-1905. *277*

—. Ohio. Sheep raising. 1807-1900. *727*

—. Oklahoma panhandle. Railroad systems, adequate. Territorial status. 1880's-1930's. *366*

—. Railroads. Social Change. Vermont. 1843-70. *314*

—. Stock Exchange. ca 1792-1977. *272*

—. Tobacco, cultivation of. Virginia. 1613-1732. *665*

—. Transformer industry. 1963-79. *974*

Economic crisis. Banks. Capitalism. Social Classes. 1974-75. *303*

Economic Dependence. European Economic Community. Multinational corporations. 1946-76. *125*

Economic Development. Banking. California. Legislation. 1890-1915. *194*

—. Banking. Cost functions. South. 1870-1976. *234*

—. Banking history. Federal Regulation. Federal Reserve System. Wisconsin. 1863-1914. *1248*

—. Banking (multivariate analysis). Business. Holding Company Act of 1956. 1970-74. *238*

—. Banks, incorporated. Mississippi. 1829-37. *190*

—. Business. Government. Planning. 1960's-70's. *168*

—. Business. Industrial Technology. Research and development. 1968-71. *113*

—. Business. Noble, David F. (review article). 1880-1930. 1977. *44*

—. Corporations. Northeastern or North Atlantic States. Relocation. South. 1970-80. *1146*

—. Cotton Exchange. Louisiana (New Orleans). 1870-81. *209*

—. Developing Nations. Multinational corporations. 20c. *146*

—. Gristmills. Missouri. Pioneers. 1820-80. *704*

—. Illinois (Chicago). Steamships. Transportation, Commercial. 1821-1949. *352*

—. Industrial Technology. Manufacturing. 1839-99. *1000*

—. Manufactures. Technology (diffusion of). 1975. *996*

—. Ohio (Wood County). Oil and Petroleum Products. Social change. 1883-1917. *1089*

—. Railroad expansion. Steamboats, decline of. Transportation, Commercial. West, ante-bellum. 1811-60. *379*

—. Railroads. Texas & Pacific Railroad. Texas (Ector County). 1881. *496*

—. Campaign Finance. Corporations. Electoral politics. Labor Unions and Organizations. 1971-76. *1048*

—. Child Labor Act (1916). Cotton. Textile Industry. 1907-16. *741*

—. Coal mines and mining. Geology. 1969-77. *654*

—. Coal Mines and Mining. Industrial safety. 1942-79. *1289*

—. Coal Mines and Mining. Legislation. Safety. 1941-70. *1253*

—. Commerce Department. Hoover, Herbert C. Licensing. Radio. 1918-22. *1311*

—. Commodity exchanges. 1922-74. *1260*

—. Congress. Food, Drug, and Cosmetic Act (US, 1938). Pharmacy. Prescriptions. Supreme Court. 1906-50's. *1333*

—. Conservatism. Esch-Cummins Act (1920). Newlands, Francis G. Progressivism. Railroads. 1888-1917. *1174*

—. Consumers. Trucks and Trucking. 1970's. *1322*

—. Corporations. Economic Conditions. 20c. *1166*

—. Costs. Industry. Occupational Safety and Health Act (US, 1970). Working conditions. 1971-81. *1293*

—. Cotton dust. Occupational Safety and Health Administration. Textile industry. 1970's. *1351*

—. Dairy industry. Food Administration. Hoover, Herbert C. 1917-18. *1212*

—. Economy. Ideas. Mass Media. 1973. *1178*

—. Electric power companies. Investments. Public Utilities. 1970's. *1245*

—. Executive power. Politics. President's Advisory Council on Executive Organization. Public Administration. Reform. 1937-79. *1345*

—. Germany. Interstate Commerce Commission. Public policy. Railroads. 1870-1920. *500*

—. Health services. Inflation. Price controls. 1965-73. *257*

—. Insurance (public provision, overinsurance). 1974. *260*

—. Intermodal rate competition. Interstate Commerce Commission. Transportation. 1963-66. *1216*

—. Interstate Commerce Commission. Motor carrier industry. Prices. Profit standards. 1970's. *1190*

—. Interstate Commerce Commission. Trucks and Trucking. 1938-76. *1277*

—. Johnson, Lyndon B. (administration). Prices. Sulphur industry. 1960's. *1180*

—. Law. Management. Railroads and State. 1885-1916. *350*

—. Mass Media. Press. 1912-73. *1165*

—. Medical care. Physicians. Professional Standards Review Organization Program. Social Security Act (US, 1935; amended, 1972). 1965-80. *1185*

—. Mineral Resources. Mining. Oceans. Seabed. 1974. *1197*

—. Northeastern or North Atlantic States. Railroads and State. United States Railway Association. 1975. *453*

—. Occupational Safety and Health Act (US, 1970). Working conditions. 1970-76. *1280*

—. Oil Industry and Trade. Power Resources. Technology. 1970-78. *647*

—. Oil Industry and Trade. Prices. 1970-79. *652*

—. Productivity. 1947-79. *1175*

—. Railroad Revitalization and Regulatory Reform Act (US, 1976). Regional Rail Reorganization Act (US, 1974). Subsidies. 1974-78. *1226*

—. Risk analysis. Technology. 1970-81. *1251*

—. Saccharin. Science and Government. 1907-80. *1302*

—. Storage and Moving Industry. 1978-80. *1278*

Federal regulatory commissions. Politics. Powers. 1961-74. *1341*

Federal Reserve System. Banking (central). Gold standard. Real bills. 1870-1930. *1342*

—. Banking history. Economic development. Federal Regulation. Wisconsin. 1863-1914. *1248*

Federal Reserve System (Board of Governors). Banking. Comptroller of the Currency. Justice Department. Mergers. 1950-66. *1202*

Federal subsidies. Air line war. Civil Aeronautics Board. Southwest Airlines. Texas. 1970's. *400*

Federal Trade Commission. Advertising. 1914-38. *1332*

—. Advertising regulation. Whealer-Lea Act (1938). 1914-71. *1329*

—. Agricultural Cooperatives. Citrus industry. Monopolies. Prices. Sunkist Growers. 1974-81. *762*

—. Competition. Meat industry. 1900-21. *1162*

—. Industry. Magnuson-Moss Act (US, 1975). 1914-81. *1282*

Federal Trade Commission, Bureau of Competition. Antitrust. Arbitration. Law. Oil Industry and Trade. 1973-75. *1215*

Fertilizers. Cotton. Farming, scientific. Furman, Farish. South. 1878-83. *818*

Fiction, romance. Harlequin Enterprises, Inc. Women. 1970's. *568*

Filene, Edward A. Industrial democracy. Massachusetts (Boston). Reform. 1890-1937. *961*

Filipino Americans. Alaska. Canneries. Labor Unions and Organizations. Salmon. 1902-38. *751*

Filipinos. Aliens. Brotherhood of Sleeping Car Porters. Labor. Negroes. Pullman Company. Railroads. 1925-55. *1110*

Film industry. 1910's-30's. *248*

—. 1950-79. *550*

—. American Mutoscope and Biograph Company. New York City. 1900-06. *569*

—. Finance capitalism (concept). Lenin, V. I. *(Imperialism: The Highest Stage of Capitalism)*. Monopolies. 1916-39. *534*

—. Multinational corporations. USA. 1949-74. *57*

Films. Advertising. Corporations. 1900-20. *206*

—. Anti-Communist Movements. Industrial Relations. Politics. 1933-53. *571*

—. California (Hollywood). Hays, William Harrison. Motion Picture Producers and Distributors of America. Sex. 1922-56. *579*

—. California (Hollywood). Jesse L. Lasky Feature Play Company. *Squaw Man* (film). 1911-14. *543*

—. Electronovision. Mark Armistead Television. Sargent, William, Jr. 1964-65. *545*

Finance. Arkansas. Construction. Little Rock and Fort Smith Railroad. Railroads. Robinson, Asa P. ca 1867-76. *495*

—. Banking (failures). Economic Conditions. 1946-76. *267*

—. Capital. New York Life Insurance and Trust Company. Ohio Life Insurance and Trust Company. 1830's. *222*

—. Citibank. Community Banking Pilot program. Economic Conditions. New York City (Brooklyn; Flatbush). 1978-82. *276*

—. Great Britain. Insurance. 1945-71. *275*

—. Indiana (Gary). Intergovernmental Relations. Minnesota (St. Paul). Negotiated investment strategy. Ohio (Columbus). Public Policy. 1979-80. *192*

—. Lumber and Lumbering. 1830's-ca 1940's. *814*

Fruit and Fruit Crops. Advertising. Agricultural cooperatives. California. Nutrition. Vegetables. 1880's-1920's. *820*

Fuel. Agriculture. Alcohol. Business. Motors. Prices. Surpluses. 1930's. *607*

—. Automobile Industry and Trade. Competition. Federal Regulation. International Trade. Politics. Working class. 1973-79. *362*

—. Behavior. Pennsylvania (Pittsburgh). Public Policy. Smoke. 1940-50. *1132*

—. Coal. Power Resources. 18c-1977. *650*

—. Hopewell Forge. Iron industry. Labor. Management. Pennsylvania. Productivity. Technology. 1750-1800. *977*

Fuel shortage. Conspiracy. Oil industry and Trade. 1972. *629*

—. Conspiracy, accusations of. Oil Industry and Trade. 1970-73. *655*

Fulmer, William E. Discrimination, Employment (review article). Negroes. Rubin, Lester. Wrong, Elaine Gale. 1865-1973. *1108*

Funeral industry. Advertising. Death and Dying. Public Relations. 1830-1980. *185*

Furman, Farish. Cotton. Farming, scientific. Fertilizers. South. 1878-83. *818*

Furniture and Furnishings. Design. Manufactures. Technological innovations. 1850-1920. *939*

—. Ledgers. Massachusetts (Boston). Mercantile Agency. 1880. *933*

G

Galambos, Louis. Business History (review article). Public Opinion. Snow, Barbara Barrow. Social Change. 1880-1940. 1975. *1103*

Galbraith, John Kenneth. Corporate state. Economic Structure. Gould, Jay. Soviet of technicians. Veblen, Thorstein. 1954-72. *103*

Galena and Chicago Union Railroad. Economic Growth. Illinois (Chicago). Ogden, William Butler. Railroads. 1836-53. *441*

Gallatin, Albert. Banking. Debt, public. Federal Government. Securities. War of 1812. 1813. *183*

Games, board. Education. Social Change. Values. 1832-1904. *1016*

Gardner, Vernon O. Banking. Brotherhood of Railway Telegraphers. Manion, Edward J. Missouri (St. Louis). Telegraphers National Bank. 1922-42. *232*

Garibaldi mill. Lumber and Lumbering. Oregon (Tillamook Bay). 1917-74. *821*

Garment Industry. 1954-77. *687*

—. Child labor. Women. Working conditions. ca 1900-20. *1100*

—. Illinois (Chicago). Men. Strikes. 1910-11. *836*

—. Location. Working class. 1950-74. *850*

—. New York City. 1979. *721*

Gas light industry. Edison, Thomas Alva. Electric light industry. Monopolies. 1879-1900. *960*

Gasoline shortage. Consumers. Energy Department. Iran. Oil Industry and Trade. 1979. *593*

—. Mass media performance. Oil Industry and Trade. 1971-74. *599*

Gates, Frederick T. Idaho. Mining. Rockefeller, John D. Washington. 1890-1905. *871*

Gellert, Dan (accounts). Aeronautics. Eastern Airlines. L-1011 (aircraft). Safety. Working Conditions. 1972-78. *1060*

General Electric Company. Coolidge, William D. Industry. Langmuir, Irving. Scientific Experiments and Research. Whitney, Willie R. 1900-16. *1007*

—. Corporate structure. New Deal. 1933-40. *962*

—. International Trade. Monopolies. 1878-1980. *957*

—. Labor Unions and Organizations. New York (Fort Edward, Hudson Falls). Pollution. Polychlorinated biphenyl. United Electrical, Radio, and Machine Workers of America. 1975. *1030*

General Motors Corporation. Accounting. Management. 1920's. *409*

—. Automobile Industry and Trade. Corporations. Corvair (automobile). Ford Motor Company. Pinto (automobile). 1959-70's. *380*

—. Automobile Industry and Trade. Design. Engines (copper-cooled). Kettering, Charles. 1919-26. *426*

—. DeLorean, John Z. (account). Executive Behavior. 1970's. *345*

—. Economic Conditions. Labor. Local Politics. Location. Michigan (Detroit). Public Policy. 1970-80. *1099*

—. Economy, international. Foreign relations. International Telephone and Telegraph. Labor Unions and Organizations. Multinational corporations. 1970's. *151*

—. Industry. Kettering, Charles. Midgley, Thomas. Scientific Experiments and Research. Sloan, Alfred. 1916-44. *427*

—. Michigan (Pontiac). Occupational Safety and Health Administration. United Automobile Workers of America. Working conditions. 1971-78. *1337*

—. Snell, Bradford. Transportation (review article). ca 1935-74. *477*

Geology. Coal mines and mining. Federal regulation. 1969-77. *654*

Georgia. Economic Regulations. Mortgages. Savings and loan associations. State Government. Usury ceilings. 1960's-70's. *253*

—. Oleoresin industry. Pine trees. 1842-1900. *699*

—. Railroads, short line. 1915-78. *442*

Georgia (Atlanta). Automobile Industry and Trade. Economic Growth. Woodruff, Robert W. 1909-20. *463*

Georgia Power Company. Atlanta Transit Company. Street, Electric Railway and Motor Coach Employees of America. Strikes. 1946-50. *437*

Georgia Railroad and Banking Company. Banking. Capital. Railroads. Taxation. 1833-1980. *481*

Georgia (Sapelo Island). Archaeology. Spalding, Thomas. Sugar industry. ca 1795-1850's. 1976. *694*

Gerber Products Co. 1927-79. *822*

German Americans. California (San Francisco). Clothing industry. Strauss, Levi. 1850-1970's. *787*

Germany. Banking. Jews. 17c-19c. *220*

—. Business. Economic Conditions. Electric power. Great Britain. Public policy. 1880-1929. *613*

—. Cartels. Corporation Law. France. Great Britain. Monopolies. 1880-1914. *1183*

—. Corporation law. Economic growth. France. Great Britain. Stock Companies. 1860-1920. *1230*

—. Federal Regulation. Interstate Commerce Commission. Public policy. Railroads. 1870-1920. *500*

—. France. Great Britain. Regulation. Stock exchange. 19c-1934. *211*

Germany, West. Competition. International Trade. Japan. Manufactures. 1970's. *117*

Girard, Stephen. Bank of Stephen Girard. Profit. 1812-31. *184*

Goebel, William. Election Laws (gubernatorial). Kentucky. Railroad regulation. Taylor, William S. 1887-1900. *1171*

Gold Mines and Mining. Alaska. California. Dredging. Environmental damage. 1905-20. *893*

—. California (Mother Lode). Eggleston, William S. Personal narratives. 1921-26. *869*

—. California (Sierra County; Allegheny). Sixteen-to-One Mine. 1890-1965. *866*

—. Colorado (San Juan Mountains). 1870's-1900. *897*

Gold production, value of. California. Economic Conditions. 1848-1900. *859*

Gold Rushes. Alaska (Kantishna Hills). National Parks and Reserves. Transportation. 1903-78. *863*

—. Alaska (Unalaska Island). Howard Company Shipyards. Howard, Edmunds J. Indiana (Jeffersonville). Shipbuilding. 1897-1901. *504*

—. Clipper ships. International Trade. Shipbuilding. 1850-57. *309*

Gold standard. Banking (central). Federal Reserve System. Real bills. 1870-1930. *1342*

Goldsmith's (department store). Ottenheimer, Ike. Retail Trade. Tennessee (Memphis). 1900-63. *994*

Gonzales amendments. Foreign aid sanctions. Hickenlooper amendment. Multinational Corporations. 1959-76. *107*

Gould, Jay. Business. Railroads. 1860's-92. *244*

—. Corporate state. Economic Structure. Galbraith, John Kenneth. Soviet of technicians. Veblen, Thorstein. 1954-72. *103*

—. Railroads. 1850-1900. *416*

Gov. Morrow (locomotive). Little Miami Line. Ohio (Cincinnati). Railroads, steam. 1837-70. *509*

Government. Agricultural policy. Capitalism. Food. 1800-1979. *1283*

—. Antitrust. Imports. Protectionism. Steel Industry. Trigger Price Mechanism. 1959-78. *1281*

—. Armaments Industry. Navy. Tracy, Benjamin Franklin. 1881-97. *934*

—. Borch, Fred. Business Roundtable (March Group). Executives. Harper, John. Public policy. 1970-79. *120*

—. Business. Cabinet. Elites. Mills, C. Wright. 1897-1973. *1057*

—. Business. Conferences. Conventions. Executives. 1970's. *273*

—. Business. Consumers. Public policy. 1974. *1291*

—. Business. Economic Development. Planning. 1960's-70's. *168*

—. Business. Economic planning. Labor Unions and Organizations. Liberalism, corporate. 1920-40. *121*

—. Business. Economic Policy. Historiography. Liberalism, corporate. 20c. *67*

—. Citizen Lobbies. Corporations. Courts. Legislation. 1980. *49*

—. Coal Mines and Mining. Health and safety regulations. Ohio. 1869-81. *1249*

—. Construction, heavy. Dams. Idaho (Boise). Morrison-Knudsen Company. Western states. 1933-40. *188*

—. Corporations. 1787-1982. *122*

—. Corporations. Economic Conditions. Research and development. 1950-79. *1161*

—. Corporations. Elites. Social backgrounds. 1939-70. *45*

—. Corporations. Political Theory. Public policy. 1970's. *1279*

—. Developing nations. Economic growth. Multinational Corporations (review article). Politics. USA. 1945-70's. *90*

—. Executive Power. Multinational corporations. 1973. *1097*

—. Foreign Relations. Industrialized Countries (cooperation). Multinational corporations. ca 1960-75. *162*

—. Multinational Corporations. Nation state. 1974. *20*

—. Railroads. Strikes. 1877. *361*

Government agencies. Corporations. Freedom of Information Act (1966). Law firms, large. Trade secrets. 1966-74. *1305*

Government Enterprise. ConRail. Northeastern or North Atlantic States. Railroads. 1970's. *1173*

Government intervention (avoidance). Commerce Department. Hoover, Herbert C. Industry. Labor. 1921-28. *1221*

Government regulation *See also* Federal Regulation.

—. Act to Regulate Public Warehouses (Illinois, 1871). Grain. Illinois. Interstate Commerce Act (US, 1887). Trade. 1870-1900. *1354*

—. Advertising. Consumers. Social responsibiltiy. 1950's-70's. *252*

—. Agriculture. Chemical Industry. Food Adulteration and Inspection. Mississippi State Chemical Laboratory. 1882-1979. *1296*

—. Arizona (Scottsdale). Cable broadcasting systems. Federal Communications Commission. 1981-82. *1222*

—. Banking. 1894-1914. *291*

—. Banking. 1933-82. *1308*

—. Business. Higher education. 1960's-70's. *1206*

—. California, northern. Construction industry. Housing. Prices. Suburbs. 1970's. *1204*

—. Citizen Lobbies. Corporations. Economic Conditions. Legislation. 1975-80. *1032*

—. Communications. 1927-80. *1300*

—. Communism. Public Utilities. Texas Public Utility Commission. 1975-79. *1218*

—. Conservation of Natural Resources. Energy. Public Policy. 1929-79. *1273*

—. Drugs. Food and Drug Administration. 1960-78. *1231*

—. Federal Communications Commission. Legislation. Radio. Supreme Court. Television. 1927-74. *1319*

—. Forests and Forestry. Oregon. Pinchot, Gifford. Washington. 1902-10. *707*

—. France. Poisons. 1899-1980. *1170*

—. Health insurance. Medical Care (costs). 1870-1980. *249*

—. Industry. Pollution. Productivity. 1972-81. *1314*

—. Inflation. Transportation. 1960-81. *371*

—. Milk. 1922-78. *1237*

—. Multinational corporations. 1960-75. *4*

—. Public Administration. US Regulatory Council. 1978-80. *1292*

—. Raw materials. 1976-80. *1353*

Government regulations, fear of. Corporations. Public opinion. Social responsibility. 1960-70's. *1044*

Government, Resistance to. Corporations. Political Attitudes. 19c-20c. *1143*

Government responsibility. Energy crisis. Multinational oil companies. Oil, Allocation of. 1973-74. *653*

Grain. Act to Regulate Public Warehouses (Illinois, 1871). Government regulation. Illinois. Interstate Commerce Act (US, 1887). Trade. 1870-1900. *1354*

—. Agricultural Production. Prices. 1970's. *691*

—. Christianson, Ivan D. (interview). Railroads. South Dakota (Granville). 1920's. *330*

—. Depressions. Livestock. McGregor Land and Livestock Company. Prices. Washington (Columbia Plateau). 1930's-82. *760*

Grain elevators. Economic Regulations. Illinois (Chicago). 1870-90. *1336*

—. Technology. 1840-1980. *713*

Grain exports. Agricultural production. Europe. Great Britain. International Trade. USA. 1770-1976. *849*

Grain mills. Economic Conditions. 1963-74. *826*

Grain production. Agricultural Commodities. Pacific Coast. 1846-1900. *797*

Grand Canyon. Arizona. Mines. Uranium. 1540-1969. *887*

Gray Goose (aircraft). Colorado (Denver). Design. *Flivver* (aircraft). Lewis-American Aircraft Co. McMahon, Bill. Mooney brothers. 1930-33. *347*

Great Britain. Adams, John Quincy. Diplomacy. Fishing. Monroe, James. Newfoundland banks. USA. 1815-18. *1208*

—. Agricultural production. Europe. Grain exports. International Trade. USA. 1770-1976. *849*

—. Agriculture. American Revolution (impact). South. Strickland, William. 1794-95. *726*

—. Alexander Brown and Sons. Cotton. International Trade. South. 1820-60. *737*

—. Automobile Industry and Trade (review article). Ford, Henry. Lewis, David. Management. Morris, William. Overy, R. J. 1903-45. *336*

—. Boston Manufacturing Company. Industrialization. International trade. Lowell, Francis Cabot. Massachusetts. 1807-20. *677*

—. Brazil. Foreign Investments. USA. 1870's. *149*

—. Business. Economic Conditions. Electric power. Germany. Public policy. 1880-1929. *613*

—. Capitalism. Latin America. Pepper, Charles M. *(Pan-American Railway)*. Railroads. 1904. *17*

—. Cartels. Corporation Law. France. Germany. Monopolies. 1880-1914. *1183*

—. Civil Engineering. Railroads. Technology. 1825-40. *490*

—. Coal Mines and Mining. Illinois. Labor Unions and Organizations. Legislation. Lobbying. 1861-72. *1209*

—. Corporation law. Economic growth. France. Germany. Stock Companies. 1860-1920. *1230*

—. Corporation Law. Management. Stock Companies. 1860-1920. *86*

—. Corporations. Economic Conditions. Inflation. Stocks and Bonds. USA. 1934-56. *41*

—. Economic regulations. 1609-1975. *1234*

—. Environment. Transportation. USA. 19c-1974. *1128*

—. Finance. Insurance. 1945-71. *275*

—. Ford, Henry. Ireland (Cork). Location, industrial. Tariffs. Tractors. 1912-26. *404*

—. France. Germany. Regulation. Stock exchange. 19c-1934. *211*

—. Industrial organization (review article). USA. 1945-72. *154*

—. Industrial technology. Iron Industry. Productivity. Profit. 1890. *921*

—. Iron industry. Middle Atlantic states. USA. 1750-1850. *1003*

—. Management. Multinational corporations. Technology. 1880-1979. *27*

—. Management, private. Oil Industry and Trade. Public policy. USA. 1918-24. *615*

—. Money (sources of). USA. 1870-1913. *196*

Great Britain (London). Cities. Industry. New York City. Office location. 1960-72. *1154*

Great Contraction. Bank deposits. Depressions. Economic Conditions. Money (demand). 1929-33. *217*

Great Lakes. Bradley Transportation Company. Limestone Quarrying. Michigan (Rogers City). Shipping. US Steel Corporation. 1912-67. *448*

—. Brown, Alex E. Shipping. Steamboats. Technological innovations. 1852-1910. *415*

—. Coal. Shipping. 1965-75. *604*

—. Shipping. Steamships. 1871-1976. *353*

Great Northern Railway. Canada. Locomotives. Railroads. USA. 1861-1970. *414*

—. Canada. Railroads. USA. ca 1850-1910. *449*

—. Competition. North Dakota, northern. Railroads. Townsites. 1905. *402*

—. Hill, James J. Milwaukee Road. North Dakota. Northern Pacific Railroad. Railroad construction. 1879-85. *451*

—. Minnesota (St. Paul). Northern Pacific Railroad. Working Conditions. 1915-21. *507*

Great Plains. Agriculture. Labor casualization. Mechanization. Wheat. 1865-1902. *669*

—. Campbell, Thomas D. Drought. Farm income. Prairie Provinces. Wheat farming. 1915-1940. *853*

—. Power Resources. 1859-1940. *589*

Greene, William Cornell. Copper Mines and Mining. Mexico (Sonora; Cananea). Multinational Corporations. Stock manipulations. Taylor, Frederick Winslow. Wadleigh, Atherton B. 1901-07. *130*

Greer, Edward. Cities. Ewen, Linda Ann. Industrial Relations (review article). Meier, August. Negroes. Rudwick, Elliott. 1900-81. *1096*

Gristmills. Economic development. Missouri. Pioneers. 1820-80. *704*

Grocery stores. Food Industry. Lutey Brothers Marketeria. Montana. 1897-1924. *955*

Gulf Oil Company. Angola. Public relations campaign. USA. 1968-74. *1116*

H

Habakkuk, H. J. Carriage and wagon industry. Labor supply hypothesis. Manufactures. Ohio (Cincinnati). 1850-1900. *357*

Haciendas. Agricultural Production. Mills. Puerto Rico, southwestern. Sugar industry. 1902. *838*

Hall, Henry. McKay, Donald. Shipbuilding. 1880-90. *421*

Hamilton, Alexander. Coxe, Tench. Manufactures. Society for Establishing Useful Manufactures. 1790-92. *1182*

Hanes Hosiery (team). Basketball. Industrial leagues. North Carolina (Winston-Salem). Women. 1940's-50's. *1027*

Harlequin Enterprises, Inc. Fiction, romance. Women. 1970's. *568*

Harper, John. Borch, Fred. Business Roundtable (March Group). Executives. Government. Public policy. 1970-79. *120*

Harris, Leon. Adburgham, Alison. Department stores (review article). Hendrickson, Robert. Weil, Gordon L. 1850-1975. *984*

Harrison, Pat. International Trade. Mississippi. Reciprocal Trade Act of 1940. Senate Finance Committee. 1940. *1301*

Harvard Business School (Baker Library). Archival Catalogs and Inventories. Business. Manuscripts. New England. 1978. *110*

Harvard University, Graduate School of Business. Environment. Labor. Western Electric Co., Inc. Workplace. 1924-33. *1153*

Harvesting. Agricultural Technology and Research. California (Central Valley). Tractors. 1850's-1920. *841*

International Cotton Textile Agreement (1962). Cotton Textiles. Trade. 1962-72. *675*
International economy. Labor. Multinational Corporations. 1975. *36*
International Harvester Company. Corporations. Henequen. Mexico (Yucatán). 1902-15. *169*
—. Henequen. Marketing. Mexico (Yucatán). Molina-Montes (firm). Prices. 1898-1915. *8*
—. Labor practices. Minorities. Race relations. 1831-1976. *1022*
International Law. Foreign Policy. Multinational corporations. 1945-78. *161*
—. Labor Unions and Organizations (international). Latin America. Multinational corporations. North America. 1937-74. *181*
International Petroleum Company. Nationalization. Oil Industry and Trade. Peru. USA. 1968-71. *132*
International Salt Co. v. *United States* (1947). Leases. Lixator machine. Monopolies. Prices. Supreme Court. 1940's. *1290*
International Steel Cartel. Foreign policy. Import restrictions. Labor. Steel Workers Organizing Committee. US Steel Corporation. 1937. *954*
International Telephone and Telegraph. Chile. Foreign policy, private. Multinational Corporations. USA. 1960-74. *12*
—. Economy, international. Foreign relations. General Motors Corporation. Labor Unions and Organizations. Multinational corporations. 1970's. *151*
—. Spain. State Department. 1924-44. *108*
International Trade. Act of state doctrine. Antitrust. Foreign Policy. Sovereign compulsion. Trials. 1965-78. *1357*
—. Agricultural production. Europe. Grain exports. Great Britain. USA. 1770-1976. *849*
—. Alexander Brown and Sons. Cotton. Great Britain. South. 1820-60. *737*
—. Antidumping Act (1921). Dumping. 1968-73. *1244*
—. Automobile Industry and Trade. Competition. Federal Regulation. Fuel. Politics. Working class. 1973-79. *362*
—. Banks. 1958-79. *243*
—. Bee, Hamilton Prioleau. Confederate Army. Cotton. Economic regulations. Texas border. 1862-63. *184*
—. Boston Manufacturing Company. Great Britain. Industrialization. Lowell, Francis Cabot. Massachussetts. 1807-20. *677*
—. Cartels. Tobacco. ca 1945-79. *33*
—. China. Pacific & Eastern Steamship Company. Ships, shortage of. USA. World War I. 1914-16. *466*
—. Clipper ships. Gold Rushes. Shipbuilding. 1850-57. *309*
—. Competition. Germany, West. Japan. Manufactures. 1970's. *117*
—. Developing Nations. Labor. Multinational corporations. Political attitudes. 1966-75. *69*
—. Developing nations. Law. USA. 1964-73. *1188*
—. Dumping. Japan. Public Opinion. Steel Industry. 1974-78. *950*
—. Economic competition. Industry. Manufactures. 1970's. *975*
—. Economic Policy. Protectionism. Steel industry. 1870-1979. *1358*
—. Energy. 1974-79. *630*
—. Energy crisis. Oil companies (independent, international). 1973-74. *657*
—. Fish. Massachusetts. Portugal. Spain. 1700-73. *747*

—. Foreign Policy. Labor Unions and Organizations. Multinational Corporations. Politics. 1966-74. *70*
—. Foreign Policy. Multinational corporations. 1974. *159*
—. Foreign policy. Nuclear power industries. Uranium cartel (possible). USA. 1970's. *174*
—. General Electric Company. Monopolies. 1878-1980. *957*
—. Harrison, Pat. Mississippi. Reciprocal Trade Act of 1940. Senate Finance Committee. 1940. *1301*
—. Merchant Marine. 1973. *386*
—. Multinational corporations. Social Problems. 1960's-70's. *1139*
—. Technology transfer. 1960-78. *114*
International Trade (competition). Economic Reform. Inflation. 1971-74. *175*
International Whaling Commission. Whaling Industry and Trade. 1975-81. *682*
Interstate Commerce Act (US, 1887). Act to Regulate Public Warehouses (Illinois, 1871). Government regulation. Grain. Illinois. Trade. 1870-1900. *1354*
—. Economic Conditions. Hepburn Committee. Northeastern or North Atlantic States. Railroad regulation. ca 1870-1910. *1265*
Interstate Commerce Commission. Baltimore & Ohio Railroad. Chesapeake and Ohio Railway. Mergers. Railroads. Transportation Act (US, 1940). 1958-62. *318*
—. Business. Federal Regulation. Freight and Freightage. Hepburn Act (US, 1906). 1905-06. *1339*
—. Chicago, Burlington & Quincy Railroad. Iowa (Mt. Ayr). Labor Unions and Organizations. Missouri (Grant City). Railroads (abandonment). 1943-44. *456*
—. Civil Aeronautics Board. Employment. Federal Communications Commission. Private sector. 1977-80. *1198*
—. Economic regulations. Social costs. Trucks and Trucking. 1978. *1199*
—. Federal Regulation. Germany. Public policy. Railroads. 1870-1920. *500*
—. Federal Regulation. Intermodal rate competition. Transportation. 1963-66. *1216*
—. Federal Regulation. Motor carrier industry. Prices. Profit standards. 1970's. *1190*
—. Federal Regulation. Trucks and Trucking. 1938-76. *1277*
—. Interest groups. Regulation. 1887-1920. *1335*
—. Labor Unions and Organizations. Teamsters' Union. Trucks and Trucking. 1973. *1158*
—. Missouri-Kansas-Texas Railroad. Oklahoma, western. Railroads (branch lines). 1969-73. *396*
—. New York, New Haven and Hartford Railroad. Railroads (freight rates). Supreme Court. 1958-64. *1252*
Inventions. Agricultural Technology and Research. California (Riverside County). Citrus industry. Mergers. Parker, George. Stebler, Fred. 1900-36. *770*
Investment behavior. Manufacturing. Tax policy changes 1971-73. *262*
Investments. Art. Internal Revenue Service. Prints. Retail Trade. Tax shelters. 1980. *562*
—. Atchison Associates. Atchison, Topeka & Santa Fe Railroad. Kansas. Railroads. 1868-69. *382*
—. Banking. 19c-20c. *283*
—. Banking (trust accounts). Corporations, control of. 1973. *227*
—. Banks, mutual savings. New York City. Portfolio management. Trustees. 1830-62. *256*

—. Multinational corporations. 1950's-70's. *72*
—. Multinational corporations. Productivity. 1950-77. *13*
—. New England. Productivity. Textile industry. 1830-60. *776*
—. Productivity. Skills. Technology. Telecommunications industry. 1970's. *529*
Labor casualization. Agriculture. Great Plains. Mechanization. Wheat. 1865-1902. *669*
Labor Disputes. Factory system (welfare work). Industrial Technology. National Cash Register Company. 1895-1913. *968*
—. Howard, Robert. Massachusetts (Fall River). Textile industry. 1860-85. *813*
—. Mine wars. Violence. West Virginia. 1912-13. 1920-21. *903*
Labor Disputes (unionization). Darlington Manufacturing Company. South Carolina (Darlington). Textile Workers Union of America. 1956-73. *671*
Labor, division of. Business offices. Economic growth, rapid. 1790-1840. *34*
Labor input. Productivity. Sawmills. Technology. 1958-75. *702*
Labor law. Industry. Management. Public policy. 1867-1927. *1275*
Labor practices. International Harvester Company. Minorities. Race relations. 1831-1976. *1022*
Labor Reform. Steel industry. Twelve-hour day. 1887-1923. *944*
Labor, skilled. Technological change. Textile mills. 1960's-70's. *848*
Labor supply hypothesis. Carriage and wagon industry. Habakkuk, H. J. Manufactures. Ohio (Cincinnati). 1850-1900. *357*
Labor Unions and Organizations *See also* names of individual unions, e.g. AFL-CIO, Brotherhood of Railway Telegraphers, etc.
—. Alaska. Canneries. Filipino Americans. Salmon. 1902-38. *751*
—. Americanization. Indiana (Gary). Polish Americans. US Steel Corporation. 1906-20. *917*
—. Bethlehem Steel Company. Daily Life. Depressions. Pennsylvania. Working conditions. 1910-50's. *990*
—. Business. Economic planning. Government. Liberalism, corporate. 1920-40. *121*
—. Calumet and Hecla Mining Company. Copper Mines and Mining. Michigan (Keweenaw Peninsula). Social Change. 1840-1968. *868*
—. Campaign Finance. Corporations. Electoral politics. Federal regulation. 1971-76. *1048*
—. Chicago, Burlington & Quincy Railroad. Interstate Commerce Commission. Iowa (Mt. Ayr). Missouri (Grant City). Railroads (abandonment). 1943-44. *456*
—. Cities. Manufactures. Skill differential. 1952-73. *988*
—. Class struggle. Corporations. Electrical manufacturing industry. 1933-50. *986*
—. Coal Mines and Mining. Great Britain. Illinois. Legislation. Lobbying. 1861-72. *1209*
—. Code of conduct. Multinational corporations. Organization for Economic Cooperation and Development. 1966-76. *65*
—. Collective bargaining. Litton Industries. Multinational corporations. Royal Typewriter, shutdown of. 1960's-70's. *37*
—. Congress of Industrial Organizations. Management. National Industrial Recovery Act (US, 1933). National Labor Relations Act (US, 1935). South. Textile Industry. 1933-41. *1349*
—. Economy, international. Foreign relations. General Motors Corporation. International Telephone and Telegraph. Multinational corporations. 1970's. *151*

—. Family. Massachusetts (Lowell). Textile Industry. Women. 1830-60. *701*
—. Foreign Policy. International Trade. Multinational Corporations. Politics. 1966-74. *70*
—. General Electric Company. New York (Fort Edward, Hudson Falls). Polychlorinated biphenyl. United Electrical, Radio, and Machine Workers of America. 1975. *1030*
—. Illinois (Pullman). Pullman strike. Railroads. 1880-94. *432*
—. Industry. Occupations. Wages. 1973-78. *1023*
—. Interstate Commerce Commission. Teamsters' Union. Trucks and Trucking. 1973. *1158*
—. Multinational corporations. 1971-73. *1029*
—. Piedmont Plateau. Textile industry. 1901-32. *777*
—. Radio Company of America (shutdown). Tennessee (Memphis). 1965-70. *527*
—. South. Textile industry. 1918-40. *710*
—. South. Textile industry. ca 1949-75. *789*
—. Stevens family. Stevens, J. P. & Co., Inc. Textile Industry. 1813-1978. *781*
Labor Unions and Organizations (black). Industrialization. Race Relations. 19c-20c. *1134*
Labor Unions and Organizations (international). International Law. Latin America. Multinational corporations. North America. 1937-74. *181*
Labor (work hours). Legislation, state. Manufacturing. 1900-30. *1243*
Laboratories. American Telephone and Telegraph Company. Bell Telephone System. Communications Technology. Competition. Industry. 1900-25. *559*
LaGrange and Memphis Railroad (proposed). Economic Conditions. Panic of 1837. Railroads. Tennessee. 1830-50. *423*
Lake Superior. Fishing. Minnesota (North Shore). 1849-70. *734*
Lamps, electric. Industrial technology. Power Resources. Productivity. 1954-77. *590*
Land. Automobiles. California, southern. Politics. Railroads. Speculation. Streetcars. 1880's-1970's. *483*
—. Coal mines and mining. Energy crisis. Federal Government. 1970's. *611*
Land boom. Migration, Internal. Railroads. Settlement. South Dakota. 1878-87. *381*
Land grants. Central Pacific Railroad. Railroads. Subsidies. 1860's. *364*
—. Joy, James F. Kansas & Neosho Valley Railroad. Kansas (Kansas City). Railroads. 1865-69. *450*
—. Political Corruption. Railroads. 1850's. *354*
—. Railroad construction. Union Pacific Railroad. ca 1860's. *365*
Land negotiations. Ewing, Thomas Jr. Indians. Kansas Pacific Railway Co. Railroads. 1855-66. *494*
Land ownership. Bibliographies. Corporations. Farms. Local government. 1969-70's. *680*
—. Michigan (Manistee County). Timber industry. 1841-70. *679*
Land (sale of). Mineral rights. Montana. North Dakota. Northern Pacific Railroad. Railroads and State. 1900-54. *340*
Land speculation. Appalachia. Coal. Economic Conditions. Iron. 1889-93. *895*
Land Tenure. Law. Lumber and Lumbering. Timber and Stone Act (US, 1878). Washington. 1860-1910. *1352*
Land use regulation. Connecticut River. Farmland, loss of. Massachusetts. 1969-74. *1297*

—. Death and Dying. Free market. Social Change. Values. 19c. *298*

Liggett & Myers. American Tobacco Company. Monopolies. Tobacco. Union Tobacco Company. 1890-1900. *684*

Limestone Quarrying. Bradley Transportation Company. Great Lakes. Michigan (Rogers City). Shipping. US Steel Corporation. 1912-67. *448*

Liquidity. Mergers. -1973. *40*

Literacy. Books, distribution of. Business History. Developing Nations. Publishing. USA. 1900's. *547*

Literature. Competition. Corporations. Economic theory. Empiricism. Invisible hand (concept). 20c. *115*

—. Economic Growth. Farmers. Norris, Frank. Social Change. 1890-1910. *1119*

—. Music. Railroads. South. 1830's-1970's. *391*

Lithographs. Advertising. California. Citrus industry. Orange crate art. 1877-1950. *717*

Little Miami Line. *Gov. Morrow* (locomotive). Ohio (Cincinnati). Railroads, steam. 1837-70. *509*

Little Rock and Fort Smith Railroad. Arkansas. Construction. Finance. Railroads. Robinson, Asa P. ca 1867-76. *495*

Litton Industries. Collective bargaining. Labor unions and Organizations. Multinational corporations. Royal Typewriter, shutdown of. 1960's-70's. *37*

Livestock. Alabama. Civil War. Reconstruction. 1850-1900. *763*

—. Depressions. Grain. McGregor Land and Livestock Company. Prices. Washington (Columbia Plateau). 1930's-82. *760*

Livestock exchanges. Cooperative Livestock Commission Company. Trans-Mississippi West. 1906-09. *732*

Livestock prices. Cattlemen (cooperative endeavors). Illinois (Chicago). Meat packing industry. Texas. 1890's. *843*

Lixator machine. *International Salt Co.* v. *United States* (1947). Leases. Monopolies. Prices. Supreme Court. 1940's. *1290*

Loans. Banking. Cities. Rural areas. 1916-40. *278*

—. Banking. Competition. Wisconsin. 1870-1900. *240*

Lobbying. Agriculture. Business. 1940-80. *683*

—. Coal Mines and Mining. Great Britain. Illinois. Labor Unions and Organizations. Legislation. 1861-72. *1209*

—. Communications Bill. Federal Communications Act (US, 1934). House of Representatives. Radio. Television. VanDeerlin, Lionel. 1934-79. *1258*

Lobbyists. Airplanes, Military. B-1 (aircraft). Rockwell International Corp. Unemployment. 1975. *971*

Local Government. Airports. Courts. Federal Regulation. Noise complaints. 1958-77. *1318*

—. Bibliographies. Corporations. Farms. Land ownership. 1969-70's. *680*

—. Hooker Chemicals and Plastics Corp. Love Canal disaster. New York (Niagara Falls). School boards. Toxic waste. 1942-80. *1151*

—. Illinois (Hennepin). Jones and Laughlin Steel Company. 1960's-70's. *1126*

Local Politics. Economic Conditions. General Motors Corporation. Labor. Location. Michigan (Detroit). Public Policy. 1970-80. *1099*

Location. Corporations. Research and development. 1965-77. *112*

—. Economic Conditions. General Motors Corporation. Labor. Local Politics. Michigan (Detroit). Public Policy. 1970-80. *1099*

—. Garment industry. Working class. 1950-74. *850*

—. Labor. Piedmont Plateau. Textile Industry. 1880-1900. *854*

Location, industrial. Ford, Henry. Great Britain. Ireland (Cork). Tariffs. Tractors. 1912-26. *404*

Lockheed Corporation. Japan. Political Corruption. USA. 1976. *307*

Locomobile Company. Automobiles. New England. Stanley Steamer (automobile). 1899-1903. *501*

Locomotive industry. Business. Economic Theory. Technological change. 1920-55. *436*

Locomotives. Canada. Great Northern Railway. Railroads. USA. 1861-1970. *414*

—. Machinery. Maine. Portland Company. Railroads. 1848-1906. *351*

Logan, Ronald R. Airplane Industry and Trade. California Aero Company. Cull, George E. Lark-95 (aircraft). Personal narratives. 1958-63. *344*

Lomen family. Alaska. Ohlson, Otto F. Railroads. Reindeer industry. 1928-31. *513*

Long, George S. Fire control. Lumber and Lumbering. Pacific Northwest. Public Policy. 1902-10. *768*

Long, Huey P. Cotton Acreage Control Law (Texas, 1931). Crop limitation. New Deal. South. 1931-33. *1343*

Los Angeles Dodgers (team). Baseball. California. Dodger Stadium. 1956-62. *225*

Louisa Railroad Co. Railroads. Virginia. 1836-1980. *499*

Louisiana. Agricultural Production. Congress. Economic Conditions. Subsidies. Sugar industry. 1860-1930. *803*

—. Environmentalism. Oil and Petroleum Products. Shrimp. Strategic reserves. Texas. 1970-79. *1313*

—. Oil Industry and Trade. Strikes. Texas. 1917-18. *632*

Louisiana & Arkansas Railway. Arkansas. Railroads. 1898-1949. *323*

Louisiana (New Orleans). Blanchard, Jim. Conventions. Economic Reform. National Committee for Monetary Reform. 1971-80. *199*

—. Communications Technology. Radio. Television. WWL (station). 1940-50. *557*

—. Cotton Exchange. Economic Development. 1870-81. *209*

Louisiana, northern. Arkansas, southern. Oil Industry and Trade. Texas, eastern. 1900-35. *619*

Love Canal disaster. Hooker Chemicals and Plastics Corp. Local Government. New York (Niagara Falls). School boards. Toxic waste. 1942-80. *1151*

Lowell, Francis Cabot. Boston Manufacturing Company. Great Britain. Industrialization. International trade. Massachussetts. 1807-20. *677*

Lucas, Anthony F. Higgins, Pattillo. Oil Industry and Trade. Spindletop Oil Rush. Texas (Beaumont). 1901-30's. *651*

Lukens Iron Works. Authority. Paternalism. Pennsylvania (Coatesville). Profit. Strikes. 1886. *992*

—. Paternalism. Pennsylvania (Coatesville). Strikes. 1886. *991*

Lumber and Lumbering. Alabama (Mobile). Export market. 1760-1860. *703*

—. Alaska. Pacific Northwest. Paper industry. 1914-71. *816*

—. Arizona (White Mountains). Economic Conditions. 1919-42. *752*

—. Bibliographies. British Columbia. Pacific Northwest. 1890's-1960's. *744*

—. California (Butte, Tehama, Shasta Counties). Sierra Flume and Lumber Company. 1875-78. *728*

—. California (San Francisco area). Oregon. Shipbuilding. Washington. 1850-1929. *341*

—. Customs district. New Jersey (Great Egg Harbor). Ports. Shipbuilding. Trade. 19c. *373*

—. Dismal Swamp. North Carolina. Virginia. 1760's-1970's. *1130*

—. Documents. Port Blakely Mill Company. Washington, University of (Library). 1876-1923. *678*

—. Employment. Pacific Northwest. Productivity. Technology. ca 1899-1973. *795*

—. Fire control. Long, George S. Pacific Northwest. Public Policy. 1902-10. *768*

—. Frontier. 1830's-ca 1940's. *814*

—. Garibaldi mill. Oregon (Tillamook Bay). 1917-74. *821*

—. Idaho (Potlatch). Potlatch Lumber Company. Social Organization. 1901-31. *1073*

—. Kinsey, Clark. Oregon. Photographs. Washington. 1914-45. *851*

—. Land Tenure. Law. Timber and Stone Act (US, 1878). Washington. 1860-1910. *1352*

—. Lutcher, Henry J. Moore, G. Bedell. Sawmills. Texas, East. 1870-1930. *753*

—. Maine (Washington County). Oral history. 1945-47. *674*

—. Michigan. ca 1840-1900. *786*

—. National Recovery Administration. 1933-35. *791*

—. New York (Rochester). 1788-1880. *761*

—. Port Blakely Mill Company. Washington (Bainbridge Island). 1888-1903. *708*

—. Washington. Weyerhaeuser Timber Company. 1899-1903. *709*

Lutcher, Henry J. Lumber and Lumbering. Moore, G. Bedell. Sawmills. Texas, East. 1870-1930. *753*

Lutey Brothers Marketeria. Food Industry. Grocery stores. Montana. 1897-1924. *955*

Lynd, Robert S. (account). Oil Industry and Trade. Working Conditions. Wyoming (Elk Basin). 1921. *1088*

L-1011 (aircraft). Aeronautics. Eastern Airlines. Gellert, Dan (accounts). Safety. Working Conditions. 1972-78. *1060*

M

Machinery. 1960-73. *1001*

—. Locomotives. Maine. Portland Company. Railroads. 1848-1906. *351*

Machinery, use of. Cotton planters. Farms, large. Technological change. 19c-1975. *796*

Magnuson-Moss Act (US, 1975). Federal Trade Commission. Industry. 1914-81. *1282*

Mail-order business. Ward, Aaron Montgomery. 1872-1919. *925*

Maine. Davis, Owen W., Jr. Katahdin Charcoal Iron Company. 1876-90. *938*

—. Locomotives. Machinery. Portland Company. Railroads. 1848-1906. *351*

Maine (Washington County). Lumber and Lumbering. Oral history. 1945-47. *674*

Maine (York County). Railroads. York and Cumberland Rail Road. 1848-1900. *460*

Malpractice suits. Consultants (business). Insurance. 1971-72. *198*

Management. Accident Insurance. Judicial process. Labor. New England. 1890-1910. *1063*

—. Accounting. General Motors Corporation. 1920's. *409*

—. Accounting (systems development). Corporations. DuPont de Nemours, E. I. (Powder Company). 1903-12. *84*

—. Affirmative action. American Telephone and Telegraph Company. Employment. Technology. Women. 1972-75. *1070*

—. Age. Coal Mines and Mining. Standard of living. Strikes, wildcat. Working conditions. 1970's. *861*

—. Alcoholism. Chicago, Burlington & Quincy Railroad. Employees. Law Enforcement. Railroads. 1876-1902. *319*

—. AMTRAK. North Central States. North Coast *Hiawatha* line. Western States. 1970's. *465*

—. Assembly lines. Automobile Industry and Trade. Europe. Values. 1950-81. *1069*

—. Automobile Industry and Trade (review article). Ford, Henry. Great Britain. Lewis, David. Morris, William. Overy, R. J. 1903-45. *336*

—. Baseball. 1961-80. *263*

—. Bevan, David. Pennsylvania Railroad. Perlman, Alfred. Railroads. 19c-1970. *476*

—. Business. Postindustrialism. 1970's. *106*

—. Business History. Railway officials, recruitment of. 1885-1940. *452*

—. Chandler, Alfred D., Jr. (review article). Communications Behavior. Corporations. Technology. 1960-79. *39*

—. Committee for Economic Development. Education, Finance. Educational policy. Higher education. 1971-74. *1046*

—. Congress of Industrial Organizations. Labor Unions and Organizations. National Industrial Recovery Act (US, 1933). National Labor Relations Act (US, 1935). South. Textile Industry. 1933-41. *1349*

—. Corporation Law. Great Britain. Stock Companies. 1860-1920. *86*

—. Corporations. Corporations, Subsidiary. Profit. 1960's-70's. *11*

—. Corporations. Marketing. Research. 18c-20c. *25*

—. Economics. Europe. 19c-20c. *6*

—. Federal regulation. Law. Railroads and State. 1885-1916. *350*

—. Forests and Forestry. Mason, David T. McNary, Charles L. Sustained-Yield Forest Management Act (US, 1944). Washington (Shelton). 1944-46. *1229*

—. Fuel. Hopewell Forge. Iron industry. Labor. Pennsylvania. Productivity. Technology. 1750-1800. *977*

—. Great Britain. Multinational corporations. Technology. 1880-1979. *27*

—. Industry. Labor law. Public policy. 1867-1927. *1275*

—. Jews. Labor. Massachusetts (Lynn). Shoe industry. 1900-55. *924*

—. New England. Slater, Samuel. Textile Industry. 1790-1835. *825*

—. Private Utilities. Public Utilities. 1970-72. *600*

—. Stock companies. 1960-77. *93*

Management organization. Business History. Ford Motor Company. Ideology. Mass-production. 1920's-40's. *484*

Management, private. Great Britain. Oil Industry and Trade. Public policy. USA. 1918-24. *615*

Management, scientific. Bethlehem Steel Company. Executive Behavior. Pennsylvania. Taylor, Frederick Winslow. 1898-1901. *969*

—. Buckeye Steel Castings Company. Bush, S. P. Ohio (Columbus). Social Work. Steel Industry. 1890-1920. *923*

—. Business. Hudson, J. L. Retail Trade. 1861-1912. *947*
—. Economic Conditions. General Motors Corporation. Labor. Local Politics. Location. Public Policy. 1970-80. *1099*
—. Industrialization. Railroads. Sawmills. Shipbuilding. Stoves. 1840's-90's. *1008*
Michigan (Keweenaw Peninsula). Calumet and Hecla Mining Company. Copper Mines and Mining. Labor Unions and Organizations. Social Change. 1840-1968. *868*
Michigan (Manistee County). Land ownership. Timber industry. 1841-70. *679*
Michigan (Pontiac). General Motors Corporation. Occupational Safety and Health Administration. United Automobile Workers of America. Working conditions. 1971-78. *1337*
Michigan (Rogers City). Bradley Transportation Company. Great Lakes. Limestone Quarrying. Shipping. US Steel Corporation. 1912-67. *448*
Michigan (Upper Peninsula). Iron mining. ca 1840-1978. *860*
Middle Atlantic states. Great Britain. Iron industry. USA. 1750-1850. *1003*
Middle East. Antitrust laws. Foreign policy. Multinational Corporations. Oil Industry and Trade. USA. 1945-61. *622*
—. Antitrust prosecution. Cold War. Foreign policy. Oil cartel case. 1950-65. *623*
—. Business. Energy crisis. Oil Industry and Trade. USA. 1960-73. *580*
—. Carter, Jimmy (administration). Foreign Policy. Oil Industry and Trade. Senate. 1947-77. *596*
—. Communications. Corporations. Diplomacy. Foreign policy. 1979. *142*
—. Foreign Relations. Natural gas. Oil Industry and Trade. USA. 1967-73. *640*
Midgley, Thomas. General Motors Corporation. Industry. Kettering, Charles. Scientific Experiments and Research. Sloan, Alfred. 1916-44. *427*
Midwest. Economic Conditions. Industry. Pork-packing. Urbanization. 1835-75. *833*
Migrant Labor. Canning industry. New York State Factory Investigating Commission. Polish Americans. 1900-35. *735*
Migration, Internal. Cities. Multinational Corporations (takeover). Wisconsin (Milwaukee). 1968-79. *1090*
—. Farmers, yeoman. Income. Kentucky. Tennessee. Tobacco. 1850-60. *802*
—. Land boom. Railroads. Settlement. South Dakota. 1878-87. *381*
Military. Economic Structure. Foreign investments. Multinational corporations. South Africa. 1945-78. *157*
Military Finance. Business. Federal Government. 1948-53. *1086*
Military intervention (sought). Fall, Albert Bacon. Mexico. Oil Industry and Trade. USA. 1919. *608*
Military spending. Capitalism, corporate. Economy. -1973. *148*
Military-industrial complex. 1861-1979. *935*
Milk. Government regulation. 1922-78. *1237*
Milk industry. Productivity. Profit. 1958-77. *784*
Milk substitutes. Developing nations. Marketing. Multinational corporations. 1970's. *71*
Miller, Franklin, and Stevenson (firm). Bancroft, Joseph and Sons Company. Delaware (Wilmington). Scientific management. Textile Industry. 1911-27. *827*
Milling technology. Flour trade. Maryland (Baltimore). 1750-1830. *808*

Mills. Agricultural Production. Haciendas. Puerto Rico, southwestern. Sugar industry. 1902. *838*
—. Cotton. New England, southern. New York. 1810-40. *746*
—. Flour. Minnesota. Research. 1880's-1930's. 1978. *714*
—. Industrial Relations. Towns. 19c. *1043*
Mills, C. Wright. Business. Cabinet. Elites. Government. 1897-1973. *1057*
Milwaukee Road. Great Northern Railway. Hill, James J. North Dakota. Northern Pacific Railroad. Railroad construction. 1879-85. *451*
—. North Central States. Railroad system. 1850-1977. *478*
Mine wars. Labor Disputes. Violence. West Virginia. 1912-13. 1920-21. *903*
Mineral Resources. Canada. Industrialization. Mining. USA. 1700-1977. *892*
—. Federal regulation. Mining. Oceans. Seabed. 1974. *1197*
Mineral rights. Comstock Lode. Law. Nevada. West. 1850-1900. *1255*
—. Land (sale of). Montana. North Dakota. Northern Pacific Railroad. Railroads and State. 1900-54. *340*
Miners. Arizona. Corporations. Hunt, George W. P. State Politics. 1915-17. *905*
—. Arkansas (Cushing). Manganese mining. Social Conditions. 1849-1959. *894*
Mines. Alaska. 1871-1975. *858*
—. Arizona. Grand Canyon. Uranium. 1540-1969. *887*
—. Conservation of Natural Resources. Energy. Western States. 1970-79. *879*
—. Hearst, George. South Dakota (Deadwood area). 1876-79. *865*
Mining. Alabama (Birmingham). Boomtowns. Cities (promotion of). Iron Industry. 1871-96. *1059*
—. Alaska. Arctic. Canada. Scandinavia. USSR. 1917-78. *883*
—. Arizona (Tucson). 1853-1920. *901*
—. Canada. Industrialization. Mineral Resources. USA. 1700-1977. *892*
—. City Planning. Company towns. Corporations. North Central States. 19c-20c. *1020*
—. Federal Government. Surface Mining Control and Reclamation Act (US, 1977). 1977-79. *1274*
—. Federal regulation. Mineral Resources. Oceans. Seabed. 1974. *1197*
—. Gates, Frederick T. Idaho. Rockefeller, John D. Washington. 1890-1905. *871*
—. Historiography. Western States. 1850's-1979. *885*
—. Idaho. Law. 1865-1935. *1350*
Mining Engineering. Blakemore, Page (interview). Utah (Alta). 1870-1970's. *880*
Mining Law (1872). Colorado (Uncompahgre Primitive Area). Nature Conservation. Wilderness Act (1964). 1973. *1330*
Minnesota. Alcohol. New York. Price controls. State Legislatures. 1947-71. *1259*
—. Bonanza farming. North Dakota. Railroads. Red River of the North. Wheat. 1870's-90's. *722*
—. Company towns. Copper Mines and Mining. Documents. Iron mining. Michigan. Wisconsin. 1845-1930. *1018*
—. Flour. Mills. Research. 1880's-1930's. 1978. *714*
Minnesota (Lake Superior area). Company towns. Iron mining. 1840's-1940's. *1019*
Minnesota (Minneapolis, St. Paul). Beck, Joe (account). Television. Twin City Television Lab. 1945-50. *519*

Newspapers. Advertising, systematic. Business History. Industrial development. Palmer, Volney B. 1794-1864. *230*
—. Antitrust. Buffalo *Courier-Express*. Buffalo *Evening News*. Courts. New York. 1977-80. *521*
—. Competition. Corporations. Mass media. Public opinion. Public Policy. Stock exchange. 1970's. *516*
—. Conglomerates, effects of. Strikes. *Washington Post* (newspaper). 1975. *1164*
—. Federal Communications Commission. *National Citizens Committee for Broadcasting* v. *Federal Communications Commission* (US, 1977). Programming. Television. 1975-77. *1348*
—. Joint printing contracts. Laws, antitrust. 1964. 1968. *1160*
—. Monopolies. New York *Tribune*. Reid, Whitelaw. Wire services. 1885-92. *566*
—. Ownership trends. Radio. 1922-70. *570*
Newspapers (circulation). Editorial content. Format characteristics. 1972-73. *575*
—. Population. 1940. 1970. *530*
Newspapers, daily. Economic Conditions. Electronics. Information. 1970-78. *539*
Newsprint. Herty, Charles Holmes. Paper mills. Pine trees. Scientific Experiments and Research. Southeastern States. 1927-40. *779*
Newton, Luke Vanderveer. Copper-facing. Printing. Typefounding. 1850-1907. *565*
Nezperce & Idaho Railroad. Camas Prairie Railroad. Idaho, north-central. Johnson, T. A. Railroads. 1910-22. *328*
Nicaragua. Bananas. Standard Fruit Co. 1921-30's. *87*
Nicholson, John. Industry. Pennsylvania. 1790's-1800. *911*
Nixon, Richard M. Japan. Multinational corporations. Politics. ca 1948-76. *80*
Noble, David F. (review article). Business. Economic Development. 1880-1930. 1977. *44*
Noise complaints. Airports. Courts. Federal Regulation. Local Government. 1958-77. *1318*
Nonprofit firms. Credit unions. Decisionmaking. Economics. 1968-69. *239*
Norris, Frank. Economic Growth. Farmers. Literature. Social Change. 1890-1910. *1119*
Norris, William. Private sector. Public services. 1900-81. *1135*
North. Agricultural Production. Farms. North Central States. Profit. 1820's-60's. *695*
—. Business. City Planning. Development. Indiana (Kingsport). Towns. 1880-1950. *1021*
North America. Farms. Mechanization. Prairies. Prices. 1896-1930. *698*
—. International Law. Labor Unions and Organizations (international). Latin America. Multinational corporations. 1937-74. *181*
North American Aviation. California (Inglewood). Communist Party. Strikes. United Automobile Workers of America. 1941. *464*
North Carolina. Dismal Swamp. Lumber and Lumbering. Virginia. 1760's-1970's. *1130*
North Carolina (Brevard). Chemicals, toxic. Health safety requirements. Occupational Safety and Health Act (US, 1970). Olin Corporation. 1970-74. *1233*
North Carolina (Wilmington). Cotton. Exports. Sprunt, Alexander and Son. 1866-1956. *736*
North Carolina (Winston-Salem). Basketball. Hanes Hosiery (team). Industrial leagues. Women. 1940's-50's. *1027*
North Central Airlines. Airplanes. 1940-76. *431*
North Central States. Agricultural Production. Farms. North. Profit. 1820's-60's. *695*

—. AMTRAK. Management. North Coast *Hiawatha* line. Western States. 1970's. *465*
—. Blacklisting. Bureaucracies. Chicago, Burlington & Quincy Railroad. Employment. Railroads. 1877-92. *1028*
—. Chicago and Eastern Illinois Railroad. Railroads. Real Estate. St. Louis-San Francisco Railroad. South Central and Gulf States. 1902-13. *454*
—. City Planning. Company towns. Corporations. Mining. 19c-20c. *1020*
—. Demand. Pennsylvania. Production. Steel Industry (location). 1910-72. *942*
—. Meat packing industry. 1840's-70's. *831*
—. Milwaukee Road. Railroad system. 1850-1977. *478*
—. Pork industry. Transportation. 1835-75. *834*
North Coast *Hiawatha* line. AMTRAK. Management. North Central States. Western States. 1970's. *465*
North Dakota. Bonanza farming. Minnesota. Railroads. Red River of the North. Wheat. 1870's-90's. *722*
—. Farmers' Railroad. Hines, David Willington. Populism. Railroads. 1894-98. *475*
—. Great Northern Railway. Hill, James J. Milwaukee Road. Northern Pacific Railroad. Railroad construction. 1879-85. *451*
—. Land (sale of). Mineral rights. Montana. Northern Pacific Railroad. Railroads and State. 1900-54. *340*
North Dakota, northern. Competition. Great Northern Railway. Railroads. Townsites. 1905. *402*
North Dakota (Ramsey, Towner counties). Farmers' Grain & Shipping Company. Kelley, Joseph M. Railroads. 1896-1945. *374*
North Dakota (Wilton). Coal Mines and Mining. Labor. United Mine Workers of America. Washburn Lignite Coal Company. 1900-30's. *906*
Northeast Airlines. Airplane Industry and Trade. Boston-Maine Central Vermont Airways. 1927-72. *422*
Northeast Corridor Improvement Project. Passenger service. Railroads. 1976-80. *315*
Northeastern or North Atlantic States. ConRail. Government Enterprise. Railroads. 1970's. *1173*
—. Corporations. Economic Development. Relocation. South. 1970-80. *1146*
—. Corporations. Fitchburg Railroad. Ownership. Railroads. 1842-1939. *370*
—. Economic Conditions. Hepburn Committee. Interstate Commerce Act (US, 1887). Railroad regulation. ca 1870-1910. *1265*
—. Federal regulation. Railroads and State. United States Railway Association. 1975. *453*
Northern Pacific Railroad. Antitrust. Contracts. Supreme Court. 1950's. *1187*
—. Great Northern Railway. Hill, James J. Milwaukee Road. North Dakota. Railroad construction. 1879-85. *451*
—. Great Northern Railway. Minnesota (St. Paul). Working Conditions. 1915-21. *507*
—. Land (sale of). Mineral rights. Montana. North Dakota. Railroads and State. 1900-54. *340*
—. Railroads. Settlement. Westward Movement. 1882. *378*
Nova Scotia (Halifax). Massachusetts (Boston). Steamship lines. 1840-1917. *406*
Nova Scotia (Yarmouth). Massachusetts (Boston). Steamship services. Transportation. 1855-1971. *407*
NOW accounts. Mortgages. Savings and loan associations. 1970's. *223*

Nuclear power industries. Foreign policy. International Trade. Uranium cartel (possible). USA. 1970's. *174*

Nuclear Science and Technology. Coal industry. Environment. 1860's-1970's. *633*

Nunn, Lucien L. Electric power. Nunn, Paul N. Utah. 1898-1912. *614*

Nunn, Paul N. Electric power. Nunn, Lucien L. Utah. 1898-1912. *614*

Nutrition. Advertising. Agricultural cooperatives. California. Fruit and Fruit Crops. Vegetables. 1880's-1920's. *820*

O

Occupational Safety and Health Act (US, 1970). Accidents. Industry. Legislation. 1877-1970. *1261*

—. Chemicals, toxic. Health safety requirements. North Carolina (Brevard). Olin Corporation. 1970-74. *1233*

—. Construction industry. Occupations (dangerous). 1972-75. *1145*

—. Costs. Federal Regulation. Industry. Working conditions. 1971-81. *1293*

—. Federal Regulation. Working conditions. 1970-76. *1280*

—. Public Administration. 1970-78. *1267*

Occupational Safety and Health Administration. California. Elliot, Robert. Lawsuits. P & Z Company. Working conditions. 1975-77. *1115*

—. Cotton dust. Federal regulation. Textile industry. 1970's. *1351*

—. General Motors Corporation. Michigan (Pontiac). United Automobile Workers of America. Working conditions. 1971-78. *1337*

Occupations. Electric power. Natural gas. Technology. 1960-77. *598*

—. Industry. Labor Unions and Organizations. Wages. 1973-78. *1023*

Occupations (dangerous). Construction industry. Occupational Safety and Health Act (US, 1970). 1972-75. *1145*

Oceans. Federal regulation. Mineral Resources. Mining. Seabed. 1974. *1197*

Office location. Cities. Great Britain (London). Industry. New York City. 1960-72. *1154*

Off-shore drilling. Alaska pipeline. Ecology. Oil Industry and Trade. 1974. *643*

Ogden, William Butler. Economic Growth. Galena and Chicago Union Railroad. Illinois (Chicago). Railroads. 1836-53. *441*

Ohio. Agricultural cooperatives. Business. Legislation. Social Organization. Woods, W. N. (reminiscences). 1907-78. *846*

—. Coal Mines and Mining. Government. Health and safety regulations. 1869-81. *1249*

—. Coal Mines and Mining (bituminous). Kentucky. Model towns. Pennsylvania. West Virginia. 1880-1930. *1101*

—. Company towns. Social Classes. Steel Industry. Strikes. 1937. *915*

—. Economic Conditions. Sheep raising. 1807-1900. *727*

Ohio (Cincinnati). Carriage and wagon industry. Habakkuk, H. J. Labor supply hypothesis. Manufactures. 1850-1900. *357*

—. *Gov. Morrow* (locomotive). Little Miami Line. Railroads, steam. 1837-70. *509*

Ohio (Cleveland). Johnson, Tom L. Managerial innovation. Street railways. 1883-98. *958*

Ohio (Columbus). Buckeye Steel Castings Company. Bush, S. P. Management, scientific. Social Work. Steel Industry. 1890-1920. *923*

—. Finance. Indiana (Gary). Intergovernmental Relations. Minnesota (St. Paul). Negotiated investment strategy. Public Policy. 1979-80. *192*

Ohio (Dayton). National Cash Register Company. Patterson, John H. Physical Education and Training. Working Conditions. 1890-1915. *1122*

Ohio (Hocking Valley). Coal Mines and Mining. Strikebreakers. Violence, absence of. 1884-85. *597*

Ohio Life Insurance and Trust Company. Capital. Finance. New York Life Insurance and Trust Company. 1830's. *222*

Ohio (Mahoning Valley). Corporations. Employment. Factories. Ownership, employee. Youngstown Sheet and Tube Co. 1977-79. *1152*

Ohio River, Falls of the. Canal. Indiana Company. Kentucky. 1804-30. *489*

Ohio (Sandusky). Automobile Industry and Trade. Hinde, James J. Production. Sandusky Automobile Company. 1896-1904. *327*

Ohio, southern. Coal Mines and Mining. Columbus and Hocking Valley Railroad Co. Industrialization. 1866-81. *498*

Ohio (Troy). Airplane Industry and Trade. Brukner, Clayton J. 1923-30. *479*

Ohio (Wood County). Economic development. Oil and Petroleum Products. Social change. 1883-1917. *1089*

Ohlson, Otto F. Alaska. Lomen family. Railroads. Reindeer industry. 1928-31. *513*

Oil, Allocation of. Energy crisis. Government responsibility. Multinational oil companies. 1973-74. *653*

Oil and Petroleum Products. Alaska. Bartlett, E. L. Naval Petroleum Reserve No. 4. Rivers, Ralph J. Vinson, Carl. 1959-62. *644*

—. China. Kerosene. Nationalism. Standard Oil Company of New York. Taxation. 1925-27. *661*

—. Conservation of Natural Resources. Economic Regulations. Oklahoma Corporation Commission. 1907-31. *1176*

—. Diplomacy. Foreign Investments. Mexico. Teapot Dome Scandal. 1926-27. *616*

—. Economic development. Ohio (Wood County). Social change. 1883-1917. *1089*

—. Economic Regulations. Prices. 1974-76. *1327*

—. Electric Power. Pennsylvania Railroad. Prices. 1913-68. *316*

—. Environmentalism. Louisiana. Shrimp. Strategic reserves. Texas. 1970-79. *1313*

—. Foreign Relations. Mexico. ca 1910-72. *585*

Oil cartel case. Antitrust prosecution. Cold War. Foreign policy. Middle East. 1950-65. *623*

Oil cartels. Antitrust. Energy Policy and Conservation Act (1975). Prices. 1950-70's. *1169*

Oil companies (independent, international). Energy crisis. International Trade. 1973-74. *657*

Oil Industry and Trade. 1950-80. *603*

—. Alaska pipeline. Ecology. Off-shore drilling. 1974. *643*

—. Alaska (Prudhoe Bay). Development. Eskimos. 1970's. *1082*

—. American Petroleum Institute. Pollution. Texas (Gulf Coast). 1900-70. *1112*

—. Antitrust. Arbitration. Federal Trade Commission, Bureau of Competition. Law. 1973-75. *1215*

—. Antitrust. State Government. Texas. Trade Regulations. 1901-11. *635*

—. Antitrust laws. Foreign policy. Middle East. Multinational Corporations. USA. 1945-61. *622*

P

Physicians. Federal regulation. Medical care. Professional Standards Review Organization Program. Social Security Act (US, 1935; amended, 1972). 1965-80. *1185*

Piedmont Plateau. Labor. Location. Textile Industry. 1880-1900. *854*

—. Labor Unions and Organizations. Textile industry. 1901-32. *777*

Pierce-Arrow Motor Car Company. Automobiles. Birge, George K. Clifton, Charles. May, Henry. New York (Buffalo). 1873-1938. *514*

Pinchot, Gifford. Forests and Forestry. Government regulation. Oregon. Washington. 1902-10. *707*

Pine trees. Georgia. Oleoresin industry. 1842-1900. *699*

—. Herty, Charles Holmes. Newsprint. Paper mills. Scientific Experiments and Research. Southeastern States. 1927-40. *779*

Pinto (automobile). Automobile Industry and Trade. Corporations. Corvair (automobile). Ford Motor Company. General Motors Corporation. 1959-70's. *380*

Pioneers. Economic development. Gristmills. Missouri. 1820-80. *704*

Pittsburgh Stock Exchange. Oil Industry and Trade. Pennsylvania. Stocks and Bonds. 1884-96. *280*

Pittsburgh Survey (1909). *Charities and the Commons* (periodical). Industrialization (impact of). Pennsylvania. Social Surveys. 1907-14. *1093*

Plains Cotton Cooperative Association. Agricultural Cooperatives. Computers. Cotton. Marketing. Telecommunication. Texas (Lubbock). 1920's-70's. *790*

Planning. Business. Economic Development. Government. 1960's-70's. *168*

—. Coal Mines and Mining. Economic growth. Employment. Illinois. 1970's. *602*

Plantation economy. Employment. Industrialization. Negroes. Social Mobility. 1860's-1974. *749*

Plantations. Brazil (Amazonia). Ford, Henry. Rubber. 1923-45. *52*

Plastics. Bag industry. Demand. Paper Industry. Productivity. Technology. 1954-77. *927*

Pluralism. Mass media. Subcultures. 1960's-70's. *526*

Pocket Books (company). Competition. Paperback Books. Publishers and Publishing. 1958-78. *561*

Poisons. France. Government regulation. 1899-1980. *1170*

Polish Americans. Americanization. Indiana (Gary). Labor Unions and Organizations. US Steel Corporation. 1906-20. *917*

—. Canning industry. Migrant Labor. New York State Factory Investigating Commission. 1900-35. *735*

—. Everett Mill. Massachusetts (Lawrence). Radicals and Radicalism. Strikes. Textile Industry. Women. 1912. *778*

—. New Jersey (Bayonne). Standard Oil Company of New Jersey. Strikes. 1915-16. *601*

Political Attitudes. Antibusiness sentiments. Federal regulation. 1968-80. *1141*

—. Corporations. Government, Resistance to. 19c-20c. *1143*

—. Developing Nations. International Trade. Labor. Multinational corporations. 1966-75. *69*

Political Campaigns (presidential). Economic concentration. Newspaper chains (endorsements). 1960-72. *1144*

Political Corruption. Antitrust. Daugherty, Harry M. Federal Government. Pennsylvania (Philadelphia). United Gas Improvement Company. 1914-24. *1205*

—. Business. Interest groups. Progressivism. 1895-1910. *1094*

—. Japan. Lockheed Corporation. USA. 1976. *307*

—. Land grants. Railroads. 1850's. *354*

Political economy. Banking. Economic Regulations. 1864-1933. *1356*

Political Leadership. Automobile Industry and Trade. City Government. Michigan (Detroit). 1910-29. *1040*

Political Theory. Corporations. Government. Public policy. 1970's. *1279*

Politics. Anti-Communist Movements. Films. Industrial Relations. 1933-53. *571*

—. Automobile Industry and Trade. Competition. Federal Regulation. Fuel. International Trade. Working class. 1973-79. *362*

—. Automobiles. California, southern. Land. Railroads. Speculation. Streetcars. 1880's-1970's. *483*

—. Automobiles. Cities. 1900-56. 1977-79. *367*

—. Banking. Crime and Criminals. Farmers and Drovers National Bank (failure). Pennsylvania (Greene County; Waynesburg). Rinehart, James B. F. 1835-1906. *212*

—. Bright, Charles. Public Policy. Rose, Mark H. Transportation (review article). 1941-72. *312*

—. Business. Corporate power. Profit system. 1970-73. *1102*

—. Corporations (distrust of). 1960's-70's. *1142*

—. Developing nations. Economic growth. Government. Multinational Corporations (review article). USA. 1945-70's. *90*

—. Developing nations. Multinational Corporations (review article). ca 1950-80. *105*

—. Executive power. Federal Regulation. President's Advisory Council on Executive Organization. Public Administration. Reform. 1937-79. *1345*

—. Federal regulatory commissions. Powers. 1961-74. *1341*

—. Foreign Policy. International Trade. Labor Unions and Organizations. Multinational Corporations. 1966-74. *70*

—. Japan. Multinational corporations. Nixon, Richard M. ca 1948-76. *80*

Politics, legislative. American Medical Association's House of Delegates. Systems analysis. 1957-74. *284*

Politics, world. Multinational Corporations. Oil Industry and Trade. 1950-76. *656*

Pollution. American Petroleum Institute. Oil Industry and Trade. Texas (Gulf Coast). 1900-70. *1112*

—. General Electric Company. Labor Unions and Organizations. New York (Fort Edward, Hudson Falls). Polychlorinated biphenyl. United Electrical, Radio, and Machine Workers of America. 1975. *1030*

—. Government regulation. Industry. Productivity. 1972-81. *1314*

Pollution control. Business. Economic incentive. Labor. 1974. *1053*

Polychlorinated biphenyl. General Electric Company. Labor Unions and Organizations. New York (Fort Edward, Hudson Falls). Pollution. United Electrical, Radio, and Machine Workers of America. 1975. *1030*

Ponzi, Charles (pseud. of Charles Bianchi). Massachusetts (Boston). Securities. 1919-20. *269*

Poor. Mass Transit. Taxation. 1970-79. *1303*

Population. Newspapers (circulation). 1940. 1970. *530*

Populism. Agricultural Commodities. Freight and Freightage. Prices. Railroads. 1870-97. *304*

—. Corporation as government. Counter-corporate movement. 1895-1975. *163*

—. Farms. Mechanization. North America. Prairies. 1896-1930. *698*

—. Federal Regulation. Interstate Commerce Commission. Motor carrier industry. Profit standards. 1970's. *1190*

—. Federal regulation. Johnson, Lyndon B. (administration). Sulphur industry. 1960's. *1180*

—. Federal Regulation. Oil Industry and Trade. 1970-79. *652*

—. Food Administration. Hoover, Herbert C. Pork-packing. Voluntarism. World War I. 1917-19. *1186*

—. Henequen. International Harvester Company. Marketing. Mexico (Yucatán). Molina-Montes (firm). 1898-1915. *8*

—. *International Salt Co.* v. *United States* (1947). Leases. Lixator machine. Monopolies. Supreme Court. 1940's. *1290*

Prices (cuts). Competition. Standard Oil Company of New Jersey. 1870-1967. *631*

Pricing structures. Advertising discounts. Television, network. -1973. *266*

Printing. California. Nash, John Henry. 1831-1930. *520*

—. Copper-facing. Newton, Luke Vanderveer. Typefounding. 1850-1907. *565*

—. Industrial Technology. Working Class. 1931-78. *289*

—. New York City. 1950-79. *573*

Printing, calico. Architecture. Cotton mills. Dover Manufacturing Co. Print Works. New Hampshire (Dover). 1820-25. *686*

Prints. Art. Internal Revenue Service. Investments. Retail Trade. Tax shelters. 1980. *562*

Private sector. Armaments Industry. Industrial Technology. 1820-60. *946*

—. Cities. Employment. Public services. Taxation. 1980. *1092*

—. Civil Aeronautics Board. Employment. Federal Communications Commission. Interstate Commerce Commission. 1977-80. *1198*

—. Norris, William. Public services. 1900-81. *1135*

Private utilities. Elites. Public relations. South. ca 1977-78. *663*

—. Management. Public Utilities. 1970-72. *600*

Production. Automobile Industry and Trade. Hinde, James J. Ohio (Sandusky). Sandusky Automobile Company. 1896-1904. *327*

—. Demand. North Central States. Pennsylvania. Steel Industry (location). 1910-72. *942*

Production, internationalization of. Economic Conditions. Multinational corporations. 1941-76. *50*

Production technologies. Cost functions. Econometrics. Electric power industry. Price indexes (hedonic). 1971. *972*

Productivity. Automobiles. Dealers, franchised. Employment patterns. Profit. 1958-75. *358*

—. Bag industry. Demand. Paper Industry. Plastics. Technology. 1954-77. *927*

—. Ball bearing industry. 1958-79. *1011*

—. Blast furnaces. Industrial Technology. Iron Industry. 1840-1913. *907*

—. Boxes, folding paperboard. Manufactures. 1963-78. *1010*

—. Buses. Industry. 1954-79. *333*

—. Business. Economic growth. 1948-77. *89*

—. Capital expenditures. Quality control. Steel Industry. Technological change. 1954-71. *930*

—. Cleaning industry. 1958-76. *203*

—. Concrete industry. Employment. Technology. 1958-71. *982*

—. Construction machinery industry. Economic growth. Employment. Investments. Technology. 1958-78. *937*

—. Corporations. Industry. 1971-72. *82*

—. Corporations, nonfinancial. 1948-73. *46*

—. Drug trade. Quality control. Technology. 1963-72. *197*

—. Drugstores. Retail trade. 1958-79. *940*

—. Electric motor industry. Industrial technology. 1954-76. *1009*

—. Employment. Lumber and Lumbering. Pacific Northwest. Technology. ca 1899-1973. *795*

—. Fabricated structural metals industry. Metals. 1958-78. *973*

—. Federal regulation. 1947-79. *1175*

—. Fuel. Hopewell Forge. Iron industry. Labor. Management. Pennsylvania. Technology. 1750-1800. *977*

—. Government regulation. Industry. Pollution. 1972-81. *1314*

—. Great Britain. Industrial technology. Iron Industry. Profit. 1890. *921*

—. Industrial technology. Lamps, electric. Power Resources. 1954-77. *590*

—. Industry. Research and development. 1920-80. *881*

—. Labor. Multinational corporations. 1950-77. *13*

—. Labor. New England. Textile industry. 1830-60. *776*

—. Labor. Skills. Technology. Telecommunications industry. 1970's. *529*

—. Labor input. Sawmills. Technology. 1958-75. *702*

—. Milk industry. Profit. 1958-77. *784*

—. Railroads. 1955-74. *329*

—. Research and development. Statistics. 1959-77. *61*

—. Soap and detergent industry. Technological innovations. 1958-77. *1005*

—. Textile Industry. Yarn. 1958-80. *847*

Professional Standards Review Organization Program. Federal regulation. Medical care. Physicians. Social Security Act (US, 1935; amended, 1972). 1965-80. *1185*

Professionalism. Advertising. Ethics. Social status. 20c. *270*

Professionalization. Business (management). Human relations consulting firms. 1973. *189*

Profit. Agricultural Production. Farms. North. North Central States. 1820's-60's. *695*

—. American Telephone and Telegraph Company. Federal Regulation. 1969-77. *523*

—. Authority. Lukens Iron Works. Paternalism. Pennsylvania (Coatesville). Strikes. 1886. *992*

—. Automobiles. Dealers, franchised. Employment patterns. Productivity. 1958-75. *358*

—. Bank of Stephen Girard. Girard, Stephen. 1812-31. *184*

—. Banking. 1965-74. *215*

—. Business. Entrepreneurs. 1940's-70's. *66*

—. Capital. Corporations. Costs. 1945-78. *74*

—. Capital. Foreign investments. Multinational Corporations. 1955-78. *187*

—. Corporations. Corporations, Subsidiary. Management. 1960's-70's. *11*

—. Discrimination, Employment. Industry. Metropolitan areas. Racism. 1973. *1037*

—. Great Britain. Industrial technology. Iron Industry. Productivity. 1890. *921*

—. Milk industry. Productivity. 1958-77. *784*

Profit standards. Federal Regulation. Interstate Commerce Commission. Motor carrier industry. Prices. 1970's. *1190*

Profit system. Business. Corporate power. Politics. 1970-73. *1102*

Programming. Business. Federal Communications Commission. Ownership. Radio. Spanish language. 1970-81. *564*

—. Federal Communications Commission. *National Citizens Committee for Broadcasting* v. *Federal Communications Commission* (US, 1977). Newspapers. Television. 1975-77. *1348*
Programming, local (regulation). Federal Communications Commission. Television, UHF. 1960's-70's. *551*
Progressive era. Industrial safety movement. Reform. "Safety First" (slogan). Young, Robert J. ca 1900-16. *1025*
Progressivism. Business. Interest groups. Political Corruption. 1895-1910. *1094*
—. Conservatism. Esch-Cummins Act (1920). Federal Regulation. Newlands, Francis G. Railroads. 1888-1917. *1174*
Property rights. Baseball. Contracts. Economic Theory. 1955-76. *207*
Property rights formation. Cattlemen's associations. Income (maximization). Range, open. West. 1860's-80's. *697*
Protectionism. Antitrust. Government. Imports. Steel Industry. Trigger Price Mechanism. 1959-78. *1281*
—. Economic Policy. International Trade. Steel industry. 1870-1979. *1358*
—. Wallpaper. 1756-1927. *956*
Protest movements. Developing nations. Food industry. Infant formula. Marketing. 1970-79. *55*
Public Administration. Antitrust. Shipping Act (US, 1916). 1916-79. *1201*
—. Executive power. Federal Regulation. Politics. President's Advisory Council on Executive Organization. Reform. 1937-79. *1345*
—. Government regulation. US Regulatory Council. 1978-80. *1292*
—. Occupational Safety and Health Act (US, 1970). 1970-78. *1267*
Public Broadcasting Service. Corporations. Philanthropy. Public relations. 1972-76. *1050*
Public Health. Agriculture Department. Dyes. Federal regulation. Food. 1913-19. *1228*
Public Lands. Capital gains. Forests and Forestry. Legislation. Revenue Act (US, 1942; amended 1944). Taxation. 1943-44. *1328*
Public opinion. Arizona. Armies. Federal Government. Railroad building. Southern Pacific Railroad. 1875-78. *305*
—. Business History (review article). Galambos, Louis. Snow, Barbara Barrow. Social Change. 1880-1940. 1975. *1103*
—. Competition. Corporations. Mass media. Newspapers. Public Policy. Stock exchange. 1970's. *516*
—. Constitutional Amendments (1st). Mass media. 1734-1981. *572*
—. Corporations. Government regulations, fear of. Social responsibility. 1960-70's. *1044*
—. Dumping. International Trade. Japan. Steel Industry. 1974-78. *950*
—. Multinational Corporations. Oil Industry and Trade. 1870's-20c. *587*
Public policy. Automobiles. Illinois (Chicago). Mass transit. 1900-50. *311*
—. Behavior. Fuel. Pennsylvania (Pittsburgh). Smoke. 1940-50. *1132*
—. Borch, Fred. Business Roundtable (March Group). Executives. Government. Harper, John. 1970-79. *120*
—. Bright, Charles. Politics. Rose, Mark H. Transportation (review article). 1941-72. *312*
—. Business. Consumers. Government. 1974. *1291*
—. Business. Economic Conditions. Electric power. Germany. Great Britain. 1880-1929. *613*
—. Coal Mines and Mining. Severance tax. Western States. 1976-78. *1210*

—. Competition. Corporations. Mass media. Newspapers. Public opinion. Stock exchange. 1970's. *516*
—. Congress (committees). Depletion allowance. Oil Industry and Trade. Subgovernment theory. Taxation. 1900-74. *588*
—. Conservation of Natural Resources. Energy. Government regulation. 1929-79. *1273*
—. Corporations. Government. Political Theory. 1970's. *1279*
—. Corporations. Industry. 1945-80. *123*
—. Economic Conditions. General Motors Corporation. Labor. Local Politics. Location. Michigan (Detroit). 1970-80. *1099*
—. Energy. Legislation. 1930-79. *1241*
—. Europe. Nationalization. Railroads. 1830-1976. *1192*
—. Farms. Market industries. Specialization. 1970's. *681*
—. Federal Regulation. Germany. Interstate Commerce Commission. Railroads. 1870-1920. *500*
—. Finance. Indiana (Gary). Intergovernmental Relations. Minnesota (St. Paul). Negotiated investment strategy. Ohio (Columbus). 1979-80. *192*
—. Fire control. Long, George S. Lumber and Lumbering. Pacific Northwest. 1902-10. *768*
—. Great Britain. Management, private. Oil Industry and Trade. USA. 1918-24. *615*
—. Industry. Labor law. Management. 1867-1927. *1275*
—. Industry structure. Market rivalry. Monopolies. -1973. *42*
—. Multinational Corporations. Oil Industry and Trade. 1945-80. *628*
Public Relations. Advertising. Death and Dying. Funeral industry. 1830-1980. *185*
—. Corporations. Philanthropy. Public Broadcasting Service. 1972-76. *1050*
—. Elites. Private utilities. South. ca 1977-78. *663*
Public relations campaign. Angola. Gulf Oil Company. USA. 1968-74. *1116*
Public service. Corporations. Massachusetts. New York. 17c-18c. *1320*
Public services. Cities. Employment. Private sector. Taxation. 1980. *1092*
—. Norris, William. Private sector. 1900-81. *1135*
Public Transportation. AMTRAK. Railroads. 1971-73. *457*
Public Utilities. Communism. Government Regulation. Texas Public Utility Commission. 1975-79. *1218*
—. Electric power companies. Federal Regulation. Investments. 1970's. *1245*
—. Federal Policy. Pacific Northwest. Power Resources (partnership concept). ca 1950-70. *1262*
—. Management. Private Utilities. 1970-72. *600*
Public Utilities (competition). Maryland (Hagerstown). Oregon (The Dalles). State utility commissions. 1910-71. *636*
Public Utility Commission. Economic Regulations. Texas. 1975-81. *1157*
Publishers and Publishing. Bean, Donald P. (report). Scholarship. University of Chicago Press. 1929. *518*
—. Books, distribution of. Compaine, Benjamin M. (review article). Marketing. 1960's-70's. *548*
—. Competition. Corporations. Mergers. 1960's-70's. *556*
—. Competition. Paperback Books. Pocket Books (company). 1958-78. *561*
—. Periodicals. 1978. *567*
Publishers and Publishing (small). 1960's-70's. *531*

Publishing. Books, distribution of. Business History. Developing Nations. Literacy. USA. 1900's. *547*

Publishing, independent. Authors. Business History. Committee of Small Magazine Editors and Publishers. 1772-1975. *535*

Publishing, Scholarly. Association of American University Presses. 1920's-1974. *558*

Puerto Rico. Industrialization. 1940-70. *936*

Puerto Rico, southwestern. Agricultural Production. Haciendas. Mills. Sugar industry. 1902. *838*

Pullman Company. Aliens. Brotherhood of Sleeping Car Porters. Filipinos. Labor. Negroes. Railroads. 1925-55. *1110*

Pullman, George Mortimer. Pullman-Standard Car Manufacturing Co. Railroads. 1860's-1936. *515*

Pullman strike. Illinois (Pullman). Labor Unions and Organizations. Railroads. 1880-94. *432*

Pullman-Standard Car Manufacturing Co. Pullman, George Mortimer. Railroads. 1860's-1936. *515*

Q

Quality control. Capital expenditures. Productivity. Steel Industry. Technological change. 1954-71. *930*

—. Capitalism. Industry. 1970-80. *1250*

—. Drug trade. Productivity. Technology. 1963-72. *197*

Quarrying. Colorado (Fort Collins). Stone industry. Stout, William H. B. 1880-1900. *862*

—. New York, eastern. Roofing. Slate. Vermont. 1850's-1970's. *882*

R

Race Relations. Industrialization. Labor Unions and Organizations (black). 19c-20c. *1134*

—. International Harvester Company. Labor practices. Minorities. 1831-1976. *1022*

Racial discrimination. Employment. Law. 1964-73. *1312*

Racism. Discrimination. Employment. Industry. Metropolitan areas. Profit. 1973. *1037*

Radicals and Radicalism. Everett Mill. Massachusetts (Lawrence). Polish Americans. Strikes. Textile Industry. Women. 1912. *778*

Radio. Business. Federal Communications Commission. Ownership. Programming. Spanish language. 1970-81. *564*

—. Commerce Department. Federal Regulation. Hoover, Herbert C. Licensing. 1918-22. *1311*

—. Communications Bill. Federal Communications Act (US, 1934). House of Representatives. Lobbying. Television. VanDeerlin, Lionel. 1934-79. *1258*

—. Communications Technology. Louisiana (New Orleans). Television. WWL (station). 1940-50. *557*

—. Federal Communications Commission. Government regulation. Legislation. Supreme Court. Television. 1927-74. *1319*

—. Illinois (Chicago). Waller, Judith Cary. WMAQ, station. 1922-57. *577*

—. Industrial Technology. Monopolies (sought). Patents. Research. 1912-26. *560*

—. National Association of Broadcasters. Self-regulation. Television. 1922-70's. *554*

—. Newspapers. Ownership trends. 1922-70. *570*

Radio Company of America (shutdown). Labor Unions and Organizations. Tennessee (Memphis). 1965-70. *527*

Radio (review article). Barnouw, Eric. Briggs, Asa. Culbert, David Holbrook. Metz, Robert. 1920-76. *563*

Railroad. Ball, Ed. Du Pont estate. Florida East Coast Railroad. Pepper, Claude. 1926-58. *492*

Railroad building. Arizona. Armies. Federal Government. Public opinion. Southern Pacific Railroad. 1875-78. *305*

Railroad Carmen's Strike (1911-15). Scientific management. Strikes. Working class. 1903-22. *1285*

Railroad construction. Great Northern Railway. Hill, James J. Milwaukee Road. North Dakota. Northern Pacific Railroad. 1879-85. *451*

—. Land grants. Union Pacific Railroad. ca 1860's. *365*

Railroad expansion. Economic Development. Steamboats, decline of. Transportation, Commercial. West, ante-bellum. 1811-60. *379*

Railroad regulation. Economic Conditions. Hepburn Committee. Interstate Commerce Act (US, 1887). Northeastern or North Atlantic States. ca 1870-1910. *1265*

—. Election Laws (gubernatorial). Goebel, William. Kentucky. Taylor, William S. 1887-1900. *1171*

Railroad Revitalization and Regulatory Reform Act (US, 1976). Federal Regulation. Regional Rail Reorganization Act (US, 1974). Subsidies. 1974-78. *1226*

Railroad stations. Atchison, Topeka & Santa Fe Railroad. Kansas. 1880-20c. *321*

Railroad system. Milwaukee Road. North Central States. 1850-1977. *478*

Railroad systems, adequate. Economic conditions. Oklahoma panhandle. Territorial status. 1880's-1930's. *366*

Railroad, transcontinental. Overland Journeys to the Pacific. Travel. 1869-90. *324*

Railroad war. Pennsylvania (Erie). Violence. 1852-55. *377*

Railroads See also names of individual railroads, e.g. Baltimore and Ohio; Atchison, Topeka and Santa Fe, etc.

—. Agricultural commodities. Alaska (Matanuska Valley). Colonization. 1915-40. *512*

—. Agricultural Commodities. Freight and Freightage. Populism. Prices. 1870-97. *304*

—. Alaska. Lomen family. Ohlson, Otto F. Reindeer industry. 1928-31. *513*

—. Alcoholism. Chicago, Burlington & Quincy Railroad. Employees. Law Enforcement. Management. 1876-1902. *319*

—. Aliens. Brotherhood of Sleeping Car Porters. Filipinos. Labor. Negroes. Pullman Company. 1925-55. *1110*

—. American Railway Union. Montana. Strikes. 1894. *510*

—. AMTRAK. ConRail. Federal Government. State government. 1971-77. *1287*

—. AMTRAK. Passenger service. 1930's-72. *443*

—. AMTRAK. Public Transportation. 1971-73. *457*

—. Arizona. Boomtowns. Copper mines and mining. 1880-86. *896*

—. Arkansas. Construction. Finance. Little Rock and Fort Smith Railroad. Robinson, Asa P. ca 1867-76. *495*

—. Arkansas. Louisiana & Arkansas Railway. 1898-1949. *323*

—. Arkansas (northern). Economic Growth. Missouri and North Arkansas Railroad. Settlement, pattern of. 1880-1920's. *384*

S

Social costs. Economic regulations. Interstate Commerce Commission. Trucks and Trucking. 1978. *1199*

Social Customs. Advertising. Consumers. Ewen, Stuart (review article). 19c-1976. *231*

—. Food Consumption. Industrialization. ca 1920-75. *745*

Social environment. Corporation training programs. Employee sponsorship. Minorities. 1960's-70's. *1039*

Social geography. Clothing industry. Employment, location of. Maryland (Baltimore). 1860-1900. *772*

Social Mobility. Clothing manufacturers. Wisconsin (Milwaukee). 1840-80. *832*

—. Corporations. Elites. Pennsylvania (Scranton). 1880-1920. *1055*

—. Employment. Industrialization. Negroes. Plantation economy. 1860's-1974. *749*

Social Organization. Agricultural cooperatives. Business. Legislation. Ohio. Woods, W. N. (reminiscences). 1907-78. *846*

—. Corporations. 1974. *16*

—. Corporations. Disney World. Monopolies. 1971-81. *236*

—. Idaho (Potlatch). Lumber and Lumbering. Potlatch Lumber Company. 1901-31. *1073*

Social problems. California (Santa Clara County). Economic Conditions. Electronics industry. Environment. 1950's-70's. *1121*

—. City planning. Indiana (Gary). Steel Industry. US Steel Corporation. 1905-30. *1059*

—. Corporations (company camps). Latin America. USA. 1950-66. *1*

—. Ford, Henry. Industry. Management, scientific. Mechanization. Taylor, Frederick Winslow. 1875-1900's. *23*

—. International Trade. Multinational corporations. 1960's-70's. *1139*

Social responsibility. Appalachia. Coal barons. Labor. 1880-1930. *870*

—. Attitudes. Business. Technology. 1950's-70's. *1123*

—. Corporations. 20c. *2*

—. Corporations. Government regulations, fear of. Public opinion. 1960-70's. *1044*

—. Multinational corporations. 1960's-79. *164*

Social responsibilty. Advertising. Consumers. Government Regulation. 1950's-70's. *252*

Social Security Act (US, 1935; amended, 1972). Federal regulation. Medical care. Physicians. Professional Standards Review Organization Program. 1965-80. *1185*

Social status. Advertising. Ethics. Professionalism. 20c. *270*

Social Surveys. *Charities and the Commons* (periodical). Industrialization (impact of). Pennsylvania. *Pittsburgh Survey* (1909). 1907-14. *1093*

Social Work. Buckeye Steel Castings Company. Bush, S. P. Management, scientific. Ohio (Columbus). Steel Industry. 1890-1920. *923*

Socialism. Antibusiness groups. Business. Capitalism. 1974. *60*

Society. Corporations. 1906-75. *1113*

Society for Establishing Useful Manufactures. Coxe, Tench. Hamilton, Alexander. Manufactures. 1790-92. *1182*

Soft drink industry. Coca-Cola. Pepsi-Cola. Seven-Up. 1880-1977. *909*

Soil Conservation Service. Agricultural Adjustment Administration. New Deal. 1933-41. *1315*

Songs. Industrial Workers of the World. Rhetoric. 1906-17. *334*

South. Aeromarine Airways, Inc. Air Lines. Seaplanes. 1920-24. *425*

—. Agricultural Production. Cotton. Economic Conditions. Soybeans. 1920's-75. *712*

—. Agricultural reform. *Debow's Review*. 1846-61. *715*

—. Agricultural Technology and Research. Cotton. Mechanization. Southwest. 1946-79. *801*

—. Agricultural Technology and Research. Cotton. Sharecroppers. Tractors. 1915-60. *773*

—. Agriculture. American Revolution (impact). Great Britain. Strickland, William. 1794-95. *726*

—. Alexander Brown and Sons. Cotton. Great Britain. International Trade. 1820-60. *737*

—. Banking. Cost functions. Economic development. 1870-1976. *234*

—. Bibliographies. Strikes. Textile industry. 1929-76. *856*

—. Boll weevil. Cotton (decline). Negroes. 1929-77. *724*

—. Brown & Root, Inc. Construction industry. Corporations. Housing. Rural areas. ca 1977-79. *177*

—. Brown lung disease. Burlington Industries, Inc. Carolina Brown Lung Association. Cotton. Liberty Mutual Insurance Co. 1970's. *1038*

—. Brown lung disease. Carolina Brown Lung Association. Textile industry. Workmen's Compensation. 1970's. *1098*

—. Central place theory. Cotton industry. Marketing. Urbanization. 1880-1930. *835*

—. Congress of Industrial Organizations. Labor Unions and Organizations. Management. National Industrial Recovery Act (US, 1933). National Labor Relations Act (US, 1935). Textile Industry. 1933-41. *1349*

—. Corporations. Economic Development. Northeastern or North Atlantic States. Relocation. 1970-80. *1146*

—. Cotton. Farming, scientific. Fertilizers. Furman, Farish. 1878-83. *818*

—. Cotton. New England. Textile industry. 1951-60. *688*

—. Cotton Acreage Control Law (Texas, 1931). Crop limitation. Long, Huey P. New Deal. 1931-33. *1343*

—. Cotton "overproduction". Farmers. ca 1880-1915. *696*

—. Cotton textiles, price of. Economic Conditions. Johnson, Lyndon B. (administration). Price controls. 1965-66. *1179*

—. Cotton-textile manufacturers. New England. Technological change. 1890-1970. *706*

—. Economic competition. Manufacturing. Market structure. 1850-60. *914*

—. Elites. Private utilities. Public relations. ca 1977-78. *663*

—. Forest Farmers Association. 1940-78. *775*

—. Forestry, impact of. 1880-1971. *754*

—. Labor Unions and Organizations. Textile industry. 1918-40. *710*

—. Labor Unions and Organizations. Textile industry. ca 1949-75. *789*

—. Literature. Music. Railroads. 1830's-1970's. *391*

South Africa. Diplomacy. Foreign Investments. Kissinger, Henry A. Multinational Corporations. 1969-76. *143*

—. Economic Structure. Foreign investments. Military. Multinational corporations. 1945-78. *157*

South Carolina. Jim Crow laws. Negroes. Railroads. Separate coach bills. 1880-98. *1091*

South Carolina (Darlington). Darlington Manufacturing Company. Labor Disputes (unionization). Textile Workers Union of America. 1956-73. *671*

South Central and Gulf States. Chicago and Eastern Illinois Railroad. North Central States. Railroads. Real Estate. St. Louis-San Francisco Railroad. 1902-13. *454*

South Dakota. Land boom. Migration, Internal. Railroads. Settlement. 1878-87. *381*

South Dakota (Deadwood). Freight and Freightage. Railroads. Stagecoaches. 1874-87. *383*

South Dakota (Deadwood area). Hearst, George. Mines. 1876-79. *865*

South Dakota (Granville). Christianson, Ivan D. (interview). Grain. Railroads. 1920's. *330*

South, New. Agricultural businessmen. Industrialization. Textile industry. Urban entrepreneurs. 1870-1900. *725*

Southeastern Carriers Conference. Discrimination. Fair Employment Practices Committee. Negroes. Railroads. World War II. 1941-45. *1074*

Southeastern States. Business. Housing. Labor. Mechanization. Mobile homes. Taylor Homes. 1972-79. *1014*

—. Cotton ginning, evolution of. 18c-1973. *666*

—. Herty, Charles Holmes. Newsprint. Paper mills. Pine trees. Scientific Experiments and Research. 1927-40. *779*

Southern Pacific Railroad. Arizona. Armies. Federal Government. Public opinion. Railroad building. 1875-78. *305*

—. California. Construction. San Diego and Arizona Railway. Spreckels, John D. 1907-19. *455*

Southerners. Columbia Broadcasting System. Discrimination. Journalism. 1970's. *1138*

Southwest. Agricultural Technology and Research. Cotton. Mechanization. South. 1946-79. *801*

Southwest Airlines. Air line war. Civil Aeronautics Board. Federal subsidies. Texas. 1970's. *400*

Sovereign compulsion. Act of state doctrine. Antitrust. Foreign Policy. International Trade. Trials. 1965-78. *1357*

Soviet of technicians. Corporate state. Economic Structure. Galbraith, John Kenneth. Gould, Jay. Veblen, Thorstein. 1954-72. *103*

Soybeans. Agricultural Production. Cotton. Economic Conditions. South. 1920's-75. *712*

Spain. California. Economic Regulations. Prices. 1768-1810. *1159*

—. Fish. International Trade. Massachusetts. Portugal. 1700-73. *747*

—. International Telephone and Telegraph. State Department. 1924-44. *108*

Spalding, Thomas. Archaeology. Georgia (Sapelo Island). Sugar industry. ca 1795-1850's. 1976. *694*

Spanish language. Business. Federal Communications Commission. Ownership. Programming. Radio. 1970-73. *564*

Spatial influence. Banking. Economic Structure. Megalopolis. New York City. 1971. *237*

Specialization. Debt. Farmers. 1860's-90's. *692*

—. Farms. Market industries. Public Policy. 1970's. *681*

Speculation. Automobiles. California, southern. Land. Politics. Railroads. Streetcars. 1880's-1970's. *483*

Sperry Rand Corp. (Univac division). Computers. Eckert-Mauchly Computer Corp. Mergers. Remington Rand Inc. 1946-55. *997*

Spindletop Oil Rush. Higgins, Pattillo. Lucas, Anthony F. Oil Industry and Trade. Texas (Beaumont). 1901-30's. *651*

Sports. Federal Policy. 1974-77. *1191*

Sports Broadcasting Act (US, 1961). Advertising. Antitrust. Broadcasting. 1961-78. *1232*

Sports, professional. Congress. Legislation. 1951-78. *1242*

—. Dallas Cowboys (team). Investments. Suburbs. Texas (Arlington, Irving). Texas Rangers (team). 1968-75. *268*

Spreckels, John D. California. Construction. San Diego and Arizona Railway. Southern Pacific Railroad. 1907-19. *455*

Sprunt, Alexander and Son. Cotton. Exports. North Carolina (Wilmington). 1866-1956. *736*

Squaw Man (film). California (Hollywood). Films. Jesse L. Lasky Feature Play Company. 1911-14. *543*

Stagecoaches. Business History. New England. Transportation, Commercial. 1800-50. *397*

—. Freight and Freightage. Railroads. South Dakota (Deadwood). 1874-87. *383*

Standard Fruit Co. Bananas. Nicaragua. 1921-30's. *87*

Standard of living. Age. Coal Mines and Mining. Management. Strikes, wildcat. Working conditions. 1970's. *861*

Standard Oil Company. Monopolies. Oil Industry and Trade. Railroads. 1880's. *638*

Standard Oil Company of New Jersey. Competition. Prices (cuts). 1870-1967. *631*

—. EXXON. Humble Oil and Refining Company. Oil industry and Trade. Trademarks. 1910-73. *605*

—. New Jersey (Bayonne). Polish Americans. Strikes. 1915-16. *601*

Standard Oil Company of New York. China. Kerosene. Nationalism. Oil and Petroleum Products. Taxation. 1925-27. *661*

Standard Oil Company of Ohio. Coopers' International Union. Industrial Relations. Mechanization. 1870's. *612*

Standard Radio. California (Los Angeles). Recording Industry. 1934-54. *553*

Stanley Steamer (automobile). Automobiles. Locomobile Company. New England. 1899-1903. *501*

State Department. Bureaucracies. Chambers of Commerce. Commerce and Labor Department (Bureau of Manufactures). Economic Policy. Exports. 1890's-1913. *170*

—. International Telephone and Telegraph. Spain. 1924-44. *108*

State government. AMTRAK. ConRail. Federal Government. Railroads. 1971-77. *1287*

—. Antitrust. Corporation law. Judicial Administration. Supreme Court. *United States v. E. C. Knight Company* (US, 1895). 1869-1903. *1268*

—. Antitrust. Oil Industry and Trade. Texas. Trade Regulations. 1901-11. *635*

—. Banking, commercial. Corporation Charters. Law. 1781-1843. *1344*

—. Coal. Environment. Montana. Strip mining. 1970-72. *1238*

—. Copper Mines and Mining. Taxation. 1970-81. *873*

—. Economic Regulations. Electric Power. Monopolies. 1907-38. *1239*

—. Economic Regulations. Georgia. Mortgages. Savings and loan associations. Usury ceilings. 1960's-70's. *253*

—. Transportation policy. 1956-80. *1235*

State Legislatures. Alcohol. Minnesota. New York. Price controls. 1947-71. *1259*

State Politics. Arizona. Corporations. Hunt, George W. P. Miners. 1915-17. *905*

—. Interest Groups. New York City. Real Estate Business. 1970's. *245*

—. Mass transit. New Jersey. New York. Port Authority (finance). 1921-74. *403*

State utility commissions. Maryland (Hagerstown). Oregon (The Dalles). Public Utilities (competition). 1910-71. *636*

USSR. Alaska. Arctic. Canada. Mining. Scandinavia. 1917-78. *883*

Usury ceilings. Economic Regulations. Georgia. Mortgages. Savings and loan associations. State Government. 1960's-70's. *253*

Utah. Electric power. Nunn, Lucien L. Nunn, Paul N. 1898-1912. *614*

Utah (Alta). Blakemore, Page (interview). Mining Engineering. 1870-1970's. *880*

Utah Northern Railroad. Business. Hatch, Lorenzo Hill. Idaho (Boise, Franklin). Letters-to-the-editor. Railroads and State. 1874. *385*

Utah, southern. Sheep raising. Wool. 1862-81. *782*

Utopian thought. Collectivism. Intellectuals. National Association of Corporation Schools. Steinmetz, Charles Proteus. 1910-17. *1065*

V

Values. Assembly lines. Automobile Industry and Trade. Europe. Management. 1950-81. *1069*
—. Death and Dying. Free market. Life insurance. Social Change. 19c. *298*
—. Education. Games, board. Social Change. 1832-1904. *1016*

VanDeerlin, Lionel. Communications Bill. Federal Communications Act (US, 1934). House of Representatives. Lobbying. Radio. Television. 1934-79. *1258*

Veblen, Thorstein. Corporate state. Economic Structure. Galbraith, John Kenneth. Gould, Jay. Soviet of technicians. 1954-72. *103*

Vegetable industry. Illinois Central Railroad. Mississippi. Railroads. 1880's-1940. *439*

Vegetables. Advertising. Agricultural cooperatives. California. Fruit and Fruit Crops. Nutrition. 1880's-1920's. *820*

Venezuela. Florida. Foreign Investments. 1973-79. *293*

Vermont. Economic Conditions. Railroads. Social Change. 1843-70. *314*
—. New York, eastern. Quarrying. Roofing. Slate. 1850's-1970's. *882*

Videorecorders. Communication satellites. Television (cable, subscription). 1980. *524*

Villa, Pancho. Cananea Copper Co. Extortion. Mexico (Sonora). 1915. *147*

Vinson, Carl. Alaska. Bartlett, E. L. Naval Petroleum Reserve No. 4. Oil and Petroleum Products. Rivers, Ralph J. 1959-62. *644*

Violence. Labor Disputes. Mine wars. West Virginia. 1912-13. 1920-21. *903*
—. Pennsylvania (Erie). Railroad war. 1852-55. *377*

Violence, absence of. Coal Mines and Mining. Ohio (Hocking Valley). Strikebreakers. 1884-85. *597*

Virginia. Chesapeake Bay area. Economic Conditions. Maryland. Tobacco industry. 1617-1710. *765*
—. Dismal Swamp. Lumber and Lumbering. North Carolina. 1760's-1970's. *1130*
—. Economic Conditions. Tobacco, cultivation of. 1613-1732. *665*
—. Louisa Railroad Co. Railroads. 1836-1980. *499*

Virginia, eastern. Coal Mines and Mining. Insurance. Investments. Safety. Slavery. 1780-1865. *625*

Virginia (Richmond, Petersburg, Norfolk). Railroads. Urban rivalries. 1830's - 1850's. *491*

Voluntarism. Agricultural Industry. Economic Regulations. Federal government. Mississippi. Prices. Texas. 1925-40. *756*

—. Food Administration. Hoover, Herbert C. Pork-packing. Prices. World War I. 1917-19. *1186*

W

Wadleigh, Atherton B. Copper Mines and Mining. Greene, William Cornell. Mexico (Sonora, Cananea). Multinational Corporations. Stock manipulations. Taylor, Frederick Winslow. 1901-07. *130*

Wage statistics. Economic Conditions. Manufacturing. Prices. 1953-70. *913*

Wage-price controls. Models. 1971-74. *1306*

Wages. Attitudes. Ford Motor Company. Labor. 1890-1915. *438*
—. Economic Conditions. Inflation. Price controls. 1971-74. *1324*
—. Electronic equipment. Marketing. Retail Trade. Working Conditions. 1970's. *978*
—. Industrial Relations. Job security. Labor. Multinational corporations. 1970's. *145*
—. Industry. Labor Unions and Organizations. Occupations. 1973-78. *1023*

Waller, Judith Cary. Illinois (Chicago). Radio. WMAQ, station. 1922-57. *577*

Wallpaper. Protectionism. 1756-1927. *956*

War of 1812. Banking. Debt, public. Federal Government. Gallatin, Albert. Securities. 1813. *183*

Warburg, James P. Banking. Monetary policy. New Deal. Roosevelt, Franklin D. (administration). 1932-41. *254*

Ward, Aaron Montgomery. Mail-order business. 1872-1919. *925*

Washburn Lignite Coal Company. Coal Mines and Mining. Labor. North Dakota (Wilton). United Mine Workers of America. 1900-30's. *906*

Washington. Bellingham Port Commission. Economic Growth. Shipping. 1920-70. *1227*
—. California (San Francisco area). Lumber and Lumbering. Oregon. Shipbuilding. 1850-1929. *341*
—. Forests and Forestry. Government regulation. Oregon. Pinchot, Gifford. 1902-10. *707*
—. Gates, Frederick T. Idaho. Mining. Rockefeller, John D. 1890-1905. *871*
—. Kinsey, Clark. Lumber and Lumbering. Oregon. Photographs. 1914-45. *851*
—. Land Tenure. Law. Lumber and Lumbering. Timber and Stone Act (US, 1878). 1860-1910. *1352*
—. Lumber and Lumbering. Weyerhaeuser Timber Company. 1899-1903. *709*

Washington (Bainbridge Island). Lumber and Lumbering. Port Blakely Mill Company. 1888-1903. *708*

Washington (Columbia Plateau). Depressions. Grain. Livestock. McGregor Land and Livestock Company. Prices. 1930's-82. *760*

Washington, eastern. Business. Columbia Plateau. Farming. McGregor family. Oregon, northeastern. Sheep. 1882-1980. *759*

Washington (King County). Coal Mines and Mining. Negroes. Oregon Improvement Company. Strikebreakers, black. 1891. *899*

Washington Post (newspaper). Conglomerates, effects of. Newspapers. Strikes. 1975. *1164*

Washington (Puget Sound area). Boeing Company. Economic Growth (linkage systems). Income generation, spatial pattern of. 1968-73. *47*

Washington (Shelton). Forests and Forestry. Management. Mason, David T. McNary, Charles L. Sustained-Yield Forest Management Act (US, 1944). 1944-46. *1229*

Washington, University of (Library). Documents. Lumber and Lumbering. Port Blakely Mill Company. 1876-1923. *678*

Washington (Walla Walla). Montana (Fort Benton). Mullan Road. Trade. Westward Movement. 1860-83. *440*

Water Supply. Cattle raising. Texas Panhandle. 1930's-70's. *840*

Waterman Arrowbile (aircraft). Aeronautics. Automobiles. Phillips, Jerry (account). 1920's-38. *459*

Watkins, Carleton E. California (San Francisco). Pacific Mail Steamship Company. Photography. Shipping. 1867-71. *505*

Wealth redistribution. Corporations. Economic theory. Taxation. 1970's. *1136*

Webb-Pomerene Act (US, 1918). Antitrust. Exports. National Commission for the Review of Antitrust Laws and Procedures. 1914-79. *1203*

Weil, Gordon L. Adburgham, Alison. Department stores (review article). Harris, Leon. Hendrickson, Robert. 1850-1975. *984*

Weir, Ernest Tener. Federal government. Foreign Policy. Pennsylvania (Pittsburgh). Steel industry. 1900-50's. *999*

Welch, Henry. Antibiotics. Conflict of interest. Federal regulation. Food and Drug Administration. Periodicals. Pharmaceutical Industry. 1959-62. *1270*

Wells, Fargo & Company. Banking. California, southern. Transportation. ca 1852-69. *233*

West. Cattle industry. Englishmen. Immigrants. 1866-79. *799*

—. Cattlemen's associations. Income (maximization). Property rights formation. Range, open. 1860's-80's. *697*

—. Comstock Lode. Law. Mineral rights. Nevada. 1850-1900. *1255*

West, ante-bellum. Economic Development. Railroad expansion. Steamboats, decline of. Transportation, Commercial. 1811-60. *379*

West Jersey. Business History. Commerce, Atlantic. Delaware Valley. Pennsylvania, southeastern. Shipbuilding. 1722-76. *343*

West Virginia. Coal Mines and Mining (bituminous). Kentucky. Model towns. Ohio. Pennsylvania. 1880-1930. *1101*

—. Labor Disputes. Mine wars. Violence. 1912-13. 1920-21. *903*

Western Electric Co., Inc. Environment. Harvard University, Graduate School of Business. Labor. Workplace. 1924-33. *1153*

Western Federation of Miners. Arizona (Globe). Copper Mines and Mining. Strikes. 1917. *890*

Western Nations. Developing nations. Foreign investments. Multinational corporations. ca 1960-75. *165*

—. Steel Industry. US Steel Corporation. 1950's-70's. *998*

Western States. AMTRAK. Management. North Central States. North Coast *Hiawatha* line. 1970's. *465*

—. Appalachia. Coal industry. Federal regulation. 1969-77. *1177*

—. Chicago, Milwaukee, St. Paul and Pacific Railroad. Curtis, Asahel. Photography. Railroads. 1909-29. *480*

—. Coal Mines and Mining. Public Policy. Severance tax. 1976-78. *1210*

—. Conservation of Natural Resources. Energy. Mines. 1970-79. *879*

—. Construction, heavy. Dams. Government. Idaho (Boise). Morrison-Knudsen Company. 1933-40. *188*

—. Historiography. Mining. 1850's-1979. *885*

—. Rivers. Steamboats (profitability of). 1850-70. *306*

Westward Movement. Economics. Railroads, land grant. 1864-1900. *445*

—. Montana (Fort Benton). Mullan Road. Trade. Washington (Walla Walla). 1860-83. *440*

—. Northern Pacific Railroad. Railroads. Settlement. 1882. *378*

Weyerhaeuser Timber Company. Lumber and Lumbering. Washington. 1899-1903. *709*

WGBH (station). California (San Francisco). Economic Conditions. KQED (station). Massachusetts (Boston). Television, public. 1945-81. *544*

Whaling Industry and Trade. Economic competition. Ports. 1784-1875. *817*

—. International Whaling Commission. 1975-81. *682*

—. New England. 1712-1924. *819*

Whealer-Lea Act (1938). Advertising regulation. Federal Trade Commission. 1914-71. *1329*

Wheat. Agriculture. Great Plains. Labor casualization. Mechanization. 1865-1902. *669*

—. Bonanza farming. Minnesota. North Dakota. Railroads. Red River of the North. 1870's-90's. *722*

Wheat farming. Campbell, Thomas D. Drought. Farm income. Great Plains. Prairie Provinces. 1915-1940. *853*

Whitmarsh, Samuel. Corticelli Company. Massachusetts (Northampton). Silk industry. 1830-1930. *800*

Whitney, Willie R. Coolidge, William D. General Electric Company. Industry. Langmuir, Irving. Scientific Experiments and Research. 1900-16. *1007*

Wichita Falls and Northwestern Railway. Oklahoma. Railroads. Texas. Townsites. 1900-20. *395*

Wilderness Act (1964). Colorado (Uncompahgre Primitive Area). Mining Law (1872). Nature Conservation. 1973. *1330*

Wildman, Perry (reminiscences). Arizona (Superior). Silver King mine. 1879-89. *904*

Wilkins, Mira (review article). Multinational Corporations. 1914-70. 1974. *5*

Williams Act (US, 1968). Business. Cash tender offers. Economic Regulations. 1968-80. *1240*

Williams school. Depressions. Diplomatic history. Foreign markets. Steel industry. 1893-1913. *1012*

Williams, William Appleman. Business historians. Expansionism. Foreign markets. Manufacturers. 1870-1900. 1970's. *916*

Wilson, John (letter). Bank of North America. Banking, commercial. Pendleton, Joseph. 1782-84. *264*

Wilson, Woodrow. Antitrust. Historiography, revisionist. 1913-24. 1960's-70's. *1321*

—. Food crisis. Price controls. World War I. 1917. *1214*

Wine. Agricultural Industry. California. ca 1830-1975. *729*

Wine industry. California. Europe. 1875-95. *689*

—. California. Oral history. Teiser, Ruth (interviews). 1890's-1977. *769*

—. California. Seghesio family. 1886-1977. *807*

Wire services. Monopolies. New York *Tribune*. Newspapers. Reid, Whitelaw. 1885-92. *566*

Wirt, George H. Forest management. Pennsylvania State Forest Academy. Rothrock, Joseph Trimble. 1870's-1903. *824*

Wisconsin. Banking. Competition. Loans. 1870-1900. *240*

—. Banking history. Economic development. Federal Regulation. Federal Reserve System. 1863-1914. *1248*

—. Food crisis. Price controls. Wilson, Woodrow. 1917. *1214*

—. Railroads. Women workers. 1917-30. *1067*

World War II. Agricultural production. Farmers. Michigan. 1939-45. *690*

—. Airplane Industry and Trade. Contracting policies. Industrial concentration. 1938-46. *981*

—. Airplane Industry and Trade. Industrial concentration. 1938-47. *471*

—. Congress of Industrial Organizations. Oil Industry and Trade. Texas. 1942-43. *618*

—. Discrimination. Fair Employment Practices Committee. Negroes. Railroads. Southeastern Carriers Conference. 1941-45. *1074*

Wrong, Elaine Gale. Discrimination, Employment (review article). Fulmer, William E. Negroes. Rubin, Lester. 1865-1973. *1108*

WWL (station). Communications Technology. Louisiana (New Orleans). Radio. Television. 1940-50. *557*

Wyoming. Electric railroads. 1900-20. *376*

Wyoming (Elk Basin). Lynd, Robert S. (account). Oil Industry and Trade. Working Conditions. 1921. *1088*

Y

Yarn. Productivity. Textile Industry. 1958-80. *847*

York and Cumberland Rail Road. Maine (York County). Railroads. 1848-1900. *460*

Young, Robert J. Industrial safety movement. Progressive era. Reform. "Safety First" (slogan). ca 1900-16. *1025*

Youngstown Sheet and Tube Co. Corporations. Employment. Factories. Ohio (Mahoning Valley). Ownership, employee. 1977-79. *1152*

Youth. Daily Life. Pennsylvania (Phoenixville). Pennypacker, John G. (memoirs). 1900-08. *1042*

Z

Zinc mining. Arkansas (Buffalo Valley). Lead mining. Transportation. ca 1720-1930's. *886*

12-hour shifts. Canada. Chemical Industry. Oil Industry and Trade. USA. Working Conditions. 1977. *1104*

AUTHOR INDEX